PAGA

RONALD HUTTON is professor (
authority on the British Isles i.
on ancient and medieval paganism and magic, and on the global context or
witchcraft beliefs. He is the author of eighteen books.

Further praise for *Pagan Britain*:

'Attempts to understand what the pagans believed, whether focusing on solar
worship, ancestor worship or the Moon Goddess, tell us much more about the
theorists than their data. Yet Hutton argues strongly that this diversity, and this
incomprehensibility, shouldn't be seen as intolerably frustrating.' Tom Shippey,
London Review of Books

'Hutton peels away the layers of so-called ancient beliefs to discover many
aren't that ancient at all ... Lively and bang up-to-date, this is a must-read for
anyone remotely interested in the subject.' Trevor Heaton, *Eastern Daily Press*

'Offers a fascinating glimpse into a world that defies the simplifications of
modern re-enactors.' *Good Book Guide*

'This is a work of great scholarship, it is also an accessible and enjoyable account
of a major part of the history of Britain. Greatly recommended.' John Rimmer,
Magonia Review of Books

'This book is a thoroughly researched, well-written, readable and balanced
history of a subject that is often associated with cranks and phantasists.
Professor Hutton is not, I think, one of them.' Lindsay Fulcher, *Minerva*

PAGAN BRITAIN

RONALD HUTTON

YALE UNIVERSITY PRESS
NEW HAVEN AND LONDON

For information about this and other Yale University Press publications, please contact:
U.S. Office: sales.press@yale.edu   www.yalebooks.com
Europe Office: sales@yaleup.co.uk   www.yalebooks.co.uk

Set in Minion Pro by IDSUK (DataConnection) Ltd
Printed in Great Britain by Clays Ltd, Elcograf S.p.A

Library of Congress Control Number: 2022942441

ISBN 978-0-300-20546-6 (pbk)
ISBN 978-0-300-26834-8 (new edn pbk)

A catalogue record for this book is available from the British Library.

10 9 8 7 6 5 4 3

CONTENTS

ACKNOWLEDGEMENTS

THE RESEARCH WHICH underpins this work was carried out over a period of two decades, in which I accumulated many debts of gratitude to librarians, archivists, colleagues and publishers, the list of which would run to many pages if expressed in full. In the short term, of the actual writing up, three stand out. The first debt is to my university, of Bristol, for awarding me a research fellowship in the final year of the process, so that my work could be completed on time following an exacting and exhilarating period as head of department. The second is to Heather McCallum, of Yale University Press, for having pursued me so relentlessly as a possible author for a long time, and treated me so cleverly once she had secured me. The third is to Ana Adnan, for her customary shrewd encouragement and advice.

After the writing, four notable scholars and friends – Joshua Pollard, Sir Barry Cunliffe, Martin Carver and Brendan Smith – read individual draft chapters, relevant to their own expertise, and provided invaluable advice. Clive Ruggles, the national expert, read the section on archaeoastronomy. To have taken the time for this work from their own concerns, to no personal advantage, especially as the sections concerned are not short, is one of the most generous acts that a fellow professional can undertake, and I shall always be grateful.

A NOTE ON DEFINITIONS

⇒◆⇐

I T MAY BE wise to define from the beginning the key words employed in this book. At no point will the term 'art' be used of the many images painted and carved during British prehistory, even though it is both convenient and sanctioned by long scholarly tradition, viz. 'Palaeolithic cave art', 'megalithic art', 'rock art', etc. This is because of the modern connotations of the word, as something intended to be decorative and inspirational, giving pleasure to those who see it, rather than functional. The prehistoric imagery may indeed have had exactly that purpose, but some or all of it may have operated as well or instead as a form of language, providing information to the observer in the form of directions, lessons, blessings, prayers, curses, prohibitions or declarations; and to use the conventional word obscures that possibility. That is why more neutral terms such as 'images', 'figures' or 'designs' will be preferred.

Next come those two old lexical friends, 'religion' and 'magic'. Both have been fought over extensively by professional colleagues in recent years, and merely to use the latter, or to use the former in the context of prehistory, may arouse the ire of some, while others may be as severely provoked by the implication that the latter has a separate identity from the former. I have argued at length in a previous publication (*Witches, Druids and King Arthur*) that they can indeed be distinguished, and have a different essence, even though they can easily overlap or blend and magic can form a category inside religion. The definitions offered and explained there will be retained here. Religion is characterized as *belief in the existence of spiritual beings or forces which are in some measure responsible for the cosmos, and in the need of human beings to form relationships with them in which they are accorded some respect*. When a group of people operates it in the same way, it becomes 'a' religion. Magic embraces *any formalized practices by human beings designed to achieve particular ends by the manipulation and direction of supernatural power or of spiritual power concealed within the natural world.* The word 'ritual' has been the subject of equally extensive and complex debate. In previous publications I have used Clifford Geertz's lovely and simple definition, of 'consecrated action', which captures perfectly its sense of action invested with an exceptional formality and freight of meaning, often expressed in repeated patterns. This puts performance at the heart of ritual, which seems correct, and enables the term both to be linked to religious behaviour and separated from it.

Finally, this book needs a definition of 'paganism', a word central to its being. There is an obvious one: that the term refers to the pre-Christian religions of Europe and the Near East. This holds the essence of the way in which it is most commonly used, and is employed here, and retains the original positioning of it as something defined by and against the Christian faith. It does, however, beg the question of what religions are, and while that has been answered above, the reply that was provided does have some knock-on effect for the matter now at issue. By highlighting relationships with spiritual beings it confines the term 'paganism' to an active worship of the deities associated with those old religious traditions. This is the 'minimalist' position, as defined by twentieth-century philosophers of religion, and one which avoids endless, and irreconcilable, arguments over the extent of the survival of the essence of a religion when the people who professed it have been formally converted to another. It draws a boundary which is at least clear and can usually be recognized in the historical record.

Throughout this book I retain the old-fashioned expression 'the British Isles' to describe the whole complex archipelago with Ireland and Britain at its centre. This is not intended as a slight upon citizens of the Irish Republic, who have long won the right not to be regarded as British, but is purely the result of geographical accuracy. The alternative term of 'Britain and Ireland' seems to forget the Northern Isles, the Hebrides, Man, Anglesey, the islets off Pembrokeshire, and the Isles of Scilly and Wight, all of which play a part – and often an important one – in the issues discussed here, and which often have a strongly marked cultural character of their own. The centrality of Britain to the expression is simply a reflection of its size, as the main island of the group, as in 'the Canaries', 'the Hawaiian Islands', 'the Maltese Islands', and so forth.

A greater personal discomfort attaches to the means of reckoning historical epochs. In a previous book of mine, *Witches, Druids and King Arthur*, I adopted the increasingly fashionable, and religiously neutral, usage of BCE and CE, to replace BC and AD, which are specifically Christian. As I explained in the introduction to that book, I myself had no strong feelings on the matter, and have an instinctual wariness of gesture politics; but, none the less, I accepted that it was a courteous gesture to make towards the ideal of a multi-faith, multi-ethnic society. My commitment to that kind of society is as strong as ever, and will feature prominently in the conclusion to the present book, but here I have reverted to the older usage. The difference is purely one of context. The new forms are most common among newer publishing houses and in disciplines such as Religious Studies, where the issues involved are most sensitive. That earlier book of mine was placed with such a publisher and overlapped with the concerns of those disciplines. The present book is devoted almost wholly to history and archaeology, older-fashioned scholarly traditions which have adhered to the BC/AD forms. Archaeologists in particular, who have most to reckon with dates BC (or BCE) have done so, not because they are usually Christian but because of the reverse consideration: that as a group (with striking individual exceptions) they tend to be less religious than most and so more indifferent to hallmarks of particular belief systems. The older usage is also the normal house style of Yale University Press, the representatives of which had accommodated my wishes in other respects and whom I was accordingly reluctant to press over this one.

The matter cost me much aching of conscience, till I discussed it with a Roman Catholic friend, an Irishman. With the wit and geniality of so many of his nation, he replied that to use the traditional forms was itself a gesture of inter-faith co-operation, because Christians like him had employed the pagan names for days of the week, months of the year and constellations, for centuries without complaint. It therefore seemed to him an appropriate gesture of gallantry on my part, this time, to accord the chronological framework in return. His argument won the day, and so during this book I record the last two millennia as Years of a Lord to whom I owe no personal allegiance, but of whose followers I am frequently fond.

Illustrations

—⇒◆⇐—

PREFACE

⇒•⇐

A T THE END of the 1980s, I wrote a book called *The Pagan Religions of the Ancient British Isles*, which was published in 1991. It had two intentions, the first of which was simply to provide an overview, for general readers and specialists in particular ages and cultures, of how experts interpreted the evidence for pre-Christian religion in these islands, from the Old Stone Age until the Middle Ages. On the whole, my task was simply to synthesize their work period by period, though at times the process did involve making choices and priorities of my own, and pointing out moments at which the views concerned seemed contradictory or problematic. The second intention represented my personal 'take' upon the whole subject, which was to emphasize more than other authors at that period the difficulty of the evidence and the large number of interpretations possible for most aspects of it. In particular, I wanted to celebrate the latter, as a strength rather than a weakness, and their utility in providing a past into which different people could read different meanings to inspire and challenge them in the present. For this reason, I gave more explicit consideration than most academic authors to viewpoints separate from, and often opposed to, those of professional archaeologists and historians, although this was more often to engage with them than to give them equal status. The book was tremendous fun to write, and enjoyed reasonable critical and commercial success, and has remained in print for over two decades.

I had always intended, providing that it provoked sufficient interest, to produce a second edition, but that project gradually turned into a different one: to replace it with a work that covered the same ground with new interests and emphases. This book is the result. It is designed to retain the basic utility of its predecessor, of introducing the current evidence for ancient British paganism

to general readers and to students and scholars with more concentrated expertise. The format is slightly different. Although a longer work, it is devoted prin-
cipally to Britain and its offshore islands, and makes only occasional and
comparative reference to Ireland, in the same manner as to Continental Europe.
This is to enable a closer and more considered treatment of the material from
Britain and its smaller neighbouring islands, which is so much greater now
after two further decades of excavation and publication. More attention is paid
to specific sites and scholars, and less to modern forms of paganism, because
I have published extensively on those during the intervening period. The
emphasis upon the potential for differing, and often conflicting, interpretations
of the same evidence remains as strong. Underpinning this new book is a great
deal more of my own work than before: indeed, some of that informs every
chapter, and the quantity grows as the volume goes on.

In addition, this book explicitly poses, and attempts to answer, four more
questions. The first is whether it is possible to have either an archaeology or a
history of prehistoric and early historic British religion, in view of the extreme
limitations of the evidence. The second is where the limits of relativism lie in
the interpretation of the data: how far the latter impose constraints on the
ability of each person to create her or his own imagined view of the ancient past
and how far experts have a right to impose theirs. The third is how much
changing cultural patterns in the present, and very recent past, have influenced
scholarly reconstructions of ancient paganism. The fourth concerns the extent
to which a broad-sweep study such as this enables useful comparisons to be
made between approaches to the study of religious activity in different periods,
the specialists in which do not normally converse with each other. In this
manner it intends to offer thoughts which may be of value to fellow professionals as well as providing information and entertainment to those general
readers who may be less interested in such theoretical problems.

1

⟫•⟪

THE PALAEOLITHIC AND MESOLITHIC
HOW RITUAL CAME TO BRITAIN

Human-like beings have been occupying the land which has become Britain, on and off, for almost a million years, and probably longer.[1] For most of that period, the land concerned was a peninsula of the European mainland, representing a remote hilly margin to the great plains which now lie under the North Sea and to which archaeologists have given the name 'Doggerland'.[2] Whether the first species of human to reach it had a capacity for what we would now call religious belief, and whether such a capacity was possessed by any of those that followed before the arrival of our own, is a disputed question. The balance of opinion currently seems to be shifting towards the view that they had, and especially the Neanderthal people who occupied Europe when anatomically modern humans arrived there. The matter, however, is far from decided.[3] What is absolutely clear is that our own species, *Homo sapiens*, manifested every sign of possessing the necessary imaginative faculty as soon as it evolved, whether as a result of evolution, as most Western scholars now believe, or as a divine gift, as is still the opinion of some adherents to certain faiths. Every test of evidence which has produced equivocal results when applied to other kinds of human has yielded an unequivocal one in the case of ours, and especially in two areas: the ceremonial burial of the dead, and the production of painted or carved representations, of animals, humans and figures which mix attributes of the two. Together with other traces of a heightened sense of imagination and of symbolic behaviour, such as the making of musical instruments and the regular development of new and better technologies of tool-making, these activities attest strongly to a capacity to conceive of worlds beyond the material and the immediate.

Such a capacity was manifested with particular strength as anatomically modern humans reached north-western Europe from about 42,000 BC onwards: indeed, the quantity of paintings that survives there from their hands is probably greater than that found anywhere else in the world from humans living more than 10,000 years ago. Why this should be has been much discussed. Some commentators suggest that unusually rich hunting grounds there generated exceptionally large and settled populations of people with a greater need to mark territory and reinforce group solidarity. Others attribute this artistic productivity to the collision of our human species in Europe with an existing one, the Neanderthals, producing an enhanced propensity on our part to engage in creative behaviour designed to affirm our identity and mark our world.[4] In the 1990s the term 'the Human Revolution' was coined to describe the quantum leap taken by European material culture with the arrival of *Homo sapiens*.[5] Whether or not it is appropriate in the world context, it vividly conveys the dramatic change in the archaeological record caused by the arrival of our kind of human. With it, the study of the earliest epoch of human prehistory, the Palaeolithic or Old Stone Age, reaches a point at which a consideration of religious behaviour needs to be part of the process.

Until recently, Britain hardly featured in such an exercise, being regarded as one of the most marginal areas of human activity in Palaeolithic Europe. Since the 1990s that position has altered dramatically, as British sites have been revealed as important even by global standards. Three in particular have been outstanding, and in each case the evidence concerned has posed problems that reach to the heart of the archaeology of the Palaeolithic and raised questions concerning the nature of perception, and of knowledge, itself.

Three Special Places: Paviland, Creswell and Cheddar

The first site is the Goat's Hole cave at Paviland, on the south-western coast of the Gower Peninsula in South Wales. It is associated with an outstanding scholar, William Buckland, the son of a Dorset clergyman who had lost his vision in an accident.[6] Buckland therefore grew up accustomed to describing the landscape around them to his father on walks, and this close observation of it gave him an interest in rock formations. It persisted when he went to Oxford University, and brought him in 1815 to fill its first full-time post in the new science of geology. He was especially inspired by the idea, currently most strongly propounded by French scholars, that rocks contained the remains of extinct species of animal and plant. This new sense of the great age of the planet gave devout Christians such as Buckland the problem of reconciling the evidence of geology with the testimony of the biblical Book of Genesis, and no British scholar attempted more fervently than he, at that period, to find the

1 Major sites in Britain for evidence of Palaeolithic ritual.

solution to the problem by practical fieldwork. In other respects he was a remarkable individual. His home was crammed with fossils and rocks, but also cages of snakes and frogs, while the vertebrae of Jurassic reptiles were used as candle-holders. Guinea pigs roamed the floor of his office, and occasionally got eaten when the jackal escaped from the living room. His star pet was a bear, which he named Tiglath Pileser after a biblical monarch, and which he sometimes took along to academic functions, dressed in a student's cap and gown. These colourful oddities were, alas, symptoms of an unstable as well as of a broad and brave mind, and towards the end of his life he went clinically mad.

In the 1810s, at the height of his powers, he embarked on a campaign of investigation of caves, which he felt to be ideal sources of evidence for past ages of the earth, as they had been least disturbed by subsequent activity. His first excavation of one, in Yorkshire, met with such success that it drew the attention of local scholars in Gower. In 1822 the doctor and clergyman at the fishing village of Port Eynon began to dig in the caves at Paviland, and found bones and flints. They informed the owners of the land, the Talbots of Penrice Castle, and the lady of the house, her daughters and her friends joined the investigations. They found so much material in the Goat's Hole that they sent a message to Buckland, who came at once, even though the season was midwinter, and set about digging in the cave himself. He found pieces of ivory, mammoth bones, flint and bone tools, and part of a human skeleton, stained with red ochre, which lacked its head and most of the right side. Because there was an Iron Age fort on the cliff top above, he decided that it had been the body of a lady of ill fame, almost literally a scarlet woman, who had kept a tavern in the cave for soldiers from the fort. The nickname 'the Red Lady' has clung to the remains ever since. Buckland's mistake may justly be attributed to his dogmatic determination to reconcile the physical evidence with the scriptural account in Genesis, which he believed forbade him to associate humans with the extinct animals now being found in the caves: by calling the remains an intrusive burial from a much later period, he got rid of the problem. Three comments may be made upon this story. One is that the Church of England did more to promote knowledge of the ancient past at this vital period than to hamper it, by providing the essential financial support for Buckland himself, as a cleric and a member of an Oxford college, and furnishing a living to amateur antiquarians such as the curate of Port Eynon. The second is that the prominence given to Buckland, though natural, highlights the problems of the emphasis on great individuals in history, obscuring as it has often done the vital role of instigation and support played by the local leaders of Gower society. The third is that by packaging the new data in a form which was not immediately offensive to Christian opinion, Buckland made the great age and complexity of the earth much easier for a contemporary audience to accept, and geology a respectable vocation.

During the following hundred years further excavations took place in the Paviland caves, and it became accepted that the Red Lady was a Palaeolithic man, and the first human fossil ever known to science. Renewed interest in him, and the site, was kindled by a project led by Stephen Aldhouse-Green in the 1990s, which carried out a fresh excavation in the Goat's Hole and a systematic re-examination of the surviving finds from it.[7] The human bones yielded ever older results to each dating process: the current one stands at around 32,000 BC, making it possibly the oldest ceremonial human burial yet found in Europe.[8] The man concerned was in his prime, between twenty-five and thirty years old, and probably stood around 5 feet 8 inches (173 centimetres) high and weighed about 154 pounds (73 kilos): not a big person for his time. He had apparently been buried in a two-piece garment dyed red, which was impractical for routine activities such as hunting, and so presumably of a ceremonial kind. With him were placed hoops of mammoth ivory which seem to have been bracelets or castanets, and ivory structures like wands or batons, which were broken before being placed with the corpse. Again, these grave goods are most easily interpreted as having a ritual function. At a point where a pocket would have been was a collection of perforated periwinkle shells, presumably either decorations for clothing or a necklace, or objects to be cast as some kind of divinatory process. From all this evidence, Stephen Aldhouse-Green and his team concluded that the dead man had most probably possessed some kind of spiritual function among his people. The basic pattern of the burial – the laying out of the body, the placement of possessions with it, and the significant presence of the colour red – is found in other graves scattered across Europe over the following ten thousand years. Such conformity to a continent-wide tradition suggests equally widespread shared belief systems (whatever they were): and the Red Lady is at present the oldest known example.[9]

The same research project revealed much more information on the environment of the Gower between 34,000 and 24,000 years ago. Today the Goat's Hole looks out from its cliff face directly on to the seascape of the Bristol Channel: very high tides enter the cave, and the waves below constantly suck and lash at a landscape of weathered limestone boulders, as though a gorgon had passed and petrified an army on the march. Thirty-four millennia ago, the land below was a frozen tundra, which bloomed during the warmer climate of the following few millennia into a range of grasses and herbs making up a

2 The Goat's Hole, Paviland. The cave shows up as a dark cleft to the right, underneath the lichen-covered crag of Yellow Top.

richer version of the historic steppes of southern Russia: if the comparison is apt, in the brief summer it would have been a carpet of brilliant flowers, with glow-worms spreading emerald fire across it after nightfall. Grazing it were stiff-maned wild horses, long-nosed saiga antelopes, red deer, reindeer, the extinct species of huge wide-horned wild cattle known as the aurochs, woolly mammoths, and woolly rhinoceroses. Mountain hares leaped among the grass, and through it wandered predators that still survive in Europe such as lynxes, red and arctic foxes, wolves and brown bears, with other, greater, beasts that have long vanished: cave bears, cave hyenas and cave lions, the largest cats that the world has ever known.

In this panorama, the Goat's Hole stood out for humans as somewhere special: the Aldhouse-Green project has also confirmed that the quantity of artefacts found in the cave far exceeds that discovered at any other site in Britain or neighbouring parts of Europe from the Early Upper Palaeolithic, the first 20,000 years in which our species is known to have been active in the region. Not even the other caves on that coast of Gower, which are numerous and include one almost next to the Goat's Hole, have produced anything like its amount of material from that period. The deposits were made in repeated visits over a long span of time, covering up to 11,000 years: among those made later than the burial were bone objects which could have been blades or stylized female figurines. Stephen Aldhouse-Green and his colleagues suggested that the key to its unusual status may have lain in its position under a prominent crag, now named Yellow Top because of the mustard-coloured lichens which cover it and seem to make it glow in sunlight. To humans approaching across the plain to the south, it would have acted as a natural beacon signalling the presence of what is now the South Welsh massif. More prosaically, the cliff would have made an ideal killing ground over which hunters could have driven herds of animals to their death. Paul Pettitt has suggested that for people moving north and west into what has become Britain from adjacent areas of Europe, a large river flowing along the present line of the English Channel represented a serious barrier. The easiest route round it was along the Atlantic coast of what is now France, which meant that their first sight of the upland area which has become the island of Britain would have been the modern Gower. Yellow Top would therefore have been a landmark of extraordinary importance.[10]

It needs to be emphasized that the earlier excavations at the site, at which many of the most significant finds were made, were extremely badly recorded, and that much of the material recovered, such as that collected by the Talbots, has subsequently been lost. This makes anything like a full reconstruction of the burial of the Red Lady impossible. It will never be clear whether the body was whole when buried or already half missing: observers at the time of excavation were indeed not certain whether Buckland had found the remains of one person or two. Some of the surviving finds made with it are still enigmatic: the segments of ivory could indeed have come from wands, but may have had quite another purpose. The role that the dead man played during life is of course entirely conjectural: there remains the possibility that his trappings had connotations of political or social power rather than of spiritual authority in particular. None the less, the Goat's Hole may be regarded as the most important Early Upper Palaeolithic site in north-western Europe, and seems to have had associations, like the Red Lady himself, which were numinous rather than merely practical. This probability, linked to the very long period during which the Goat's Hole was in use, now makes it a prime candidate for the reputation of being the first great sacred place thought to have existed in what are now the British Isles and the adjacent parts of Europe's mainland. Its growing significance has as yet made little difference to it as a physical entity. The cave itself is effectively now a shell, completely dug out, and its position has not become any more accessible since Buckland described it as 'altogether invisible from the landside, and ... accessible only at low water, except by dangerous climbing along the face of a nearly precipitous cliff'.[11] In many ways, its wild and lonely situation enhances its dignity, in contrast to sites more open to tourism.

The second outstanding site is Creswell Crags, a gorge just over half a mile long upon the border between the counties of Derbyshire and Nottinghamshire. Buckland made cave-digging, in search of human prehistory, an enthusiasm among British scholars, and the caves of the Creswell gorge were emptied in a series of campaigns between the 1870s and 1920s. Large quantities of animal bones and flint tools were discovered, and also, most exciting, the only figurative pieces of Palaeolithic mobile art yet uncovered in Britain, to compare with the large amount found on Continental sites. Two in particular drew attention, on segments of animal rib bone. The first was the front half of a horse's body, covered and preceded by a series of vertical lines, the second an upright shape interpreted by the discoverer as 'a masked human figure in the act of dancing a ceremonial dance'.[12] As humans are relatively rare in Palaeolithic paintings and carvings, this made the discovery all the more important, especially as it seemed to have a connotation of ritual. In 2003 the site became the focus of a major research project based in the universities of Sheffield and Hull and led by Paul Pettitt and Paul Bahn, which immediately achieved spectacular success by revealing the existence of the very first Palaeolithic pictures ever found on the walls of British caves.[13] They had been there all the time, carved on the interiors but unnoticed by scholarship, partly because they are visible only from certain angles and partly because they are obscured by Victorian graffiti. Britain had been presumed to possess none of the celebrated Old Stone Age pictures with which French and Spanish caves are decorated: suddenly it had proved to contain fine examples.

The same project revealed much about the environment in which the depictions were made. Around 20,000 BC a new Ice Age began, rendering the land mass which became Britain too cold for human habitation for over five thousand years. Dates from the Creswell caves range between 13,700 and 10,600 BC, a period when the climate had warmed again to a point at which temperatures were similar to those of today. The vegetation, however, had not caught up with the change, so that the region still consisted of open grasslands with spruce, birch, pine and juniper growing in sheltered places. All of the animals that had thronged the region during the last warm period had returned, except the bison, rhinoceros, hyena and lion, making the new hunting grounds safer places for humans than the old, while still abundant with game. The gorge was occupied only in spring and early summer, when it formed an ideal migration route for reindeer, and the caves there were mostly used for the processing of meat. Significantly, that called Church Hole, which contained most of the carvings, was the only one not employed for such mundane purposes: facing north, which made it colder and so less attractive for such work, it seems to have been turned instead into a sort of shrine. The choice of subjects is standard for the art of the time, animals predominating – especially deer, horses and bison – with a set of more enigmatic shapes over which modern observers argue. Surfaces were selected with care, just one wall of Church Hole being used although both were suitable. One picture was so deep inside that artificial light must have been needed to create it, and it could have been seen by only a single person at a time, lying on one side and looking up.

The same research project, however, met with difficulties as well as successes. If it brought cave depictions dramatically into the record, it also seemed to cast doubt on the engraved bones from Creswell. It revealed, more comprehensively than before, that ever since the discovery of the carving of the horse had been announced, accusations had been made that it had been planted by one of the excavators. It certainly seems to be a genuine Palaeolithic artefact, but appears different in colour and form from the other finds in the caves; and the matter remains unresolved and perhaps insoluble. The dancing masked man has also been re-examined, and there is now no definite evidence that the figure was either dancing or a man: it could, for example, be a bear. Other pieces of stone found in the 1920s, in which the discoverer had claimed to find etchings of animals, may just have natural markings. Nor is there agreement on the actual number of carvings on the walls of Church Hole, for the same reason, that natural cracks are not easily distinguished now from deliberate etchings: earlier estimates reaching over two hundred have now been reduced to just twenty-five absolutely certain images. Interpretation of those is also sometimes controversial. Some consist of a triangle with a vertical line through it, a symbol common on the Continent, which may represent the female sexual organs and thus be a potent symbol either of human fertility and eroticism or of a goddess. On the other hand, that image may represent an animal footprint instead, or something altogether different from both. Swaying, intertwined lines, also with Continental parallels, might be the shapes of dancing, naked women, perhaps indicating some springtime fertility cult; but they might as easily be the necks of birds. The Creswell cave pictures remain, for reasons that at present elude everybody, the only body of such pictures yet found in Britain, despite an immediate and intensive hunt through other sites. A possible outline of the head and back of a mammoth was found in Gough's Cave, Cheddar, in 2007, but is regarded by some experts as a natural marking.[14] In 2011 the figure of a single reindeer was identified as carved on the wall of a Gower cave, not very far from Paviland, and seems to be receiving more general acceptance: at a dating of 13,000 to 12,000 BC it is the oldest design on rock yet found in the British Isles.[15]

The practicalities of conservation at Creswell have also been problematic. Nobody had expected the new research project to make such dramatic discoveries there that the site would be catapulted into a place of global importance. Its physical condition at the moment of its scholarly elevation was one of the worst possible for such promotion: on the boundary of two county jurisdictions, with a public road running straight through it and a water filtration plant at the top. There was little room for a visitor centre, and none of the finds made in the caves previously were held locally, being divided between the British and the Manchester Museums. As a result of a considerable joint effort by the local councils, and a large National Lottery grant, several million pounds have been raised to remove the road and the plant, and to construct a large heritage centre at the end of the gorge, from which parties of visitors can be conducted into the site by official guides. At the time of writing, the displays set up at the centre are already impressive, and sensitive to the difficulties of interpretation, outlined above.

The third site has already been mentioned: Gough's Cave, in Cheddar Gorge which cleaves through the western side of Somerset's Mendip Hills. Unlike the other two, it has been one of the nation's major tourist attractions ever since Victorian times, because of the natural beauties of its stalactite and stalagmite formations. Ever since then, also, Palaeolithic bones and flints have been found in it. In 1986, the owner, the marquis of Bath, embarked on a major new programme of redevelopment to enhance its attraction to visitors and so its capacity to generate income, and as part of this a team from the British Natural History Museum was called in to conduct further excavations. These were completed by the end of the 1980s, together with a fresh consideration of the surviving finds made earlier, and the result was to reveal Gough's Cave as having provided the richest single concentration of objects yet known from the late Palaeolithic in Britain. Among them were about seven thousand flint tools,

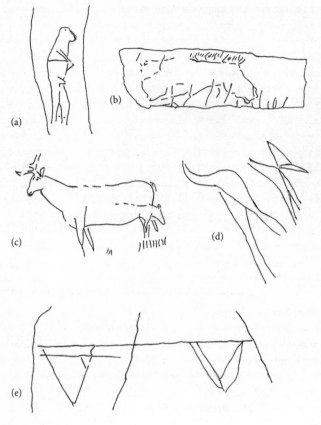

3 Images from Creswell Crags
(a) 'Dancing masked man' found in the 1920s, all details of this interpretation are now in doubt.
(b) Horse's head found in the 1870s and considered to be a genuine Palaeolithic engraving, but one possibly planted on the site.
(c) Stag, first of the wall-carvings found in 2003. Not everybody is convinced of the existence of the engraving of the smaller animal on its right.
(d) Shapes taken by some to be dancing women, and by others to be long-necked birds.
(e) So-called 'vulva' figures – female genitalia or animal tracks, or something else altogether.

left there by hunters who had occupied the gorge seasonally at some points between about 13,800 and 11,400 BC in order to hunt a range of mammals and birds, but especially horses. They used the same kinds of tools as those at Creswell and may indeed have been the same people. If so, they seem to have left no equivalent carvings on the cave walls, but instead two particular kinds

4 Gough's Cave, Cheddar Gorge.

of deposit which have created excitement in recent years: decorated objects and pieces of human body.

The decorated objects were leg bones of hares, ribs of wild cattle, and pieces of mammoth ivory marked with straight lines along the edges in groups varying in number from eight to sixteen. Commentators have interpreted these as tallies for keeping count, message sticks, equipment for games, rulers for measuring, and lunar calendars. Clearly, the seriousness of the purpose varies greatly between these explanations, and with it the views taken of Palaeolithic society: and there is no definitive way of choosing between them.[16] Four similar objects were found at Kendrick's Cave, overlooking the resort town of Llandudno in North Wales, which also produced a horse's jawbone incised with zigzag lines and nine perforated deer or cattle teeth etched with lines at their roots. It is usually assumed that some symbolic meaning was conveyed by these decorations, but it likewise remains elusive. Nor is it even certain that the Welsh horse jaw is Palaeolithic: it might date from the subsequent Middle Stone Age.[17]

The human remains, dating to between 13,000 and 12,000 BC, consisted of bones from at least four adults and a child, found in the 1980s, and from two more adults and a child dug up in the 1920s. They had been systematically defleshed: first dismembered, then skinned, and then the meat cut from the bones and the tongue from the mouth.[18] In the cave, they were mixed together with animal remains, as if treated equally, and so immediately and at points ever since, they have been considered as evidence for cannibal feasts. Other commentators, however, have pointed out that the interpretation of cannibalism is unproven: the bones were not broken to extract marrow, or burned or snapped as the animal remains had been. An alternative explanation for them is that these were individuals who had died on migration, and whose bones had been cleaned on the spot so that they could easily be transported to a sacred place, Gough's Cave, and interred there.[19] In 2011, after further analysis of the bones, it was found that three of the skulls had been reshaped like drinking vessels, by cleaning, removal of facial bones and bases, and grinding of broken edges: the oldest such skull-cups known in the world.[20] It has been noted that, just as human activity in Church Hole seems to have ceased after the pictures were made there, as if it had now been consecrated to deities or spirits, so occupation of the Cheddar cave seems to have ended once the dead were placed in it.[21] Fairly obviously, the debate over the significance of the human bones from Gough's Cave has acted as a projection on to them, by modern authors, of general attitudes to human nature. Those with a more pessimistic attitude have tended to favour cannibalism as an explanation, and those with a more optimistic one to favour a burial rite; while others have tended to keep options open. Understanding was increased at the end of the 2000s by experiments which proved that the marks on some of the toe bones and one of the ribs exactly matched those made by human teeth: so the parts concerned had been chewed by people, making the explanation of cannibalism more likely. On the other hand, as said, the skull-cups were not cleaned to provide food but for fashioning into cups. Where examples of this activity have been recorded among different peoples in historic times (and it has always been rare), it has been for two completely different reasons: to humiliate dead enemies, who provided the heads which were turned into vessels, and to honour dead ancestors, from the source of whose wisdom, the head, their descendants drank. Either could fit the evidence at Cheddar, and if the latter was true, then we circle around again to the idea of a funeral rite, of which cannibalism may have formed a part. Whatever the exact reason for the treatment of these particular bones, it should be emphasized that the burial of human remains was extremely rare across Europe and the Near East in the later Palaeolithic, just as in the earlier. Most pieces of human skeleton found on those sites are fragments apparently used for personal ornaments, suggesting that burial of bodies was an exceptional procedure reserved for people who had been unusual in themselves or died in unusual ways.[22]

The division of opinions over Gough's Cave bones provides the context for the public representation of the remains. In 2005 a new visitor centre was opened opposite the cave entrance, dedicated to the Palaeolithic material, which played up the interpretation of the bones as evidence of cannibalism as proven fact and in the most gruesome and sensational fashion. The opportunity to suggest that ancient evidence may be interpreted in different ways was firmly rejected. In Torquay Museum, by contrast, reposes a piece of human arm bone found in 1866 inside the famous nearby cave of Kent's Cavern, another notable source of Palaeolithic remains though not hitherto as strongly associated with ritual as the other three sites. It has seven cut marks upon it exactly like those upon the Cheddar skeletons, and may indeed have been deposited by the same people. The interpretative label carefully avoids advocating any one view of the exhibit, citing both the possibility of a funerary rite and of cannibal activities.[23] Visitors to the museum, however, tend to be fewer than those to Cheddar Gorge and are mainly individuals there specifically to learn about the past, whereas the director of the Cheddar caves has the challenge of persuading huge numbers of people in search of the entertaining and the spectacular to take an interest in the ancient finds from the site. This has obviously been met, because the new museum has attracted a million visitors in its first five years, and this has been largely due to its promotion as the only one in Britain to be dedicated to cannibalism.[24]

In all three cases, of Paviland, Creswell and Cheddar, the recent discoveries have resulted from a re-examination of sites that were made famous by work in the nineteenth and early twentieth centuries, and largely stripped of archaeological material then. It may be, however, that they will be succeeded by investigations of Palaeolithic ritual behaviour in places hitherto untouched by excavation and so capable of revealing the very finest results provided by the latest techniques for recovery of data. Recent surveys of the ridge which contains Creswell Crags have revealed more than 160 caves, shelters and fissures with a high archaeological potential.[25] If that is realized, and reproduced in other promising locations across the country, an understanding of the British Palaeolithic may only now be commencing.

The European Context

It is time now to relate these discoveries in Britain to the wider picture of Palaeolithic Europe that has been developed over the same period. This is the more important in that there has never been an age since in which Britain was so completely integrated with the major European land mass: not just physically, but culturally. The lifestyle, artefacts and pictorial designs of the people who wandered over what would be Britain are precisely those of the nearby parts of the Continent, and theories concerning the nature and meaning of them, developed in and for other European nations, are equally applicable to the British context. The people concerned arrived in Europe already making stone tools of great beauty as well as of utility, variety and specialization. They were already at the top of the local food chain, bringing down large grazing animals such as horses and deer, and perhaps mammoths and rhinoceroses, and capable of keeping predators such as wolves and hyenas away from their carcasses until the work of butchery was complete. The first human beings to arrive in the north-west of the Continent, long before *Homo sapiens* evolved, left remains of hunting camps where the discarded bones bore the marks of their tools underneath those of the teeth of scavenging beasts: the humans had made the kills and then protected them, rather than coming later to bodies abandoned by more effective kinds of carnivore. Our own species was more lethal still: Palaeolithic hunters stampeded a total of 10,000 horses over a cliff at Solutré, France. From its first appearance in the Continent, therefore, *Homo sapiens* had the potential to reshape its world in a manner possessed by no other animal: when it wished, it could destroy with the power of a forest fire or an earthquake rather than of just another predator. After 20,000 BC Europeans acquired the use of the eyed needle, allowing them to create clothing with several layers, suitable for almost any climate, and developed the spear-thrower, greatly increasing the range of their missiles. Before the end of the Palaeolithic they acquired bows and arrows. Although meat made up a large part of their diet, as in the case of Arctic peoples today, they also harvested wild plants, with sickle-shaped flints. By the end of the period they had constructed systems of exchange which could carry flint up to 250, and shells up to 400, miles: they had started to trade.[26]

In attempting to discover how they conceived of their place in the natural or divine order, scholars have focused in the main on the painted and carved images that Palaeolithic Europeans left behind them. Interpretation of these passed through three phases during the twentieth century, each of which reflected changing modern concerns with the nature of humanity and with the human past. The first, which dominated in the first two-thirds of the century, centred on the undoubted truth that most of the figures carved or painted in Old Stone Age Europe were of animals. It was the great French scholar Salomon Reinach, in 1909, who characterized the main purpose of these as aids to hunting magic: in other words, ceremonies were performed around the pictures of animals to ensure that they could be successfully tracked and killed in real life. A subsidiary theory that accompanied this one was that the images were also associated with fertility magic, rites designed to increase the numbers of the beasts concerned and so the supply of food which they represented. One or both of these ideas was adopted by most of the leading figures in the field until the 1960s, when it became apparent that the animals represented did not usually match the diet of the people who made the images, as suggested by the bones left on their living sites. Nor do the pictures normally portray animals in the process of being hunted or caught: markings on some images have sometimes been interpreted as traps, spears or arrows, but the cases where these appear are few, and this interpretation of the marks may itself not be accurate. Animals are never shown in the act of mating, and rarely as pregnant or with young, so that the explanation of fertility magic has no clear justification. Old Stone Age picture-makers, in fact, seem to have been remarkably uninterested in the act of sex: there is not one definite representation of human or animal copulation in any of the images which they have left.[27] The twin explanations of hunting magic and fertility magic were products of an age deeply concerned with science and technology, and predisposed to interpret ancient ritual as an attempt to secure the practical benefits eventually produced by those forces instead.

The second model of explanation was more short-lived, and associated with another leading scholar, André Leroi-Gourhan, who published between 1963 and 1994. It drew its inspiration from the prevailing intellectual movement of structuralism, which was especially influential in anthropology, and its guiding principle from the undoubted truth that Palaeolithic figures of animals are very often paired: horses with bison, ibex with cattle, or cattle with mammoths. This organization of imagery is part of a broader preoccupation with space, distinctive designs or groups of designs being associated with particular areas on cave walls. From this Leroi-Gourhan developed a theory that the images represented an elaborate system of matched feminine and masculine symbols, intended to promote the fertility of both human and animal populations. This had the merit that it seemed to explain much of the layout of the figures, and the drawbacks that it was completely incapable of proof and seemed to impose a single crude scheme upon a wide variety of imagery spanning two score millennia. It also failed to account for the number, posture, shape and rendering of the animal designs.[28]

During the later twentieth century, admiration for scientific and technological achievement, and faith in the ability of the European mind to impose structure upon, and discern true meaning in, the beliefs of traditional peoples, began to be tempered. A growing concern about the materialist preoccupations of the developed world, and a sense of the potential value of pre-industrial concepts and customs, led to a new interest in the spirituality of indigenous cultures. Largely because of the influence of a Romanian refugee to France and then America, Mircea Eliade, this came to focus on the notion of shamanism, usually broadly defined as apparent contacts with a spirit world made by humans in an altered state of consciousness. Eliade himself applied this to the interpretation of Palaeolithic imagery, and found some followers in this enterprise among German scholars in the 1950s and 1960s. The idea met with little enthusiasm outside Germany, however, and more or less slipped from view after 1970.[29] It reappeared dramatically in 1988 with the work of two South Africa academics, David Lewis-Williams and Thomas Dowson, which brought

two major pieces of new evidence to the support of the idea that shamanic practices formed a 'significant component' of Palaeolithic rock paintings and carvings. The first was that the pictures created by the San, the hunter-gatherer
peoples of South African commonly called Bushmen, bore a similarity to those
of the European Palaeolithic and were the work of a people who employed
shamanism as a central part of their spiritual and therapeutic practices. The
second was gained from psychology, and consisted of the discovery that human
beings entering 'entoptic' states (trances or drug-enhanced visions) often see
the material world disintegrate into a sequence of increasingly abstract forms
such as those found in the Old Stone Age images of Europe. Both authors developed these ideas further over the following ten years, and Lewis-Williams
teamed up with Jean Clottes, a French expert in the Palaeolithic, to sum them
up in a book for a general readership.[30] The new theory accomplished two
things that those before it had not: it provided a convincing parallel for the Old
Stone Age figures and symbols among humans whose beliefs and motivations
could be studied, and it reintegrated study of the abstract figures of the
Palaeolithic with the animal representations. Almost half of all the imagery left
in Europe from the Old Stone Age is in fact abstract, consisting of about sixty
basic motifs, and this large number of designs had been neglected in comparison with the famous animal pictures. Indeed, most Palaeolithic images in the
world are abstract: Europe is most unusual in the high proportion of 'realistic'
figures among them.[31]

The new model of explanation accordingly attracted many enthusiastic
responses, which in turn provoked increasingly passionate rejoinders from
specialists who felt that it was being accepted too rapidly and comprehensively.
Some in South Africa emphasized that San paintings themselves embodied a
range of cultural meanings, of which shamanism was only one; nor was it quite
certain that those San groups who had made the images had also practised
shamanism. Experts in native Australian rock pictures doubted that these were
entoptic, while those in the Central Asian equivalent could not agree upon
whether those were a reflection of shamanism or of Indo-Iranian religion.
Neuroscientists insisted that the model of stages of trance used by Lewis-
Williams and Dowson, with its specific imagery, was not found in the natural
state of the human brain but generated only by certain hallucinogenic drugs
not obtainable in Palaeolithic Europe. It was also pointed out that animal
images of the San and Palaeolithic kind, and abstract designs with allegedly
entoptic associations, are also produced by surviving human societies that do
not practise what scholars define as shamanism. Conversely, living peoples
who do place an emphasis on altered states of consciousness can make designs
which include none of those associated with entoptic trance by scientists.
Visionary experiences may be similar, other arguments ran, but take place in

particular cultural contexts, so that similar sorts of drawing and painting can have very different meanings.[32]

The most attractive feature of the argument made by Lewis-Williams and Dowson is that it seems to account for certain forms of Palaeolithic imagery better than any other. Lewis-Williams and Clottes took pains in their book to point out that the range of concepts, subjects and techniques found in the Old Stone Age pictures of France and Spain alone make it 'naïve to hope for one complete explanation'.[33] An American anthropologist, Randall White, has suggested that the shamanic theory can account for perhaps 10 per cent of Palaeolithic figures, and this has been echoed by Stephen Aldhouse-Green, the project leader of the new study of Paviland.[34] More generally, however, the shamanism hypothesis has served a useful purpose in emphasizing the nature of the pictures in caves as images associated most commonly with some form of spiritual experience. This would explain why they are often hidden deep in interiors which can only be reached after much effort, and with a journey using artificial light. It would account for why some were positioned to be viewed by quite large numbers of people and some by only one at a time. It would also explain the careful combination and composition of pictures, creating spaces for the performance of different rites or engagement with different sorts of experience. If the cave walls were indeed seen as membranes between human and other worlds, then much of the patterning and location of the figures makes sense. They may have given expression to spirit forms thought to exist in the world beyond the membrane, or have been offerings to these beings. The debate over the shamanism model has drawn attention to the large number of images which are sketchily produced and hard to reach, suggesting that the act of creating an image was more important than the act of viewing it afterwards. It has also concentrated thought on the fact that caves with plenty of images resonate well, with the implication that singing or chanting was a part of the rites conducted in them.

Ultimately, however, the significance of most of the images in the caves, as upon mobile objects, must elude us. Randall White has pointed out that research among living tribes who have carried on a hunting and gathering life-style in the Arctic, such as the Aivilik of the Inuit people, has proved that accurate interpretation of their painted and carved representations depends on a comprehensive understanding of their belief system and environment. In the case of the European Palaeolithic, we can reconstruct the latter, but not the former; and there has been no hunter-gatherer people in modern times that has possessed a culture exactly like those of Old Stone Age Europe. The consistency with which similar images, locations and activities were reproduced there over twenty millennia argues for a very strong framework of beliefs, but one completely lost to us.[35] We can be more or less certain that people who left so many pictures and shapes on rocks and stone, bone, clay or antler objects would have decorated their own bodies, clothes, baskets and wooden possessions with many more: but all these are also lost to us. Since the 1990s experts have increasingly argued that grand schemes of explanation are not appropriate for Palaeolithic images, and that researchers should concentrate instead on asking why the making of them should have been meaningful to certain people at certain times in certain places; which induces a greater concentration on the setting and experience of particular sites.[36] An alternative but complementary approach is to recognize that they may have had multiple and diverse meanings, only some of which we may ever understand.[37]

In these discussions, images in human or near-human shape have often been given special prominence and divided according to gender. Among the female representations, particular attention has been paid to a group of about thirty-five statuettes, usually relatively small and portable, produced – as far as dating evidence for them exists – between 26,000 and 19,000 BC. They are fashioned in clay, ivory or stone, and all are footless, faceless, and wholly or mostly nude, with pronounced breasts, buttocks and/or abdomens, though some seem plump, some pregnant and some to have breasts and buttocks alone emphasized. They are found across Europe, though those from the western and central regions tend to lack an exact context, and those from Russia are found more often in groups and upon settlement sites, against interior walls or in pits. When they first began to be identified, in the nineteenth century, they were nicknamed 'Venuses' after the nude statues of the Roman goddess of love; and the label has stuck. They have been interpreted as images of goddesses, or of a goddess, or of spirits, as magical objects used in healing, fertility, funeral or contraceptive rites, as marriage tokens, and as ideals of female beauty, general symbols of womanhood or vehicles for female self-expression.[38] Female, or apparently female, figures are also carved on plaques of stone, or bones, or carved or painted on rock walls, and these representations are found on sites datable down to the end of the Palaeolithic. Occasionally these resemble the famous figurines, the best known of which is the 'Venus of Laussel', one of three female forms holding objects, carved into a French rock shelter. Another celebrated set of female images is the pair carved upon the entrance to the cave of La Madeleine in the Aveyron Valley of central France. Each is large, naked and reclining, with the head only partially and sketchily indicated but the pubic triangle deeply etched. One has a bison drawn below her, and the other a horse. The Abri du Roc aux Sorciers, the 'overhanging part of the Magicians' Rock', also in central France, is etched with the loins, bellies and legs of three naked females standing above a bison, their genitalia again clearly marked.[39]

Since the European Palaeolithic first began to be studied, it has been obvious both that human figures in general are much rarer in its carvings and paintings than those of animals, and that among the small minority of human representations females are more common than males. The iconic masculine images on which attention has been concentrated are all on cave walls, apparently dancing, and either dressed up as animals or part animal themselves. Three of the four most famous are found in a single cavern, Trois Frères, the Cave of the Three Brothers, in the French Pyrenees. One has a bison's head, forelegs and body and human hind legs, and seems to dance and play a musical instrument in the middle of a herd of bison: though it may have had no connection with the latter, and the instrument may be a cloud of steam from its nose, or the manifestation of a spirit form. A second has the horned head of some similar animal. The third is the single most famous male figure from the whole of the Palaeolithic, nicknamed 'the Sorcerer' and known generally from the drawing made of it by Henri Breuil, the greatest expert in Palaeolithic cave pictures in the early twentieth century. He portrayed it as having the head of a stag, the eyes of an owl or cat, a long beard, the body of a horse or deer, a deer's ears, the legs of a man, the tail of a horse or wolf, animal forepaws, and the genitals of a male feline. In the cave of Le Gabillou in the Dordogne is the fourth famous image, of a being with a male human body and the head of a bison or bull. Scholars have interpreted these beings as different gods, a single god, spirits, monsters, priests, jesters, witch doctors or shamans, or hunters disguised as animals to deceive their prey.[40]

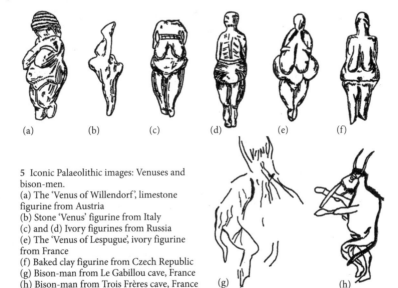

5 Iconic Palaeolithic images: Venuses and bison-men.
(a) The 'Venus of Willendorf', limestone figurine from Austria
(b) Stone 'Venus' figurine from Italy
(c) and (d) Ivory figurines from Russia
(e) The 'Venus of Lespugue', ivory figurine from France
(f) Baked clay figurine from Czech Republic
(g) Bison-man from Le Gabillou cave, France
(h) Bison-man from Trois Frères cave, France

6 Iconic Palaeolithic images: The 'Sorcerer' of Trois Frères.
The illustration (a) is the famous one by the Abbé Breuil (redrawn after R. Bégouën and
H. Breuil), while (b) shows the features visible from the floor of the cave. The contrast could
be regarded simply as one between painted and carved features, the latter being visible only at
close quarters and so to the artist: but there seems to be no general agreement upon exactly
how many of the body parts drawn by Breuil are actually present.

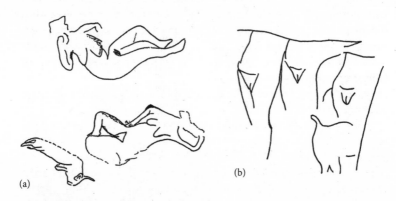

7 Iconic Palaeolithic images: carvings of females.
(a) Reclining figures from the cave of La Madeleine.
(b) The three from L'Abris du Roc aux Sorciers, who were giantesses if the bison below was
associated with them: but was it?

Since the 1990s, it has become increasingly obvious that the emphasis on these celebrated images may be misleading, and that the human form in Palaeolithic images needs to be approached from other perspectives. In part this shift has been propelled by the first systematic attempts to catalogue the representations of human-like figures, which have brought a realization of the impossibility of such a task. One problem in attempting it has already been stressed: the difficulty of distinguishing very ancient carvings from natural lines in a rock or bone. This has some interesting implications for the manner in which the human-made images were produced. To take one of the most famous examples, the 'Sorcerer' of Trois Frères is partly painted and partly carved, and the carved portions are invisible from the cave floor, the position from which anybody entering the cave would be likely to view it. Other people would therefore effectively be seeing a different image from that represented by the person who made it; a point which drives home the message that Palaeolithic caves cannot be equated to modern art galleries and that the act of making a picture may have been the really important rite associated with it. More worrying is that there seems to be no general agreement on how many of the features of the figure shown in the famous drawing by the Abbé Breuil are actually present in the original.[41] Another difference between Palaeolithic compositions and what Europeans have historically called art is superimposition: very often different pictures were made one on top of another until it is now both very hard to tell which line belongs to which figure and how much particular images in the whole mix were ever related to each other. Even when superimposition did not take place, the portrait is rarely a clear and simple one. Ann Sieveking examined engravings upon pieces of stone, bone and antler made in Europe between 30,000 and 8,000 BC, and found that most of the human or animal figures had additional lines added to them, often very numerous. The significance of these is unknown: to the modern eye they have no obvious purpose.[42]

Where there is absolute confidence in the shape and form of what is being represented, complete disagreement can remain as to the meaning. A classic case here would be that of the triangular designs at Creswell mentioned above, common among Palaeolithic rock images, which were interpreted by Breuil as symbols of female genitalia and by others – most notably of late, Steven Mithen – as animal footprints, while yet others simply declare them impossible to interpret. The same sort of basic shape occurs in many different forms, square, round, broken and oval. If they were indeed vulvae, then the number of references to the human female form on Palaeolithic sites would be greatly multiplied; but nobody can be sure.[43] Another such case arising at Creswell, also mentioned above, is the impossibility of deciding whether certain wavy figures are dancing women or waterbirds: similar shapes are known from different regions of the Continent, and the same argument takes place over them in each location.[44] One researcher into native Australian rock paintings, N. W. G. Mackintosh, identified twenty-two different animal images in them. In this case, however, he was later able to ask a native belonging to the culture that made the pictures what they meant, and discovered that he had been wrong about fifteen of the animals and only partly right about the rest.[45]

What is more significant is the growing realization that while much of this kind of ambiguity is a product of our own ignorance, much is also inherent in the imagery. Modern Western culture has long drawn a sharp distinction between human and animal, and female and male but, in pictures at least, the Palaeolithic did not. Furthermore, modern Westerners like to classify things by type, in a way that more traditional peoples do not: Jean Clottes has pointed out that those who have hunted the bison in recent centuries have not viewed it as a single category of animal but as one with many attributes.[46] This way of looking at the world made it easier for Palaeolithic people to blur the boundaries between species as well as making the nature of a species itself multi-faceted: fantastic beasts, which mix the attributes of actual animals, are well represented in their imagery. The cave of Trois Frères alone has deer-birds, bear-wolves and bear-bison, so it is hardly surprising that it should also have beast-men (if indeed the bison-headed human shape is in fact male).[47] There now seems to be a consensus among experts that no effective criteria exist for distinguishing human and animal figures in Palaeolithic imagery.[48] Similarly, the traditional scholarly habit of dividing the apparently human figures of the period into female and male misses the point that such a division was not seemingly important to the people who fashioned them. Ann Sieveking and Rosemary Powers have made surveys of these figures, the former on the engraved plaquettes and the latter in all media. Their findings agree that apparently female forms are more numerous than apparent males, but that the majority cannot be assigned to either sex. Most are slim, and only about half of the female examples possess the accentuated breasts, hips or stomachs of the 'Venuses'.[49] Human figures are usually very stylized, lacking hands and feet and with faces hardly indicated; most are incomplete.[50]

It is helpful in this context to take another look at the 'Venus' figurines themselves. Doubt hangs over the number that can be accepted as authentic pieces of Palaeolithic craft, as opposed to the products of modern forgers: some authorities would consider that only those from central and eastern Europe, which have precise find-spots, should be regarded as certainly prehistoric.[51] At the opening of the twenty-first century, a fresh look was taken at those with an apparent secure context by three scholars who pointed out that the obviously female figurines had been overemphasized at the expense of others from the same sites. Taken together, the whole collection from each site was remarkable for its number of hermaphrodites, or beings not fully human or clearly part-animal. They seemed to illustrate not only different types of being but relations between beings; a world in which the human form, or at least the female one, could shift from one kind of reality to another.[52] At Dolní Věstonice in the Czech Republic, a total of fifteen clay human figurines were found, of which eight were female, two male and five of neutral gender, among a much larger number of clay animals. One of the female statuettes was a classic example of the 'Venus' kind. The figurines, human and animal, had been deliberately blown to pieces by being placed wet in a hearth or kiln, and the 'Venus' one appeared to have been stabbed: it was apparently for this act of ritual destruction that all had been made.[53] Once again, the figures seem to be associated with transformation, rather than with static identities. Now that modern Western culture is itself starting to abandon rigid gender divisions and polarities, to challenge its customary sharp distinction between animal and human, and to admit to fluidity in the making and remaking of individual identity, it is beginning to perceive the same patterns in the creations of the Palaeolithic.

A few further observations can be made. The first is the great importance that the people of the period attached, in ritual contexts, to the colour red. It is, of course, that of the vital fluid of life, which is also, in menstruation, the sign of human fertility. The costume of the Red Lady has already been noted, and other burials from the European Old Stone Age were given the same hue, either by sprinkling or painting with red ochre or likewise by being interred in red clothing. Some figurines were coated in that colour, and it features commonly in paintings on rocks. The attribution of a special significance to it is a human trait that long predates our species, as red pigments are found on sites used by human-like

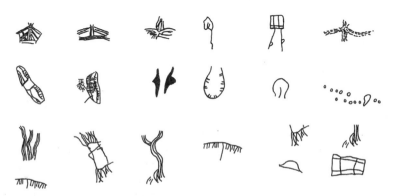

8 Less familiar Palaeolithic images: abstract forms
No one theory of interpretation has as yet comprehended all of the symbols shown here, which form less than a third of the stock abstract repertoire of Palaeolithic Europeans.

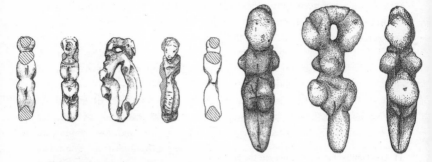

9 Less familiar Palaeolithic images: figurines
Carved figures found at the Balzi Rossi caves in Italy with a 'Venus' statuette. Neglected in
comparison to the 'Venus', they seem to show the human body, perhaps specifically the
female body, undergoing a series of transformations. Redrawn after M. Mussi *et al.*

10 Less familiar Palaeolithic images: fantasy and reality?
The eight forms on the left, are typical representations of human or quasi-human figures
made in the Palaeolithic – rarely complete, rarely more than sketches, and moving easily
between human and animal shapes. On the right, engraved on a stone plaque in France, and
redrawn here after J. Airvaux and L. Pradel, a wholly realistic human face, showing that it was
quite possible to produce both types at the same time.

beings in Africa a million years ago, and in Neanderthal burials: in this as in
other respects *Homo sapiens* greatly multiplied and intensified older behavioural
patterns. Red ochre certainly had several practical virtues which may have reinforced, or at times supplanted a ritual one, including treating and colouring
animal skins, decorating the human body, cleaning wounds, repelling insects,
protecting skin against sunburn or frostbite, and disguising bodily odours, both
of the living and of decomposing corpses. How far the presence of the colour in

11 Less familiar Palaeolithic images: the problem of the extra lines
Limestone block from France with an engraving of two apparently male figures. It is accompanied by a large number of the mysterious, and seemingly superfluous, swirling additional lines so common in Old Stone Age pictures. Redrawn after L. Pales.

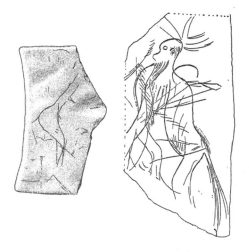

12 Less familiar Palaeolithic images: female and male?
The figure on the left, carved on the bottom of a stone lamp found in France, is typical of the shapes usually interpreted as human or humanoid females: but were they? On the right, also French, a schist plaque. This may show a bearded man wearing a plumed headdress and horse's tail. He could, however, also be a god, or a beast-man, while the usual superimposition of lines means that plumes, tail and beard could all actually belong to another figure. Redrawn after H. Breuil.

apparently ritual contexts is the result of a projection of these attributes, and how much it relates to the deeper, vital associations mentioned above, is probably impossible to tell, and almost certainly varied from case to case.[54]

There may yet be a way of getting inside the Palaeolithic religious mindset, which has hitherto not really been systematically attempted: to compare the cosmologies and mythologies of native peoples in Siberia and the Americas, recorded as close to first contact with Europeans as possible. If these show certain abiding common features, among ethnic groups too far from the straits dividing the continents for direct contact and diffusion of ideas to be a likely explanation, then it is possible that we are looking at concepts carried from the Old World to the New during the great human migrations of the Old Stone Age. So far only a little pioneering work has been done in this area.[55] Anthropology has been of help in establishing that hunter-gatherers in general make no firm distinctions between humans and other animals, give great importance to animal spirits and spirits that control animals, and treat the making of pictures as a revelation of the workings of nature, an extension of ecology and subsistence rather than an activity separate from lived experience.[56] All this is of relevance in providing a context for the mindset of Palaeolithic Europeans, even if it cannot explain the specific images and forms which they have left behind.

The Mesolithic

Until quite recently, the end of the last Ice Age was portrayed as a smooth and gradual process, in which temperatures, vegetation and sea levels all rose together millennium by millennium. Towards the end of the twentieth century, new scientific processes – the analysis of pollen and that of ice samples extracted from the polar ice sheets – provided better evidence against which to test this supposition. In addition, moreover, a powerful emotional impetus to do so was provided by the recognition of increasingly dramatic and disturbing climate change in the present, creating a new interest in it during the past. The result was a cascade of information which revealed how erratic and disruptive a process the warming of Europe had been. Between 13,000 and 12,500 BC, summer temperatures in north-western Europe doubled, to a point that was, as has been said, similar to or slightly higher than they are today. By 12,000, tree cover was advancing into northern Europe at the rate of about a mile per year, and birch forest covered much of what was to be England. Around 11,000, temperatures fell again, almost halving in perhaps as little as fifty years, so that the trees died and arctic conditions returned to what is now Britain for more than a millennium. From about 9500 the warming resumed, and by 8000 the trees had begun to return: within two thousand years they had covered much of what would be Britain in forests of oak, lime, hazel, elm and alder, though areas of open grassland survived. Sea levels also rose as the ice caps melted, Ireland breaking away in about 7500 BC. Between then and 6200 the spreading Atlantic finally turned Britain into an island and drowned 'Doggerland', which had perhaps been the richest hunting ground in Europe. This influx of cold water brought down temperatures again, to those of present-day southern Scandinavia, for about four centuries. After that, the warming resumed until around 4000 BC Britain enjoyed something like a modern north Mediterranean climate.[57]

Inevitably, such a colossal alteration in environment meant an equivalent change in human lifestyles, great enough for archaeologists to label the coming of forests to north-western Europe as the opening of a new era of prehistory: the five millennia which have been generally known since the 1930s as the Mesolithic or Middle Stone Age. The vast herds of grazing animals vanished with the steppes, and mammoth, bison, reindeer and horse became extinct in Britain. Red and roe deer, wild cattle, elk and wild boar either adapted to the woodlands or came north with them, but were harder to see among the trees than the wildlife of the plains had been. Lynxes, bears, red foxes and wolves survived as competing predators. Plant food – nuts, fruit, fungi, seeds, seaweeds, cresses and tubers – became much more important to diet, and the spreading forests and waters meant that much human occupation was relocated to the margins of lakes, rivers and the sea. This in turn made fish and shellfish a further major source of food, along with waterfowl. People accordingly laid a new emphasis on woodworking tools, archery and artefacts made of wood and plant fibres, domesticated the dog and adapted flint-working to create smaller blades. By the seventh millennium BC they seem to have acquired the ability to burn areas of forest in order to create clearings in which game animals could graze. By the fifth, some communities in what is now central southern England may have settled down, ceasing to move around even seasonally. The elk and lynx apparently disappeared from Britain by 4000 BC, and may have been hunted to extinction. The new climate and terrain seemingly suited humans well enough, because they supported a much larger population: one estimate is that the inhabitants of Britain multiplied by a number between three and five between 9000 and 5000 BC, to somewhere between two and a half and five and a half thousand. All the technological and cultural innovations were developments of existing Palaeolithic skills and practices rather than dramatic breaks with the past.[58]

In pictorial expression, however, the break was dramatic: the Palaeolithic enthusiasm for carving and painting figures, which had flourished for 20,000 years, completely disappeared. Indeed, until the 1990s the British Mesolithic was commonly treated as almost barren of evidence for ritual behaviour. The single site left from it of which the world had heard was Star Carr, in eastern Yorkshire, excavated by Grahame Clark between 1949 and 1951. It had been a lakeside hunting camp during two different periods in the early ninth millennium, for the pursuit of forest animals and waterfowl, and particular interest was generated by the discovery here of twenty-one skull frontlets of red deer with antlers attached. They had been adapted to be worn on human heads, masking the face, and Clark proposed that they had been the costume of priests or shamans: there is a famous seventeenth-century drawing of a Siberian shaman wearing just such a headdress. On the other hand, he admitted that they could also have been disguises used by hunters of the deer; and those two possibilities have been cited, without resolution, ever since.[59]

From the 1990s, new evidence began to be assembled, and old data reassessed, for ceremonial activities. It began to be appreciated that the Palaeolithic custom of cave burial had been continued and amplified during the British Mesolithic, between the years 9000 and 5000 BC, and indeed at some of the same sites: Gough's Cave was reused, as were other Mendip caverns which had yielded Old Stone Age material such as Aveline's Hole and Badger's Hole, and also Kent's Cavern in Devon. The body found in Gough's Cave, nicknamed Cheddar Man, achieved celebrity in the 1990s when DNA from him was found to match that of two pupils and a teacher in the local school, proving the length of some British bloodlines; but he was dug up so long ago and so carelessly that there is no absolute certainty that he was deliberately buried. Aveline's Hole, in a smaller gorge on the opposite side of the Mendip Hills, seems to have been a cemetery, for at least fifty bodies were found there in 1797, sealed by calcium dripping from the limestone ceiling and walls. Most were removed without being properly recorded, but at least thirty-one more were excavated there between 1914 and 1924, some with grave goods such as seashells, animal teeth and fossils. These might have been decorations for clothing, as they were drilled or notched for fastenings, and further continuity with the Old Stone Age was provided by a deer bone with marks notched upon the edge, like those at Gough's Cave, and red staining on a few skeletons. In 2003 two rows of engraved diagonal crosses were found in the cave, which were thought possibly to be Mesolithic, and so a continuation of the older tradition of abstract carvings.

The Aveline's Hole burials have now been dated to between 8400 and 8200 BC, making them the largest assemblage of Mesolithic human remains in Britain and one of the most important in Europe; and, indeed, Britain's oldest cemetery. Further analyses of the finds show that the people concerned had hunted red deer, wild boar, wolf, lynx and bear, amid a landscape of birch and pine woodland with open stretches of grass.[60] The markings, however, cannot be dated and could well be overlapping V-signs, a motif well known from the Tudor and Stuart periods and believed to give protective power, and known from other Mendip caves: more will be heard of it later in this book. The problem with this interpretation is that there is no evidence that the cave was open between the Middle Stone Age and the eighteenth century; but here we start to travel in circles, because if the marks are of early modern style, then this in itself would be possible evidence that people had entered the cavern at that time. In 2005, in another of the many caverns of Cheddar Gorge, the Long Hole, more putative Mesolithic art was identified consisting of three engraved rectilinear designs, all apparently very old. They, might, however, be of any date before the last few hundred years, and the site has yielded no Middle Stone Age finds.[61] Seven Welsh caves have produced Mesolithic remains, and at Rhuddlan in north-east Wales six pebbles were found incised with lines making patterns that may be geometric (or may be random); another echo of the past, recalling the marked bone from Kendrick's Cave. Twelve of the fourteen sites from which Mesolithic human bones have been recovered in Britain are caves, all but one of which had been used in the Old Stone Age: they were apparently still regarded as places of natural power and ancestral mythology. It is possible that the newly powerful and intrusive medium of water was also used for burial at this time: human bones from the period have been found in a former watercourse in the Trent Valley and in Norfolk's River Yare, but they seem to be the only securely dated example of their kind.[62]

Further interest has recently been provoked by the analysis of mounds of food waste – middens – found on the Scottish mainland and islands. They could be huge: one at Morton, in Fife, was made up of 10,000 shells. Three on the island of Oronsay, in the Hebrides, were several yards or metres high and contained human bones, especially from the hands and feet. One purpose of the mounds may have been to lay out dead bodies so that they could be picked clean by animals before burial: it is notable that most of the skeletons found in the caves were disarticulated and incomplete. Chantal Conneller has proposed that this may have been one aspect of living in a hunting society: just as humans cut up animals for food, so after death humans themselves were left to wildlife to be taken apart in turn. In one sense, the middens were simply rubbish dumps, but they were carefully placed out of reach of storms and tides and used over many seasons. As such, they may have been used to mark territory, or at least a sense of group continuity and belonging in the landscape, and so functioned, in effect, as monuments.[63] If so, they were not the only monumental structures from the period. In 1966 a new visitors' car park was built next to Stonehenge, and in the process three large holes were discovered in an irregular line, which had held pinewood posts two and a half feet (0.6 to 0.8 metres) thick. In 1988–9 the car park was extended, and a large pit, dug by humans, found near the post holes. In the 1990s all of these were securely dated to between 8500 and 7500 BC. If they were all erected at once, the posts may have been intended to line up with a large tree, perhaps regarded as sacred, of which the root-pit remains; it is also likely that the place was made special in human eyes by the presence of lines of grooves dug in the chalk rock by glaciers during a preceding Ice Age, aligned on the midsummer sunrise. The natural tendency has been to conclude that the posts were equivalents to Native American totem poles, and probably carved and painted in the same manner: they have no apparent practical function. A very similar pair of posts, from the earlier eighth millennium, stood at another spectacular Neolithic site, the enclosure at Hambledon Hill in Dorset: like those at Stonehenge, they commanded a wide view and would have been visible from some distance. It is highly significant that the presence of these great posts was only detected because they were on the sites of impressive later monuments, raising the question of how many more are as yet undiscovered.[64]

In recent years pits containing Mesolithic deposits have been identified up and down Britain, from Dorset to northern Scotland. Most impressive are the sixteen in Warren Field at Crathes, up the Dee Valley from Aberdeen. They were dug in an irregular line in two phases between about 8120 and 6690 BC, and contained charcoal-rich material, perhaps left by people fishing for salmon and trout in the Dee. At Down Farm on the Cranborne Chase chalklands of Dorset, now home of the farmer archaeologist Martin Green, a deep natural hollow was opened in the fifth millennium and given deposits of animal bones for centuries after.[65] As Richard Chatterton has pointed out, although the contents of Mesolithic pits can look like mere refuse, it would have been far easier to dispose of that by dumping it in the forest. The opening of pits and hollows not only required more effort but was a purposeful, ritualized act suggesting greater respect for the material buried and also associations with fertilization and regeneration.[66] Moreover, an increasing number of Mesolithic wooden structures has been identified in Scotland, the Isle of Man and northern England. Some were substantial, that at Howick in the Scottish Borders consisting of a roughly circular foundation cut into the ground about 19.7 feet (6 metres) across, with timber posts erected inside. It was first made around 7800 BC and then rebuilt or mended repeatedly for up to two hundred years. All may have been dwelling places – Britain's earliest houses – but they may have been ceremonial buildings as well or instead: another form of monument.[67] On the whole, the cave burials tend to come from earlier in the Mesolithic, and the pits, posts and buildings from later, but there is a large overlap between them.

Joshua Pollard and Richard Chatterton have gone further, to suggest that accumulations of Mesolithic deposits in watery places, which had hitherto been interpreted as mere disposal of rubbish, had in fact been ritually made. They point in particular to accumulations of animal bones put into water at various sites across England and Wales; above all in the lake at Star Carr, where they were accompanied by 191 barbed antler points, made as hunting weapons and many unbroken. The animals, they suggested, had been put into the lake after butchery, as a sign of respect to protect their bodies from scavengers and perhaps as a rite of regeneration. The points, by the same logic, would have been part of this ceremony of renewal, and perhaps in addition were subject to a prohibition against their further use once they had taken life.[68] This idea was developed into a proposal that the wooden platform on the lakeside, which had

hitherto been regarded as a jetty, might have been a walkway for putting offerings into the water.[69] As noted, until 1990 it seemed that there was almost no
evidence for ritual activity in the British Mesolithic: suddenly vestiges of such
activity seemed to be everywhere, simply because archaeologists were now
looking for it strenuously. Not everybody, however, was prepared to go that far:
in 2009 Paul Mellars objected that the items recovered from the lake could
indeed have been casually discarded there.[70] Likewise, in 2007 Graeme Warren
wondered whether the importance of the Scottish middens might have been
overstated, as few of them are large and we do not know how they would have
looked in the prehistoric landscape; and if human bone was found in them, so
it has been on Mesolithic sites in general.[71]

The people of the period must have had a vivid repertoire of myth and religious belief connected to their landscape and its past. As Vicki Cummings has
suggested, inherited stories almost certainly referred to, and explained in
mythological terms, the dramatic changes in terrain at the end of the Ice Age,
while the forests among which people dwelt must have made trees prominent
beings in their spirituality.[72] Spirits of water would presumably also have been
important to them. It can be said too that by the end of the Mesolithic humans
in Britain were still engaging with their environment in such a manner as to
leave the smallest possible lasting evidence of their presence in it. None the
less, they had already made a number of major conceptual innovations, in
keeping with our species's unique capacity for symbolic action, of which religious activity is one dimension. Immediately after arriving in what was to be
Britain, they had begun to hold funeral ceremonies for their dead and to desig-
nate certain natural places as spiritually numinous – consecrated – and so to be
set apart from everyday activities and dedicated to ritual. In some of these they
had left a permanent sign of those rites, in the form of carved figures and
designs that could be viewed ever after by any person capable of recognizing
them. During the Mesolithic they had started to impose their own structures
on the landscape in general, in the form of buildings, posts and mounds, which
would leave a testimonial to their presence even when the builders had
wandered on or died out. The wooden structures would decay away, but the
mounds remain as permanent features. All the ceremonial activities and monuments that would follow during the next six millennia were already present in
embryo, even though their range and scale were as yet modest.

2

THE EARLIER NEOLITHIC
A CRAZE FOR MONUMENTS

DURING THE CENTURIES around 4000 BC, Britain passed into the New Stone Age, or Neolithic. As a concept, this is a Victorian creation. The basic modern division of European prehistory, based on the nature of tools, was worked out in Denmark in the early nineteenth century, as one of successive Stone, Bronze and Iron Ages. It was Sir John Lubbock, one of the founders of the modern British discipline of archaeology, who divided the Stone Age for the first time, into Old and New, in 1865 (the Middle Stone Age did not push in between for another seventy years).[1] The idea of a Neolithic has lasted because it makes such good sense, describing as it does the adoption of a package of new activities which between them radically changed human life. By the 1950s this was agreed to consist of the cultivation and harvesting of crops (types of wheat, barley and pulses); the keeping of livestock (cattle, pigs and sheep); the making of pottery; the production of polished stone tools; deep mining; and the building of large structures of earth, wood and stone. All of these developments first appeared in the Near East, and spread slowly westwards across Europe. Together, they meant that human beings were no longer only living upon and off the land, but reshaping and redeveloping it as well: they marked the shift from a hunting and gathering lifestyle to a farming one. They also, unsurprisingly, produced some radical changes in ritual behaviour.

Archaeologists at present divide the period in two different ways. One is into an Early (4000–3300 BC), Middle (3300–2900 BC) and Late (2900–2400 BC) Neolithic, the other more simply into Early (4000–3000 BC) and Late (3000–2200 BC).[2] The proponents of each seem to regard it as normative. Both have relevance to the subject of this book, but the second a greater one, the reasons for which should become obvious in the course of the next two chapters.

The Coming of the Neolithic

No period of British history or prehistory has been so dramatically recon-
figured than the New Stone Age. In the mid twentieth century it was thought
to have lasted for a few hundred years, and to have commenced after fully
developed urban civilizations had arisen in Egypt and Mesopotamia, relegating
Britain to the status of a barbarous frontier. During the 1970s, improvements
in dating techniques (based on the analysis of radioactive carbon in ancient
deposits) revealed that it lasted about two thousand years, and that its monuments rank among the most impressive achievements of humanity at that
period. The same developments in dating have shown that the spread of the
Neolithic lifestyle across the European Continent was a process of relatively
brief and rapid spurts of expansion, followed by lengthy periods of consolida-
tion. In the Near East this lifestyle had been formed by around 9000 BC, but it
took over three millennia to reach the centre of Europe. Between 5500 and
5100 BC it spread from the Balkans to what is now eastern France, but there it
stuck for almost a thousand years, before appearing all over western France,
the British Isles and the Baltic region in the couple of centuries on either side
of 4000 BC.[3] Furthermore, it has recently been agreed that there was in fact no
homogeneous Neolithic 'package' which people adopted in its entirety.[4] Rather,
different communities selectively adopted aspects of the new lifestyle which
appealed most to them, resulting in a range of different cultural experiences.
Across the Continent, this produced spectacular variations: for example, on
the eastern extremity of Europe, between the Carpathian Mountains and the
River Dnieper, towns appeared, with populations of up to 10,000 people and
laid-out streets, while between Hungary and France villages of small family
houses were common; but neither form of settlement was found in the north-
west of Europe, including Britain.[5]

Smaller, but still very significant, differences were found within the British
archipelago itself. The 'Celtic Tiger' boom in the Irish economy in the years
around AD 2000 resulted in a large amount of developer-led excavation, which
produced a sudden new flood of information on the Neolithic of Ireland. It was
revealed to have been characterized, from the beginning, by widespread
building of houses, cultivation of cereal crops and making of fields. The same
pattern seems true of the Western and Northern Isles of Scotland. By contrast,
across most of Britain there is comparatively little evidence of either dwellings
or cereals, and instead the economy seems to have come to depend mainly on
herding, especially of cattle, by people with a nomadic or semi-nomadic way of
life. The amount of grain found is so small that it has been suggested that
consumption of it was reserved for ceremonial occasions; it may even have
been brewed into ale.[6] Dramatic evidence of a highly mobile Early Neolithic

British lifestyle was provided in 2000 by analysis of the remains of a woman and three children who had been buried in a pit in the chalk hills of Dorset during the late fourth millennium. Lead and strontium isotopes, accessible by means of new technology, proved that all of them had lived at some point in a non-chalkland environment, while the adult had grown up in the Mendip Hills, at least 50 miles (80 kilometres) away.[7] Isotope analysis led to a yet more remarkable result around the same time, when it was revealed that the Neolithic British seemed to have consumed virtually no marine food, in contrast to those of the Mesolithic. This result seemed not to match the material evidence from the Scottish islands, and coastal areas of western Britain, where fish bones and seashells are often found on sites from the period. Some commentators therefore questioned its accuracy; but it has been accepted, provisionally, as true for most areas, and prompted speculation as to the reason. It has been suggested that a herding lifestyle may have made fishing for and gathering seafood difficult, or else that some kind of religious taboo was imposed on its consumption, perhaps (for example) because the sea had become associated with the dead. Whatever the answer, it is a powerful indication that the transition to the Neolithic brought considerable disruption of traditional world views.[8]

If that transition in Britain was both rapid and dramatic, this begs the question of how it was accomplished. For most of the twentieth century a simple and confident answer was applied: that the Neolithic was brought by colonists from abroad. This was a Victorian idea, expressed most fully and influentially by Sir William Boyd Dawkins in 1880: that the Palaeolithic inhabitants of Britain had been of the same race as the modern Inuit or Eskimo, whose lifestyle they had shared and who were driven north into the Arctic by warlike newcomers who had introduced the Neolithic lifestyle. These he pronounced to have been destroyed in turn by later, more technologically advanced, invaders, leaving the Basques as their only modern descendants in Europe. They had therefore been, he declared, a small dark people even as the Basques were today.[9] This preoccupation with racial differences, and the superiority of some races over others, was a hallmark of late Victorian thought, and its source of inspiration is obvious: the spread of Europeans in general, and the English-speaking peoples in particular, over vast expanses of North America, Australia and New Zealand during the nineteenth century, subduing and sometimes exterminating the native inhabitants. The same inspiration is equally obvious in a much later popular work on British prehistory, by Jacquetta Hawkes published in 1945, which declared that, without this Neolithic invasion, the Mesolithic inhabitants of Britain might well have indefinitely 'remained as primitive as those of North America, Africa or the Pacific at the time of their discovery by Europeans'.[10] The heavyweight scholarly texts on Neolithic Britain that appeared in the mid twentieth century carried the same message in more detailed and forensic terms, using local differences in Neolithic culture to plot the arrival of separate groups of colonists from France and the Netherlands, most having travelled from the more civilized Mediterranean and brought some of its inventions. As late as 1954, the greatest contemporary British expert on the Neolithic, Stuart Piggott, could portray the island as being settled piecemeal, by 'intrusive agricultural colonies established in areas uninhabited, or at most populated by a small number of hunter-fisher groups', like so much of the land occupied by modern British colonists.[11]

In the course of the late twentieth century, this portrait disintegrated, as the British Empire disappeared, emigration to colonies came to an end, and the United Kingdom turned instead into a multi-racial state belonging to the European Union. The notion that the Neolithic British had been similar to Basques was never based on good evidence, and there remains no means whatever of judging the colour of their complexions. As for their size, their skeletal remains had always suggested that they were only slightly shorter than present-day people (about the same height, indeed, as most of the British until the nineteenth century), and of about the same build.[12] Less securely based was the new orthodoxy, dominant at the end of the twentieth century, that the Neolithic lifestyle had in the main been adopted by the Mesolithic natives, who chose to take on new ideas and techniques from abroad.[13] It was admitted that there must have been some influx of newcomers, if only because the new techniques of farming needed to be taught by experts. Moreover, none of the domestic breeds of cattle and sheep could have come from wild species in Europe, let alone Britain: they had all descended from Near Eastern strains, and been driven across the Continent. Indeed, it might be objected that the new orthodoxy was as much rooted in contemporary cultural experience and assumption as the old: in the Britain of the decades around AD 2000, an existing population learned new and imported technologies just as their Neolithic forebears were now presumed to have done. Another recently developed scientific technique did, however, weigh in upon the side of this idea: that of genetics, using a technique developed at Oxford University to recover DNA from ancient bones. Different projects of analysis converged to suggest that, all over Europe, the majority of the female bloodlines of the modern population derived from women who had lived in the Continent before the Neolithic began. The male lines pointed to a much more significant arrival of foreigners from the Near East as part of the adoption of farming, but in Western Europe that proportion was less than a third. The British evidence seems to testify to a complex addition of new female and male genes in the Neolithic, amounting to 10 to 30 per cent of the modern population, with southern England having the highest levels and the rest of Britain much lower.[14] By 2006 one author on genetics, Robin McKie, could declare that 'farming was an idea, not a people'.[15]

Britain seemed always to have done what it was doing at the beginning of the twenty-first century: absorbed immigrants who brought useful ideas and skills and could be granted work permits and then residency.

Actually, things are not that simple, because the genetic record cannot tell us how that 10 to 30 per cent of Neolithic newcomers arrived in any district: as traders, marital partners, preachers, instructors, welcome new neighbours, or conquerors. There is a considerable difference between those roles. Not a single archaeological site has yet yielded good evidence for this problem, and by the end of the first decade of the new century two of the most prominent experts on Neolithic Britain, Richard Bradley and Timothy Darvill, had acknowledged that no variant of the two basic models of explanation – that the new lifestyle was adopted by natives or brought by new settlers – fitted the data really well.[16] In 2010 a study of apparent population densities concluded that the seeming growth in the number of inhabitants of Britain between 4100 and 3400 BC was too sudden and dramatic to be accounted for except in terms of large-scale migration from the Continent.[17] It is, however, very hard to compare shifting and mobile populations, and to distinguish an increase in people from an increase in the activities of those people; and to succeed in both would still leave open the question of the relationship between newcomers and existing inhabitants. In 2011 a comprehensive comparison of more than 1,500 statistically modelled dates for Early Neolithic sites in Britain and Ireland yielded the conclusion that the Neolithic lifestyle had arrived there just before 4000 BC, probably in the Thames Estuary. By 3900, aspects of it could be found all over south-eastern Britain, and within another hundred years they had covered much of the rest of the island, save for the extreme west and north. By 3700 the lifestyle had more or less spread across the archipelago.[18] This would suggest that farming had originally been brought from Europe by colonists who arrived in the Thames, and that it had swiftly been adopted by the natives: but none of this is securely proved by the better dating. All told, the problem of how the Neolithic arrived in Britain does not seem to have been solved at the time of writing; and with that admission, it must be acknowledged, any chance of reconstructing the manner in which attitudes to the cosmos were altered by the change has been immediately much diminished.

Thinking Monumentally

One aspect of the classic Neolithic lifestyle, as defined in the 1950s, was the erection of large human structures upon the land: for the first time in prehistoric Europe, people articulated their ideas about the world in great building works. The making of large monuments has not been confined to farming peoples – hunter-gatherers have raised them in Canada and Australia – and in this as in all other respects the European Neolithic was diverse and selective, the communities in the centre and south-east of the Continent investing much effort in domestic buildings but little in ceremonial structures.[19] Those of western Europe, however, coupled the adoption of farming with the creation of a completely unprecedented number, range and scale of ritual constructions, making a new and dramatic distinction between human and non-human elements in the landscape.

Christopher Tilley, an archaeologist who has thought even harder than most about how Neolithic people viewed their world, has highlighted the difference in attitude that the clearing of land for farming would have made. It revealed contours and profiles fully, in many cases for the first time in several millennia, and so perhaps inspired those who carried out the work to reconstruct the land itself for the first time, shaping it even as natural forces had done before.[20] Although much of Britain seems to have remained wooded in some measure throughout the fourth millennium, the Western Isles and the extreme north of Scotland were apparently denuded of trees by 3500 BC, while much of the eastern Dorset chalklands were open by the end of the millennium.[21] This did not mean that the land itself ceased to matter as a spiritual entity, or a mass of them. Natural marks in it – such as rock outcrops, pools and great trees – that had been important to nomadic hunter-gatherers, would have retained their sense of the special and powerful for people wandering with livestock or tilling fields nearby. Inevitably, much of this sense of significance is lost to archaeology. For example, the prominent hill of Caburn in the South Downs of Sussex was surrounded by activity in the New Stone Age, yet carefully avoided, its summit being covered by yew trees.[22] Caburn is now perhaps the most heavily excavated site in Britain, with no fewer than 170 trenches dug into it by archaeologists to date, so there can be little doubt of this avoidance, but why was it avoided? Were the trees a sacred grove, the main religious centre of the district? Or were the shadowy stands of yew regarded as spiritually menacing, a place to which entry was under taboo, or was the tough wood of this species of tree simply too much of a deterrent for stone axes when there was easier terrain all around? This draws attention to the wider problem that we do not know how far the coming of farming changed people's attitudes to the land. It is entirely possible that woodland, which had hitherto been an indivisible part of the human world and a vital economic resource, began to be seen as a separate and alien realm; but we cannot tell.[23]

What is abundantly evident from the archaeological record is that the natural world continued to play a very important part in spiritual life. Burials were still sometimes made in caves, as they had been since humans first appeared in that part of Europe, and often in the same areas as before, such as the Mendip Hills and North Wales. Caves were indeed used for this purpose more often in the Neolithic than previously, and continued to be employed for it during the whole of the remainder of British prehistory.[24] In the southern chalklands of England, and the Breckland heaths of Norfolk, the people of the New Stone Age found deposits of flint on the surface of the ground which were quite good enough for tool-making. Yet they took the difficult and dangerous course of sinking shafts to dig out the glossy, lustrous stone found deep underground. Its beauty was no doubt an attraction, but it may also have been thought to carry arcane power from having lain at such a depth: a possibility reinforced by the fact that the miners left deposits of pottery, tools and animal and human bones behind them, as if making offerings to the subterranean powers into whose realm they had intruded. It is possible that the flint thus obtained was thought to act as a transmitter between human and spirit realms. Miles Russell has noted that the mines tended to be sunk in places apart from any other human activity and which commanded impressive views: his suggestion is that they may have been settings for rites of passage as well as industrial activity.[25]

This sense of negotiation, by which humans gave presents to special places and received rewards from them in return, is even more evident in the industry of axe production. Axe heads of extraordinary stone, valued more for its aesthetic appearance than its practical utility, were prized objects in the period, often kept as sacred or artistic objects instead of being put to work. They were traded over long distances: those made of dolerite rock in Brittany are found from Gloucestershire to the Pyrenees, while those of the jadeite of the Western Alps were traded across an area from Ireland eastwards to the Danube and Elbe basins, and south into Italy and Spain.[26] Even those that were suited to heavy use as tools evidently had more than straightforwardly practical associations. Repeatedly in the British Isles, axes were made not from the most accessible deposits of a particular sort of stone but from those in dramatic natural settings, such as islands and mountains, which were apparently seen as charged with supernatural power.[27] One of the most important factories was in the Langdale Pikes, some of the highest peaks of the Cumbrian Mountains or Lake District. The climb to the site is still long and hard, and anyone who makes it enters a world where wisps of clouds drift along the surface of the land, and silence is usually absolute save for the voices of wind and of thunder, and where pieces of rock, broken by frost and storm, come loose from their places and roll crashing down the slopes of scree. It is a place where the majesty of stone is most evident, united with that of the heavens themselves.

Furthermore, even when detached from the locations which provided them, building materials and artefacts were themselves not necessarily seen as inanimate. Posts could remain imbued with the spirits of the trees that they had been, and to build with stone could be to fill structures with the spirits of those stones. Studies of traditional peoples in modern times have revealed that they commonly viewed stoves, weapons, tools and ornaments as living entities. They believed that material things create persons as much as persons make them, and that they likewise have life phases. Non-human bodies such as pots or houses were readily seen as the outward forms of non-human beings, which transform the social contexts in which they move and change their own meanings as those contexts are transformed. This makes the fashioning of a tool or a vessel very much akin to a magical act: a rite in itself, as well as the production of a functional object. It is notable, indeed, that in many periods of British prehistory before the Iron Age, pottery was buried on ceremonial rather than domestic sites. This has made one archaeologist, Ann Woodward, wonder if much, if not all, Neolithic ceramics were produced for special purposes such as ritual deposition or great feasts, instead of regular use. Traditional peoples also commonly lack the modern sense of the human self as indivisible, seeing it instead as penetrating and being penetrated by other beings in the world around.[28] It is possible, or perhaps even likely, that the Neolithic inhabitants of Britain shared this mindset, though this can probably never be proved.

All these reflections provide a framework for considering the way in which those inhabitants might have conceived the monuments they built with such zest; and before going on to consider what those structures were, it may be worthwhile to think a little further about the nature of monumentality in a prehistoric society. Richard Bradley set the pattern for this exercise in a series of studies which emphasized the novelties, rather than the continuities, which the adoption of farming has commonly brought to attitudes to the land. Farmers exploit nature rather than belonging to it, and enclose and own resources, rather than making paths through them and using them. To erect monuments can be one way of stamping that sense of ownership on the land's surface, reordering and dominating it. They ground space in an entirely new, deliberate and human, sense of construction; endure to become highly visible representatives of the past; and can change their meanings to succeeding generations, while remaining in the same form. They orchestrate human experience, operating sometimes as stages and sometimes as screens.[29] In the British Neolithic in particular, they are so common, while the remains of daily life are so few and transitory, that it is possible that the people of the period viewed life itself, to an unusual degree, as a brief journey to a different, and eternal existence.[30]

None the less, it is possible to exaggerate the role of Neolithic monuments both as a means of possessing and dominating land, and as permanent structures. Joshua Pollard has agreed that they were rarely an imposition of built forms on an empty landscape and were instead a new form of working with places which had already seen some kind of previous activity and so accumulated a sense of being special.[31] This observation would harmonize well with the pattern noted by many archaeologists, that Neolithic monuments were frequently reshaped, and sometimes apparently deliberately destroyed after construction, rather than left in an enduring form once built. Julian Thomas in particular has drawn attention to this as suggesting that it was the places concerned which were really important, and that the human works placed upon them were different ways of drawing attention to them and facilitating specific activities there.[32] This still allows for an interpretation of those activities in terms of the control and exploitation of a piece of land, but it also recognizes a strong possibility that the land concerned was regarded as powerful in itself and as an active agent in human affairs. The pattern of construction and reconstruction, moreover, invites a different form of reflection: that the act of making a Neolithic monument may have been the vital activity in itself, a prolonged ritual of tremendous importance for religious and social life rather than simply a process aimed at an end result: a structure which would stand as witness to its makers and their beliefs.

Now that these preliminary considerations have been made, it is time to survey what is presently known and thought about the kind of monuments which the people of Britain during the fourth millennium actually erected.

The Tomb-Shrines: General Reflections

One type of construction in particular defines the Early Neolithic of Western Europe. It consists of a chamber of large stones ('megaliths'), usually formed of uprights holding up one or more big rocks acting as a covering, and usually covered or supported by a mound or cairn. In regions without supplies of stone, timber chambers were sometimes made instead. This basic kind of structure is found all around the western seaboard of the Continent in the fourth millennium, from south-eastern Spain to southern Sweden, and including most of the British Isles. Even now, after tens of centuries of destruction, about 40,000 examples still survive, none identical in form but most falling into clear regional traditions of architecture. Naturally enough, these monuments have been known for centuries by names native to the languages of the countries in which they stand, though the Breton term dolmen, 'table-stone', has become widely used internationally for many. Scholars were stuck for something to call them which accurately sums up their nature, and the generic name 'chambered tomb' was gradually adopted in the early twentieth century. It was based on the fact that many of these constructions contained the remains of human beings, often in great quantity. On the other hand, it has frequently been acknowledged that some seem never to have done so, and that the people deposited in most were too few to have represented more than a selection of the population at the time when they were used.[33] The present tendency among current experts on the Neolithic is to continue to employ the term 'tomb' for lack of any better, while acknowledging its limitations in this context. An attempt will be made here to overcome the problem by adopting the expression 'tomb-shrine', which recognizes the presence of the dead at most of these monuments, but also the equally apparent fact that the structures were not simply receptacles for them, but functioned as sites of ritual in their own right. Often, indeed, they are the only ceremonial sites of which we have evidence in the landscape of their time.

Tomb-shrines have long been recognized as some of the most impressive prehistoric monuments in Europe, and in many areas the most impressive. Until the 1970s, however, they were regarded as the comparatively primitive products of a savage backwater, ultimately inspired by the much more impressive, and older, constructions of the Near East. It was frequently stated that Egypt's Step Pyramid, dating from the mid third millennium BC, was the oldest stone building in the world. That honour still belongs to the Near East, currently being held by the temple complex at Göbekli Tepe in Turkey, erected about 12,000 years ago by a culture that was in European terms Mesolithic.[34] The tomb-shrines of the Atlantic coasts of Europe, however, have now been relocated by improved carbon dating to a period one to two thousand years older than the pyramid. They represent the first widespread stone constructions of the human race. Where the tradition of making them began is still not agreed, except that it was plainly not in Britain. Megalithic tomb-shrines in Spain, Portugal and western France have all produced dates going back to the mid fifth millennium, and probably earlier.[35] In general, these monuments seem to appear in Britain, and rapidly become widespread, in the first half of the fourth millennium, soon after the adoption of farming, or in some areas perhaps just before it. In northern Europe they appear to have arrived later still: those of the Netherlands, for example, date from the second half of the fourth millennium.[36]

The building of this style of monument therefore seems to have spread from south to north along the Atlantic coasts, at what in prehistoric terms was a fast pace, as part of the equally rapid importation of the Neolithic lifestyle into each region. Where it began, within a vast span of land stretching from southern Spain to Brittany, is at present unknown. Nor is it possible to identify a single style of tomb-shrine as being the primordial one, because as soon as the tradition was taken into any new area it seems to have flowered there almost immediately into a variety of different forms. Moreover, the source of inspiration for it is equally unclear, natural rock outcrops and houses being the most popular candidates.[37] It is distinctly possible that the long mounds which covered tomb-shrines in large areas of Britain and France were inspired by the long houses built by Neolithic people in central Europe in the preceding period.[38] This was something like an orthodoxy by the 1990s, but it has recently been challenged by the fact that better dating has revealed a seven-hundred-year gap between the end of the long houses and the beginning of the long mounds.[39] There was a general tendency in the late twentieth century to speak of the tomb-shrines in general as 'houses of the dead' (or at least of the special dead), but they resemble the shapes of actual dwellings only in certain areas.[40]

In view of all these uncertainties, it is not surprising that no clearly agreed explanations currently exist for the meaning and purpose of this first great European monumental tradition. For most of the twentieth century, the tomb-shrines were regarded as the holy places of a new religion spread by settlers or missionaries; which, as they are plainly ceremonial rather than practical constructions, and usually dominated their landscapes, made good sense. Their different styles and sizes would therefore correspond to the different kinds of church and chapel within which the Christian religion has been practised; and the simile here was the easier to accept in that the megalithic faith concerned was thought to have spread to Western Europe from the Near East.[41] Very occasionally this notion has still been heard in the twenty-first century, for example from a leading scholar of Neolithic Ireland, Michael O'Kelly, who declared that the tomb-shrines of his land were 'implanted here and there by a small group led by an accomplished preacher'.[42] Significantly, O'Kelly was at the end of his life when he wrote these words, and in general in the 1970s the concept of a megalithic religion was abandoned by most specialists. The occasion for this change was the realization that the tomb-shrines were in fact older than the eastern monuments from which they were supposed to have derived. None the less, the change in dating did not in itself invalidate the idea that they were expressions of a particular form of religion. That idea disappeared because it was replaced by another, which became dominant in the 1980s and 1990s: that this kind of monument was developed as part of the transition to a farming economy, and represented a new way of looking at the land resulting from that alteration.

In this formulation, tomb-shrines were built as territorial markers, by farming groups who were dividing up an area between them and warning off newcomers: as most were striking and novel additions to the landscape, they visually expressed the fact that the surrounding area was now occupied, exploited and controlled. The human bones which most of these monuments contained were, according to this view, those of the first farmers to occupy that plot, who were then revered as ancestors by their descendants as part of a continuing process of affirming group identity and asserting rights of possession.[43] This concept was certainly based on sound anthropology, as traditional peoples in other parts of the world sometimes used monuments, combining the functions of tomb and shrine, in just this way. It also, however, represented a secularization of prehistory, depriving religious belief of any status as a force in itself and grounding all ideology ultimately in economic needs and the power politics which these generated. Consciously or not, it owed much to Marxism, and there may be no coincidence in the fact that its popularity peaked as British archaeology came to be dominated by a generation who had been students at the apogee of Marxist ideology around 1970. The concept has tended to die away in the twenty-first century, largely because of the change in the understanding of the Neolithic British economy. If that depended on wandering with herds and flocks rather than tilling and grazing a specific block of farmland, the tomb-shrines became markers along paths (initially through woodland) rather than the spiritual centres of family plots. The notion of them as territorial boasts and warnings also failed now to explain why they often clustered closely together in certain areas. It would have worked if their landscape had been full of static farmsteads, to each of which one was attached, but no trace of such farmsteads has been found across most of Britain.

The concept of these monuments as centres for ancestor worship has been more durable, but can no longer be stated without difficulty or challenge. In 2002 James Whitley launched a direct attack on the manner in which ancestors seemed to have become the defining entities of the British Neolithic. He cannily related the development to a modern yearning for contact with a national past from which the tremendous changes of modernity had left his contemporaries feeling severed and bereaved. He pointed out that while some agricultural societies studied by anthropologists had maintained shrines to ancestral spirits, many had not, while pastoral peoples, such as those who seemed now to be typical of Neolithic Britain, generally did not. He added that the presence of the dead at ritual sites did not in itself prove that the dead concerned were regarded as ancestral. Moreover, where traditional peoples did venerate ancestors, they commonly did so in special shrines away from burial sites.[44] The effect of such criticisms was rapidly to dilute the usage of the term 'ancestor' when applied to such monuments. Alasdair Whittle, in particular, redefined it as signifying 'any forebears who are remembered', whether generalized or individual.[45] In 2011 he and a team of co-workers decided that the tomb-shrines were markers of place, but more of places connected to cosmology and spirituality than just territory.[46] It seems therefore that scholars are circling round towards a vaguer version of the twentieth-century orthodoxy: that these monuments were centres for ritual activity which was commonly mediated, at least partly, through the dead.[47] Such general reflections on their nature cannot, however, even begin to do justice to the true complexity and variety of these monuments as a type. For that, detailed local case studies are needed, and it is time to proceed to a selection from the British evidence.

The Tomb-Shrines: Four Case-Studies

The first regional study to be offered here is that of the long barrows of Sussex. The term 'long barrow', so frequently employed by scholars and general public alike for the most common kind of southern British tomb-shrine, is almost as old as England itself. 'Barrow' is simply the southern English dialect word for a burial mound, from the Old English *beorg*, a hill, and an Anglo-Saxon charter distinguishes one such mound as a *longnam beorge*. It was the seventeenth-century antiquary John Aubrey who first used the term specifically to describe extended mounds or cairns made in the Early Neolithic. Some cover stone chambers of the classic tomb-shrine kind, while others do not, and to these Stuart Piggott gave the name 'earthen', which has stuck: the Sussex examples are of this kind.[48] Over 300 earthen long barrows have been identified, across most of the eastern half of Britain from Aberdeenshire to the South Downs, with western projections into Dorset and Galloway: most of the surviving speci-mens are found in English chalk country, though aerial photography is now revealing an increasing number in river valleys that have been ploughed away above ground level. They range in length from about 154 feet (14 to 125 metres, averaging 47), and can be rectangular, oval or trapezoidal in shape. Fourth-fifths have flanking ditches. They have yielded (crude) dates from around 3800 to around 3000 BC, with most clustering in the centre of the millennium.[49] These massive whale-backed mounds, grown with tall grasses, yellow and blue flowers (buttercups and harebells) and fragrant wild thyme, are among the most imposing prehistoric monuments of the English chalklands. When freshly made, they would have been a brilliant white from the chalk rock, and shone beneath sun and moon.

At first sight (and in much traditional writing by archaeologists), they could be seen as an outgrowth of the tomb-shrine tradition, as most which have been excavated have yielded human remains. They tend to occur, moreover, in regions which lack the large surface rocks needed to build megalithic cham-bers. Some look like perfect matches for that tradition, such as Fussell's Lodge in Wiltshire, where the mound covered a timber chamber which had held the bones of over fifty individuals. Most, however, contained the burials of only a few people, and scattered across southern England are some which had none at all.[50] The extreme case here is that of Sussex, where long barrows are found at both ends of the county's chalk hills, and only one out of a dozen has proved to contain any human remains (and those consisted of just three fragments). This has propelled one archaeologist, Miles Russell, into suggesting that any

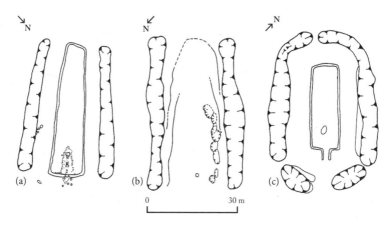

13 Earthen long barrows: (a) Fussell's Lodge (Wiltshire); (b) Horslip (Wiltshire); (c) Wor Barrow (Dorset). The long mounds lie between or within ditches represented by hatching on the plans. The Horslip mound had been ploughed down more than the others, but seems to have contained no structures or human remains. Wor Barrow held burials, and Fussell's Lodge about sixty of them in a wooden chamber. Redrawn after Timothy Darvill, Miles Russell and Julian Thomas.

association between such monuments and the dead was incidental. He has pointed out that more human bone has commonly been found on other kinds of Neolithic ritual sites, as will be described, and in places assumed to have had a practical primary purpose, such as the flint mines. Instead he emphasizes the mound itself as the essential part of the monument, as a structured assemblage of soil, timber and stone to which deposits of special material had been added, often in the ditches: occasionally flint arrowheads and knives, and pottery, more commonly the bones of cattle, pigs, birds and humans. Russell suggested that the mounds represented a code or language, each embodying the identity and memory-bank of a particular community, and perhaps also containing offerings to their deities. Certainly they were colossal investments of energy: to put up an average one, ten people would have needed to work eight hours a day for three to seven months.[51] It is also certain that there were strong regional variations in the components of commemoration put into the mounds or over which the mounds were erected. In eastern and southern Scotland they were commonly built over large post holes, the posts in which were allowed to rot before the long barrow was constructed. Gordon Noble has suggested that the posts represented trees, which were not only important elements in the Early Neolithic landscape but potent symbols of birth, death and degeneration. The posts would therefore decay like the human bodies which were added after they had gone.[52] This metaphor reappears much further south, at Haddenham in the Cambridgeshire Fenland, where a long barrow covered a long, low timber structure (at most three feet, or just under a metre, high), in which at least five people had been interred. The authors of the excavation report suggested that it would have been like burial within a tree trunk.[53]

Thus far, Russell's argument that the mound itself was the essential feature of the monument seems well sustained. It becomes more contentious when considering the second case study: that of the Cotswold–Severn group of long barrows. These are very similar to the earthen kind in size, shape and orientation, and where the two kinds overlap, as they do on the north Wiltshire and Dorset chalk hills, they are now sometimes indistinguishable to the eye. What marks them off as a separate group is that they cover megalithic chambers, often lined with dry-stone walling and with more such walling stretching around the mound and defining a forecourt at the broader end. As their name implies, their epicentre lies on the limestone Cotswold Hills, stretching from north Somerset through Gloucestershire into Oxfordshire: a total of 140 of them once existed there. They are also found on the other side of the Severn Estuary, along the coastal plain of South Wales as far west as the Gower Peninsula, and in parts of the Black Mountains. In the Cotswolds, their long, sloping green mounds, often now surrounded by modern walls and grown with beech trees, are the most characteristic prehistoric monuments of the region, rising out of green pastures or from fields of red earth in winter and waving cereals in summer. When first made, of piled-up, newly cut limestone blocks, they would have gleamed like freshly minted gold, making as glorious a sight in the wider landscape as the white mounds of the chalk hills. A few of this group were restored as visitor attractions in the nineteenth and early twentieth centuries, followed by a spate of others in the mid twentieth, most of which ended up in the care of English Heritage. Inevitably, those chosen for this treatment were the largest and most impressive, above all those with passages entered from the forecourt and side cells leading off these. The latter actually represent a rare variety of design within the group, and their disproportionate occurrence among the selection preserved for public view tends to give many visitors a misleading impression of the whole. Most have smaller chambers, entered from the side of the mound or completely enclosed within it.

It was Glyn Daniel who first defined the group, in 1937, and Timothy Darvill who has produced the most recent comprehensive study of it.[54] The long barrows comprised by it possess one more distinctive characteristic: that their stone chambers almost always contained human bone, and usually – for the space – in large quantities: an average of forty to fifty people in each. Often bodies were placed there whole and decayed inside the barrow, and sometimes they were cleaned down to bone elsewhere, by being exposed to the attentions of animals or buried temporarily. In both cases, once inside, the remains

14 Classic whale-backed mound of a Cotswold–Severn long barrow, in this case Hetty Pegler's Tump on the Cotswold Edge of Gloucestershire.

15 Another Cotswold–Severn long barrow, from a greater distance: even a mile off, the huge mound of Adam's Grave dominates the skyline above the chalk scarp plunging to the Vale of Pewsey in Wiltshire.

usually became mixed with each other, in an apparently deliberate merging of the individual with the collective, though there was sometimes segregation by sex or age in different chambers of the same mound. Both sexes, and all ages, were indeed represented by the bones, and in some cases certainly, and in most cases possibly, burials within the chambers took place successively, at intervals. In some proven cases, and perhaps more generally, the entrance to the chambers was closed and then reopened, at various times, and individual bones look to have been removed, perhaps for use in ritual. Timothy Darvill has calculated that the number of people found in each well-preserved barrow means that it could have functioned as a family vault for a group of ten to fifteen people over a period of about a hundred and fifty years.[55] In that case, they would have been true tombs, and Russell's interpretation, so cogent for the Sussex long barrows, has to be reversed for those of Gloucestershire and its neighbours: the large shining mound would have been there to advertise, glorify and protect the chambers which it covered, and the humans lying within them.

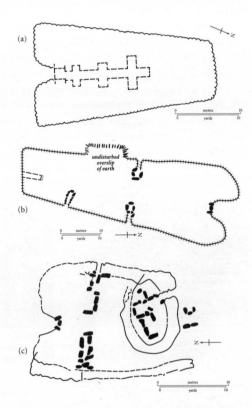

16 Cotswold–Severn long barrows, with differing arrangements of stone chambers (a) Stoney Littleton, near Bath; (b) Belas Knap, near Cheltenham; and (c) Ty Isaf, between Talgarth and Abergavenny in the Black Mountains of South Wales. (a) and (b) have been restored and are maintained for public access; (c) is now just a low mound in a field. Redrawn after Glyn Daniel.

Few goods were ever deposited with the bodies: some pottery, worked flints, exotic pebbles, stone discs, beads, bone pins, and the bones of dogs and (above all) cattle. Animal bones are also common in the forecourts, especially the skulls of pigs and cattle. They may have functioned as protective talismans or totemic symbols, but they may also be the remains of feasts, as bonfires were often lit in the same spaces before the mound.[56] The orientation of long barrows of all kinds, chambered and earthen, calls out for some explanation, as in every county the higher and broader end of most faces between north-east and south-east, and most of the remainder face other parts of the eastern or southern quadrants. This suggests some alignment on the sunrise at different times of the year, but a large minority of the mounds are orientated outside this span. In the 1980s, Aubrey Burl, using the earthen long barrows of Salisbury Plain as his sample, decided that they were aligned instead upon the movements of the moon.[57] There remain, however, a number, even in Burl's original sample let alone in other areas, that face in directions outside the moon's range as well. In the 1990s, a historian of astronomy, John North, surveyed a large sample of such barrows in southern and eastern England and decided that they were orientated upon the rising and setting of some of the brightest stars; an idea which has not caught on, perhaps because it does not seem wholly to rule out coincidence.[58] Experts in these monuments therefore now speak vaguely of a possible or probable connection with sun or moon.[59]

The most exciting recent development concerning the Cotswold–Severn long barrows relates to their dating. Since 2000, the existing carbon-based dates have been refined, applying a statistical method, Bayes' theorem, which allows a much greater precision in the results when derived through computer modelling. This procedure was applied to a sample of Cotswold long barrows, and the Fussell's Lodge earthen one, and it was revealed that they had been a

17 Entrance and passage of Stoney Littleton.

relatively short-lived phenomenon, all having been built and used between 3800 and 3350 BC, and most between 3750 and 3600, and each one active only for a period corresponding to from one to five generations of people. This would make a fit with Timothy Darvill's theory that they were family vaults, and opens up the possibility that the same social group might have constructed and put burials into a number of these monuments in succession. In that case, the clustering would be explained, and once more the suggestion that they marked particular territories, even for people with a nomadic lifestyle, would be strengthened; but, once more, not proved.[60] What the new evidence does erode is the idea that the barrows were centres of ancestor worship, if the people whose bones went into their chambers had been members of a living community. Access to the interior of the barrows to make new burials, or (perhaps) to take out bones, must have been a ghoulish business, because the entrances to most needed a crawl, the chambers within were not large and many would have contained decaying corpses. We cannot tell at this distance whether it would have regarded as an honour or an ordeal, and whether it was confined to special persons or taken in turn by all in the group.

The third case study consists of the megalithic tomb-shrines of West Wales, that part of the land beyond the Gower Peninsula and south of the River Teifi contained in the old counties of Pembrokeshire and Carmarthenshire. These

18 Forecourt and chambers of Nympsfield Long Barrow, on the Cotswold Edge. The barrow lost its capstones centuries ago and has recently been tidied up as a visitor attraction.

twenty-eight monuments are mostly classic dolmens, consisting of a capstone supported by uprights. They have in the past been classed in different ways according to form, but the most recent and simplest classification, that of Alasdair Whittle and Vicki Cummings, recognizes just two basic types: simple box-like chambers, sometimes with a short passage and generally with a large capstone; and a smaller kind of chamber in which a thinner capstone rests upon the earth itself at one end.[61] Some caution is needed in accepting even this distinction, for it has been pointed out that some of the examples of the second, 'earth-fast', variety may have lost uprights or collapsed at one end.[62] When both apparent varieties are included, twenty-eight survive at the present day, standing like giant grey stone mushrooms or bracket fungi in meadows, moorland or clumps of bracken. They cluster thickly in coastal regions of Pembrokeshire but are spread along the whole Welsh coast between the Gower and the mouth of the Teifi, with many outliers inland. The largest, finest and most famous is Pentre Ifan among the gentle slopes of the eastern Preseli Mountains: the gazelle of dolmens with its tapering uprights on which the tilting main capstone appears to float rather than rest, and a broad, curving façade of megaliths on either side. No reliable dates have been obtained for the 'earth-fast' chambers, which seem unique to the region and may be Late Neolithic; but a single one, of *c.* 3500, exists for the chambers with a complete set of uprights, and indeed they belong to a class of tomb-shrine found all round the Irish Sea, which elsewhere has been dated to the fourth millennium.[63] In major respects the West Welsh monuments make a contrast with the Cotswold–Severn long barrows. It is now generally thought that they were never covered by mounds or cairns, but were at most supported by piled stones for some of their height. Furthermore, the dominant burial rite within them was cremation, and human bones have indeed rarely been found inside the chambers.

These distinctive characteristics have naturally produced much recent discussion of their nature and purpose. Alasdair Whittle and Vicki Cummings have argued that these monuments were not straightforward chambers for burials as the Cotswold–Severn barrows have been thought to be, but huge stones raised up on supports for display and contemplation: in Whittle's lovely phrase, 'stones that float to the sky'.[64] Colin Richards has agreed that the capstones could have been sacred rocks, connected to mythology, that were lifted up in just this manner; in which case the scraps of human bone, pottery and flint found inside the chambers would not have been burials but offerings to the holy stone. He has also noted that at one of the few such monuments to have been scientifically examined, Carreg Samson on the north Pembrokeshire coast, the uprights seem to have been brought from different localities, suggesting that separate communities had come together to build the

19 Arthur's Stone, or Maen Cetti, on the Gower Peninsula, the most easterly of the West Welsh dolmens.

structure.[65] It is difficult, however, to know how paltry the contents of the chambers actually were. If they always stood open, much might have been removed in the millennia since they were deposited, and the acidic soil of the region destroys bones.[66] Only ten of these monuments have any recorded excavation, and most of that took place in the nineteenth and early twentieth centuries, under relatively primitive conditions. Six show signs of having been dug over in even earlier periods, and 'charcoal' or 'rich black earth' was recorded at the same number.[67] This last detail matters a lot, because a newly developed technique of phosphate analysis, applied to an Irish tomb-shrine on similar acidic terrain, yielded just a few small fragments of human bone but a dark layer of soil.[68] It proved the 'soil' to consist entirely of eroded skeleton: so the present state of the evidence may seriously underestimate the number of burials that were once placed inside the West Welsh tomb-shrines.

There is another contrast between these monuments and the English long barrows: the scholarly attention which has been dedicated to finding possible connections between the latter and heavenly bodies has been devoted in the case of the former to possible connections with the surrounding landscape. This debate was started by Christopher Tilley in 1994 when he pointed out that

20 Carreg Samson, a dolmen on the Pembrokeshire coast, with its capstone on a hoist to protect archaeologists during the excavations of 1968 (which the author attended).

just over half of the Neolithic tomb-shrines of Pembrokeshire were located near dramatic natural outcrops of rock. He proposed therefore that their primary purpose had been neither as places of burial nor as markers of territories, but to represent ceremonial meeting points along pathways, which drew attention to important natural features.[69] His suggestion provoked a significant amount of criticism, centring on the objections that ancient stone structures would tend to survive better near rock outcrops, which could be more easily quarried for building stone; that the ancient landscape itself continually altered; and that it is impossible to determine how it appeared at any one point, as so many features, such as trees and ponds, cannot be precisely reconstructed from the surviving evidence.[70] As a result, the significance of position in the terrain has been reformulated, especially by Vicki Cummings, to emphasize instead a more general manner in which most tomb-shrines along the British shores of the Irish Sea, not merely in West Wales but in Gwynedd, Galloway and the Isle of Man, were built on slopes that provide views of the sea or of mountains, and often of both. The sea is in fact visible from 82 per cent and mountains from 78 per cent of the West Welsh examples. This observation caused Cummings to speculate that places which combined water and stone were appropriate for spiritual transformations, perhaps including those of humans after death.[71]

Vicki Cummings has gone on from this to suggest that the sites of the tomb-shrines of western Britain were also remarkably well chosen for visits – effectively pilgrimages – by Neolithic seafarers, who might have carried out ceremonies at a succession of them along the same stretch of coastline, depositing objects or human remains at some as they went.[72] Combined with the idea that the capstones represented rocks which were already sacred, and famed in story, this is a very radical departure from the concept of these monuments as territorial markers and centres of ancestor cults for specific communities. It might indeed rebound upon the interpretation of the Cotswold–Severn barrows to the east. It has been noted that those barrows were built from a collection of carefully selected materials, brought at different times to the construction sites and woven into the growing structures: apparently taken from special places or associated with special people.[73] In this case, the long barrows might themselves have been the results of collective effort, bringing together different social groups rather than marking differences between them,

21 'The gazelle of West Welsh dolmens': Pentre Ifan in the Preseli Mountains of Pembrokeshire.

and become places of seasonal or occasional pilgrimage for these wandering bands. The notion that special landscape settings were needed for the placement of the Irish Sea tomb-shrines would also help to explain why they are missing from large areas of central and north-eastern Wales and north-western England, which have signs of Neolithic occupation but lack the necessary dramatic combinations of sea and high ground. It does not, however, account for their striking absence from Cumbria, where the coastline has exactly the features of other parts of the Irish Sea coast where tomb-shrines clustered thickly, and where the mountains were – to judge from the importance of the Langdale Pikes axes – regarded as special and powerful places during the period. Seemingly more subtle complexes of attitudes were at work, which are even more difficult to recover.

It may therefore be seen that, across this zone of southern Britain, from Pembrokeshire to Sussex, the basic components of the tomb-shrine model – the mound, the chamber and the dead – were apparently treated in three very different ways, which in turn have called forth very different interpretations from archaeologists. Likewise, still in the extreme south of Britain, Kent was the location for another distinctive variation, while the equivalent monuments in Cornwall bear more resemblance to those of West Wales than do those of other parts of the West of England. The same pattern is reproduced across the northern two-thirds of Britain: nearly two hundred megalithic tomb-shrines of different styles survive in the topmost quarter of Scotland, from the Great Glen northwards, alone. How far any general religious idea united all the variations on the basic architectural language of the form, even within Britain and its neighbouring islands let alone across Western Europe, is impossible to say. Many shapes and usages of sacred building can of course be generated by the same basic set of beliefs, as has been demonstrated not merely in theological faiths such as Christianity but in others such as the paganism of ancient Greece. On the other hand, it is equally possible for the same basic form of structure, such as the late Roman basilica, to be employed for very different purposes. To which of those patterns the tomb-shrines of the fourth millennium corresponded is at present anybody's guess.

Causewayed Enclosures

Tomb-shrines are today the most widespread visible monuments of the western European Early Neolithic, but a different kind of structure was even more common in Europe at the period, and found much deeper into the interior of the Continent: the enclosure of land by the digging of a ditch and often the piling up of the earth from it into a bank. This is as true of Britain as elsewhere, but here the fourth millennium produced a particular variation on this pattern:

the definition of a special piece of land by the digging of curving, sausage-shaped ditches with gaps between them. The result was to create a broken ring of excavated earth in the landscape. Sometimes one such ring was enough, but often others were added. The circular shape was almost always a very rough one, of crude ovals dug in straight sections, and frequently incomplete circuits of ditch were dug, to produce semicircles. Only 35 per cent of those recorded, in fact, had complete circuits; but the open portions of some rested on hill slopes or watercourses which provided natural barriers, and hedges or woods might have served the same function at others. They vary in size from roughly 1.25 to 25 acres (0.4 to 10 hectares), and both large and small examples are sometimes found in groups. Because of the gaps between the ditches, since the 1920s this sort of monument has been given the standard name, among archaeologists, of 'causewayed enclosure'.[74] When freshly dug, they would have been quite dramatic sights, especially in chalk country where both the segments of ditch and the low banks piled beside them would have been a fresh white against the green terrain. The sheer labour needed to construct them – thousands of hours – makes them important monuments.

At the present day, unlike the megalithic tomb-shrines, causewayed enclosures are mostly invisible: at Windmill Hill and Knap Hill on the north Wiltshire chalk hills, the broken circuits of ditch and earthwork can still be discerned in the turf, but nobody could call these impressive relics of prehistory. For the most part, they can only now be discovered from the air, as crop marks in fields, and this process has revealed a rapidly increasing number, the tally of them having doubled since 1970. They are found as far west as Ulster, Anglesey and the Isle of Man, but are generally a phenomenon of the southern two-thirds of England. Of more than a hundred known or suspected by 2010, almost all are on English soil, mostly in the Wessex chalk hills, the south-east, East Anglia, the Thames Valley and the East Midlands. They show up so much better on light upland earth like chalk, however, that this may massively distort their perceived range, and it may be noted that the densest concentration of them yet discovered is actually in the lower Welland Valley in the East Midlands.[75] Often they were made to the side of prominent natural features, such as a hill crest or a river bend, which may already have been seen as sacred or otherwise significant. They occur in much the same terrain as earthen long barrows, though rarely very close to those: they were usually the first monuments in their own (generally wooded) landscapes. They represent the first human enclosure of open space in the story of Britain. The developments in dating of Neolithic sites, based on computer use of Bayes' theorem, have had an important impact on knowledge of these structures. They appeared in *c.* 3700 BC around the Thames Estuary, and spread out from it so rapidly that between 3650 and 3550 they seem to have been the favourite monumental form of the south-eastern British

Distribution of
causewayed enclosures

22 Distribution of causewayed enclosures in Britain.

Neolithic, starting later than the long barrows but then running parallel to them in use. The largest may have been built in stages, over anything from five to seventy-five years, and used for three to four centuries. Most, however, were abandoned after shorter periods of between one and forty years.[76]

Some sense of the variety that the enclosures represent, as a phenomenon, can be captured by looking at a few of the most famous examples. The most celebrated of all – virtually the definitive one in the mid-twentieth century – is also the largest: that on Windmill Hill, which was excavated in the 1920s and has been analysed at times ever since.[77] Large amounts of carefully deposited material were recovered from the ditches, of which most was animal bone, primarily cattle but also pig and sheep or goat, with some of dog. The cattle were sometimes buried whole rather than being the remains of feasts, as were

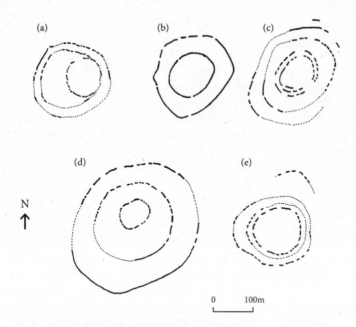

23 Plans of British causewayed enclosures. (a) Briar Hill, Northamptonshire; (b) Robin Hood's Ball, Wiltshire; (c) Whitehawk Camp, Sussex; (d) Windmill Hill, Wiltshire; (e) The Trundle, Sussex. Redrawn after Timothy Darvill.

dogs, and cattle skulls were put against the causeways. There was also pottery, worked flint, worked stone of different types, some imported from abroad, worked animal bones and chalk blocks, and deer antlers. Thirty-four pieces of human bone were among the assemblage, as were two pieces of chalk carved like penises and more possibly worked into figurines, balls and cups. The authors of the most recent study have concluded that while it would be hard to prove that the burial of these objects was a religious activity, it was certainly a 'meaningful social practice', helping to create meaning and sustain values: virtually all aspects of Neolithic life that are accessible through archaeology are represented there.[78] Another large and famous site is that at Hambledon Hill, where the Dorset chalk hills prepare to drop into the West Country lowlands: like Windmill Hill, it commands a fine view. It was excavated by a team led by Roger Mercer between 1974 and 1986. Again, the ditches were full of deposits, having been carefully scoured before items were placed in them, and there were ninety-seven pits inside with more carefully structured placement of items. There were, however, two separate enclosures on the hill, which had been used for different purposes, creating a total complex which is to date the biggest yet uncovered to be based on this sort of monument. The main one was given deposits of human bones (some from complete burials but most weathered or carefully scraped pieces of skeleton), flint nodules, foreign stones, and pottery. The human remains were, indeed, so common and prominent – skulls, some of which were already old by the time of burial, were placed at points in the ditches – that it was proposed that the enclosure had been a place where bodies were exposed in order to clean the bones. It was therefore a site for ritual and the dead, whereas the smaller enclosure produced plenty of flint-knapping debris and deer bones, suggesting that it was used for activities associated with the living.[79] The Sussex sites also all contained human bones – in contrast with the local long barrows – suggesting that like the main Hambledon enclosure they were to some extent concerned with the dead.[80] At Windmill Hill, by contrast, dead humans were barely present.

These large and long-famous monuments can be compared with smaller examples from further east in England. One that has achieved archaeological celebrity is Etton, near Peterborough, built on what was then an island in the flood plain of the River Welland. Francis Pryor oversaw the excavation, and found that it was divided by a fence into east and west halves with their own entrances. The eastern one had pottery, tools and animal and human bones

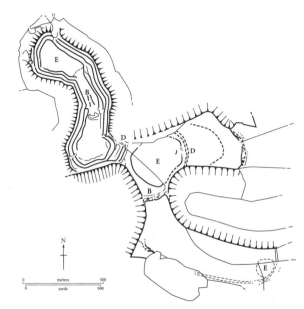

24 The huge complex around the enclosures on Hambledon Hill, Dorset, redrawn after Roger Mercer and Frances Healey.
E = enclosure
B = long barrow
D = dyke

interred in pits and ditches, with human skulls at the ditch ends. The western side contained the remains of feasting and woodworking, though human bones were present too, which had been exposed and gnawed by dogs or wolves. Dung traces indicated that some livestock had been kept there. The eastern half therefore seemed concerned with family ties and the relationship between life and death, and the western with daily living: so the enclosure was a world in miniature. The wood found at the enclosure had been cut in late summer or autumn, indicating seasonal gatherings towards the end of the grazing and growing season.[81] The second example consists of a pair of causewayed enclosures discovered in the 2000s by developer-funded excavations on the Isle of Sheppey in the Thames Estuary. They seem to have been built one after the other in the century 3700 to 3600 BC, and each was used at most for two generations. One had two or three circuits of ditch, and the other a single one. The latter was made first, for small, apparently individual, deposits of objects, and the larger one followed, for larger-scale activity which apparently included feasting. Neither included human burials. They were dug to face away from each other, commanding different views, perhaps by different communities with contrasting needs, or by the same people with changing needs, or who used each space for particular purposes or seasons.[82]

Unsurprisingly, in view of this range of examples, experts currently consider that the segments of ditch were dug, and consecrated with deposits, to define

25 The causewayed enclosure at Knap Hill on Wiltshire's Marlborough Downs, one of very few at which the broken banks still show above the surface.

special places into which people could go for special purposes at special times. The range of those purposes, however, seems potentially at least to cover every aspect of Neolithic existence: religious ceremonies (including those relating to death), trade, manufacturing, discussion, stock-breeding, feasting and celebration. What is missing is much sign of continuous domestic activity.[83] Perhaps these monuments were places where different groups could meet and interrelate; it remains a distinct possibility that each segment of ditch was dug by a different one, as its contribution to the common effort. On the other hand, some at least could well have been made and used by a single set of people. Although the ditches and banks would have provided slight physical barriers, and the gaps between them afforded easy entry, we know so little about Neolithic mentalities that it is possible that the consecrated ditches represented spiritual defences, which would slow down and channel attackers and so afford some protection to people gathered within. As in the case of the tomb-shrines, a basic architectural idea seems to have been rapidly adapted to a range of local needs.

Cursuses and Other Types of Monument

Soon after long barrows and causewayed enclosures were being constructed across parts of Neolithic Britain, a third major category of monument appeared in much the same regions. It consisted of long, linear paired ditches, which usually joined at their terminals and contained banks thrown up from the ditch-earth. Both banks and ditches were small compared to the area of ground which they enclosed: the shortest were 164 feet in length (50 metres), while the longest snaked over the chalk hills of north-east Dorset for over six miles (almost ten kilometres). This huge construction would have needed about half a million hours of work, though an average-sized monument of this class could have been dug by a hundred people in a week. They often cluster in groups, though it is not clear whether the individual structures in these were all in use at once or constructed in a sequence. These constructions are called 'cursuses', a term coined by the great antiquary William Stukeley in the early eighteenth century, for the large one near Stonehenge, because it reminded him of the type of ancient Roman racetrack that bears the name cursus. It took almost two hundred years, however, for it to be applied to a category of structure, this step being taken by O. G. S. Crawford in 1935, after aerial photography had begun to show up more and more of these lines on the landscape.[84] They make up the largest class of Neolithic monument: the huge Dorset one is in fact the biggest known Neolithic earthwork in Western Europe, and the largest Christian church of Europe, St Peter's in Rome, covers only slightly more ground than the smallest cursus. They had no mundane role, having no signs of domestic rubbish and no impressive structures inside, so that they seem to have been made to set a space apart from the landscape around it. Nothing like them has appeared before or since, and they represent the first specifically British sort of monument, spreading westward into Ireland but otherwise marking the point at which the Neolithic of Britain began to diverge from that of the Continent. Recent estimates of their possible number in Britain have come to just over a hundred.[85] Over half are in England, especially in its eastern and southern parts, with a few in Wales and the rest in Scotland (mostly in the Tay basin and the south-west), where the cursus shape was usually defined by pits or wooden posts rather than earthworks. Some, like the monster in Dorset, seem to have been maintained for centuries, while others, like the smaller of the two near Stonehenge, were allowed to start disappearing just after they were completed. Disappear they have, as completely as most causewayed enclosures. The banks of a few of the biggest, such as the Dorset one and the larger near Stonehenge, are still just visible in places, but most have now only a phantom existence, as crop marks visible from the air in the right seasons and weather.[86]

The revised system of dating has not yet been properly applied to cursuses, but a rough sense exists of how they relate chronologically to other monuments. Some of the Scottish timber examples seem to have been started early, in the first half of the fourth millennium, if they were indeed the same kind of structure as the earthen variety in England. They played the role in Scotland of causewayed enclosures in England. The English cursuses appeared around 3550 BC, just as the enclosures were going out of fashion, and were built throughout the second half of the millennium, with the Dorset giant being one of the latest: so they came after the long barrows and causewayed enclosures and were made alongside the last of the former but seem largely to have replaced the latter.[87] There is absolutely no agreement on their purpose, or purposes. The obvious human activities in a space of that long and comparatively narrow shape are processions or races, but some cursuses cross watercourses or bogs which would have interrupted these. They may have functioned to honour and celebrate the natural environment, by linking parts of it together, or to express human triumph and dominance over it. Some, though not most, incorporate older monuments such as long barrows into their structure: again, this might have been to acknowledge the people who built these and to draw upon the spiritual power which they embodied, or to slight and deface them, and so deliver an opposite message. They may not have acted as connecting mechanisms or channels of movement at all, but as barriers across the land, consecrated buffer zones separating different territories or areas of activity. They could have represented symbolic rivers. Some are apparently aligned on movements of the sun, the central section of the big Dorset one on the midwinter sunset, that at Dorchester on Thames upon the midwinter sunrise,

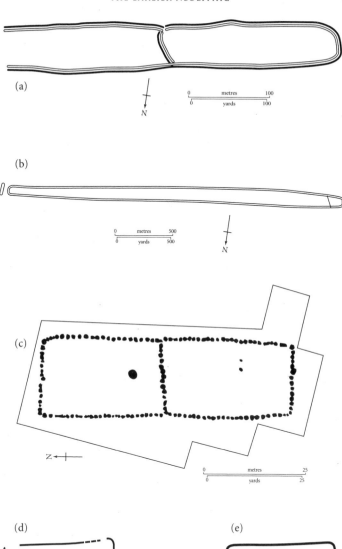

26 Cursus monuments. (a) Smaller cursus of two near Stonehenge; (b) The Great Stonehenge cursus; (c) timber cursus, Douglasmuir, Scotland; (d) Dorchester-on-Thames cursus, Oxfordshire; (e) Raunds cursus, Northamptonshire. Redrawn after Timothy Darvill, Alasdair Whittle and Julian Thomas.

and the larger one near Stonehenge on the equinoctial sunrise and sunset. Most, however, are not. All would, in the nature of the sky, point towards some groups of stars, but this inevitability in itself rules out much proof of intention. One interpretation, which is just as feasible as the others, turns the concept of heavenly alignment round, by suggesting that cursuses were signalling devices to be read by deities looking down from above. Another is that they were indeed processional ways, but for the dead and not the living, which would explain the lack of concern about physical barriers along the route.[88] The existing evidence does not prioritize any of these suggestions over the others. They were usually built to harmonize with older structures but not, apparently, used as part of a single system with them: for example, the largest of the five cursuses at Stanwell, Middlesex, now under Heathrow Airport, which was over one and a half miles (3.8 kilometres) long, followed lines of Mesolithic pits and earlier Neolithic post holes, and was aligned with an existing cursus.[89]

Tomb-shrines, causewayed enclosures and cursuses were the main architectural forms of the early British Neolithic, all apparently concerned with ritual and symbolic, rather than straightforwardly functional and practical, behaviour. In addition, however, there were many other types of structure made in the island during the fourth millennium; and here the whole notion of categories of monument starts to break down. The classification of phenomena into families and types has been one of the essential techniques of modern scientific enquiry – to start to see a pattern in things is often the first step to understanding them – and this is as true and natural in the discipline of archaeology as in others. By the mid twentieth century, however, certain kinds of monument from the British Neolithic were already emerging as anomalous, and difficult to categorize, and an appreciation of this problem has increased in recent years as many new sites have been revealed by aerial photography or construction work. Large timber structures, for example, have been excavated at three places in Scotland, along the Dee Valley and in the Central Lowlands, since the year 2000, and over a dozen more are suspected from crop marks: two isolated similar monuments have been found in Oxfordshire and Kent. All those excavated have been dated to the early fourth millennium and interpreted as roofed, rectangular wooden halls, where cereals were stored or consumed. They have been interpreted as places for ceremonial gathering rather than as houses, and all were burned down, in what have been taken to be ritualized acts of decommissioning.[90] Gordon Noble has pointed out that in all key respects – the timber construction, the rectangular shape and the end in flames – the so-called halls were remarkably similar to other Scottish monuments of the same period or slightly later. These are also found in the Lowlands, from Aberdeenshire across to Galloway, and comprise the post-defined Scottish cursuses and long enclosures sometimes associated with human remains. Noble has suggested that all were essentially different varieties of the same structure, which used wooden posts to enclose a rectangular private space for special activities, and were dramatically ended, by burning, in what could have been a rite which fixed them in memory.[91] It is possible that these early Scottish monuments provided the idea for the later earthwork cursuses of southern Britain (whatever that idea actually was).[92] Down the eastern side of Britain from the Dee Valley to the southern English chalk country, however, other sorts of rectangular wooden structure were also built in the early to mid fourth millennium, consisting in essence of large boxes. More than fifty are known: many contained human remains, and long barrows were sometimes built over them later, so they have generally been interpreted as timber equivalents of the megalithic tomb-shrines. They could, however, also represent just another use of the rectangular timber enclosure, an association strengthened by the fact that they too were sometimes burned down, while in Scotland the human bones placed inside them had usually been cremated, in a different employment of the transformative effects of fire.[93]

All these kinds of structure were invisible above the ground surface before excavation, but other kinds of unusual monument have always been highly visible. Among these was a class defined by Sir Mortimer Wheeler, in 1943, as 'bank barrows', very long, narrow, rectangular mounds apparently all dating to the period between 3600 and 3000 BC. They seem to have taken centuries to build, being slowly heaped up, sometimes by joining long barrows together: the largest, at Cleaven Dyke in the Perth and Kinross district, consisted of a total of thirty-four segments, added together to make a mound about a fifth of a mile (at least 2,085 metres) long. About a dozen are known or suspected, thinly scattered across the range of earthen long barrows and cursuses from central Scotland to the south coast with a particular concentration in Dorset. At first they were treated by archaeologists as exceptionally extended long barrows, from which they are divided by a purely arbitrary unit of measurement: a long barrow becomes a bank barrow if it is longer than about 430 feet (140 metres). Recently, the lack of burials or other deposits beneath them has caused a reconsideration of their role, towards viewing them more as solid forms of cursus monument. As such, they share most of the possible roles of cursuses, with the additional option of providing a raised platform for rites.[94]

In much of Scotland and north-eastern England, and a few areas of the Midlands and south, the most common fourth-millennium burial monument was a circular mound, or round barrow. These were made by piling up earth or stones, sometimes in careful layers, over a central burial pit, cremation trench or wooden or stone chamber: the later to be built often contained just one to three complete bodies. Hitherto little studied, they may have been yet another local variation of the tomb-shrine tradition, commencing soon after the long barrows and continuing alongside them.[95] The catalogue of unusual mounds also contains oval barrows, a variant of either long or round barrows found in central southern England. In addition, throughout the fourth millennium people were buried singly or in small groups in simple pits.[96] Indeed, the careful deposition of a range of objects in pits was a Mesolithic tradition that continued, on a larger scale, all through the Neolithic.[97] Jan Harding has suggested that to return things to the earth – usually animal remains, pottery and flints – was a way of celebrating and renewing the relationship between the objects, the cosmological forces responsible for their creation, and human life cycles, as an intrinsic part of everyday practice.[98] Furthermore, monuments could be erected in such a way as to mimic the shape of the land around and to complement, and engage with, the surrounding environment. Kirsty Millican, considering ways in which this is true of post-defined cursuses and other timber monuments in the Nith Valley of south-western Scotland, has pointed out that this makes any strict division between landscape and monument unwise, so that both together formed a ceremonial setting.[99]

Certainly, however, the early Neolithic British were flamboyantly capable of changing the earth as much as honouring it. Not only did the work of stripping it of woodland continue through the millennium – cursus monuments, in particular, would have made no sense in a landscape which had not become largely opened up – but, whatever the purpose of these different kinds of monument, they all imposed a dramatically visible human presence on the land. It was being transformed to the eye, on a large scale, and the speed with which varieties of impressive ceremonial structure appeared and mutated, all requiring enormous investment of energy, bears testimony to the confidence and exuberance with which Britain's first farmers imposed their identities and beliefs upon it.

Designs on Stone

At the end of the twentieth century, experts in British prehistory became more conscious of the presence of motifs which were carved or pecked into stone monuments and natural rock surfaces. The most common consisted of simple hollows, called cup marks, often with one or more rings made about them. Some panels on natural outcrops were much more elaborate, with rosette, keyhole, grooved and spiral forms, sometimes interlacing with each other and with the cup-and-ring design. There are distinctive regional styles: multiple concentric circles in Argyll and Galloway, Scotland, rectangles in Northumberland and rosettes in Northumberland and Yorkshire. Such markings show up on exposed faces and boulders of stone in certain parts of Britain, suddenly glimpsed by the hill walker among heather, bracken, gorse and broom. As they could not be readily dated and there was no apparent means ever of understanding the meaning of the markings, they were long neglected by archaeologists, being vaguely assigned to the Bronze Age. In 1996 Richard Bradley could comment that research into them was still regarded as 'the open-air equivalent of brass-rubbing'.[100] This vacuum of attention was filled in the later twentieth century by dedicated amateurs, in particular a solicitor, Ronald Morris, who concentrated on the designs in Scotland, and a school-master, Stan Beckensall, who surveyed those in northern England. They carried out the essential preliminary work of locating and cataloguing designs and commencing analysis of the data.[101] During the 1990s, archaeologists began to take a sustained interest in the phenomenon, mainly because of the new impor-tance attached by their discipline to the study of landscapes and symbols. As part of this, the sense of the age of the designs began to shift. A Neolithic enclo-sure at Milfield in Northumberland was shown to be connected by a trackway to a carved outcrop, and as the enclosure was dated to 3800 BC and disappeared from view relatively quickly, this suggested that the carved designs were as old or even older. Cup marks on fourth-millennium tomb-shrines, which had been assumed to have been added in the Bronze Age, were now reassessed as contemporary with the monuments. It was noted that the curved arrowheads and pottery designs of that millennium were closer in form to the motifs than the more angular shapes of later Neolithic pottery decoration and tools. By contrast, it became apparent that none of the designs could securely be dated to a Bronze Age context except some on slabs which were reused in funeral monuments and therefore had been decorated at an earlier time. It is currently agreed, therefore, that the designs are a Neolithic tradition, though there is less consensus on whether most date to the earlier or later part of the period, and whether they continued to be made into the Bronze Age.[102]

Traditional peoples all over the world make or have made paintings and carvings on rock, but over 70 per cent of them are hunter-gatherers, to whom this sort of activity seems to come more naturally.[103] It is true that farmers in all periods of European prehistory did produce such designs, especially in Scandinavia, Estonia, France, Italy, Switzerland, Germany and Spain. The problem here is that this Continental work is mostly figurative, creating a contrast with the abstract motifs which make up the British equivalent. Nor is the latter found throughout the island. It is almost confined to the northern half, with its main concentrations in West and North Yorkshire, County Durham, northern Northumberland, the Forth–Clyde region, Galloway, central Argyll, and the Tay Valley. Of about eight thousand sites in Britain, over 1,300 are found in Northumberland. In Cumbria, Wales and the English West Country, although there are plenty of suitable rock surfaces, this type of decoration is both much

27 Most common repertoire of designs on rock faces in Britain, certainly or probably Neolithic. Redrawn after Ronald Morris.

rarer and appears mostly on monuments.[104] It seems to occur along natural route-ways and very often in restricted, borderland zones between rich soils on the one side and infertile uplands or the sea on the other. Such decoration clusters in particular, and with unusual elaboration, around entrances to valleys and basins, and prominent viewpoints, but is not itself usually positioned to be seen from a distance: people had to know that it was there. Like monuments, it recognized certain places as special and made them more so.[105] Almost certainly, it would have taken its place among a much wider making of designs and figures – on trees, tents or yurts, wooden structures, clothes and human bodies, and indeed on rock surfaces that weather more severely – which have disappeared without trace.[106] Andy Jones has noted that the motifs were carved to take account of natural cracks and veins in the rock surface, which were effectively treated as pre-existing designs fashioned by non-human hands.[107]

In 1979 Ronald Morris could list a total of 104 possible explanations that had already been offered for the designs, and it remains generally recognized that no certain one can ever be reached.[108] None the less, it is possible to suggest plausible ways in which they may have been used. One is that they conveyed information, through a symbolic language, to people moving through the locations in which they were made: and the British Neolithic lifestyle seems, as said, to have been a very mobile one. In other words, they acted as signposts, boundary markers and noticeboards. Alternatively, or additionally, they could

Carving from Woodhouse Crag, West Yorkshire, usually, for convenience, described as a swastika

A patch of cups and rings from the Badger Stone boulder, West Yorkshire

Cup and ring from a rock face at Achnabreck, Kilmartin Valley, Argyll

Pattern from part of a rock outcrop at Baluacraig, Kilmartin Valley, Argyll

Cups, rings and ladders from the Panorama Stone boulder, Ilkley Moor, West Yorkshire

28 Complex designs on rock faces.

have been religious images and altars, or (harking back to the explanations of Palaeolithic cave designs) the result of visions induced by trance. In historical times, cup-marked stones in Scandinavia were used for offerings of grain, meat or milk to ancestral and land spirits. At places in the Hebrides, Argyll and West Yorkshire, prehistoric designs were filled with milk in modern times as gifts to the fairies. It would be wonderful if these practices had come directly from ancient times, but this cannot be proved. In the Hawaiian Islands a cup mark is traditionally made to mark the birth of a child, while Australian natives still create them to release a spirit from the stone to bless the surrounding land. Robert Wallis has proposed the exciting theory that the prehistoric British designs were indeed messages, but not for humans; instead they may have been made to be viewed by beings living below the surface of the land. Just as tools were often made of 'special' stone, the boulders and faces selected for carving may already have been regarded as sacred. In general, traditional peoples elsewhere in the world tend to make images on rocks for a variety of purposes, undertaken by different groups within the same community, some openly and some secretly. So it may have been in prehistoric Britain.[109]

The Great Goddess

Since the 1970s, British archaeologists have, apparently universally, paid no attention to the nature of the deities venerated during the Neolithic era of their islands, as part of an assumption that nothing can be known about them. For a century before then, however, they were increasingly inclined to credit the period with having venerated, above all other divinities, a single goddess, representing the sustaining and regenerating powers of the earth, who presided over the religion of the tomb-shrines. The story of the rise and decline of scholarly belief in this religion is one which certainly provides important insights into the nature of modernity, whether or not it tells us anything about the nature of the New Stone Age.[110]

This goddess appeared in the minds of poets before she did in that of scholars, as one aspect of the Romantic Movement, that great rebellion against an excess of civilization, rationalism, urbanization and industrialization which swept Europe in the decades around 1800. As part of this, creative writers, especially in Britain which was most affected by the last two processes, lost much of their traditional interest in the classical Greek and Roman pagan goddesses, who were mostly patronesses of human communities and activities. Instead, they personified the divine feminine increasingly in terms of the natural world, and commonly with broad and simple labels such as 'Mother Nature' and 'Mother Earth' rather than any of the specific classical deity names. This newly popular nature goddess was identified especially with the moon and with wild, green and growing things. As such, she was celebrated in English by John Keats, Percy Bysshe Shelley, Charlotte Brontë, Robert Browning and Algernon Charles Swinburne, to name only the most prominent. The appearance of this figure as a major literary motif ran parallel to an emerging theme of German Romantic thought: that very ancient human beings, being closer to the fount of creation, had been possessed of sublime truths concerning the nature of the cosmos which had degenerated or been forgotten by subsequent peoples. The biblical roots of this idea should be obvious, as well as the assumption by the same thinkers, such as Johann Herder and Johan Ludwig Tieck, that one of those sublime truths had to be monotheism. It is not surprising, therefore, that in 1849 another German intellectual, Edouard Gerhard, hypothesized that behind all the various goddesses of ancient Greece stood a single great one, who had originally subsumed all of them within her being.

As the nineteenth century progressed, other German classicists, and some in France, took up the idea and began to apply it to prehistoric locations: in particular, when female figurines began to emerge in significant numbers on Neolithic sites in Greece and the Balkans, these were sometimes interpreted as images of this presumed deity. By the end of the century it was starting to be embraced by some in Britain, of whom the most important was Sir Arthur Evans, the discoverer of the Minoan civilization of Bronze Age Crete. In 1901 he published the idea that the main deity of that civilization had been the Great Goddess, and continued to develop it thereafter. At the same time the concept of the goddess began to merge with a different nineteenth-century theory, first fully articulated by J. J. Bachofen in 1862: that the earliest human societies had been woman-centred, altering to a patriarchal form before the beginning of history. The union of the two ideas in Britain was made most prominently in 1903 by the Cambridge classicist Jane Ellen Harrison, who posited the existence of a peaceful and intensely creative woman-centred Greek civilization in prehistory, in which humans, living in harmony with the natural world and each other, had worshipped a single female deity, representing the earth. This happy state of affairs, she suggested, had been destroyed by invaders from the north, who had brought male rule, warfare and dominant male deities.

Thereafter the idea of the universal ancient goddess grew still stronger among experts in the prehistory of south-eastern Europe and the Near East. In 1929 one of them in Britain, G. D. Hornblower, gave it an important projection by proposing that the so-called 'Venus' figurines of the Palaeolithic had also been images of that deity, pushing her worship back to the earliest human settlement of Europe. In the same period, anthropologists took up the image and incorporated it into their own work, claiming to detect belief in a Mother Earth in all traditional human societies; a theory first fully articulated by the German scholar Albrecht Dieterich in 1905.[111] At the same time, the literary invocation of Mother Nature, the Great Mother, the Earth Mother or the Mother Goddess remained as powerful as ever, having now as great a presence in prose as in poetry and featuring prominently in the work of such authors as D. H. Lawrence, H. J. Massingham and Robert Graves, while Rudyard Kipling wrote of a priestess-centred prehistoric British religion. As the leading late twentieth-century scholar of comparative religion Mircea Eliade was to note, by the early twentieth century a 'search for the Mother' had become a major component of the 'unconscious nostalgias of the Western intellectual'.[112]

Experts in the British Neolithic, however, reserved judgement, largely because their sites lacked the figurines which were the main pieces of evidence for a goddess-centred religion at the other end of Europe. The barrier appeared to be removed in 1939, when A. L. Armstrong claimed to have found unequivocal proof of such a religion at the bottom of one of the flint mines called Grimes Graves, in the Norfolk Breckland. He announced the discovery there of an altar, with a bowl for offerings before it and a crude female figurine, carved of chalk, seated upon it. From that moment onwards, the statuette appeared in books on the British Neolithic, interpreted as a goddess. Rumours circulated among archaeologists that it was a fake, but such was the discretion of their community that not until 1986 did one of them, Stuart Piggott, print the possibility. In 1991 Gillian Varndell examined the case and found that Armstrong had never recorded the discovery in his site notebook and had ordered all other experienced excavators to leave the location on the day on which it was made. The figurine and bowl looked suspiciously freshly carved, and Varndell concluded that they could no longer be accepted on face value as Neolithic. At the time, however, they removed from some writers on British prehistory the restraint previously shown regarding acceptance of the religion of the Great Goddess in Western Europe. The most prolific and enthusiastic of these was Jacquetta Hawkes, who developed further Jane Ellen Harrison's view of a peaceful, woman-centred, goddess-worshipping early Europe. In her opinion the early Neolithic tomb-shrines had been the temples of the goddess, brought to the Atlantic coasts of Europe as part of her worship by missionaries from the Near East. To her way of thinking this admirable religion and society had been eradicated by the Indo-Europeans, warriors from the East who had introduced a male-centred society and the worship of sky gods, and ushered in the Bronze Age. She was, however, only the most passionate and populist exemplar of a broad trend. Whether or not there was ever an 'Age of the Goddess' in Neolithic Europe, there certainly was one among European intellectuals in the mid twentieth century. Between 1954 and 1958 three giants of British archaeology, O. G. S. Crawford, Gordon Childe and Glyn Daniel, all declared their belief in the veneration of a single female deity by Neolithic cultures all across Europe and the Near East. Specialists in the history and theory of religion now took this belief as proven fact, as did psychologists, above all Erich Neumann, who proclaimed that such a figure was embedded in the human subconscious.

Leaving aside the possibility of divine revelation, which a historian can neither confirm nor disprove, there are fairly clear reasons why such a figure should have strongly appealed to the modern Western imagination. It served two very different purposes. One was to bring the divine feminine strongly back into the consciousness of Western intellectuals, as part of the de-Christianization of society and as a balance to the male-centred nature of traditional public and religious life. The fact that the image of the prehistoric great goddess corresponded quite closely to a biblical model, as that of a single and universal primeval deity, the worship of whom later shattered into historical polytheism, would have made it easier to absorb. The figure of the nature goddess of the earth and night sky had appeared as part of a movement which questioned some of the basic traditional assumptions of Western civilization and represented a major shift of consciousness. On the other hand, whereas certain writers, like Harrison and Hawkes, portrayed the world of goddess-worship as a superior one to later prehistory, others, who included Neumann, suggested that the move from it to worship of male deities had been a sign of human progress. Moreover the image of the Neolithic Great Goddess, concerned with fertility, maternity, earth and nature, propagated a limited and restrictive set of associations for female identities, and could be as readily used to disseminate traditional gender roles as to question them.

It is not uncommon for ideas to achieve this kind of apogee before a fall, and so it was in this case: belief in the Neolithic goddess began to wane among specialists in the period from the mid 1960s, and within ten years it was more or less gone. Specific attacks on aspects of it were published by Peter Ucko and Andrew Fleming, both, significantly, young scholars just commencing their careers, but in themselves these were not sufficient to have caused the change. The willingness to believe simply ebbed away, and, as one of the rising generation involved in British archaeology at that time, I myself can testify to some of the developments behind the change. One was that great questioning of traditional assumptions that was a feature of the time: directed against the construct of the Great Goddess, this revealed that there was in fact no solid evidence for it, only data which might possibly be interpreted to support it. With the tide of archaeological thought running strongly towards social and economic models, the construct seemed old-fashioned as well as unnecessary. Furthermore, the discipline of anthropology was making a major impact on archaeological theory, and the monotheistic goddess religion posited by the theory bore little resemblance to the very complex spirit worlds, teeming with different entities, which formed the belief systems of actual traditional peoples studied by scholars. Instead the concept of a faith focused on a single benevolent deity, preached by missionaries from the Near East, began to look very much like a projection from Christian models, at the same time as the new dates for the Western European Neolithic proved that its monuments could not have been copied from the presumed Eastern models after all.

To British liberals, socialists and feminists, moreover, an image of a female deity which emphasized motherhood, nurturing and nature over intelligence, ambition and vocational skills did not seem an empowering one for women. By contrast, anthropologists were shaking up received concepts of gender, let alone gender roles, so that by 1975 one of them, Shirley Ardener, could ask whether our very categories of 'women' and 'men' might not be cultural constructs that would one day disappear. At the same time, other anthropologists were questioning the earlier assertion, within their discipline, that the belief in a Mother Earth was universal among traditional peoples. In 1966 a Continental scholar, Olaf Petterson, launched a general attack upon it, followed by specific deconstructions based on particular parts of the world.[113] Samuel Gill suggested that where such a figure featured in accounts of Native American mythology she had been imposed on them by the European and European

American authors, while Tony Swain declared that European scholars had done the same thing for native Australian tradition.[114]

To many British prehistorians, therefore, it came as a shock when the old image and the old framework around it were reintroduced from the United States in the years around 1980, if in a newly radicalized guise. American writers such as Mary Daly, Susan Griffin and Adrienne Rich had taken up the traditional, conservative idea of an essential female nature, and simply reversed the sympathies, attaching a positive value to those qualities which the traditional language had defined as negative. British liberals had dealt with an inconvenient old idea by deconstructing it, while the Americans had done so by reversing it. Both responses are excellent strategies in their own right: but unfortunately completely incompatible with each other. One result in the USA was the Goddess Movement, a modern religion devoted to counteracting the perceived ill effects of centuries of male domination of Western society by reasserting the divine feminine, usually embodied directly or ultimately in a single great deity identified with the natural world. Its most distinguished convert among archaeologists was Marija Gimbutas, the foremost American expert in Eastern European prehistory, who published a series of popular books between 1982 and 1991 which reasserted the arguments of authors such as Jane Ellen Harrison, Jacquetta Hawkes and Erich Neumann in updated form. Like them, she envisaged a woman-centred Neolithic Europe, devoted to a single goddess, but remoulded the latter to stress creativeness and universal capability rather than maternity and fertility. Although the epicentre of the Goddess Movement remained in the United States, and indeed it could be viewed as a product of the American evangelical tradition, it found some adherents in Europe, including Britain, who reproduced its emphasis on the Neolithic as a feminist golden age, in society as in religion.[115]

One effect of the Goddess Movement, especially as reflected in the work of Marija Gimbutas, was to make archaeologists in the 1990s look explicitly and systematically at the evidence for the veneration of a single great deity in the Neolithic. The result was generally to confirm the impression that had been gained implicitly two decades before: that it could not be proved, because the data could be interpreted in other ways. One by one, centres of Neolithic and Bronze Age culture that had been prominent in the works of authors who had propounded the concept of the goddess were examined and this conclusion was drawn: for Turkey (and above all the remarkable Neolithic urban site of Çatalhöyük), Greece and the Balkans (the epicentre of Marija Gimbutas's archaeological work), the Aegean Islands, Cyprus, Crete, Malta, Spain, Portugal and France.[116] The very concept of a prehistoric great goddess was considered anew and problems found with it.[117] In Britain the record looks particularly bare, because of the almost complete absence, among Neolithic objects and images, of gendered human-like forms. Now that the Grimes Graves figurine is removed from the bank of reliable data, as discussed above, the clearest example of one is a block of wood found beneath a portion of a wooden trackway across the Somerset Levels. It is roughly carved into the form of a hermaphrodite, having a head, two large breasts and a huge erect penis (the suggestion that this member is a remaining leg seems to be refuted by the lack of any mark where another limb was broken away). It is dated to a period around 3800 BC, and the leading experts on the archaeology of the Levels, Bryony and John Coles, concluded that it might have been a toy, a piece of gross humour or a potent ritual object deposited beneath the track to strengthen it.[118] It would perhaps be a little easier to distinguish between these options if we knew what the raised wooden way, known as the Sweet Track, was actually for: whether a practical means of crossing wetland, or a corridor into a spiritual otherworld, to be walked on vision quests or to worship water spirits.[119]

Two aspects of this poverty of evidence should perhaps be highlighted. The first is that it is virtually certain that Neolithic Europeans venerated goddesses, or at least powerful female spirits, because traditional peoples always do. The worship of such beings is well established, everywhere, as soon as each area of Europe and the Near East emerges into history: and they are generally potent figures in their own right rather than being subservient to gods. The problem is with the concept of a single great goddess, venerated across the whole region. The whole tendency of religious development in the recorded history of the

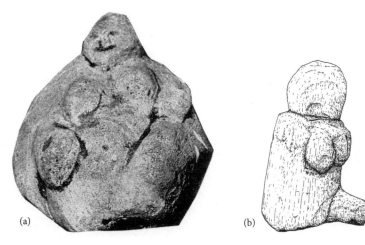

(a)
(b)

29 Neolithic British figurines actual and reputed. (a) Grimes Graves chalk 'goddess'; (b) carved wooden figure from the Sweet Track, Somerset Levels. The former is drawn from life, the latter redrawn after Bryony and John Coles.

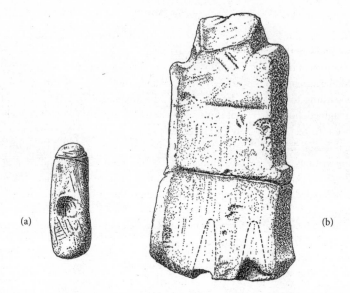

(a)

(b)

30 Carved pieces of chalk from British Neolithic sites. (a) probable phallus from Thickthorn Long Barrow; (b) possible figurine from Maiden Castle, Dorset.

ancient world is that of a primeval situation in which a very large amount of local deities coexist, which later become reduced in number by identification with each other and combination into pantheons. For Sumer during the early third millennium BC, the earliest recorded civilization of Mesopotamia and one contemporary with part of the British Neolithic but possessed of written texts, about four thousand deities can be identified. Only in later millennia, and by succeeding imperial states, were they brought into a single system, and grouped or blended into a family or polity.[120] Eventually, late in pagan antiquity, first some philosophers and then some worshippers were able to conceive of an essential unity of the divine. The concept of a profoundly good primeval religion, centred on a single great deity, which degenerated over time into a polytheism associated with a much worse kind of human behaviour, is a Judaeo-Christian one with no support from the historic or archaeological record. None the less, it is not decisively negated by the evidence of prehistory either. This introduces the second point: that just as the Goddess Movement is a perfectly viable modern religion, so it is still possible to interpret the data from any part of Neolithic Europe as conformable with the worship of a (or the) great goddess. It remains an acceptable reading of the record, though now one among many others.[121]

Warfare

In the present state of the evidence, and probably that of most states to come, we know nothing certain about the social and political structures and gender relations of the British Neolithic, any more than we can of its religious beliefs. Modern people are therefore able to imagine those in many different forms, according to their own beliefs, values, dreams and ideals. What cannot be imagined, however, is that this era was peaceful. To conceive of it as such has been, in fact, a relatively recent development, for the Victorian pioneers of modern archaeology mainly saw it as a period of savagery and bloodshed: in the writings of the two most influential of all, Sir John Lubbock and Sir William Boyd Dawkins, it is more or less a chamber of horrors.[122] Where the great scholars led, creative writers followed, such as the essayist Grant Allen, who considered the disarticulated human bones found in the chamber of a Cotswold–Severn long barrow and imagined them to be the refuse of rites of human sacrifice and cannibalism, enacted to honour a chieftain interred among them.[123] In part such hostile attitudes were based on the premise that people who seemed primitive in technology must also be debased in morality. They also, however, drew directly and heavily on accounts of traditional peoples in the tropical world, produced by the spreading forces of European imperialism and evangelism and often subject to distortion and exaggeration in the reporting. The same sources underpinned the attitudes of the founder of the discipline of anthropology in Britain, Sir Edward Tylor, who portrayed indigenous cultures elsewhere in the world as being given to hideous rites, which he attributed also to the early British.[124] Such a view largely died away in the course of the twentieth century, with the waning of the missionary and supremacist spirit that had produced it, and a growing respect for native peoples. By the end of the century, virtually every piece of data that the Victorians had interpreted as evidence of atrocity was viewed benignly: the human bones mixed together in the long barrows as the results of a social view which erased the individual to glorify the community, and honoured ancestors; the presence of more skeletal material on ceremonial sites as part of a package of deposits intended to venerate all aspects of life; and the similar treatment of the bones of people and animals in such contexts as proof of the harmony in which the societies of the time lived with the natural world.[125]

A concomitant of this set of attitudes was a strong tendency among historians of war, especially the Americans Quincy Wright and Harry Turney, to emphasize the ritualized and limited nature of conflict in 'primitive' societies. They held that wars were fought for prestige and social solidarity, not for gain or power, and so avoided casualties and stressed individual combat in such a way as to turn military action into a sport or a form of gesture politics rather

than a means to conquest and bloodshed. As a result, most textbooks of archaeology published across the Western world in the 1980s made no reference to
warfare.[126] It is difficult to uncouple this development from the complete cessation of conflict between states throughout the Western world in the second half
of the twentieth century, and the relative demilitarization of its societies: people
living in this new condition wanted to have a nicer prehistory, or at least earlier
prehistory, in which war was no longer seen as natural. A challenge developed
in the 1990s, most prominently made by two other Americans, Laurence
Keeley and Raymond Kelly. They conducted systematic studies of the by then
considerable amount of anthropological data for societies which had remained
at a stage of development before the evolution of a state structure, and found
war to be very frequent among them: in one sample of fifty, forty-five often
engaged in it, while in another sample of ninety, seventy-eight did. The exceptions tended to be living under the jurisdiction of modern states, or in isolation
from other humans. Of the tribes of western North America at time of first
study by Europeans, 86 per cent had made war more than once annually: a
higher rate than the ancient Roman republic. There was no evidence that
battles between peoples who had no state apparatus were proportionately less
lethal than those between peoples who had one. Indeed, it was much rarer for
the former to take male prisoners than the latter, which had a stronger interest
in acquiring new subjects. The most peaceful peoples were those who lived in
low numbers in a region of generously distributed natural resources: but they
tended to have above average homicide rates, so that violence among them was
often simply expressed in a different form.[127]

It seems doubtful whether warfare would have existed in the European
Palaeolithic, as the small, highly mobile groups roaming the rich hunting
grounds of the time would not seem to have had much occasion for it. On the
other hand, the areas of France and Spain that have produced the famous cave
pictures may have held much denser and more settled populations; and indeed
the paintings and carvings could have been one expression of rivalry among
them. One French cave, at Cougnac, has two apparent portrayals of human
bodies pierced by many spears, and one in Italy held the body of a child with
an apparent projectile wound; but it has been acknowledged that these may be
manifestations of violence between individuals.[128] It may be added here that
the pictures could also have other meanings, for example showing a shaman in
trance with rays of spiritual power radiating from the body. The Mesolithic
looks different. The world's first known war grave is at Jebel Sahaba in the
Sudan, dated to between 12,000 and 10,000 BC and containing fifty-nine
people, 40.7 per cent of whom had clearly suffered violent death, most by flint
projectiles, probably arrowheads.[129] In European terms, this was a Mesolithic
society, and indeed the cemeteries of the Continental European Mesolithic

contain many examples of individuals who had sustained violent injuries to their bones. A Bavarian cave has disclosed a collection of severed heads, about half bludgeoned to death, from the period. In the Neolithic the Continental evidence apparently becomes yet more dramatic, with more damage to bodies as well as mass graves and fortifications.[130] No attempt is made here to determine whether such interpretations of the evidence are in fact correct: recognition is simply made that this is how some experts – apparently at present without much opposition – have viewed it.

In Britain, most attention has been focused on two causewayed enclosures, at Hambledon Hill, and at Crickley Hill on the Cotswold Scarp of Gloucestershire, and on a stone enclosure on Carn Brea, a dramatic hill in the west of Cornwall. At the first two, systems of timber palisades with gateways, apparently fortresses, had been built in the later fourth millennium. That at Hambledon was burned down at least three times between 3700 and 3300 BC, and two male skeletons were found in the ditches with arrowheads at their throats. At Crickley Hill, over 400 arrowheads littered the perimeter, apparently the product of two attacks, the first of which had ended in a massive strengthening of the defences and the second in their complete abandonment. The wall at Carn Brea had been constructed to a height of six feet (180 centimetres) in about 3700 BC to protect a settlement inside, established near a good source of stone for tools. Roger Mercer's excavations found a total of 751 arrowheads stuck in it and in the ground inside, while the houses had been destroyed by fire. Another causewayed enclosure, at Maiden Castle on a chalk hill in Dorset, had seemingly also been attacked by archers, as there was a concentration of broken arrowheads in one ditch. An enclosure built to protect a promontory at Hembury in Devon had been burned, and at least 120 arrowheads were clustered around a gateway.[131]

Recently a study of 350 Early Neolithic skull-caps, mostly from southern Britain, has revealed that at least 7.4 per cent show evidence of serious injuries, made by heavy blows.[132] As most war wounds would have injured soft tissue and left no trace on skeletons, this is quite a significant figure. In 136 cases arrowheads have been found among the remains of British Early Neolithic burials, and may well have been the cause of death: in five this role was certain, because they were actually sticking into the bones.[133] Some long barrows yielded more concentrated evidence of violence. At Boles Barrow on the edge of Wiltshire's central chalk plateau, many of the bones had suffered traumatic injuries compatible with axe blows.[134] At Wayland's Smithy on the Berkshire Downs, several men seemed to have died 'in a storm of arrow shot'.[135] The weapons that fired these projectiles had the same length as a medieval longbow and could hit a target over 100 yards (100 metres) away. The bone assemblages from British Neolithic sites do not suggest a hunting of large wild animals regular enough to warrant such powerful equipment: their most obvious use is in warfare, and the heavy leaf-shaped arrows that they shot are of a remarkably uniform design and are found commonly all over the British Isles.[136] It is important not to exaggerate the significance of all this evidence: most causewayed enclosures show no sign of violence, nor do most of the bones from tomb-shrines. None the less, there actually seem to be more signs of active warfare in the Early Neolithic than in any other period of British prehistory.[137] This is perhaps not very surprising, as the economy of the time was apparently centred on cattle and sheep, highly mobile forms of wealth which are particularly vulnerable to raiding. Among the handful of societies in the anthropological record that did not practise war, none had a pastoral way of life.

This has some implications for views of British Neolithic ritual practices. Societies that practise warfare regularly tend to ritualize it to a considerable extent and integrate it into their religious traditions, especially in matters such as victory celebration, launching of expeditions, trophy-taking and the treatment of prisoners. It may be that we need to reconsider some of the familiar evidence from sites of the period. Miles Russell has suggested that the human bones put into long barrows could have come from human sacrifices, selected from captives, slaves or superfluous members of the community.[138] Rick Schulting and Michael Wysocki have raised the possibility that the bones gnawed or pecked by animals, found in some of the barrows, had actually been retrieved from battlefields, and represent either the heroic dead of the community or vanquished enemies. They have further asked whether the skeletal material found in the ditches of causewayed enclosures, such as the weathered skulls at Hambledon Hill, might not have been military trophies rather than the remains of venerated ancestors.[139] It is perhaps time to look again at other aspects of the period, such as the number of timber monuments destroyed by fire in Scotland and parts of eastern England. What was going on there may well have been a rite of closure; but it could also have been straightforward enemy action. There is no need to make a full circle back to the Victorian portrait of savagery, but if there is truly to be a just and impartial consideration of the nature of Early Neolithic ritual and religion, then the range of plausible speculation must now readmit the possibility that some of it was bloodthirsty.

3

⇒◦⇐

THE LATE NEOLITHIC AND EARLY BRONZE AGE
THE TIME OF THE SACRED CIRCLE

I N SEVERAL IMPORTANT senses, the transition from the fourth to the third millennium, and from the Early to the Late Neolithic, was one of continuity, the abiding characteristics including an economy based on progressive clearance of woodland and a reliance on herding livestock across much of mainland Britain; a more or less mobile lifestyle across the same range, with little evidence of permanent settlement; a technology centred on the use of stone and flint which made the bow its main weapon and the axe its main tool; and an appetite for the construction of ceremonial monuments which remained as strong as before. The nature of those monuments, however, underwent a profound alteration throughout the southern and eastern parts of the island. Most of the favourite forms of the fourth millennium – long barrows, causewayed enclosures and cursuses – ceased to be built, and in most cases apparently to be used, by 3000 BC. Instead new types of ceremonial enclosure appeared, followed by new settings for the burial of human remains, which had in common a general taste for the circle as the basic unit of shape.

Round monuments had been built in the Early Neolithic, but were, as noted, outnumbered by rectangular and trapezoid forms. Now they became the norm across most of Britain. In the rest of the island, and its offshore isles to west and north, and in Ireland, the old forms persisted, but even there circularity became a prominent feature, as they were developed to a new apogee of size and sophistication. In many ways the circle is one of the great primal units of nature: it reflects the horizon, the sun and moon, the cycle of seasons and the concept of eternity. It is also the simplest geometrical shape to lay out, and the most economical, in terms of the ratio between length of perimeter and area enclosed.[1] It can be one of the most democratic of monumental forms, if all people present are positioned at equal spaces around it, and one of the most hierarchical, if a special person or persons occupy the central point. This shift is the most obvious alteration in monumentality that distinguishes the two millennia from each other, and the two divisions of the New Stone Age. The Late Neolithic in Britain, however reckoned by individual archaeologists, was shorter than the earlier part, as around 2500 BC a copper-based technology entered the island; by the end of the millennium it had developed into a dominant bronze-based one.[2] This made very little difference to ritual behaviour: whereas the advent of the Neolithic had brought about a profound change in the British ceremonial landscape, thereafter alterations in material culture and expressions of spirituality were largely uncoupled from each other. For anybody interested in ancient religious behaviour, the distinction between the New Stone Age, Bronze Age and Iron Age, so handy at a time before the advent of radiocarbon dating when the relative age of sites could only really be judged by artefacts, is now more or less irrelevant in Britain. It survives mainly because of a wholly understandable intellectual inertia, but may also do so because the primacy of technological development as an index of progress in the human story, so dear to nineteenth-century writers, still retains much potency today.

Developed Passage Graves

In Ireland, the new concentration on the circle was married to the older tradition of the tomb-shrine, and produced the most magnificent expression of the latter in a style of monument commonly known to archaeologists as the developed passage grave, or passage tomb. This consists of a large round mound, entered by a long passage of megaliths leading to a stone-built chamber, usually with side cells or recesses. It was a natural elaboration of a type of tomb-shrine common in Western Europe in the fourth millennium, which had embodied a smaller and simpler combination of the same components: the round mound, the passage and the chamber. What distinguished the developed version, in addition to sheer size and multiplication of chambers, was the frequent presence of carved or pecked designs on the stones and the fairly common one of alignment of the passages on the rising or setting of the sun at midsummer and midwinter. The finest examples are now the most celebrated of Irish prehistoric monuments, especially the three in the bend of the River Boyne west of Drogheda: the huge mounds and superb chambers of Newgrange, Knowth and Dowth, constructed around 3300 to 3200 BC.[3]

The famous Boyne Valley passage graves also have the largest number of decorated stones, the 250 surviving at Knowth representing almost half of those found at such monuments in Ireland, and over a quarter of those found in them in Western Europe. Altogether, the designs concerned include about 130 different motifs, of which the most common are circles, dots, cup marks, U-shapes, spirals, radials, parallel lines, chevrons, zigzags, lozenges and triangles. Ireland has the greatest variety of them as well as the greatest quantity, and although a few of the designs overlap with those found in the tomb-shrines of France, Spain and Portugal, most do not. Nor do they have much in common with those carved or pecked into natural rock faces, which tend not to occur in the same areas and apparently have a much broader chronological range, spanning the Neolithic instead of, as in the passage grave art, concentrating in the centuries around 3000 BC.[4] In the mid 1990s, following the interpretation of Palaeolithic cave designs in terms of altered states of consciousness associated with shamanic rites, Jeremy Dronfield proposed a similar explanation for those in the tomb-shrines, as induced either by hallucinogenic drugs or conditions of trance. A parallel debate ensued to that over the Palaeolithic, with an equally indeterminate result.[5] Richard Bradley has argued more recently that there is no single style of passage grave decoration, and so there cannot be a single sort of experience behind it, as even motifs which are common between regions are used in different ways at different sites. He has emphasized instead the dramatic sensory experience of entering a passage grave as warmth and light ebb away and those walking towards the chamber encounter the designs sequentially and in single file.[6] Doubtless an altered state of consciousness would enhance the effect, but would not have been necessary to appreciate it. How people would have qualified for it – whether it was open to all who wished, or to people chosen in turn, or confined to a political or religious elite – we simply cannot tell.

The western side of Wales had belonged, since the Neolithic began, to a cultural province which spanned both sides of the Irish Sea, and its tomb-shrines had similarities to those in Ireland. It is not surprising, therefore, that the developed passage grave crossed the water, to the important offshore island of Anglesey which was already thickly set with tomb-shrines, to produce the finest Welsh examples of the tradition. It is possible that another was constructed further east, on the shores of the Mersey in what is now Lancashire, which included the six decorated stones now preserved in Calderstones Park, Liverpool. These bear the most complex carved megalithic designs in Europe, with concentric circles, grooves, lines and spirals, arcs, cups, footprints and a wheel.[7] They, however, have no certain provenance and may have been taken from a rock outcrop, so at present there are no certain examples of the developed passage grave on mainland Britain. The Welsh representatives are the two in Anglesey: Bryn Celli Ddu, sitting in a field behind a farmyard within the island, and Barclodiad y Gawres, at the end of a promontory jutting out from the western coast. Both have been much reconstructed in modern times, after

(a)

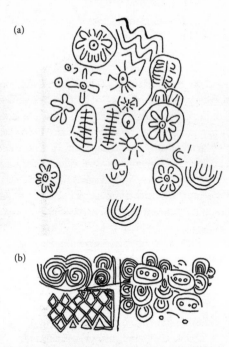

(b)

31 Classic designs from Irish developed passage graves, drawn from life:
(a) in the rear of the chamber of Cairn T at Loughcrew, County Meath;
(b) on kerbstone 52 at Newgrange, in the same county.

excavation, and are kept open to the public by Cadw, the Welsh heritage conservation body.

Bryn Celli Ddu was a large circular cairn of stones covering a passage 27 feet (over 8 metres) long, leading to a central, polygonal chamber. This had a small spiral carved into one upright, visible only by artificial light, while a megalith with an elaborate serpentine design was put face-down over a pit in the centre of the site before the monument was constructed over it. The passage points at the midsummer sunrise, which lights up a quartz-rich monolith at the back of the chamber.[8] Barclodiad y Gawres (meaning 'the apron-ful of the giantess' in reference to a local legend) had a mound mainly composed of earth, with turf – carefully taken from marshy ground – piled over it; as in the case of many tomb-shrines, including the Boyne passage graves, the covering structure was made up of materials brought from more than one location. The mound was 90 feet (27 metres) across and a passage 23 feet (7 metres) long led into it, to a cross-shaped chamber with three smaller cells opening off. It lacks an apparent orientation on the sun, but has more decorations:

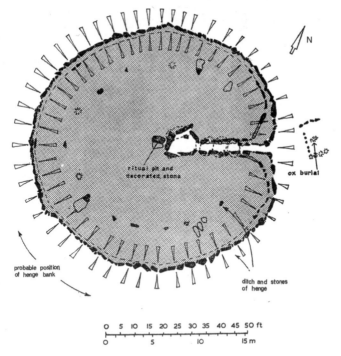

32 Bryn Celli Ddu developed passage grave: exterior and plan. The plan is redrawn after T. G. E. Powell *et al.*

(a)

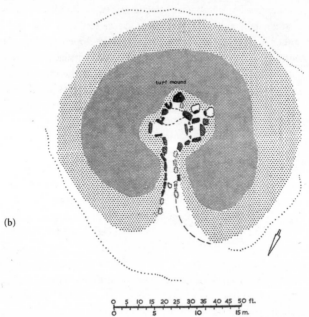

(b)

33 Barclodiad y Gawres developed passage grave: interior and plan. The plan is redrawn after T. G. E. Powell *et al.* One of the decorated stones can faintly be seen in the left-hand upper portion of the photograph.

concentric circles, chevrons, lozenges, zigzags and spirals appear on seven of the stones. The burial mode at both of the Anglesey passage graves was cremation, as it was in the Boyne Valley, but the central area of the Barclodiad y Gawres chamber had been used for a much more enigmatic rite, in which a fire had been quenched with a 'stew' containing frog, toad, snake, mouse, eel, and two types of small fish.[9] At both monuments, fires had been burned in the passages and chambers, which would have lit them up and shown the carvings.[10] The two are perhaps the most sophisticated and elaborate Neolithic structures in the whole of Wales.

That honour among Scottish monuments is commonly given to the finest expression of the developed passage grave tradition there, Maes Howe in the Orkney Islands to the north of the British mainland. The islands concerned were exceptionally well fashioned by nature to provide settings for monumental construction in the period, being composed of sandstone rock which weathers to fertile soil, supporting a large human population, and also splits easily into slabs perfect for use as megaliths. The building of tomb-shrines there began intensively in the middle of the fourth millennium, until about eighty were constructed across the archipelago. They seem to fall into two main varieties. One is the 'stalled cairn', a long, rectangular chamber, subdivided by upright slabs into separate stalls and set in a rectangular or round mound of piled stones. The other is the local development of the developed passage grave, having the central chamber of the type, entered by a long passage from the side of a circular mound, and usually with cells opening off the chamber. This second kind is much rarer, known from ten to twelve examples. Both seem to have become larger over time, Maes Howe, built in the early third millennium BC, being the largest and most beautifully formed of the passage graves. It is set, appropriately, in the centre of the biggest island, Orkney Mainland.

Maes Howe shows several features that indicate direct inspiration by the slightly older Boyne Valley monuments. One is the sheer scale: the grassed-over, dome-like mound being over 110 feet (35 metres) across, the passage 54 feet (over 18 metres) long, and the chamber 15 feet (over 4 metres) square. The stones making up the passage and chamber weigh as much as 30 tons each, and are highly polished and carefully fitted together. The second Irish feature is the making of a precinct around the mound, which sits on a platform bounded by a ditch 35 feet (nearly 14 metres across). The third is a probable orientation on the sun, which sends a beam of light straight down the passage as it sets at midwinter, and would have done even when the entrance was blocked because the closing stone left a gap at the top to emit the sunbeam. The outer part of the passage was rebuilt in the nineteenth century during the modern restoration of the monument, so it is not absolutely certain that this feature is original; but the rebuilding seems to have followed the original

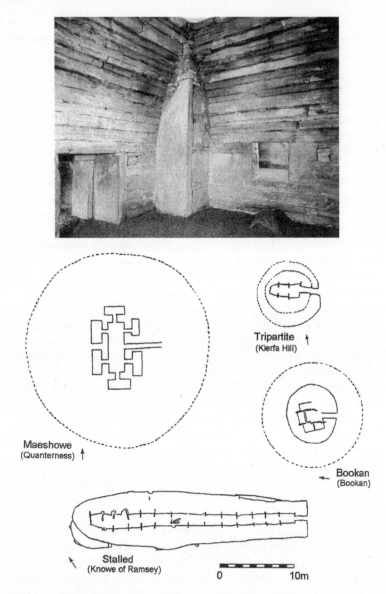

34 Orkney tomb-shrines. Above is a photograph of the chamber of Maes Howe, below are plans of the two main types of design, and two lesser varieties which may have grown out of these, redrawn after Audrey Henshall.

line. Most Orcadian tomb-shrines, however, face points between north-east and south-east like English long barrows. Colin Richards has suggested that this formed a deliberate calendar whereby a succession of monuments was illuminated by the rising sun at different times of the year, which is an enticing idea; though we would still have to reckon with the minority of tomb-shrines which face away from this span. The fourth Boyne Valley feature at Maes Howe is the presence of engraved designs on ten stones, of triangles, lozenges, diamonds and chevrons. They were not noticed until the 1980s, being lightly incised: perhaps they were bases for paintings that have disappeared, or perhaps the act of marking the megaliths was more significant than the finished result. Six other Orkney tomb-shrines have or have had decorated stones, mostly similar pecked angular designs but also a set of linked spirals. All these similarities to Ireland are, however, approximate and not exact, and the Orkney monuments lack the Irish customs of grouping passage graves in cemeteries and cremating the dead placed in them: as usual in the Neolithic, a basic architectural and ritual idea was being adapted to local tastes and traditions.[11]

The tomb-shrines of Orkney have naturally been subject to changing patterns of interpretation within recent British archaeology. Those on the island of Rousay are spaced fairly evenly along the southern shore, facing the channel that divides it from the main island. In the 1970s, Colin Renfrew took this as evidence that each marked the territory of a different social group. By 2005 Vicki Cummings and Amelia Pannett could see them instead as a succession of sacred sites easily visible and accessible to people travelling by boat along the channel; the settlements of the island are on the opposite coast, so that this one would have been set aside for ritual. Cummings and Pannett found water, indeed, to be a key reference point in the setting of all Orcadian tomb-shrines, as in many of those in western Britain.[12] Making sense of these monuments as burial places has become increasingly problematic. Some held very large quantities of human bone. Isbister, a hybrid variety of tomb-shrine overlooking the shelving cliffs and seabird roosts of South Ronaldsay, contained at least 338 people, whose bodies had been stripped of flesh and dismembered beforehand, and whose skulls and long bones were stacked in different areas. Quanterness, a developed passage grave on the main island, held fragments of at least 157 individuals, whose bones had been scorched and then pulverized. As it could have been built by twenty people, this might represent the burial place of an entire community. On the other hand, it is an easy walk from there to Cuween Hill, a passage grave with just five human skulls, and then to Wideford Hill, another which seemed completely empty. The same pattern is repeated across the archipelago. Leaving aside Isbister and Quanterness, the average Orcadian tomb-shrine held remains of eleven people,

deposited over thirty to fifty generations. Clearly most of the Neolithic
inhabitants of the islands were not interred in these monuments. This has led
John Barber to wonder if they were indeed primarily shrines, with burials as
incidental to their purpose as they are to a Christian church, and Timothy
Taylor to suggest that they were reserved for a social elite, just as the inhabitants of certain Melanesian islands used to preserve the bones only of the most
important families. Colin Richards has proposed that parts of body were
moved between tomb-shrines, to forge relationships between different groups
in the islands.[13]

Certainly human bone was nearly always part of an assemblage in the
chambers, with material goods – especially pottery – and animal bone accompanying and sometimes outnumbering it. The most celebrated site to be associated with animals is Isbister, which contained pieces of forty-five pots and
bones of cattle, sheep, deer and sea eagles, the largest birds of prey found in the
islands at that time. It is special in that it was excavated by the farmer who
owned the land, Ronald Simison, between the 1950s and 1970s, and it remains
open to the public, with a fine little museum that displays the finds that are
retained in the hands of his family.[14] It became famous because of a popular
book published in 1984, by John Hedges, which dubbed the site the 'Tomb of
the Eagles' and suggested that these birds had been the totems of the community which had built the monument. It is true that twenty-four dog skulls were
found at Cuween Hill, while the tomb-shrine at Knowe of Yarso mixed the
bones of humans with those of red deer; and two other such monuments
contained, respectively, remains of songbirds and cormorants. On the other
hand, many had no animals inside, while that at Blackhammer contained,
with human beings, sheep, cattle, deer, gannet, cormorant and geese, and that
at Point of Cott had sheep, dog, cattle, deer, otter, rodents, birds and fish as
well as people. Some of the animal bones at the latter site were modern, and an
unknown number had been intruded during the millennia since the Neolithic.
More significant still, the tomb-shrine on the Holm of Papa Westray,
re-excavated in the 1980s, was proved to have been used as a lambing pen for
sheep in between burials, even when it was still active as a ritual monument.
This shows that at least some of these monuments were kept open for at
least some of the time by their builders, making possible all manner of intrusions by domestic and wild creatures. Furthermore, the dating of the various
chamber deposits needs refining, and it may well turn out that the eagles from
Isbister and dogs from Cuween Hill were centuries younger than the human
bones, and not related.[15] Once more, a neat and exciting interpretation of the
Neolithic evidence does not match up to its sheer complexity.[16]

All in a Ring

From the opening of the Neolithic, Ireland and Britain had been different in their relative choices of both farming methods and monumental forms, and one such distinction had been the much greater interest shown by the inhabitants of Britain, east and south of the Scottish Highlands, in ceremonial enclosures open to the sky. Unsurprisingly, with the coming of the third millennium and the new emphasis on circularity, they applied this to the concept of the enclosure, to produce rings of earth, timber and stone, usually surrounding open spaces, in large numbers. Although only some of these were true circles, many being ellipses or ovals, or formed of a series of more or less straight segments joined in the round, or simply roughly and unevenly circular, all looked more or less like circles to the eye. They seem, like the monuments before them, to have been associated with a mobile lifestyle of herders and graziers, and concentrate along natural routes across the landscape, the larger and more numerous where two or more of those converge, to create places where different groups might gather from separate directions at special times.[17]

The earthen circles could consist of a ditch, a bank, or both. In most of the latter cases the ditch was dug inside the bank, with one or more entrances through both, to produce a kind of monument customarily called a 'henge'. The name, as archaeologists have always recognized, is anomalous, being taken from Stonehenge itself, the most spectacular Neolithic circle of all, even though the bank around Stonehenge is inside the ditch. It was developed as a label for this sort of monument between 1939 and 1951, by Stuart Piggott and Richard Atkinson, for lack of any better, and has stuck.[18] The recurrent form of henges, which is unique to the British Isles, seems to imply some basically similar purpose for them, and they are the archetypal ritual sites of the third millennium. Some 120 were recorded across the archipelago by 2002, twenty-seven in Ireland and the rest in Britain, mostly in the south and east, but they varied greatly in size, the nature of the defining enclosure, and internal features, throughout the time in which they were built. The range of size is anything between less than 30 feet (10 metres) across to almost 1,300 feet (400 metres). Some contain settings of pits, wooden posts or standing stones. In the Thames Valley they are usually small, but on the Wessex chalk hills they tend to be huge, while on the chalk upland of the Yorkshire Wolds, apparently ideal terrain for them, they are almost absent, as they are from south-eastern England, the Welsh Border and the West Midlands. In Scotland they are found mostly in the same regions as the earlier Neolithic enclosures: in the Borders and the Tay Valley, Fife and Angus. Even very large specimens sometimes congregate together, such as the six near Thornborough in Yorkshire's Ure Valley, so they were not spaced out between territories, and look more like pilgrimage centres than cathedrals or centres for chiefdoms. None shows any sign of consistent domestic occupation: they were gathering-places for particular times.[19] Jan Harding, perhaps the leading British expert in them, has suggested that their variety of size may represent a hierarchy from small specimens used by individual groups to large constructions designed for mass seasonal gatherings. Clearly the sheer effort needed to build the larger presupposes that they had relatively large catchment areas. On the other hand, as Harding as also suggested, the smaller could have been made to serve moments of religious, social or political difficulty, or to mark the forging of alliances, or to cater for seasonal cults; which may explain which henges sometimes occur in groups. The larger could have allowed the expression of a range of social identities (and, one might add here, a range of religious activities).[20]

The timber rings were even more varied in form – some having one or two circles of posts and some multiple circuits – and in size. Alex Gibson has been the archaeologist most closely associated with their investigation. It is very likely that some or many were joined together at the top, like the lintels of doors, and some may indeed have been roofed.[21] Others took the form of palisaded enclosures, the uprights being close enough together to form a continuous wall. Twenty have been discovered in Scotland since the 1970s, and are among its largest prehistoric monuments. That investigated in the 1990s at

35 A small henge, excavated and restored by farmer and archaeologist (and celebrated flint-knapper) Martin Green, on his land in Cranborne Chase, Dorset.

36 Entrance to the large henge, preserved by being turned into a Roman amphitheatre and then into a Civil War fort, at Maumbury Rings, Dorset.

Hindwell in the Radnorshire region of eastern Wales is potentially the biggest Neolithic enclosure in Britain, covering 74 to 86 acres (roughly 28 to 35 hectares) and made of posts probably almost 20 feet (6 metres) high.[22] The most famous of all prehistoric British timber circles, however, is now the small one constructed towards the end of the third millennium near the Norfolk coast, not far from what is now the settlement of Holme-next-the-Sea. It was one of dozens of prehistoric circular ritual sites being excavated each year in the nation during the economic boom of the 1990s, and what made it special was simply that it was exposed by the action of the sea, next to a bird sanctuary. First the winter, and then the need to let the birds breed, delayed excavation for almost a year, until the summer of 1999, by which time the mass media had turned the find into a national sensation. Though it was not originally by the sea, and was not a henge, it was dubbed 'Seahenge' by journalists, and had attracted 16,000 visitors before excavation began. When that took place, it was caught up in a controversy over the nature and purpose of the process, generated by the different claims and perceptions of archaeologists, local communities and members of modern pagan traditions. After removal and conservation, it is now the single biggest attraction of the King's Lynn Museum.

It was erected in 2049 BC, in a marsh, and consisted of the bole of a large oak tree inverted into a hole in the centre of an elliptical palisade of timber posts taken from the same wood, with one narrow entrance which was blocked off after the structure was completed. The tree rings of the oak permit the exact dating. The oak itself could have been the point of veneration in the monument, which may have been a shrine to its spirit, or those of all the trees employed in construction. On the other hand, it may have served as an altar to different spiritual powers or as a platform for a human body during an elaborate funeral rite. The ring was possibly aligned on the midsummer sunrise or midwinter sunset, and so may have been designed for a seasonal festival. All that is certain is that it could contain a relatively small group of people, who were admitted for a brief period to an enclosed world of inverted space. The posts were, however, shaped by between fifty and sixty bronze axes, so that a sizeable number of individuals, perhaps from different communities, seem to have been involved in the making of the monument.[23]

Timber circles, and most henges, are now visible only as crop marks, but the third kind of circle, that made by standing large stones up on end, maintains a great presence in the British landscape. Indeed, it is virtually indestructible, save by human effort, and the stone circle makes up with the tomb-shrine one of the two most famous classes of monument from earlier British prehistory. For many people these rings of grey megaliths, whether set in lush valley pastures, limestone ridges or wilder moor and mountain scenery, sum up the imaginative power and physical presence of the remote past. They have been studied as a group since the 1970s by Aubrey Burl and then John Barnatt. Some 702 were recorded as surviving in Britain in 1976, with another 261 in Ireland, and a few more have been discovered since: like henges, they are almost exclusively a feature of the British Isles. Their distribution, however, is broader, covering most regions of the island in which stone is available, save for the south-eastern corner. The highest concentrations are in the south-western peninsula and in the north-eastern horn of Scotland around Aberdeen.[24] Many are only a dozen feet across (almost four metres), while the largest of the three in the valley of the River Chew at Stanton Drew in Somerset is almost 340 feet (about 110 metres) wide. One reason for their abundance may have been that, compared with making a long barrow or an earthwork, they were relatively easy to construct. Tom Clare has estimated that four to five adults, effectively a family group, could have erected any of the forty-six circles in Cumbria using the materials available in the third millennium.[25]

Linear monuments continued to be made alongside the round, though in stone or wood rather than in earth as before. Scattered up and down western Britain among stone circles, with (as in the case of the latter) a special concentration in Devon and Cornwall, are lines of megaliths, mostly single but sometimes double. In the south-west they are found most often on the boundary between summer and winter pastures, pointing from one to the other. Perhaps they were intended as paths for spirits – some of the double rows are too narrow

37 Upland stone circle, Trowlesworthy Warren, Dartmoor, Devon, superbly photographed in mist by the historian Matt Kelly, and reproduced here with his permission.

38 A lowland stone circle, the Nine Stones at Winterbourne Abbas, Dorset, enclosed in their Ministry of Works precinct from the mid twentieth century.

to be easily trodden by humans – and the higher ground was associated especially with the supernatural and with the human dead. Peter Herring has
noticed that those on Bodmin Moor tend to highlight sudden dramatic views,
especially of prominent hills, and wondered if they did not mark special routes
for groups engaged in seasonal migration.[26] At the same time, single standing
stones were erected, or continued to be erected, in many parts of the island.

For much of the late twentieth century, archaeologists were routinely
employed in counting and classifying the monuments in each of these categories, as part of the process of discovering, labelling and designating intrinsic to
modern science. This activity has faltered in recent years, as the utility of the
classes concerned has been increasingly called into question. For one thing,
they tended to be combined: most timber circles, for example, were enclosed
by earthen banks.[27] Henges often contained wooden rings, and sometimes
those of stone. For another, sites were often revealed by excavation to have
passed through different stages to reach their enduring form: thus, a stone
circle at Meini Gwyr, in a meadow south of the Preseli Mountains of
Pembrokeshire, started as a ring of pits, became an enclosure and turned into a
henge within which the stones were erected.[28] Timber circles were often subsequently encircled by henges, and sometimes rebuilt in stone.[29] At Forteviot,
beside the River Earn in Central Scotland, a timber circle was erected, only to
be knocked down and replaced by a set of small henges. These were then
surrounded by one of the largest Neolithic enclosures in Europe, a circular
earthwork over 800 feet (265 metres) across, with an entrance avenue of oak
posts, some 7 feet (over 2 metres) wide.[30] Furthermore, even when structures
were single-period, those of very similar form could be given quite different
sorts of deposit and so apparently be used in distinct ways. Julian Thomas has
emphasized this pattern in the particular case of henges, and also noted that
some henges contain material similar to that found on other kinds of Late
Neolithic site, arguing from this that function was not derived from form, and
henges were not a coherent and bounded tradition of construction. Gordon
Barclay has agreed, noting that the category of 'henge' monument was an
artificial construct created by comparing only individual elements of sites
which often had long and complex histories of development.[31]

Dating the timber and earthen circles is relatively easy, once they are excavated, because they are composed of or made by materials that are susceptible
to the necessary analysis. The problem is the relative lack of excavation: only
twenty-three henges had provided dates for initial construction by 2002. That
said, those dates have at least been consistent, the 'classic' form of henge
becoming standard from about 2800 BC and apparently no longer built in most
regions after 2000, which makes it a securely Late Neolithic tradition across
most of Britain. The exception is the far north of Scotland, where diminutive

henges were built well into the second millennium, perhaps as short-lived family shrines.[32] Timber rings seem to appear earlier, around 3300, and go on much longer, until around 1000, although becoming largest, most common and most complex in the mid third millennium.[33] Single standing stones, circles and rows are much harder to date, because stone itself carries no indication of one and the few excavations have revealed surprisingly few deposits within or around them. They can mostly be placed in time only by association with other kinds of monument, though the temptation is to assume that since they follow the same basic pattern as timber rings, they probably cover the same period.[34] None the less, some recent discoveries seem to extend their range still further. A row on Cut Hill, Dartmoor, was discovered to have been sealed by peat which apparently dates its erection to some point in the fourth millennium, so it must be Early Neolithic.[35] At the other end of the timescale, a stone circle at Croft Moraig in Perthshire, which had been given an inner ring of timbers and then replaced by a ditched enclosure, was redeveloped around the year 1000 BC into an oval of megaliths orientated on a mountain pass and the midwinter sunset. So, in a few places in Britain at least, such sites were being reused and reconstructed as late as the final millennium of prehistory, whether or not the beliefs and rites enacted at them were similar to those engaged in before.[36]

This of course begs the question of what those beliefs and rites had ever been. It is impossible at present to tell whether the banks of henge monuments were intended to exclude or include: whether they screened off activities inside from anybody on the exterior, or provided grandstand seating for people to watch those activities. It may be also that the design of henges reflected the landscape, and so an entire cosmology, the shape representing the horizon, the banks encircling hills, and the ditches watercourses. It remains unclear whether they had any defensive function, although this would be more obvious if the ditch were outside the bank. A radical alternative to all these ideas has been to note that the construction of a henge was often the final activity upon a site, and may have been an act of closure in itself. In this view the surrounding of the ground would have been intended to pen in the spiritual power associated with it or formerly raised upon it, and keep people on the outside safe for ever from it when it was abandoned.[37] In general, timber and earthwork constructions of the third millennium are full of deposits similar to those from causewayed enclosures – flints, pottery, animal bone, and sometimes that of humans – which suggest gatherings, and probably feasting as an important element of those. The stone monuments, by contrast, show little sign of human visitation, and, once a timber or earth structure was given standing stones, activity seemed to cease there. In 1998 this pattern was formalized by Mike Parker Pearson into a theory that wood symbolized the world of the living in Neolithic Britain, and

stone that of the dead. He had worked in Madagascar, an island where this
belief is securely recorded, and proposed, in partnership with one inhabitant,
an archaeologist called Ramilisonina, that it could be applied to British prehistory. This provoked an immediate debate, in which colleagues argued that to
emphasize the human dead, rather than deities and other supernatural beings,
was to narrow the interpretation of the monuments excessively, while to other
traditional peoples, such as some Native Americans, wood represented human
ancestors.[38] None the less, in its broader sense that wooden structures were
places for the human and the stone equivalents were associated with the supernatural, and largely reserved for it, the interpretation has found some influential endorsement in the years since.[39] Colin Richards has even suggested that
the stones of circles represented individual dead people, or kin groups or
ancestral bodies, and acted as their memorials.[40] At its most extreme, this idea
invites us to regard the stone rings of Britain, for centuries imagined as places
for gathering, ceremony and celebration, as having been designed as silent and
empty monuments reserved for the deities and the dead, for at least most of the
time. The alternative is that they were used for rites that left no material debris;
but this explanation still recognizes a significant contrast between them and
the monuments of wood and earth.

Combinations and Collisions

It has already been noted that different kinds of circular structure could be
combined in various ways, and the relationships between the monuments of
the fourth millennium and those of the third were still more complex. On the
whole, the builders of the rings were not only reluctant to demolish or injure
the older structures but often chose to site their creations close to them. Long
barrows occasionally received intrusive burials or deposits of artefacts, and the
great Dorset cursus was given the latter at times throughout the third millennium.[41] Generally, however, the constructions of the Early Neolithic were
abandoned, and it is impossible to tell whether the placing of those of the Late
Neolithic in proximity to so many signified a continuing reverence for the old
monumental forms, a continuing reverence for the location itself, or a triumphant assertion of new ideas over those of the past. In places a more adversarial
relationship may have been present. The developed passage grave of Bryn Celli
Ddu was apparently built over a henge monument containing a stone circle,
which was destroyed to make way for it, the stones being removed, broken or
toppled.[42] At Callanish, on the island of Lewis in the Outer Hebrides, Scotland's
finest single megalithic complex was built, in the form of a small stone circle
amid a cross-shaped pattern of stone avenues which may have echoed the
chamber plan of a developed passage grave. If so, this reference to older forms

did not save it, because a miniature passage grave was then built in the centre of the circle, preventing any further easy use of it.[43] In both cases – which alike date from the middle of the third millennium – it looks as if old traditions were being violently reasserted against new, though it is possible that both also represented attempts to reconcile them.

If so, a much more extensive and imposing reconciliation of the forms from the different millennia was achieved in Orkney, in a basin of land near the centre of the main island, where two lakes, Lochs Stenness and Harray, meet. There a chain of monuments was built at the end of the fourth millennium and the first half of the third, of which the westernmost was a large stone circle, the

39 Callanish, the striking complex of stone circle and radiating avenues on the Hebridean island of Lewis. The plan is redrawn after E. Haddingham, and both it and the photograph clearly show the miniature tomb-shrine intruded into the centre.

Ring of Brodgar, contained within a rock-cut ditch. Next, on the peninsula called the Ness of Brodgar, sticking out into the lakes, came a settlement, which was succeeded by a single large building, with walls over 15 feet (5 metres) thick and a cross-shaped chamber. To the east of that, just across the narrow arm of water joining the lakes, was another settlement, Barnhouse, also dominated by a single large building which seems to have had a ceremonial purpose. Later an enormous circular building succeeded it. Individual standing stones were placed in this sequence of major constructions, to the east of which were the Stones of Stenness, a henge with an internal ring of megaliths, smaller than that of Brodgar but with even taller stones. To the east of that in turn stood the great passage grave of Maes Howe. More of the complex may remain to be discovered: though the stone circles and tomb-shrine have been famous for over three centuries, the buildings at Barnhouse were only found in the 1990s and those at the Ness of Brodgar in the 2000s. Together they make up the single most imposing and celebrated megalithic complex in Scotland, and some of the finest structures in the care of the nation's heritage agency, Historic Scotland: they are, indeed, now a World Heritage Site.

40 An arc of the Ring of Brodgar stone circle on Orkney.

Colin Richards has pointed out the common links between them, which seem to make them function as a single ideological unit. Stenness is a stone circle that mirrors the form of a circular house with a single entrance and central hearth, of the sort most common in Neolithic Orkney, all features reproduced at the final ceremonial building at Barnhouse nearby. Both Stenness and Barnhouse contained evidence for feasting. Maes Howe is a passage grave which imitates the house-like concept as well, being circular with a single entrance and passage; furthermore, the chamber incorporates four standing stones which make it into a stone circle as well. Only the hearth is missing, perhaps because it was a place of the dead, not the living. The dominant Ness of Brodgar building, and that in the initial Barnhouse settlement, had cross-shaped interiors like that of Maes Howe. The final building at Barnhouse faced the midsummer sunset, as Maes Howe apparently does the midwinter one. The ditches of the circles of Brodgar and Stenness would have filled with water at most times of the year, turning them, as Richards has suggested, into ceremonial spaces surrounded in concentric circles by stones, water, earth, water (the lochs), and earth (the encircling hills) All therefore look like different expressions of the same set of ideas, seemingly turned into physical form in a great spurt of construction between about 3300 and 2800 BC. The stones in the circles were of different forms of geology, indicating that they had been brought from separated parts of the island by distinct groups, acting in a concerted effort. Colin Renfrew saw this as a harmonious enterprise reflecting a newly centralized authority, such as of paramount chiefs, while Colin Richards views it as a feverish competition for status between still independent groups from different districts: the choice between them must be a matter for personal taste. Richards has noted that the stone circle at Stenness was never completed, and that at Brodgar may never have been, so that the actual value of such monuments could have lain in the building of them, and not in any subsequent use.[44]

The discovery of the settlement sites in the complex has invited reconsideration of what is known of the other Neolithic settlements found in the Orkneys, of which the most famous – and indeed the best-preserved Neolithic village in northern Europe – is Skara Brae on the coast west of the Ring of Brodgar. Exposed by a storm in 1850 and excavated in three successive campaigns between the 1850s and 1970s, it is noteworthy not merely for the richness of the finds within the houses, but for their stone furniture of beds and dressers. Gradually, however, a dozen other settlements have been discovered in the islands, of the same age, and it has increasingly been questioned whether they should be regarded as domestic structures at all. Some contain incised designs of the same sort as those found in the local tomb-shrines, and mirror the chamber shapes of the latter in the houses, while Skara Brae also had burials: perhaps those dressers held ancestral skulls instead of the household objects presumed in traditional reconstructions. Two of the houses at the Ness of Brodgar also had zigzag patterns painted on the walls, in yellow, red and black; the first evidence for houses decorated with paint from anywhere in northern Europe. Furthermore, the so-called settlements have Grooved Ware, a kind of pottery decorated with similar designs, which appeared around 3200 BC and is found throughout Britain at ceremonial rather than living sites. As such, it is probable that they were themselves ritual spaces, or – for those who wish to think in terms of elites – the homes of the special class of people who officiated in ritual.[45] Further attention has been focused on this issue by the discovery of the latest Orcadian settlement site, at the Links of Noltland on Westray island, where excavation began in 2009. It was certainly occupied by people who engaged in regular practices of farming, hunting, shellfish-gathering and craftwork, but also contained at least one massive building with inverted cattle skulls placed within its structure. The site yielded the only known carvings of the human form from Neolithic Scotland, two small pieces of sandstone and one of clay in rough human shapes with rudimentary facial features and (in two cases) circles which may indicate female breasts or clothing fasteners: despite the doubt about their sex, the national press immediately dubbed the first to be found 'the Orkney Venus', showing how conservative the public perception of prehistoric artefacts can remain.[46]

41 House Seven in the Skara Brae settlement, Orkney.

The people of Neolithic Orkney created some of the most splendid prehistoric monuments in the world from a fusion of vision which incorporated circles, tomb-shrines and houses. This activity seems to have ceased, however, by the middle of the third millennium, and thereafter no more were erected. Burials became individual, in a new tradition, although deposits were still made outside the blocked entrances of the old tomb-shrines, and a cluster of the new-style burials was put around the Ring of Brodgar.[47] In Ireland, henges appeared but remained rare, while stone circles were adopted enthusiastically. At the same time the tomb-shrine tradition remained buoyant there, and generated a new and widespread form, known as the wedge tomb, which became the most common kind of all in the island and flourished well into the second millennium.[48] The situation in Wales is less clear: henges and timber circles are found in the north and east and small stone rings across the western half of the country, but it is uncertain how these interrelated with the tomb-shrines where they feature in the same district. In West Wales the dolmens were given some new deposits towards the end of the third millennium, but may have been long disused when those were made.[49] In the extreme west of Britain, in the Isles of Scilly and the toe of Cornwall, a return to the old tradition occurred in the second millennium, with the building of entrance graves. These were chambers consisting of a single broad passage, entered from the side of a small circular mound. The deposits inside usually consist of dark earth mixed with potsherds, charcoal and ash, rather than burials as such, suggesting that this apparent revival of the tomb-shrine put an emphasis on the shrine rather than the tomb component (unless, as has been suggested for West Wales, the earth actually consists of cremations).[50]

In north-east Scotland, new mixtures were made around the same time, with the appearance of two new kinds of spectacular construction, both of which have recently been much illuminated by the investigations of Richard Bradley. Around the head of the Moray Firth were built the Clava Cairns, about fifty passage graves surrounded by stone rings, two with entrances aligned exactly on the midwinter sunset and most possibly facing the movements of the moon. These were conscious imitations of Neolithic monuments, but built a thousand years later, in the early second millennium, and used once more at the end of that millennium: they thus span the Bronze Age.[51] In the equally fertile coastal lowlands of what became Aberdeenshire, during the late third millennium, appeared the recumbent-stone circles, close-set rings with the megaliths graded in height, and one massive horizontal slab positioned between two tall flankers in the southern arc. They were probably the first stone circles in the British Isles, apart from Stonehenge itself, to be identified by scholars as human-made monuments (in the early sixteenth century).[52] Seventy-one survive, though only nine are intact, and Bradley's excavation of

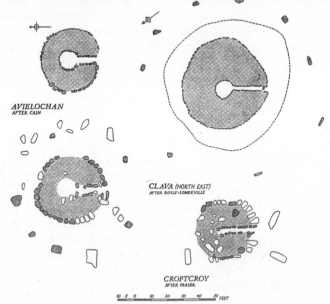

AVIELOCHAN
AFTER CASH

CLAVA (NORTH EAST)
AFTER BOYLE-SOMERVILLE

CROFTCROY
AFTER FRASER

10 5 0   10   20   30   40   50 FEET

42 Clava Cairns. The photograph shows one of the group at Balnuaran of Clava, while the plans, redrawn after the scholars named by each, are taken from a representative sample of the group.

three revealed that the circles represented the last activity on each of the sites concerned: they had been built to surround stone cairns, at least one of which held cremated human bone. The recumbent stone in each was placed along stages of the moon's progress across the sky, but also aligned on a prominent mountain in the vicinity. The stone made actual observation of the moon difficult or impossible in some of the circles, and the internal cairns would have exacerbated this problem. Bradley has therefore suggested that the orientation was symbolic rather than a component of active ritual, though he has also pointed out that the cairns would have made good platforms for bonfires, perhaps cremation pyres, which would have lit up the circles from inside and made them appear alive. Further recent work has suggested that winter sunsets, rather than the moon, could have been the reason for the orientation of the

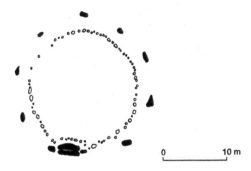

43 Plan, redrawn after Aubrey Burl, and photograph of an Aberdeenshire recumbent stone circle, Loanhead of Daviot.

rings.[53] The Clava Cairns shared with the recumbent-stone circles' graded megaliths the same orientation on the sky, and the erection of the stone ring as the final act of construction. Essentially, however, they were using the same ideas in different ways, to make distinct kinds of monument on opposite sides of the Grampian Mountains.[54]

Other parts of Britain went through the third millennium without bothering about the new forms of ceremonial site. Kent and Sussex had contained causewayed enclosures and stone-chambered and earthen long barrows, but apparently did not adopt stone or timber circles and had only one certain henge. The Cheshire basin is another area where Late Neolithic people were present but did not raise monuments. None were erected on Exmoor, the upland which spans the border of Devon and Somerset, in the Neolithic, and although geometric settings of stones were created in the Early Bronze Age, they were of very small boulders. Christopher Tilley has suggested that they marked territories for the hunters of the red deer that still roam the moor.[55] On the other hand, where impressive monuments were constructed, which after all was still across most of the British Isles, the memory of their former presence could be surprisingly long. On Machrie Moor in the Isle of Arran two timber circles were constructed and then rotted away, the ground in which they had been set being then put under cultivation. Several centuries later, however, a pair of stone circles was erected on the same site: somehow, stories, songs or rites had preserved the tradition that the place had been special, and perhaps even the recollection of what had stood there.[56]

The Wessex Superhenges

The term 'Wessex' is commonly used in British archaeology for the chalk hills of Wiltshire, Dorset and western Hampshire, those gently rolling uplands associated with grass (often cropped to turf by sheep), flowers, blue butterflies, the spiralling songs of skylarks and the mewing of hunting buzzards. Its use is in fact a classic example of the power of literary fiction over the human imagination, for, while it originally signified the Anglo-Saxon kingdom covering south-western England, its application to the chalk country alone is ultimately the work of the nineteenth-century novelist Thomas Hardy. Hardy's coinage itself covered a slightly wider area than the chalk hills, but narrowed to them the name is a convenient one, providing a label where none had existed for a distinctive region in geology, natural history and archaeology, in which ancient monuments survive unusually well because of a relative lack of dense later settlement and intensive arable farming. Furthermore, its Neolithic inhabitants consistently showed a taste for grandeur and complexity in the construction of monuments which surpassed that of any others in Britain. In the fourth millennium they built the largest chambered long barrow, causewayed enclosure and cursus, and in the third, the largest henges. There were four of these, spaced out at intervals across the region: at Avebury, in a hollow of hills around the headwaters of the River Kennet in north Wiltshire; at Marden, in the Vale of Pewsey in the centre of the county; at Durrington in the Avon Valley upon the far side of Salisbury Plain from the Vale; and at Mount Pleasant above the River Frome in central Dorset.

Of these, Marden was possibly the biggest, but is now the least known, having been largely destroyed by farming. In 2010 excavations began there, led by Jim Leary and David Field, and found that it may have contained standing stones and certainly had a huge mound, over 45 feet (up to 15 metres) in height, near its centre. A smaller henge also stood in the interior, with a house containing a central hearth on the bank. The hearth was so large in relation to the building that normal occupation may have been impossible, and the excavators have suggested that it was a sauna for ritual cleansing, like the American Indian sweat lodges.[57] Even less remains now above ground level of Mount Pleasant, excavated by Geoffrey Wainwright in the early 1970s. It was started around 2800 or 2700 BC, as a circular henge with a large mound, like that at Marden, on the western bank. Multiple timber circles were erected inside, and replaced later with a rectangular setting of megaliths. Between 2200 and 1900 BC the whole enclosure was given a palisade of 1,600 strong oak posts, which may or may not have been a fortification: at any rate, around 1900 this was burned down, the megaliths inside wrecked and the site abandoned. There is no way of telling whether this was the result of enemy action, or a ritual decommissioning of the place.[58]

By the end of the first decade of the twenty-first century the sequence of events at Avebury had been reconstructed as follows. At the beginning of the third millennium, settings of huge local stones were erected in the hollow among the hills, including one of three massive blocks in the form of an open-ended rectangle, a type of monument which William Stukeley, in the early eighteenth century, called a 'cove'. To the south went up an exceptionally tall and broad monolith, and other megaliths were put round both of these structures, probably in circles. A small earthen bank was dug to surround all of these stones. In the middle of the millennium, most probably between 2600 and 2500 BC, this bank was replaced by an enormous henge monument, with a ditch 35 feet (about 13 metres) deep – the largest made at any henge. A proportionately massive bank was heaped up outside it, which would have needed a million hours of labour. In the remainder of the third millennium, the world's largest stone circle, of about a hundred megaliths, was erected inside the ditch, to surround the smaller rings within, and at least two avenues of standing stones were pushed out from the henge, one to a small double stone circle a mile and a half (about 2.5 kilometres) to the south-east and another which apparently ended at another 'cove' an equivalent distance to the west. Stones continued to be erected and re-erected in various parts of the whole complex, and burials, human bones and pottery were put in beside them and into the ditch, in the early second millennium. During medieval and modern times, and perhaps before, almost all of the western avenue and cove, and most of the other avenue and the outer and inner circles of the henge were destroyed or buried. Many of the megaliths, however, survive, as does most of the great bank and ditch, to make up one of the most spectacular prehistoric monuments accessible to visitors today and the core of another World Heritage Site. For many visitors, a large part of its charm lies in the fact that the Anglo-Saxons built a village in and around the henge, much of which still exists as a functioning rural community. In the 1920s and 1930s it was owned by Alexander Keiller, who had inherited a large family fortune based on the making of marmalade and set about using it to investigate and restore as much of the monument as possible. As part of this process, many buried or broken stones were uncovered, repaired and re-erected in the circles and eastern avenue, and concrete markers placed where destroyed megaliths were thought to have stood. The whole great enterprise ended when Keiller's fortune ran out, and the monument is today very much as he left it: more of the great stones have been located where they were interred centuries ago, but there is currently neither will nor funding for further restoration.[59]

44 The surviving portion of the stone avenue leading to the Avebury henge, mostly restored by Alexander Keiller in the 1930s.

45 The south-western arc of the Avebury henge, showing the bank, ditch and outer circle of megaliths. The village is in the background.

Only about 8 per cent of the henge has been excavated, so that any suggestions as to its purpose lack basic evidence, though further examinations were carried out on the avenues and 'cove' between 1997 and 2003 by the Negotiating Avebury research project. So far, investigations have revealed a striking lack of debris associated with feasting or other human occupation. Instead, at the time of construction, flints were placed along the western avenue and antler picks and stone discs in the henge ditch. The central 'cove' was completely clean of any sign of activity other than construction, though it was the most enclosed and secluded, and so perhaps the most sacred, part of the whole monument, providing a perfect screen or stage for ritual. This has naturally now raised speculations that the 'cove', and perhaps the entire complex, was never designed for human activity, but reserved for supernatural beings. If the individual stones did represent ancestors or earth spirits, then the circles and avenues were not built for them but actually 'of' them. If ceremonies did continue in them after they were built, then the existence of two avenues, and two stone settings within the henge, could indicate a dedication of each to a different deity, heavenly body, season, clan, tribe, gender, act of commemoration, or mode of ceremony. Moreover, as the whole complex was developed in stages over about a thousand years, the meanings and activities with which it was invested may well have changed profoundly during that time.[60]

Both of the Avebury avenues not only framed views of older monuments, such as causewayed enclosures and long barrows, but ended at or near sites of previous Late Neolithic activity, an earthen enclosure in the case of the western one, and a timber monument in that of the south-eastern. They were connecting with a remembered or legendary past. The timber monument was replaced by the double stone circle, which William Stukeley recorded just before it was destroyed in the 1720s, and to which he gave the evocative name, which has stuck, of 'The Sanctuary'. It was re-excavated in 1999 by Mike Pitts, who found that what had earlier been presumed to have been a single wooden building had been a mixture of pits which may have held nothing, and posts which were constantly being replaced. In his words, 'it was not a monument at all – it was a process' – of digging, planting of wooden uprights, and then their removal, in a cycle lasting for perhaps a generation and accompanied by feasts of beef and pork. Then the stones arrived, and literally petrified the place.[61] The process was repeated in the early twentieth century, when concrete markers were placed on the sites where stones, posts and pits alike had been, to create an impression of a single design which had in fact never existed. An excavation by Alasdair Whittle in 1987 revealed a pair of important monuments nearby of which hitherto nothing had been known: large timber enclosures near the young River Kennet in the valley below the Sanctuary. They were 600 and 900 feet (over 200 and 300 metres) across respectively and made of high, solid palisades of oak posts with narrow entrances, one in a double concentric circle and the other forming a single oval. They had been built and used for a few generations in the late third millennium, posts being replaced as they rotted. Pigs had been slaughtered there in large numbers, for meals or sacrifices, or both, by seasonal gatherings of people who also left pottery there: the contrast with the absence of such activities inside the great henge, which was being elaborated at the same period, is striking.[62]

The Avebury monuments were completed by the construction, a short distance up the River Kennet, of Silbury Hill, probably (at almost 100 feet or 31 metres) the tallest prehistoric mound in the world, and also (being about 410 feet or 135 metres across the base) the second largest after one in the United States. Its profile, of a massive flat-topped cone, has become one of the icons of British prehistory, but the present shape is the result of its modification for use as an Anglo-Saxon fortress, and we may never know how it corresponds to the original form of the monument. It has been the object of repeated investigations between the late eighteenth and early twenty-first centuries, of which the most recent and productive have been those conducted between 2000 and 2008 by Jim Leary and David Field for English Heritage, to stabilize the mound after one of the earlier tunnels driven into it, by a Georgian antiquarian, partly collapsed. They revealed that it had been built, like the other outlying monuments of the henge, in the late third millennium, probably somewhere between 2400 and 2300 BC. It was not planned from the beginning to take its final form, but developed instead through rapid stages from a single hearth through a complex series of mounds, sometimes single and sometimes multiple and composed of different kinds of material. Eventually it reached its present vast scale, not a true circle but nine-sided, and made mainly of successive banks of chalk with sandstone boulders embedded in it, and surrounded by a ditch and bank which were themselves recut into different forms over time. Set in open chalk grassland, it commanded wide views. The builders therefore kept changing their minds regarding what and how Silbury should be, and as the exact external form of the final monument is not now ascertainable, neither is its purpose.[63]

Leary and Field have noted that the material in the mound was carefully chosen from different locations, like the stones in the great Orkney circles, and suggested that it could have been the work of separate communities engaged in a work to confer luck and health upon themselves, or acting out a myth. The huge ditch, unnecessary in practical terms, may have been intended to keep out evil spirits.[64] Logically, if the whole structure had any purpose once it reached its final size, this must fall into one or both of two categories: that it was a symbol, embodying an idea; or a platform to raise a group of people a very long way above the ground. The most famous proponent of the former idea is Michael Dames, who has claimed that it represented the body of the

46 The classic, crème caramel profile of Silbury Hill.

Great Mother Goddess of the Neolithic, especially with relevance to the harvest season.[65] The difficulties with the concept of this goddess have been discussed earlier, but as it is still one tenable reading of the evidence, so must this interpretation of Silbury be, although the presumed connection between the hill and harvest has not stood up to scrutiny.[66] Another reading of Silbury's symbolism is that, if stones represented spirits, those inside the mound made it a home for dead ancestors.[67] If the primary function of the eventual monument was as a platform, this could have been to observe celestial events, or be related to the fact that the Avebury henge, and the ends of both its avenues, can be seen from the summit. It could therefore have been a signalling station from which rites could be activated in those different places, to mesh in a synchronized pattern.[68] It has some parallels elsewhere, in the large mounds found at the Marden and Mount Pleasant henges, while the four or five henge monuments of more normal size clustered at Knowlton in Dorset, on the chalk between Mount Pleasant and Durrington, had another beside them. All of these, however, are small compared with Silbury, and the latest team of archaeologists to consider them together has concluded that they do not at present seem to form a coherent group.[69] However, there is one other monument that does seem to be directly connected with Silbury, five miles down the Kennet Valley at Marlborough, where a conical mound 62 feet (19 metres) tall has long stood in the grounds of the famous school there, and had been part of a medieval castle before then. Hopes had often been voiced that it might be still older, and Jim Leary at last led an investigation in 2011 which proved that it was indeed Late Neolithic, yielding various dates spanning the mid to late third millennium. These suggest that it was built at roughly the same time as Silbury and by a similar process of repeated reconstruction. Though only two-thirds of the size, it now appears very clearly to be the companion of the great structure a short distance upriver.[70]

Today, the Avebury monuments are awkwardly divided, the National Trust having custody of the henge itself, the eastern avenue of stones and the building which contains the museum of finds from local excavations, while English Heritage is responsible for the contents of that museum and also the outlying sites: the Sanctuary, Silbury, and the West Kennet long barrow.[71] In addition, the county and parish councils must also have a voice in management, as has the national authority which cares for highways, as a major public road runs through the centre of the henge. It is a situation tailor-made for confusion and tension, which so far have been avoided by the careful co-operation of all parties. During the 1990s Avebury at last began to attract so many visitors that the impact on the monuments became dangerous, but that was partly remedied in the 2000s by the simple if ruthless expedient of making car parking more restricted and expensive.

The last of the Wessex 'superhenges', Durrington Walls, lies near the River Avon several miles downstream from Marden. It is larger than Avebury – 1,680 feet (over 560 metres) across – and visitors can easily mistake the surviving arc of bank for a natural feature. In 1966–8 it was partly excavated by Geoffrey Wainwright, who found pits with deposits of pottery, tools and animal bones and two large circular timber structures which have been interpreted as free-standing posts defining ceremonial areas. The southern one alone had six rings of them and was over 120 feet (40 metres) in diameter.[72] In the mid 2000s the monument was further examined, by the Stonehenge Riverside Project, prob-ably the largest university-based archaeological field enterprise ever seen in the United Kingdom, involving five academic institutions and including Mike Parker Pearson and Ramilisonina, Joshua Pollard, Julian Thomas and Colin Richards. It showed that, like the palisaded enclosures near Avebury, Durrington Walls had been used for tool-making and for feasts of beef and pork, which featured large amounts of Grooved Ware. The cattle had been driven there for hundreds of miles, perhaps from Wales or the West Country, and the thousands of pigs slaughtered at an age which, given their season of birth, indicated that the festivities were held at midwinter. The axis between the southern timber circles and the south-eastern entrance to the earthwork is, indeed, aligned on the midwinter sunrise. The new excavations also uncovered inside the henge the largest Neolithic settlement known from north-western Europe, with up to a thousand houses handsomely made with chalk floors, wooden beams, large central hearths, and markers for furniture. They were, however, still flimsy structures, made for seasonal gatherings of thousands of people, with five more substantial buildings, contained within ditches, lacking occupational debris and possibly representing shrines, in the western half of the henge. A roadway of packed earth and flint – the only one from the third millennium yet known in Europe – ran from the south-eastern entrance to the Avon. The whole great complex was built in the middle of the third millen-nium, the village and timber circles first and then the henge around them.[73]

Just outside Durrington Walls to the south was built another, smaller, struc-ture, which was discovered by aerial photography in 1925 and excavated over the next three years by Maud Cunnington. It was promptly dubbed 'Woodhenge', because it had a henge's bank and ditch, which had enclosed six concentric rings of wooden posts. In 1970 it was examined again and dated to the late third millennium. The Stonehenge Riverside Project dug there in 2006 and found that stones had once stood inside as well as posts, while many of the pits may never have held either. Rather than being a single, planned out, structure, the site had constantly developed, like the Sanctuary, with stones succeeding posts and posts succeeding each other, and deposits of pottery, animal bone, flints and carved chalk objects put into the holes that had held them, and into

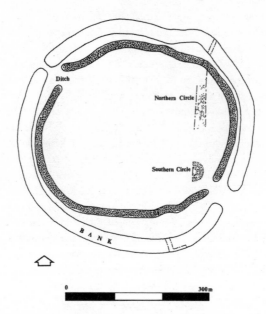

Ditch

Northern Circle

Southern Circle

B A N K

0   300 m

47 Plan of Durrington Walls henge, redrawn after Geoffrey Wainwright.

the ditch. Its entrance was aligned on the midsummer sunrise.[74] How it related to the older and much bigger henge of Durrington Walls, beside it, is not known. Durrington had, moreover, another satellite structure, about two miles (almost three kilometres) to the south-west, which has eclipsed its huge neighbour in all historic times to become the most famous prehistoric monument in the world: Stonehenge. It is not merely a product of prehistory but an icon of cultural history in itself, with a continuous record of admiration and investigation going back almost nine centuries before the present, long before most of the other relics of ancient Britain began to be given attention.[75]

This pre-eminence has been due to three different factors. The first is that the appearance of Stonehenge is unique, representing a lone experiment in working stone as if it were wood, with the planning and smoothing of surfaces and the making of classic carpenters' joints. Probably, the wooden building that it copied was the southern circle inside Durrington Walls which was the same size. The result is the famous settings of three stones joined like doorways with jambs and lintels (or, in more brutal times, like a gibbet to hang criminals, which is what a 'henge' originally meant in medieval English). They make a logo or brand symbol, instantly recognizable. Its second reason for fame is its accessibility, in the heartland of a leading modern nation. By the 1840s the

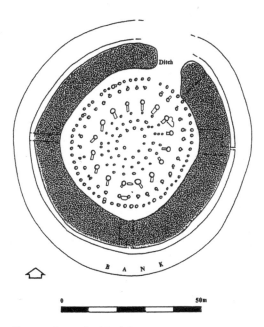

48 Plan of Woodhenge, redrawn after Maud Cunnington.

main London to Exeter highway had been built right past it, and it has since been contained within a junction of arterial roads, the removal or reduction of which is a major current project of heritage managers trying to improve presentation of the site: English Heritage is responsible for the stones themselves, but the National Trust for the surrounding land, and once more local and highway authorities are involved in any developments. The third factor in its importance is the element of mystery: from the publication of the first major survey of British antiquities by William Camden in the reign of Elizabeth I, books on Stonehenge have emphasized the lack of a generally agreed explanation of its purpose. It has been accepted as possessing some kind of ritual significance, but the nature of that remains open. This in turn has encouraged individuals to produce self-proclaimed 'breakthrough' hypotheses, which have achieved celebrity at particular periods. The most successful to date has been that of Geoffrey of Monmouth, published in the twelfth century – that it was a war memorial constructed by the wizard Merlin – which was dominant for about five hundred years. In the 1740s William Stukeley proclaimed it a temple of the Druids, an idea which achieved pre-eminence for one century and remained popular for another. During the twentieth century, when it was firmly dated to the Late Neolithic and Early Bronze Age, the element of mystery was stressed still further and has enabled the monument to function as a people's temple, apparently outside the power of learned archaeologists and historians to appropriate and explain, in which anybody is free to see what she or he wills. This populism is exemplified by the custom of crowds of ordinary people gathering at the stones to witness the midsummer sunrise. This developed spontaneously around 1870 when transport improvements made access easier; Stonehenge attracted thousands by the 1890s, and this has continued, subject to fluctuations in popularity and official tolerance, ever since.

For centuries, Stonehenge has effectively functioned, even more intensively and effectively than other relics of prehistory, as a mirror in which modern people can reflect and justify their own prejudices, ideals and expectations. Those who find their own time, and society, wanting have seen in it the work of ancestors of a superior knowledge and morality. Those who preach the creed of progress, or their own religion, or else the folly of religion in general, have filled it in their imagination with gory, barbaric and orgiastic ancient rites. In the 2000s it became, uniquely, the focus of two different projects of investigation, equally well funded and led by equally distinguished archaeologists. The result was a complete, if good-natured, disagreement. To Timothy Darvill and Geoff Wainwright, who led the SPACES Project, it was a place of healing, the stones being believed to possess magical curative properties which attracted pilgrims seeking relief.[76] The Stonehenge Riverside Project adopted the theory of Mike Parker Pearson and Ramilisonina, two of its leading members, that timber symbolized the living and stone the dead. In their eyes, Stonehenge was a shrine to the ancestors, visited at special seasonal times in order to honour them, after the parties and pig roasts at Durrington Walls, the place of timber, and life.[77]

Certainly, there is now some agreement as to the sequence of construction on the site. It commenced soon after 3000 BC, with a circular segmented ditch between two banks, similar both to a henge and to one of the older causewayed enclosures. Pits were dug in a circle within this earthen ring, which may have held timbers or stones: if stones, then these may have been the smaller megaliths still visible at the monument, nicknamed bluestones. Whatever they had held, the pits, called in modern times the Aubrey Holes, were later emptied and given cremation burials instead. These continued through the early and middle third millennium at the average rate of one every two years, making the site the largest cemetery yet found in Britain from the Late Neolithic. Mike Parker Pearson and his team from the Stonehenge Riverside Project have suggested that it was the burial ground of a ruling family, and continued to be so as the monument took the form evident today. Between 2650 and 2480 BC a double setting of bluestones was erected, surrounded by a circle and (inside that) a horseshoe-shaped setting of huge sandstone blocks, worked like wood as has been described. Either soon after that, or in the later third millennium, the bluestones were rearranged to match that, into an outer circle inside the sandstone one and an inner horseshoe within that of sandstone. The entrance of the monument was aligned on the midsummer sunrise, like that of 'Woodhenge', and banks and ditches dug to create an avenue running from it down to the River Avon. The result was a monument unique in prehistoric Britain for its combination of design, survey and construction skills. It made up a series of stone screens confining a relatively small central space, reserved either for an elite or for all members of a community in succession or rotation, at special times of their lives. In the early second millennium, two rings of pits were dug between the stones and the encircling bank but never seem to have held anything, so that their purpose and significance remain baffling. Around the same period, eleven of the stones were lightly incised with the largest group of prehistoric rock decorations in southern England, mostly showing axe heads, but also a dagger, a knife, and quadrilaterals.[78]

Of course, things are not as simple even as the limited amount of information provided above would seem to imply. Beneath the topsoil, the interior of the monument is pockmarked by hundreds of holes which apparently once held stones or timbers, very badly disturbed by excavations carried out between

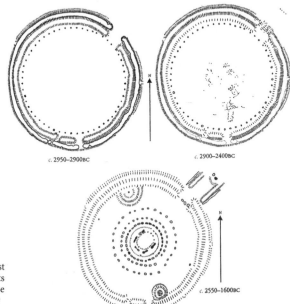

c. 2950–2900BC   *c.* 2900–2400BC

c. 2550–1600BC

49 Plans of three successive phases of Stonehenge, redrawn after Ros Cleal *et al.* The post holes shown as dots in the middle phase belong only highly conjecturally to it.

the seventeenth and twentieth centuries, so that the precise sequence of construction may never be known. Furthermore, fresh discoveries are at present constantly being made in and around the site. In 2008–9 the Stonehenge Riverside Project dug at the point at which the avenue running from the monument met the Avon and found that a henge almost 80 feet (over 24 metres) across had already existed there before the avenue was made, and had itself apparently succeeded a bluestone circle. The following year, the newly formed Stonehenge Hidden Landscapes Project announced the existence of a possible miniature henge between the stones and bank of Stonehenge itself, and of a former mound within the stones.[79] It is also not clear that Stonehenge was ever completed. The south-western arc of megaliths is missing, and from Sir Flinders Petrie in the nineteenth century to Paul Ashbee in the 1990s there have been competent scholars to suggest that it was never present, and that the space there was either always empty or was finished in wood, not stone.[80] It is possible that the builders just ran out of stones, or else that the monument was actually designed to have a superb north-eastern façade but to be open on the opposite side. If so, this would have reinforced the greatest single solar alignment of the developed phase of the monument: not on the midsummer sunrise along the avenue and through the north-eastern entrance, but on the midwinter sunset. This would have sent a narrow ray of light between the uprights of the Great Trilithon, the largest of the three-stone, doorway-like settings of sandstone blocks in the interior (and the tallest single prehistoric stone structure in Britain) on to the so-called Altar Stone which lay near the centre of the monument. Such a superlative effect was lost because at some unknown time before the Middle Ages, one of the uprights of the Trilithon – which had never been long enough to be securely anchored – fell and broke, part-burying the Altar Stone and wrecking the central space of the site.[81]

The biggest of the current problems hanging over Stonehenge, however, concerns the so-called bluestones in its structure. Forty-three of these survive out of an original sixty to a hundred. In 1923 Herbert Thomas confirmed what had been suspected since the nineteenth century: that they could probably all have come from South Wales, and most could only have originated in the Preseli Mountains in northern Pembrokeshire. The point of contention, which has been constant and sometimes bitter since the 1980s, is whether they were brought to Wiltshire by human action or that of a glacier during a recent Ice Age. In favour of the latter theory is the sheer physical difficulty of the transportation process involved. The large stones used to build every other megalithic monument in north-western Europe were found within less than six miles (around ten kilometres) of the site. Most of the Stonehenge bluestones would have had to travel at least 250 miles (400 kilometres), mostly by sea around some of the most dangerous coastlines in Britain. In favour of human

50 Stonehenge (of course), the surviving upright of the Great Trilithon, with its woodworker's tenon joint, showing on the right-hand side.

transport is the fact that no trace of glacial action has been found in Wiltshire; though it should be added that no search for any has yet been made in the western parts of the county, from which stones might still have been moved across Salisbury Plain with relative ease. Still, none of the bluestones at Stonehenge is marked by glacial action. Moreover, the much larger sandstone blocks at Stonehenge undoubtedly broke the six-mile rule, being dragged at least 20 miles (around 32 kilometres) from the north. In the 2000s the SPACES project investigated Preseli with the problem in mind and found that the geological patterning of the rocks there was mirrored in the way in which the identical kinds of rock were placed around Stonehenge. They also discovered evidence for quarrying, a possible sacred precinct and possible healing wells at points on Preseli where stone outcropped of the sort found at Stonehenge; but so far none of these features have been proved to be prehistoric. The category 'Stonehenge bluestone' in fact covers thirteen different types of rock, not all of which are found in Preseli. The Altar Stone, for example, is of a type which occurs most commonly across a broad zone of south-eastern Wales, mostly far inland.[82] At present we know much more about the bluestones than we did in 1990, but are no closer to solving the problem of how they reached Stonehenge.

What has been proved is that all of the Wessex 'superhenges' were constructed, and in use together, around the middle of the third millennium BC: a huge investment of labour and belief representing the apogee of the Neolithic monumental tradition in Britain. They followed no standard plan and were not conceived as single projects; rather, like earlier monuments, they showed how the same basic architectural language could be deployed repeatedly in different ways, and represented a constant reworking of original ideas until at last the process ended and they were left in a final form. This, and the fact that they were spaced out across the chalk country, invites the conclusion that they represented separate, and competitive, communities. Back in the 1970s Colin Renfrew suggested that they signalled the emergence of chiefdoms in the region, led by powerful rival leaders who could draw upon greater resources than the smaller and more numerous groups who had made the long barrows.[83] Such an interpretation fitted the evidence, but also owed much to the modern interest in mechanisms of state-building, and the focus upon economic and social evolution as the main force of historical change which had been invited by the challenges of Marxist theory. It has since been pointed out that there is little evidence of an elite in Late Neolithic British society – few rich grave goods and no high-status dwellings – and that elsewhere in the world (such as in Madagascar) impressive monuments have been constructed by egalitarian societies. If charismatic leaders did direct the work which made the huge Wessex monuments, then they are more likely to have been religious functionaries than chiefs.[84]

If they led groups that were competing with each other to raise magnificent and enduring structures, then it is noteworthy that the process seems to have proceeded without violence, unless the burning of Mount Pleasant is actually evidence of this. It seems at present as if there is much less evidence of warfare during the later Neolithic of Britain than in the earlier: no apparent fortifications, and no concentrations of arrow shot. There are certainly individual cases of homicide. In 1978 the body of a young man equipped as an archer was found in the bank of Stonehenge; he had been interred there in the late third millennium. He had been hit by between three and six arrows, and finished off with one at close range. A cremation burial within a timber circle near Welshpool in the Upper Severn Valley of eastern Wales contained four arrowheads. One of the few human bones found by the Stonehenge Riverside Project inside Durrington Walls had been shot by an arrow (and preserved for a long time before being buried). These may, however, have been not war heroes or victims but human sacrifices or else the casualties of private murders or blood feuds.[85] The explanation in terms of sacrificial victims may be weakened by the fact that in recent years what had been one of the most famous pieces of evidence formerly produced to argue for the practice of human sacrifice in British prehistory has been removed from the record. It was the body of a small child, found near the centre of 'Woodhenge' by Maud Cunnington and declared to have been that of a three-year-old girl, buried as a foundation deposit at the building of the structure after her skull had been split by an axe. This innocent little victim subsequently featured in works of archaeology and of fiction alike as a classic reason to regard ancient Britain as a place of sustained barbarism.[86] Only in 2000 did Mike Pitts point out that the skull could have fallen apart naturally along the unclosed suture lines found in the cranium of a child. Moreover, the excavation of the Stonehenge Riverside Project has now raised the possibility that the burial was not Neolithic at all, but intruded at a later period.[87] As a result, the record of apparent casualties of violence from the third millennium in Britain is even sparser than was previously thought. Indeed, Mike Parker Pearson has suggested that the building of the Wessex 'superhenges' – above all, Stonehenge – was itself a process of union, creating or formalizing a collective identity for the people of southern Britain, and perhaps of the whole island, after the turmoil and localism of the fourth millennium.[88]

In recent years, the period of globalization and of the European Union – and of the analysis of chemical isotopes in teeth – attention has shifted from the local to the Continental context of Stonehenge. In 2002 the richest grave ever found from the time when the monument was in use was excavated on the far side of the River Avon, and the occupant dubbed, from his equipment, 'the Amesbury Archer'. His teeth revealed that he had grown up on the Continent (though in many possible locations), and the burial, with its profusion of fine ceramics, and gold, copper and stone objects (almost a hundred items in all), was made in about 2300 BC. The special honour shown to him might have meant that he was a king or chief, or a skilled metalworker who had helped to foster this new technology in Britain, a wealthy pilgrim, an ambassador from a powerful people, or just a very popular individual. Another grave rich in goods was found fairly close to that of the Archer in the following year, of three adult men, a teenage boy and three children, perhaps a family group, who had grown up in a region of old rock: probably Brittany, Portugal or central France. Three of the bodies were incomplete, and the bones weathered, suggesting that they had been transported from some distance. The adults were nicknamed 'the Boscombe Bowmen'.[89] These people are evidence that by the later third millennium individuals from far across Europe were travelling to Britain, and perhaps that the great complex of ritual monuments based on Durrington Walls had acquired a reputation which penetrated deep into the Continent. It provides a useful balance to an emphasis upon the huge Wessex henges as products of rival local territories, even though this is equally well based on the archaeological data.

The Circles and the Dead

It was said earlier that the new interest in rings as standard units of sacred space was combined in Ireland and the far north and west of Britain with the older architectural form of the tomb-shrine, to produce the developed passage grave. Across most of Britain the application of circular space to the ritual disposal of human remains took a different form: that of the interment of those remains in individual burials under round mounds, which were then sealed and not touched again. The mounds concerned, smaller than those of the long barrows, have come to feature alongside stone circles as the most familiar British monuments from the late third and early second millennia. On the uplands of southern Britain, especially on the chalk, they stand out like green bowls, and have in modern times been given the name of round barrows. In the harsher hills and mountains of the north and west they are formed of piled stones, and given the modern label of round or ring cairns.

The use of round mounds as burial monuments was nothing new in the Neolithic, and nor were individual burials: indeed, the two were sometimes combined. The circular mounds had been built for most of the fourth millennium, especially in Yorkshire where at the end of that millennium they grew to impressive size, to produce such famous examples as Duggleby Howe in a valley of the eastern chalk hills, the mound of which contained 5,000 tons of chalk and clay. It eventually covered nine complete burials and over fifty cremations, with yet more individual human bones piled around with those of wild and domestic animals. Three of the complete burials, all adult men, were given grave goods, one of them a rich assemblage of arrowheads, knives, ox bones, beavers' teeth, boars' tusks and a bone pin. The first interments were successively burials in a pit, between about 3450 and 3300 BC, some of which showed signs of violent death: as stated above, this has become recognized as a significant feature, though a minority one, of fourth-millennium bodies. More were added between 3000 and 2900 BC, and the great mound built in the early twenty-ninth century BC, interments in it continuing for the rest of the millennium. It is just possible that it was influenced by the massive coverings of developed passage graves, as it is more or less contemporary with Maes Howe and younger than those of the Boyne Valley. Chemical tests reveal that none of the people in the mound had lived in the surrounding chalk country, so either the chalk hills were a place to which people came from elsewhere to bury their dead or else dwellers upon the chalk reserved burial for distinguished strangers, or even enemies killed in war or human sacrifices, with whom the objects buried were not grave goods but offerings to deities.[90] The great change that came in the early third millennium was that this complex of fourth-millennium features – the round mound, the individual interments of complete bodies which were often multiplied over time within the mound, and the placing of possessions with some burials – ceased to be a regional and a minority tradition and became dominant throughout Britain.

This being so, it may be wise at this point to consider some of the general problems of interpreting the meaning of placing objects with the dead, problems that are going to recur throughout most of the remaining chapters of this book. Grave goods may have been intended to equip the dead person for the next life, but may equally well have been especially favoured possessions of that person, placed in the grave lest the ghost should linger near them and trouble the living. Alternatively, they may have been gifts made to deities or spirits to persuade them to favour the spirit of the person laid with them, or gestures of generosity on the part of guests at the funeral, presented to do honour to the deceased. Where they consist of knives and/or of pots and other vessels, they may have been involved in the funeral feast and then been interred as polluted by that event. All these are very different motivations for an act which leaves the same material remains. Likewise, funeral rites may have been intended to remove the dead from the society of the living or to reintegrate them, placing them in a new and different relationship with the living.[91]

Only a fraction of the prehistoric round barrows that once existed in Britain survive as visible monuments, as they were relatively easy to demolish to make way for farming. As such they are now found mostly in uplands where agriculture was less intense, though even there a lot have been flattened; an aerial survey of the Dorset chalk upland of Cranborne Chase, made in 2006, doubled the number known to have existed there by finding the marks of many in fields.[92] More formerly existed in lowlands than on hills, and over four hundred of them, now levelled, have been identified in the Great Ouse Valley of Cambridgeshire. The greatest concentration in Britain seems to have been on the Isle of Thanet, then a fertile islet off the Kent coast and now merged with it.[93] It is difficult to determine why particular locations were chosen for the mounds. Sandy Gerrard, noting that the round cairns on Dartmoor are mainly found in the upland grazing zones, offered six different reasons why this might have been so: because those areas were of low economic value; because the cairns built lower down have been destroyed; because the prime grazing lands were especially honoured as sacred; because the uplands were regarded as the home of the deities; because placement higher up made the cairns look more impressive; and because the cairns represented territorial markers establishing grazing rights.[94]

The chronology of round barrows in southern England is easiest to establish. Between 2500 and 2150 BC they were relatively small and mostly covered individual male bodies with grave goods. Between 2150 and 1850 BC they became larger and more varied in form, and contained a greater proportion of women and children, while bodies were treated in more diverse ways and cremation grew more common. Mounds were often reopened and rebuilt, with insertion of fresh burials. They were often placed close to Neolithic monuments, and grave goods were abundant. From 1850 to 1500 formal cemeteries of round barrows developed, each often placed over a central cremation burial, which was sometimes accompanied by rich goods. Big mounds, however, did not necessarily mean rich graves, and vice versa. The barrows were usually built in a single operation and not reopened, and were constructed over a much larger area of terrain. Finally, between 1500 and 1200, they continued to be built in a single phase, but were smaller and simpler and reused repeatedly for cremation burial, and more cremations were also placed around them, while grave goods died out.[95] What seems at first sight to have been a consistent tradition, spanning more than a thousand years, turns out to have been subject to constant development and mutation.

Timothy Darvill has mapped out six main regional styles for the making of round burial mounds by the early second millennium, within each of which the basic similarity of model comprised a wide range of actual structures.[96] The barrows on the Wiltshire and Dorset chalk were most often bowl-shaped (in Dorset 94 per cent of those surviving), but could also take the form of bells, discs, ponds and saucers.[97] In Wales, and England west of the River Severn, mounds and cairns could be bowl-shaped, sometimes with stone kerbs, or else given the form of rings of heaped stones with central spaces. On the Clwydian Mountains of north-eastern Wales, the many cairns were based on the concept of the round pile of stones above cremations, which were often placed in urns. Some, however, covered single burials, others multiple burials made at the one time, and yet others multiple burials made successively.[98] In the south-western peninsula of Britain we find simple earthen bowls, kerbed cairns, cairns on stone platforms, platform cairns with rims, platform cairns with central mounds, kerbed platform cairns, ring cairns, and cairns including natural rock outcrops. On one upland region of the peninsula, Dartmoor, the ring cairns alone divide into simple circles of piled stones, standing stone circles with linking banks, piled-stone circles with kerbs, circles of piled stones built on platforms, and circles of piled stones with piled-stone mounds in the centre. Excavation usually reveals their structure to have been even more complicated.[99] In Orkney the tradition of burial under a small round mound, usually with a single original grave, likewise became general around 2000 BC; but the burials could be either cremated or unburnt, and placed in pits, pockets of rock or stone coffins.[100] Sometimes sites that look like levelled round barrows turn out to be something else: one in Derbyshire and one in Hampshire turned out to be round platforms, surrounded by ditches, which were apparently used for feasts in the Early Bronze Age. The former had cremated human bone scattered at points on it, as if the dead were invited to join the meals, or to consecrate the space.[101] Human remains continued to be placed around monuments that seem to have been gathering-places, and in the later third millennium were found inside timber circles more often than before. They were also put into rivers during the third and second millennia, and cave burial remained a custom. Nor were mounds needed for burial, cemeteries of flat graves being found in parts of Britain north of the River Tees.[102]

The round barrows most celebrated in British archaeology are those of the Wiltshire and Dorset chalklands, and especially a few which covered very richly equipped burials from the early second millennium. In 1938 Stuart Piggott described these as being the work of a 'Wessex Culture', a label which has stuck: the 'type specimen' of it was the Clandon Barrow excavated in southern Dorset in 1882, where the burial was accompanied by an incised gold lozenge, a shale mace head with five gold bosses, an amber cup, an incense cup and a dagger with a wooden sheath.[103] About a hundred such richly furnished graves under round mounds are known from the region, a dozen of which included gold objects.[104] The Wessex round barrow cemeteries seem to have been the burial grounds of people drawn from a wider area than a local community: the number of barrows found along the South Dorset chalk ridge is too large to have taken the dead from the surrounding area alone.[105] The more exotic grave goods were selected mainly for qualities of colour and texture, being shiny, lustrous or cool, and so made of gold, amber, jet, faience, bone or shell; the most common type of all was beads.[106] The individuals interred with them – usually male where the bodies were unburnt – might have been chiefs, or priests or shamans, or simply unusually respected family or clan elders.[107]

Once more, our complete ignorance of the nature of the society which made the graves leaves each possibility open, though there is now broad agreement that, in Wessex as across Britain, those mounds which received successive burials were probably used by particular lineages or kinship groups.[108] There is also an increasing tendency to reject the idea – which Piggott himself favoured, and which was dominant until the 1970s – that the people given these rich assemblages of goods were warrior aristocrats. There was always the possibility that the burial of such valuable objects could itself have prevented an accumulation of wealth and power by inheritance, and that the people given them were individuals who had gained especially good reputations among clusters of equally important family-based groups. A recent study of the objects from the 'Wessex Culture' graves has revealed that some were freshly made but others had been in use for long periods. This does make it less likely that the goods were all the property of the people with whom they were buried and more that some at least were put into the graves by mourners or ritual specialists (who can be termed priestesses, priests or shamans according to taste). Some seem to have belonged to ceremonial costumes and equipment rather than having been simply tools, which makes that last possibility, of ritual deposition, the more likely.[109]

It also seems that in some areas round barrows were used as territorial markers, in the manner which was once suggested of the long barrows. Along the valley of the River Welland, near Peterborough in the East Midlands, large specimens, often within multiple ditches, were constructed evenly at half-mile intervals; as if the lush pastures there were divided up equally, and the dead positioned to oversee this agreement.[110] The barrows that the Wessex culture created were linked directly to the older ceremonial monuments left by the Neolithic, clustering notably around the great stone structures of Avebury and Stonehenge. In the Nene Valley of Northamptonshire, round barrows were also placed near older structures, in great number: hundreds of mounds, or ring ditches without mounds inside, were made there in the centuries around 2000 BC. A few had no human remains at all, and animal bones and pottery were put into others without any reference to the burials. It seems as if the mounds and circular ditches were becoming shrines in their own right, replacing the henges which were no longer built as the main communal places for religious ceremony.[111]

Some round mounds in England were built to make reference to surrounding geography, so that one at Towthorpe, on the East Yorkshire chalk hills called the Wolds, was made of earth from the immediate vicinity and from two other areas a mile or two to the north and west. Joanna Brück has suggested that these locations may have been significant in life to the person buried there, or to specific groups of mourners; it may also be suggested that the mound could have been a sacred entity in itself, embodying particular spirits of place.[112] The groups of small round cairns common in the uplands of northern England and southern Scotland sometimes cover burials but frequently do not, having deposits of flint and charcoal instead. The latter kind have commonly been thought to have been mere dumps of stones cleared from pasture land nearby to improve grazing, but this would not explain either the material laid in them or the fact that they were built with the same care, and in the same style, as the burial cairns.[113] Sir Cyril Fox's perception that round barrows were more than just burial places, published back in the 1950s, seems justified now more than ever before, and can indeed be applied to the whole phenomenon of the round mound by the second millennium BC.[114]

Interpretations

It is time to ask what explanations experts have offered for the apparent large-scale changes in ritual behaviour between the fourth and third millennia, and to do that involves first taking a wider view of the approaches to the interpretation of the evidence for ritual in Britain in recent years. Two converging movements, both under way by the 1980s but becoming fully developed in the 1990s, have been most influential in this respect. The first is cognitive archaeology, the study of ways of thought of past societies based on their material remains, which can provide the symbols used by people in those societies to depict their world. It does not claim to recover the meaning of those symbols, but to demonstrate how they were used in a particular context: in other words, to show how the people concerned had been thinking even if it is impossible to know what they actually thought. Since much religious behaviour leaves evidence of symbols behind it, this methodology held out the hope of providing insights into the nature of that behaviour, even if the belief system behind it might be lost.[115] Ironically, the second movement, post-processual archaeology, was initially conceived as a reaction against an older school of scholarship, which viewed archaeology primarily as an anthropological science and of which cognitive archaeology was itself one of the most recent outgrowths. It tended to call for a plurality of interpretations, which put the modern interpreter into the foreground of investigation and called into question the ability of archaeology to produce final and definitive accounts of the past.[116] None the less, it also took a keen interest in symbolic behaviour, and believed that operations of the human mind could be perceived at work in material remains, even if in most cases the meaning of those operations could not be recovered. By the mid 1990s the two sub-disciplines were effectively working together or being combined.[117]

The effect of these developments was greatly to quicken interest in ancient ceremonial monuments, and the apparent remains of ritual, in Britain, and to encourage a large quantity of new investigations of them and publications on them; but there were limits to the effect. For one thing, the impact of theoretical developments on the practice of archaeology has always been muted: the author of one justly popular and admired textbook on the discipline commented in 2010 that most of his colleagues across the world probably retained a 'crude and reflective empiricism', holding that data could speak for itself without the need of an intervening theory.[118] For another, the archaeology of religion tended by its very nature to become essentially what Colin Renfrew, its main exponent, dubbed the archaeology of cult. In other words, it could recover the material remains of ritual action – special buildings, furniture, equipment, images and decorations, and traces of feasts and offerings – but not (usually) the ideas which inspired them or even the actions, let alone the words, associated with them.[119] To recover that much is still, as Lord Renfrew emphasized, a considerable accretion to knowledge – the solution to the question 'how' – and yet the 'why' ultimately remains the more important puzzle, and the answer continues to elude us. The traces of religious rites are moreover often not easily distinguished from those of political, social and festive ritual; if indeed there was ever a distinction to be made. In the case of periods near the end of prehistory, or in the early centuries of the historic period, textual evidence, contemporary or back-projected, has regularly been used to interpret physical remains.

One of the themes of this book is, however, that such attempts are usually fraught with peril, while another is that material objects of an apparently religious nature for which there is no known written explanation continue to feature far into the historic period; indeed, until modern times. No wonder, therefore, that 'religious' material culture is a category of great ambiguity, little amenable to definition, and that an expert could still describe the archaeology of religion in 2004 as 'the poor cousin of archaeological research'.[120]

With this in mind, the examination of explanations for the great changes in ritual that seem visible in Britain from around 3000 BC can commence. The traditional one, which was based on nineteenth-century scholarship, is that they were caused by the arrival of a new people, who brought the use of metals and various novel kinds of artefact as well as a new religion. The Victorians established that the tomb-shrines were earlier than the henges, stone circles and round barrows, and decided, on inadequate skeletal evidence, that the former were the work of a smaller and more primitive people. Both of these ideas, the former indisputably correct and the latter not, were proposed between 1869 and 1871 by a doctor, John Thurnam, and by the 1880s his model had become orthodoxy. It was embodied in the major survey of British prehistory conducted by Sir William Boyd Dawkins, who cobbled together the speculations of the ancient Roman historian Tacitus with shaky comparative evidence from linguistic and ethnic patterns in historical Europe. On the basis of this work he awarded dark hair and eyes as well as small size to the Neolithic builders of the tomb-shrines, and gave blond hair and blue eyes to the Bronze Age race which he held to have conquered and dispossessed them. These newcomers he identified as the Celts, and declared that they had brought a religion based on the worship of fire, evidenced in their introduction of cremation and of round shapes for monuments which imitated the solar orb: fire was, he argued, crucial to the metal-working technology which they also brought.[121] By the 1940s the Celts had been reallocated to the Iron Age, as a fresh wave of invaders during that epoch, and, for lack of any historical label for them, the conquerors who introduced bronze and the solar religion had now become the Beaker People. This name derived from the distinctive tall ceramic pots, used as drinking vessels, which were commonly deposited in graves under some of the earlier round barrows: they were a truly pan-Continental style of artefact, being found in the third millennium from Ireland to Hungary and Denmark to Morocco. These so-called Beaker folk retained their primacy as the presumed agents of religious and technological change until the 1980s.[122]

What removed them from the record was largely the achievement of more precise dating for prehistoric remains, which revealed that the new forms of ceremonial monument appeared, as described, at the beginning of the third millennium, while metal artefacts and the other new forms of good arrived

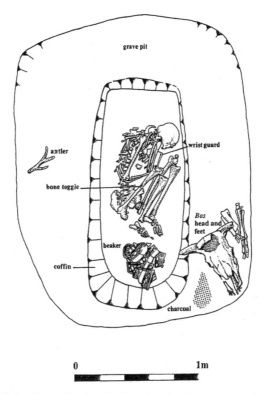

grave pit

antler

wrist guard

bone toggle

Bos head and feet

beaker

coffin

charcoal

0   1m

51 Excavator's plan of one of the classic Beaker-culture burials, at Hemp Knoll, Wiltshire.

gradually in the second half of the millennium. There was no evidence whatever for the sudden incursion of a new culture from abroad, and in the early twenty-first century the application of genetics as an archaeological science has reinforced this conclusion, producing no sign of significant racial alteration in Britain during the Neolithic and Early Bronze Age.[123] Single burials, cremation, round barrows and the first appearance of metal all predated the arrival of the Beaker style of pottery. That came round about 2400 BC, with finer metal tools and pins, gold earrings and button covers, bone belt-rings and stone guards to protect the wrists of archers from the lash of their bowstrings. Even so, all remained rare until around 2250 BC, when they were joined by a range of bronze artefacts, plus flint daggers, stone battleaxes, antler spatulas, whetstones to sharpen metal tools, and tanged and barbed arrowheads.

The process of development of new goods continued at the same rate into the second millennium: by 1900 BC beakers were already going out of fashion, to be replaced by successive new forms of impressive pottery vessels. In the course of the new millennium bronze spears, daggers and dirks were adopted, followed by rapiers around 1400 and swords, shields and harness for horse-riding about a century later. The wheel arrived in the same millennium. All these developments, however, took place in a religious landscape that was little altered in its essentials since around 3000 BC: even if henges were no longer built in the early second millennium, new round barrows continued to be erected near them. If there was a particular style of pottery associated with the new circular monuments of the third millennium it was not beakers but Grooved Ware, that form of native ceramic which has already been noted in Orkney and which during the first half of the millennium is found throughout Britain on ceremonial sites. With its distinctive linear, lozenge-shaped, zigzag, triangular, spiral, square, cross-hatched and chequerboard designs, this ware was the dominant elite pottery of the Late British Neolithic.[124]

Just as in the case of interpretations of the Early Neolithic tomb-shrines, so in that of the round monuments of the third millennium; as race and religion departed as explanatory devices in the 1980s, so economic and social deter-minism moved in. The new forms of monument and of burial custom were read as marking a shift from a society based mainly on collectivism to one in which individuals were more prominent. The former was thought to have been exemplified by the making of big communal structures and the blending of skeletal material within the tomb-shrines; the latter by the widespread adop-tion of single burial and the prominence of new kinds of prestige goods.[125] The problem with this model was that single burial, either as a one-off action or as successive interments in the same monument, had already existed in the fourth millennium (and indeed long before), while the construction of huge communal monuments continued after the adoption of the new goods. Julian Thomas has pointed out that traditional societies studied by modern anthropologists, such as Bali, are often very complex in the significance which they attach to ritual, so that (for example) an offering deposited in one sort of place by a member of one sex may have a completely different meaning from exactly the same kind of offering made in a different kind of place by somebody of the opposite sex. Reading simple explanations from Neolithic material is therefore likely (though not certain) to be wrong.[126] John Chapman has emphasized that a desire for exotic objects is evident in Europe since the Mesolithic, if not earlier, and merely elaborated as the Neolithic went on and developing technologies and trade allowed a greater diversity of desirable products. Even societies with few apparent inequalities have valued unusual and attractive possessions. As a result, the concept that the Neolithic produced the birth of the individual in Britain has lost favour since the 1990s. None the less, the greatly increased number and complexity of commodities in the third and second millennia would have demanded a much greater number of specialist craftspeople, and of traders, than ever before; creating, if not necessarily the individual, at least more varieties of individual.[127]

It is possible to discern, behind these changing views of the problem, major shifts in modern British culture. One of the obvious experiences that underlay the picture of invasion by a superior race with a more effective technology and a (literally) more elevated religion was that of the nineteenth-century European colonization of huge expanses of the globe: its influence has already been suggested in the Victorian portrait of the arrival of the Neolithic. The consciousness of the threat of invasion from the European mainland was, however, also a powerful theme in the British mentality between 1800 and 1945 (and indeed long before, and perhaps, in Cold War terms, for some time after). One of the most popular authors on British prehistory during the mid twentieth century, Jacquetta Hawkes, explicitly stated that the fear of the landing of Hitler's army in 1940 greatly reinforced her sense of the importance of violent newcomers in the ancient story of her island.[128] The same model, however, of significant change being produced by the arrival of new conquering peoples, had long been built into the legendary history of the peoples of the British Isles, such as the Irish *Leabhar Gabhálá* or Book of Invasions or Geoffrey of Monmouth's *History of the Kings of Britain*. It is embedded in the Christian religion, in the account of the Israelite conquest of Canaan in the name of a divinely chosen people, and in classical literature, in the tradition of the Dorian invasion of Greece and the migration of Aeneas's Trojans across the Mediterranean to found the Roman race.

More worrying, in view of the complete abandonment of the invasion hypothesis during the later twentieth century, is that invasions are a major theme of actual ancient history. As soon as Britain emerged into history, parts of it were occupied successively by Romans, Anglo-Saxons, Irish, Vikings and Normans. The Roman Republic was troubled by attacks from wandering and warlike peoples from the north, including Gauls, Teutones, Cimbri and Lingurini, while the Roman Empire had to fend off more, until it famously succumbed to such incursions. Phoenicians and Greeks established maritime colonies across the central and western Mediterranean. Conquest by one set of invaders, the Hyksos, brought down the Middle Kingdom of Egypt in the early second millennium BC, and attack by another, the Sea Peoples, fatally wounded the succeeding Egyptian New Empire at the end of the same millennium; likewise, migrations and invasions from the neighbouring mountains and deserts – by peoples such as the Amorites, Kassites and Aramaeans, destroyed successive states in ancient Mesopotamia over the same period. Ethnic groups in Europe and the Near East seem, in fact, to have been in episodic motion and turmoil throughout the recorded ancient world. The undoubted arrivals of new goods and technologies in third- and second-millennium Britain, however, are now ascribed wholly to travelling salespeople, traders, friendly foreigners looking for work, or foreign brides or bridegrooms; pretty well much as such novelties arrive in Britain at the present day. This picture certainly fits the apparent archaeological and genetic record, and it may well be that everything did change as soon as history began. If such a remarkable change did occur, however, it deserves more consideration, and explanation, than it has so far received.

The socio-economic model of explanation for the changing styles of monuments can in turn be related to contemporary concerns. One of the features of British (as of wider Western) society in the 1970s and 1980s was a sense of the breakdown of former collective and communal systems of behaviour and sartorial styles, in favour of a rampant individualism largely based on new and rapidly changing fashion accessories. This same development seems to have been perceived – if not projected back onto – the third millennium BC. Since the mid 1990s, there has been no widely accepted grand model of explanation for the changes of that millennium to replace those that have gone before, but a series of different conceptualizations instead. John Barrett has suggested that the very process of constructing the huge Wessex monuments of the mid third millennium, requiring as it may have a continuous succession of project leaders, acted to create a new elite who ended up in the rich graves under some round barrows.[129] Julian Thomas has reformulated the notion of the emergence of the individual into one in which simple fourth-millennium transmissions of authority through kinship lines fragmented into multiple connections between humans and the material world.[130] Jan Harding has proposed that a sense of the sacred which had been centred on special places, and concentrated in the ceremonial structures built there, gradually became refocused upon humanity: in that sense, round barrows would have been temples built by people to themselves.[131] Andrew Jones has viewed the transition from the fourth to the third millennium as one from the honouring of multiple forebears to that of a lineage traced to a single ancestor, and from the circulation of human bones to remember the dead to the use of goods for the same purpose. Cremation and inhumation (the burial of complete bodies) were likewise, in his vision, just different techniques for fixing the deceased in memory. In other words, the apparent changes were really just alternative ways of doing the same thing.[132]

Around the end of the first decade of the twenty-first century, older notions began to resurface as well, though in different forms. Race has remained resolutely unfashionable as an explanatory mechanism, for obvious reasons, and so has invasion. Richard Harrison and Volker Heyd have, however, drawn attention to the pan-Continental scope of the changes that appear in the British archaeological record, so that round barrows and single graves were adopted all the way from the Ukrainian steppes to the British Isles during the third millennium BC. They have linked these, and the spread of the beakers and other new kinds of good, to a new ideology, spread by wandering individuals and not invading groups. In their reading, this underlined the basis of personal identity and social position in an individual person's material trappings, especially if those were exotic and imported objects, and venerated the sun as the focus of religion.[133] Sir Barry Cunliffe has also stressed that the same changes occurred all over Europe, and indicated a common set of new values, based on the individual and the specific kin group, which were both powered by and stimulated further the development of social elites, larger and longer trade networks, and competition for luxury commodities.[134] Timothy Darvill has maintained a larger space for religious factors, drawing attention once more to the sudden predominance of circles as significant units of space and the greater concern for celestial movements, especially sunrise and sunset, in Britain from about 3000 BC. He goes further, to find solar imagery in the motifs of designs carved on stone and incised on pottery in the same period, and even more obviously after 2500 BC in the making of golden discs, which were apparently worn on clothing like badges. He perceives a stronger interest in the moon around the year 2000, a suggestion already strongly made by Richard Bradley.[135]

Such a plurality of opinions suits well a contemporary Britain based on a multiplicity of ethnic, linguistic, gendered, religious and other identities, linked by the concept of individual choice. It makes another good fit with recent modernity that most of them are essentially secular in nature, and implicitly celebrate individualism and diversity. Ideology is given more credit than before as a force in itself, which is appropriate to a world in which it has come once more to feature as a motivation for conflict, replacing class divisions; though there is still a reluctance to give too much credit to religious ideology in British prehistory, despite (or because of) its potency in much of the ultra-modern world. This reluctance leaves much of the changing symbolism of the Neolithic, such as the emergence of the circle as the dominant shape, hard to explain, and when explanations are offered in religious terms, they tend to be in the form of heavenly bodies, rather than of the deities to whom such bodies are commonly related in traditional societies. Not surprisingly, changed modern times also find different ancestral figures to admire. If there were heroic figures in the archaeology of the mid twentieth century, they were the people buried with rich goods in Wessex round barrows, seen as representatives of a warrior nobility influenced by the famous civilizations of the Bronze Age Near East and equivalent to the figures of classical Greek mythology. Now the best-known person in third-millennium Britain is the Amesbury Archer, generally viewed as a friendly European immigrant, expert in practical skills and knowledge which the British natives found of exceptional value. His crippled leg, moreover, has given his image an additional poignancy, by enabling him to be regarded as an example of how a person with a physical disability could – even in prehistory – emerge as a leading figure not merely in a parent society but in a foreign one.

Alternatives

Virtually all of the interpretations of the ancient British past summarized hitherto in this book have been those of professional scholars, most operating within an academic environment or in public employment. In the late twentieth century there was also a flourishing complex of different readings of British prehistory, which shared certain suppositions, publications and leading figures, and which self-consciously set itself against the mainstream view. It gave itself the name of 'alternative archaeology' or the 'earth mysteries'. A consideration of it is a natural component of the work undertaken in this volume, which is concerned as much with the manner in which the evidence for ancient ritual and religious belief has been regarded as with that evidence itself. As such, this exercise offers not only further insights into the relationship between archaeological data and modern societies, but insights into the manner in which orthodox and unorthodox readings of prehistory have interrelated since the professionalization of archaeology.

Logically speaking, an unorthodox attitude to the prehistoric past could only develop once an orthodox one had done so, which took a very long time. In the first two hundred years during which British antiquarians took a sustained interest in ancient monuments, between the early sixteenth and early eighteenth centuries, there was no clear solution to the basic question of who had erected them: the main contenders were the pre-Roman British natives, the Romans, the post-Roman British and the Vikings. Between the mid eighteenth and mid nineteenth centuries something like a consensus was achieved, that they were the work of the ancient British, led by their priests, the Druids, though also great argument over whether the latter were to be regarded as admirable or barbaric, and how they fitted into the account of human development provided in the Bible. The first genuine 'alternative archaeology' arose in the mid nineteenth century, in the form of a tradition of writers who argued that Britain's megalithic monuments had been made by the post-Roman British after all. Its greatest proponent was an architectural historian called James Fergusson. By the end of the century it had disappeared, having been crushed by the increasing evidence that the monuments concerned dated to the Neolithic or Bronze Age, articulated by an ever more cohesive and determined group of established experts.[136] In the 1920s a new dissident group arose, inspired by Alfred Watkins, a wealthy citizen of Hereford and respected local antiquarian, who thought that he had discovered a network of ancient straight trackways, which he called 'leys', across the British landscape. His suggestion came to be rejected by most experts in prehistory: not merely by those in the emerging national cohort of recognized scholars, but by his fellow local enthusiasts of the sort who filled up county archaeological societies. They thought his straight roads to be impractical ways of crossing hill country, and the monuments and other landscape features which he took as their markers to date from too many different periods. Instead Watkins attracted a following among people interested in esoteric spirituality, mainly from the affluent middle class, who saw a pattern of ancient wisdom in his lines; and, having initially regarded the latter as trade routes, he himself came to give this new idea cautious encouragement. The group concerned, however, disappeared in the 1940s.[137]

During that decade and the two following, a major shift occurred in the professionalization of the practice of archaeology. For the first time, it became a widely taught academic discipline, which provided a university degree as the most obvious route to a career in the subject. Over the same period, amateurs, including landowners, lost most of the initiative in excavating ancient sites, which was reserved increasingly to the university-based or university-trained experts. This emerging near-monopoly had the effect of making the professionals concentrate primarily on the actions and objects over which they exerted such novel control: excavation and the finds which it turned up. Individuals with a keen interest in the ancient British past, who were unwilling or unable to ascend the academic stepladder, were presented with the choice of becoming employees and assistants to the new professionals, joining local societies which were still able to engage in excavation (but tended to follow the views and agenda of the professionals) or else of striking out on their own. The third route could only lead into areas of activity which were relatively or absolutely neglected by the newly formed archaeological establishment. There were really just two of those that had any importance: a study of astronomy and mathematics, and a consideration of landscape features as these related to ancient sites.[138] Such a course did not necessarily end in confrontation with orthodoxy, as the development of the study of prehistoric designs on rock faces – a very important enterprise conducted mostly by amateurs – makes clear. It would do so, however, if it were combined with a self-consciously countercultural movement which rejected most forms of traditional and official authority, and that is exactly what arose in the late 1960s, to produce the most striking British manifestation to date of 'alternative archaeology'.[139]

It actually arose as a spin-off from one of the most dynamic areas of unorthodox scientific enquiry in the 1950s: an interest in Unidentified Flying Objects. In 1961 a young man called Tony Wedd published the idea that Watkins's leys might have been markers for the flight paths of alien spacecraft, which must therefore have been visiting our planet for many millennia. There was, from the start, a strong religious and apocalyptic tinge to his thought, as he declared that the extraterrestrials were now multiplying their visits to prepare humans for 'a Golden Age of Peace and Justice' much like angels or gods; indeed, he subsequently referred to them as 'gods'. He became friendly with a Surrey schoolboy, Philip Heselton, who founded a Ley Hunters' Club and a *Ley Hunter* magazine to propagate it. Heselton in turn inspired a fellow pupil, Jimmy Goddard, who lectured on the subject for the next few years, and in doing so attracted the attention of a Londoner, John Michell.[140]

It was Michell who brought these ideas to a much wider public. His first book on them, *The Flying Saucer Vision*, in 1967, restated Wedd's views at much greater length, holding that the development of the human race had been influenced by 'gods' from the sky, who had rejected it when it turned too greedily to material and technological goals. Those, he preached, were now bringing it close to self-destruction, which could be prevented by renewing contact with the gods, and in the process reactivating the ancient holy centres which had promoted such contact.[141] Two years later he published the book which, more than any other, defined and energized the earth mysteries movement, *The View over Atlantis*.[142] This combined Watkins's leys with the Chinese mythology of *lung mei*, lines of energy which run across the surface of the earth and with which humans need to live in harmony if they are to prosper, especially when placing buildings. In Michell's portrait, the leys had been laid out to harness this energy, which was magnetic and rose naturally from the ground. They had been the work of a scientific and religious elite that had visited almost every corner of the planet and constructed a network of megalithic structures upon it to channel the earth energy for the good of humanity. This vision, like Wedd's, embodied a fervent religious feeling, which though not Christian was heavily influenced by Christian models. It had the biblical belief in a former universal, good and true system of belief and knowledge, which had decayed because of the unworthiness of later generations. Its tone was evangelical and apocalyptic, announcing the dawning of the Age of Aquarius, in which tyrants would fall, the power of 'old magicians' be destroyed, and the ancient wisdom be restored. It presented the ancient knowledge of the earth energies as having been granted by 'revelation', and the book concluded with the promise that a return to it would enable 'the rediscovery of access to the divine will' and 'the restoration of the Holy Spirit'. This religious rhetoric was combined with the spirit of 1960s' 'Big Science', for to Michell the ley system had been both a partnership with divinity and a 'great scientific instrument' which united all races and nationalities.[143]

John Michell viewed professional archaeologists as active forces of opposition to this vital work of recovery, engaged in mere 'treasure hunting and grave robbery' and so personifying the evils of modern materialism.[144] He was, in fact, opposed to everybody who accepted the Victorian revolution in attitudes to prehistory, which had overturned a view of the ancient past centred on the Bible and Druids and introduced Charles Darwin's theory of evolution and the division of the past into successive ages (Stone, Bronze and Iron) based purely on technological achievement. By contrast, he honoured scholars from the seventeenth and eighteenth centuries, who had emphasized the primacy of religion as a force in human affairs, and writers since then who had continued to believe in a universal, or at least pan-Eurasian, system of ancient wisdom.

The View over Atlantis provoked a rush of publication in the 1970s and 1980s, and with it an upsurge in ley-hunting. Two books from the early 1970s may be regarded as especially important works in the maturation of the earth mysteries movement. One was *Mysterious Britain*, by Janet and Colin Bord, which embedded Michell's ideas, and those of contributors to the *Ley Hunter*, in a gazetteer of ancient sites.[145] As the title suggests, it stressed the mystery presented by such places rather than preaching a message drawn from them. None the less, one of the authors was certainly inspired by personal religious feeling, having published a magazine article three years before which informed his readers that they faced destruction unless they repented their ways and accepted once more their place as 'an integral part of the Creator's concept, with a definite purpose which he will eventually fulfil'.[146] The other book was *Quicksilver Heritage*, written by the new editor of the *Ley Hunter*, Paul Screeton, which developed Michell's view of prehistory to suggest that the Neolithic had been an era in which humanity devoted itself wholly to spirituality, only to fall from grace with the invention of metal-working. He suggested that the New Stone Age golden age could now be restored, as a 'new breed of Britons look to the countryside for a true vision of the past and find themselves also exploring the infinity of the mind's inner space'.[147]

The concept of earth energies blended well with other esoteric traditions, such as a belief in the magical properties of numbers, and practices such as dowsing.[148] Yet the leys remained the central idea and symbol of the movement, and 'hunting' them its most popular activity. The basic tool was a detailed map of a district, normally the one-inch version published by the Ordnance Survey, across which lines were drawn to connect ancient and medieval structures, mostly but not necessarily religious in nature: the classic medieval monument concerned was a parish church, assumed to have been built on a pre-Christian sacred site. Ley-hunters were not, however, usually armchair theorists, but avid explorers of the rural (and occasionally urban) landscape. It may be suggested here that leys had a powerful symbolic significance: in a modern age which drove straight lines to connect centres of economic and political power, in the form of railways and major roads, leys linked up centres of spiritual power from different periods. The movement spanned the British class system, from John Michell, educated at Eton College and Cambridge University and possessed of an unmistakable patrician hauteur, to Paul Screeton, a working-class northerner. It also spanned the political spectrum, from the radical right to the radical left wing, and covered a range of other attitudes, from members primarily interested in prehistory to those primarily interested in alien spacecraft to those concerned above all with the presumed earth energies. Another spectrum ran between the extremes of those who wanted to convince orthodox scholars of the merits of their beliefs to those who felt that communication with established authorities was pointless and that (perhaps) a revelation or a revolution would overthrow those authorities in any case.[149] However, the pace and excitement of the movement during the 1970s generally rendered such differences relatively unimportant.

One of the most prominent individuals within it by the end of the decade was Paul Devereux, who succeeded Screeton as editor of the *Ley Hunter*. He was among those who were most anxious to produce objective evidence that unusual geological or atmospheric emanations congregated at certain points on the earth, and that these tended to be made the sites of ancient sacred centres. To this end he became a founder member of the Dragon Project, established in London in 1977 to carry out ultrasonic and radioactivity tests at selected prehistoric sites, mostly stone circles. These continued through the 1980s, and generated suggestive but not conclusive results: some circles (or parts of them) produced unusual pulses or higher or lower than usual radiation, but some did not, and there was no consistent pattern between those that did; nor did the latter do so reliably. The presence of these anomalies at particular sites seemed to match reports of strange lights being seen there at night, but a connection between the two phenomena was not decisively demonstrated.[150] If professional scientists were difficult to attract to ideas concerning the earth mysteries, then the attention of professional archaeologists was more easily gained: the problem was that it was hostile. Practitioners of archaeology and history, confronted by an enthusiastic amateur or set of amateurs with an unorthodox idea, have virtually no practical incentive to test it. In most cases they may feel instinctually that there is something wrong with it, based on their knowledge of the context concerned, but to disprove it usually requires a significant amount of work, which must be subtracted from their own research, and – if the result is negative, as expected – will attract no interest, and win no regard, from their professional peers. The only people certain to be interested in such a process of testing are those who propound the idea in the first place, and who are likely to be aggrieved and resentful if the end result reached by the professionals does not confirm their hopes. It is far easier to ignore or deflect the challenge from outsiders, or to dismiss it in general terms.

This is what happened to the ley theory. In 1970 John Michell challenged the profession of archaeology to test it in the particular case of the westernmost peninsula of Cornwall, a self-contained area with many ancient sites. He offered to donate a large sum to charity if proved wrong, but could find nobody willing to take on the work.[151] Instead, the editor of the main journal of British archaeology at that time, *Antiquity*, took to condemning ley-hunting along with other heterodox approaches to the past. This was Glyn Daniel, who was with Stuart Piggott and Richard Atkinson one of the three leading experts in the British Neolithic and Early Bronze Age during the mid twentieth century. He emphasized more than most of his profession the need for its members to patrol the boundaries of acceptable thought, and to refute false ideas, but did not seem to recognize that he himself never took the time and trouble actually to refute them.[152] In the words of Adam Stout, who has made the best study of the relationship between orthodox and unorthodox archaeology of this period, Daniel thereby became a 'Demon King' to those in the latter category. In the early 1980s professional archaeology did begin to engage with ley-hunters, Richard Atkinson writing for the *Ley Hunter* and Aubrey Burl, who was emerging as a leading author of popular as well as scholarly works on British prehistory, debating with John Michell and other leaders of the archaeological counter-culture, in print and in person. They did not do much more, however, than state their general reasons for rejecting the ideas of those with whom they debated.[153]

This situation ended dramatically in 1983 when two young archaeologists, Tom Williamson and Liz Bellamy, published *Ley Lines in Question*, a full-length consideration of, and reply to, the evidence provided in favour of the existence of the lines. They pointed out that not only were the markers chosen for leys constructed in many different periods of prehistory, but that when the monuments concerned were excavated, they very rarely proved to have been built on the site of one from an earlier age. Although most ley-hunters assumed that the alignments were Neolithic, most of the structures which they took as markers for them were Iron Age or medieval. The two authors went on to argue that human occupation of the landscape had littered it so densely with ancient and medieval constructions that the statistical chance that any line drawn between two would strike some more was high enough to put apparent leys within the bounds of possible coincidence. They directly tackled Michell's case study of westernmost Cornwall, accusing him of including medieval crosses and natural outcrops in his definition of Neolithic and Bronze Age monuments. They concluded by stressing the ideas and characteristics that orthodox and unorthodox attitudes to archaeology had always possessed in common, but the overall message of the book was still that the concept of leys, as developed in the 1960s and 1970s, lacked any basis in reality.[154] The book provided the detailed and careful response of professional archaeology to the challenge of ley-hunters that the latter had been demanding, and logically left them in turn with two different kinds of response. One was to redefine earth mysteries as pure mysteries, and the belief in earth energies which underpinned them as a matter of faith, which could be very real to believers who personally sensed those energies as palpable and direct phenomena. This simply rejected further dialogue with orthodox views of prehistory, on the grounds that those who held them were too wilfully blind ever to perceive the truth. The other response was to accuse Williamson and Bellamy of failing to keep up with the latest findings and arguments of researchers into the earth mysteries, and strive to renew the challenge to archaeologists with still better data. Each was entirely viable in itself: the trouble was that they pulled in different directions, along a potential fissure between rationalism and mysticism which had always been inherent in the movement.

The former approach was immediately articulated by some responses to *Ley Lines in Question*, notably by Anthony Roberts, who had emerged as the most outspoken proponent of the earth mysteries in Glastonbury, the town which had turned during the 1970s into the national centre of avant-garde spirituality. He declared that objective proofs of the ley system were not needed if 'the whole geomantic/geomythic rationale is the crystallization of the Divine patterns projected on to creation from the all-encompassing Will of God', which only intuition could sense.[155] Indeed, a vague but deeply embedded belief in energy-bearing leys became an enduring feature of some brands of esotericism, occultism and paganism associated with the British counter-culture, though not a fixed tenet of any one tradition among them.[156] The other approach was urged most swiftly, lengthily and forcefully by Paul Devereux.[157] In 1989 it was pushed much further in a book which he jointly authored with another leading figure in the earth mysteries movement, Nigel Pennick, which argued that the movement could regain credibility among society at large only if it abandoned mysticism. They proceeded to offer a survey of the use of straight lines in the landscape for religious purposes in different parts of the world, to suggest that such a comparative study might provide telling insights into visions of the cosmos which emphasized linear connections.[158] In doing so, they were starting to veer away from a primarily structural investigation of leys and a scientific monitoring of megalithic sites to an interpretation of ritual lines as features belonging primarily to the realms of religion and folklore. This not only involved less of a collision with archaeologists but proved in itself a more immediately productive area of research. Devereux published a succession of books, which still continues, on this theme, but also on aspects of ancient ceremonial sites, in different parts of the world, which reflected their relationships with landscape features, folk tradition, skylines and acoustic properties; all matters that could make a direct and relatively uncontroversial contribution to knowledge.[159] In 1991 an article by him on the manner in which sightlines from Silbury Hill connected with the surrounding landscape was published in *Antiquity*, the scholarly journal in which, only a decade before, Glyn Daniel had been publishing tirades against earth mysteries researchers.[160]

Likewise, Nigel Pennick went on to co-author a scholarly history of paganism in Europe, for a mainstream publisher, and is the sole writer of a continuing series of well-researched shorter books and pamphlets on European mythology and folklore, with the focus on geomancy and esoteric craft traditions.[161] Jeremy Harte, who had been the editor of the *Wessex Earth Mysteries* magazine, has established himself as a distinguished historian of folklore and religious tradition, winning the Folklore Society's annual prize for his book on fairy lore.[162] Bob Trubshaw, former editor of the equivalent magazine in the Midlands, has published erudite books on mythology and folk custom as well as performing valuable work as a publisher and editor for others.[163] This convergence of their work with that of archaeologists and academic historians was made easier by the new interest taken by those groups, from the 1990s, in subjects and approaches previously more associated with earth mysteries researchers. In particular, archaeology had broken out of the mid-twentieth-century straitjacket of preoccupation with excavations and artefacts to embrace a relation of ancient sites to their surrounding landscapes and ecologies and an exploration of the cognitive effects of colour, movement, sound and other sensory experience involved in encountering them: the former interest has been considered above, mainly in connection with the work of Christopher Tilley, and the second will be treated in due course. Those earth mysteries researchers who had embraced Paul Devereux's route out of the apparent impasse produced by *Ley Lines in Question* would feel a great deal more welcome, and at home in, the archaeology that flourished around the turn of the twenty-first century than they had in the world of its predecessor. Moreover, the earth mysteries movement had itself changed, as its key preoccupations of the 1970s ebbed gently away. It is not surprising that the *Ley Hunter* ceased publication in 1999, when the internet was providing an easier forum for the expression of views than magazines; but it is still noteworthy that its last editor, Danny Sullivan, proclaimed leys to be 'dead'.[164]

Of course this is a story which can be told in several different ways, even by the present author. From one perspective, the tale of ley-hunting is one of a classic modern religious movement, arising with an apocalyptic language which appropriated some of the tropes of evangelical Christianity, flourished for a brief time, and then subsided into a set of motifs and assumptions retained by a particular subculture of believers. From another, it is a frustrating tale of missed opportunities. The neglect of landscape and sensory experience by mainstream archaeology in the mid twentieth century was indeed a serious omission, which earth mysteries researchers could well have remedied to the lasting benefit of knowledge. They might have carried out the sort of invaluable fieldwork that actually was conducted by amateurs such as Ronald Morris and Stan Beckensall, in pioneering the study of prehistoric designs on rock faces. Misled by a fixed and dogmatic set of ideas, however, they passed this by to focus on an attempted proof of beliefs which were ultimately based on faith alone. It is no coincidence that the writers who came to be seen as the worst enemies of ley-hunting, Tom Williamson and Liz Bellamy, were among the first of the new generation of archaeologists who did explore landscape as a vital component of their work. Williamson was to become one of the leading practitioners of this sub-discipline. In an article which defended their book, they expressed a wish that ley-hunters would turn to promoting an understanding and defence of the English countryside and of the human forces which have shaped it; they had set out not to destroy a belief in leys as a rival to their profession but to give it a fair trial as part of their attempt to promote the development of better attitudes to the study of the land on the part of archaeologists.[165] They also commented, however, that the concept of leys had a 'poetic truth' to it, which related to an older literature of love and nostalgia for rural England, and this is surely correct. Even those earlier works of the earth mysteries movement which now seem most outdated and over-enthusiastic are still recognizable as possessed of a genuine poetic power, reflecting both a key moment in twentieth-century British cultural change and a long-term process of the re-enchantment of the land which is one aspect of late modernity. Furthermore, the activities that they represent functioned as an indispensable training ground for a small but important group of non-academic scholars who have made a genuine contribution to the study of folklore and mythology.[166]

What is very much a live issue is the potential set of relationships between professional archaeology and those members of the public who are drawn to the ancient past by feelings of religious and moral kinship: the very people among whom a literal belief in earth energies remains one possible subset of ideology. For much of the twentieth century relations between the two were adversarial, and especially between experts in British prehistory and modern people who had taken the name and identity of Druid.[167] Since the 1990s it has been feasible to propose a mutual understanding between them, based on the more or less undoubted fact, strongly argued in the present book, that it is impossible to determine with any precision the nature of the religious beliefs and rites of the prehistoric British. It may fairly be argued, therefore, that present-day groups have a perfect right to recreate their own representations of those, and enact them as a personal religious practice – of the sort now generally given the name Pagan – providing that they remain within the rather broad limits of the material evidence (or, if they choose not to remain there, honestly to acknowledge the fact). If there are many plausible ways in which prehistoric attitudes to the divine and supernatural may be imagined, then the reconstructions made by modern Pagans can represent viable, and even valuable, conjectures. If treated as such, by both parties, then there is no necessary reason for conflict between Pagans and archaeologists. Indeed, there is much potential for a creative and benevolent partnership, if the former – while not able to claim any inherent wisdom or knowledge that automatically renders them superior to other members of their society – prove their worth by making exciting, creative and inspiring use of the data steadily generated by the latter.

The Strange History of British Archaeoastronomy

Closely bound up with the story of the earth mysteries movement is that of an academic one which, although quite different in its origins and nature, came to share a similarly fraught relationship with mainstream archaeology and to form something of an alliance with the earth mysteries as a result. This is the study of ancient responses to the heavens, known as archaeoastronomy or astro-archaeology. It was established in the 1970s and 1980s, on a wave of excitement created by pioneering works in the 1960s. It was expected at that time to become an integral and important part of the investigation of British prehistory. Instead it shrank into a small sub-discipline, isolated both from most archaeologists and from amateurs who possess the same enthusiasm for the study of the celestial alignments of ancient monuments. This is despite the fact that archaeoastronomy flourishes at the present day in university departments in North America and the European mainland, and that two of the most influential developments in British archaeology since the 1990s should have fostered a regard for it. One of those developments is the rise of landscape archaeology; and the sky is not only a major component of any landscape but the only one which remains substantially as it was during prehistory. The other is the rise of cognitive archaeology, the study of the way in which ancient people perceived and experienced their world, and the sky must, again, have formed a major aspect of both processes. However, astronomy usually plays, at present, a minor part in the interpretation of archaeological sites.

The professional archaeologists of the early twentieth century were certainly aware that some of Britain's prehistoric monuments had important alignments on the sky. The most famous were Stonehenge and Maes Howe, and there were others that have been noted in the present book. None of the leaders of the new profession, however, were much interested in astronomy, mathematics or engineering. This was partly because these are simply different disciplines, but also because the elements of them in prehistoric structures seemed simple enough to require no special study. Occasionally an outsider had taken an interest in them, sometimes with spectacular results. The most distinguished was the famous scientist Sir Norman Lockyer, the discoverer of helium, who published a series of works on the astronomical significance of ancient monuments between 1894 and 1907. By studying the layout of ancient buildings he declared his discovery of a universal ancient religion of sun worship, carried across Europe, as far as Britain, by the Phoenicians.[168] In making this assertion he got various things wrong, including the misdating of Stonehenge by almost a thousand years, and the declaration that the ceremony which opened the Welsh national cultural institution, the Eisteddfod, was four millennia old (it was actually invented by a brilliant fantasist, Edward Williams, in the late eighteenth century). There is no evidence that the Phoenicians ever got near Britain, and the buildings which Lockyer linked together in his universal solar religion are actually unrelated.[169]

However, the decisive evidence to disprove each suggestion was not discovered until the late twentieth century, and in addition Lockyer found a number of apparent alignments between specific monuments and the movements of the sun which may be correct. The archaeologists of the early twentieth century did not know what to make of any of his ideas regarding the human past, and most ignored them. A few dismissed them, and went further, to reject all attempts to characterize ancient monuments in terms of astronomical orientation.[170] This approach seemed effective: as the century wore on, such ideas slipped from public view. None the less, Lockyer had inspired a number of amateur astronomers to turn their attention to ancient sites, the most significant of whom was Rear-Admiral Boyle Somerville. He found solar, lunar and stellar alignments from several prehistoric Irish and Scottish monuments. He also identified a problem for archaeoastronomy which had appeared as soon as Lockyer wrote, and has shadowed it ever since. In his words, 'discredit and derision' had already been brought on it

through the visionary ideas of some enthusiasts, who have tried to import into the subject far more than the cold facts of science can sustain; so that with them, we become confronted by numbers of 'astronomer priests', sacrificing to the Sun, singing psalms to the Moon, and saluting the Stars. Even the number of stones compassing a Circle, and the 'cubits' that are comprised in its dimensions, have been called upon to provide mystical figures and proportions – an entire prehistoric arithmetic and astrology. It is no wonder, then, that the unmathematical, but otherwise scientific, archaeologist has repelled any suggestion of orientation in these ancient structures.[171]

Somerville published in the main journals of archaeology, but after his death this momentum died away: by the mid twentieth century a few people were still submitting articles on the subject to science periodicals and local newspapers, but they received little attention.[172] This situation ended dramatically between 1963 and 1965, with a series of publications by Gerald Hawkins, a professor of astronomy at an American university, which culminated in a book entitled *Stonehenge Decoded*, which Hawkins co-wrote with his friend John White.[173] It became a rapid bestseller on both sides of the Atlantic, and continued to be one into the 1970s. Deliberately pitched at a popular market, its claim to fame was that it represented the first attempt to apply computer technology systematically to a British prehistoric site. The authors declared Stonehenge to have been built with extraordinary skill as a calendar, and perhaps as a sort of computer itself, aligned precisely on the movements of sun and moon and intended (among other things) to predict eclipses. They were respectful to archaeologists, and used their work, but clearly believed that it had now been surpassed, in determining why the world's most famous prehistoric monument had been built. They also suggested that the prehistoric British had possessed scientific knowledge and ability unequalled until modern times. The result was a division of expert opinion. One of the most respected British astronomers, Sir Fred Hoyle, disagreed with the book's calculations, but made some of his own which confirmed the conclusion that Stonehenge had been a major scientific instrument of great sophistication.[174] Some prominent archaeologists, especially Richard Atkinson, condemned Hawkins and White for making constant mistakes in their use of archaeology and employing inaccurate plans of the monument. They could not, however, refute the mathematical and astronomical reasoning itself, arguing only that it was not certain, and that different scientists seemed to be reaching different conclusions, based on a selective use of data.[175]

The archaeologists concerned failed, moreover, to express their objections in populist works to rival *Stonehenge Decoded*, leaving a growing general readership to assume that the book's ideas were correct. In addition, they had almost immediately to reckon with a more formidable challenger in the same field, a retired Oxford professor called Alexander Thom. He was a very distinguished scholar, of engineering science, who had been interested in the astronomical and mathematical aspects of prehistoric monuments ever since the 1930s, and devoted many university vacations to surveying them, especially in his native Scotland. From 1954 he began to publish his ideas on the subject, but in journals where only astronomers and statisticians read them.[176] Hawkins cited them and called for more publications from him, and it was probably the example of *Stonehenge Decoded* which made Thom decide to write books on the subject himself.[177] These were the first works to support the hypothesis that

British prehistoric monuments were aligned on the heavens with statistical evidence from many sites, produced by extensive fieldwork of high quality. What he argued from this was that the stone circles and rows of Neolithic and Bronze Age Britain had primarily been observatories, for studying the night sky in particular with considerable sophistication and precision. He also believed that these observations were used to construct and maintain a general prehistoric calendar, of eight annual festivals. Furthermore, he contended that the monuments had been laid out with marvellous mathematical ability, using a standard unit of measurement which he termed the 'megalithic yard'.

Thom did not mock archaeologists for failing to perceive all this, but nor did he make any attempt to integrate it with their reconstructions of prehistoric culture and society. Instead he left it to his readers to decide whether or not the two could be reconciled, and many decided that they could not, especially members of the burgeoning earth mysteries movement. To John Michell and his fellows, Thom provided a classic example of an outsider who had shown the whole of orthodox prehistory to be flawed. His apparent proof of an immensely learned and sophisticated ancient Britain made an excellent fit with their quest for the rediscovery of primeval wisdom, and they took him up as a hero.[178] Thom's own relationship with them was complex. He lacked their mysticism and their contempt for most academics. On the other hand, his ideas, consciously or not, sometimes drew on those of the counter-culture associated with the earth mysteries or reinforced them. For example, his Neolithic calendar of eight festivals, based on perceived alignments in prehistoric monuments, corresponded exactly to that used by modern Paganism. Although claimed by Pagans to be prehistoric by the time that Thom was publishing his books, it had actually been developed by the first modern Pagan tradition to appear, Wicca, in 1958.[179] Its component parts were indeed found in Lockyer's work, but divided into two calendars, which he held had been used in successive prehistoric ages; and there is no evidence that Wiccans had used Lockyer when developing their own system of festivals.[180] Thom also gave support to the idea of leys, by declaring in 1971 that Neolithic engineers could survey straight between mutually invisible points.[181]

His claims were of course a great deal less convenient to professional archaeologists, especially as they had no skills with which to test them. To do that required expertise in astronomy, mathematics and statistics, and these were all separate sciences. In 1975 Richard Atkinson became the first leader of his discipline to declare acceptance of Thom's basic principle that megalithic monuments were bound up intrinsically with astronomical observations.[182] John Michell swiftly took full advantage of this opportunity, in a book in which he exulted over what he called Atkinson's 'public confession of his former errors' and termed him the first to abandon the 'sinking ship' of conventional archaeology.[183] Michell made archaeoastronomy his key example of an apparent heresy which had turned out to prove established scholarship completely wrong, and become orthodoxy itself. The lesson was that other unorthodox theorists, like Michell himself, would become the acclaimed experts of the future. By the late 1970s, therefore, two things had become clear. The first was that Thom's claims needed to be examined properly, by experts in all of the necessary branches of knowledge. Thom himself was now leaving the field, for in the mid 1970s he became too old to engage in further research. The second lesson was that established experts in prehistory now had the strongest possible reason to hope for a disproof of his ideas. As the latter had been set up, especially by earth mysteries authors, as the test case of the value of professional archaeology, archaeologists needed to face up to the test. None the less, two further factors weighed against any simple need, desire or ability on their part to defend their traditional attitudes against Thom's ideas. One was that, contrary to the assertions of some of their critics, they could actually adapt to fundamental changes to understanding of the past both speedily and well. In exactly the same period during which Thom published his books, the revolution took place in the dating system for the ancient past, enabled by radiocarbon, which altered the whole prevailing interpretation of European prehistory. This was also brought about by external, scientific, research, and it was rapidly and effectively assimilated by archaeologists. The second point to be emphasized is that a decision on the worth of Thom's theories could not be made by archaeologists alone. The span of expertise necessary for it required a coalition of practitioners, most of them trained in disciplines other than archaeology.

It was this requirement that engendered the new academic discipline or 'interdiscipline' of archaeoastronomy. It secured something like official recognition in 1979, when the *Journal for the History of Astronomy* created a supplement for it. The first full-scale conference officially devoted to the new subject was held at Oxford in 1981, and in the course of the 1980s a set of leading figures emerged within it. Some, like Douglas Heggie, were respected scientists, and some, such as Aubrey Burl, had an existing fame in archaeology. Others, like John Barnatt, Gordon Moir and Clive Ruggles, were scholars who were in the process of establishing careers. None could be considered as belonging to any existing archaeological 'establishment': the nearest to such a figure was Burl, who held a post at what was then a polytechnic. By contrast, Lockyer, Hawkins, Hoyle and Thom were all, or had been, prominent members of the 'establishment' of academic pure or applied science. A few of the new group of archaeoastronomers had personal connections with Thom; indeed, Burl had collated some of his work for publication, with approving comments.[184]

Despite this, in the first half of the 1980s the group seemed to reach a consensual, and negative, verdict on Thom's conclusions.[185] The whole of his mathematical theorizing was called into question. Stone circles which he claimed to have been laid out with marvellous precision could, it seemed, have been built without that; and nor was good evidence found for his common system of megalithic geometry or measurement. The findings concerning his astronomical alignments were more mixed. Many stone circles and rows seemed to have no sightlines on any heavenly bodies, which in itself seemed to overturn his central thesis. The associations between megaliths and stars could not be tested adequately because the latter move so frequently and swiftly that no correlation could be proved without having a more precise date for the construction of the final phase of a monument than present techniques permit. On the other hand, a significant number of structures did seem to correspond to the movements of sun or moon, and some to both. This, however, fitted the traditional model of prehistoric society perfectly well. It had always been recognized that certain monuments had clear alignments on heavenly bodies, especially the sun. The difference was that these alignments were accepted as a component in the religion or religions that had inspired the monuments, while Thom argued instead that the latter had been primarily observatories erected in accordance with a scientific knowledge astonishing even by modern standards.

A close examination of the critiques suggests that Thom's claims were not, in fact, positively refuted. What they reveal is that, at each point, those claims were susceptible to challenge and alternative readings of the same evidence: they were not 'hard' science of the sort represented by the correction of the radiocarbon dating process. For virtually all professional archaeologists, this was sufficient to make it permissible for them to discard the claims as a contribution to the study of prehistory, and a signal to get back to business as usual. By the end of the 1980s, the coalition of experts that had investigated Thom's ideas more or less dispersed, and only one member remained to make a continued reputation in the field. This was Clive Ruggles, who became the most respected archaeoastronomer in Britain during the 1990s. As well as proving to be the most dedicated academic practitioner of the subject, he had also been the most inclined to emphasize the difficulties and subtleties in it. He had pointed out, for example, that there are actually two different kinds of basic theoretical approach to statistics, which get significantly different results. He had recognized that apparent scientific conclusions may not always match up to cultural realities. When he investigated the stone rows and aligned pairs of standing stones in the northern part of the Hebridean island of Mull and in the Kilmartin Valley in nearby Argyll, he found that all had a similar orientation. The only celestial event which matched it was the major southerly lunar standstill. What worried him about this was that there are no traditional peoples on earth who have shown an interest in the movements of the moon along the horizon. In this he perceived what he called 'the fundamental problem . . . that evidence acceptable to a numerate scientist is of a very different nature from that acceptable to his counterpart trained in the humanities'.[186] This is a point of central importance to the whole subject.

By the end of the 1990s Ruggles's work effectively summed up archaeo-astronomy in Britain for his academic peers.[187] He declared decisively against any high-precision alignments on heavenly bodies in British or Irish prehistoric monuments. Instead he found evidence for rough or symbolic alignments on either the sun or the moon, with regional traditions which inclined to one or the other. These were fairly clearly expressions of a belief system based on ritual and cosmic truths rather than scientific observation for its own sake. He also pointed out a logical flaw at the heart of Thom's labelling of megalithic monuments as observatories: prehistoric farmers could determine the time of year quite easily by watching the horizon. They had no need for any markers to do so, let alone massive stone structures requiring considerable effort to build. In addition, Ruggles possessed the knowledge of anthropology needed to raise one further concern: that many recent indigenous peoples have taboos against pointing directly at things, so that all of the apparent alignments may have been deceptive. Equipped with such arguments, he opened the new century by becoming Britain's only Professor of Archaeoastronomy, a fitting symbol of his pre-eminence in the field.

It seems that to many British archaeologists, Clive Ruggles's views represented not just the end of the debate but the end of the subject, an effect neatly illustrated in the case of Stonehenge itself. In 1996 a respected academic historian of astronomy, John North, published a huge book in which he suggested that most Neolithic monuments were aligned with precision on heavenly bodies. Those from the fourth millennium, his argument ran, were linked to stars, while the enclosures of the third millennium, including Stonehenge to which he devoted most attention, were orientated more on sun and moon. North emphasized that the essential purpose of the structures was religious but still insisted that they embodied a scientific knowledge extraordinary for the time.[188] The next year, a compilation of essays on the scientific aspects of Stonehenge appeared under the auspices of the British Academy, and Clive Ruggles was invited to write that on astronomy. Without concentrating on North's book, he still managed to answer all its arguments, holding that they were hard to prove and suggesting that Stonehenge had only one undoubted axis, based on the solstices, and a possible lunar component; and that neither required much grasp of science.[189] In 2007 Julian Richards, a leading archaeological authority on Stonehenge, produced a book on the monument aimed at a broad readership and subtitled *The Story So Far*. This did not mention North at all: he was evidently not part of 'the story'. Instead it summed up the views of Lockyer, Hawkins and Thom as misguided, and introduced Ruggles as 'the voice of reason', before quoting him at length.[190] Two years before, Richards had written the latest version of the official guidebook to the monument, and summarized Ruggles's ideas as all that needed to be said about its astronomical aspects.[191] In 2009 the Royal Astronomical Society issued a booklet for the general public which summed up the relevance of astronomy to Stonehenge; it was written by Ruggles and colleagues who agreed with him.[192]

To his credit, Clive Ruggles himself was clearly uneasy about the situation which had developed, and especially about the lack of interest in astronomy that British archaeologists had displayed since 1990. Many had ceased, in fact, to give any special consideration to possible heavenly alignments at the sites they investigated.[193] He suggested three reasons for this. One was that archaeologists had a new enthusiasm, for landscape, which had distracted their attention. A second was that archaeoastronomers drew their language from modern Western science, and so it grated on the ears of archaeologists as both ethnocentric and anachronistic. The third reason was that academic archaeoastronomy was contaminated in the eyes of professional archaeologists by confusion with what Ruggles termed a booming 'popular archaeoastronomy', associated indissolubly with a counter-culture.[194] It may be suggested here that there is truth in all three, but that each can bear some further consideration. Ruggles himself noted the logical flaw in the first: that the sky is part of the landscape which archaeologists claimed to be studying. The language of archaeoastronomy may well grate on the ears of professional archaeology. What is possibly more significant, however, is that so many aspects of archaeoastronomy itself seem conjectural and inconclusive by now that archaeologists in general – in the experience of the present author – shy away from it. A major exception to this rule in the early 1990s was the interpretation of an Early Neolithic enclosure lined with wooden posts, discovered at Godmanchester near Huntingdon. The excavators proposed alignments from several of the posts upon movements of the sky, only to have their suggestions slammed by Ruggles himself as 'ill-advised', 'dangerous' and 'unconvincing', thus providing an example potent enough to deter others.[195] In this situation, it is all too easy for archaeologists to leave the whole problem to archaeoastronomers, even forgetting in the process to supply the latter with data. If they take any notice of archaeoastronomy, then the default position is to repeat the views of Ruggles, not because he is seen as occupying an extreme, sceptical end of a spectrum but because he is regarded as the opposite: as the main representative of a cautious and consensual position with which virtually all archaeoastronomers should agree, even if some would like to go much further. Articles on the astronomical alignments of monuments have continued to be published in British archaeological journals ever since the 1980s, though they have been rare.[196] Occasionally, a new expert in archaeoastronomy has even appeared within a British university.[197] What is most significant is the lack of impression made by such writings on mainstream works of archaeology.

The terms which Ruggles used for the more unorthodox forms of archaeoastronomy may also need some refinement. To call them 'popular' is perhaps questionable, as there is no sign either that they attract more public interest or enthusiasm than mainstream archaeology, or that they are representative of the populace as a whole. Rather, they are generated by a relatively well defined minority interest and subculture within the nation, which indeed overlaps with counter-cultural movements but is distinct from the mainstream of them. The obvious source of this subculture is in the former earth mysteries, of which in some ways it is a continuation: now that ley lines, drawn straight between ancient monuments on the earth, have largely fallen out of fashion, interest has shifted to straight lines in the air, drawn between monuments and heavenly bodies. This interest is propelled by the same impulse which gave rise to a new interest in archaeoastronomy in the 1960s: that to survey the sky is one apparent way of coming up with new ideas about the prehistoric past which requires no excavation and no acquaintance with current thinking about prehistory. The force that has given it fresh vigour is the microchip revolution, which has provided exciting new tools such as software which represents the configuration of the night sky during different eras of prehistory, and satellite pictures of sites. To give some sense of the current range of approaches, three different bodies of work will now be considered as examples.

The first is that of Robin Heath, the most prominent and prolific recent figure in the field, author of a series of books since the late 1990s, and a website.[198] He is an engineer who has taught at various colleges of further education and recently held an honorary research fellowship at the University of Wales, Lampeter: a reminder that the boundary between mainstream and 'alternative' archaeoastronomers is not straightforwardly one between academics and non-academics. His heroes are Hawkins, Michell and Thom, and in his earlier work he restated their claim to have proved the existence of a worldwide ancient scientific wisdom of awe-inspiring magnitude. From the geometrical and mathematical properties of stone circles, especially Stonehenge, he concluded that the builders used them to predict eclipses, calendar dates, tides and phases of the moon. He also asserted, in partnership with John Michell, that Neolithic people accurately calculated the dimensions of the planet. In that earlier work he made no attempt to integrate any of this information with the findings of archaeologists, and indeed had no time for the latter, dismissing them, collectively, as characterized by 'ignorance and prejudice'.[199]

Instead the supporting evidence that he employed for his interpretations of measurements and calculations was taken from a personal reinterpretation of medieval Christian legends and of selected parts of the Bible and Apocrypha. In many ways his work has been firmly in the older earth mysteries tradition, arguing both for an equal validity of the insights of 'dowsers, ley hunters, sacred geometers, psychics and shamans' with those of archaeology.[200] His most substantial recent book, published in 2007,[201] is an extended defence of the work of Alexander Thom. It is much more respectful to archaeologists, though still interested in them only inasmuch as their work relates directly to Thom's ideas. Moreover, he still clearly regards rejection of those ideas as a sign of moral failings rather than simply a difference of scholarly opinion, and other authors are treated in relation to them as heroes, villains and collaborators with villains. His principal villain is of course Clive Ruggles.

Heath is, in my opinion, the most typical as well as the most prominent of my three case studies. The others, in different ways, buck the normal trend. One is a recent arrival on the scene, a computer programmer called Thomas William Flowers Junior, who has published two booklets and more information on a website since 2008.[202] His starting point is also the work of Thom, but he has attacked it as inadequate and set out to demonstrate his own surveys of Stonehenge and other major Neolithic sites to be superior. In particular, he wishes to establish a theory that the monuments concerned were designed to bring the sun and moon together to produce a baby sun. He in turn shows no interest in the recent findings of archaeology. Instead he has announced that, on sending his conclusions to English Heritage, the administrative body which cares for Stonehenge, he received a polite acknowledgement but not an acceptance of his views. This caused him to condemn archaeologists (in general) as 'stuck in the past'. It does not help the cause of 'alternative' archaeoastronomy in the world of professional archaeology that its practitioners seem to disagree with each other, while being equally hostile to mainstream scholarship if it does not give in to their demands.

The last category presents a different sort of exception to the rule. It is represented here by two works, one a lengthy study of the developed passage graves of the Boyne Valley which appeared in 2006.[203] The authors are Anthony Murphy and Richard Moore, a journalist and an artist from that district. In many ways it makes a fit with the other case studies offered here. Its inspiring figure is, again, Thom, and it proposes, after his manner, a large number of alignments between the various monuments and the sun, moon and stars. It is also rooted firmly in the earth mysteries tradition, drawing straight lines on the ground between the sites and finding a giant figure picked out in the landscape. Likewise, it treats the ancient world as having wisdom to teach the present. It also, like Heath, places an emphasis on medieval legends as supporting evidence for its claims. What is so unusual about it is that the authors have made every effort to understand archaeologists, to incorporate their findings, and so show respect for them. They never, in fact, abuse any opponents, and their work is proportionately free of evangelical rhetoric; instead, they admit that their arguments are speculative and offer them as a contribution to a general debate.[204] The other work in this category is a careful and detailed study of the astronomical alignments of the Avebury monuments, made by Nicholas Mann, another independent researcher.[205] Once again, its inspiration lies in earlier authors in the tradition, above all Thom and including Hawkins, North and Heath, but it is generally respectful to and conscious of the contributions of archaeologists, and incorporates their data with its own. It presents its suggestions modestly and temperately, treating knowledge about the past as a holistic enterprise.

There is no attempt made, as part of this treatment of the debates over archaeoastronomy, to offer any contribution to the field itself: the author lacks the necessary scientific qualifications. It is instead an exercise in cultural history, focusing on what those debates tell us about the modern British, and perhaps even about the processes of history themselves. One suggestion to be made here is that the debates concerned provide support for the concept of great person-alities as motive forces in human development. Without the towering figure of Alexander Thom, neither academic nor popular interest in the field would have taken off as it did. The same story also acts as a reminder of the differences between approaches to data on the part of scientists and of scholars in the humanities. It throws into high relief the basic problem of how truth can be established in scholarship, and especially in the study of the remote past, which is a major theme of this book. Perhaps, however, it is most revealing as a lesson in the power politics of knowledge in the modern age, expressed here in the relationships between different kinds of professional scholar, between main-stream and fringe cultures, and between secularism and religion.

The Archaeology of Experience

One aspect of the recent sub-discipline of 'cognitive archaeology', has been to encourage a more sensual and imaginative attitude to the analysis of prehis-toric sites. Francis Pryor, for example, has suggested that Neolithic tomb-shrines were probably brightly painted, and filled on feast days with perfumed smoke, drumming, horn-blowing, cries and incantations.[206] One does not have to be a spoilsport to point out that this is a highly speculative picture: the paint is unproven and many chambers were too small to accommodate more than one or two living people at a time. It is just as likely that the Neolithic experi-ence of these monuments consisted of a crawl into silent darkness full of the spirits of the dead. None the less, to think about them in such terms as Pryor did is in itself refreshing, and suggestive.

The sense of prehistoric monuments as places to be experienced as well as studied has manifested in different ways in the years since 1990. One is as a component of the surrounding terrain, which intersects with the parallel new interest in landscape as a feature of archaeological investigation. In 1996, Timothy Darvill summed up a growing mood by urging archaeologists in general to stop regarding landscape as a purely physical entity, and to view it as 'socially constructed sets of values, categories and understandings that individuals and communities develop and impose on the environment', which were constantly mutating and being contested as relationships between people and their perceptions of the world altered.[207] At this time Christopher Tilley was also developing his studies which highlighted the manner in which monuments related to the surrounding land. In addition to those cited already, attention may be drawn here to his study of Bodmin Moor in Cornwall, in which he suggested that the Neolithic ritual structures on this upland, long cairns and enclosures, were placed to draw attention to the rocky outcrops, or 'tors', which crown it. To him, therefore, tors were 'non-domesticated megaliths'. The largest of the moor's Bronze Age round cairns, by contrast, were placed on hill crests themselves, as if to mimic or enhance the tors: in his view, the Neolithic marked out powerful rocks but the Bronze Age 'captured' them.[208]

Similar recent attention has been paid to the use of colour on megalithic sites. At the Scottish Clava Cairns, grey or white stones were placed in the fabric of the mounds to face the directions of sunrise, red stones to face the sunset, and black stones in the rear of the chambers.[209] In earlier Neolithic tomb-shrines along the western British coast from Galloway to Pembrokeshire, there is a common alternation in the composition of the chambers between rough and smooth, and rectangular and triangular, stones, as well as of different colours; so texture and shape mattered as well as hue, even if there is no overall pattern, or 'code', in the oppositions across the region.[210] This is a fine example of the realization of Colin Renfrew's hope that cognitive archaeology will reveal how ancient people thought, if not what. Attention has also been paid since the 1990s to the acoustic properties of megalithic monuments, and here much of the significant work has been carried out by one researcher, Aaron Watson. In his person and his interests he is a perfect example of an individual now occupying a space between what had been the different concerns of professional archaeology and the earth mysteries in the 1980s. He has found several remarkable effects at different sites, though – once more – without a standard pattern. At the stone circles of Stenness and Brodgar, sound was reflected back from the megaliths to the centre of the rings, while the chambers of some Orcadian tomb-shrines enhanced the effects of drums and voices. At an Aberdeenshire recumbent-stone circle, the recumbent megalith generated echoes, while the huge earthwork of the Avebury henge prevented sound from the interior from reaching people outside, and vice versa. The inner surfaces of Stonehenge amplify sound and produce notable fluctuations in it.[211] There are obvious problems in building all this data straightforwardly into an interpretation of a site: prehistoric people may not have sensed things quite as we do today and there is the major obstacle of proving that any of these effects were intentional. Joshua Pollard has summed up both the potential importance and the limitations of 'acoustic archaeology': that a Neolithic world without music is 'inconceivable', but that actual instruments have not apparently survived and that sites such as Stonehenge may have been places of quiet veneration.[212] Yet he agrees fully that sound was always a part of prehistoric sites and deserves study with every other aspect of them.

As a result of the new interest in the colour and texture of British prehistoric monuments, one material has emerged as especially prominent, and apparently numinous: quartz. It has been noted that white was a favoured colour in general during the Neolithic era in Britain, mounds being commonly constructed of chalk or other pale rocks, and chambers or circles built of pale stone. The big henges at Thornborough in North Yorkshire, where the soil is dark, were coated in gypsum to lighten them. Of a piece with this tradition, quartz pebbles have been found on many sites, especially in tomb-shrines all around the Irish Sea, and also in many Bronze Age burial monuments. Timothy Darvill, who first drew systematic attention to this phenomenon, pointed out that although white quartz was preferred, red and speckled varieties were deposited as well. He wondered whether quartz represented a link to water, as its pebbles were usually found on beaches and in river beds and springs, and so to the moon.[213] Ffion Reynolds has taken this further by pointing out that the same mineral has a sacred significance for traditional peoples in the Americas, Africa and Australia. Another of its properties is that it emits flashes or glows when rubbed, so appearing to be alive, and this would powerfully have reinforced its significance as a numinous material.[214] Vicki Cummings has noted that in the tomb-shrines of the Irish Sea coasts quartz was often used to mark out important parts of the chambers: entrances, rears or sides. She has repeated the possible associations with water and the moon, while adding that the pebbles may also have represented skulls or eyes and that they would have reflected light, and sparkled, if the monuments were used at night.[215]

All of these subjects for study impinge on the larger question of states of consciousness, dramatically highlighted by experts in the Palaeolithic in their debate over the shamanic interpretation of cave paintings and carvings. The new popular taste for hallucinogenic drugs in the Western world during the late twentieth century engendered an interest in their possible use in European prehistory, where again the work of orthodox archaeology and earth mysteries researchers converged. A representative of the former, Andrew Sherratt, and of the latter, Paul Devereux, proved especially active in this.[216] Results were suggestive but inconclusive, as traces of opium poppies and hemp were found on Continental sites but not proven to have been used for ritual, as opposed to medicinal, purposes. In Britain, small ceramic vessels commonly called 'incense cups', found with many Early Bronze Age burials, may have been used to burn such substances.[217] Pollen and seeds from henbane, a native hallucinogenic (and very poisonous) plant, were found on Grooved Ware sherds at the complex Late Neolithic ceremonial site at Balfarg, in the Fife region of Scotland, but may have been intruded on to them rather than contained within them.[218] Since the turn of the twenty-first century less has been heard of the subject, but attention should still be paid to the almost certain presence of the mind-altering substance most widely used by historical Europeans, including the British, and indeed most commonly found among our species in general: alcohol.[219] The prominence of drinking vessels, such as beakers, among Neolithic and later prehistoric artefacts suggests that the owners had something consciousness-transforming to put into them for special occasions. This, however, is still apparently lacking in absolute scientific proof, and it is notable that historic European pagans employed strong drink much more often for nutritional and recreational than ritual purposes, and in the latter it featured more in the form of libations than for the specific aim of altering consciousness.[220] Moreover, other liquids, such as milk, may well have enjoyed a greater importance both in diet and symbolism.

All these examples of a new taste for an 'archaeology of experience' raise the question of whether the convergence at many points of the concerns of professional archaeology and the earth mysteries represents a coincidence or an imitation. Since the 1980s, there have been occasional attempts by archaeologists to give space in edited collections to 'alternative' viewpoints on their subject. These have partly been made in the cause of inviting better relations between the two traditions (especially over flashpoints like access to Stonehenge), and partly because of the growing general consciousness in Western intellectual culture of the importance of a plurality of views on any subject, which is integral to the project of postmodernism.[221] More recently a few academics, bridging the disciplines of archaeology and religious studies, have made a speciality of comparing and contrasting the viewpoints of prehistorians, heritage managers, Pagans and practitioners of New Age spirituality, and enabling dialogues between them.[222] It is difficult to see, however, any clear examples of the transference of ideas and attitudes between them, as opposed to a greater understanding and acceptance of different ideas. The new interest in experiential aspects of archaeology, after all, apparently arose as a subset of the new cognitive sub-discipline, which was itself an academic reaction against older models of enquiry based on a growing sense of their inadequacy for changing generations. Yet it may still be argued that there is a relationship, in that the earth mysteries arose partly as a reaction against the perceived limitations of concern, and sensual aridity, of mid-twentieth-century professional archaeology, and so did the cognitive strain of enquiry among archaeologists, a decade or two later. Both therefore actually do have more in common than a subject matter and a set of interests and responses, so it is hardly surprising that there have been so many correspondences between them.

A Time without Tombs or Temples

It has been noted that there was no sharp division in Britain, in terms of either social and economic structures or ritual activity, between the technological epochs which archaeologists have termed the Stone Age and the Bronze Age. It has become increasingly obvious, however, that such a division did occur in the course of the Bronze Age, and in the second millennium BC. As Richard Bradley has recently stated, all experts now agree that the Bronze Age no longer forms a single useful unit of British prehistory, but not on how it should be split up. The problem is that the making of metalwork, the nature of burial rites and patterns of settlement and land division all altered profoundly in the course of the period, but not at the same time. Bradley himself suggested that the Early Bronze Age had more things in common with the Neolithic, and the Middle and Late Bronze Age with each other. He dated the three periods of the Bronze Age as falling between 2150 and 1500 BC, 1500 and 1100 BC, and 1100 and 800 BC, respectively, and therefore suggested that the main cultural watershed of the period should be placed around 1500 BC. This latter suggestion seems now to be generally accepted.[223]

Bradley also stressed that none of the developments which made the period after about 1500 BC look different were themselves new, all having made their appearance in the earlier second millennium or even before then. What changed was that in the second half of the millennium they became dominant. The generally mobile pattern of life, across open landscapes, which had been carried on since the beginning of the Neolithic, largely became replaced by settlements of permanent houses, some of which probably deserve the name of villages or hamlets. The landscape was increasingly divided up, first into small fields and then by long banks which seem to mark off territories or ranches. Round barrows became smaller and then vanished, to be replaced by flat cemeteries of cremation burials placed in ceramic urns. Goods, especially metalwork, were placed much less often with the dead and much more often in pits in the ground or (particularly) in watery places. Ceremonial monuments, of the sort that had dominated many landscapes since the coming of farming, became scarce or died out. Henges were apparently no longer built in much of Britain by the second millennium, and there is little sign of continued use of most. Stone circles, which are much harder to date, seemingly continued to be made in northern and western Britain (and in Ireland) throughout the Bronze Age, but more and more rarely, until their construction, and any activity at them, appears to have ceased by its end. The same can be said of timber circles. Activity continued in and around the great monumental complexes of Stonehenge and Avebury during the early part of the second millennium, but not beyond it. Orkney, which had produced the most spectacular achievements of Neolithic Scotland, turned into a backwater. For two and a half thousand years, from around 4000 to around 1500 BC, ritualized activities had largely been bound up with the making of monuments, but thereafter they almost wholly parted company with it.[224]

There are signs that this process may have involved the abandonment of systems of belief as well as modes of expression of them. In previous shifts of fashion between forms of monument construction, such as those around the junction of the fourth and third, and the third and second, millennia, the new forms of ceremonial structure were often built close to the old, and little attempt was made to degrade or demolish the latter. As said before, this need not be an indication of continuity and respect, as the incoming ideologies may have been appropriating sites associated with ideas that had been held before, as part of the process of replacing them. However, the overall action was one of recognition and preservation of the old. From the later second millennium, this tradition was increasingly abandoned, as farming first encroached upon and then demolished earlier sacred sites. Where the latter were respected, they were also neglected: by the Iron Age the whole Avebury complex seems to have been overgrown. During that age, across Britain, henges, round barrows, cursuses and ring cairns were destroyed or mutilated wholesale wherever they got in the way of agricultural or industrial activity. Richard Bradley has made the most systematic survey of this process, in southern England, and found that the pattern of disrespect and demolition was constant from the Late Bronze Age to the beginning of the modern period. He found not a single clear example in his region of continuous use of a ceremonial site throughout the last two millennia BC.[225]

Such a rupture with traditional ways demands explanation, and one of the first areas in which to seek it might be environmental and economic determinism: a cataclysmic shift in the natural order could well provoke a proportionate alteration in belief systems. Certainly the weather deteriorated in later British prehistory. Between the Late Mesolithic and Early Bronze Age it had been warmer and drier than at the present, perhaps equating to that of the modern south of France. From around 1800 BC it began to get colder and wetter, a trend accelerating after 1400 to reach a point around 700 at which the British climate was apparently worse than at present. From 500 BC it began to recover. This long process of declining temperatures and increasing rainfall made its impact on landscapes which were already being eroded by tree clearance and farming. The long process of removing woodland, which had commenced at the end of the Mesolithic, continued steadily through the Neolithic and Early Bronze Age until by the middle of the second millennium BC most of it was gone. With it were disappearing large animals that competed with humans, such as the bear and the species of huge wild cattle known as the aurochs: the bear would probably survive until the end of the Iron Age but the aurochs does not seem to have got that far. In places the very soil was disappearing too, being washed away from kinds of terrain as different as the North Yorkshire Moors and the Cotswold Hills by the second millennium BC. Complete new landscapes were being created, such as heather-clad moors, and chalk downs of bare green turf. Sea levels began to rise and bogs to form, and human occupation receded from areas of upland in the northern and western parts of the island.[226]

Profound as these changes were – and, indeed, many of those in the natural environment have proved to be lasting – they were also slow, and allowed the peoples of Britain time in which to adapt. There is no definite evidence that the climatic change resulted in an overall drop in population, as opposed to a redistribution of it. The inhabitants of Britain do not seem more impoverished at the end of the second millennium than at the first: indeed the reverse, as continuing technological innovation produced ever more elaborate kinds of bronze ware, and styles of pottery continued to mutate. It is hard to say whether the societies of which they were the creations altered significantly, simply because there is no certainty as to the nature of those societies in earlier times. The abandonment of barrows, cairns and burials with goods, and the appearance of flat cremation cemeteries in their place, looks like a shift to greater social equality, but the increasing numbers of valuable bronze goods, many obviously items designed for warrior elites, suggest the opposite. What does occur, quite dramatically, is a gradual but steady shift from putting energy into the construction of ceremonial monuments to investing it in the making of domestic and agricultural units, such as houses, field walls and boundary earthworks. As people increasingly settled down, the need for spaces set apart for ritual and assembly, in which migrating groups halted at special times of the year, seems to have died away.[227] It is possible to argue that the special significance of the circle, so evident in the ceremonial monuments of the third millennium, just became transferred to the domestic sphere in the second, as henges and stone or timber circles were replaced by the roundhouse as the dominant form of the new, permanent, dwellings. It was in the Bronze Age that this sort of construction first became widespread and common, continuing to sustain its popularity for the remainder of British prehistory.[228] Such a hypothesis gains some strength from the example of Leskernick, a settlement on Bodmin Moor apparently occupied from around 1525 to around 1265 BC and excavated in the late 1990s. It was built near a set of stone circles and rows put up in the earlier second millennium, and included three circular structures which have been interpreted as shrines open to the sky. A corridor running through the centre of the settlement site was marked with standing stones and may have been a processional way: it is as if the activities formerly carried out in the special monuments nearby had been relocated to the heart of everyday life.[229] Likewise, the disappearance of metalwork from graves may only have represented a similar transference of traditional rites, if it was now taken from the dead as they were prepared for burial and placed separately in the ground or in water.[230] The apparent dramatic change of belief represented by the abandonment of monuments as settings for ritual may be illusory, with the same supernatural beings and forces continuing to be honoured in similar ways within new contexts.

What needs to be emphasized here is that the inhabitants of Britain, from the moment at which they began to reshape the landscape and erect impressive structures upon it, had never been truly static or conservative in their ritual behaviour. Even when lifestyles, technologies and environments were barely altering at all, they carried out dramatic revisions of their ceremonial architecture. The latter had, indeed, been in a state of more or less constant development and mutation ever since it appeared. After two and a half millennia in which so many varieties of monument had been created, it may be that the only further innovation which could be envisaged was to abandon monumental constructions almost completely and redirect creative attention to the home and the farm. Certainly it can be argued that the change to a new and sedentary way of life invited such a reconsideration, but settled peoples have proved themselves repeatedly, and in many parts of the world, to be more capable of constructing massive temples and tombs than mobile populations. In one sense it is lame, but in other salutary, to emphasize that the shift in the expression of ritual behaviour which took place in the second millennium BC was just the latest in a series which had commenced as soon as the prehistoric British became builders, and had gone on incessantly ever since. Their Christian successors were to observe a basic continuity in the form and use of ritual space, enforced by doctrine, which was unknown before the beginning of history.

4

⫸━◆━⫷

LATE PREHISTORY
EARTHWORKS, PITS AND BONES

I N 2011, THREE experts on the Early Neolithic declared that the precision
with which dating could now be determined was so great that the fourth
millennium BC might soon be deemed to belong to history rather than prehistory.[1] As a rhetorical statement it makes an excellent point, but many historians
may be tempted to reply that it would only be true if henceforth we knew what
the peoples of Britain in that millennium called themselves or were called by
others; what kind of political, social or religious beliefs they held; what had
motivated them to construct the monuments which they left behind; and
(ideally) the names of some individuals among them and a narrative of
the actions in which they engaged. Such data is only available with the appearance of written records of some kind, which by definition mark the transition
from prehistoric to historic times, and, this being so, history securely begins
for the British in the twenty-first century exactly where it has begun for them
ever since the Middle Ages: with the landing of the Roman general Julius
Caesar in 55 BC.[2] Caesar departed for good in the following year, and the
Romans did not return, bringing back history with them, until AD 43, but
the gap is plugged partly by the existence of a native British coinage bearing the
names of tribal leaders, matched very slightly by occasional Roman references
to these figures.

The appearance of the Romans and of the coins are interlinked, and mark
the development of a new and distinctive phase in the development of British
society, poised between the prehistoric and historic and known generally in
recent years by the cumbersome name of the Late Pre-Roman Iron Age.
Whether it is still useful to speak in terms of such an epoch as the Iron Age in
Britain, however, is a debatable point. It has already been observed that the

Late Neolithic and Early Bronze Age have in many ways more in common with each other than the former has with the Early Neolithic and the latter with the Late Bronze Age. Writing in 2007, Richard Bradley drew attention to this, and suggested that, likewise, the Early and Middle Iron Ages formed one period with the Late Bronze Age, while the Late Iron Ages was better joined to the succeeding Roman epoch.[3] There is undoubted truth in this perspective, and yet it will be argued here that, in terms of ritual activity, there is still merit in treating late British prehistory as a unit, although one which adopts half of the proposed model and defines that unit as starting with the Late Bronze Age and ending with the Roman conquest. As the context to such a treatment, a sketch will be provided now of what is currently thought to be the sequence of economic and social developments over that span of time.

Technological developments could themselves be related to aesthetic and spiritual factors rather than to the purely functional: thus, the appearance of metal in Britain during the third millennium BC was not only a slow business but one in which the new medium was at first often used for jewellery rather than tools. It is by no means obvious that gold or copper objects were superior for the performance of everyday tasks than flint, wood, bone or pottery, but they were attractive for their colour and sheen.[4] Bronze, however, was both beautiful and stronger and more versatile than flint, and by the Late Bronze Age, commonly thought to run in Britain from about 1200 to about 800 BC, it had come to dominate the economy and its working had reached a peak of technical perfection.[5] Just as before, it was employed for a succession of new goods: by the thirteenth century, socketed axes and hammers, saws, chisels and anvils, by the twelfth, leaf-shaped swords and circular shields, and by the eleventh, sheet-metal cauldrons.[6] As Sir Barry Cunliffe has emphasized, the warrior equipment thus developed, of spear, slashing sword, socketed axe and round shield, was found all over Europe at this period, reflecting a new degree of interconnection across the Continent. A shield retrieved from an Irish bog is identical to one carved upon a stone slab in Spain, while a sword found in the Shetland Islands is very similar to one depicted on the same Spanish slab. This must reflect an intense mobility, of people, objects and ideas, which was itself probably driven by the strongly restricted occurrence of the ores needed to make bronze (copper and tin) and so the need to gain access to them and their products.[7] In 2010 one of the wooden ships that had carried them was found in the bay at Salcombe, Devon, where it had sunk in about 900 BC. It was up to 40 feet (about 12 metres) in length and still held a cargo of copper and tin ingots, and a sword and ornaments, which together derived from Iberia and the Alps, and possibly from France as well.[8] Rivers would have functioned as the main highways of the time, along which goods could be moved easily by boat, but wheels are recorded in Britain from around 1300 onwards and would have assisted mobility by land: landscape archaeology has now detected many droves and trackways dating to the period.[9]

It is possible that the need to acquire bronze by trading other commodities compelled the increasing intensification of farming which is plain in the record of the time, as the Late Bronze Age landscape was divided up ever more carefully into fields, ranges and settlements. Fortified circular enclosures appeared in areas of southern and eastern Britain, which may have been residences for local leaders, or else trading posts for the locality. More clearance of woodland took place on good soils, and beans and rye were introduced, with new species of wheat and barley. A salt industry developed to preserve food for travel, and tools suggest increasing textile production. All this activity took place against a background of continuing climatic deterioration, which forced agriculture out of more areas as the ground became waterlogged, forming peat bogs in uplands and coastal marshes in lowlands.[10] It is still not easy to decide how society was organized, because the lack of richly furnished burials or obvious high-status dwellings seems to imply a lack of social hierarchy and distinction, and there is little evidence of active warfare, but the large quantity of carefully made bronze weaponry indicates the presence of a warrior elite. As a result, experts have divided over the matter, Francis Prior arguing strongly for an egalitarian and peaceful British Late Bronze Age, and Timothy Darvill and Timothy Champion for one dominated by a warlike aristocracy.[11]

There is no greater agreement on the transition to the Iron Age. To John Gale in 2003, the distinction between the two ages was meaningless, as the landscape of 700 BC was the same as that of 1200, while to Stuart Needham four years later, 800 BC was 'the great divide' of later prehistory.[12] Once more, they were looking at genuine differences in the data. The adoption of iron was certainly a slow business: it was worked in Britain from about 1000 BC at the latest, and not fully adopted throughout the island until the fourth century.[13] On the other hand, the years between 800 and 600 BC were pivotal in its impact, because it was then that the bronze trade collapsed, taking with it the international networks on which it depended. Iron was not, initially at least, an obviously superior metal, but it had the single considerable advantage of depending on one type of ore, which, in Britain as in many other places, was found in many more localities than copper and tin. Whether growing shortages of the latter caused a shift to iron, or iron production undercut bronze, is not known, but the result was a transformation of Western Europe, including Britain, into more localized and inward-looking societies. The change co-incided with the nadir of the apparent climatic deterioration to produce about two centuries of apparent dislocation. New centres for intermittent gatherings appeared in southern Britain, represented by feasting sites which left large deposits of animal bone, pottery and metalwork, and large, lightly defended hilltop enclosures. The round forts had been abandoned after 1000 BC, and now many field systems and settlements were left derelict as well, with new linear earthworks cutting across the fields. There was a movement of population out of the East Midlands and Fens of England, which had thrived on the waterways which carried the bronze trade, and from the uplands of Britain, which bore the brunt of the climatic downturn. Prestige goods declined in quantity and variety, for the first time in two millennia, and an emphasis was placed instead on the control of land and of food production as the main source of wealth. Domestic buildings, the roundhouses, grew larger and more important.[14]

After about 600 BC the climate seemingly turned drier and warmer again, never returning to the maximum achieved in the Mesolithic and Neolithic but reaching about the levels of the present day by the last century BC. Lowland settlement and agriculture expanded again, on to the heavier clay soils and into more areas of the chalk hills, indicating a growing population.[15] Increasing grain production meant that mice appeared in Britain, followed by domestic cats, brought in to hunt them, while the open landscapes allowed the brown hare to arrive in the island.[16] Settlements became more numerous than ever before, so that tens of thousands are now recorded from the British Iron Age as a whole, and fortified enclosures of many kinds were constructed in many parts of the island. Manufacturing became increasingly complex, although only a minority of those engaged in it are thought to have become full-time specialists. Lathes and potter's wheels were introduced, and glass beads and bracelets made. Rotary quern stones were developed to grind grain, and iron-tipped ploughshares allowed deeper cultivation.[17] Society is generally agreed to have been relatively communal and egalitarian, the absence of rich burials, already apparent in the Late Bronze Age, now being accompanied by a lack of high-status goods, and individual fields being replaced by common land associated with settlements, in which people lived, or at least worked or traded, as groups.[18]

All this, however, involves a very large amount of generalization, and the new emphasis on localism encouraged an even greater degree of regional variation than before. Timothy Darvill, with his keen sense of this factor, has identified five regions in Britain by the fifth century BC.[19] Between what is now the Welsh borderland and Kent, including the Cotswolds, Wessex and Sussex, was a zone full of fortified enclosures, with linear earthworks and scattered farmsteads and hamlets. Southern Scotland looked very much the same. The Central and East Midlands and East Anglia were dominated by villages, hamlets and farmsteads, with few forts, and most of what is now northern

England was similar, but with linear earthworks and more enclosures, of walls or palisades, around settlements. The Atlantic coast of Britain, from Cornwall up Wales to western and northern Scotland, was characterized by fortified homesteads and different kinds of stone fortress. Such distinctions in the human landscape imply social differences as well, but how these can be determined from the physical remains is not clear.

Every specialist on the period agrees that the British Iron Age should be divided, but there is no accompanying consensus on where the division should fall. Some commentators partition it into two periods, with the line falling, according to individual taste, anywhere between about 400 and 200 BC.[20] Others insert a Middle Iron Age within that span, with its own characteristics.[21] What everybody accepts is that Britain changed significantly between about 400 BC and the Roman invasion, with the alterations speeding up towards the end of that time. Iron artefacts at last became common, and gold and silver objects were increasingly used, above all coins, which arrived from the Continent in the second century BC and were being manufactured in most areas of lowland Britain within two hundred years. Manure and crop rotation became features of farming, drainage ditches were dug and the manufacture of ironware, textiles, pottery, and glass and shale ornaments turned into full-time occupations for specialists in several lowland areas. Valuable personal goods were multiplying, and both objects and customs were showing an ever greater tendency to be imported from the Continent or influenced by styles from there. Forts were generally abandoned, but those still used were made larger and more elaborate and imposing. Differences in wealth and social status emerged very noticeably within communities, especially in the south-east where kingdoms and aristocracies had developed by the time the Romans arrived there. The Romans must, in fact, have been ultimately at the back of most of these developments, as their cultural impact on peoples on the Continent, and then their direct conquest of them, remodelled native societies neighbouring Britain to make them more akin to those of the Mediterranean.

Once again, regional differences were considerable, and once more it is Timothy Darvill who has produced the most elaborate mapping of them, dividing Britain into three zones, radiating out from the point of closest contact with Romanized Europe in the south-east of the island. The south-east itself, up to the lower Thames Valley, had coinage, many imported Roman or Roman-style goods and customs, a rich agriculture, and the largest settlements, including some that functioned as combined political and industrial centres. North and west of this area, as far as the limit of the Midlands, and the Yorkshire Moors and Bristol Channel, was a zone that had smaller settlements and farmsteads, numerous enclosures, and a greater emphasis on pastoral farming.

Coins and objects of precious metal were present, but goods tended to be locally manufactured. The rest of the island exhibited much more continuity with the earlier Iron Age, lacking coins and Continental manufactures, and indeed large central places of assembly. The main social unit was still the homestead, with fortified enclosures being used for gatherings, while ornaments emphasized local and personal identities. Recent specialists have tended to stress how much of the island remained immune to Roman ways, and how even those who adopted some in the south-east adapted them to local circumstances rather than simply copied them; but the reconfiguration of British cultural regions which resulted from the impact of Roman fashions is still apparent.[22]

These changes in economic, technological, environmental, cultural, social and political activities, over more than 1,200 years, had major implications for patterns of ritual behaviour, which will be discussed in the remainder of this chapter. First, however, it is necessary to consider a few conceptual problems that have emerged among those working on the British Iron Age since the 1980s. Between them these problems set the context for the manner in which much of the material data which has just been outlined may be, and has been, interpreted.

The Problem of the Celts

For over a hundred years, until the 1990s, British scholars had no difficulty in characterizing the Iron Age of their island as 'Celtic'. This was because, at the end of that age and the opening of history, all of the languages that can be identified as spoken in the British Isles belong to the Celtic family group. According to nineteenth-century notions of nationalism, the three factors of language, race and culture intertwined to define an ethnic group, and they certainly performed this function for the Celtic peoples of modern Western Europe in their struggle to preserve their own identity in the face of the English and French. British scholars in general, therefore, accepted that the Iron Age British Isles had been Celtic in all three respects, and the only thing that changed between the nineteenth and twentieth centuries was the date at which the Celts were supposed to have arrived there. In the 1880s, according to the scheme of the leading archaeologist, Sir William Boyd Dawkins, the Celts had ended the Neolithic and brought in the Bronze Age (as described earlier). This was refined before the end of that decade by an equally eminent philologist, Sir John Rhys, who divided them into a more primitive wave, the Goidels, who had introduced the Bronze Age, and a more technologically advanced and powerful one, the Brythons, who had arrived later, in the Iron Age. As the former were the ancestors of Irish-speakers and the latter of Welsh-speakers, this had the effect of dissociating all of the British from the Irish at a time when the wish of so many of the latter to leave the United Kingdom was creating considerable tension between them and the British.[23] This concept of the two successive Celtic invasions then fossilized in textbooks of British prehistory, save that the honour of introducing bronze technology passed to the Beaker People in the early twentieth century. The arrival of the Goidels was relocated to the Late Bronze Age, the Brythonic Celts being credited with introducing a full Iron Age technology to Britain between 450 and 100 BC, together with that curvilinear style of decoration known on the Continent as La Tène art. In 1945 the author of popular works on prehistory Jacquetta Hawkes could compare the Brython warlords to the Norman barons who conquered much of medieval Britain and Ireland.[24] For most of the late twentieth century, even though faith in the model of invasions as the force which powered British prehistory waned, the concept of an Iron Age in which the British Isles were occupied by ethnic and cultural Celts remained standard. In the epoch of growing European unity, the concept of an ancient 'Celtic world', covering most of Western and Central Europe and with colonies as far as Asia Minor, had a new attraction. The fact that the epicentre of this world, from which people and ideas had radiated out, was in the area between the Rhineland and the Upper Danube basin, seemed to lodge the ancient Celts firmly in the heart of the Continent. The character-istics of ancient Celticity were assembled from a mixture of archaeological data drawn from all over this range, medieval texts in Celtic languages, and the comments of ancient Greek and Roman authors.[25] They were applied to religion as much as to any other area of belief and activity.[26]

Disquiet concerning this intellectual construct began to be expressed in Britain in the late 1980s, when a few archaeologists questioned whether it might not be impeding the interpretation of Iron Age data.[27] During the mid to late 1990s, a full-scale attack on it developed, led above all by John Collis and Simon James. The essence of their case was that the word 'Celtic' had come to be applied to three different phenomena – to an ancient racial group, a set of languages, and a style of curvilinear decoration – which interlocked to create the modern concept of ancient Celticity. The problem was that the three did not correspond exactly to each other in geographical area, and that they had been developed as mental constructs independently and at different times. Ancient Greek and Roman authors had spoken of Celts as a category of people, but generally used the term vaguely to indicate barbarians living north of the Rhine delta, Alps or Danube; none provided any criteria for it and they dis-agreed over where the people for whom they used it should be located. The employment of the word 'Celtic' to describe a group of languages had occurred only at the beginning of the eighteenth century, by the Welsh scholar Edward Lhuyd; and most of the languages concerned survived in the British Isles, where no ancient writer had placed Celts. The category of 'Celtic art' was a nineteenth-century one, first defined by the Englishman John Kemble in 1856 and achieved by linking designs found on Iron Age artefacts and monuments (from all over north-western Europe) with those in medieval manuscripts and metalwork (mostly Irish). It was only in the early twentieth century that the three semantic fields became combined to define a single ancient pan-European culture and people, a step taken in 1914 by the Frenchman Joseph Dechelette. It was this combination that had become so deeply troubling to the revisionist writers of the 1990s, and especially questionable as a framework for the automatic interpretation of archaeological evidence. It seemed too obviously a product of nineteenth-century attitudes of racist stereotyping which had continued under its own momentum into the succeeding century. None of these points undermined the validity of modern Celtic nationalism: the problem was that a thousand-year gap divided the people called Celts in the ancient world from those who called themselves Celts-in the modern one, and they hardly overlapped in geography. It seemed best, therefore, for experts in Iron Age archaeology to abandon the term.[28]

Reactions to these arguments were complex. The most immediate and vociferous opposition to them was mounted by a pair of Australian historians of art. They did not, however, produce more than articles and reviews to counter the large books of the revisionists, and by the mid 2000s were falling back on the risky argument that archaeologists were still using other terms for ethnic groups culled from ancient literature, which were just as open to challenge, and so 'Celtic' should be retained as well.[29] By the 2000s British archaeologists generally accepted the revisionist argument, in some cases explicitly.[30] More often, they did so implicitly, by dropping the C-word and adopting some other term for the period, most commonly (as said) the colourless but exact one of the Late Pre-Roman Iron Age. In the latter part of that decade geneticists weighed in, and pronounced that the evidence of DNA showed no sign of any mass migrations from Central to Western Europe during the last millennium BC. On the other hand, they did not rule out smaller movements of peoples, or think the data wholly conclusive.[31] The new concern about the use of the term 'Celtic' for the Iron Age remained largely a British phenomenon, although at least one prominent German scholar swiftly came to share it, and opinion among Irish colleagues was divided.[32] British specialists in medieval literatures in Celtic languages were initially placed in what seemed to be a difficult position, but it was largely resolved by an influential essay published by Patrick Sims-Williams in 1998. He recognized that Celticity was apparent to linguists but invisible to archaeologists and that Celtic Studies needed to question all stereotypical assumptions. He also, however, asserted that linguists could indeed use the term 'Celtic' with precision, even if it was not adopted for a class of languages until modern times. To apply it to art or archaeology was more risky, even though it might possibly have some useful results; but the real trouble started when scholars tried to synthesize the languages, the art and the archaeology into a single construct, as had often been done. He concluded that the label should not be used as 'a short-cut from one discipline to another, or from one region to another, or from one millennium to the next'.[33]

Perhaps the most creative reaction to the pressure of the revisionist case was that of Sir Barry Cunliffe, the archaeologist who had established himself during the late twentieth century as the leading expert on the British Iron Age. He long placed his work within the traditional model of a Celtic world covering much of ancient Europe, but in the early 2000s he declared himself firmly against the idea of Celtic migrations or invasions, and a single Celtic culture, and above all against that of a Celtic race. On the other hand, he argued from good evidence for a kaleidoscope of cultures across Western Europe, sharing a broadly similar set of languages and values, to which Greek and Roman observers gave the name of Celts; the language group, in turn, was that to which modern scholars later applied the term Celtic. He then set out to propose an origin point for these languages and values, and found one in the trading networks which spanned Western Europe during the Bronze Age, for which a common language would have provided a vital component. He believed that the differences between historic Celtic languages, and especially those between the Goidelic and Brythonic branches, would have been the result of the shattering of the Late Bronze Age trading system into more detached local communities at the beginning of the Iron Age. He was now on a convergence course with an American linguist, John T. Koch, who had likewise decided that the languages later called Celtic were fundamental to a new and better concept of ancient Celts. He also believed that the most likely place and time for their development was along the Atlantic seaboard during the Late Bronze Age, spread by networks of gift exchange and travelling craftspeople, musicians and poets through a patchwork of differing communities. In 2010 the two of them produced a joint manifesto that summed up these ideas to create a new model of ancient Celticity, which avoided all the problems of the old. Instead of movements of peoples from Central into Western Europe it proposed the spread of a language, carrying with it some common cultural traits and values and brought by traders, performers and artisans, from the Atlantic seaboard eastwards through Europe in the Bronze Age. One of its cultural traits was the form of decoration known as La Tène, which had been the classic ancient component of the construct of 'Celtic art' in the old model. The modern analogy used by the two authors was not that of the European Union but of the United States, where different linguistic, genetic and ethnic groups are brought together within a single culture, many aspects of which have been adopted far beyond its national frontiers. The word 'Celtic' was thus fully restored to the Iron Age map, shorn of all the accretions which revisionists had found most disturbing: in particular Cunliffe and Koch declared that 'the notion of race is unscientific nonsense' in this context.[34] How far their new framework for the concept of ancient Celts will become standard remains to be seen, but it represents the most valuable and interesting attempt to date to find a fresh utility for the name.[35]

The departure of the idea of Celtic invasions or migrations has removed the disposition to believe in mass movements of people during later British prehistory. The landmark publication which dissolved faith in this belief has often been identified as an article by Grahame Clark which appeared in 1966.[36] This, however, was intended to stop the convention of ascribing virtually every cultural change in prehistoric Britain to the arrival of newcomers. It still declared that 'invasions and minor intrusions have undoubtedly occurred', and proposed two major migrations as probable, that of the Beaker People in the second millennium, and that of the Belgae in the later Iron Age. The reason why this latter people was given a particular name was that Julius Caesar, describing Britain after his own two expeditions to it, stated specifically that the coastal areas of the island were inhabited by tribes who had invaded and settled within historical memory from the neighbouring part of the Continent. The ethnic group from which they derived (the homeland of which Caesar himself conquered) was the aforesaid Belgae, whose name has been revived for the modern state of Belgium.[37] Caesar's information on Britain was of varying quality: for example he stated that the natives in the interior wore skins instead of textiles and did not have agriculture, both statements being disproved by archaeology. As he did not himself enter the interior, but remained among the coastal tribes, it was their history that he was reporting when he spoke of invasions. He did not say, however, whether he was repeating what they themselves believed or surmising their origin from the fact that – as he pointed out – they shared the same names as Belgic groups across the Channel. Either way, his testimony was taken literally by earlier experts in the Iron Age and is now disregarded by most of those at the present day. This is partly, perhaps, because invasions are unfashionable as motors for change in British prehistory in general, but also because (as said above) the undoubted importations of Continental goods and customs during the later Iron Age seem to have been adapted to existing native ways rather than imposed wholesale as might be presumed to be the result of settlement. This conclusion, though reasonable, does beg the question of how far settlers might adapt to the habits of the peoples among whom they settled, especially if the latter were not too different ethnically. Some specialists remain a little uncertain on the matter: Colin Haselgrove, for example, has left room for the possibility of 'limited' immigration from Belgic Gaul.[38] How limited immigration can be before it becomes the movement of a tribe, or a section of one, is probably another question that is impossible to answer; and there at present the issue seems to rest.

The Problem of the Druids

The Druids were the leading experts in religion, magic, and other matters concerning the supernatural among the Iron Age peoples of north-western Europe who spoke Celtic languages, including the British; and that is all that can be said about them with absolute certainty. As such, they have exerted a powerful hold on the modern imagination of the British, Irish, Germans, French and Dutch, and their descendants in the New World. With the exception of the Irish, who kept Druids embedded in their native literature, none of these ethnic groups paid much attention to them in the Middle Ages, when they served no useful ideological purpose. Their emergence as major figures in national histories was very much a product of Renaissance humanism, with its heavy emphasis on the recovery and close study of ancient Greek and Roman texts. These provided scholars in north-western Europe with the only written sources for their own early history (aside from the more generalized narratives of world creation in the Book of Genesis), and Druids featured in them as among the most colourful and (at times) impressive characters in the region. Accordingly, they became prominent in the histories that early modern writers developed for their nations at a time when national self-consciousness was being sharpened by cultural change. The Georgian British came to take an especial interest in them, treating them as the central figures of the religion that had inspired the megalithic monuments in which parts of the island abounded. They remained so until the nineteenth century, when the developing discipline of archaeology, with its Victorian emphasis on race and invasion as motors of change, turned them into the priests of the last wave of prehistoric invaders, the Celts. The presence of Druids, indeed, became one of the features of the 'Celtic world' to which twentieth-century scholarship allocated much of Western and Central Europe.[39]

The Druids are therefore very important characters in the cultural history of modern Britain: but the place which they should have in its Iron Age archaeology is a much more contentious question. The problem is one of source material, which falls into three categories. The first consists of the Greek and Roman writers mentioned above, who present a number of difficulties in this respect. Their descriptions of Druids are brief, and in only two cases may have been eyewitness accounts. One was provided by the leading Roman politician

Cicero, who met a single Druid when the latter visited Rome. The other was from Cicero's still more famous contemporary Julius Caesar, the single ancient author whose work has survived and who himself had the opportunity to observe Druids in their own society. His description is therefore the most valuable, and also the most detailed, and refers to Gaul, the large region bounded by the Atlantic, the Pyrenees and the River Rhine, which he conquered for Rome. It has, however, long been regarded by some scholars as beset by difficulties of apparent contradiction and possible distortion and misrepresentation. As a group, the ancient sources portray Druids in contrasting ways, while always making them colourful. To some, such as Dion Chrysostom, Clement of Alexandria, Hippolytus, Diogenes Laertius and Ammianus Marcellinus, they were impressive philosophers and scientists, in some respects superior to those of the more conventionally civilized Mediterranean world. To others, notably Diodorus Siculus, Strabo, Pomponius Mela, Pliny, Lucan and Tacitus, they presided over a savage and bloodthirsty religion with a special emphasis on human sacrifice, which any civilized person should regard with horror and revulsion. Caesar combined features of both pictures, portraying them as having at least ambitions for great learning but exerting a dominant power in Gallic society which was essentially malign because of the brutal and superstitious nature of the religious rites in which they engaged.[40]

The variety of portraits of Druids thus provided by the Graeco-Roman texts, all eye-catching, provides a large part of the reason for their attractiveness to the modern European imagination, as they could be turned into heroes or villains according to national, political or sectarian taste. Caesar stated that the system of Druidry originally arose in Britain and spread out from there, but only one ancient author mentions any as active there: Tacitus, who describes the Roman conquest of the large island off the North Welsh coast which is known to the Welsh as Môn and the English as Anglesey. On reaching its shore, the invaders encountered an opposing army which included 'Druids, raising their hands towards the sky and shouting dreadful curses' and 'women clad in black attire like Furies, with hair dishevelled, waving flaming torches'. The Roman soldiers were initially frightened by these displays, but recovered their nerve and launched a successful attack. Their brutality in crushing opposition was justified in their eyes by their discovery of sacred groves 'dedicated to inhuman superstitions' such as the sacrifice of prisoners on the altars there and the use of human entrails to divine the future.[41] The problem with this famous passage is that we have no certainty of its reliability. Tacitus himself was not a member of the Roman expeditionary force, and the nature of his information may be located anywhere on a spectrum running from an accurate eyewitness report made to him by the observer or observers, to a fiction composed by him in order to embellish his narrative.[42] At the least, the reported amazement of the Romans on that occasion seems to suggest that they did not often encounter Druids as opponents during their conquest of Britain.

The second category of material consists of medieval Irish literature, in which references to Druids are much more abundant than in the Greek and Roman sources, and which was, moreover, composed in a society to which Druids had been native. None the less, it has been used less often in the composition of modern images of Druidry, partly because it is not as familiar to most Europeans (including the British) as the ancient texts, and partly because it was not composed until Ireland had been converted to Christianity; in most cases, centuries after that event. The authors were reconstructing a vanished pagan world, and there are no means now of knowing how accurate was the information which they employed in doing this. The spectrum of possibility stretches from a situation in which the writers concerned were possessed of a full and reliable memory of ancient Irish society, conveyed through the intervening period by oral tradition, to one in which they had no real information at all and were relying mainly on their own imagination. In recent decades, experts in the subject have engaged in prolonged debate over the matter, and, although agreement appears impossible, the sceptics have grown more prominent and confident during this time.[43] The third category of evidence, that of archaeology, suffers from the problem of all material evidence: that it is of at best limited value in reconstructing belief systems, whether religious, social or political. The ancient Druids have, as far as anybody is aware, left no writings of their own, and not a single artefact has yet been discovered which can be unequivocally linked to them. Modern scholars have, inevitably, interpreted the material record in accordance with the written sources described above, filtered through their own beliefs and prejudices. As a result, their portraits of Druids have been as varied, and as lacking in objective proof, as those of other kinds of author.[44]

Since the twenty-first century began, there has been no sign that these difficulties are any nearer resolution. It may be argued that a continuing preoccupation of archaeologists with Druids as charismatic and alluring literary figures can have the effect of closing down discussion and narrowing intellectual horizons. In 1996 a cremation burial was discovered at Stanway, near Colchester, in part of a cemetery used by local aristocrats in the years around and just after the Roman conquest. It was notable for being accompanied by a set of surgical instruments, making it the earliest unequivocal evidence for a medical practitioner in Britain, and some of the oldest in the world; as such, it is of international importance. With the instruments were a set of rods, which *might* have been used for divination, as part of the diagnosis of an ailment. The various goods in the grave combined native British objects with some which were clearly imported from the Roman world and some which mixed the styles of both: and the surgical instruments had features derived from British, Gallic and Roman culture. A number of possible cultural identities might have been determined for the owner, each set in the context of the partial adaptation of the native aristocracy to Roman ways during the period of conquest. The excavation report, published in 2007, chose however to draw specific attention to just one – that he could have been a Druid – and this was taken further in the publicity which attended the launch of the report.[45] At the same time, commentators on classical literature have inclined increasingly to highlight the untrustworthiness of the Greek and Roman texts on which archaeology has mainly relied for the identification of sites and objects as Druidic, and for their characterization of Druids.[46] What is needed is a proper discussion by specialists in Iron Age archaeology of the place of Druids in the interpretation of material evidence, which takes fully into account all of the problems stated above, and is informed by the recent studies of the literary sources and aware of the modern cultural context of varying reconstructions of the ancient evidence. All of the necessary components now seem to be in place for such a development.

It has not, however, yet commenced.[47] Instead, many experts in the Iron Age have tended increasingly to ignore Druids, and interpret the material remains of the period without reference to them.[48] Two of the greatest established scholars of the period have indeed taken account of the difficulties of integrating them into the evidence, but not – at least to the mind of the present author – in a wholly satisfactory way. The first is Sir Barry Cunliffe. He has argued that, as some of the information on Gaulish society provided by the classical authors can be borne out by archaeology, their portraits of Druids may be considered plausible. He has also suggested that although four of the best-known of those authors seem never to have visited north-western Europe themselves, they may all have relied for their passages about Druids on a lost text by a traveller called Pytheas. He certainly made a journey across most of the region at the end of the fourth century BC, and so his reports would have been eyewitness accounts.[49] The first suggestion is valid, but no more than suggestive, and the second raises an interesting possibility which may never be confirmed. The second of the two distinguished recent writers is Miranda Aldhouse-Green, currently the leading expert in British Iron Age and Roman-period religious iconography, who has published a large and exciting book which shows, with the greatest of erudition, how everything that Greek and Roman writers said about Druids can indeed be matched to archaeological evidence left by the societies which had contained these figures.[50] The problem, as she herself acknowledges, is that every single piece of the material data concerned can also be interpreted in other ways. The argument of the book is really that although the deductions made are merely suggestive and speculative, and incapable of proof, if enough of them are offered then an impression of probability will gradually be built up. Both works are full of fascinating ideas and evidence, and certainly contribute to discussion; but neither engages in a proper re-evaluation of whether (and if so, how) literary evidence and the material remains can be reconciled in a manner which takes full account of the problems of both and which can achieve a proper working consensus among experts. They are more likely just to reassure those who do not want to engage in such a re-evaluation.

One starting point for a reconsideration of the place of Druids in Iron Age society might be to compare the accounts provided by the ancient writers, which mostly refer to Gaul, with those in the medieval Irish texts. The Gaulish Druids, especially as portrayed by Caesar, are very much members of a national order, produced by a long and rigorous system of training and meeting in an assembly which represents all the Gaulish tribes. In the Irish texts, however, the word *druidecht*, literally 'druidcraft', is simply a general term for magic. Anybody who works magic can be called a Druid while they are doing so, irrespective of what they are in the rest of the story. Full-time magicians are therefore full-time Druids, but the category is extremely vague, as other kinds of professional, notably poets and smiths, can be the equals of full-time Druids in wielding magical skills. The Irish category of Druids is therefore extremely porous in a way in which the Gaulish one, at least as defined by Caesar, is not.[51] It may well be that *drai* or *drui* was an ancient root word, in Celtic languages, for somebody who deployed and understood supernatural power; and was therefore applied by the Iron Age to a range of specialists in the various societies that spoke those languages. Such a possibility is lent greater weight by the parallel example of native Siberian cultures, as encountered by European travellers and conquerors between the sixteenth and twentieth centuries AD. Each had a number of magical specialists with distinctive functions and often different names, to whom European scholars proceeded to apply the blanket term of 'shaman', taken from just one of those peoples to describe just one of those specialists within it.[52]

Here again, the medieval Irish literature is of interest, for it contains several terms to indicate varying sorts of magical practitioner and activity; and whether or not they accurately characterize those that had operated in an earlier pagan period, they do embody a sense of the complexity of the use of arcane power in a culture which had once contained Druids.[53] If Caesar was not exaggerating the power and sophistication of the Gaulish Druid organization for his own ends – and for more than a hundred years some scholars have suggested that he was – then the Druids of Gaul were uniquely highly developed; which would accord with the material and social culture of Gaul in general. It is the glamour of his Gaulish Druidic society that scholars have often projected on to Britain and Ireland in the past five hundred years. This is, not least, because Caesar's Druids make the best equivalent to the Christian clergy that the later British and Irish felt to be normative for a religion worth respecting. One archaeologist, Andrew Fitzpatrick, has recently suggested that there is plenty of evidence for people with religious knowledge and skills in Iron Age Britain, but little for a specialist priesthood.[54] This sort of insight chimes well with some of the thoughts offered above, and may represent one route past the difficulties of dealing with the term 'Druid' in any meaningful way as part of Iron Age studies.

It may be, however, that no consensus can be achieved over the matter. During the past half-millennium, the British have tended (as most Western Europeans have done) to draw upon the ancient images of Druids and emphasize their benevolent and malevolent qualities according to taste and to political or religious purpose.[55] Twentieth-century scholars, including archaeologists, continued this tradition in an only slightly more muted form.[56] There is nothing inherently wrong with a situation in which different writers prefer instinctually to believe different things about these enigmatic and controversial figures, to attach differing degrees of importance and interest to them and to link them to different pieces of material evidence; as long as the essential subjectivity of this exercise is fully recognized.

The Problem of Hill Forts

The most familiar and impressive monuments of late British prehistory are large enclosures, made by digging ditches and heaping up the earth or stones extracted into banks inside these. The dates that they yield span the first millennium BC, from the Late Bronze Age to the period just before the arrival of the Romans, and they are a strongly regional phenomenon. To be precise, they are found thickly in two zones: in England and Wales south-west of a line drawn between Ipswich and Chester, and across southern Scotland from Galloway to Angus, overlapping into the northernmost parts of England. The Isle of Man represents an extension of this second zone. In both areas they look quite similar, but the Scottish and Manx examples tend to lack ditches and consist of earth and rubble ramparts faced with stone. In the westernmost parts of the southern zone, in Devon, Cornwall and West Wales, the jagged coastline produced a preference for 'promontory forts' or 'cliff castles', where banks and (sometimes) ditches were used to cut off pieces of land protruding into the sea. Throughout their range, the different kinds of Iron Age structure called forts are some of the most spectacular surviving structures of the ancient British past. On the chalk and clay lands, the contours of their earthworks often crown hills and ridges like huge piled cheeses or coiled serpents. On granite, grit,

52 A fairly typical hill fort, crowning the Malvern Hills which divide Herefordshire from Worcestershire. The inner and outer circuits of bank and ditch can clearly be seen terracing the slope.

limestone and sandstone uplands, the piled stone blocks of their walls loop around slopes under a coat of heather, gorse or broom, or still show bare beneath the sky. Walkers in woodlands find their banks and ditches suddenly blocking the way. To most of the heritage-conscious public, they are the definitive monuments of the British Iron Age. In 1931 Christopher Hawkes gave them the label of 'hill-forts', which has stuck ever since.[57]

It is hard to put an overall figure on their number, because the smallest of them can barely be distinguished from the enclosed farmsteads which were another feature of the age. A. H. A. Hogg's study, published in 1979, seems to have been the most authoritative, and gives a total of 3,840 sites, making up a small but notable proportion of the 20,000–30,000 such large and defended Iron Age enclosures found across non-Mediterranean Europe.[58] The most famous in Britain is also one of the largest and most complex: Maiden Castle, with quadruple ramparts which hug the contours of an isolated chalk hill south of Dorchester, and mighty and elaborate outworks for the entrances. The total area enclosed is 120 acres (over 48 hectares). It is one of the prizes of English Heritage's National Monuments Collection. To archaeologists, the most significant is probably another fort on the Wessex chalk, this time to the north-east in Hampshire: Danebury, near Andover. In 1969 it was placed at a potent convergence of developments – the death of many of the trees inside from Dutch elm disease, the establishment of a dynamic new department of archaeology at the nearby University of Southampton, and the decision of the county council to develop the site as a country park – which enabled a major research project there. This consisted of excavations lasting for twenty seasons in succession, directed by Sir Barry Cunliffe, followed by seven more seasons in which the surrounding district was studied with reference to the fort, and trial excavations mounted there. Its actual name was Dunbury, the dark fortress, and the Danes were only brought in as a romantic Victorian alteration. In all, about half of the total interior was examined, making it the most thoroughly studied hill fort in Britain, and arguably the scene of the most important investigation to date into the British Iron Age.[59]

There is a fairly clear overall sequence in the construction of these monuments. They were built in great numbers in the Early Iron Age, and then many were abandoned in the middle portion of the period, while the survivors were usually enlarged and elaborated, sometimes dramatically. In the Late Iron Age most of these were forsaken in turn, except in southern Wessex, though some new double-banked enclosures were constructed.[60] Until the late twentieth century, archaeologists usually viewed them as the prehistoric equivalent of medieval baronial castles: fortresses which dominated their areas politically, socially and militarily and formed the homes and power bases of local chieftains, supported by war bands. Their number, and the strength of the defences

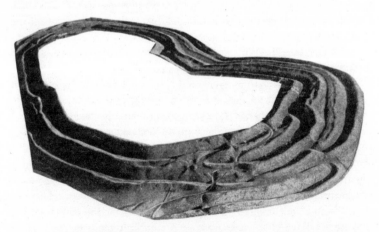

53 A drawing, from a 1930s aerial photograph, of the defences of Maiden Castle, the most famous of the 'developed' hill forts and one of the largest. The sheer complexity of these defences, especially at the end shown, the western, is brought out from this angle, as is the manner in which they hug the contours of the entire hill.

of many, suggested that they were the product of intense competition between such petty rulers, in a world in which social and political success were measured by military prowess: an Iron Age indeed.

From the late 1980s this picture began to be questioned. It was noted that several of the hill forts that have been excavated showed no sign of occupation; that some were built in such high and exposed places – on ploughshare escarpments, bare peaks and open plateaux, all raked by wind and rain – that they could hardly have been used in most seasons of the year; and that others were constructed in positions where they could be overlooked from higher ground, rendering them vulnerable to missiles. As said above, for most of the Iron Age, including the period in which most of these structures were built, there is no evidence of an elite group of chieftains and warriors. They seem instead to have been the work of peasant farmers who lived in scattered holdings and came together periodically for joint enterprises like the making of these enclosures. Certainly towards the end of the age, when social, political and cultural traditions were changing under the impact of Continental models, especially in south-eastern Britain, there is much more evidence of kingly figures and their retinues. By that time some hill forts were clearly used as fortresses; but this was after most had been abandoned. Moreover, the strongly regional nature of the tradition argues in itself against a purely functional explanation for the structures: from all the material evidence, the peoples living in the East Midlands, Norfolk and the Yorkshire Wolds (among other places) had the same kind of society and military technology as those who made the 'forts', but got along perfectly well without building them.[61] Similar discussions developed over the purpose of the 'promontory forts'. It was noticed that some were too limited and exposed to be good defensive positions, and the fortifications too meagre; and it was suggested that they might have been places set aside for ritual instead.[62]

A consensus is currently emerging that variety is the key to the purpose of hill forts, and that their use both differed between sites and altered over time. Some look like enclosures employed mostly for ritual, some resemble fortified villages, and others seem to have been places for seasonal assemblies such as fairs or lawcourts. Some were occupied for long periods, others but briefly or intermittently. It is fairly clear that their often massive defences were in many if not most cases intended more for display than for practical military strength. Maiden Castle is so big that it is hard to imagine how its district could have supported a population sufficient to defend all its circuits of walls. On the other hand, some hill forts were, at least for periods, genuine fortresses: the 11,000 sling-stones found stored in an ammunition dump inside Danebury were obviously not there just for show. The ramparts and ditches of most could be formidable military obstacles. However, as was apparently the case in the making of

so many earlier kinds of prehistoric monument, the act of communal
co-operation involved in their construction may have been the most important
factor in the enterprise, leading as it did to greater social cohesion and closer
personal alliances. This would explain the number of hill forts that were apparently left unfinished: by this reckoning, they would still have served their
purpose. According to this view, areas which did not make the forts were occupied by communities that were normally more closely knit, and did not have
the same need to band together formally for specific purposes and times.
Although no overall model of use for hill forts is possible, most that seem
to fit the description converge on three purposes proposed by Sir Barry
Cunliffe: assembly, settlement and storage. None the less, the patterning of
them in the landscape does point to a desire to control major economic operations, above all farming, trade and mining. This is a functional field in which
power and intimidation remain crucial, so that the term 'hill forts' may not be
so inappropriate after all.[63]

What relevance, then, do these impressive monuments – the greatest
construction works in Britain for a millennium – have for a book mainly
concerned with ritual? The answer is already perhaps implicitly obvious in
what has been said above. Some of these enclosures seem to have had functions

54 One of the banks and ditches at the western end of Maiden Castle photographed to show
their size and strength: the flock of sheep at the left-hand side gives some sense of relative
scale.

that were primarily concerned with ceremony, such as Ingleborough in West Yorkshire and Carrock Fell in Cumberland – high, open and remote places not much suited to practical purposes but excellent for rites; especially in the former case, as it also contains cave systems. A few forts, like Figsbury on the Wiltshire chalk, had ditches inside the banks like Neolithic henges.[64] The broader purpose attributed to most of these monuments – as places for periodic assemblies of people drawn from a surrounding region – would almost certainly have included religious rites, and indeed the assemblies were probably at seasonal festivals. The cattle and pig bones found at Danebury seem to have been the remains of animals killed in early summer, probably at that great celebration of the coming of the warm season which is found in historic times under various names across northern Europe, and is known in Gaelic as Cetsoman or Beltaine, in Welsh as Calan Mai, and in English as May Day.[65] Moreover, as shall be considered in later sections of this chapter, hill forts are often rich in ritual deposits and also contain structures which are interpreted as shrines.

There is, however, a wider frame of reference within which hill forts may have things to teach about the mode of ritual thinking in the parts of Britain in which they occur: that they are simply the most visually impressive aspect of a more general tendency of people in their areas to enclose places of significant activity. Farmsteads were given the same treatment, although their encircling earthworks were often dismantled after construction or remade in successive phases. These actions and those which made hill forts seem to have in common a symbolic and physical rite of inclusion and exclusion, defining those who carried it out as an independent and separate group.[66] Niall Sharples has recently taken this insight further, to argue that in Wessex a Late Bronze Age of open settlements and small farms, in which enclosures were rare, turned into an Iron Age obsessed with boundaries and barriers. He sees in this a fractured society filled with fear, and draws on the work of anthropologists such as Mary Douglas, who have studied such cultures in the recent world. They use ritual to constrain both contacts with outsiders and individual behaviour, and are characterized by tensions which commonly manifest not only in a general suspicion and hostility towards other groups but in accusations of witchcraft against members of the same community.[67] Whether or not this interpretation is overstated, it makes a viable fit with the evidence.

In the currently prevalent view, therefore, the hill and peninsular forts of Iron Age Britain may to some extent be equated with the causewayed enclosures of the earlier Neolithic, the henges of the later Neolithic and the stone circles of the later Neolithic earlier Bronze Age, as enclosed ceremonial spaces used mainly for occasional gatherings. In that sense they were the last and the most imposing of these structures to be built in British prehistory.

The parallel is not quite exact, as unlike those earlier classes of monument they were quite frequently used as settlements and (probably) for practical purposes such as the storage of grain, and their enclosing banks and ditches were usually stronger, with a clear military potential and sometimes a proven military role. None the less, it is close enough for them to be regarded, to some extent, as ceremonial monuments. With that conclusion, it is time to commence consideration of the actual evidence for ritual behaviour during the period.

Deposits in Water

One of the most poignant moments in the cycle of stories surrounding King Arthur, and one of the most famed in modern times, comes right at the end, when the faithful Sir Bedivere throws the king's sword Excalibur into the lake from which it first came, and back into the keeping of the supernatural female figure who presented it to Arthur. At first sight, a lake is an odd place in which to find or deposit a sword, but it reflects a prehistoric reality, of the placement of weapons, and other pieces of metalwork – often very beautiful – in many watery places in the British Isles. The presence of this motif in the Arthurian legend is probably not in itself a direct memory of ancient custom, because it appears relatively late in the development of the legend, in the final part of the Middle Ages. It reflects instead a practical reality, of the finding of ancient bronze and iron objects in lakes and other wet places. The apparently deliberate casting of valued items into water was not something new in itself by late prehistory, for more Neolithic flints have been found in British rivers than can be accounted for easily in terms of accidental loss. None the less, the scale, and seeming careful patterning of the deposits made from the Late Bronze Age until the Roman period were genuinely novel.

The patterning is partly geographical, because the finds concerned are concentrated in England in some of the rivers that flow eastwards into the North Sea: the Thames, Trent and Welland are all notable for them. On the other hand, other eastward-flowing Midland rivers, the Ouse, Nene and Cam, are not, and those that discharge into the English Channel, Bristol Channel and Irish Sea have produced very few such objects, despite as thorough an amount of dredging. Similar artefacts are found in former wetlands in the East and West Midlands, but not in the bogs of the West Country. In Wales, the same sorts of deposit are found at the bottom of a few relatively small lakes, and in Scotland in the River Tay and its tributaries (again, flowing east into the North Sea) and some wetlands in the Borders region. Even in rivers rich in such finds, they are concentrated at particular points: along the Thames, where field systems came down to the river, and not in the open country between, as if they consecrated sites of intensive human activity. The kind of object deposited is also specific to place: shields and cauldrons are found mostly in bogs and pools, swords in rivers, and spears and body ornaments in both: though not the famous Iron Age neck ornaments of twisted metal known as torques, which were clearly prized but rarely ended up in water. There is also a chronological patterning, for the water hoards become frequent after 1200 BC, and remain common, with swords as the most favoured item, until about the year 400. There is then a notable reduction in them (and this is the time at which hill forts were also being abandoned in the uplands), before a further expansion after 100 BC, with cauldrons now being most favoured.[68]

Two famous sites, on opposite sides of southern Britain and excavated in different halves of the twentieth century, may be used to exemplify the phenomenon. One was discovered in the Second World War, when an airfield was being extended in Anglesey, a process which required peat to be cut from the fringe of a small lake, Llyn Cerrig Bach. A tractor needed a tow rope, and the driver noticed a chain opportunely sticking out of the peat concerned. It worked perfectly for the purpose, and two of the supervisors of the work, thinking it rather curious, sent it to the National Museum of Wales for examination. It turned out to have been made over two thousand years before, to shackle slaves, and to have been one of a total of ninety metal objects, with a mass of animal bones, which people had thrown into part of the lake in ancient times. The metalwork, with a few of the bones, was sent in turn to the National Museum, and the report written on them there by Sir Cyril Fox became a landmark in British Iron Age studies, as he revealed that they had originated across an area extending from north-east Ireland to south-east England. Many had been broken or damaged before deposition, and some were simply well used, but others (like the slave chain) had been in excellent working condition. More recently the animal bones sent to Fox have been carbon-dated to the fourth to the second centuries BC, suggesting that they began to be thrown into the lake before the artefacts, which dated from the third or second century BC to the second century AD. The animals had not been butchered beforehand, and so appear to have been genuine sacrifices rather than the remains of meals, even consecrated meals: it was rumoured at the time that human bones were also present, but this remains unconfirmed. The material therefore represented offerings made at the lake over a period of up to five hundred years, probably (though not certainly) in successive small acts of deposition. Whether they were the work of local people, or of pilgrims, is impossible to determine, as all of the metal objects could have been acquired by the island's social elite.[69]

The second site was discovered in 1982, when archaeologists started to examine freshly cleaned drainage ditches in a patch of reclaimed marshland called Flag Fen, on the outskirts of the East Midland city of Peterborough. Led by Francis Pryor, they eventually dug out some three hundred pieces of metal-work, plus shale bracelets and pottery, which had been put into water there over a period between about 1200 and 200 BC. The metal objects included weapons and ornaments, most of which had been broken before deposition, either to 'kill' their indwelling spirits symbolically, or simply to diminish the probability that somebody else would fish them out and steal them. Some were very fine, others so badly made that they may have been fashioned simply to be cast into the water. They were part of a monumental landscape, for a line of about two thousand large oak posts had been driven into the shallow water between an island and the nearby mainland which had existed on that spot at the time. The objects had been placed on either side of this construction, while the posts themselves had been 'consecrated' with deposits around their bases, which included loose human bones, a boar's tusk and the bodies of dogs. The post alignment was erected in stages between 1350 and 950 BC, so that the placing of objects on the spot clearly continued for a long time after the posts had decayed. The monument might have been orientated upon some heavenly feature or towards a direction made significant by mythology. It could have been a boundary marker intended to deter other humans, or else a magical protection against rising water levels (which were indeed a threat to the district

55 Reconstruction of one section of the alignment of posts at Flag Fen, provided at the heritage centre constructed on the site and set in a marsh landscape similar to that which would have existed at the time.

at this time). It may even have been a funerary monument, centred on the human bones, if they had belonged to very significant individuals. A museum and heritage centre were duly built at Flag Fen, which became the best place in England for visitors who wished to learn about the Late Bronze Age; but they closed (perhaps temporarily) in the economic recession at the end of the 2000s. Only a portion of the site has been examined, and Francis Pryor has estimated that the total number of objects deposited there may number between three and five thousand.[70]

In 2001 Colin Pendleton launched a full-scale attack on the interpretation of Iron Age metalwork found in watery locations in Norfolk, Suffolk and Cambridgeshire as ritually deposited, which had some knock-on implications for the same idea as applied elsewhere. He described, in detail, how recent that interpretation was, gaining momentum only from the 1960s and becoming an orthodoxy only in the years around 1980. He pointed out that only about 1 per cent of the total number of artefacts from the period which had been found in the region had been recovered from rivers or pools, and in only one case were those concentrated in what could be called a hoard. The rest were individual finds or in small groups, from dredged material and banks, and just one of these had beyond doubt been placed in water at the time of deposition: the rest might have been eroded or washed into it. If they were not, then many or most might have been casually lost overboard from river craft. He concluded, resoundingly, that 'there is no evidence to support ritual deposition of metalwork in Northern East Anglia during the later Bronze Age'.[71] He may well be correct for his chosen region, and his cautions could also act against too easy an acceptance of a ceremonial origin for much of the ancient metalwork from other rivers in eastern England. Clearly, however, mass deposits such as those at Flag Fen and Llyn Cerrig Bach survive them, and the selective and patterned nature of the deposits, discussed above, would also work against a general application of such a dismissal.

Several possible explanations can be provided for the ceremonial placement of objects in water. They could have been part of a funeral rite, accompanying or in place of human remains; and where these wetland deposits are found, burials do indeed tend to be absent. It is also notable that most of the swords dating from the Early Iron Age that have been found in Britain were dredged out of rivers, while most from Europe had been placed in graves, suggesting that the two may have been equivalent. As stated above, actual human bones were among the deposits at Flag Fen, and many skulls have been found in the Thames, a river rich in late prehistoric metalwork, and its tributaries. Those from the Walbrook, in London, were dated firmly to the Late Bronze Age, but, unhappily, most are not assigned to any period, and many have been lost. Over a hundred were found in the Thames itself together with

56 A representation of a Late Bronze Age funeral beside the River Thames, as imagined in the mid twentieth century by the artist Alan Sorrell. The mode of burial is cremation, as fits the period, and the implication is that the burnt remains will be consigned to the river together with the gleaming bright (and so newly made) sword being brandished to the left. This is one plausible explanation for the presence of Late Bronze Age metalwork in watery deposits.

one of the most magnificent, and famous, of all the late prehistoric artefacts and works of art pulled out of British rivers, the Battersea Shield. All, however, may be from a different date or dates.[72] It is true, moreover, that human remains were present with only a minority of the artefacts recovered from watery places, even when the latter have been carefully excavated; and they become much rarer in the course of the Iron Age.

It is also possible, therefore, that the placing of the objects in water (including the pieces of human being) could have been an act of worship, directed to water spirits or deities, at a time when the climate was indeed becoming cooler and wetter.[73] Indeed, they could have been offerings to a broader spectrum of deities and spiritual beings, if water was regarded as a portal between the terrestrial and human world and other kinds of world in general. There is a specific reference in a contemporary text to just such a custom among a tribe in contemporary Gaul, who occupied the area around what is now Toulouse. It occurs in the work of the Greek geographer Strabo, who was quoting an older book, famous in its time but now lost, by the traveller Posidonius. The cult concerned the throwing of treasure into sacred lakes, 'by way of invoking and propitiating their god'.[74] The account does not explain who the god concerned was, nor why water seemed to be a medium which he favoured, but it is valuable in establishing the existence of such a practice. Posidonius visited the area himself, and also had access to a record or records left by the Romans who had conquered it and looted the bullion from the lakes. It may therefore be given better credence than Greek and Roman accounts of tribal peoples that were based on less secure sources or experiences. However, this does not necessarily mean that the peoples of Britain had the same motivation, of worship. To continue the catalogue of alternative explanations for the placement of objects in wetlands, they may even have been cast away as ritualized acts of destruction, rather than dedication, to prove the wealth and power of the owner, especially if they had been captured from rival peoples who had themselves been punished or destroyed. Rivers can furthermore act as natural barriers as well as routes for travel and trade, and the placement of offerings in them might also have been an act intended to consecrate and strengthen them as frontiers which separated rival tribal territories.[75] It could have functioned also as a propitiation of the powers of water by people who were embarking on a journey across it and wished for good fortune. There is even a possibility that it was not the element which mattered but the location: Posidonius recorded that at Toulouse precious metals were thrown into the pools and piled up on dry land nearby, both being within a sacred precinct. Treasure in water is much more likely to survive the centuries until modern times than that deposited on the surface of the ground, rendering the former visible to archaeology but the latter not. Readers may choose whichever kind of explanation makes best sense to them, or pick and mix, as all may have obtained at different times and places and they are not mutually incompatible.[76]

The landscapes of the waters of lowland Britain have perhaps changed more since prehistory than any other rural environment. A few pockets of undrained marsh survive as nature reserves, but gone for ever, to rich farmland, are the vast expanses of fenland, with the sighing of the wind in millions of green reeds and the feathery blond heads of sedge, and the whistling wings of mighty waterfowl flocks; and encounters with more spectacular wildlife such as the swoop of the osprey or fish eagle, the booming of bitterns, the strut of courting cranes, the heavy flight of a pelican, or the slap of a beaver's tail as it dives in the pool beside its dam. By sunlit day, they would have glittered with some of Britain's most brilliant butterflies, the swallowtails and large coppers, while by night the pale flames of ignited marsh gas, the will o' the wisps or punkies, would have danced above them instead. Lowland rivers, often dredged, embanked and straightened, bear only occasional resemblance to their ancient selves when they would have been looped and braided watercourses, with many more islets, channels and meanders, and aquatic plants. The pools and lakes of the highland zone are less altered, but by definition most of the specific

examples in which ancient deposits were found have been drained or remodelled, which is why the discoveries were made in the first place. Of famous sites,
one of the least altered is Llyn Fawr in the Black Mountains of Glamorgan,
where cauldrons, axes, sickles, horse harness and cart or chariot fittings were
thrown in about 600 BC.[77] It still lies in wild scenery, set among clumps of coni-
fers with a tall crag beetling over its quiet waters; but it now has a concrete lip
because it was converted to a reservoir. This was how, of course, the hoard was
noticed. The ancient objects presented to watery places were probably once
incidental accretions to numinous landscapes: now they are themselves often
the most tangible and evocative testimonies to the vanished primordial power
of those aspects of British nature.

Deposits in Earth

Iron Age objects which may have been ritually placed in pits or shafts dug into
the ground are much more common in Britain than those in water, or formerly
watery places. At first sight, the chances that they were accidental losses, or
displaced to the locations in which they were found by natural processes, are
much less; but there are still major problems of interpretation. Where pits have
very clearly been dug and then goods deliberately placed inside them, this
could have been to store or hide the objects concerned, which were then left
there because the owners never returned. Where artefacts and bones are mixed
together, they may simply represent the burial of rubbish, and an apparent
careful structuring in the layers of this could simply be the result of the sequence
in which different types of it were interred; or they may, on the other hand,
bear witness to a rite in which an entire cosmology was portrayed by the burial
of different sorts of material.

In the case of deposition in pits, even more than in that of the placing of
things in water, late prehistory carried on a custom which had long been
enacted in Britain: as must be clear from earlier parts of the present book, it
had existed since the Mesolithic, and was one of the main expressions of ritual
behaviour in the New Stone Age. It has been given more prominence in
accounts of the Late Bronze and Iron Ages largely because of what was long
presumed to be an absence of ceremonial and funerary monuments during
that period, but the burial of selected objects was another of the main features
of the age. Many more pieces of its metalwork have been recovered from the
ground than from water: just one hoard, at Isleham, where the hills of East
Anglia come down to the edge of the Fens, contained 6,500 items.[78] Thousands
of buried collections of Bronze and Iron Age artefacts and bones are known
from the British Isles. Francis Pryor has suggested that many of the tools in
them may never have been made to be used at all, because worn-out items are

rare and so are finds of tools in domestic buildings: this suggests that many of the items recovered from hoards may have been created purely to be buried.[79] Richard Bradley argues instead that some of them seem like stores of unfinished objects, perhaps pieces of scrap metal awaiting the forge. He urges the abolition of any boundary between a ritual and a utilitarian purpose when interpreting them: objects found in ritualized contexts had often played practical roles. Nor is it certain that metal-working was regarded as an everyday and secular activity. It if were not, then hoards associated with industrial processes may have carried a numinous charge just as those placed in pools or rivers did. The blacksmith's craft could have been accompanied by rites which required that a certain proportion of the material used was turned into a religious offering. Bradley suggests that as both ritual and functional aspects of metal deposits often involved broken objects, it is impossible to distinguish between them.[80] This view of smithcraft has also found support with Richard Hingley, who has drawn attention to the fact that in some recent African societies it is still regarded as a magical and impressive process. He thinks it likely that the process of iron-making, from the gathering of the ore to the end of the artefact's use, was seen, like agriculture, as a cycle of regeneration.[81] Francis Pryor has noted that Late Bronze Age swords which had broken along flaws in the casting were not just melted down again, but deposited, as though the object had acquired a proper identity and required burial.[82]

The locations in which objects were placed in the earth had strong regional variations. On the coastal plain of Sussex and Hampshire they were laid near settlement sites, while on the chalk downs behind they were normally along watercourses, but never (in sharp contrast to the situation further north) in water itself.[83] Deposits were also made frequently in eastern and southern Scotland and the north of England, personal ornaments predominating in the north-east of Scotland and weapons in the English northern zone, while the south of Scotland had a great variety of metalwork and pottery. In the Scottish north-east they were mostly interred in settlements and in the south of the country in water, while in northern England they are found in both, and in caves and on beaches. The north-eastern Scottish and northern English finds are in small quantities, and so perhaps the work of households, while those further south are much larger, and hence may have been the work of tribes or tribal confederacies.[84] In northern Scotland objects were laid over long periods at certain special locations. One was High Pasture Cave, a complex, stream-fed cavern on the Isle of Skye, where domestic material was left in careful deposits between the fifth and first centuries BC. It included crafted bone and antler objects (including a bridge from a lyre and tuning pegs for it, the oldest stringed instrument yet found in Western Europe), animal skeletons, especially of pigs (split into right and left halves) and pottery and stone instruments. In the fourth century a stone stairway was built into the cave, to facilitate visits, and when it was finally sealed up around 100 BC, the body of a young woman with a newborn baby and a foetus was left among the blocking earth and stones.[85]

In Wessex and the West Country, deposits have been found inside pits within hill forts, and in their ditches and under their ramparts, as well as at various places on settlements. They often consist of the skulls or other pieces of animals, and sometimes whole bodies, especially those of horses and dogs, the two kinds of beast most faithful to, and beloved of, humans. Cattle, pigs and sheep are most common, horses and dogs rarer, and wild animals even scarcer, perhaps because they were not regarded as sacrifices or because they had not made personal relationships with people. There are also quite a lot of human bodies or bones.[86] A total of 2,399 pits was identified by Sir Barry Cunliffe's excavations at Danebury, meaning that the whole site probably had around five thousand. Of these, 1,707 were examined and about a third of them were found to have held deposits: the latter included a quarter of a million animal bones and a similar number of potsherds. It is possible that those that were apparently empty had been given libations of beer or mead as offerings instead. Sir Barry noted that pits inside hill forts were not identified as associated with ritual until the 1940s, having formerly been taken for dwellings, and then for granaries. They seem often to have been used for storage, presumably of grain, and the deposits were generally made when the use of them ceased, as if to thank the divine powers of the earth for protecting the commodities temporarily placed in them. When the offerings had been made, the old pit was filled in and a new one dug and put to practical use. Grain keeps well in the ground, but equally so above it, and for less effort if the ricks that hold it are well maintained, prompting Sir Barry to suggest that storage underground might have seemed attractive because it symbolically returned the harvest to the care of the deities or powers that had grown it. Such pits tend to be found in areas which in the Iron Age were dependent on agriculture, while water deposits are found in those where trade was apparently more important; but grain was also grown in the West Midlands, Wales and the Scottish Borders, and storage pits are rare there. Those at Danebury were especially abundant in sheep bones, but also held significant quantities of cattle, pigs, horses and dogs, and had single or group burials of humans, either interred whole or represented by a part or parts of the body. The animals were sometimes not even skinned, let alone butchered, so that they must have represented true sacrifices; unless they had died of diseases that made their hide and flesh suspect to their owners.[87] Less than 2 per cent of the bones found in the Danebury pits were of birds, but of these almost three-quarters were ravens, and most of the rest belonged to the closely related carrion crow; and these two species were deliberately interred in at least twelve other English Iron Age sites. They are the most intelligent and among the largest of British birds, and have spectacular flight displays: ancient and medieval myth make them symbols of communication. They are also traditionally associated with battlefields, because of their taste for carrion, which in addition caused them to keep close to human settlements where they fed off some of the organic rubbish. They may even have had a funerary function, in picking clean human bones before burial.[88] These overall patterns are highly suggestive, but it is worth bearing in mind that no two hill forts may have been alike in their deposits. At South Cadbury near the southern fringe of Somerset, 362 pits were located in the interior and a sample of them had animal bones and human skulls. At Hunsbury in Northamptonshire about three hundred were discovered in the nineteenth century and found to contain huge quantities of bronze and iron metalwork, plus glass and pottery, and over 150 stone querns for grinding grain.[89]

During the 1990s, late prehistoric rubbish itself came under scrutiny as evidence for ritual behaviour. David McOmish looked at Late Bronze Age and Iron Age sites in Wessex which had been interpreted simply as middens, and decided that they were deliberately preserved and deposited accumulations of debris from feasts. A wide range of materials had been selected from these special events and piled up in carefully structured mounds, challenging both traditional concepts of ceremonial deposits and those of monuments.[90] This theme was matched on a larger scale by J. D. Hill's celebrated study of materials placed in pits and ditches on Iron Age settlement sites in Wessex. He noted that what had been treated as refuse had been deposited with as much care and structuring as hoards, or grave goods. Pottery, loose animal bones and small artefacts had been put into the earth as meticulously as the human bones and whole animal carcasses often found in the same places. He concluded that this was not part of a daily disposal of rubbish, but of 'irregular rituals which engraved a cosmology into the physical setting and daily lives of Iron Age people'.[91]

These patterns enable a relationship between hill forts and settlements to be mapped out in Wessex, with further clues to the purposes of the former. At Danebury the deposits must have been at least annual, while on the farmsteads excavated they were apparently made only every five to ten years. The human bones found on settlements were mainly those of babies and children, while those at hill forts tend to be of adults, with an almost complete monopoly on skulls and partial skeletons. The former seem therefore to have had rites celebrating the family and individual household; the latter to have focused on the wider community and the preoccupations of mature people.[92] Iron objects have been found especially often in the physical boundaries of settlements, as if playing a significant role in their definition and perpetuation: perhaps they helped symbolically or magically to defend them.[93] Such neat conclusions, however, still rest on a relatively small sample of evidence, and there have been cautions against any simple recognition of 'structured depositions' as resulting from ritual. It has been pointed out that deposits of Late Bronze Age pottery are so complex and variable that they cannot be reduced to distinct categories, while human bone is very commonly found on settlement sites of the period as well as in hill forts and caves. At some in Bedfordshire, discarded debris, including the bits of human skeleton, was apparently moved around the settlements rather than given a single, ceremonial, deposition.[94] James Morris has emphasized that the burial of animals or portions of animals could still be the result of butchery, and the disposal of animals dead of disease or of meat gone putrid, as much as that of ceremonial acts. He points out that butchers' refuse was still deposited in an apparently deliberate and structured manner in the Christian Middle Ages, when pagan rites could no longer provide the motive. To Morris, it remains true that 'one archaeologist's rubbish is another's ritual deposition.'[95]

The same diversity of interpretation hangs over another form of late prehistoric 'rubbish': burnt mounds. These are found all over northern Europe, including most parts of the British Isles, and consist of heaps of shattered stones, in contexts mainly dating from the Late Bronze Age but also from the Iron Age and, more rarely, as far back as the Neolithic. There is no doubt concerning how the stones were broken: they were first heated and then either had water poured over them or were dropped into it. The debate concerns why this happened. A functional explanation is that to drop hot rocks into water was the easiest way of bringing the latter near the boil, to cook food, when to put pots or cauldrons directly on to a fire would risk damage to them. In this scenario, the mounds would represent the refuse either from domestic meals or from special feasts on such occasions as ceremonies to mark boundaries: and this idea was favoured in the 1980s.[96] They would also, however, take exactly the same form if they were created by ancient European equivalents to the Native American sweat lodges: timber and canvas structures within which people underwent ritual purification and trance experiences by sitting in steam released by sprinkling water over hot stones in a central hearth. On the other hand, there was no necessary ritual component to the use of this technique to induce sweat: it operated perfectly well as a means of getting clean in cold weather when bathing in the open was uncomfortable, and the modern sauna is an exact equivalent. The sweat lodge or sauna explanation for burnt mounds, propounded in the 1990s, seemed to have become dominant among experts in turn by the opening of the twenty-first century, because of the absence of evidence for actual feasting near the mounds.[97] Then, in 2009, it was reported that one at the tip of the Lleyn Peninsula of north-west Wales was associated with a wooden trough and a water channel, which had been preserved by unusually good local conditions. Grain remains were discovered in the mound itself, and a residue of burnt stone and charred chaff and seeds in the trough. One obvious interpretation of all this evidence was that the complex had been used for brewing, and a replica was tested with this activity and found to reproduce precisely the same remains.[98] For a while it looked as if the shattered stones were testimony not to prehistoric spirituality or hygiene but to the enduring northern European taste for beer. The whole matter was, however, opened out again by a survey published in 2011, of evidence from the five thousand or so burnt mounds known to exist in Ireland. This found that many were discovered with troughs – rock-cut, wooden or clay – like that in the Lleyn, so that the brewing hypothesis stood up. However, a few sites had large quantities of cattle bone, and so feasting comes back into the frame, while a few others had evidence of small timber structures nearby which might have been sweat lodges.[99] It seems as if everybody was right after all, and the same features could be produced by different processes.

That may be a salutary verdict on the whole issue of careful depositions of material in dry-land contexts during late prehistory, which occupy a spectrum from near-certain evidence for spiritually motivated activity at one end to the practical dumping of refuse at another: different kinds of rubbish, gathered from different places on living sites and removed at different times, would give a very convincing appearance of structuring. Not even the most hardened cynic would term High Pasture Cave a straightforward rubbish dump, and it is quite possible that it was the setting for ceremonies concerned with encounters and symbolic oppositions between light and dark, life and death, water and earth, and animal and human, with that lyre being played to enhance an altered state of consciousness on the part of the worshippers.[100] On the other hand, it is also possible that the cave system was a dumping ground of a kind, for objects and beasts (and eventually people) who had become contaminated by bad associations and needed to be placed well out of the way of normal activity. When dealing with most of the other deposits, it is well to remember James Morris's caution about the manner in which experts still differ in their understanding of them: which means that people in general are free to do so as well.

Human Remains

Pieces of human bone have regularly featured in the discussions above, as common in the deposits from late prehistory found in water and land. There is nothing unusual or new in this pattern: after all, from the Neolithic onwards, this sort of material appeared on both ceremonial and domestic sites, and it has been found associated almost casually with camps and settlements in Europe since the Palaeolithic. What has frequently distracted attention from this fact, at least in the public eye, is its simultaneous presence, during most periods, in contexts that look to modern eyes more like formal burial: from the cave at Paviland through the tomb-shrines of the earlier Neolithic and the round barrows of the later Neolithic and Early Iron Age, to the cremation urn cemeteries of the Middle Bronze Age. The difference in later British prehistory, and especially between the years 1000 and 600 BC, is that there is very little evidence of ceremonial burial, and of tombs or graves, and so the bodies or individual bones recovered from other places become the more prominent.

A number of explanations have been advanced for this pattern. One is that human remains were disposed of in water, as whole bodies, cleaned bones or cremations. As said above, some of the artefacts laid in wet places at this time may have been the equivalent of grave goods. There is a little direct evidence for this: as also said, pieces of human skeleton are sometimes found with the water deposits, and in the Thames, at Eton, the skulls and bones of up to fifteen people, who died at some time between 1300 and 200 BC, were found weighted down in the river. Some had been defleshed beforehand.[101] However, this may have been a punishment for transgression rather than a normal rite, and hoards left in still water, where bones would be preserved, are rarely accompanied by human remains. Cremation, followed by the scattering of the burnt bones, is another possible explanation for the apparent absence of burials. This rite certainly continued into the Late Bronze Age, when a few little circular ditches with cremated remains inside were dug in southern England. Small quantities of burnt human bone have been found in pits inside settlements from the period, perhaps token deposits from funeral pyres.[102]

In the 1990s and 2000s Joanna Brück made a special study of the presence of the dead on Late Bronze Age sites, and noted that not only humans but houses and artefacts were fragmented at the end of their active lives in an apparently common process of transformation. The pattern, in her reading, calls into question the existence at the period both of the concept of a bounded and indivisible human self and of formalized and static political and social hierarchies. As houses were abandoned, they were often given deposits of human bone or tools, and freshly broken pottery or quern stones, and then dismantled or burned down. Human remains were often put at boundaries between different sorts of space, such as ditches, entrances, water and caves, as were objects, themselves often broken. They were placed in middens of domestic refuse, which were in turn sometimes apparently spread on fields as fertilizer, so continuing the cycle of death and rebirth. They were also fashioned into objects that appear to have functioned as amulets, and in general a human being seems to have been regarded as an assemblage of separable parts.

Similarly, Brück noted that it was rare for the whole of a socketed axe to be deposited in the same hoard, suggesting that such pieces of equipment were likewise dispersed at the end of their cycle of use, as part of the same process of regeneration.[103]

Such reflections remain relevant to the succeeding period, in which the Bronze Age gave way to the Iron, cremation apparently disappeared (though burnt remains may have been dispersed in air and water rather than buried), and unburnt human bone continued to feature in deposits on living sites and in hill forts. Its presence has led to a widespread feeling among archaeologists that the predominant burial rite for most of the British Iron Age was excarnation, by which bodies were exposed until they disintegrated and disappeared under the impact of the forces of nature. The individual bones and partial skeletons found on many sites were supposed to have been unusual examples of the retrieval of remains from this process and their employment for particular purposes.[104] The excavation of partial or whole human bodies, or single bones, on Iron Age sites can be explained in a number of different, often contrasting, ways. It is clear that the people represented could have been only a small proportion of the population – at most 5 or 6 per cent – and so the key question is how they were selected. They may have been especially honoured individuals, who were worshipped after death as heroic or wise ancestors, and whose bones were venerated in the manner of the relics of Christian saints before being interred to consecrate or protect a space. Alternatively, they may have been enemies, killed in battle or after capture, or criminals executed for heinous offences, whose corpses or body parts were displayed for a time at the settlement or fort concerned before being cast into a ditch or pit. The Greek traveller Posidonius witnessed at first hand how the tribes of southern and central Gaul collected and treasured the severed heads of foes as trophies; but the British may have been different.[105] The pieces of body found in Iron Age contexts in Britain may have been used in religious or magical rites, before being replaced by others and discarded.[106] Where human and animal bones are found deposited in the same or similar places, having apparently been treated in the same or similar ways, differing interpretations are again possible. The beasts concerned may have been especially precious to, or symbolically or spiritually associated with, the dead person or persons. They may have been intended as food for the dead on their journey into the next life; or they may all have been sacrifices, offered up to deities or spirits. There is really no decisive means of distinguishing between these options.

Two regional case studies, taken from opposite ends of the island, may illustrate the problems and opportunities of the evidence. At a Late Bronze Age settlement at Cladh Hallan on the Outer Hebridean island of South Uist, a team led by Mike Parker Pearson dug up what seemed to be two human bodies in the floors of roundhouses. They had apparently been laid there as dedicatory deposits when the houses were constructed, and the people concerned had lived locally but been dead for centuries before burial. They had been preserved during that time by soaking in a peat bog, the acidity of which would kill the bacteria that normally decompose soft tissue: in effect, they were mummies, the only examples known so far from a Bronze Age society in the Old World outside Egypt. Parker Pearson suggested that they had been retained and venerated as ancestors, and interred when the world of the living altered at the building of the settlement.[107] There are other more sinister possibilities, such as that they were the remains of enemies kept as trophies, object lessons or oracles, with stories attached to them, but these are probably less likely. They came to seem even more remarkable subsequently, when they were examined in detail and each was found to consist of parts taken from three different people assembled to make an apparent whole: the significance of these 'jigsaw mummies' remains unclear.[108]

Iron Age settlements in northern Scotland often contain small amounts of human skeleton, usually as individual bones, and especially skulls, placed under floors and in walls or in storage places, or on display. Some were pierced to be hung up prominently. The people represented by these remains could have been admired forebears, victims of head-hunting or sacrifice, or ordinary individuals whose parts were selected for use in rituals after death. They could have been used to consecrate buildings, especially at their construction or abandonment. The flesh was usually left on the skulls, most of which were those of women and children, which might argue against the idea of ancestor worship, as does the fact that animal remains were treated in much the same way on the same sites. Evidence of violence is, however, rare, the exception being a child with a chop mark to its spine, who was dismembered and placed under a newly built roundhouse with butchered parts of animals. We do not know if the burial was the work of the killers or of grieving relatives. Occasionally ancient bones were used: one in the foundations of a wheel-shaped house on the island of Lewis, in the Outer Hebrides, had been dug out of a nearby cemetery over a thousand years older. At Rennibister in Orkney skulls were defleshed and displayed, with apparent pride or respect.[109] Caves were also used for such deposits: the closing burial at High Pasture is one case in point (and a rare one of bodies being interred whole). At another northern Scottish site, Sculptor's Cave on the Moray Firth, the Late Bronze Age deposits included large numbers of human bones together with exceptionally rich metalwork. There was no sign of domestic occupation, and it seems to have been a sacred place visited at intervals. Severed children's heads were displayed at the entrance, apparently associated with some of the skeletons inside. Ian Armit, who has studied these remains from northern Scottish sites most consistently, has suggested that they might have been the result of human sacrifice or of the processing of the bodies of people who had died normally: a third possibility is that they were enemy war dead, dedicated at the cave along with booty. In the second to fourth centuries AD, the cave was reused for ritual, more personal ornaments and accessories being deposited along with seven headless bodies, victims of sacrifice, execution or war.[110]

At the southern end of Britain, in the Wessex chalk hills and neighbouring areas of the West Country, a very similar pattern obtains: a scatter of human bones and parts of bodies across settlement sites; and individual bones, especially skulls, sections of skeleton, and some complete burials, placed in disused pits in hill forts. Some of the partial and whole bodies were interred in groups, and the skulls were generally of men.

At Danebury the complete bodies were often weighed down by large blocks of flint and chalk, as if to deter them from rising again: indeed this, and the fact that whole human corpses are so rarely found, suggests that the burial of whole corpses was reserved for criminals and other outcasts from the social group.[111] Most of the human remains were apparently perceived and treated in similar ways to those of animals, objects and materials, being commonly dismembered, modified and interred in a deliberate and structured manner. There were, however, some limits to the similarities, as the animal bones show signs of having first been exposed in the open air, while the human were not, presumably having been buried for a time beforehand or protected by shelters or suspended in shrouds. At seven places in the southern English chalk country pieces of skull have been found which were fashioned into amulets or pendants for use by the living. The choice of people to go into pits and ditches on Wessex sites was highly selective – at Danebury, bones from about three hundred people have been identified to date, laid there over 450 years, out of a total occupying population which would probably have been around three hundred strong at any one moment.[112]

The picture is therefore fairly consistent across Britain, and admits of the same very broad spectrum of interpretation, with one end resting on an assumption that the individuals whose bones were left on Iron Age sites were sacrifices, criminals, transgressors or enemies, or simply had their remains arbitrarily selected for magical or religious rites, and the other on the view that they were beloved friends and relatives, admired leaders or forebears, or the mourned victims of tragic ends. Even those corpses weighted down at Danebury were not necessarily treated in this way because they were hated in life: they may have been acceptable enough persons who perished in especially disturbing and unfortunate ways, which created a fear that they would be restless after death. A mixture of all these contexts may have obtained at the same site. All that can be said with confidence is that for much of the Iron Age, the people who left physical remains must have been remarkable in some fashion.

Once again, however, archaeology may prove capable of altering apparently well founded conclusions with just a few new excavations. In 1991 and 1996 an enclosed settlement, dating from *c.* 700 to *c.* 300 BC, was investigated at Suddern Farm, near Danebury. It showed the classic pattern of deposits in pits: some seventy-eight of the latter were found, of which 44 per cent contained animal bones or pottery. All the domestic species of the time were represented, plus a few pieces of red deer and fox, and 126 bird bones, of which over half were of ravens. There were also two partial human skeletons and some isolated bones. So far, so normal, but Sir Barry Cunliffe and his colleagues also found a cemetery on the edge of the site which, extrapolating from the sample excavated, could have contained 300 adults, 80 children and 180 babies, buried between about 500 and 300 BC: a representative population.[113] In the same decade a similar cemetery was unearthed connected to a settlement at Yarnton, near Oxford, and a small one has also been found to the west of that in the Cotswold Hills at Kemble.[114] All were of crouched complete bodies, flexed so tightly that they were probably tied. It has begun to seem possible that, by (naturally enough) failing to excavate the edges or environs of settlements as well as the core sites, archaeologists have so far missed the major burial rite of the Early to Middle Iron Age. If this is the case, then the bones or bodies found in settlements or forts would be people either denied interment in the usual cemeteries, or dug up later so that the skeletons, or pieces of them, could be brought back into places of regular activity by the living, for some symbolic or ceremonial purpose. They still look special, but the context of their treatment may have altered.

Certainly from the Middle Iron Age onwards, normative burial sites began to reappear very obviously in a few regions of Britain, taking highly distinctive local forms which multiplied in the later part of the period. The earliest and most spectacular – starting in the third century BC – were on the chalk hills of eastern Yorkshire, where cemeteries of mounds inside rectangular ditches appeared, covering individual crouched burials. They were huge, numbering up to 500 graves in each, and organized in a clear hierarchy. Most of those buried had no goods, some had pottery, ornaments and joints of pork, and a few were given swords and knives. Nineteen of these were buried with carts, which might have functioned as chariots, and two in this number were female, with ornaments and a mirror instead of weapons: in addition isolated cart-burials of this kind have been found at Ferrybridge in the Aire Valley of West Yorkshire and much further off at Newbridge, near Edinburgh. The people singled out for this elaborate kind of rite might have been royalty, aristocrats or religious leaders, and it seems to have been practised for a relatively short period around 200 BC. Different styles of burial were adopted in different cemeteries in East Yorkshire: in some the bodies were extended, in others flexed, and in yet others crouched in the form of a foetus, though this was probably also the normal sleeping position of the time. Yet, there were different traditions concerning which goods were favoured for the dead, and whether meat was put with them. Most of the corpses were laid out on a line north to south, but those with weapons had a special, east to west, alignment. Likewise, the animal part laid beside most bodies was the left foreleg of a sheep, but some had that of a pig. These burials were laid according to the predominant custom of putting their faces to the east; but a minority faced west, and in that case the leg of the pig was taken from the right side of the animal. Similarly, in the cart (or chariot) graves the only animal parts found are from the front of a pig,

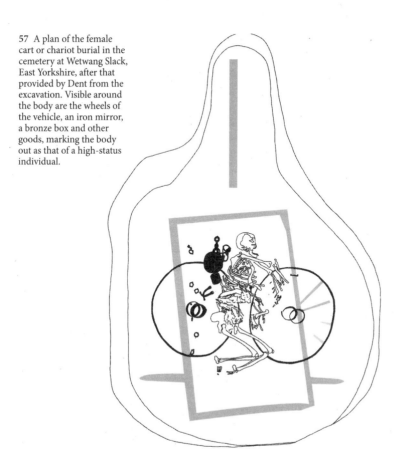

57 A plan of the female cart or chariot burial in the cemetery at Wetwang Slack, East Yorkshire, after that provided by Dent from the excavation. Visible around the body are the wheels of the vehicle, an iron mirror, a bronze box and other goods, marking the body out as that of a high-status individual.

joints cut from the left side being put to the north of the body and those from the right side of the beast being put to the south. As Mike Parker Pearson has noted, encoded in this pattern is a cosmology of associated directions and cardinal points. These cemeteries flourished on the Yorkshire chalk for about one and a half centuries, and then died out.[115]

In the third century BC, the people of what are now Devon and Cornwall began to produce cemeteries of stone coffins, with mostly crouched burials and few goods: the largest yet found, at Harlyn Bay, Cornwall, had 130 bodies. From the last century BC, fields of cremation urns were created in Kent and Sussex, and in Kent people were also laid extended under square barrows similar to those which had been made in Yorkshire. The largest Iron Age cremation cemetery yet discovered in England is at Westhampnett near Chichester, which had at least 161 burials, cremated on pyres near the graves. Only a minority of the burnt bones were in urns, though the rest may have been buried in bags, some of which could have been highly decorated as some of the urns were: this is another example of the manner in which the survival rate of different materials may skew the archaeological record. Few graves contained all the human remains from the pyre, many had less than 5 per cent of them, and some had none, showing that the older custom of interring parts of the human body persisted in a new guise, and that the very term 'grave' may be inappropriate here: 'memorial' or 'cenotaph' might be better. Likewise, though almost all the deposits included goods, they were never weapons and rarely ornaments or tools; most consisted of pottery and animal bones, so were perhaps food offerings. The same rites were used for all people, as if a community based on dispersed farms was being brought together in death. In the same period mass cemeteries without coffins appeared in Dorset, of people laid crouched on their right side with heads towards the east, often with pots and joints of meat and some with jewellery and weapons. Some men, however, were interred on their backs, with heads to the south-east: so even now, as in the earlier hill forts, a distinction was made between different kinds of dead. Across most of southern England, cremation burials were now dug, with or without urns, or single complete burials with weapons put alongside the men and rich goods – mirrors, bronze bowls and beads – with the women. At Basingstoke in the Hampshire lowlands, a young woman was interred in a pit with two sheep, two horses, joints of beef, four weaving combs, two rings, and an older woman, whose head rested on the pelvis of the younger. Perhaps she was a devoted servant who had died naturally at the same time, or who had chosen, or been compelled, to accompany her mistress into death.[116]

Each of the distinctive regional customs corresponded to a territory occupied by a particular tribe at the time of the Roman conquest: eastern Yorkshire by the Parisi, the south-western peninsula by the Dumnoni, and Dorset by the Durotriges. Similarly, the most spectacular of the Late Iron Age burials were found in the Hertfordshire and Essex heartland of the richest and most powerful of the kingdoms which had formed in Britain before the Romans arrived: the joint one of the Catuvellauni and Trinovantes. There members of the elite were put into deep burial pits with imported wine jars, drinking vessels, foodstuffs and firedogs for spit-roasting. At Welwyn Garden City in Hertfordshire, close to one of the main royal residences, a young man had been cremated in a bearskin and laid in a pit with five wine jars, Italian bronze and silver drinking bowls and glass gaming pieces. It seems that he was expected to do some entertaining in the next life, unless the objects were so polluted by his person that nobody else dared use them, or were gifts made by mourners to show their generosity. At another royal centre, which became Colchester, dead aristocrats were apparently laid in state in wooden chambers during the early first century AD. They were then burned on pyres close by, with various goods, and the ashes were put back into the chambers, with smashed dinner services – perhaps from the funeral feasts – before the structures were themselves burned.[117] Such elaborate burials spread southwards, as a fashion among the elite, into the south-eastern corner of England, so that the last graves at the Westhampnett cremation ceremony in Sussex were of this kind.

The new fashions in burial were accompanied by a proliferation in southern Britain of distinctive new regional styles of pottery: indeed, the two largely, though not entirely, matched each other.[118] Clearly, important marks of local group identity were being set up by them. All of the new treatments of human remains seem to have arrived from the Continent. Indeed, the Yorkshire square-barrow cemeteries are so similar to those found around Arras in northern France that it was formerly thought that they must have been made by invaders from that region. The differences in detail in the nature of the burials have now substituted the idea that the custom was imported and combined with native traditions. These imported traditions of how to treat the dead either fed upon or themselves helped to inspire a new system of social inequality among the southern British, with a clearly different rite accorded to superior individuals: the development of the Westhampnett cemetery, from the standard and universal system of cremation burial to the appearance of large chambers containing individuals with rich goods, is a striking illustration of this change in one community. To state this is not to suggest perfect equality in the earlier Iron Age – the selection of certain people for whole or partial burial in pits rules this out, and Niall Sharples's portrait of a fractured Wessex culture deeply suspicious of strangers and transgressors should not be forgotten – but there is patent evidence for the emergence of aristocracies in the south by the start of what is reckoned to be the Christian or Common Era. In this sense, the southern British were Romanizing before the Romans arrived, and the point is made even more obvious by the contrast with their northern neighbours, for in Scotland, beyond the limit of Roman rule, the old treatment of human remains continued for over half a millennium more.[119] What is completely unknown is how far these changes in social structure and burial rite reflected altering beliefs with regard to the nature of the afterlife and the fate of the soul. The only general comment that can be securely made about these developments is that by the end of the prehistoric period in southern Britain, formal burial was once more becoming the norm, but according to a sharply distinctive range of regional traditions.

The Problem of Human Sacrifice

Repeatedly, in this chapter the possibility has been acknowledged that human remains recovered from various Iron Age contexts had been the victims of sacrifice. The latter term originally just meant 'consecration' in the sense of being dedicated to a religious purpose, and has been narrowed to its modern sense of being put to death as part of such a purpose.[120] Such a rite has been recorded in relatively recent times, and by reliable observers, in North and South America, Africa, Asia and Oceania, and in various forms: killing a person or people so that they can accompany a powerful individual into the next world; or to give strength to the foundations of a building; or as a means of predicting the future; or, most commonly, in the belief that the action gives pleasure to the deities worshipped by the community concerned. Despite this wide distribution across the globe, most human beings in recorded time have shunned all forms of human sacrifice. For present purposes it matters greatly that the ancient cultures that have been most influential in forming the world view of the Western world – the Hebrews, Greeks and Romans – abhorred such practices and regarded them as a hallmark of barbarism and bad religion.

Here lies something of a problem, for the ritual killing of human beings has often taken other forms, which are easily confused with sacrifice. One is the execution of individuals convicted of serious crimes, which has been a custom of most societies and has generally been invested with a large measure of cere-mony and often with religious trappings, right up to to the presence of a clergy-man to afford prayers or rites for the condemned in the modern West. Likewise very many communities have put prisoners of war, especially captured enemy warriors, to death, and have done so with a strong element of ritual. This includes cultures that formally denounced human sacrifice as an unacceptable component of religion. The greatest of Greek poets, Homer, admiringly portrayed his mightiest hero, Achilles, as killing twelve captive noblemen to decorate the funeral pyre of his friend Patroclus. Indeed, his warriors operated in a world in which the adult male population of a captured town was routinely slaughtered. The Old Testament approvingly records several episodes of similar treatment of tribes defeated by the Israelites. The Romans used arenas for the destruction of both criminals and war prisoners, in highly theatrical displays, and in 97 BC put a set of foreign captives to death in order to avert danger, following the advice of a soothsayer. The only reason why they, and the Greeks of the classical period, had discontinued the earlier wholesale murder of males in a conquered population was that they had developed an economy based on mass slavery. To outsiders, the three forms of ritualized killing – execution, slaughter of prisoners, and sacrifice – could look extremely similar, and archaeologically they can appear identical.

In this context, it is crucially important that a number of ancient Greek and Roman texts – by Julius Caesar, Diodorus Siculus, Strabo, Pomponius Mela, Suetonius, Pliny and Lucan – accused the tribes of Gaul of killing human beings as an integral part of their religion, closely associating this with the Druids. Another Roman writer, Tacitus, made the same charge against the native British, specifically on the island of Anglesey, and a later one, Dio Cassius, described it as a component of Boudicca's Rebellion in south-eastern Britain. Most of these authors used it as a means of justifying the Roman conquest of the peoples concerned, and only one of them, Caesar, had firsthand experience of the tribal cultures which he described. Three, Caesar, Diodorus and Strabo, discuss the motivation behind the custom, in all cases in Gaulish society. Caesar said that it was employed only in times of mortal danger, when it was believed that by offering up the life of other human beings, the people making the offering would themselves be spared. He added that condemned criminals were the victims, but that innocent individuals were used if no malefactors were available. Diodorus and Strabo, both living far from Gaul and after the Roman conquest, said that people were killed as offerings to deities at the beginning of harvest, but the former said that prisoners of war were chosen for the purpose, and the latter specified that criminals were. It may readily be seen how much the three models of ritual killing outlined above overlap in these texts, and how only a little misunderstanding or misrepresentation may produce a major shift of perception in them.[121] Two recent essays are of relevance here in constructing a framework of interpretation. One is by J. Rives, who notes that Greeks and Romans deployed the charge of human sacrifice against foreigners in order to confirm their own sense of cultural superiority. Moreover, pagan Romans also levelled the same charge against groups within their own state whom they regarded as suspect, including Jews and Christians.[122] Modern scholars have tended automatically to disbelieve it in the latter context, while being much more ready to accept it in the case of

foreign peoples, who have left no records of their own. A similar pattern is
found in the second essay, by Lautaro Roig Lanzillotta, who has studied how
Christian Romans, in turn, employed the same accusation to attack Jews and
heretical sects within their own faith. He has emphasized that historians have
usually rejected it when used against Jews and members of mainstream
Christian denominations, and believed it in the case of heresies which have left
no writings of their own and no modern descendants.[123] Such insights may
caution scholars against too ready and literal an acceptance of the accusations
against the ancient Gauls and British.

For much of the late nineteenth and early twentieth centuries, it seems that
medieval Irish literature weighed in on the side of belief in the custom in the
Iron Age British Isles, for a few texts, notably the prose and metrical
Dindeshenchas, testify to the existence of human sacrifice in pagan Ireland.
Recently, however, Jacqueline Borsje has made a thorough study of these works
and concluded that they reflect a new interest in the subject by Irish scholars in
the period around 1100, inspired by accounts of it in the Bible and ancient
Roman texts and having no demonstrable link to any ancient Irish reality.[124] In
view of all this, it is hardly surprising that, over the past five hundred years,
writers on ancient Britain in general, and the Druids in particular, have
accepted or rejected the belief that they offered humans as sacrifices, with
varying degrees of fervour, according to their own dispositions and polemical
purposes.[125] During the twentieth century, a notable chasm opened up within
the discipline of archaeology itself, concerning the treatment of the issue in
different periods. As discussed earlier, Victorian scholars frequently interpreted Neolithic burials as evidence of human sacrifice, but their professional
successors largely abandoned this tradition for more benign interpretations of
the same evidence. This is despite the fact that the evidence concerned shares
several features with that found on Iron Age sites: the presence of human bone
in ceremonial contexts; the mixing or close proximity of human and animal
remains, with some similarities of treatment; the fact that only a small
percentage of the likely population can be represented by the surviving skeletal
material; and the frequent deposition of only parts of bodies or even single
bones. By contrast, while the majority of experts on the British Iron Age have
tended to ignore the question of human sacrifice since the 1990s, some of the
most prominent have continued to argue for its existence in the period.[126] The
difference seems explicable only in terms of the survival of texts, for the later
Iron Age, by the Greek, Roman and Irish authors who seemed to record the
practice in Iron Age Britain: it is a specific literary tradition.

In 1984 that tradition appeared to have found a clinching piece of evidence
in its favour, with the discovery of the 'bog body' known as Lindow Man. It
consisted of the head, neck, arms and upper torso of a man (and, in a later

discovery, part of his leg), dug out of a peat bog called Lindow Moss, Cheshire. This was arguably the most sensational find made by British archaeology in the decade, and the man's remains became one of the most carefully investigated human bodies of all time.[127] The key member of the investigating team was Iain West, a leading criminal pathologist from Guy's Hospital, London, who concluded that the man had suffered a triple execution, his skull being broken by two blows, his throat cut, and his neck broken by a cord still fastened around it, which had been twisted tight like a garrotte. This strongly suggested a ritual killing, an interpretation reinforced by two other factors. The first was contributed by Anne Ross, the leading expert on Iron Age religion in Britain during the 1960s and 1970s, who pointed out that triple deaths were recorded in medieval Celtic literature, where they could represent a memory of just such a sacrificial practice in pagan times. The second consisted of four grains of mistletoe pollen found in the stomach contents of the body. The Roman writer Pliny had asserted that mistletoe was held sacred by the Druids when it was found growing on an oak tree, and its presence in the man suggested that he might have been given a drink containing it as part of his consecration as a sacrifice.[128] The cumulative evidence thus assembled appeared to justify the action of the British Museum in putting the body on display, as one of its best-known exhibits, with a label declaring that the evidence 'strongly suggests' that it had been subjected to 'ritual sacrifice'. As such, it rapidly took its place in works on the British and European Iron Age, as the near-solid proof that had been needed that the ancient authors who had accused the British and their neighbours of engaging in this practice had been telling the truth.[129] It also found its way into popular culture as a cathartic force for religious intolerance: fundamentalist Christians and irresponsible journalists alike used it as a means to denounce ancient Druids, and then turn on their modern counterparts for attempting to revive a religion tainted by atrocity.[130]

Behind such an interpretation lay a text a great deal more recent and directly influential than anything written by a Greek or Roman: the best-selling English translation, published in 1969, of a Danish book by Peter V. Glob, which had revealed to a large public the importance of human bodies preserved in peat bogs as source material for prehistoric cultures.[131] Glob drew attention to the large number of such finds made by that time, in Denmark, Germany and the Netherlands, dating from late prehistory. Some had suffered violent deaths and seemed to have been ritually deposited. He suggested that these had been human sacrifices, linked specifically to the cult of a fertility goddess to whom they had been ceremonially wed before being sent to join her. This idea was speculation based ultimately on one custom which one Roman author, Tacitus, had recorded (on unknown authority) as being practised by one (remote) group of German tribes, and for which there is no solid evidence.[132] There may have been no common reason for the presence of these corpses in northern European bogs. Some may have been murder victims, and those killed with signs of ritual may all have been criminals, found guilty of heinous crimes which were deemed to merit special punishment and exclusion from the human world in death.[133] A total of 184 sets of human remains had been recovered from British wetlands before Lindow Man, but few had been securely dated, and none had been susceptible to a full measure of modern scientific analysis.[134] The Lindow body was not only substantial and well preserved, fitted for such treatment, but may have been the first bog body ever discovered with its stratigraphic context intact. As almost all the British peat levels old enough to preserve such finds had then been dug out, he also represented one of the last chances to carry out any such work. Unsurprisingly, his discovery was hailed as a British example of the tradition highlighted by Glob, and interpreted according to Glob's ideas.[135]

On closer inspection there are serious problems with the interpretation. The greatest was that before Iain West saw the body, it was inspected by another expert, an anatomist from Liverpool University and coroner's pathologist called Robert Connolly, who was then recruited to the investigating team. He and West agreed that the man had been in his twenties and completely unused to hard manual work, suggesting high social status. He had been put into the bog naked except for a fox-fur armband around one arm, and his skull had been fractured by heavy blows. Connolly, however, thought that the cord around the throat was a necklace, from which the pendant had been removed by the man's killers or had corroded away.[136] He pointed out that the cartilage and muscle showed none of the usual trauma of strangulation, and that the tightness of the cord had been caused by the swelling of neck tissues in the peat. He likewise believed that the deep cut on the throat had been caused after death, perhaps by peat-cutters, and the broken neck by another of the blows that had smashed the skull; a broken rib might have been caused by a further blow, and there also seemed to be a stab wound in the chest. That turned a highly ritualized killing into a more mundane one.[137]

Anne Ross's parallel cases of triple deaths in medieval literature were also less helpful than had at first appeared. Leaving aside the bigger question of whether that literature contains any accurate information about ancient British or Irish paganism, which will be considered later, the deaths in the medieval texts were never sacrifices: instead, the people who suffered them were accidentally killed three times over and so fulfilled apparently impossible predictions that they would die in each of those ways. The stories concerned were intended to illustrate the power of prophecy, or of destiny.[138] As for the mistletoe in the man's stomach, even accepting that Pliny's assertion had any basis in truth, no remains of the plant itself were found with the four pollen grains, and four grains is too a small quantity to make ingestion in a drink probable. They could have got into the man's system accidentally, by blowing on to his last meal.[139] In 1987 parts of a second ancient male body were found in the same bog, which contained good evidence of that man's last meal, and it had not included mistletoe. Both scientists who made this analysis put on record their disbelief that there had been any ritual significance to the final food eaten by either person.[140] A different problem concerns dating, which in the case of the Lindow bodies is made problematic by contamination by peat, so that the radiocarbon results obtained may too easily reflect the time at which the peat developed, rather than that at which the human remains were put into it. After three successive attempts to reach a reliable date, by two different laboratories, the British Museum accepted the last, which gave a cluster of dates between the early first century AD and the early part of the second, but with a 30 per cent chance that the body was up to a few hundred years more recent. The museum disregarded that chance, and declared officially that the man had died in the mid first century, which represented the medium point on the cluster of dates and was still before the Roman invasion of the region.[141] However, a human head had already been found in Lindow Moss in 1983 and dated firmly to the Roman or post-Roman period, and the second body found there, in 1987, achieved the same result.[142] In 1958 a severed head, which had also been tied about the neck by a cord and had a fractured skull, had been found in another bog near Manchester, Worsley Moss: its radiocarbon likewise made it Romano-British.[143] When the dates from the different body parts are all put together, they cluster in Roman Britain, when human sacrifice was formally illegal. Some scholars have sought to reconcile this with the sacrificial theory by suggesting that the nefarious practices of the preceding Iron Age had continued in secret.[144] This is a tenable hypothesis, the evidence for which will be considered in the next chapter, but a circular one, because of the lack of solid proof that such practices had ever existed: Lindow Man was supposed to *be* that proof.

It may therefore be proposed that the identification of the body as the victim of a highly ritualized killing, let alone of human sacrifice, is still possible, but insecure. There is no doubt that Iain West was an excellent pathologist, but he had never before examined a body which had lain in peat for almost two thousand years. No modern British court of law would accept the conclusions of a single medical expert, when another had challenged them right at the beginning, and there was a chain of cases during the late twentieth century which revealed the dangers of relying on one such expert when unchallenged. What has been especially interesting, in the context of modern cultural history, has been the manner in which the original, hegemonic, propagation of the interpretation of Lindow Man as the victim of a ritual death has broken down.

During the first ten years after the publication of the British Museum's report, a few experts in prehistoric religion who did not specialize in the Iron Age commented briefly on the possibility that its conclusion – in favour of the sacrificial hypothesis – was insecure.[145] They were ignored, as was a BBC television programme in 1998, in the *Horizon* series on current scientific developments, which drew attention to problems in the pathological and the dating evidence: a very rare case of an attack by television journalists on an archaeological orthodoxy.[146] In the mid 2000s controversy broke out at last, in the pages of the *Times Literary Supplement* and *The Times*, which provoked first a restatement of the official line from the British Museum and then a possible acknowledgement that it might have flaws; but nothing was done to alter the labelling of the exhibit.[147]

The turning point came when the body was loaned to the Manchester Museum for a temporary exhibition in 2008. It had been there before, when the interpretation of ritual killing had been stated as orthodoxy, but this time the staff at Manchester mounted a display which highlighted the many different ways in which the significance of the body could be viewed.[148] The exhibition was accompanied by a conference, at which virtually all speakers argued for a similar openness of vision, including Jody Joy, who was the spokesperson for the British Museum and had just taken charge of the gallery in which Lindow Man usually resided.[149] Subsequently he published a booklet with the museum's press, intended for visitors, which candidly acknowledged the difficulties in interpreting the body, and entered an open verdict.[150] When the corpse was returned to the museum from Manchester, it was given a new label which took the same line. In 2010 the second edition of Timothy Darvill's classic textbook on prehistoric Britain stringently questioned the original interpretation of the find.[151] A similarly wide survey published by an equally prominent expert in the Neolithic, Richard Bradley, had already declared the sacrificial explanation for bog bodies unlikely.[152] The new tendency towards pluralism has, however, not completely overtaken the old hegemonic emphasis on sacrifice, for the latter was restated in 2010 by some of the most eminent experts in Iron Age ritual practices, in books intended for a popular market and without recognizing any challenges to the old orthodoxy.[153]

In other nations, the application of the sacrificial interpretation has continued to be applied to newly found bog bodies as if no others were possible or necessary, most obviously in Ireland, where remains of two more men were dug out of peat at Oldcroghan in County Offaly and Clonycavan in County Meath during the year 2003. They bring the total of bodies recovered from Irish wetlands to 130, dating from the Neolithic to the Middle Ages, but clustering, like those from elsewhere in northern Europe, in late prehistory. Both had been young, muscular and of high status, and had been savagely battered and mutilated as part of the process of being killed and consigned to the bogs, perhaps around 300 BC. Their presence close to what have been identified as the boundaries of early medieval Irish kingdoms was used to strengthen the assertion that they had been victims of pagan religious rites, ignoring the fact that such frontiers were also appropriate as execution sites for criminals or political enemies, or points at which to despatch captured enemy warriors. This single reading of the evidence was conveyed not only in print but on television and in a permanent exhibition of those and other bog bodies at the National Museum in Dublin, entitled 'Kingship and Sacrifice'.[154] In Britain, however, we seem to be reaching a situation, at least for the present, in which a multiplicity of readings of the evidence can be made officially as well as in practice. In these, Lindow Man may have been a human sacrifice, willing or not, a member of or a stranger to the people who put him into the Moss, a victim of violent crime or an individual himself condemned and executed, justly or not, for a serious crime. He may have been Iron Age or Romano-British, or even, by a long stretch of the possible dates, post-Roman. He may have been laid in the bog with the other people found there, and for the same reasons, or at a very different time and as a result of very different motives. He can be used to exemplify the triumphs or failures, the prowess or the limitations, of modern archaeology.

As such, he stands for the nature of the evidence for human sacrifice in Iron Age Britain as a whole. It should be obvious from what is argued above that to suggest that there is none would be very wrong: there is plenty, both textual and material. The problem is that all of it can be interpreted in a different way, negating its status as proof. The progress of knowledge in this area can perhaps best be characterized not as producing a 'better Iron Age', or a 'new Iron Age', but as generating a series of different possible Iron Ages, existing in parallel. This is, of course, a larger theme of this book as an approach to the study of prehistory, but whether readers will find it attractive or not will depend upon their natures and habits of thought.[155]

Sacred Places

It used to be a truism of Iron Age studies that Britain lacked ritual monuments from the period, in sharp contrast with those of the Neolithic and Early Bronze Age but in conformity with the Late Bronze Age. Only in the last centuries of the period, ran the argument, did detectable ritual structures reappear, in the southern part of the island and probably under the same Continental influences which encouraged the return of burials to the same region. Even then, they were not very impressive, in number or size. By 2009, eighteen had been identified, at fifteen sites. Their form made another break with the earlier

58 Reconstruction of the Iron Age shrine identified at Heathrow, Middlesex, under the site
of the present airport, as imagined in the mid twentieth century by Alan Sorrell and
reproduced here with the permission of the Museum of London. It was larger than most. The
sacrifice of a bull is being represented here, with a presiding pair of figures who may be
intended as Druids.

prehistoric past, because they were rarely circular, 70 per cent being rectangular or square and the rest a variety of shapes. They were, moreover, rather flimsy timber buildings, most of which could only have accommodated a dozen people and a quarter of which were large enough for just one worshipper, though a few could have taken up to fifty. Almost all were isolated from other buildings, and almost half had an enclosure to set them further apart. Virtually all had doors facing between north-east and south-east, towards the sunrise (but not quite all). Over half were inside settlements or hill forts, but the rest stood in open countryside and needed a special journey. Eight have produced deposits of objects when excavated: brooches at seven, coins at seven, animal bones at four, and real or miniature weapons at two.

The most elaborate interments of objects known to date were probably at Hallaton on a Leicestershire hilltop, where the shrine was set within a ditch, and probably a palisade, with a processional way running east to west. The local tribe, the Corieltavi, buried a total of 5,294 coins there, in fourteen hoards, just before the Roman invasion of their territory. Some 6,901 pieces of animal bone were also found, almost all from pigs which had not been butchered before burial and so look like genuine sacrificial offerings. There was a strong tendency at Hallaton to give special significance to the right-hand side: the right forelegs had been removed from most of the pigs, perhaps to be consumed by special people, and most of the coins were on the right-hand side of a ditch in the entrance which funnelled worshippers round to the right. It is very likely that offerings of food, drink or cloth were made at most of these sites, but these leave no trace in the archaeological record. There is no clear indication of the nature of the deities venerated though the presence of weaponry at two sites might argue that they were sacred to a warrior cult. Distinguishing these so-called shrines from other features represented now only by post holes is difficult without the presence of apparent offerings (and such deposits were of course common in forts and settlements in general). Their main qualification for the label is often simply that they seem to have had no other discernible purpose.[156]

The apparent absence of impressive ritual monuments in Britain during the period seemed more surprising in view of the increasing evidence for them in surrounding lands. In Ireland, huge ceremonial enclosures were erected in the last millennium BC. Some, such as at Tara in Leinster and Rathcroghan in Connacht, occurred in clusters and were rectangular, round or oval and made of low walls or banks. Others, such as at Navan Fort in Ulster and Dún Ailinne in Leinster, consisted of rings of massive timber posts, which in the latter case were almost certainly free-standing and in the former may have supported a wooden building, surrounded in turn by a bank with an internal ditch. These constructions would have been as imposing as anything erected earlier in Irish prehistory and were sometimes set in landscapes with prominent Neolithic monuments, as if to maintain a deliberate continuity with a remembered or legendary past; the placing of the ditch inside the bank at Navan and some of the Rathcroghan enclosures may have imitated henges.[157] In northern France, large rectangular enclosures of wood and mud brick were constructed around 300 BC; the most celebrated are at Gournay-sur-Aronde and Ribemont-sur-Ancre. Within them were quantities of animal bones – cattle, pigs, sheep and wild game – and Gournay had about two thousand iron weapons and pieces of armour hung from poles inside the precinct or from the gateway. More weapons were piled around the outer wall of Ribemont, with eighty headless skeletons, and the bodies of nearly a thousand young men had been burned inside the inner precinct. They seem to have been associated with war, but which of the human bodies represented enemy dead found on the battle-field, or prisoners who were later killed for entertainment or sacrificed, and which represented the honoured war casualties of the community, is anybody's guess.[158] Again, nothing like these precincts has been found in Britain.

The perceived barrenness of the British Iron Age of impressive ceremonial monuments has largely evaporated in recent years with the realization that hill forts were enclosures within which people gathered, often episodically and seasonally, for a range of purposes, of which ritual was one. Some, as has been said, seem suited only for occupation for specific ceremonies. If they are admitted to the ledger of consecrated structures from the period then it becomes crowded with sacred sites as impressive as anything before. Furthermore, the existence of substantial timber alignments and avenues is increasingly being recognized, in that earlier time around the junction of the Bronze and Iron Ages in which hill forts were not yet common. That at Flag Fen has already been described, and not far away, at Barleycroft Farm in the Great Ouse Valley of Cambridgeshire, over a thousand posts were set up during the Late Bronze Age in a series of rows, often with T-shaped terminals. They were erected amid farmland but could have served no practical purpose, and required a great communal effort: the obvious conclusion is that they formed a vast ritual landscape.[159] Similar long and mysterious lines of posts were found around a settlement of about 1000 BC near Upper Bucklebury above the Kennet Valley in Berkshire. This was not just any community, but one associated with the earliest evidence yet found for iron-working in Britain, and the alignments may have marked it out as special.[160] That similar traditions persisted into the Iron Age seems indicated by the now celebrated site of Fiskerton, on the River Witham east of Lincoln, where a timber causeway ran down to the water. It was composed of 195 vertical posts with brushwood and plants laid between, which were originally erected in the early part of 457 BC (dated by the tree rings) and repaired at intervals for one and a half centuries. Around and beneath the causeway was a classic ritual wetland deposit, of swords, spearheads, axe heads, metal-working tools, files and saw, with three fragments of human bone (one from the skull of a young adult, with an unhealed sword slash in it) and some from both domestic and wild animals. The structure could have served a practical purpose as a landing stage, but the length was in excess of that needed for one, and the deposits were commenced after the causeway was finished. Great interest has been generated by the discovery that forty-four of the timbers were felled in episodes spaced nineteen years apart, six of which coincided with total eclipses of the moon. This suggests that the posts were being replaced at special times, but it is as yet no more than an exciting suggestion, needing to be tested at other sites. As things stand, Fiskerton is the pre-eminent riverside site with ritual deposits yet to be dated to the British Iron Age.[161]

It may be observed that one problem in detecting sacred places in that age is the manner in which ceremonial and practical uses of constructions seem often to overlap. This has been discussed with relation to hill forts, and to

Fiskerton, and it becomes acute, and controversial, when discussing the structures to which archaeologists have given the French name 'souterrain'. They consist of underground chambers with passages leading into them and with an entrance or entrances significantly smaller than the space inside. They are found over much of Ireland, northern and western Scotland and its islands, western Cornwall and Brittany, usually in settlements and forts. In this sense they look like a feature of 'Atlantic' Britain, France and Ireland, but they are missing from Wales and Galloway, a pattern which has never been explained. In Ireland, where they are one of the commonest kinds of archaeological monument – over three thousand are known, all across the country – there has been little doubt about their purpose. The early medieval texts there spell it out: they were temporary refuges for people and their most portable possessions if raiders attacked and were too numerous to be repelled in a straight fight. They were ideal for the purpose, as enemy warriors would be obliged to enter their chambers one by one, exposing head and arms as they did so. Concealed air vents made it difficult to smoke out the occupants, who would have to be starved or dug out, and both operations were too lengthy for the classic hit-and-run tactics of a raid, to which the same early literature also testifies. Archaeology has supported this interpretation, as the elongated chambers seem to have an odd shape for storage places and have no layer of dust from regular opening and no trace of storage containers. Finds within them have been few and, as the texts suggest, of relatively small and valuable items, such as coins, a beaker, a bell or a brooch.[162]

Some authors, reasonably enough, have projected the Irish use of these structures on to their whole range.[163] There is, however, a problem of dating, because the Irish examples all seem to date from between AD 500 and 1200, while those elsewhere mainly belong to the pre-Roman Iron Age: in Brittany they were built between 600 and 100 BC, and in Cornwall between the fourth century BC and the second century AD, and in Scotland between the first and third centuries AD.[164] Despite the basic similarity of form, they may therefore have had different purposes, and they also have different scholarly traditions of interpretation. The Scottish structures are locally known as 'earth houses', and they vary in form between different regions: those around the Tay basin and Firth of Tay are larger, tend to curve and sometimes have side chambers, while those in northern Scotland and Orkney are smaller and simpler. The traditional interpretation, which is still dominant, is that they were storehouses for agricultural produce, although recently it has been suggested rather tentatively that they might also at times have been refuges (on the Irish pattern) or shrines.[165] In Cornwall, the same structures are called 'fogous' (from the Cornish word for a cave), and form one of the most interesting classes of ancient monument in the westernmost third of the peninsula, their entrances showing up in cattle pastures, by the walls of farmyards, in the parkland of mansions, in woodland glades and among the bracken and boulders of uplands. There the prevailing explanation has been that the souterrains were ritual structures, one proposed in the 1960s and 1970s by Evelyn Clark and Patricia Christie: although the dominant figure in Cornish archaeology at the time, Charles Thomas, suggested that they might also have been byres for farm animals, or larders (he noted that they were used as storehouses in modern times), he was positive in rejecting the Irish interpretation that they had been used for refuge.[166] In 1992 this tradition was challenged directly by Rachel Maclean, who eliminated the explanation that they had been storage places on the grounds that they were both damp and difficult of access, while structures above ground would be better for meat and grain. Dairy produce would fare better in them, but could be more easily kept in barrels, and beer casks would have needed to be small in order to get through the entrances. She also opposed the idea that they had been made for ritual, because no deposits had been found in them of the sort familiar from ceremonial sites of the period, while they were not separated from the surrounding settlements in the manner of the shrines identified elsewhere in southern Britain. She urged instead the explanation that they had been refuges in time of attack, for which she thought them splendidly suited.[167]

By that time, however, the idea that fogous were religious structures had been taken up enthusiastically by the growing number of modern Pagans and goddess-worshippers in west Cornwall, some of whom indeed used them for ceremonies and meditations. It was this community that generated the finest field study yet made of these monuments, the work of an artist called Ian Cooke who in 1993 published a first-rate gazetteer, with (as one might expect from somebody of his profession) superb visual aids, including many drawings by antiquarians as well as plans, and photographs, some of which had never been published before. He also advanced a fervent defence of the concept of fogous as sacred sites, using the particular argument that their northern ends were aligned with the midsummer sunrise or sunset.[168] In a review of the book, an archaeologist, Peter Herring, warned that the definition of a fogou adopted in it skewed the evidence in favour of the conclusion drawn, and that the solstice alignments proposed by Cook were not proven. He followed Rachel Maclean in rejecting the theory that fogous were designed for storage of food or drink, but instead thought it possible that they were refuges, stores for tin (in which the region is rich and which was certainly mined at the time) or cult centres.[169] With that pleasingly indeterminate conclusion, the debate seems to have petered out, though in 2001 Sir Barry Cunliffe glanced at the matter and revived the idea of storage of agricultural produce, with some 'ritual protection' of it, as the most likely purpose of the structures.[170] In Britain, at least, there is now even less certainty as to the meaning of souterrains than there was thirty years ago.

The problem of distinguishing sacred from secular use of space in the British Iron Age has recently extended to the heart of apparent domesticity in the period, the roundhouses which were the main dwellings. It was noted earlier that their shape may have mirrored that of the ceremonial monuments of the third millennium BC, and that their increasing adoption could have represented a greater importation of ritual into the home environment. This idea was given further impetus in 1995, when a team of archaeologists in the Wessex region pointed out that the house entrances often faced between east and south-east, the positions of the equinoctial and midwinter sunrises. This was the orientation of the Late Iron Age shrines, and both settlement gateways and hill-fort entrances tended to face 'broadly' east or west, while most bodies were laid in graves facing east. Furthermore, the team suggested, the areas for activities in the roundhouses were generally on the southern side of the interior, and the sleeping space on the northern, which seemed to mimic the movements of the sun.[171] Four years later, Mike Parker Pearson reinforced these points, and suggested that in the 'wheel houses' of the Hebrides (named after their structure) the tasks of the day were generally carried out in the southern sector of the building.[172] A pan-British solar cosmology, tied into daily life, seemed to be taking shape. It was swiftly pointed out that many Iron Age houses do not face south-east, so that the lie of the land could be as important to their construction as cosmology.[173] None the less, the idea of dwellings as imbued with ritual and symbolism caught on. Francis Pryor emphasized that the burials of babies and children were sometimes found near house doorways, as if to link youth with the rising sun which so many of the doors faced.[174]

At the same time, reservations about this kind of interpretation continued to be expressed. Leo Webley argued that in southern England most round-houses showed no apparent division of activity between different halves, and those that did were concentrated around the borderline between the Bronze and Iron Ages, and were unusual cases. These were, in particular, buildings which were burnt or demolished (activities which seemed to be relatively infre-quent) and the deposits at them were more likely to have been left by feasts which accompanied the destruction rather than routine activities.[175] Rachel Pope echoed the point that the placement of roundhouse doorways was appar-ently dictated by the surrounding landscape as well as the movement of the sun. Even the many that faced its rising positions, she suggested, could have been intended to admit the maximum amount of light into the interior rather than reflect any symbolic significance.[176] This last argument was challenged, on the grounds that if light and warmth were the paramount factors, then the

doorways should mostly have faced south, not east.[177] To this Pope riposted by
considering the evidence for the layout of domestic space in tribal cultures
studied by anthropologists, and finding that only a few adopted binary oppositions of the sort suggested in the British case. Most mixed practical and
symbolic factors. She acknowledged, however, that the doorways of British
roundhouses did generally face points between east and south, and while still
suggesting that the need for light may have played a part in this, she also noted
that ceremonial monuments from the Neolithic long barrows to Christian
churches had a similar orientation.[178] Ann Woodward and Gwilym Hughes,
revisiting the evidence for deposits within both houses and shrines, found a
strong preference for leaving them in the right-hand (usually the southern)
side of both (facing the entrance), but that this was not a strict rule even within
any one period of use. They concluded that the matter was 'very complex'.[179] In
the years around 2000, it seemed as if a key had been found to a general
symbolic code for the British Iron Age. A decade later nothing seems so simple,
although there remains a strong feeling that, for much of the time, the daily
course of the sun, and the right sides of objects and places (which mirrored the
rightward movement of that course), had some significance in the layout of
human spaces.

Much of the earlier disinclination to look harder for ceremonial monuments was another consequence of the former tendency to rely on the writings
of ancient Romans for information on pre-Roman societies. Three of them,
Lucan, Pliny and Pomponius Mela, wrote that the peoples of Gaul worshipped
in sacred groves of trees, while Tacitus and Cassius Dio said the same of those
in Britain. This gave rise to a long-lasting modern belief that the Druids, and
those to whom they ministered, preferred to hold ceremonies in natural places
rather than to build temples or shrines.[180] This was plainly not true of the
peoples of southern Gaul, especially in the region now called Provence, who
have long been known to have constructed substantial stone sanctuaries decorated with sculpture; and the recent discovery of timber and earthen equivalents in northern France, as described, discredits it there as well. The Roman
authors may, however, not have been wholly wrong. It is possible that the
Druids themselves preferred to hold rites in natural places, especially if Roman
persecution, following conquest, drove them away from settlements. It is also
extremely likely that the British had continued to find a sense of the sacred in
atmospheric parts of the natural landscape, as well as constructing monuments, ever since the Neolithic. The presence of ritual deposits in water, of
which so much has now been said, is proof that this was true of certain lakes,
pool, rivers and bogs. Sacred groves may well have stood around some of the
shrines that have been identified, and the deposits in pits, and they were indeed
recorded as a feature of ancient European paganism everywhere that trees

could flourish, both north and south of the Alps, so the British are likely to have had them.[181]

Having said this, it is notable that ritual deposits have not been found at most of the more eye-catching and majestic landscape features of Britain, such as rock outcrops, and that, despite the widespread modern talk of 'Celtic holy wells', there is not much sign of religious significance being attached to springs. The main exception is the most spectacular of these in Britain, the hot one at Bath which still pumps steaming water from the ground at the rate of half a million gallons each day. We know that this was sacred to the Iron Age British, because the Romans recorded the name of the goddess to whom they dedicated it, Sulis, but the quantity of objects which they actually deposited in it, or around it, still seems small compared with those in other kinds of water.[182] Recently experts in the British Iron Age have tended to play down the veneration of natural places, and one author, Jane Webster, has done so explicitly. She has emphasized that the Celtic word 'nemeton', formerly taken to mean a sacred wood, simply means a sacred place, and that there is much less sign of a cult of either springs or wells in pre-Roman Britain than elsewhere in the ancient world, including Greece and Rome.[183]

Current perceptions of the use of consecrated space in the period are therefore both dynamic and mutable. Almost overnight entire new categories of monument can appear as candidates for admission: in Cornwall, for example, four embanked circular enclosures which had been assumed to be Neolithic were dated in 2010 to the first millennium BC. It has been suggested that they could have been local copies of the great round ceremonial structures of Iron Age Ireland, and that crop marks recently identified in Cornish fields may indicate the existence of hundreds more.[184] Connected to discussions of where and how the Iron Age British held rites are others, of how the beliefs of the time accommodated the presence of the, by then, considerable number of monuments left in the landscape from earlier phases of prehistory. These discussions tend to occupy points on a spectrum of emphasis stretching between the work of two Richards, Bradley and Hingley. The former has made a survey of the use of English ceremonial monuments which suggests that there was virtually no continuity between the Neolithic and the Iron Age. Even at places such as Tara in Ireland, where impressive Iron Age monuments were deliberately constructed among those of earlier millennia, the latter had been disused for long periods between. Bradley concluded that a distant and now legendary past was being incorporated into the empowerment of later rulers.[185] A stress on discontinuity would be reinforced by the evidence from the most spectacular of all British Neolithic sites, Stonehenge and Avebury, which seem to have both been abandoned and neglected more in the Iron Age than in the periods either before or after: they seem, indeed, to have been actively avoided.[186] Richard Hingley, by contrast, has drawn attention to the interest taken by Iron Age people in the remains of earlier times, including several hundred Bronze Age weapons and tools, collected and carefully deposited in Iron Age contexts. Some had been curated, and may have been venerated as ancestral or magical objects, and used as amulets. He has also noted the reuse of Neolithic tomb-shrines in Scotland – especially on Orkney and the Outer Hebrides by the leaving of pottery and other 'domestic' objects in them and the building of houses at them. Some pottery styles at these places apparently imitated those of the Neolithic, and the new houses followed the plans of the tomb-shrine chambers: the Iron Age people themselves may have viewed the older monuments as houses.[187]

In reality there is no necessary contradiction between these positions, for they illustrate, between them, that the Iron Age British reacted selectively to relics of the past, avoiding or demolishing some and adopting others. This could happen according to marked regional traditions (Wessex compared to Orkney, for example), but also within the same district: Tim Mallin's study of the Ouse Valley in Cambridgeshire showed how some of its many Neolithic ceremonial complexes may have been employed for ritual purposes in the Iron Age, but others were converted to agricultural use.[188] Richard Bradley himself acknowledged that Britain has a few cases in which Iron Age enclosures or possible shrines were imposed upon or incorporated those of the Neolithic, as what he termed a process of legitimization by linkage with the remote past.[189] What is missing in all this is any indication that the people of the later period had any memory of what had happened in the earlier monuments or why they had been constructed. Instead their attitude seems better to correspond to the Iron Age world proposed by John Barrett, in which the old monuments had become part of a mythical past, belonging to a different order of existence but used to explain and justify present social and political relationships, in the manner of myth and legend everywhere.[190]

Images and Interpretations

Back in the days – only in the recent past, but now seeming so distant – when the label 'Celtic' was applied without hesitation or definition to the British Iron Age, the material evidence for religious activity and belief was generally interpreted within a framework created by mixing elements from four different kinds of source: medieval Irish literature; medieval Welsh literature; the writings of ancient Greek and Roman authors about the peoples of Gaul, Britain and Germany; and inscriptions and dedications from the Roman provinces that were established in those regions. This tradition was established in the late nineteenth century, by an international alliance of scholars of whom the most prominent British representative was probably Sir John Rhys, and continued and elaborated by a similarly broad network of distinguished academics for most of the twentieth century.[191] During the 1960s and 1970s the most eminent British practitioner of it was Anne Ross, whose wonderfully rich and exciting book, *Pagan Celtic Britain*, which appeared in 1967, revealed to a new generation the extent of the material evidence for the subject.[192] In the 1980s Miranda Green emerged as the foremost scholar to apply it.[193] Since the mid 1990s those working in the field have become more cautious about using the fourfold system of interpretation, and that tendency will be continued in the present book. The special difficulties of employing medieval literature for the purpose will be discussed in its final chapter, and those of the Graeco-Roman sources have already been mentioned. While the Romano-British evidence is still of crucial importance for an understanding of the Iron Age, and more abundant than ever, it will be considered in the next chapter, as a treatment of the manner in which Roman and native cultures interacted after the conquest of the province. For a while longer, the prehistoric British material will continue to be analysed in its own right, in order to see of what it consists when viewed without the use of perspectives gained from other periods and cultures.

One major and celebrated limitation in doing this is the reluctance of the prehistoric British to create physical representations of the divine beings whom they venerated. As a result, the possible religious images that we do possess from the last phase of prehistory in the island are few and enigmatic. By far the most spectacular is the White Horse carved on to the northern scarp of the Berkshire Downs above the village of Uffington by stripping away topsoil to reveal the chalk rock beneath. Having been celebrated since the Middle Ages as one of the great ancient monuments of Britain, it was finally dated in the late 1990s, using a brand new method to determine the age of chalk figures (optically stimulated luminescence), to between 1740 and 210 BC, with a 68 per cent chance of a time between 1380 and 550. The archaeological evidence favours a point towards the end of that latter span, because there is little sign of activity on the hill where it was made during the Late Bronze Age, whereas at the opening of the Iron Age a fort was built directly above where the figure now sprawls.[194] Strictly speaking, it may not be a horse, as its stylized shape could conceal a dragon, cat or dog, but a horse remains the most likely, not least because a fairly similar image appears on the coins of the three tribes which, by the time that the Romans arrived, occupied territories that met roughly where the carving is situated, the Catuvellauni, Atrebates and Dobunni. That image is certainly equine, because the make of coin is derived in each case, by various stages across Europe, from the Macedonian currency which displayed the sun chariot of the god Apollo. By the time it reached Britain, nothing was usually

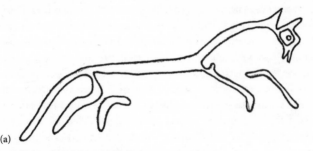

(a)

59 Figure (a) is the form of the famous, and unique, Uffington White Horse (or cat, dog or dragon). Figure (b) is taken from a coin, in the author's possession, minted by the Dobunni, one of the Iron Age tribes that may have occupied the territory in which the horse was carved. There is a basic artistic similarity, but not a close one. The image on the coin derives originally from a chariot horse on the Macedonian currency which was ultimately the inspiration for the British one, and only one wheel of the vehicle remains; that may have been repaired because the spoked wheel was a symbol of the sun, or of the sky, in northern European cosmology at the time.

(b)

left of this but a horse and a wheel, which may have had its own resonance in northern Europe as the wheel appears in Bronze Age Scandinavian rock carvings as a clear solar symbol, carried in a cart or chariot across the sky.[195] What the White Horse itself meant, however, is anybody's guess: it may, for example, have been associated with a deity, or been a banner flaunted by a particular people on their border, or a common symbol for a number of peoples, marking a place at which they could meet to trade and negotiate.[196] Nor is there any solution to the associated problem of why this particular hill figure managed to survive into the Middle Ages and beyond and how many others, like or unlike it, were allowed to become overgrown and be lost along the way.

Talk of coinage raises another difficulty: that the first coins struck by the British do show many images that are clearly those of goddesses and gods. We can be sure of this because they were copied from Continental originals, mostly Roman, and may have had no significance to the British other than indicating money. This is not to say that the coins themselves necessarily had the status of currency in the strict commercial sense. They were so limited in distribution and so often associated with ritual deposits that they may have been tokens given by rulers to their followers rather than a medium for buying and selling commodities. Indeed, it is possible that the British fully recognized the Graeco-Roman deities on the coins as divine beings, and had even become familiar with the myths and rites that the Romans attached to them, which would have given the objects themselves a further spiritual value.[197] There are also abstract designs on the coinage, and John Creighton has suggested, following the relevant tradition of interpreting Palaeolithic images, that they are like those images similar to shapes perceived by humans in altered states of consciousness; for this reason, he thought they might have been associated with Druids in their capacity as seers. It is a plausible and attractive idea, but not susceptible to proof.[198] Yet, occasional images do appear on them which seem to be those of native deities, and perhaps the most striking is on a silver one dating to the early first century AD, found in England and now in the National Museum of Wales. It shows a bearded male head with a crown bearing a wheel – perhaps once again a solar symbol – and apparent antlers rising from the sides. The antlers may, however, be part of the crown, and the wearer a king or priest rather than a god. None the less, it is a remarkable personification of the symbols which the makers associated with masculine power, human or divine.

None of the possible ceremonial sites datable to the British Iron Age has yielded a single generally agreed visual representation of a deity.[199] The figures that have sometimes been regarded as religious icons have come from other

60 This enigmatic face, god, king, chief or Druid, adorns a silver coin from the first century AD, found in Hampshire. It is now in the National Museum of Wales. The crown upon the head is decorated with antlers and a mounted wheel, perhaps a solar or celestial symbol. Around the head are abstract designs of the sort common on Iron Age coinage.

contexts, especially taking the form of wooden figurines retrieved from the locations, mostly wetlands, which have preserved them. There are just three British sites that have produced such finds with a proven date in late prehistory: Ballachulish in Argyll, Roos Carr in East Yorkshire and Kingsteignton in south Devon, spanning between them a maximum period between 728 to 352, and a minimum between 524 and 426 BC. The one from Scotland is of alder wood, and may be female although the sex is hardly empha- sized, while that from Devon has been called male and is of oak; sexual ambiguity seems the case at Roos Carr. The Ballachulish image had agate eyes and may have stood in a wicker hut in the bog where it was found. All have been taken as divine beings, but there may be other explanations, such as that they were effigies of enemies who were being symbolically drowned or interred by being deposited in such places or of criminals who should have been killed and dumped there but had escaped. The wicker structure apparently surrounding the example from Argyll may have been intended to confine it or weigh it down, rather than representing a shrine.[200] In 1967–9 about fifteen small, crudely carved stone figures were found at Garton Slack in the East Riding of Yorkshire, not far from Roos Carr. Over half had swords, and there were holes in their bases as if to

61 The carved wooden statuette found in the bog at Ballachulish, Argyll, and now in the National Museum of Antiquities of Scotland. Its appearance conveys well the difficulty of establishing the sex, let alone the nature and purpose, of these images, though this one seems to have been fashioned to be mounted on a stand.

steady them when they were set up for display. All but one lacked a head and others were badly scratched, so that their condition points to deliberate damage, before all were left in a ditch. Melanie Giles has plausibly suggested that they might have been made as dolls, gaming pieces, or images of enemies to ensure their destruction, but favours the explanation that they represented household gods or ancestors, because they had been displayed before burial. This is entirely possible, but all of the other explanations also favour a need for them to have been set upright.[201]

Anne Ross gave fresh impetus to an earlier idea that the Iron Age British, and their Irish and Continental neighbours, had a cult of the human head, as symbolic of divine and spiritual power. The evidence for this consisted of the prominence of heads on decorated metalwork and on stonework; of the existence of complete carved stone heads; and of the occurrence of human skulls in ritual deposits and apparently as decoration of some hill fort defences.[202] It remains a tenable hypothesis but thus far lacks proof, as the undoubted frequency with which the motif appears could have other explanations. Posidonius, our ancient eyewitness cited above, stated firmly that head-hunting in Gaul was simply a by-product of warfare, intended to provide trophies. Anthropological studies of recent tribal peoples who have conserved and displayed human heads have found that the practice is either explained by the same impulse or by a wish to preserve and revere parts of ancestors. Sarah Ralph and Ian Armit, who have made recent studies of the evidence – the latter more extensively – have agreed that a special treatment of the human head is apparent in Iron Age art and deposits in north-western Europe. Ralph has suggested that it could be accounted for in terms of trophy-taking, while Armit's view is that it can be explicable as that activity, but also in other contexts and periods as associated with rites of fertility and renewal, and veneration of ancestors.[203] Like so many others, therefore, this matter remains open. So does the different question of whether certain objects from the period were functional or ritual, or both, such as the polished metal mirrors, often beautifully engraved, found carefully deposited in graves, wetlands and pits. Jody Joy, who has published the best study of them, suggests that they could equally have been used for personal vanity, or in rites of divination, or to reflect the sun's rays in ceremonies.[204]

Among those who have considered the possible meanings of Iron Age imagery since the 1990s, none has continued to do so with such determination and energy as Miranda Aldhouse-Green, who has made constant attempts to break out of the constrictions of the traditional fourfold methodology outlined above. Her focus has remained on the iconography of north-western and Central Europe during the prehistoric Iron Age and the succeeding Roman period. Most of her material has been drawn from the latter, but she can easily point to continuities between the two epochs and across the different Roman provinces of the region that can be argued to represent particular styles of native imagery which mark it off from other areas of Europe. Among the common themes that she has noted are the deposition of cauldrons in marshes, perhaps holding offerings of food or drink and seeming to show a link between these objects and water with a symbolic pairing of life and death; an interest in shape-shifting between human and animal, so that motifs often combine the two forms; and a particular significance accorded to the number three, so that some kinds of object, being and character (but not all) often appear in triple form. She has shown how the blurring of lines between species was accompanied by an equivalent ambiguity in representing gender, and a disinclination to distinguish clearly between the human and divine. When human and animal were combined, special types of beast were chosen, namely horses, dogs, stags and bulls, and the stag above all: indeed, its antlers were sometimes given to female human-like figures as well as male. At the least, all this plausibly suggests a spirituality which depended on a regular sense of crossing 'natural' boundaries and of fluidity of identity, and perhaps the special status of individual experts within it who mediated between the human and other worlds. Another of Miranda Aldhouse-Green's insights is that ancient images were probably not passive objects to be contemplated and consumed as works of art, but 'dynamic tools used by the communities which produced and consumed them'. Thus the same image may have had different meanings in different contexts, while apparently similar shapes and forms could have belonged to completely different symbolic categories.[205] Such acute observations reinforce an impression that much of the content of Iron Age belief must remain forever unknown, although (and this also needs to be emphasized) the forms and imprints of it can be recovered in better and better detail.

Final Thoughts

In keeping with the general tone and preoccupations of this book, the present chapter has stressed the intractable nature of much of the evidence, and the diversity of conclusions that can be drawn from it. Despite this, it is possible to mystify Iron Age religion too much, for certain broad conclusions can be drawn with a fair degree of safety. We can be certain that the pre-Roman British believed in and honoured a large number of goddesses and gods, with powers and functions related to the natural world or to human concerns and activities, and often particular to specific localities and peoples. This is partly because the British are revealed as doing exactly this as soon as the Romans arrived among them, and partly just because all European pagans did so. Likewise, we can be sure that they practised animal sacrifice, in at least its minimal form: that the beasts consumed at festivities were consecrated to deities before being slaughtered and eaten; this is, again, because it was a universal custom across pagan Europe.[206] The remains of livestock found on Iron Age ceremonial sites, and often on other kinds of site, would probably have been the consequence of this rite. It is also possible to reconstruct the festive calendar of the ancient British, in outline, from historic records and comparative data.[207] We can be positive that it included feasting and merrymaking at midwinter, because this season was observed all over Europe as it emerges into history, and an equivalent celebration at midsummer which included protective and blessing rites involving fire, because this too was found throughout the Continent. There would also have been festivals and ceremonies to open the four seasons, and especially summer and winter, for these too were observed across large areas of northern Europe. This would represent a cycle of six major annual points of festivity, and there would probably have been others tied more functionally to the completion of especially demanding and important agricultural processes such as sheep-shearing and the grain harvest.[208]

The emphasis on the right side in burial customs and (perhaps) domestic layout is almost certainly related to a belief that it is lucky to turn to the right when moving, in the direction in which the sun moves in this hemisphere and which the modern age calls clockwise. This remained widespread in northern Europe until recent times: the Gaelic term for the sunwise – fortunate and proper – direction for ritualized movement is *deosil*. There is eyewitness testimony to its use in ancient north-western Europe from the Greek traveller Posidonius, who stated that the people of Gaul thought it reverent to turn to the right.[209] It may be noted once more, however, that no general application of it is visible in the British evidence: some burial patterns emphasized the left, perhaps because it indicated the world of the dark and the dead. We can also be certain that the pre-Roman British possessed some sort or sorts of belief in the survival of the soul after death, not only because this is also general among traditional peoples but because Greek and Roman authors noted that such a belief was held with unusual fervour among the natives of north-western Europe. They did not, however, agree on its actual content, some asserting that those natives thought souls were expected to be reborn in different bodies on this earth, while others reported a conviction that people would continue to exist with their accustomed identities and bodies, but in a parallel world.[210]

It can thus be proposed that the modern age need not be wholly ignorant of the religious system of the British upon the edge of history. We possess an outline of its most important aspects, which is coherent enough and can be sustained from historical sources. Within that, however, are still many blank spaces, which can be filled in according to individual and subjective taste, using an ever expanding body of material evidence. This is arguably not a bad point to have reached, in which all interested in the subject have both some essential common ground, and a very large remaining potential for personal instinct and inclination to operate freely in reimagining the past.

5

THE ROMAN IMPACT
TEMPLES, STATUES AND INSCRIPTIONS

THE MODERN BRITISH have always expressed mixed feelings about the Roman conquest of most of their island. On the one hand, the Romans possessed many attributes – and introduced them to large areas of Europe – which have defined progress and civilization, and indeed modernity, for most Europeans: a fully developed state with law codes, coinage, a professional army and civil service; proper towns with large public buildings built enduringly of stone; and a sophisticated literature. For their medieval successors across most of the Continent, they provided the model of what a proper form of government and culture should be. This deep respect for them, and tendency to identify with them, only increased as the modern replaced the medieval, because of three factors which affected the British more than most other peoples. The first was the growth of a standard system of collective education for the elite (which increasingly included ambitious members of the middle classes), that placed a heavy stress on Roman texts. The second was the acquisition of a colonial empire containing huge numbers of peoples with more traditional societies and cultures, the moral justification for which was one that the Romans had articulated to explain and extol their own conquests: that incorporation into that empire brought the blessings of civilization to humans who otherwise would have continued to live with all the shortcomings of savagery or barbarism. The third was the industrialization of Britain, a process in which it led the rest of the developed world, which induced a still deeper respect for the Romans' undoubted skills in engineering and mass production.

The problem with all this, which remained significant even at the apogee of the British love affair with Rome, was that the Romans had still arrived in Britain as foreign and often brutal conquerors, who slaughtered and enslaved those who resisted them and compelled obedience to a distant ruler over whose opinions and actions the natives had no control. It was very tempting to feel sympathy for the leaders of resistance to this invasion, such as Boudica, Caractacus and Calgacus, a reaction aided by the fact that the Romans themselves – whose histories are the only source of information on these figures – depicted them as heroic adversaries. During the Victorian period in which the reasons for admiration for Rome were most compelling, and the long cultural hangover from it which lasted until the middle of the twentieth century, the British provided a range of solutions to the conundrum. Some were unequivocally supportive of the Romans, and some as completely hostile to them, while many settled on a compromise, of praising them for their discipline, sophistication and technological prowess, and the British for their courage and love of freedom. In some works this took the form of a suggestion that the subsequent inhabitants of Britain had combined the best of both sets of qualities, while in others it became a classic contrast between civilization and noble savagery, with a yearning for the liberty and colour of the latter coupled with a grudging recognition that the former would, and should, always prevail. Such difficulties were always strongest when the arrival of the Roman presence in Britain was considered, and largely disappeared when attention shifted to the final phase, of its collapse. By then the Romans were Christians, a fact which caused most of the modern British to identify still more readily with them, and they could credibly (if still not to the satisfaction of everybody) be regarded as the defenders of most of the island against new, savage and heathen, attackers. Such a view of them intensified during the mid twentieth century, with the dissolution of Britain's own empire and the disappearance of several other familiar features of the nation generating profound fears among many Britons of a loss of role and identity.[1]

The passage of the world into a post-colonial phase, in the second half of the century, intensified hostility to the Roman occupation, even while it continued to play a prominent part in the British historical imagination: novelists in the 1990s and 2000s regularly treated the subject as a means of exploring the relationships between civilization and barbarism; social control and social freedom; and mainstream society and its critics. Rarely, now, did they accord the Romans much sympathy.[2] Unsurprisingly, the same pattern revealed itself in the publications of archaeologists. Few were as blatant in their linkage of past and present politics as Francis Pryor, who declared that both the Roman and British empires had 'offended against all concepts of natural justice', called the Roman conquest of Britain a 'black moment' and claimed that prehistory had given the British 'a belief in individual freedom'.[3] A different depreciation of the Roman role in Britain emphasized that the coming of imperial rule left the daily lives of the great majority of the native population completely unaffected.

It suggested that all the manifestations of Roman civilization in the island were superficial foreign importations which collapsed and disappeared as soon as imperial rule was withdrawn, leaving native customs and institutions to re-assert themselves.[4] The most common reaction to such views has been to stress the complexity of Romano-British colonial identities and reject the concepts of 'Roman' and 'native' as static, monolithic and homogeneous categories. This was a concomitant of a general scholarly tendency in the years around 2000 to regard ethnicity and identity as actively created traits, specific to particular situations. Not only did the British participate in Roman behaviour in different ways, but there was no single Roman way of life to be resisted, adopted or adapted. Roman habits were only one component of the manner in which people in the province would have constructed their own image and self-image, along with region, gender, age, occupation and class. The process by which they were adopted depended on many kinds of actor, including imperial officials and merchants, retired soldiers, and allied native rulers and nobles, who oper-ated in different ways. There could have been no common set of values and understandings that mapped out exactly what was needed to 'become Roman', let alone any agreement that one should, because Roman culture was itself a cosmopolitan fusion of influences with very diverse points of origin.[5]

When all this is acknowledged, however, there are still certain broad chrono-logical and regional patterns to be discerned. As should be obvious from the previous chapter, Roman cultural influence was already having a profound impact on south-eastern Britain, and so dividing the island into more and less Romanized zones, before the conquest. The conquest merely represented a dramatic acceleration and intensification of this process, not the commencement of it. The broad history of the occupation is also clear. Within fifty years of arrival, Roman rule had reached its greatest extent, halting at the edge of the Scottish Highlands; after that its northern frontier wavered between the Forth–Clyde and Tyne–Solway lines for another century, before finally being drawn along the latter, marked by Hadrian's Wall. This left two-thirds of Britain, including most of its mineral resources and agriculturally profitable lowlands, in Roman hands, along with the islands of Wight and Anglesey, and the Scillies. Most of what is now Scotland, and Man and the Hebrides, remained outside them, and retained a native culture little affected by Roman goods or customs: effectively, those regions were prehistoric until the early Middle Ages. Roman Britain itself is only partly within the bounds of historical time, as the relevant texts are too few and episodic to allow a full narrative of political and military events there. On the other hand, the archaeology is so rich that a social and economic history of the province can now be provided, and reveals certain major features.

One is the great size and importance of the military garrison, concentrated overwhelmingly in the north, where most of the land itself may have remained in state ownership. In the second century it numbered 55,000, making it the largest permanently stationed in any Roman province, and so it is possible that, quantitatively and perhaps qualitatively, the army was proportionately more significant to British life than it was to any other part of the empire.[6] We know more about it than any other aspect of Roman-British society, because it has left the most evidence, in histories, inscriptions and material objects. It introduced or increased the quantity of Roman goods in many parts of the island, stimulating local industries and attracting imports.[7] Another spectacular aspect of Roman rule was the foundation of planned towns across the lowlands, with a street grid, ruling councils, and imposing public buildings of the classical Mediterranean style. A third consisted of the network of state-built and state-maintained roads, linking towns and forts and equipped with milestones and rest-houses. It remains true that even wealthy rural householders showed little sign of buying or being given Roman objects during the first two centuries of imperial rule, a fact which fits the argument for superficial Romanization. Another point in favour of that is the apparent failure of the planned towns. In comparison with those elsewhere in the empire, they attracted few public constructions or inscriptions, and their existing communal buildings were decaying badly by the third century, when they were also in serious decline as commercial and industrial centres. None the less, even in this earlier period Roman government would have altered the existence of all its British subjects in certain respects, disarming them, replacing their accustomed rulers, imposing systematic and formal taxation upon them, and perhaps placing them in contact with large numbers of foreign peoples, constructions and institutions. They would also have been submitted to, or enabled to embrace, a widespread process of continued farming improvements, including further woodland and marsh clearance, deeper ploughing and an expansion in both the quantity and diversity of cereal crops. This, and prolonged internal peace, allowed the population of the province to increase to what was almost certainly a new level, of three to four million, which would probably not be surpassed again until the Tudor period. Such a conclusion has been made possible by recent aerial surveys which have revealed a hitherto unsuspected density of settlement.[8]

During the third and fourth centuries, the economic and social underpinning of the province altered significantly. Britain became one of the most peaceful and prosperous parts of an empire beset by civil war and invasion, and the institutions which had been the most obvious markers of the Roman presence there changed in nature and relative importance. The size of the garrison fell to between ten and twenty thousand, but it also became more static and hereditary, producing a civilian community numbering 50,000 to 200,000 in the northern military zone which was devoted to supporting and producing soldiers. While the planned towns lost importance as commercial, industrial and civic centres, they retained it as administrative foci and gained some as gathering places for the local aristocracy. Increasingly, the lowlands were divided up into estates based on large country houses, the villas, of which around five hundred existed by the fourth century and which were decorated and equipped in the manner of the Roman elite throughout the empire. Across the lowland areas small towns also appeared, which had considerable importance as commercial and industrial centres and dealt in goods, especially pottery, which were increasingly produced in the province but made in the Roman style. By the fourth century, these goods were found even in ordinary dwellings in the countryside, as were coins, as low-value currency issues now penetrated most parts of British society and brought it into a money economy for the first time. Villages multiplied as part of the same process, and it could be said that by the middle of the fourth century Britain had become as Romanized as any other province, retaining a tincture of native culture but recognizably part of a system of loyalties, attitudes, commodities and values which extended as far as the Sahara, the Euphrates and the Danube.[9]

This, then, is the context for a study of Romano-British religion. There is reasonably good evidence for the nature of that in Rome itself, and the same religion suffused the political, military and administrative structures that the Romans brought to Britain, and the lives of many of the personnel who operated them.[10] It depended on the concept of a huge number of divine or semi-divine beings, some of which were attached to particular peoples and human activities and some to particular natural forces or places. It was safe for a Roman to assume that an individual guardian was associated with each significant feature of a given landscape and that, if her or his local name were not known, this being should be honoured simply as the *genius loci*, the spirit of the place. An individual *genius* also attached itself to every man between birth and death (and a *juno* to every woman), acting as a divine counterpart and guardian. This made it a natural duty for all inhabitants of the empire to honour and encourage the guardian spirit (in this case usually called the numen) of the reigning emperor, both to care for him and to enable him to rule well. An especially good ruler was revered upon death by the belief that he had become one with his numen and could now be granted the honours of a divinity (a distinction also accorded to a few empresses). Houses and fields had their attendant spiritual guardians, the lares and penates, to whom each household would pay regular respects. Roman deities tended to be functional: thus, there were ten goddesses (or perhaps ten aspects of the same goddess as the distinction is not made clear), who presided over different processes in cereal farming. Five more deities, goddesses and gods, were concerned with the broader activities of agriculture, down to Sterculinus, the god who had a special care for manure. Childbirth, often a complex and potentially lethal business, attracted the protection of seven goddesses and a god, who specialized in different moments and aspects of it. Each military unit was expected regularly to honour a list of about a dozen divinities with a particular interest in war. There was, strictly speaking, no native Roman mythology about divine beings – no home-grown traditions of their origins, deeds and family relationships – although Greek myths about equivalent deities became attached to those of Rome as part of the general Roman acquisition of many traits of Greek culture. The Greeks themselves had acquired this way of thinking about divinities from the Near East, and it therefore seems likely that the peoples of north-western Europe, including the ancient British, were no more inclined to make stories about their deities, spontaneously, than the Romans had been.

New cults were welcome in Rome, as long as they did not break the law or keep the neighbours awake, and were formally approved by the Senate. These could take the form of the worship of long-revered deities from foreign lands, arriving in the city, or of new forms of reverence paid to divinities who had just revealed themselves to devotees. Likewise, Romans travelling abroad would both take with them the rites dedicated to their familiar divine patrons and expect, very often, to honour the deities of the lands which they entered. This general tolerance of religions not their own came during the imperial period to have one notorious exception: Christianity, because it rejected the whole premise upon which the pagan Roman religious system depended, by condemning all spiritual beings except its own god and his servants as demons. The Christians' hostility extended to a refusal to honour the emperor's numen, which to most Romans was to disown membership of the state. Such a direct clash of ideologies sometimes resulted in savage persecution of Christians, but this seems to have been officially directed in a total of less than ten of the two hundred and fifty years in which Christianity existed under pagan rulers in the western half of the empire. Roman paganism had no theology in the normal sense of the word, the great questions about the nature of the cosmos being left to philosophers, who were divided between competing schools which provided different answers. The most pressing question, for most humans, of the fate of the individual person-ality after death, was likewise answered in many different ways. Between them the schools covered most of the answers proposed by humans throughout recorded time, including oblivion, a passage to a place of reward or punishment, rebirth in a new body, or a universal journey to a spirit world.

Participation in religion was very much an individual choice. People could ignore it more or less completely, as long as they did not attack or mock the rites of others. Most would honour their household spirits and take part in the great seasonal festivals of their community, dedicated to particular local deities. In addition, they would probably try to contact one in moments of particular need related to issues of health, occupation, family, movement or general fortune. The most critical of these moments would provoke votive offerings, gifts promised to an individual divine helper if the latter granted a request. Some people, in whom the religious instinct was especially strong, would place themselves for life in the care of a specific goddess or god, or a specific set of deities. Such a spectrum of dealings was a perfect reflection, in the divine sphere, of relations with powerful human beings. Increasingly, as the imperial epoch progressed, the most dedicated of these inherently devout individuals entered the growing number of mystery religions, centred on a particular deity or divine couple, such as Mithras, Isis and Serapis, Dionysus, or Cybele and Atys. Unlike other forms of religion, these were carried on in private shrines, by worshippers who underwent training and initiation, and sometimes progression through a series of grades to which learning was incrementally revealed. Their rites were usually secret, and those who engaged in them could not merely achieve an unusual intensity of religious experience and feel themselves to be part of a spiritual elite, but could receive assurance of a better chance of well-being in both life and death. These mystery religions would also have afforded the practical comfort, for individuals who had a mobile lifestyle – soldiers, administrators and merchants – of a group of companions with common interests and experiences, in most parts of the empire to which they were posted or needed to travel; an ancient equivalent, to some extent, of Freemasonry.

The variety of deities was to some extent balanced by a greater conformity of sacred places and actions. Places of worship generally consisted of an enclosure, separating off the mundane world, which contained a platform on which was erected a temple, with a cult statue of the deity to which it was dedicated. The temple itself was regarded mostly as a local home for the goddess or god concerned, and as a setting for prayer but not for routine ritual. That was usually concentrated on a stone altar built inside the enclosure and away from the temple, at which the key rite of Roman paganism was performed: sacrifice. This was in essence the presentation of a gift to the deity concerned; this could consist of the burning of incense, or the offering of flowers, fruit, or libations of wine, honey and other fluids. Blood sacrifice, the giving of an animal life, was the most prestigious, as meat was the most expensive and valuable food. Very little of it was sacrificed in the modern sense, because generally only the least edible parts of the animal, and some of the internal organs, were burned as offerings to the deity in whose honour it was slaughtered. The rest was consumed by the worshippers, so that the rite was in fact the consecration of a feast. Moreover, the animal was expected to be killed without showing either pain or fear, so that the act of slaughter was probably a good deal more humane than those inflicted in the normal processes of preparing domestic animals for the table. Blood sacrifice was in theory a ritual carried out only by men, who were responsible for the conduct of all public religious ritual, but women could officiate for themselves or each other and assist or accompany male rites.

This was a form of religion which embodied no divine revelation and depended on no books, dogmas or orthodoxy, resting instead entirely on prescribed ceremonies. It had no specific founder or leader, no concept of conversion, made no demands on foreigners and was centred on the community and not on the individual. It left ethics to society to prescribe, freed worshippers to decide how to venerate their own deities, and aimed for earthly well-being, not salvation in the next life. It had no concept of sin, though a very active one of blasphemy and impiety. Every citizen could act as a priest, and every public act was a religious one. Though there were specialist priests and priestesses who offered their skills for hire or as a social duty, they did not act as mediators or theologians and had no personal sanctity; indeed, they usually had mundane daily occupations. In the mystery religions they seem to have needed a greater sense of vocation and to have acted more as mentors, but this was apparently only a difference of degree. Although the religions of Rome are better recorded than those of anywhere else in ancient Western Europe, there is not much sign that they were significantly different from those in the rest of the Continent.[11] Apart from the greater enthusiasm for mythology, Greek religions – about which we know at least as much – were very similar in all basic respects, and indeed, save for a greater emphasis in places upon a professional priesthood, so were those across the entire ancient Near East. To the British, there would have been nothing very alien about the essence of the religious system that their Roman conquerors brought with them.

Given this context, it is time to examine some of the practical problems involved in determining the nature and extent of the Roman impact on native British religious beliefs and practices. Guy de la Bédoyère has assembled a checklist of these, beginning with the problem, general to archaeology, that so much of the evidence consisted of materials which would not survive in the record: altars of wood or turf, wooden vessels, and offerings of food, drink, blood, incense, ashes or crops.[12] He also warned that the evidence for Britain may be distorted by the concentration of it in the most Romanized of sites, above all military stations but also towns and villas. It may be added that the nature of the concentrations are mismatched, as most of the inscriptions are from the north and west of the province and most of the temples and burials in the south and east. Guy de la Bédoyère's conclusion was that 'religion in Roman Britain is a subject we barely understand'.[13] On the other hand, there is certainly plenty of data, for more temples and shrines are mentioned in inscriptions from the province than any other class of building, and altars and tombstones account for the vast majority of its inscribed stones. Large numbers of structured deposits have now been discovered, and extensive cemeteries, with an array of other material finds that may be related to ritual. With all the caveats that have just been entered, an attempt can now be made to ascertain what is currently known of Romano-British religion.

Deities

During the 1980s and early 1990s, experts in that religion were divided over the emphasis that should be placed on the Roman and British components of it: Miranda Aldhouse-Green, Graham Webster and Guy de la Bédoyère were of the opinion that the conquerors merely laid a classical Mediterranean veneer over the native system, while Martin Henig and Joan Alcock believed that the latter was more thoroughly Romanized.[14] The debate petered out inconclusively, largely because of the nature of the evidence. The bulk of this comes from the most Romanized sites, as said, and not enough is known of pre-Roman British religion to allow Romanization to be measured against it with any precision. There is no way of knowing whether it was a Roman or a native who carried out a particular religious act, or erected a particular religious structure, unless the person concerned recorded her or his identity. In the majority of cases that did not happen, and where it did, a Roman name may hide a Romanized Briton. With regard to a question which lay at the heart of the debate – that of which deities were honoured in the province – the archaeological record shows a mixture of native and imported cults, varying not just by the ethnic identity of the worshipper but by social class, region and even individual. The result is to provide enough material to support either side of the debate, and not enough to resolve it.

Certainly Roman deities are well represented in Britain, above all Jupiter, Mars and Mercury who between them covered most human concerns including government, weather, trade, travel, farming, war and death. Hercules, Venus, Diana, Silvanus and Minerva also occur. They are found most often in East Anglia and the Midlands and the northern military zone – the most Romanized areas – but are scattered across most of the province.[15] The imperial cult also features to an extent fairly typical of an outlying part of the empire, with colleges established by merchants to carry it on in the cities of London, York and Lincoln, dedications to it in East Anglia, Sussex and Oxfordshire, and small busts of emperors proving that it was maintained in rural areas of what is now eastern England. A massive temple was constructed at the town of Colchester to honour Claudius, the ruler who had ordered and presided over the establishment of the province.[16] Some of the mystery cults also entered Britain during the period of Roman rule.[17] That of the Asian goddess Cybele and her son Atys is attested at London by finds in the River Thames, a bust of the god and a serrated bronze clamp decorated with busts of the two deities,

62 A classical Roman deity: the god Mars, represented in a bronze figurine commissioned by the Colasuni brothers, Bruccius and Caratius, who also dedicated it, loyally, to the guardian spirits of the emperors of Rome. Found in the East Midlands.

63 This image illustrates well the difficulties of interpreting many representations of deities in the province. Found on an altar in the northern military zone, it must therefore depict a god. Is it, however, Mars, and the protrusions on the head a helmet; or wings, in which case he would be Mercury; or horns, for a local divinity who bore them; or none of the above? It is impossible to tell. Drawn from an exhibition in the Carlisle Museum.

which may have been used to castrate the priests of the cult; this surrender of their manhood would have been the focal event of initiation into its service. The Graeco-Egyptian religion of the goddess Isis and her consort Serapis was given a temple at York, while an image, an inscribed jug and an amulet all dedicated to Isis may point to its presence in and around London. Most firmly established was the cult of the saviour god Mithras, which was said to have come from Persia. In the Western Roman Empire it was a closed religious society of men, especially soldiers, and its characteristic long rectangular shrines have been found at London and York, on Hadrian's Wall and at the fort which guarded the Menai Strait between Wales and Anglesey and was the forerunner of the medieval town of Caernarvon. Altars dedicated to Mithras have been found at Musselburgh, to the east of Edinburgh. The deity associated with a mystery religion who was apparently most widespread in Britain was the Greek god Dionysus, under his Roman name of Bacchus, who is represented by statues and statuettes and on incised vessels, mirrors and mosaics. However, as patron of wine, he may simply have been celebrated in the province as a general symbol of festivity and encouragement to it, rather than as a focus for special rites. It seems likely, however, that it was his mysteries that were being indicated in a mosaic in the villa at Brading, on the eastern side of the Isle of Wight, because another mosaic pavement there seems to portray the mysteries of the

64 A thoroughly Roman figurine of a thoroughly Roman goddess: the 'Venus of Verulamium', found in the ruins of that city and now in the museum there, near St Albans. Drawn from a replica in the possession of the author.

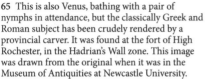

65 This is also Venus, bathing with a pair of nymphs in attendance, but the classically Greek and Roman subject has been crudely rendered by a provincial carver. It was found at the fort of High Rochester, in the Hadrian's Wall zone. This image was drawn from the original when it was in the Museum of Antiquities at Newcastle University.

goddesses Demeter and Persephone at Eleusis in Greece, and yet another the rites of Cybele: the owner was clearly a connoisseur of initiatory traditions.

The mention of Asiatic, Egyptian and Greek divinities signals another aspect of religion in Roman Britain: that many goddesses and gods arrived in it from parts of the empire far distant from Rome. A few came directly from the east to the northern forts and the settlements that served them, such as Hercules of Tyana, who was honoured, with an attendant priestess, at the town that became Corbridge, near Hadrian's Wall.[18] Many more derived from the other northern provinces, such as Gaul and Germany, which provided many military units and settlers to Britain, both because of their relative proximity to it and because their people were better accustomed to the climate. The most important were the Matres, the 'Mothers', who were venerated across a wide expanse of the northern Roman Empire with an epicentre in the Rhineland. Images of them took the standard form of three stately ladies, standing or (more usually) seated in a row, and often holding dishes, bread, fruit or flowers. Sometimes one of them, in the same form, was shown alone. They were especially popular with soldiers serving in the British garrison, all but eleven of their fifty or so dedications or representations from the province having been found on military sites; and indeed no other deities attracted such spontaneous enthusiasm among the occupying army. It seems that they functioned as protecting and

66 The famous relief of Mithras, the deity at the centre of the most celebrated of Roman mystery religions, slaying the bull which represented cosmic darkness, which once decorated the temple of Mithras at London. It was the gift of a veteran of the Second Legion.

nurturing figures, perhaps of a kind profoundly reassuring to people caught up in the mobility and insecurity of military life. There is, however, no literature on them which could explain their nature and popularity, and this lack also prevents certainty as to whether it is always the same goddesses who are being represented: inscriptions often honour them as specifically the Mothers of particular countries or institutions.[19]

Another importation from the Rhineland and who seem to have originated in the district around Trier and were sometimes associated in carvings with one of the Mothers, were the enigmatic *Genii cucullati* or 'hooded spirits'. These were also usually shown as a trio of figures, standing facing the viewer and characterized by the fact that all wear the hooded cloak or *cucullatus* popular in the northern provinces of the empire. About twenty reliefs of them have been found in Britain. At times, across their whole European range, representations of them carry swords, eggs or loaves, and their associations seem, like those of the Mothers, to have been with benevolence and protection.[20] Precisely the same qualities were manifested by another divinity apparently imported from Gaul, the goddess Rosmerta, 'the Good Giver', who was represented with an axe, apparently to sum up her role as a guardian, and a barrel of food or drink or a butter churn, representing her provision of plenty.[21] Images that strongly resemble her have been found in and around the Cotswold Hills,

67 A typical icon of the enigmatic Matres, or Mothers, shown in characteristic bountiful mode seated with trays of what look like loaves of bread upon their laps. This one was found at Cirencester and is now in the Corinium Museum there.

68 In contrast to the 'classical' image of the Matres at Cirencester (left), this one, from the precinct of Sulis Minerva, at Bath, seems to show the same sort of goddesses in a much cruder form more native to north-western Europe. It is now in the Roman Baths Museum.

which is also the area in which the Matres and the *Genii cucullati* are most commonly recorded outside the northern military zone. Why civilians should have adopted these Continental deities in that particular western region of Britain is a question to which there is no easy answer. The area concerned was the heartland of a British tribe called the Dobunni, who may have taken especially to these foreign deities, perhaps because they had some of their own who corresponded to them. On the other hand, wealthy refugees from Gaul and the Rhineland may have settled in the Cotswold region in the third century, when their own provinces were badly disrupted by invasion and civil war, and brought their divine protectors with them. The problem sums up in miniature the whole difficulty of using the occurrence of deities as evidence for the extent of Romanization. Some goddesses and gods from northern Europe made an impact more broadly in the civilian areas of the south and east, and perhaps the most important of these was that represented by the figurines known to scholars as 'pseudo-Venuses'. They were small statuettes of a pretty nude woman, standing coquettishly like the Roman goddess of sexual love, Venus, and her Greek counterpart Aphrodite. They were mass-produced in Gaul, apparently for purchase by individuals, and are found in Britain in houses, shrines and graves.[22] Their nature and purpose are unknown: it could be, for example, that they were images of a Gaulish love goddess, or even of Venus herself, and believed to confer success in romance or sex; or aids to rites

69. These are the mysterious *Genii cucullati*, or 'hooded spirits', who, despite their sombre garb and expressions, seem always to have a benevolent and protective nature. On this relief from Daglingworth, in the Cotswolds, now in the Corinium Museum, they seem to be carrying swords and guarding one of the Matres.

of religion or magic intended to assist with specifically female medical problems. The god from northern Europe who is best recorded in the civilian zone was Toutatis, whose name seems to mean 'protector of the people' and whose cult was found all along the Danube and Rhine frontier. His name is found in Britain on two plaques and a potsherd, from Hertfordshire, Hadrian's Wall and Essex, but above all on rings, upon which he was recorded more than any other deity in the province. Sixty-eight have been found so far, all produced in British workshops and almost all from the East Midlands, above all Lincolnshire.[23]

In contrast, it is notable that not all of the favourite divinities of the northern Roman provinces achieved a significant presence in Britain. Belenus, the chief god of Noricum, the region which essentially became modern Austria, was popular westwards as far as Gaul but represented in Britain only by one engraving on a tile.[24] Sucellus, 'the Good Striker', a much-loved Gaulish god whose symbols were a hammer and a barrel, is mentioned on a single ring found at York.[25] Another major god of the Gauls was one depicted seated with his legs crossed under his body, large stag's antlers, one or more of the heavy twisted neck ornaments called torques, and a heavy sack or purse (though not all these features appeared in every one of his images). He strongly moved the imagination of

71. Another divine Continental enigma who achieved popularity in Roman Britain: one of the clay 'Venus' figurines mass-produced in Gaul. This one was found in the Walbrook at London and is now in the Museum of London.

70. To judge by her usual trappings, of axe and tub, and her association with her Roman consort Mercury, this is the Continental goddess Rosmerta, transplanted to the Roman colony of Gloucester, where this relief is now in the city museum.

nineteenth-century French scholars, who gave him the name 'Cernunnos', probably meaning 'the Horned One', from a relief found underneath the cathedral of Notre-Dame at Paris.[26] Some doubts have been expressed about this identification, on the grounds that the Paris relief shows a figure with short horns unlike the spreading antlers of the cross-legged god (and may have, indeed, lacked the crossed legs, as he is shown only from the chest up). Nor is the name itself certain, as the slab is broken on one side, and it will never be known if there was a letter 'C' at the beginning.[27] None the less, a widespread impression of his importance – by that name – pervaded the English-speaking world, largely because of Margaret Murray, in the 1930s, who made him the best known of the horned (or antlered) gods of north-western Europe to modern people.[28] In Britain the cross-legged, antlered god is represented only by a single, possible, relief, from Cirencester. It is in the right area – the Cotswolds – for a Gaulish deity, and has some of the characteristics of the one (rightly or wrongly) called Cernunnos, but the identification is not certain, not least because the relief is very worn.[29] Britain also almost lacked Epona, a divine patroness of horses from Gaul who achieved great popularity in the Western Empire, especially among cavalry regiments: inscriptions to and images of her are found as far south as Africa and as far east as Hungary.[30] Only two dedications are recorded to her in

72. This relief was discovered at the shrine of Coventina at Carrawburgh on Hadrian's Wall, and may portray three different aspects of the goddess herself, or the goddess flanked by attendant nymphs, or three nymphs who were honoured as separate divinities within Coventina's complex. It is now in the museum at Chesters fort, in the care of English Heritage.

Britain, however, both from northern forts, plus two probable and two possible images of her from the southern half of the province.[31]

One of the most interesting aspects of Romano-British religion is that newcomers from the rest of the empire commonly honoured many of the native deities of the British and encouraged the natives themselves to continue to do so. The arrival of the Roman custom of regularly making images of divine beings in stone and metal, and written dedications to them in the same durable materials, effectively reveals these Iron Age goddesses and gods to history. Graham Webster has drawn attention to a sequence of them, spaced out along the Hadrian's Wall zone. The god who represented the River Tyne was honoured where the frontier highway crossed it at modern Chesters, as a reclining, mature, bearded male with flowing robes. The goddess Coventina was the centre of another aquatic cult at the fort at Carrawburgh, where a clutch of springs sacred to her received intense devotion from all ranks among the soldiers stationed there. A probable icon of her from the site shows her reclining in stately classical fashion, with a similar robe to that of the river god. The Irthing Valley to the west was the territory of the god Cocidius, whom the army along that stretch of the wall identified with Mars and Silvanus, the Roman gods of war and wild nature respectively. He is portrayed as a stout figure in armour and bearing arms. Still further west in Cumbria was Belatucadrus. His name means 'the bright beautiful one' in the native Brythonic language, though the probable pictorial representations of him (admittedly not absolutely certain) show a

73. Given the appearance of a bird in armour by crude craftsmanship, this is in fact the warrior god Cocidius, from the Irthing Valley of the Hadrian's Wall zone, as portrayed on a silver plaque found at the Bewcastle fort. It is now in the Carlisle Museum.

crudely depicted naked horned being with a huge nose and penis, carrying spear and shield: dedications to him suggest that he attracted a following from a lower social class than Cocidius. At the fort of Benwell, on the eastern stretch of Hadrian's Wall, was the only known shrine to Antenociticus, another horned god, but with gentler features; and one adopted by high-ranking officers.[32] The pattern seems to be one of intense localism, with deities of different sex and personality being associated with territories which could be a score of miles wide or confined to a single site. The military men stationed across it perhaps adopted the worship of the divinities whom they encountered there from a mixture of personal liking for them as characters and a belief that they would afford good protection and favour in the terrain over which they presided.

Surveying the evidence for native British deities, as revealed on Romano-British sites, it is possible to make a case, that goddesses tend to be associated more with the natural world and gods with human activities and functions. Certainly female divinities seem to be more closely linked to water: Coventina has been mentioned, while Sulis was honoured as the indwelling spirit of the hot spring at Bath; Verbeia of the River Wharfe; Belisima of another Pennine river, the Ribble; while the medicinal wells at Buxton in the Peak District were Aquae Arnemetiae, 'the waters of the goddess of the sacred precinct'.[33] However, there were also water gods, such as that of the Tyne, and Condatis, who presided over a meeting of rivers in what is now County Durham, and others connected to natural places, such as Rigonemetis who was associated with a patch of land in what became Lincolnshire.[34] Furthermore, the evidence itself is too patchy to allow of any certainty. Most of the deities revealed by Roman-British inscriptions are merely names, and most of the pictorial representations of them are anonymous. The identities and roles of the individual goddesses portrayed with a palm branch at Caerwent, or with apples at Cirencester, or with a horn of plenty at Gloucester, or with a spear at Lemington in the Cotswold Hills (to choose just four examples from one region, around the lower Severn basin), are equally mysterious.[35]

Understanding the functions of native divinities is usually very difficult, even when there is plenty of evidence. It has often been presumed, for example, that Sulis was a patron of healing, because her spring at Bath was frequented in later historic times by people seeking cures from its mineral-rich waters. This may well have been the case, but there is actually no firm evidence of it in the many finds from the site. All testify, instead, to her association with a much fiercer nature, such as the many lead tablets which call on her to curse enemies, and the miniature replica of a war catapult found with them in her spring. It may be that she was thought to personify the fiery spirit which heated up the water, and so was considered an appropriate deity for war or vengeance (which would itself make the apparent absence of military goddesses more doubtful). The Romans associated her with their own Minerva, goddess of both war and handicrafts. Similar problems attend horned gods, of whom the British seem to have been fond. They are recorded especially well on the northern frontier, where three have already been noted, and the incoming soldiers seem to have found such aggressive figures attractive; but they are also found across the centre and south of the province. The horns that they wore were those of bull, ram, goat or (much more rarely) stag. The Greeks and Romans also had horned gods, such as Pan and Faunus, but these were deities of the remote countryside, much less prominent in worship than other forms of divinity. What is less easy to conclude is what the horns signified. They could be simply symbols of strength and power; or of wild nature; or of a pastoral economy based on herds and flocks. In some of the cruder or more weathered images, they could indeed be intended to represent helmets or wings, so that a number might even be icons of the Roman wing-headed god Mercury.[36]

Apparent native war gods such as Belatucadrus and Cocidius were honoured in Roman Britain apparently without difficulty, although they had presumably once been invoked against Rome. War goddesses seem harder to find among the British, though Sulis may have been one, and so may Brigantia who will be discussed below: certainly they were prominent in many ancient European and Near Eastern religions. The one most famed in traditional histories of Britain is also the most problematic: Andate or Andraste, the favourite deity of Boudica, queen of the Iceni tribe of East Anglia, who launched the greatest rebellion against Roman rule in the island. This goddess features (under both names) in a history written by an aristocrat living in southern Italy called Dio Cassius, a century and a half after Boudica's time; or rather, in a summary of that history made at least seven centuries later still. This text stated that the goddess's name meant 'Victory', and that captured Roman women were sacrificed to her, with barbarous tortures, in her sacred grove.[37] None of these details is found in the account of the rebellion by Tacitus, writing a hundred years closer to the event (but still a generation later), and there is no way of knowing how reliable Dio Cassius's source of information was, or indeed what it was. When the surviving versions of his history can be checked against earlier texts, the distortions in his version are very apparent: a comparison of his account of Julius Caesar's Gallic War with Caesar's original one is a case in point. The historical status of this goddess therefore remains unconfirmed, and the two contexts in which the references to her appear in the history – in a reported speech which no Roman could have heard, and an atrocity story – are among those in which truth was most likely to be embroidered or evaded by ancient writers.

One means of assimilating native and Roman religion, which has attracted much attention from scholars in recent years, was to produce hybrid deities, in which a native one was identified with a Roman one with equivalent character-istics. Cocidius has already been cited here as an example of this practice. The most popular Roman divinity in the pairings was Mars, who functioned in Roman mythology as a general protective figure associated with war, farming and government. The Roman god of healing, music and the arts, Apollo, was coupled in the northern forts with Maponus, who was presumably another such deity of skills. The woodland and hunting god Silvanus was linked to three British or Gaulish gods, and Mercury, patron of commerce, travel and educa-tion, with one. This was a decidedly British patterning, for in Gaul, where the same tactic was adopted, Mercury was by far the most popular Roman divinity for identification with local gods. As he was also found quite widely in Britain by himself – and was made the consort of the goddess identified as Rosmerta – this may simply mean that the Britons had fewer divinities of Mercury's kind than the Gauls. The tactic was much rarer in the case of goddesses, but Minerva, Roman patroness of war and handicrafts, was twinned prominently with Sulis at the great temple complex built around the hot spring at Bath; her dedications furnish eight of the eleven known cases of a linkage of a native with a Roman female deity. As Jane Webster and Amy Zoll have emphasized, this sort of pairing was a relatively rare exercise, representing just 8 per cent of the more than 900 references to deities from the province recorded by the mid 1990s. On the other hand, it was found in a quarter of those from its southern half, and, to play the game of statistics from a different starting point, 65 of the 246 deities with names in Celtic languages recorded in Roman Britain were paired with a

Mediterranean deity (26 per cent). Twelve more were portrayed beside such a
deity, in a visual if not a written linkage. Jane Webster has suggested that the
pairing of deities may have been an imposition by Rome, and thus a demonstration of its power, rather than a dialogue between native and newcomer.
Amy Zoll has drawn attention instead to the lack of any evidence for official or
social pressure to match divine beings in this way, and of much for the fact that
the process was a matter of choice for individuals and small groups.[38] We have
in fact no reliable evidence of how this occurred, or the reasons for it.

A final complication in the exercise of determining what the treatment of
deities can tell us about Romanization is that of knowing which divine figures
actually were native to Britain. Along the whole northern frontier of the Roman
world, the wheel was the symbol of the sky, representing either the sun in
particular, or the whole circle of the heavens. When associated with a god in
this huge zone, from Britain to the Danube Valley, it indicates very firmly that
the deity concerned is a celestial one; and indeed at two military installations in
the Hadrian's Wall complex, and one site in the Cotswolds, it is found with
images of divine males. The problem is that in no case is the god concerned
named. Conversely, at two places in East Anglia, the wheel motif was found on
metalwork associated with a cult of the Roman sky god Jupiter.[39] In the other
cases, therefore, we may be looking at good evidence for a native British equivalent, or for one or more imported from other northern provinces of Rome, or
simply at a linkage of the northern European symbol of the sky with Jupiter
himself, who would then be the god represented in every case. Similarly, the
direct association of Coventina with the springs at Carrawburgh would seem to
suggest a cult concentrated on that single natural feature; but dedications have
now been found to her at Narbonne in southern France, and in north-west
Spain, while all her worshippers in Britain who identified themselves on dedications came from Germany or the Netherlands.[40] Either she was a Continental
deity who came to be transplanted to the Cheviot Hills, or else her worship was
taken over from Britain to the European mainland. Likewise, more inscriptions
survive to Maponus in Britain than on the Continent, but in the former they all
derive from the northern military zone, and most are the work of high-ranking
officers, while in the latter they were dedicated by civilians. His cult may therefore have been imported to Britain.[41] Under Roman rule a goddess called
Brigantia was venerated in the northern part of the British province, as
patroness of the dominant tribe there, the Brigantes. She may indeed have been
its main deity before the Romans arrived, but it is also possible that Rome itself
created the cult of Brigantia, as a personification of the new unit of local government that it imposed upon the tribe.[42] Even the origin of Sulis, the goddess
of the hot spring at Bath who was twinned with Minerva, has now been cast
into doubt; Guy de la Bédoyère, noting the lack of conclusive evidence for a

prehistoric cult at the spring, has suggested that she might have been first recognized and named by the Romans themselves.[43]

It must now be fairly clear that there is ample evidence for the importation of deities from elsewhere in the Roman Empire into Britain: above all those from the nearest provinces, of Gaul and Germany, but also from Rome itself and, to a lesser extent, the eastern parts of the Roman world. There is equal proof that native deities continued to be honoured under Roman rule, in large numbers, and that quite frequently these were identified with Roman divinities in an act of cultural syncretism. What cannot be decided, from this data, is how far the cults of imported goddesses and gods remained confined to worshippers who had arrived with them from outside Britain; how far the movement to 'twin' deities was encouraged or imposed as a manifestation of imperial rule; and what a relationship with most of the divine beings recorded in the province meant to most of those who engaged in it. Too often the inscriptions now preserved in museums or recorded by early antiquarians feature mere names, with no sense of context or function; while the images of deities that have survived to the present, most of them mutilated or broken, or with features dissolved by weathering, are usually even more enigmatic. Just as in the case of the pre-Roman religion of the island, we have a framework which sets out the main outlines of a system of belief and behaviour, but must rely on speculation to fill in the many gaps.

Sacred Places and People

There is a reasonable degree of certainty regarding the physical form of at least the most impressive and public settings for Roman-British worship, for between 140 and 150 temples belonging to the period have been identified. They were built in various styles, of which the classical Mediterranean one, of a large rectangular stone box fronted by a triangular pediment and bordered by columns, was the rarest. The only known example in Britain is the temple to the deified emperor Claudius at Colchester, the platform of which still supports the medieval castle; although various urban holy places had classical façades, with columns and a pediment. The most common style, used in about 45 per cent of known temples in Britain, was found across the north-western provinces of the empire and consisted of an inner stone precinct built inside an outer one of the same shape. The shape itself took various forms, of which rectangular and polygonal were the most common. It was a mode of architecture which gave good protection from the weather, and so was well suited to a more northerly climate than that of Greece or Rome, but it also continued the Iron Age tradition of sacred enclosures, found in the same region. Another form of continuity is that wherever a native shrine is known to have been still

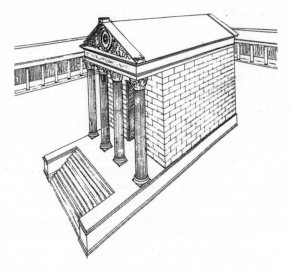

74. A conjectural restoration of the temple of Sulis Minerva at Bath, based on the classical Greek and Roman design but lacking the border of columns all about the building: those are reserved for the front, to give it a perfect façade in the Mediterranean style.

in use when the Romans landed in Britain, worship was kept up there after the conquest and generally the structure was rebuilt in stone. Most of the temples in the province were small, having comfortable space for no more than a dozen people: this would fit the pattern of seeing them as houses for deities in which one or a few worshippers might pray with the main rites taking place outside.[44]

They were initially found as commonly in both urban and rural settings: the main town built to serve the eastern sector of Hadrian's Wall, and now called Corbridge, had a whole street of them.[45] During the third and fourth centuries, however, the construction of temples in towns and cities virtually ceased, and what seem to have been rural pilgrimage temples were constructed in large numbers across southern Britain, especially in the West Country. Often these were in striking natural positions, and seem to have been established to welcome worshippers from outside their immediate vicinity. Some were near roads, while others were deep in remote countryside. Their appearance was one aspect of that boom in the economy of the Romano-British countryside in the period, of which the multiplication of villas and market towns was another. They appear to have been constructed by the owners of the land on which they stood, presumably propelled by a mixture – in varying personal degrees – of piety, a desire for prestige, and a wish to profit financially from the pilgrim traffic which they created. Although some appear to have been dedicated to a dominant goddess or god, a range of other deities was usually honoured at them as well. A sample of three such sites, chosen from a fifty-mile span of the West of England, may serve to typify their kind.

The first was in a valley of the limestone Cotswold Hills, which holds natural springs and lies in what is now north-west Wiltshire near the village of Nettleton Shrub. The presiding deity was a local one called Cunomaglus ('lover of dogs'), who may – given his canine associations – have been a patron of hunting and was identified by the Romans with their god Apollo. Also honoured there were Apollo's sister Diana, another dog-lover and a huntress, and the god of woodlands, Silvanus, who was likewise a favourite of hunters; but also Mercury and Rosmerta. The temple itself was one of a complex of buildings, of which others may have been a dormitory and a theatre.[46] The site is now just an open field. Another such field of red Cotswold earth lies on the western fringe of the hills, where their steep escarpment plunges to the Severn Valley above the village of Uley. An Iron Age shrine once stood there, where miniature spears were dedicated, perhaps to a local war god, and which was refashioned into a stone temple under Roman rule. Spears were also placed in that new building, but by the fourth century the main deity, who had a handsome cult statue, was not a military one but Mercury. Goats and cocks were offered to him, as his special animals, and also coins and rings, perhaps as suitable gifts to a god who included commerce among the activities for which he had a special care. Another of those activities was crime, and this may have combined with the fierce reputation of the original, native, divinity to make the Mercury of Uley a particular patron of devotees who wanted to curse those who had injured them: above all, thieves. He also seemingly gave shelter to a range of fellow deities, including Mars, Silvanus, Sol (the sun god), Jupiter, probably Bacchus, and a being who was either Cupid or Victory. Once more the temple stood at the centre of a set of buildings, which may have included a hostel and a shop (for the purchase of votive offerings).[47]

The third site lies on a spur of high ground on the edge of the Forest of Dean, above the village of Lydney on the opposite side of the Severn to Uley. It was excavated at different points in the nineteenth century, and again in the 1920s by the celebrated husband and wife team of Mortimer (later Sir Mortimer) and Tessa Wheeler. They left the ruins laid out for public instruction and enjoyment, which is still possible in a short period each year by permission of the landowner who maintains the lovely park around the hill and the museum which contains the finds. The Wheelers interpreted the temple as a cult centre of a British healing god called Nodens, whom the Romans twinned with Mars: he is otherwise known only from two statuettes found in Lancashire (and now lost).[48] Some of the surrounding structures were identified as a set of baths and a guest house, while the temple had a system of cubicles which were thought, on the basis of a Greek parallel, to have been places where devotees could seek divine messages

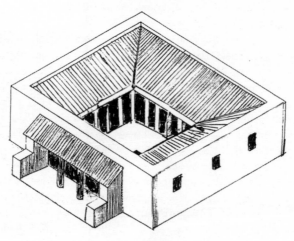

75. A conjectural restoration of the temple of Mercury at Uley in Gloucestershire which conforms to the more native form of Romano-British sacred architecture.

which came in the form of dreams as they slept. Fifteen statuettes or carvings of dogs were found in the precinct, which the Wheelers (using Greek and Italian examples) suggested might have been kept there to lick the afflicted parts of sick pilgrims, and so heal them.[49] All this remains possible, but also speculative. The cubicles may not have been used for dreams, but for private worship, or as shrines for different deities, or for insulation; or they may even have been a Christian addition to the structure after pagan worship ended there. The evidence for the site as a healing shrine consists of a miniature arm, a bone figurine of a woman with hands on waist, and an eye doctor's stamp. The arm matches the models of body parts dedicated at such establishments on the Continent by those healed in them, and the figurine is of a sort left at these places by women cured of their ailments. The arm also, however, may have held an apple, and so have been part of a statuette of Venus, while the figurine could have nothing to do with medicine and the eye doctor could simply have been looking for trade. Nodens was (as said) identified with Mars, whom the Romans did not regard as a healer, and none of the votive messages to him at Lydney mention healing: the single one which specifies a service asks him to curse a thief. His identification as the main deity at Lydney may itself be an accident resulting from the greater survival of inscriptions to him there: a bronze relief of a sun god and a stone statuette of a goddess holding a horn of plenty were also found on the site. The dogs may have been general figures of protection, or guidance, rather than associated with the curative properties accorded to them at a few places in the Mediterranean.

76. The foundations of the temple at Lydney, as preserved for visitors at the present day.

77. A drawing of the finest of the images of dogs found at the Lydney temple, a magnificent bronze deerhound, now exhibited in the museum at Lydney Park.

    Despite their more recent date, and sophisticated construction, the temples of Roman Britain are more badly ruined than many of the island's prehistoric sites, consisting – where anything now appears above the ground at all – of foundations of brick and stone. This means that the original physical experience of them is lost, let alone that of the rites conducted in or outside them. We have little sense of their height, inside or outside; of whether they were shadowy places or filled with natural or artificial light; and of what their roofs looked like. Indeed, there is no certainty in some cases whether we should be imagining a large, completely roofed building, or a cloister around a central open space. It is probable that they were equipped with lamps or torches, draperies, paintings, cut flowers and reflecting surfaces (a pool for water was laid in the Uley temple), but this remains supposition. We do not know how well heated they were, or whether music, dance, singing, chanting and the sharing of drinks went on inside. There are hints of rites by which visitors were received on arrival. At Bath, the sacred spring was enclosed in the second century to create a shadowy and private space, approached along a narrow passage which would have given access to worshippers only singly or in pairs. Brean Down is now a steep limestone peninsula jutting out into the Severn Estuary in Somerset, but in Roman times the marshes on its landward side would have effectively turned it into an island. Pilgrims to the square fourth-century temple built on its crest, where stag antlers were kept as cult objects, would probably have had to be rowed across to it, before commencing the steep climb to its precinct.[50] We do not know if these places were wrapped in reverent silence, or if their environs were surrounded by a hubbub of stalls selling refreshments, sacrificial animals and incense, and votive objects.

We are also unsure of the nature of the staff who carried out the rites at Romano-British temples and maintained them from day to day, or of how these people were supported. Haruspices, or professional diviners, are recorded at Bath, where they would have served the considerable pilgrim traffic to the sacred spring, and the name of a priest is also recorded there. Otherwise, priests are only named at two sites on Hadrian's Wall, with a 'master of ceremonies' cited in an inscription at Greetland in a West Yorkshire dale. A fine relief carved on a slab on the temporary, second-century frontier in central Scotland shows a priest clad in the classic Roman costume of a toga, pouring a libation over an altar while a pig, sheep and bull are being led towards it by an assistant.[51] Ceremonial trappings have been found at Lydney, Bath and places in Surrey, rural East Anglia and the East Midlands, which have been identified as the garb of religious officials: they consist of spiked or arched metal crowns, silver-plated diadems, headdresses with bronze chains suspended from them, metal masks, sceptres, ornamented staves, and rattles (used elsewhere in the empire to drown out distracting noises). The supposition that they were religious costumes and accessories is credible, and indeed likely, but none has so far been found in a context which firmly proves their use. In addition, the temple precincts have been found to contain axes and knives (presumably for animal sacrifice); flagons and bowls (presumably for cleansing and libation); spoons and plates (presumably for ritual feasts); metal burners (presumably for incense); and metal standards (apparently for display in ritual). All these

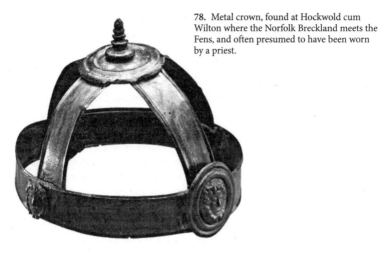

78. Metal crown, found at Hockwold cum Wilton where the Norfolk Breckland meets the Fens, and often presumed to have been worn by a priest.

attributions are logical, and may be correct, but any of them may embody a basic misunderstanding of the function of the object concerned.[52]

Just as the sites of Iron Age shrines were perpetuated as holy places, so cults located at special points of the natural landscape continued. There was no general rupture in the custom of venerating particular pieces of water, as the Romans themselves, and many peoples of their empire, fully shared the concept of sacred springs, lakes and pools. In certain areas the deposition of objects in wetlands did decline, the classic case being Wales where almost none of the pools and lakes in which deposits were made during the Iron Age seems to have continued to receive such attention: the main exception is Llyn Cerrig Bach.[53] Elsewhere, some waters marked out for attention in prehistory continued to be honoured. The Thames, beside the newly founded Roman city of London, was given metal figurines of animals, birds and deities, and thousands of coins. The Walbrook stream, which flowed into it next to the city, received more coins, ornaments and tools. Nothing had changed, except that the nature of the deposits now reflected civilian life instead of a warrior aristocracy.[54] Moreover, vigorous new aquatic cults developed under Roman rule. The reverence paid to the spring at Bath, and those of Coventina at Carrawburgh, and the goddess at Buxton, and to the deities of the Tyne and Wharfe, has already been mentioned. At Piercebridge, where a major Roman road crossed the River Tees, divers have now recovered about two thousand objects dropped into the water. They span the period of Roman rule, with a peak in the middle, and include coins, rings, brooches, and images of various deities, especially the staple Roman gods Jupiter, Mars and Mercury.[55]

The deposition of objects in pits dug into the ground also continued. Human bones became rare among them (though not, as shall be seen, wholly unknown), but the other kinds of material persisted. In the precinct of the temple built on Jordan Hill, above what is now the Dorset port of Weymouth, a chest of crude stones was placed at the bottom of either a shaft or a dried-out well, with two pots, a short sword, a spearhead, a knife, two pieces of iron and a steelyard. The shaft was then filled with seventeen successive layers of ash and charcoal, and of tiles, the latter containing the bodies of ravens, crows, buzzards and starlings, each accompanied by a coin. Just as in the Iron Age, these scavenging and carrion-eating birds, associated with death and war but also daily cleaners at human settlements, retained symbolic potency.[56] At Ashill on the clay plateau of central Norfolk, two shafts and a pit were dug into the interior of two circles of ditches. In the lower part of the deeper shaft were placed a hundred pots, almost half of them broken but the rest whole, embedded in hazel leaves and nuts. With them were a boar's tusk, pieces of antler, a whetstone, bronze clasps, fragments of wall plaster and of a wooden basket, broken sandals, charcoal, stones and a knife blade. The shallower received more pots, an ox skull and red deer antlers, and the pit a goat's skull and other animal bones.[57] They would perhaps be written off as rubbish pits were it not for the sacrifice of so much fine and intact pottery. Most of this assemblage would have been familiar from ritual depositions made at any time since the beginning of the Neolithic, and some of it from even earlier.

Rites

Only one description has survived of an actual ritual in Roman Britain, or at least one among the native British, and it may be a complete invention. It is the famous passage in the work of the naturalist Pliny, who wrote in the later first century, which asserts that 'at certain sacred rites' the wives and daughters-in-law of the Britons 'march along naked', having stained the whole of their bodies almost black with dye from the woad plant.[58] Pliny presented this as an example (among many in his work) of the folly of 'remote tribes', and there is absolutely no means of knowing how reliable his information was. He never went near Britain himself, and as he scrupulously provided source references for material which he took from earlier texts, this was clearly a piece of news that he had picked up, from a person or persons unknown. It may be a valuable piece of anthropological information, or a salacious myth concocted to mock the British at a time when the province established among them was undergoing a fresh period of expansion.

This being so, the only solid evidence for ritual behaviour in that province is provided by archaeology, and consists of special deposits of the sort made all through prehistory, and susceptible to much the same range of possible interpretations. As indicated above, these were made in familiar kinds of location, and often indeed at the same places as earlier. Coventina's springs received around 1,600 coins, thirteen altars, jewellery, figurines, pins and a human skull. The altars may have been thrown in to destroy or decommission the shrine at the end of its use, but the other items all seem to have been deposited as a part of regular worship. Those of fragile material were lowered in carefully, though whether this was to ensure that they passed to the goddess intact, or whether to immerse them in this way was believed to drown their indwelling spirit and so make them the equivalent of blood sacrifices, is unknown. Nor is it clear what the point of such devotion was, for the water of the springs has no medicinal properties, and none of the offerings was attended by inscriptions declaring their purpose. It is not really known what sort of goddess Coventina was, and all that can be securely attested is her association with water and the popularity of her cult at Carrawburgh. All that is visible there now is a bog overgrown with cotton grass and other moorland vegetation, through which the wind courses.[59] Not much more can be said about the nature of other Romano-British water deities. The case of Sulis Minerva has been considered, while at Piercebridge it has been noted that a sixth of the coins thrown into the River Tees featured imperial women. This could indicate that the ruling spirit of that water was a goddess, or that an unusual number of the devotees there were women, but nothing is certain.[60]

The appearance of towns under Roman rule, and an associated growth of population and intensification of farming, led to a much greater digging of wells, thus providing new linkages of water and ritual. The latter was particularly evident at the construction of a well and at its termination, when it was filled in or covered over, and abandoned. In general, pottery was deposited in the former stage, and pottery and animals during the second. There were clear sanitary reasons why animal matter was not put into a well before or while it was used, but the choice of beast is significant, as dogs were especially favoured, and above all in pairs: a well at Staines in the Surrey part of the Thames Valley had no fewer than eight couples. Offerings to wells at their termination could be both varied and extensive. When one was filled in at the great coastal fortress at Portchester, which dominated what would be Portsmouth Harbour in the fourth century, the soil put into it contained another pair of dogs, but also three sheep's skulls, thirteen of oxen and a Great Northern Diver, a kind of large wild bird associated with water.[61]

Much the same kind of deposits as those put into watery places were placed in pits dug into the ground, of the sort noted at Jordan's Hill and Ashill, the two cases mentioned above.[62] Once more, pots, dogs and coins predominate; and it is possible that the pottery, whether interred whole or smashed, contained offerings of food or drink.[63] As these two cases indicate, however, the pits with apparent ritual deposition vary greatly in location and contents, most having their own idiomatic character. Animal remains buried at temples contained fewer dogs and horses than at Iron Age shrines and more sheep and goats than seem to have been the rule in the actual economy of the province, though cattle and pigs were also represented. The animals were generally butchered for feasts, presumably after sacrifice at festivals, and most seem to have been killed in early summer and late autumn, the times when young and mature animals tended to be slaughtered, respectively. Some holy places showed remains of large-scale sacrificial activity, such as Uley, while others, such as Bath and Lydney, had little.[64] The pits next to a temple at Great Chesterford, a market town on the chalk hills of what is now the north-western corner of Essex, had repeated deposition of ironwork and animal remains, above all newly hatched chicks and the right sides of lambs. Young animals, therefore, were chosen for sacrifice there, and delicate pieces of gold and silver, which may be termed 'leaves', were also buried, presumably by worshippers.[65] Once more, local patterns were individual and idiosyncratic.

Towns also had such pits, of more or less the same kind as in the country-side, and a particular study of them in an urban context has been made by Michael Fulford, the most recent excavator of the city of Silchester in Hampshire, the site of which was never subsequently built over and can there-fore be intensively examined. Once more animal remains, pottery, metalwork and coins were the favourite kinds of deposit (and pots and dogs most common of all), but the forty pits and shafts which contained them varied in size and richness of material, so that some were apparently created by large and communal rites and others by small, private, equivalents. They span in date the whole of the life of the city, but naturally enough are most abundant during the peak period of its population and economic vitality.[66] Villas were another site for such apparent offerings, and indeed the boundary between these kinds of building and temples is a hazy one, as it has been argued that some, such as at Lullingstone in the Darent Valley of Kent and Chedworth in the heart of the Cotswolds, may either have been designed primarily as shrines or converted to them.[67] The usual pit deposits are found at them, but again with distinctive individual variants: one at Lullingstone contained a lamb's head, lots of pottery, thirty-four leather sandals and a complete sucking pig.[68] Boundary ditches were ready-made receptacles for such material, and those that ran outside the city wall at London and along the roads leading in and out of the city itself received clusters of it, mostly pots and animal bones (above all of dogs) as usual. The thresholds and walls of buildings were also favourite locations, and here, as in the case of wells and all the kinds of site listed above, these deposi-tions were especially common at the beginning or end of a structure's working life. Some such rites survived to modern times: in the twentieth century, and perhaps even now, shipwrights still put coins into the mast steps of new boats, following a widespread Roman custom.[69]

Despite all this richness of evidence, for the Romano-British period as for the preceding one, it remains true that one archaeologist's ritual deposit is another's rubbish pit. Guy de la Bédoyère has sounded the alarm in this case, pointing out that it is impossible to distinguish dogs deposited as offerings from those simply affectionately buried; and rites of consecration and termination from a straightforward disposal of garbage. 'Structured deposits', to him, could merely indicate an organization of waste material before it was buried: he notes that rubbish dumps of some sort had to be an intrinsic part of every settlement, and burial represented the most sanitary and easy method of getting rid of the refuse. Pits containing objects could also be hiding places for goods. De la Bédoyère therefore concluded that pit deposits did not provide evidence from which ritual activity in Roman Britain could be safely reconstructed.[70] Certainly the spectrum that runs from an undoubted landfill of waste at one end to apparently unequivocal evidence for ceremony at the other is a frighteningly complex one. In the Romano-British town of Godmanchester, next to the later county town of Huntingdon, pits were dug which were interpreted as straightforward rubbish dumps, yet at the foot of each at least two dogs were always interred, perhaps as guardians or offerings.[71] Here the opposite ends of the spectrum form a single unit.

One category of deposit in earth has attracted particular attention of late in the case of Roman Britain: the hoard of buried valuables. As seen, this was a feature of British behaviour from the Late Bronze Age onwards, and it retained or resumed its importance under Roman rule. Traditionally the hoards of fine metalwork and jewellery from the Roman province were regarded as caches of personal valuables, buried for safe keeping in difficult times and never retrieved by the unfortunate owners (or thieves). From the 1990s it became increasingly common for experts to raise the possibility that these had been interred as offerings to spirits or deities. This suggestion reflected an ever growing body of evidence, consequent on the invention of the metal detector, and one of the strongest arguments in favour of it was that the dates at which the treasures concerned were buried were usually too early – from the second to the early fourth centuries – to match times of civil war or raiding in the province that could induce such precautions. More Roman coin hoards have been found in Britain than in any other part of the empire – well over two thousand to date – and almost six hundred consist of issues minted in the late third century, when the province was a haven of peace and security. The largest ever found, at Mildenhall, where the Suffolk heathland meets the Fens, had 54,992 coins, of which the latest was minted in the year 273. The second largest hoard was detected near Frome, in the East Somerset farmland, in 2010, with 52,503 specimens of which the most recent dated from 293. By the time of its discovery the concept of such deposits as sacrifices – the Frome treasure would have represented about four years' worth of pay to a common Roman soldier – was becoming paramount.[72] None the less, it was not universally accepted, even those who emphasized it agreeing that some hoards might indeed have been personal safe-deposits, especially those from near the fall of the empire. Some scholars pointed out that buried collections of Romano-British valuables are especially common in East Anglia, one of the parts of the province most vulnerable to raiding and invasion.[73] Then in 2012 the whole dating system was thrown into confusion, as another pot full of third-century coins was reported from Bredon Hill, which rises from the Severn Valley in Worcestershire. What made this one different was that the context proved that it could not have been buried before the late fourth century, meaning that these collections of currency minted in tranquil and secure times may have been put into the ground in much more perilous circumstances a century later.[74] What this realization does for the theory of ritual deposition is yet to be seen.

The material placed in water and earth spans the spheres of communal and personal religious behaviour. The two are often difficult to disentangle, but at times it is possible to identify the relics of an act as belonging firmly to the latter sphere. At Wasperton, for example, beside the River Avon in central Warwickshire, a sandstone block was uncovered in 1983. Somebody had carved the word *Feliciter* (For luck) upon one side, and placed the stone with the carved part facing down. Then a fire had been lit on the upper one, within red deer antlers set in a square, before the stone, antlers and ashes were buried.[75] They are clearly remnants of a rite designed to bring personal good fortune, perhaps from underworld beings, but how, or why, or by whom, can never be known. Other forms of personal religion are embodied in portable objects, such as rings, amulets, bracelets, gems and pots, or house decorations such as mosaics. These are inscribed with the names of a large number of deities, all from outside Britain. Some are from Rome itself, such as Minerva, Bacchus, Hercules, Fortuna, Ceres, and the Dea Panthea (a figure developed under the empire who represented all goddesses), while others, such as Zeus of Heliopolis, Serapis, Isis and Zeus Ammon, came from the eastern provinces; above all, Egypt. The only possibly British figure to feature in such private settings is Brigantia, who, as mentioned, might have been a Roman creation; though a number of anonymous images of goddesses and gods in such contexts may conceal others. A lot of the jewellery may have been brought into Britain by people arriving from the Mediterranean basin, who wanted their familiar divine patrons with them; and much of the rest, and the pottery, may have been inscribed by them once they were in Britain. The mosaics, however, were all or almost all made in the province, and so the designs on them must have been commissioned by wealthy people who were either of immigrant stock or wished to be identified with the wider Roman world. Certainly the mosaic factories at Cirencester, capital of the Romano-British West Country, used images of Orpheus and Venus as their trademarks, so the purchase of them need not have indicated religious belief. Some motifs were very standardized, and given different attributes by the vendors or purchasers: the same armed female figure, for example, could in different contexts be labelled Minerva, Brigantia, Victory or Dea Panthea.[76] Another possible form of portable religious icon may have been coins, which often bore images of deities and were, as said, deposited on sacred sites in large quantity. At some, those bearing particular goddesses or gods were chosen; but it is usually impossible to tell whether the value of the currency or the figure upon it was more important in the use of coins as offerings.[77]

Likewise, the frequency with which hunting scenes and gladiatorial combats appear on the mosaic floors of villas could signify an interest in themes of life and death, or simply pleasure in these forms of entertainment, the most exciting available to the wealthy. Decorations on pottery may represent religious belief, scenes of actual ritual, episodes from popular myth or legend, or mere excitement or humour. Any of these explanations could account for the men in animal skins and antlers, within a woodland setting, on a sherd from Colchester. Another, from Horsey Toll in Cambridgeshire, made at a factory in the Nene Valley, is etched with a man running towards a naked woman who is holding a huge penis. She is pointing to her genitals, he is ejaculating; the scene could span a huge spectrum of explanation, from the deepest solemnity to the greatest ribaldry. The penis is a common symbol in Roman-British culture, fashioned in stone or pottery or carved as amulets or hung from necklaces. In many contexts it evidently encouraged strength, virility, or the ability to stand strongly upright or grow. As such, it was often carved upon buildings to encourage them to stand long and well: at the Hadrian's Wall fort now called Chesters, they were put on to the bridge abutment, bath-house and headquarters.[78]

Quite frequently, dedications to deities are inscribed with the names of those who made them. It is much rarer for these people to explain why they did this, but such moments do, invaluably, occur. We can, perhaps, share in the exhilaration of the prefect of a cavalry detachment, Gaius Tetius Veturius Micianus, who set up an altar to the Roman god of hunting, Silvanus, on the open moor of Bollihope Common, above Weardale in the Pennine Hills. He had killed a huge wild boar which had escaped all those who had hunted it before.[79] Another officer and huntsman, the centurion of infantry Julius Secundus, set up an altar in honour of Silvanus on another Pennine moor, near the fort at Bowes. This officer, however, knew that the land concerned belonged to a native god, Vinotonus, and took care to honour him in an inscription as well.[80] Other soldiers were inspired by more peaceful experiences. At Carvoran, a fort in the Hadrian's Wall zone, M. Caecilius Donatianus had a vision – perhaps in a dream – of the goddess Virgo Caecilius ('the heavenly virgin'), whom he equated with Cybele, the Asian goddess who presided over a mystery religion, and (loyally) the empress Julia Domna. He recorded his gratitude to her on stone.[81]

It was not only men who left expressions of devotion to deities in the northern military zone. In 1963 a sandstone altar was revealed by ploughing on the site of a fort at Westerwood in Dunbartonshire, near the western end of the short-lived second-century frontier between Forth and Clyde. It had been erected by Vibia Pacata, the wife of a centurion of the Sixth Legion stationed there, to repay a vow, in the presence of her family. The dedication was 'to the celestial goddess of the woodlands and the crossroads', who was probably Diana, and it seems most likely that the vow was made to this goddess in her role as supreme patroness of childbirth, in the course of a difficult labour. The mention of crossroads, however, recalls a different goddess, Hecate, supreme deity of magic; in which case Vibia Pacata may have been living an even more interesting life up there above the River Clyde. At any rate, it evokes a wonderful picture of an indomitable Roman matron, keeping a promise to her goddess.[82] A different sort of testimony to personal faith was found in 1979 near Thetford, on the Norfolk chalk heaths, which seemed to consist of the ritual impedimenta of a local cult of Faunus, the Roman god of the countryside. This appears to have been carried on by a male club, for it included thirty-two spoons, each inscribed with an epithet of the god and the name of an individual devotee. Faunus was clearly identified here as a patron of agriculture, because he got names like 'Long Ear', 'Fosterer of Corn', 'Mead-Maker' and 'Giver of Plenty'.[83] The odd thing was that the farmers whose names were inscribed were native Britons, and the divine epithets were also in the native language: a rare proof of how far Roman religion could be assimilated by the conquered people.

The most vivid examples of personal acts of religious ritual to survive from Roman Britain are probably the lead tablets upon which curses were written, which invoked the help of a deity against human beings who had done the writer wrong. They have been found at half a dozen places, above all at Bath, where about 130 were thrown into the sacred spring, and Uley, where about 140 were either fixed to the temple wall or collected in a special room. The most common wrong concerned was theft, whether of a material object or of a loved one. Sometimes the name of the offender (or a list of them) was recorded, while at others the aggrieved party called down (or up) divine wrath against an unknown adversary. The precise nature of the punishment was usually left to the goddess or god, though the degree of it requested could range from repentance and restitution to a lingering death. More or less typical of those at Bath was one written by Solinus, who sought the aid of Sulis Minerva to recover the bathing suit and cloak with which he had come to the baths fed by her sacred waters, and which had been stolen there. He beseeched her to allow no 'sleep or health to him who has done me wrong, whether slave or free, unless he reveals himself and brings these goods to your temple'.[84] The author of perhaps the most famous of all such tablets in Britain was Saturnina, who went for help to Mercury at Uley. She had lost a linen cloth to a thief, perhaps from a washing line (the value of the item indicates how slender her means were), and wanted the god's aid to recover it; but was not sure which god she was addressing. First she addressed Mars and Silvanus, and only after crossing them out did she get the right name, and call on Mercury to curse the criminal. Did she start to write on the tablet and then have difficulty in finding a shrine to the first two deities? Or did she find all three honoured under the same roof at Uley, and have difficulty in making up her mind which would be the most effective? Or, faced by the handsome limestone statue in the Uley temple, did she fail at first, being unfamiliar with Roman iconography, to realize whom it represented? We cannot know, but her anger and pain, consequent on the loss, ring out from her writing.[85]

Burial

One very important and ritually loaded placement of material in the earth remained the disposal of human corpses: and here the Roman invasion brought two major changes. The first was the banning of burials inside settlements, as the much greater size of urban centres in the empire made them into a health risk. Instead, they were placed, usually in cemeteries, outside the occupied zone, and these graveyards could be very large if they served proportionately big towns. The one to the east of Roman London probably accumulated around 100,000 bodies.[86] The graves were often so neatly arranged alongside each other that their outlines must have been marked; and they usually contained an entire local population, apparently the first time since Britain was settled that whole communities were frequently buried together. As few rural burial grounds have been identified, however, and as it is not clear what percentage of the population of a town the known cemeteries around it held, it is not yet certain if wholesale burial had indeed become the rule. The second reform was to disarm the civilian population, including retired soldiers, so that weapons largely vanished from graves and the native warrior aristocracy, with its military trappings, mutated into a colonial nobility accompanied by goods suited to a peaceful and luxurious lifestyle. One special mark of this was the making of large, decorated, stone chests – sarcophagi – of the Mediterranean style, to contain the bodies of the wealthy. None the less, these reforms were imposed on a network of local traditions, developed (as described earlier) in the centuries before the Romans arrived, which still showed through Roman custom and law. Elaborate chambers with rich goods were still found in the former kingdom of the Catuvellauni, mass cemeteries with similar graves in that of the Durotriges, and cremated bones in urns in that of the Cantii.

Indeed, the overlap was the more evident in that Rome took some time to convert friendly members of the native royalty and aristocracy to its customs. The most celebrated recent example of continuity of practice, as manifested in burial, was found in 1991–2. It was the grave of a man who was probably a client king who died around the year 50, excavated at Folly Lane, St Albans, beside the new Roman-style city of Verulamium. It was inside a large enclosure, and consisted of a pit in which his cremated bones were buried with silverware melted in his pyre. Beside it was a shaft leading to a wooden chamber in which the body had apparently been laid in state with the metalwork and a valuable Roman pottery dinner service and wine jars. A mound was erected over both. Also, early in the province's history there may have been some self-conscious antiquarianism, as large round mounds resembling Bronze Age barrows were built to cover the cremated bones of aristocrats. Over a hundred are known, especially in the south-east, and the most impressive are the three survivors of a cemetery of seven in a woodland glade near Bartlow among the chalk hills at the south-eastern corner of Cambridgeshire. One of these is in fact the tallest ancient burial mound in England, and the group was the biggest one of Roman tumuli in northern Europe, raised over cremation burials put inside glass urns within wooden chests, and surrounded by handsome bronze and ceramic objects mainly associated with feasting. The nineteenth-century excavators found that lamps had been left burning inside the chests. Such big mounds were, however, also raised at Rome itself over the cremated remains of early emperors, such as Augustus, so that the custom may have been a direct imitation of the most distinguished Roman practice and not one of prehistoric British monuments.[87] None the less, older traditions certainly did linger in the geography of funerary habits: outside military sites, formal burials remained as rare in the western and northern parts of the Roman-occupied area of Britain as they had been in the preceding period. Where they are encountered, they are commonly in boundary ditches, another link with prehistoric custom.[88]

On the other hand, in the matter of funerary custom as in others, the province was linked into wider developments in the empire, of which the greatest was that cremation was the prevalent fashion during the first and second centuries, to be succeeded by inhumation in the third and fourth. They were very different modes, as the body was kept entire in the latter form, while in the former it was not only altered by fire, but in most if not all Romano-British cremation burials (as in those of the Iron Age), many – even the majority – of the burnt bones were left on the pyre, and only some buried.[89] The shift to inhumation affected everybody from emperors to poor, but was as silent and

(a)

(b)

79. Two groups of Romano-British burial mounds:
(a) The largest, in original number of mounds and in their height, the Bartlow Hills. This is the southernmost, with the next one adjoining it to the left.
(b) A pair of more usual size but still colossal by the standards of prehistoric round barrows, in a meadow above Thornborough Bridge, Buckinghamshire.

little explained as the manner in which British men moved from wearing beards to shaving cleanly, and then back again, between the seventeenth and nineteenth centuries: even highly literate societies rarely seem capable of accounting for changes of fashion.[90] The province followed imperial practice, also, in that the move to inhumation took the form of bodies stretched out on their backs, instead of crouched on their sides as in the British Iron Age, though the crouched burials had lingered in some rural areas. At some places, such as Colchester, the change from cremation to inhumation was so sudden, in the mid third century, that it looks like an official move; but no decree for it has survived anywhere.[91] There are indeed no surviving written sources which explain funeral customs and grave decorations in Roman Britain, and so the evidence is all material, with every attendant problem in the interpretation of it. We still have no idea who arranged the funerals, whether professional undertakers, priestesses or priests; nor do we know the last wishes of the deceased, or the mourning family. We have no means of reconstructing most funeral rites: the laying out of the body, its progress to the grave, and whatever happened at the burial, are all lost to us. We do not know what funeral pyres looked like, though so many objects were buried from some of them that they may have been multi-tier. What is evident is the great fund of symbolism drawn upon for imagery in and around graves. Deities themselves are rarely represented, although the different religious traditions of the empire furnished at least a dozen with special responsibility for the dead. Instead, the only divine being commonly associated with Romano-British burials is Venus – if the clay figurines, which seem to be found mainly in female graves, do indeed represent the goddess. Instead, a range of motifs is associated with tombs, such as cupids (perhaps as soothing companions for the dead on their journey); axes (perhaps symbols of power and protection); dolphins (perhaps for a journey across some otherworld ocean); poppies (perhaps as givers of sleep and banishers of pain, if they were the opium-bearing kind); stars (maybe as symbols of eternity); pine cones (from the dark evergreen tree which was associated with mourning); and lions (which could be protecting figures or devouring symbols of death).[92]

Grave goods – found with both cremations and inhumations – provide a similarly provocative and tantalizing set of possible suggestions. Those most frequently deposited were lamps (perhaps to light the tomb for the dead on their way to the next world); food vessels (either to nourish the deceased or as offerings for guardian spirits or deities, or as the containers for the funeral feast, contaminated by the act beyond reuse); keys (perhaps to open ghostly doors); stones and pebbles (possibly good-luck charms); animals' teeth (which could be the same); coins in the mouth or hand of the corpse (which would, if following Mediterranean precedent, be to pay the ferryman of the dead to transport the spirit into the next world); and hobnailed boots (suggesting that the deceased was expected to go on a long walk into that world). The only category of these objects which had Iron Age precedents in Britain were the pots. The sheer variety of grave goods seems to bear out what Greek and Roman literature infers: that the peoples of the empire had a great diversity of opinions concerning the fate of the dead, even within the same ethnic and cultural groups. It was particularly uncertain whether the spirits of the departed remained near their bodies, or passed away from them. The combination of material placed in graves was as individual as the choice of objects itself: there were sixty different such assemblages placed with eighty-nine burials surveyed in a study of cremation cemeteries in Essex, London and Kent. It should also be emphasized that most burials had no goods at all, so that coins – among the most fashionable of objects to place in graves – were found with only 2 per cent of the bodies excavated in a large cemetery at Chichester.[93] As in the case of other kinds of ritualized behaviour, burial customs were often highly individual and even idiosyncratic. One man who died in what is now Kent was cremated sitting in a chair with a cockerel in his lap, perhaps as a gift to Mercury, or as a meal, or to wake him up when the time came to start his journey. Five wine jars were then smashed around the charred remains, as libations to deities, provision for the next world or just the remains of an impressive wake, and the Holborough round barrow was built over the site.[94]

Some unusual kinds of burial strike a modern observer as sinister. Also in Kent, one cremation urn was sealed with cement, while another was packed with sharp flints: both acts could have been to confine the dead or to protect them.[95] Beheaded bodies are quite common in the second half of the period, usually with the heads laid in the grave: 24 of more than 200 Romano-British inhumations recorded along the upper Thames fall into this category. A quarter of the bodies were headless in cemeteries at Chignall St James, in the clay country of central Essex, and on Winterbourne Down in the Wiltshire chalk hills. They tend to be found in graves that are otherwise normal in their position in a cemetery, in their layout and in the provision of goods and coffins. Some heads had clearly been removed after death, though it is difficult to ascertain this in most cases.[96] It is possible that some of the bodies were those of executed criminals, as beheading was the normal mode of lethal punishment for Roman citizens, after which they were returned to their relatives for burial. On the other hand, the act of removal of the head might have been a reverent one, to free the spirit from the body and help it on its journey. A third possibility is that it was inflicted on individuals whose mode of life or death had created a fear that they would return to haunt the living: in which case the act may have been believed to silence and immobilize them for good. A fourth is that it was not the product of fear but of contempt, an insult inflicted on the corpse of a person who had incurred great unpopularity in life: the statues of public figures in the Roman world whose memories were hated were beheaded in similar manner. It seems likely that all or most of these explanations account for the custom in Britain, but they cannot readily be distinguished.

The same problem of interpretation attends prone burial, bodies laid on their front instead of their back in the grave. In Christian times this became regarded as a terrible punishment, seriously harming the person's chances of eternal life. It was fairly common in Roman Britain, especially in the country-side of the south of the province, being found (for example) in a quarter of the seventy-eight inhumations in a graveyard near Fairford beside the Thames in Oxfordshire. All sexes and ages were affected by it, but especially adult men. Some may have ended up in that position by accident, because they were clearly flung carelessly into the grave, but others were carefully laid out. They tend to have no or few goods, but occasionally they are the most richly endowed with objects.[97] The custom may have been intended to assist the deceased to go faster into the underworld, or to prevent them from returning to haunt the world of the living (again), or to damage chances of a new life in the manner of what became the Christian belief. It may simply have marked out the person thus treated as guilty of deviance or transgression in some way: and indeed many of the prone bodies, unlike the headless kind, tend to be found on the edge of a cemetery or beyond it, as if segregated. Once again, actions of dismemberment or positioning in burial followed general rules but had an individual character. At Kimmeridge, beneath the Purbeck Hills of Dorset, a group of elderly women were interred in the late third century with their heads severed and placed by their feet, after the lower jaws had been detached. Each was given a spindle whorl. The whole rite may have been intended to honour a group of weavers and set free their spirits at maximum speed, or to humiliate the corpses of women executed for suspected harmful magic (the whorl being the symbol of the Fates) and prevent them from cursing even in the grave.[98]

A discussion of apparently disturbing burials leads inevitably back to the issue of human sacrifice. At Plaxtol in Kent a body was laid out with a large stone on its breast, as if to pin it down, and cremated remains with rich goods were then placed around it. This looks like a foundation deposit, to consecrate an elite graveyard, and the question arises of whether the person concerned died naturally.[99] At the end of the fourth century, a coffin containing only coins was put into a grave in the Lankhills cemetery at Winchester, and over that were laid the bodies of two dogs and the decapitated corpse of a young man, whose head was set at his knees with a coin in its mouth.[100] The site looks like a cenotaph for somebody lost at sea or in war, who had been given two animal companions and a human one. Perhaps the latter was a beheaded criminal, or a slave or servant who had died opportunely, or whose death had been inflicted for the rite, with or without his consent.

Such suspicious burials are also found outside cemeteries. The deposition of human remains with the material placed in water or pits was much rarer in the Roman period than in the Iron Age, but it continued. Mention has been made of those in Lindow Moss, most or all of which seem to be Romano-British. Ten wells, scattered from the West Country to Hadrian's Wall and including Coventina's, contained human heads. Some were already skulls when put there, but others were freshly severed, and some were obviously associated, like other deposits, with the digging or the closure of the shafts. A cistern in Caerwent, the main Roman town of South Wales, had two skulls placed in it and a complete skeleton laid over it as if to seal it.[101] Human bones were also put into the boundary ditches at London and Canterbury, and into pits or ditches. Headless babies were laid in the foundations of a temple complex at Springhead, Kent, and whole babies inside the walls of the strong third-century coastal fortress of Reculver which guarded the southern flank of the Thames Estuary. Their small bodies are also found buried at villas, in much the same manner as animal bones.[102] Parts of six individuals, mostly limbs and heads, were interred outside the main gate of Roman Colchester. Temple buildings and precincts occasionally held human remains which had seemingly been given ritualized, but not reverent, treatment. The enclosure of one at Lowbury Hill, Oxfordshire contained the grave of a woman whose facial bones had been removed, while the temple precinct at Folly Lane, St Albans had pits in which pots in the shape of human heads had been placed, along with one real, defleshed, head, of a youth killed by a savage blow to his skull. This temple was built on the site of the funerary enclosure of the first-century nobleman or king mentioned earlier and when he was buried three women, all with disabilities which would have affected their mobility, were interred at its entrance. Another temple at St Albans had a pit associated with it which contained the head of a teenage boy who had been battered to death, after which his skull was apparently skinned and mounted on a pole. A religious precinct in the city of Wroxeter, Shropshire yielded fragments of human skull which had been cleaned of flesh and then oiled. One had been scalped, and another apparently mounted on a bronze base.[103]

These finds have long prompted speculation that they may be of victims of a tradition of sacrifice which continued clandestinely under Roman rule even though the latter officially forbade it. In recent years this possibility has been raised especially by Miranda Aldhouse-Green, R. M. J. Isserlin and Alison Taylor.[104] It runs up, however, against now familiar problems of interpretation. As Guy de la Bédoyère has pointed out, there is a world of difference between the sacrifice of a child to consecrate the foundation of a new building, and the use of a child who had died of natural causes for the same purpose, but the archaeological remains are identical.[105] Indeed, even human bodies laid in foundations may simply have been there because a building site made a conven-ient dumping ground for them. The parts of skeleton found in wells, city or fort ditches and temple precincts may have been those of criminals, which had been put on public display as object lessons before being disposed of in these different ways. It could indeed be that bits of corpse were thought to possess magical properties, but the rate of death, natural and by execution, in Roman Britain should have ensured a supply of them without the need to kill the owners for no other reason. When all this is said, the hypothesis of lingering and clandestine human sacrifice remains tenable; but a further problem with it is that it has often been articulated with the presumption that a native tradition of the practice had existed in pre-Roman Britain to be perpetuated. As suggested above, this is itself not proven.

It is perhaps salutary to emphasize at this point that most treatments of the dead in the province testify to the abiding affection of those responsible and their determination to ensure the best future for those whom they buried. Among many moving memorials that survive from the province, the personal favourite of this author is that erected at Bath by Magnius, for his 'freedwoman and foster-daughter' Mercatilla. It is in the Roman Baths Museum, and records that the girl died aged one year, six months and twelve days. The precision with which her short life was recorded testifies to her father's love, as does the fact that he had theoretically owned her as a slave, presumably with her mother (of whom he must also have been fond), and had both given her legal freedom and adopted her as his own child. His affection and generosity were ill served by fate, and it is possible that he brought her to the temple and sacred spring in a plea for her recovery when she fell ill, only to give her a tombstone there as a final testimony to the strength of his feeling. The hearts of most fathers must go out to him.

Retro-paganism

A theme which has been sounded with mounting force during the course of this book has been the manner in which successive ages of prehistory have appeared to engage with the monuments left to them from earlier times. The increase in such engagements of course, has been proportionate to the growth in the number and range of such monuments over the millennia, creating an inherited human landscape ever more complex and ever more challenging to the imagination. It is possible, indeed even likely, that a process as dramatic as that of the Roman occupation of most of Britain greatly compounded this response. It created a visible break with many aspects of the past which may have provoked the natives, as well as the incomers, to relate more intensely to previous human activity in the land, and especially to ceremonial activity which seemed to connect with that land's numinous power or powers. The radical alteration of the political, ideological, social and economic context to life in most of the island would have had dramatic implications for the ways in which people won legitimacy for their actions and formed their own identities; and the vestiges of the human past have usually played a major role in both enterprises.

Between 1988 and 1993, two archaeologists, N. B. Aitchison and Ken Dark, drew attention to the large amount of Romano-British pottery, coins and burials found on or in Neolithic and Bronze Age barrows, and suggested that these structures were regarded, in that later period, as sacred places.[106] In 1998 Howard Williams took this idea further, to find seventy-nine cases of Romano-British burials in or near prehistoric sites, although in only eighteen was the association clearly direct and deliberate. He linked these with the deposition of objects at prehistoric monuments and the construction of thirteen Roman-British temples and amphitheatres at or near pre-Roman structures or graves, to argue that these places had become foci for cults of the dead, and through them of supernatural beings.[107] Such insights made a good fit with Richard Hingley's observation that Bronze Age weapons and tools were sometimes recovered from Romano-British sites, and Paul Robinson's that miniature axes of a Bronze Age style seem to have been used as amulets in Roman-period Wiltshire.[108] All this was highly suggestive, but, as the archaeologists concerned were careful to stress, not conclusive. More recently, a further study of the Romano-British reuse of prehistoric sites has supplied more data and made conclusions easier to draw, even if the matter cannot yet be resolved with perfect confidence.[109]

This study made a close examination of three very different classes of site. The first of these consisted of the cave systems of the Carboniferous limestone landscapes on either side of the Bristol Channel, in South Wales, North Somerset and the islands off Pembrokeshire. They are some of the most impressive and abundant in Britain, and by the Roman period their natural attributes would have been enhanced, as sources of wonder, by the evidence in them of human occupation stretching back for tens of millennia and of animal occupation, often by magnificent extinct beasts, extending for hundreds more. These relics would have been exposed, at many caverns, by further human or animal activity or by the action of streams or tides. Any assessment of the extent of a Romano-British presence at them presents special difficulties, and any interpretation of it has to reckon with more. Most of the sites concerned were dug out by antiquaries in the nineteenth and early twentieth centuries, who were often deficient in care and in the keeping of records even by the standards of the time, and little interested in periods after the Palaeolithic. Even caves which they did not touch have normally been visited and disturbed by local people in modern times, and the action of water has ruined deposits at more. Even when all these problems are taken into account, it can be claimed that about half of the caves of the South Welsh and Somerset limestone regions which have been submitted to extensive archaeological examination have shown traces of activity in the Roman period. In most cases this took the form of relatively limited deposits of portable objects, above all coins, pottery and small personal ornaments. On the whole, the more heavily a cave had been used during prehistory, the more likely it was to attract interest; and this factor took precedence over more practical considerations such as the size, accessibility or dryness of the site. Although this activity spanned the Roman occupation, there was an apparent concentration in the last two centuries of it. A much more rapid look at cave systems elsewhere in the province – in the Wye Valley, Peak District and Pennines – showed much the same pattern.

The second kind of site considered consisted of prehistoric burial mounds, and especially of the Cotswold–Severn group of Neolithic chambered long barrows. As some of the most impressive monuments of British prehistory, often dominating the landscapes in which they stood, these could move the ancient imagination as much as the modern. In both cases, also, it would have counted that when the interior of their chambers was exposed by weathering or human or animal excavations, they often contained masses of human bone. Once again, they were attractive to Victorian excavators who were often hasty and careless and left no or inadequate reports; and were moreover much more interested in the original nature of these monuments than in relics of later activity at them. Furthermore, they usually dug straight for where chambers would most probably be, and ignored the rest of the mound, which is very commonly the location of Romano-British material. When all this is said, a similar pattern of deposition is found to that in the caves: of coins, pots (whole or smashed), beads, tiles and pieces of metalwork. It has been detected in the majority of Cotswold–Severn long barrows which have received careful and well-recorded excavation. By contrast, the smaller Bronze Age round barrows of the Cotswold region received less attention. A slightly different pattern was revealed in Derbyshire, where the Neolithic tomb-shrines had round mounds which were not much more striking than some of those built in the same region during the Bronze Age. The largest of the Neolithic monuments were therefore given a considerable number of Romano-British objects, along with some of the most impressive of the Bronze Age round barrows. Coins predominated, followed by pottery and then brooches and pins. Again, a more cursory survey of other evidence shows up the same pattern: earthen long barrows have frequently yielded Roman material, above all coins. By contrast, the exposed Neolithic stone chambers of Wales attracted almost no attention: the people of Roman Britain were drawn to substantial ancient mounds.

The final category of site considered was made up of some of the most spectacular prehistoric monuments of the Wessex chalk hills: Stonehenge, Avebury and the Uffington White Horse. At Stonehenge much evidence must have been lost, because of repeated poorly recorded excavations there in the seventeenth and eighteenth centuries: but none the less, more Roman pottery has been found there than that from the Neolithic or Bronze Age, together with coins and ornaments. Much less has been found at the Avebury henge, but then that has been much less investigated, and the megaliths at the end of one of the stone avenues leading to it seem to have been adapted to make a Romano-British shrine, while a second cult centre was established at Silbury. Three shafts have been discovered to the east of that great mound, filled with Roman-British deposits, and may have been part of a ring of them dug around it. There may also have been a stone temple built nearby. At Uffington the hill fort immediately above the White Horse was given quantities of coins, metalwork and (above all) pots, spread across the interior, and the long barrow near it was turned into a cemetery. This was all reuse of the sites rather than continued use, for Stonehenge and Avebury show very little sign of Iron Age activity, and the Uffington fort had been disused for at least eight centuries before the Roman Britons began to leave objects there. Moreover, activity at all three seems to have been most pronounced later, rather than earlier, in the Roman period.

It looks, therefore, very much as if the people of Roman Britain took a widespread interest in both the most impressive of the ritual monuments which survived from earlier periods and in imposing natural places which had been frequented by prehistoric humans and animals. As yet no inscriptions or objects dedicated to fulfilling specific vows have been found at these sites, and so the focus of this interest is not recoverable. We do not know if it was formal or informal, public or private; if it involved individuals, families or larger social groups, or was dedicated to specific deities, or to spirits connected to the place, or to dead human beings. The objects found at these sites were mainly personal possessions, and of relatively low value. In general, they resemble those deposited in what seem to have been ritual contexts elsewhere, in water, pits and ditches, save for a greater prominence of coins and a relative absence of animal bones (though these were numerous at Silbury and also found in some caves). As such, they point up the whole problem of determining significance when considering these sorts of deposit in general, the most common trace of apparent ceremonial behaviour in Roman Britain. As in the case of the prehistoric evidence, we can only speculate about the mass of biodegradable offerings which may have been made in the same places and left no evidence: of food and drink, and of wooden or textile objects. The pottery found in those places could have been important because of its contents (before or during the rite in which it was deposited), its association with past or present owners, the human activity with which it had been involved, the material of which it was composed, or its capacity to resist decay, even when broken into fragments. Coins could be, as pointed out earlier, not merely objects of intrinsic value (though those chosen for deposition were usually low-grade) and of social currency, but religious items charged with the power of the deities and inscriptions placed upon them, and of course symbols of human authority as well.

Returning to the specific context of the leaving of such objects in caves and at prehistoric sites, it is easy and important to note the element of continuity in such behaviour: after all, the ritual burial or placement and abandonment of human possessions has been an activity identifiable in every period of British prehistory, and especially in the Iron Age. On the other hand, the people of Roman Britain were not carrying on the same practice at the same places as their immediate predecessors. Instead, it seems that they were deliberately enacting rites at a large number of prominent prehistoric monuments, and in caves which had formerly been frequented by humans, including many which had attracted no interest in the Iron Age, or even been actively avoided. Moreover, this activity did not peak in the earlier years of the Roman occupation. Wherever it can be dated (and here coins are especially helpful) the same pattern obtains: such deposits were made throughout the Roman period, and began quite soon after its commencement, but the great majority were made in the last hundred and fifty years, from the mid third century to the abandonment of the province by Rome.

This has important implications for an understanding of their meaning. The context is at least relatively clear: the great expansion of activity and prosperity in the countryside during the later years of the province's existence, illustrated by the multiplication of villas, market towns and – perhaps most relevant in this case – the temples which have been termed probable sites of pilgrimage. This abounding wealth and energy in rural Roman Britain may well have manifested also in a further sacralization of the landscape, in which some of the increasing, and increasingly affluent, population chose to honour monuments and places associated with earlier ceremonial activity, which offered a link to the remote past and with it perhaps a stronger relationship to a spirit world, divine or ancestral. It is interesting in this connection to consider the study made by Chris Gosden and Gary Lock of the archaeology of the chalk hills known as the Berkshire Downs. They noted that the Iron Age enclosures there were built on top of Bronze Age predecessors, despite long gaps in occupation of the sites, and suggested that the memory of those predecessors was preserved in genealogical histories. By contrast, in the Uffington area the Roman Britons linked together monuments of all ages around the White Horse as if they had become part of a generalized sense of a mythical past.[110] The booming economy and society of the late Romano-British countryside is not sufficient in itself to account for such a shift, nor indeed for the ever growing, and perhaps unprecedented, amount of attention given to sites of earlier activity: an apparently religious form of ancient antiquarianism. It is easy to hypothesize that the shock of the Roman conquest might well have served to cut the British off from a sense of easy belonging to their own land and its monuments, and encourage a need to reconnect with it in new ways. If the effect concerned seems very delayed, in that this apparent urge to reconnection was at its strongest in the final centuries of Roman occupation, this may have been because it was only in that later period that the countryside became effectively Romanized for the first time, producing the necessary sense of cultural dissonance and dislocation. There is, however, one further factor which may be taken into account, that from the mid third century the empire experienced increasing religious tension and division, culminating in the official adoption of Christianity and (decades after that) the official condemnation of paganism. It is possible – though no more – that this atmosphere evoked in some British pagans a need to reconnect with the roots of their religions, through the apparent relics of those who had venerated the traditional deities of the island in previous times. It may have been the first point at which those pagans embraced the totality of their own heritage, and with it a mythical past which embodied and mediated a relationship with the land.

6

THE CONVERSION TO CHRISTIANITY
A CLASH OF RELIGIONS, A BLEND OF RELIGIONS

THE PEOPLES OF prehistoric Britain could well have undergone experiences of religious conversion, if the cultural changes that ushered in tomb-shrines, stone circles or hill forts were accompanied by major alterations in the way in which human relations with divinity were conceived. In the historic ancient European world, however, such fundamental shifts of mentality were not a part of religious behaviour. A world-picture which conceived of the existence of many deities allowed people to form intense personal attachments to particular goddesses and gods, and sometimes to relinquish them, without causing any fundamental movement in the manner in which they viewed the cosmos, and the nature of religion. The appearance of the faith of Christ required and produced just such a seismic change, by breaking most of the conventions of religious culture as they had existed in Europe and the Mediterranean basin since history began. It claimed the existence of a single, all-powerful, all-knowing, universally present and totally good deity, who had created the world and directed its fate. It also preached the existence of a force of cosmic evil in the universe, inferior by far to the single god but powerful in worldly affairs and set on subverting the divine plan for the universe. All creation was therefore polarized between those two forces, and human beings were offered the stark choice of salvation, by embracing the worship of the true deity and obeying his rules and commands, or damnation, by ignoring or opposing them and choosing other religious loyalties. The divine beings of other religions were regarded as non-existent, having the status of lies, deceptions or allegories, or of personifications and servants of the force of evil: effectively, as demons. The divine will was expressed through sacred writings, which true believers had to understand and expound correctly, creating the new discipline of theology, which replaced philosophy as the main means of understanding the universe and the human place in it. The central mystery of this religion was the insistence that its god had incarnated in human form, just once, in the person of Jesus Christ, through the agency of a mortal mother, in order to bring a clearer revelation to humanity and offer it a better chance of salvation. Acceptance of all these tenets, and entry into the community of those who believed in them, was signalled by baptism, an initiation rite requiring immersion in, or sprinkling with, water. These essential characteristics are common to all forms of the faith concerned, and justify the umbrella term of Christianity for it.

The vast and unified polity of the Roman Empire favoured the spread of this new religion from its birthplace in Palestine, but the utter rejection of the legitimacy of other religious loyalties, embodied in the Christian claim, made it impossible for Rome to assimilate it peacefully. Local persecutions of Christians occurred, sporadically and briefly, in the first and second centuries, to be succeeded by more general attempts to repress them in the mid third and early fourth. In the fourth century, imperial policy altered first to accepting Christianity as the dominant faith, and then as the only one, which increasingly involved the official curtailment, and then the extirpation, of older religious traditions, to which the new Latin term of paganism was applied.[1] As the new religion reached peoples who spoke Germanic languages, an equivalent word, 'heathen', was used for adherents to the old religious ways.[2] The progress of the faith of Christ from persecuted minority to triumphant and intolerant establishment was a fitful and uneven one, but none the less spanned just a single very long lifetime, effectively the length of the fourth century. In the first decade of that period, it was subjected to the most widespread and serious of the official proscriptions, with many Christians put to death. Between 312 and 337 the emperor Constantine the Great gradually established it as the most favoured religion in the empire, and suppressed a few pagan cults. His sons continued this work by imposing increasing restrictions upon specific aspects of pagan worship. In 361, however, the last of his family, Julian, revealed himself to be a pagan, and set about the restoration of the old religions. Julian was killed in battle by the Persians after just two years, and was succeeded by Christian emperors who returned their faith to supremacy but were tolerant of others. From 380 onwards, this tolerance was steadily eroded, until in 394 Theodosius the Great ordered the closure of temples and the cessation of pagan rites across the whole empire.[3]

This story is one familiar to anybody acquainted with late Roman history, as is its ironic sequel: that the triumph of Christianity coincided with the beginning of the disintegration of the Western Roman Empire. Britain was the first province to be lost, between 407 and 410. However, Christian success in converting the northern invaders who had brought down the Romans, and then in carrying the faith into their homelands and beyond, ensured that the whole of Europe was at least nominally converted by the end of the Middle Ages, and most of it by the end of the first millennium. The British Isles had apparently all embraced the new religion by the year 700. Such is clear: what is not clear is the process by which this latter result was achieved. Before the year 597 there is virtually no reliable data; after then, we have a story, or set of stories, for most of the archipelago, but puzzles and disputes still abound.

Evidence for Romano-British Christianity

Four centuries of the most diligent and intelligent scholarly investigation have failed to establish any consensus concerning the extent, nature and success of the Christian faith in Roman Britain. In the period since 1980, William Frend, Martin Henig and Dorothy Watts have argued for a resurgence of paganism in the late fourth century, commencing with the accession of Julian, which rolled back the early successes of Christianity under Constantine and his sons. Ken Dark and Martin Millett have contested this idea. Edward James and Kenneth Hylson-Smith have concluded that it is unlikely that the bulk of people in the province had converted before the empire fell, while Michelle Brown, David Petts and Barbara Yorke have emphasized instead the flourishing nature of the late Romano-British Church, and its permeation of all levels of society. Neil Faulkner, however, has declared it to have been a religion of the Romanized upper class, with no large popular following, a view which echoes that of Frend. Malcolm Lambert has called it the faith of a minority, but one that was well established and especially strong in the south-east.[4] To some extent these are differences of emphasis, though important differences: Lambert's formula, for example, could reconcile a number of the other views stated above. Still, there is a distinct gap between David Petts's conclusion that Christianity was a dynamic and successful force in Britain by the time that Roman rule ended, paving the way for its success in subsequent centuries, and the one proposed by Faulkner, Frend and Watts, that it was dependent on imperial sponsorship and enfeebled as soon as the empire fell.

The reason for the difficulty is (of course) the nature of the evidence, which is almost wholly archaeological. There is a little textual material. Three British martyrs were later remembered as victims of pagan persecution, Aaron and Julius at Caerleon (or perhaps York) and Alban at Verulamium, whose shrine later became the focus of the new town of St Albans.[5] Malcolm Lambert has concluded that these saints attest to a Christian presence in Britain by the third century, while David Petts has commented that all may be mythical.[6] We are on firmer ground with the list of churchmen who attended the Council of Arles in 314, which included three British bishops from different cities: a higher number than that sent from the northern half of Gaul. The council concerned was held soon after the cessation of the biggest of all the official persecutions of Christians, when their numbers should have been reduced and their hierarchy disrupted; so this is good evidence for a well-established and widespread presence of the religion in Britain by this date.[7] It might be expected that imperial support would have subsequently greatly expanded it, but here direct written evidence runs out. Certainly by 396 British bishops were numerous enough to hold a council, at which a Gaulish churchman arbitrated in a quarrel between them.[8] None of the major players in the province's politics in the last fifty years of Roman rule is noted as having been pagan, while two – Gratian and Gerontius, who were prominent in the final decade of the 400s – were specifically characterized by commentators as natives.[9] Suggestive as this is, it does not do much to reveal what was actually going on in the province.

Here the material evidence comes into play, and is divided into several categories. Decorations in fourth-century villas have been treated as testimony to a Christian presence, especially the chi-rho symbol, or cross with a loop on the upper end, which all over the empire stood for that faith. The problem is that it was also, under Christian emperors (who ruled Britain in all but two of the years after 312), a sign of imperial authority. While the prestige conferred upon a sectarian image by this sponsorship is significant in itself, it tells us nothing of the degree of personal conviction held by the people who used it.[10] Much excitement was created in 1963, when a mosaic pavement was found in a villa at Hinton St Mary, in the Blackmoor Vale of northern Dorset. It showed a male head with the chi-rho behind it, and was hailed as the earliest depiction of Christ in north-western Europe; but it was also suggested that it could be a portrait of an emperor, and the matter is unresolved.[11] It may be significant that the same building also had a mosaic representing the pagan hero Bellerophon. Another Dorset villa mosaic, at Frampton among the chalk hills further south, was discovered and drawn in the eighteenth century and is now lost. It had the chi-rho, along with representations of or references to pagan deities (Neptune, Dionysus and cupids), and Bellerophon again. Such a combination of motifs could mean that the owners of these villas held an eclectic variety of religious beliefs, or that they were part of a sect (heretical to orthodox Christians) which did so, or that they were Christians with a continuing love of classical pagan literature, or that they were employing images of pagan deities and heroes as allegories of moral qualities, or simply that they had both bought their mosaics from the same manufacturer, who used this combination of symbols as a trademark. Neither the Hinton nor the Frampton mosaic seems to have been laid in a setting which could have been used for worship.[12] The only good evidence for a church or chapel in any of the scores of villas which have now been excavated is at one of the finest maintained by English Heritage, at Lullingstone beside the River Darent in northern Kent. There the plaster coating the walls of one room had been painted with two chi-rho symbols, and with figures standing with arms upraised in the manner of Christian prayer. The antechamber had another chi-rho and the Greek letters alpha and omega, echoing the description of the Christian god in the Book of Revelation. However, not only are these paintings, as yet, unique in Britain, but the nearest parallels in the entire Roman world come from Syria. Furthermore, the chapel was constructed over another room which had been used for a pagan cult of water nymphs, followed by one of ancestors or the numen of the emperor. This was renovated in the mid fourth century, with the vessels for offerings renewed, which suggests that the pagan worship may have continued even while Christian services were conducted overhead.[13]

80 The mosaic floor from the villa at Hinton St Mary, Dorset, as reassembled in the British Museum. The head in the centre, with the Christian chi-rho symbol behind it, may well be Christ himself, or perhaps a Christian Roman emperor.

Dorothy Watts proposed in 1991 that a specifically Christian kind of ceme-tery could be identified in Roman Britain, characterized by the presence of infants as well as other age groups; whole bodies buried extended and on their backs; separate graves aligned so that the dead person could sit up and face the east at the coming of the Last Judgement; and an absence of grave goods. Upon that basis a total of fourteen such cemeteries was proposed, most common in the West Country but also scattered across East Anglia and the East Midlands: one, at Poundbury, by Dorchester, held over a thousand graves.[14] The problem with this checklist is that it certainly fits what would be expected of Christian burial, but that its separate components, with the possible exception of infant graves, are also found in burial grounds which have been thought to be pagan: they were common fashions in fourth-century Romano-Britain.[15] Moreover, the incidence of prone and decapitated bodies increased in cemeteries as the fourth century went on, though both practices were abhorrent to Christians.[16] Both problems would be solved if the characteristics of a Christian grave were adopted by pagans because of Christian influence, and if Christians had inflicted the prone and headless burials on individuals of whom they vehe-mently disapproved; but neither solution is at present certain.[17] As for Christian churches, not one has been securely identified on a Romano-British site, though a score of possible examples have been noted in forts and towns and in former temple precincts, from Canterbury to Hadrian's Wall. The essential difficulty is that there was no plan, orientation or size that was particularly associated with a building dedicated to Christian worship at this period, and much of that worship may well have taken place in people's homes.[18]

Some of the same problems attend personal objects as attend villa decora-tions. Where the chi-rho symbol appears on them it may only be a symbol of imperial authority, and Christian and pagan motifs are sometimes found together: for example, in the fourth-century Mildenhall Treasure found in west Suffolk in 1942, three silver spoons bore the chi-rho but a silver dish was engraved with the god Bacchus and an oceanic deity. Indeed, items decorated with Christian symbols or inscriptions have frequently been found deposited in watery places and pits, as if continuing the prehistoric pagan rite of offering objects at such places.[19] By 1995 a total of seventy portable items had been recorded from Roman Britain which bore clear evidence of association with Christianity, and sixty which had a possible association. This is not a large percentage of the overall haul of small and movable objects from the period, but the finds concerned were well distributed across what is now southern and eastern England, with an especial concentration in Cambridgeshire, Essex, Kent and Suffolk, while there are a few from the military zone of the north. Moreover, the texts and illustrations engraved on them exhibited a sophisti-cated kind of Christianity, with a good knowledge of the Bible and of liturgy, and a full hierarchy of officials.[20] It becomes easy to understand, in view of this evidence, how Britain could have produced a first-rate theologian by the late fourth century, Pelagius, even though his career is only recorded after he reached Italy (where his ideas were eventually condemned as heretical). On the other hand, these finds still do nothing to disclose the relative popularity and scale of the religion of Christ in the province. It is striking that not a single object has yet been dug up at London, the largest city in Britain and a major seat of government. The most significant large objects which seem to connect with Christianity are a set of (to date) twenty-eight circular lead tanks, some decorated with Christian symbols. They are almost unique to Britain, and found mostly in East Anglia and the East Midlands, with a few outliers. Traditionally, they have been interpreted as settings for baptism, and though they are not large enough for a person to be immersed in them, it is possible that they contained the holy water used in the rite, or that the postulant stood inside one and had the water poured over her or him.[21] Their very distinctiveness raises the question of whether they merely represented a British innovation to implement a normal Christian rite, or whether they embodied beliefs or practices peculiar to the province. Belinda Crerar has, however, recently emphasized that only some have clearly Christian decorations, and others may have functioned in industrial production, bath heating systems or pagan worship.[22] Put together, all these kinds of material find argue for a Christian presence in both town and country over much of fourth-century Roman Britain, and among a range of social classes; but the issue of its relative strength, and its nature or natures, is still not resolved.

One further means of approaching the problem is from the other side: an assessment of the strength or weakness of forms of paganism in the course of the same century, if practicable, would effectively provide the answer to the status of Christianity. The crucial test here is that of the survival of pagan cult centres. The continued deposition of objects in natural places and at prehistoric

81 A reconstruction, redrawn from that by Charles Thomas, of the decorative frieze from the lead tank found at Walesby, Lincolnshire. It may be our only representation of Christian baptism from Roman Britain, showing a female postulant being brought to the ceremony by two Christian matrons, undressed for immersion in or sprinkling with the holy water. It could also, however, portray the pagan goddess Venus, between two nymphs.

monuments, which – to judge from the evidence of coins – indeed went on until the very end of Roman rule, and probably beyond, is not sufficient evidence in itself. There is a chance that those carrying out these acts were Christians who still sought to propitiate nature spirits at these spots in much the same way as their descendants in the British Isles left out food for fairies. If so, this would be important and significant in itself, but there is no way of ascertaining whether it is true; and, as said, Christian objects were themselves left in earth and water and may represent a translation of this practice to the new faith. The fate of temples and shrines is a much more objective test of the fate of the old religion(s), and here there is plenty of evidence. Buildings of pagan worship continued to flourish until the middle of the fourth century, though the complex of Cunomaglus at Nettleton Shrub was replaced by a cross-shaped building which may have been a church. In the 360s Brean Down and another Somerset temple seem to have ceased to function, but Nettleton Shrub reverted to pagan use (if that had ever ceased there) and a new pilgrimage shrine was constructed within the huge abandoned hill fort of Maiden Castle, with dedications to Diana and Minerva. At some point in the mid to late fourth century the precinct of Sulis Minerva at Bath and a column dedicated to Jupiter at Cirencester were officially restored after being damaged; but whether this damage was by Christians or barbarian raiders is not known. Only from the 380s do temples everywhere fall into ruin: at Uley, for example, the buildings were demolished, the cult statue of Mercury broken and the votive objects thrown out. At four West Country sites small buildings were erected in the former sacred enclosures, which may have been Christian churches but also may have been farms. At Uley a new building was installed which contained apparent stone altars with no trace of pagan votive material, and so was possibly a church; but the altars may not have been added until long after the end of imperial rule. However, to judge from coin deposition, Lydney, Bath, the shrine at Maiden Castle and other sites (up to fifteen in the south-east) may have continued in some form of pagan worship up till the end of Roman rule, and beyond it.[23]

This pattern of decline, therefore, fits that of growing Christian intolerance of other religions during the final quarter of the century, ending in complete proscription in the 390s. The problem with it is that the timescale also precisely fits a different, and even more relevant, phenomenon: the collapse of Roman culture in Britain. In the early fourth century the province had reached the apex of its prosperity, especially in the countryside, but from the 340s, and even more from the 360s, periodic but serious raiding by Irish, northern British and Germanic war bands both disrupted the economy and drove up the cost of defence to an ever more onerous level. Round about 370 a tipping point was reached, after which economic activity, and everything that depended on it, went into rapid and terminal decline. All the things that made Britain look

Roman – towns, villas, local commerce, mass industrial production and heavy use of coinage – were increasingly abandoned, and the process was complete within a decade or two of the end of imperial rule. It is small wonder that temples shared in the wreckage; and, significantly, none of the stone buildings which some have thought to have been Christian churches were erected in this period of almost universal decay.[24] There are some signs that the abandonment of the pagan holy places was accompanied by violence. Uley was one such case. The shrines of Mithras seem to have been attacked collectively in the early fourth century, and by some kind of official order as the cult statues were often broken while the buildings were preserved; save at the fort above modern Caernarvon where the whole of one was burned and razed.[25] At Southwark and in Gloucestershire, broken statues of deities and other debris from demolished cult centres were dumped in wells, and many damaged bronze figures have been found in the Thames near the bridge that served the Roman city of London. One was the severed head of a monumental statue of the deified emperor Hadrian, while limbs broken from other statues have been found in wells in the city. When the cult statue of Sulis Minerva at Bath was destroyed, its head was cut off, slashed about the face, and thrown into a sewer where it was found in 1727.[26] There is no indication of the date and circumstances attached to these acts. It is telling that the metal of which such artefacts was composed was intrinsically valuable, and yet it was thrown away, as though used for an unclean purpose, instead of melted down. It remains possible that these acts were the work of barbarian raiders who mutilated items which they could not carry off; but it seems unlikely that London, at least, would have been captured by them and no trace of the act left in any records.

On the other hand, there is also evidence for peaceful coexistence of religions in the province, especially on the curse tablets thrown into the sacred spring at Bath. Some called down divine vengeance on offenders 'whether pagan or Christian', while the author of one actually identified himself as a Christian as he made his plea to the goddess of the spring.[27] It is possible, as has been said, that some of the mixture of motifs from the different religions on personal objects and mosaics testifies to such a genial partnership between them. The temple of Mithras at London collapsed naturally in the first quarter of the fourth century, because of unstable foundations, and its icons were buried in the floor. The building was not, however, abandoned, and seems to have been converted to a new cult, probably of Bacchus, which ended with no sign of violence many years later.[28] It has long been noted how fragmentary Romano-British religious statuary seems to be, compared with that from some other parts of the empire, and this has been ascribed to the fury of Christian iconoclasm. However, recently Ben Croxford has noted that the pieces were often buried in a manner which suggests structured ritual deposits, and that

82 The head of the cult statue of the goddess Sulis Minerva, which once stood in her temple at Bath. It had been hacked from the statue and then about the face, before being thrown into a sewer, and is now in the Roman Baths Museum.

they had been pulled apart rather than hewn into bits. He has proposed that, as the temples fell into ruin with the economy, their cult figures were ceremonially dismembered, with some parts retained as portable images or amulets until they were reverently interred.[29]

In 2006 David Petts revisited the question of how Christian late Roman Britain had been, and concluded simply that we don't know.[30] It seems hard to dispute this verdict. Together with the ability to decide, at least as the evidence stands, has been lost any knowledge of the experience and meaning of conversion during the period, and its implications for the different religious communities within the province. As so often in the story of ancient British religion, such questions are amenable to a wide variety of individual answers.

Evidence for Post-Roman Christianity

Modern scholarship has traditionally termed the early medieval period in Britain 'the Dark Ages', an expression which gives a great deal of entirely understandable offence to specialists in the history of the island from the seventh century onwards, of which a great deal is known. It also does a further injustice to this later period, of applying a label which suggests barbarism and

regression for the often highly creative, literate and culturally sophisticated
people who were active in it. For the years between 410 and 597 the second
consideration is still relevant, but the first, alas, is not. Some kind of history
exists for the whole of Roman Britain, in the sense that it is possible to know
who was ruling the empire of which it formed a part, and how, and to place the
individuals commemorated in the province in a political, administrative and
social context. Buildings can also usually be dated, by the evidence of coins and
sometimes of inscriptions, to within a portion of a century. By contrast, for
most of the two hundred years after the end of imperial rule, there is no real
political, administrative or social history. The names of many individuals can
be retrieved from it, especially from memorial stones, but virtually nothing can
be known of their lives. It is a perfect illustration of the extent of this problem
that the most famous of all the figures traditionally associated with it, Arthur,
may either have been one of the greatest people in the story of Britain, or have
had no historical existence at all.[31] The sudden absence of a money economy
and the mass production of artefacts mean that material remains often cannot
be assigned to one century or another; and although it is likely that this situation will be improved by the recent developments in the modelling of radiocarbon dates, discussed with relevance to the Neolithic, their effects have as
yet to be felt.

The lack of reliable and agreed history for the period is especially serious in
the field of religious studies, because it leaves us without any understanding of
one of the pivotal changes in the nature of British religion. At the end of Roman
Britain, as explained, it seems likely that both paganism and Christianity still
existed in the former province. When adequate information begins once more
to be available, near the end of the sixth century, the former Roman territory
has been divided into half. The western part is still occupied by the descendants of the colonial population, who are now apparently all Christian. The
eastern part seems once more to be pagan, but honouring a new set of deities
and rites derived from Germany and Scandinavia. What have apparently
vanished, throughout, are all active forms of the kinds of paganism previously
found in the large area of Britain once ruled by Rome, both of those forms
native to the island and those imported by settlers or visitors from other parts
of the Roman Empire. No solid evidence survives to enable an understanding
of how and why they disappeared, though the current scholarly consensus
seems to be that they did so rapidly, before the end, or even by the middle, of
the fifth century.[32]

This is a conclusion that is strongly indicated by the few sources that do
survive from the period. In Britain, that period is woefully lacking in the three
categories of written evidence which enable a modern person to track the
progress of conversion in other parts of the former Western Roman Empire:

lives of saints composed relatively soon after their deaths; sermons and edicts of leading churchmen; and decrees of church councils. There are several biographies of saints who operated in the former province in the fifth or sixth centuries, but virtually all were written after the middle of the eleventh century, and so are hardly reliable evidence for events in the age which they describe; and, perhaps unsurprisingly in view of the time lag, they provide little information on the process of conversion.[33] From the period under consideration, just three witnesses survive. The first is a Gaulish Christian called Constantius of Lyon, who wrote a life of a saint from his province, Bishop Germanus of Auxerre. He probably did so in the 480s, describing events in the first half of the century, and his relevance here is that those include two visits by Germanus to Britain. Both were on missionary work, to convert the inhabitants back to orthodox Christianity from the Pelagian heresy, and paganism is not mentioned as a problem, save as the religion of the barbarians who are raiding the former province. At one point Germanus conducts a mass baptism, but the reader is not told of whom; whether of pagans, heretics or just orthodox Christians who had not yet taken up the custom of baptizing infants. Had the subjects of the act been brought into Christianity for the first time, it is strange that Constantius does not mention the fact.[34] He certainly knew very little about Germanus's visits to Britain, in comparison with his activities on the Continent, but the purpose of the first one is confirmed by a near contemporary. This is the Gaulish chronicler Prosper of Aquitane, who wrote only four years after the event, which he dated to 429, with the information that it was indeed directed against Pelagianism.[35]

Our second witness is the most famous of all Irish saints, Patrick, whose lifetime cannot be dated but which is generally agreed to fall wholly or mainly within the fifth century. He left two letters, one of which contains an autobiographical sketch revealing a childhood in a western part of post-Roman Britain which was, in his recollection, securely Christian. His father held the lesser clerical office of deacon, while his grandfather had been a priest, and as a boy he had been made a deacon himself. He was captured by pagan Irish raiders, thereby launching his career as the most famous missionary to Ireland, but while he is naturally much concerned with Irish paganism, he never mentions a surviving British counterpart. Instead, in all his references to Britain he assumes a dominant Christian religion with a full ecclesiastical hierarchy.[36] The third author is Gildas. It is not certain who he was or where he lived, and he may have existed at any time between 450 and 550, although more probably in the second half of that period. His purpose was to castigate for their sins the British clergy of his time, and five petty kings, who ruled territories stretching from Cornwall to North Wales. What is highly significant is that he never included paganism among the misdeeds of the people whom he condemned, faulting them instead for moral offences such as greed, worldliness, marital misconduct, the murder of political rivals, and attacks on fellow Britons. Indeed, he explicitly considered paganism to be dead in his society, its memorials consisting only of the icons of Romano-British deities, still visible within and without the ruined cities. He recalled that his compatriots had once worshipped divine powers inherent in the natural world, but stated proudly that in his time they regarded that world merely as created for the use of humans.[37]

It is possible to enter cautions against the impression conveyed by these texts. Constantius, as said, plainly knew little about Britain, and Germanus may have been concerned only with a Christianized elite, and have ignored the mass of the inhabitants who could still have been pagan; it is interesting that he has curiously little to say about British church buildings or bishops, though he gives prominence to the shrine of St Alban.[38] Patrick may have grown up in a Christian enclave, and in his later dealings with fellow Britons simply not been interested in their problems with their own pagans. It is harder to present a counter-argument to the assumptions of Gildas, not least because he was dealing with a large region of the former province which had been one of the least Romanized and urbanized. Still, there may have been areas elsewhere with which he was less familiar in which the old religions lingered. None the less, when all of these doubts have been raised, it remains true that the picture provided by the only contemporary writings which deal with the religion of post-Roman Britain is a remarkably consistent one: that paganism had already lost its dominance there by the early fifth century, and was gone by the early sixth. It is notable that the early sixth century was also the time in which later authors located Arthur, and that the first of those to mention him, the ninth-century writer of the *Historia Brittonum*, portrayed him as a Christian warrior leading a Christian people against pagan invaders.[39]

On the whole, archaeology confirms the picture presented by the literary sources, in that if any pagan rites continued at the increasingly ruined temples by the beginning of the fifth century, they seem to have ceased at some point relatively early in it.[40] This impression may, however, be deceptive, because of the problems of interpretation and dating. The final abandonment of the temple of Sulis Minerva at Bath has been put by different experts at various times between the fourth and the seventh centuries, because the evidence is so complex: six layers of sediment accumulation and repair are visible in what appear to be the late and post-Roman levels. Radiocarbon dates for cattle bones now, however, suggest that the last attempt to repair the building was over by 430, and that soon after then it was deliberately demolished, with great effort. No more coins were put into the sacred spring after the late fourth century, although a late fifth-century brooch was added, perhaps as an accidental loss by a bather, or perhaps as one last gift from a devotee.[41] At Uley the front of the temple fell in the late fourth century, and the surviving portion was apparently converted into a smaller building, either a scaled-down pagan shrine or a church. That was replaced, probably in the fifth century, by a large wooden structure, from its shape and altars likely a church, which was succeeded in turn by a smaller stone one in the late sixth or early seventh century; after which the site was abandoned. When that final stone building was erected, pieces of the broken cult statue of Mercury were buried in the floor, the handsome classical head being placed carefully outside the junction of the body of the church and an apse.[42] Was this to venerate it, as a mixture of pagan and Christian loyalties; or to neutralize its pagan power; or because it had become mistaken for a representation of Christ or a saint? We cannot tell.

What is apparent is that British Christianity had already acquired enough confidence and momentum to become a missionary religion by the fifth century. It was during that period that it was given a bridgehead into Ireland, in the shape of Christian British slaves taken back to that country by raiding parties, as in the case of Patrick. The new religion seems to have become dominant, or even universal, in Ireland by the mid sixth century, and from there its adherents joined forces with British Christians to evangelize the northern extremities of Britain itself.[43] By the beginning of the sixth century, the new religion had spread beyond the limits of the former Roman province; and at some time in that century, and probably an early one, it had crossed southern Scotland to reach the Forth–Clyde line. The evidence for this is archaeological: the appearance of engraved marker stones of the kind associated with post-Roman Christianity in Wales and south-west Britain, and of cemeteries of unburnt burials, extending east to west, of the late Romano-British kind. Later tradition gave a particular prominence in this region to a saint called Nyniau, who became Ninian by the twelfth century. He is currently identified with a Briton named Uinniau, who also operated in Ireland where he was revered as Finnian, but became especially associated with the community of Whithorn near the south-western Scottish coast. Nothing certain is known of him except his date, which the Irish connection can place in the early to mid sixth century.[44] This is too late to make him the evangelist of southern Scotland, as tradition did, if the engraved stones genuinely predate this period. Whithorn, however, does seem to have been a very early Christian site, to judge by the preservation there of a stone inscribed with a sophisticated Christian statement in Latin, which has generally been dated to the first half of the fifth century.[45]

To the north of the Forth and Clyde lived the Britons who had never been Romanized, even to the extent of being occupied for a generation or turned into client kingdoms. All through the centuries of imperial rule elsewhere in the island, they had continued in a prehistoric Iron Age culture. From the end of the third century the Romans gave them a new collective nickname, of 'Picts', meaning 'painted people'. It probably referred to their habit of decorating their bodies, perhaps with tattoos, and summed up their barbarism, being at once redolent of contempt and fear. This was because the tribes concerned had begun to raid the wealthy and vulnerable province to their south, and continued to do so for about a century and a half, with increasingly serious effect. The name, however, stuck long after the raids had ceased, and by the end of the sixth century had come to have a more limited and important application. The inhabitants of Argyll and the southern Hebrides were closely connected to Ireland, sharing a common social, religious and political world with the kingdoms of Ulster and using the Irish (Gaelic) language; either because their area had actually been colonized by Irish invaders or because they had always belonged to the same linguistic and political zone.[46] They were given the Roman name for the Irish, 'Scots', which they eventually bestowed of course, upon the whole of northern Britain. The remaining British of the north, occupying the Northern Isles, northern Hebrides and the rest of the mainland, retained the nickname of Picts, and developed a distinctive and striking identity of their own. It was expressed especially in the production of upright stone slabs, carved with a standard repertoire of animal and abstract symbols which were later combined with explicitly Christian imagery as the slabs became crosses. Hundreds of these stones survive, displaying their carvings in churchyards, on road verges and in fields from Angus to Orkney.

During much of the nineteenth and twentieth centuries, there was a strong scholarly tradition that the Picts had been ethnically different from the rest of the Iron Age British, with a separate language and the custom of inheriting property and titles through the female rather than the male line. It was accordingly believed that they were an older race, perhaps descended directly from the Neolithic inhabitants of Britain and preserving in their inheritance traditions echoes of a former universal adherence of the very ancient British (or Europeans, or humanity) to matriarchal rule. Much ingenuity was expended on attempts to crack the code governing the symbols on the stones, in the belief that to do so would provide a unique insight into a lost world of prehistoric thought and belief. From the 1980s, this complex of scholarly beliefs dissolved. The Pictish language was identified as merely a regional dialect of Iron Age British. The belief in matrilineal inheritance proved to have been based on a credulous modern reading of just two sources. One was an origin myth, which was not composed until around 700, and seems to have been developed to justify the ability of one Pictish king to claim a realm through the female line. The other was a single Pictish king-list, which was apparently not composed until after the origin myth. As for the symbols, no attempt to decode them has so far met with general agreement. What is certain is that the symbol stones seem to have developed during the fifth and sixth centuries, as the peoples who adopted them separated off, culturally, from the Scots in Argyll and the rest of

(a)

(b)

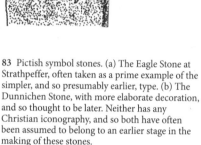

83 Pictish symbol stones. (a) The Eagle Stone at Strathpeffer, often taken as a prime example of the simpler, and so presumably earlier, type. (b) The Dunnichen Stone, with more elaborate decoration, and so thought to be later. Neither has any Christian iconography, and so both have often been assumed to belong to an earlier stage in the making of these stones.

the British to the south. The royal centres which the Picts established in the same period tended to be associated with impressive monuments from prehistory, and especially the Neolithic, as if to root the new kingdoms, dynasties and ethnicity in the ancient past. This was a pattern also found in Ireland in the same period, and among the Scots, to whom, as stated, the Irish were linked.[47]

The main question remaining from these discoveries is whether the symbol stones were a pre-Christian tradition which was subsequently linked to Christianity, or a Christian tradition in themselves. If the first is true, then the stones would have been developed as a defiant pagan gesture in the face of the approaching new religion, and were subsequently appropriated by it. The present answer is that the symbols seem to have predated conversion by a short time: the earliest that can be dated is on a small stone reused in the floor of a settlement at Sanday, Orkney, around 500.[48] They also reproduce styles which were already present on the metalwork of the northernmost British during the Roman period.[49] The erection of most of the carved slabs seems, however, significantly to post-date the adoption of Christianity. The Scots of Argyll had converted to Christianity by the mid sixth century, as an apparently integral part of the conversion of Ireland, with which they were so closely associated. It was at that time that the most famous of all their saints settled among them: Colum, whose name was Latinized as Columba. He did not come from Ireland

84 The full range of Pictish symbols as found engraved on the upright stone slabs and identified by Romilly Allen and Joseph Anderson.

as a missionary, but an exile, and his task was initially to establish a network of monastic communities within Christian Scottish territory, spreading out from the base which the local king gave him on the isle whose Irish name was Latinized to Iona. He was not, moreover, the only Irish churchman to found an important religious centre in Scottish territory at the time, as an independent one was established on another small island, Lismore, in the Firth of Lorne to the north. Another was founded later at Applecross up on the coast of Wester Ross, in 673 by the Irishman Maelrubha. Whether Columba conducted any actual missionary work himself, and where, is unclear, as the earliest account of his life, composed at a time within living memory of it, claims that he preached in the Tay basin, while the most detailed and famous, written about a century after his death, sends him to the Inverness region instead. So it looks as if he did operate among the Picts, but in which region, and whether the communities which he visited were already converted, are difficult questions to answer.[50] Later tradition preserved the names of actual Pictish saints, Drostan, Nechtan Ner and Servan, but no solid information on their careers.[51]

It is at present impossible to say how and by whom the Picts were converted, and whether the process was gradual or rapid, or easy or contested. Around the opening of the seventh century another Irishman, Donnán, established another large monastic community on the island of Eigg in the Central Hebrides. In 615–17 he and 150 followers were burned to death there by attackers. This fact is recorded in early and generally reliable Irish chronicles, along with the information that the killers went on to ravage parts of Ireland. The atrocity on Eigg was therefore one act of a large-scale raiding expedition, but the annals concerned do not identify the raiders or their motive: centuries later, a story was developed to account for the event which takes the form of a personal revenge drama and does not accord with some of the details of the chronicle entries.[52] If Donnán and his people were not slaughtered for religious reasons, then there is not a single reliably attested case of a Christian being martyred for her or his faith by pagans in the whole of the British Isles throughout the period 312 to 800, in which the conversion of most of the peoples of the archipelago took place. However, our lack of information concerning the process, in virtually every region, may caution against too ready and absolute a drawing of conclusions from that fact. Archaeology, once again, greatly enriches our sample of evidence without making it much easier to fashion into a historic narrative; and the classic case in point here is Martin Carver's recent excavation of the major Pictish monastery at Portmahomack, sited at the end of the Tarbat Peninsula on the Moray Firth. It seems to have been founded in episodes between about 550 and 675, but there is no indication of how or by whom, and when in that period it became a fully functioning monastery. Portmahomack, evidently a very important Christian centre which produced liturgical artefacts and books for daughter institutions, is itself apparently unknown to history.[53]

Before the end of the seventh century, the whole of the British Isles seems to have converted to Christianity, in the crude and external sense that it was the official faith of every community. We shall probably never know which was the last district to adopt it, though the balance of probability is that it was somewhere in the north of Scotland. On the map, the Northern Isles appear to be the most remote corner, but the sea lanes around Britain mean that they were almost certainly more receptive to new ideas than many places in the interior of the mainland. Orkney may be a good case study with which to close this survey. The late Iron Age and early medieval periods there are characterized by rectangular burial cairns orientated east to west, which may be pagan or Christian. There are also some small round or oval buildings without domestic features or artefacts which could be the first churches, or pagan shrines. Not only is any certainty of religious association lacking for all these material remains, moreover, but so is any certainty of date. As a result, although Christianity probably reached the islands in the sixth or seventh century, there is no reliable textual or archaeological evidence for it there until the eighth.[54] This kind of vagueness sums up most of our knowledge of the conversion of western Britain and Ireland to the new religion, and of the end of official adherence to paganism there: we lack a history of it.

It may be worth emphasizing here that there are still some positive things to be said about the subject. The very paucity of reliable data and interpretation means that different historians are free to put together their own stories, filling the gaps with their imagination and personal choices and with material selected from the work of later medieval authors of histories and saints' lives, who purported to provide the information missing from the earlier surviving sources, and may in some cases actually have been doing so.[55] It is also important not to miss the fact that, while the details are mostly lacking, the main features of these areas of the British Isles are clear. Their adoption of a Roman religion was one aspect of a process by which they, having lain either at the margins of the imperial province or outside it altogether, finally Romanized. They did so on their own terms, once the army that had guarded the province was gone and the frontier had dissolved. Christianity arrived as part of a package, which included literacy (in Latin as well as the local vernacular), a closer cultural and personal connection with the Mediterranean world, technological improvements in industry and agriculture, and the formation of larger political units. Its basic beliefs, its set of holy writings, its organizational structure and its framework of ceremonies remained standard, and by the end of the eighth century (and usually long before) all parts of the archipelago were to some extent part of a supranational Church. Even so, and especially in the first stages of adaptation to the new religion, different regions were able to develop individual emphases and idiosyncrasies in their employment of texts and adoption of ritual. They were also able to choose between modes of local religious leadership which were dominated by bishops, monasteries and secular rulers, or rather (and most of the time) make different relationships between those three.[56] They were able in the process to create strikingly different expressions of religious culture, the Picts for example rejecting Roman forms of literature, art and monument, although they eventually embraced the doctrinally Roman form of Christianity, and preferring distinctive alternatives such as the symbol stones.[57] The Christianity of north-eastern Britain, therefore, looked as different from that of the south, in some ways, as its paganism had done from that of the Roman province four to five hundred years before.

Adventus Saxonum

As stated above, in the course of the fifth and sixth centuries, native paganism disappeared in the eastern half of the former Roman province as well; but so did Christianity, both being replaced by a new kind of paganism, imported from German and Scandinavian lands. This was, of course, one important aspect of the phenomenon by which Romano-British culture was succeeded in this broad region by the Anglo-Saxon, as the crucial development which was to lead to the creation of the nation and identity of the English. A number of ancient and medieval texts, now long familiar to scholars, provide between them an account of how this occurred. Two, Constantius and Gildas, have already been cited: the others are a Gaulish chronicle, the main Anglo-Saxon one, the English historian Bede, and the Welsh *Historia Brittonum*. Although the product of three different cultures, the story that they tell between them is remarkably coherent and sustained, of an invasion by foreign war chiefs, leading shiploads of followers, who formed a spearhead for a mass movement of incoming peoples. It is a dramatic and traumatic narrative, of the violent dispossession of the post-Roman British of what proved in the end to be most of their land, marked by battles and the taking of towns and fortresses. It is true that some of these sources were compiled so long after the events concerned that their authors had to rely on traditions and texts handed on to them, of varying and often doubtful quality: the *Anglo-Saxon Chronicle* was commenced in the late seventh century (and its Dark Age material may have been inserted later), Bede wrote in the early eighth, and the *Historia Brittonum* was not compiled until the ninth. Some of the information conveyed is obviously invented: notoriously, the *Anglo-Saxon Chronicle* derives the names of Portsmouth and the Isle of Wight from those of their Saxon conquerors, when they plainly come from Roman originals.[58] On the other hand, there are balancing moments of attractive precision, such as the same chronicle's entry under the year 491 of the storming of the massive Roman coastal fortress of Pevensey in Sussex, given its correct Roman name. Furthermore, the Gaulish chronicle was almost contemporary to the relevant developments that it records (though with frustrating brevity), while Gildas's parents would have lived through the most intense part of the struggle between Britons and Anglo-Saxons that he records.

During the nineteenth century several prominent English historians identified passionately with the Anglo-Saxons as the ancestors both of their race and of all that was most noble in its national character and achievements.[59] They, and their colleagues, still disagreed profoundly over how much the conquest had consisted of acts of genuine ethnic cleansing, and how much it had absorbed large numbers of the British and habituated them to the ways and beliefs of the newcomers. By the 1920s and 1930s, also, doubts were frequently being expressed concerning the reliability of much of the written evidence for the process. None the less, there remained a dominant view that the arrival of the English (the 'Adventus Saxonum' in Bede's phrase) had consisted of a series of military campaigns associated with a mass movement of settlers from Germany and Jutland.[60] This doubtless derived much of its force, for some authors at least, from the persistence of the late Victorian preoccupation with race and invasion as the principal forces for change in prehistory and early history, discussed earlier in the present book. It was also, however, rooted in the available texts and in the apparent message of archaeology, as a Germanic culture became the dominant, or indeed the only visible, one across most of eastern England during the period concerned.

This view began to erode from the 1950s onward, as new archaeological techniques uncovered evidence which seemed seriously at odds with it. Aerial photography and landscape archaeology revealed that there had been no dramatic change in land use between Roman and Anglo-Saxon times, while the written evidence of charters suggested that some estates had been passed on intact from one period to the other. Field and enclosure systems in Kent and East Anglia, areas which were supposed to have been conquered first by the English, showed continuity from the Iron Age to the Middle Ages, and would have depended on hedges which needed regular maintenance. No fifth- or sixth-century cemetery contained bodies showing extensive evidence of violence.[61] None of this accorded well with a large-scale and brutal replacement of the native population, and the discrepancy was magnified when genetics added its contribution to the database. An Anglo-Saxon incursion was more or less invisible in matrilineal DNA, and though it was more apparent in male sequences, it was hard to disentangle the early English strain from that of later medieval settlement by Germanic and Scandinavian peoples such as the

Vikings. The possible influx of male Anglo-Saxons varied from a maximum of 20 per cent in East Anglia, 15 per cent in the North and East Midlands and 10 per cent in the south, to a minimum of 9 per cent in East Anglia and still lower totals elsewhere, making up an average of 5.5 per cent in England as a whole.[62] If the picture painted by the literary sources matched up to any kind of reality, the conquest would apparently have taken the form of an invasion by war bands which drove out or destroyed native British elites and took over the mass of the native population intact, to exploit it economically and impose their own culture, including their religion, upon it.[63]

The trouble with this otherwise neat explanation is that there is actually no evidence for a well-defined military elite, or any other kind of distinctive elite, in the early Anglo-Saxon settlement record. A possible further means of escape from this set of contradictions is to imagine a limited settlement of the eastern parts of the former province by Germanic farmers who coexisted with a larger but demoralized British population and converted it to a new culture suited to different times.[64] An extreme version of this hypothesis, advocated by a few scholars, is to discount the importance of a movement of peoples more or less completely, holding that it did not occur to a greater extent than in periods before or after, and to emphasize instead the willingness of British natives in the east to adopt Germanic ideas and artefacts for themselves.[65] To do this, of course, is to throw overboard the textual evidence and rely entirely upon that of archaeology and genetics.

If genetics and landscape studies indicate a basic continuity of population all over Britain, however, linguistic studies do not.[66] Old English replaced both the main languages of Roman-Britain – the native Celtic one and the official Latin one – completely in the areas that later became England. It did so, moreover, while taking on virtually no loanwords from either tongue. The areas most readily settled by invaders from the Continent (the south-east, East Anglia and the East Midlands) did not contain a hybrid culture in the late fifth and the sixth centuries, but a thoroughly Germanic one. The latter may have produced artefacts in strongly marked local styles, which showed some Roman influences at times and were deposited in greater quantity and value than was usual in the Continental homelands of Angles and Saxons; but these goods still derived unmistakably from Germanic and Scandinavian originals, as did the form of the houses of the owners. The burial rites were mostly unlike those of either late Romano-British Christians or pagans, and included the reintroduction of cremation, a practice abhorrent to Christianity, on a large scale. Romano-British cemeteries very rarely contained Anglo-Saxon graves, even when the latter existed in the same neighbourhood.[67] If there were native Britons in the eastern and south-eastern parts of the former province by the end of the fifth century, then they seem archaeologically invisible to most experts. A continuity of occupation of the same land was therefore accompanied by an absolute and abrupt discontinuity of language and culture, with no transitional period visible by which Roman Britons turned into Anglo-Saxons.[68] Such a discontinuity is commonly the hallmark of genocide, something which the evidence of the genes, bones and landscapes seem to have ruled out. Furthermore, those authors who have preferred that evidence to the testimony of the written sources, such as Gildas, have not so much explained the discrepancy of that testimony as disregarded it. What all of the literary texts which refer to the period embody, from the fifth to the ninth century, is an acute ethnic hostility between Britons and Anglo-Saxons. Furthermore, absolutely none describe any of the latter as former natives who had taken on foreign trappings: they are always characterized as invaders. Even in the late seventh century, when both were Christian, English kings who captured land from British rulers would still drive the native clergy off it and transfer the latter's endowments to their own churchmen; something that they did not do when warring against other Anglo-Saxon kingdoms.[69] Furthermore, Brittany, the westernmost peninsula of Gaul, was given its enduring character in the post-Roman period by being heavily settled by British refugees, the presence of whom would have been inexplicable had they not fled from a disaster at home. The genetic data should not be discounted, but it may be misleading. After all, the Norman Conquest, which is securely historically recorded and had dramatic political, social and cultural consequences for England, is genetically invisible.[70] If we relied on the evidence of DNA and archaeology alone for a knowledge of eleventh-century England, it would be possible to mount a very plausible argument that the Anglo-Saxons had simply imported Continental fashions on a huge scale in the 1060s and 1070s, and to point out that this was presaged in trends of cultural change already discernible in previous decades.

Considering possible answers to this critical issue of conflicting evidence, Nicholas Higham remarked in 1994 that 'it has become obvious that archaeologists are capable of producing an almost infinite succession of models, each of which is more or less incapable of either proof or refutation'.[71] This situation has not altered very much since. It is worth emphasizing also, in view of the number of times in this book at which a plurality of explanations for the same evidence has been suggested as possible, what an extreme state of affairs this one actually is. When the historical evidence for other conquests and occupations of parts of Britain in the ancient and medieval periods – the Roman, Viking and Norman – is compared with the archaeological, it makes a reasonably good match. There are arguments over whether the material data corroborates the textual and linguistic with regard to particular events and people, and the cultural implications of what occurred, but in general the two different kinds of source are compatible. In the case of the arrival of the Anglo-Saxons, the two are at present bewilderingly adrift, and lost in the gap is the reality of what happened to Romano-British religions in eastern Britain.[72]

Anglo-Saxon Paganism: The Written Evidence

As long as they remained pagan, the Anglo-Saxons were illiterate, and so by definition all the textual evidence for their religion is retrospective. It is also fragmentary and incidental, for after they converted none of them were interested in preserving a full portrait of their former beliefs and practices. Enough scraps of information survive to enable some such picture to be reconstructed, but for lack of any fresh written data that remains very much now the one assembled by the late nineteenth century. Indeed, much of the scholarship carried out since the middle of the twentieth has served to raise doubts concerning the utility of some of the traditional literary and linguistic material as a source for the matter. None the less, there remains reasonable certainty about some aspects of the religious system or systems of the pre-Christian English.

It is clear, for example, that like the great majority of other pagans they believed in a range of deities, and the names of some of those survive. The most important was Woden, who occurs most frequently both in place names, scattered across southern and midland England, and in royal genealogies, all but two of which feature him as an ancestor. He was given the day of week associated by the Romans with Mercury, god of travel, commerce and communication, and linguistically and in his attributes is clearly the English equivalent of the German Wotan and the Scandinavian Odin or Othin. This would make him a patron of rulers, wisdom, voyages and skills. A verse homily of the tenth century, indeed, calls him king of the deities and a cunning deceiver, at home on hills and at crossroads. A charm calls him an enchanter. The place name evidence gives second place to Thunor, who indeed features as more important in parts of southern England such as Essex. He got the day dedicated by the Romans to Jupiter, to whom the homily explicitly compares him. In name and character he equates to the Scandinavian Thor, German Donner and Rhenish Taranis, and all these parallels plainly make him a god of storms and rainfall, and (so) of farming. His symbols were the hammer, found as miniatures in graves, and the swastika, carved on cremation urns: they apparently stood for thunder and thunderbolts, respectively. A lesser but still broad scatter of place names indicates the presence of Tiw, who must have been a war god because he was given the day allotted by Romans to Mars (Tuesday), while the T-rune, a symbol with which he was apparently associated, was carved on weapons as well as urns. Finally, the goddess Frigg was given the day of the Roman Venus (Friday), and so presumably equates with her, and the Scandinavian Freya, as a patroness of love, passion, sexual satisfaction and abundance: she seems to feature in one place name, in Derbyshire. In addition to these there are faint traces of other divinities. The kings of Essex traced descent from a different god, Seaxnet, and a runic poem mentions one called Ing. Asser, the biographer of Alfred the Great, speaks of Geat, and Bede mentions two goddesses, Hretha and Eostre, associated with spring.[73]

There are difficulties attached to most of this information. Swastikas are found on cremation urns across a much greater area than place names which apparently commemorate Thunor, so may not be strictly associated with him; likewise there is no proven consistency of connection between the T-rune and Tiw.[74] Some of the names that could derive from Thunor might equally well come from later Viking settlers whose names had the prefix 'Thor' or 'Thur'.[75] These names of deities seem generally to be attached to natural places and prehistoric monuments, rather than to those of human use and habitation, raising the possibility that by the time that the attachment was made, the divinities had shrunk under Christian influence into demons, ghosts or legendary human figures, rather than actually being worshipped at those spots. Certainly Woden features in the royal genealogies as a descendant of Noah. How far he can be understood simply by comparison with the much better recorded Scandinavian Odin is a difficult matter. Odin, to take one instance, is one-eyed, having sacrificed the other in a successful quest of wisdom, while Woden, as portrayed in Anglo-Saxon genealogies, has both eyes: so they cannot have shared exactly the same mythology.[76] Various scholars have cast doubt on Bede's two goddesses, as they are mentioned nowhere else, and the source of his information is unknown. He speaks of them only because of his belief that the Anglo-Saxon months equivalent to March and April, Hrethmonath and Eosturmonath, were named after them, while linguistically the former could simply be 'the loud month' (because of its winds) and the latter 'the opening month' (because of its leaves). R. I. Page, for example, calls the goddess Eostre 'an etymological fantasy' of Bede's, while being no kinder to his identification of Hretha, and added that Bede's explanations for place names are sometimes definitely mistaken.[77]

There is also a larger problem attached to our knowledge of Anglo-Saxon deities. As has been described, the inscriptions of Roman Britain reveal an abundance of local goddesses and gods, as do those of the Western Roman Empire in general. Ancient Greece and the Near East had in most of recorded history more limited pantheons of a dozen or so major deities, particular to each major cultural area and often in a family or political relationship. These were, however, assembled early in the historic period from a much larger number of local divinities, as part of the construction of states and alliances between them: the enormous total of goddesses and gods originally honoured in Sumer was noted in a previous chapter, and the process of assemblage and reduction of divine figures to pantheons has been studied elsewhere.[78] In

Ireland the medieval epics similarly contain a small number of deities, gathered under a king in the Mesopotamian and Greek manner, the Túatha Dé Danann; this model was almost certainly taken by the Irish from the Greek and Roman literature with which they became familiar. The collections of medieval Irish place name lore contain, however, the names of several goddesses and some gods who do not feature in the stories. They therefore begin to look very similar to the Iron Age British, as revealed by the Roman gift of writing, and had the pagan Irish left inscriptions to their divinities then still more of the latter would probably come to light. This all makes the relatively small number of Germanic and Scandinavian deities recorded in the medieval sources look anomalous. It is telling that Tacitus, in his short account of first-century Germany, mentioned some as worshipped there who are apparently not found in the medieval texts, unless much transformed. There is thus at least a possibility that the Anglo-Saxons initially honoured many more divine figures whose names have been lost: unless they are concealed in those of settlements, usually thought to commemorate human landowners, just as lost Scandinavian deities may be hidden in names in medieval Norse verse which are usually treated as poetic doubles for the well-known figures from the standard divine pantheon.[79]

Place names also provide some evidence for holy places.[80] *Hearg* has been taken to indicate a place on a hill, and one rendering of it into modern English is Harrow. The Harrow on the Hill which is now in the north-western suburbs of London, and is the site of the famous school, features in early legal documents as the *hearg* of the Gumenings, a Middle Saxon people. The hill concerned still rises impressively above the surrounding land. So does that at Harrow in Sussex, where a dump of a thousand ox skulls has been found, presumably the remains of sacrificed animals. Ten other places with the *hearg* root have been identified, in the East Midlands, East Anglia and the south-east. *Weoh*, by contrast, has been taken as meaning a sacred site on any kind of ground, and sixteen place names embodying the word have been identified, scattered across the midland and southern counties of England, especially near roads. Sarah Semple has found that three *hearg* sites were places of extended former ceremonial activity, especially in the Romano-British period: they include the Sussex Harrow, where the ox skulls seem to date from that earlier age. Though this does not necessarily mean that the Anglo-Saxons did not carry on worship there, in turn it does away with the idea that the word refers purely to a pagan English holy place.[81] Indeed no Anglo-Saxon temple or shrine has yet been securely identified anywhere, and by the 1990s many archaeologists had come to doubt their existence.[82] The Roman historian Tacitus had spoken of the Germanic peoples in general as preferring to worship in natural groves of trees, and John Blair has noted that many early English place names suggest a possible veneration of trees, posts, pillars and mounds.[83] Sarah Semple has pointed out that the evidence of names and ecclesiastical decrees suggests that the supernatural was associated with such a wide array of natural features that the whole landscape appeared sacred to some extent.[84] This being so, *hearg* and *weoh* may also have referred to sites of special sanctity with no human structures on them at all.[85]

Of actual buildings, the best candidate for a temple to date is at Yeavering in the Cheviot Hills of Northumberland, a seat of the seventh-century kings of Northumbria. Within the palace complex was a large wooden rectangular building, with a pit beside it full of animal bones, almost all of oxen. It showed no sign of domestic use, but neither were there traces of any altars or votive offerings inside. Three posts had stood near the southern end, five more in a fenced enclosure outside, and another huge one to the north-west: perhaps they were carved with symbols or as deities, or hung with trophies, though some at least might also have been Christian crosses put up after the conversion of the kingdom. The whole structure had been burned, as if by Christians immolating one centre of a rival religion; but the bones may have been the remains of royal feasts, and the destruction an act of war or merely an accident. Another possible Anglo-Saxon shrine has been excavated at Blacklow Hill in Warwickshire, and three others have been proposed in other parts of England. It may well be significant that all seem to date from the late sixth or the seventh century, at the end of the pagan period in England, when followers of the old religion may have been starting to construct special places of worship in rivalry with Christian churches, or in imitation of Iron Age or Romano-British shrines.[86] Certainly two of the most enduringly famous figures concerned with the conversion of the English, Pope Gregory the Great who ordered it and Bede, who wrote its history, both spoke of the existence of pagan temples. It may be objected that Gregory never went near England, while Bede wrote in the next generation or two after paganism had officially disappeared. Being based in a monastery near Hadrian's Wall, Bede could, indeed, have been misled by the ruins of Romano-British holy places in his neighbourhood.[87] There is, however, no indication that he suffered from any such confusion. On the contrary, he spoke of the former site of one of the main temples of the English kingdom of Northumbria as still being shown to visitors in his own lifetime, while he had spoken to a man who had seen an actual one of an East Anglian king.[88] In the 670s a leading abbot, Aldhelm, rejoiced that 'where once the crude pillars of the same foul snake and the stag were worshipped ... in profane shrines', monasteries and churches were now built.[89] This has sometimes been read as good evidence for serpent- and stag-worship in Anglo-Saxon temples with sacred pillars. The 'foul snake', however, is here a euphemism for the Devil, so this might mean any pagan image, while there are no other certain references to a stag cult in Anglo-Saxon England. Aldhelm may indeed have been referring to the ruins of a Romano-British temple with a stag-antlered god depicted there; his monastery of Malmesbury was not far from the remains of Roman Cirencester (where such a god was carved), Bath and Nettleton. On the other hand, the mention of pillars brings to mind those posts at Yeavering. Perhaps the most reasonable conclusion is that there is some quite good textual evidence for temples and shrines in seventh-century England, but that archaeology has yet to identify these securely.

Bede also spoke of his people as having had idols, by which he meant images of their deities. In this they would, again, have been similar to other pagans, but presumably the statues and carvings concerned were of wood and would have rotted away even if they were not burned by zealous Christians. The only places where they would have been preserved were bogs and gravel terraces, and none have yet been found there; but then fewer than two dozen such timber images have been recovered from the whole of British prehistory, and not all of those may have religious significance. Bede mentions his pagan forebears as having priests, and indeed refers specifically to a high priest for his own kingdom, of Northumbria. This individual was prohibited by his office from riding a stallion or bearing weapons, a system of taboo which accords well with similar ritual restrictions placed on the leading priest at Rome and (at least in legend) on Irish kings.[90] Another such figure features in the Life of the Northumbrian saint Wilfrid, which records that when its hero and his companions were shipwrecked

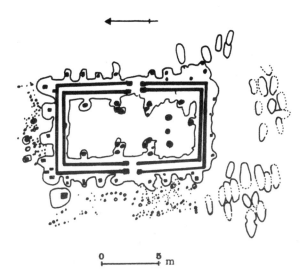

0 ____ 5 m

85 The structure at Yeavering which has been identified as a possible pagan Anglo-Saxon temple. The line of three posts in the interior is clearly picked out, as are those outside the northern end and the big one outside the north-western corner.

on the coast of Sussex, local pagans attacked them in order to steal their posses-sions, while the 'chief priest' of the locality cursed Wilfrid's people from the top of a mound, to aid the attack.[91] This account was written only a decade after the death of Wilfrid, by a monk of his abbey who should have known him person-ally. Textual sources similarly have a few traces of pre-Christian belief. There are references to divination and the taking of omens, which are easily to be believed because all ancient societies of which we have knowledge shared this interest. An early eighth-century text tells of how the whole retinue of a pagan Northumbrian king halted because a crow cawed from an unlucky section of the sky.[92] Bede has a famous story of how a councillor of the Northumbrian king Edwin, faced with the Christian message, compared the pagan view of life to the experience of a sparrow flying through a feasting hall from one door to another on a winter night, and so experiencing a brief moment of warmth and light before returning to the dark and cold. The main point of the anecdote was that pagan Anglo-Saxons, unlike Christians, did not claim any certain knowledge of what follows death; which would accord with the variety of their burial rites, shortly to be considered. It has often been considered, also, that Anglo-Saxon literature, long after the adoption of Christianity, displays an unusually heavy emphasis on the working of a predestined fate, known as *wyrd*, in human affairs, which may be a carry-over from native paganism.[93]

Again, it is possible to point out problems in this material. No bodies in Anglo-Saxon graves have been securely identified as having any trappings to pick them out as priests, though one at Yeavering had what may have been a standard or staff which might have served as one.[94] If it is a standard, however, the man in the grave may just have been its bearer. More convincingly, a number of female burials, with collections of small objects of no obvious practical or decorative use, have been identified as possible cunning women, sorceresses or female shamans.[95] The story of the fight on the Sussex coast goes on to relate how the pagan high priest was killed marvellously by a flung stone, in the manner of David slaying Goliath, and the whole altercation is compared to Gideon's exploits. The portrayal of the episode is therefore heavily influenced by biblical models, and it is hard to know how far even eyewitnesses coloured their memories in accordance with a desire to emulate those. With a greater lag in reportage the problem of reliability increases. The story of the crow's effect on the royal retinue took place, on the admission of the author who recorded it, 'long before the days of any of those who are still alive'. It was of course told to make a polemical point, of how a Christian missionary had the bird shot to show the power of his god over the forces of nature, and the folly of pagan forms of divination.[96] On the other hand, many pagan Europeans did divine the future from the cries and flight of birds.[97] Bede's accounts of the high priest of Northumbria and of the simile of the sparrow in the hall derived from a time over a hundred years before he wrote it. He quite carefully identified both information which he had received from eyewitnesses of events or from people who had spoken to those. He makes no such claim to either source in this case, so this pair of stories would have come to him through a communal spoken tradition of unknown reliability. Richard North has suggested, in fact, that Bede's account of the actions and taboos of the high priest might have been concocted by somebody using various literary and folkloric motifs.[98] S. D. Church has noted that it echoes the account of the conversion of the Frankish king Clovis, given in an earlier text by Gregory of Tours.[99] On the other hand, the metaphor of the bird in the hall is a credible one, even if it is not provable. Linguistic evidence strongly suggests that the Germanic paganism of which the Anglo-Saxon was an offshoot placed a much heavier emphasis on ritual acts than on beliefs concerning the nature of the cosmos and the fate of the soul: all early Germanic languages have many words for precise ceremonial actions, rather than for cosmological concepts.[100] As for *wyrd*, a number of scholars have argued that it was an abstraction drawn from Christian, rather than pagan, sources, and especially the sixth-century Italian writer Boethius.[101]

Bede also provided a sketch of the pagan English calendar, identifying six festivals in particular.[102] One was at the winter solstice, which he termed 'Modranect', the 'Mothers' Night', and said that it opened the New Year. The month of February was given the name of Solmonath, 'Cake Month', because (he added) people baked cakes then and offered them to deities. September was 'Halegmonath', 'Holy Month', indicating a focus of rites then, perhaps to close the harvest season. November was 'Blotmonath', 'Blood Month', and here Bede was explicit that this was because of the annual slaughter of fattened live-stock before winter set in, with a dedication of the lives of the animals to deities: one naturally thinks here of the ox skulls at Harrow and Yeavering. In addition there were the spring months, and feasts, of Hrethmonath and Eosturmonath, discussed above. There is no sign that Bede knew what rites had been carried out at these festivals, or whether his interpretation of the names of the months was a well-informed one: according to linguists, his derivation of Solmonath from 'cake' does not work.[103] Even so, there is nothing inherently unlikely about his basic information, because northern European peoples in general, including the others in the British Isles, tended to hold festivities at these times of year. The main problem with Bede's commentary is, indeed, that it is incomplete as it stands: it is barely possible that the Anglo-Saxons would not have held a festival to mark the summer solstice as well, because – again – northern Europeans in general have done so since the beginning of recorded time.[104]

The most famous single piece of early English literature is *Beowulf*, which is also the longest poem surviving in the Old English language and indeed the longest in any vernacular language of Western Europe from before the twelfth

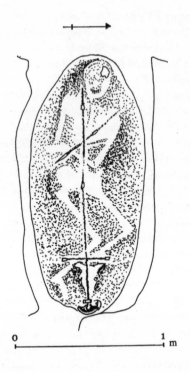

86 The burial at Yeavering with a possible staff, which may indicate that the person interred there was a priestly figure.

0 ━━━━━━━━━━━━━━━━━━━ 1 m

century. It is set in Scandinavia in pre-Christian times, but any attempt to define its relationship with historic pagan beliefs and practices is vitiated by a lack of context: after two hundred years of intense study, experts still cannot agree on when, where, for whom, or by whom, it was written. What is now consensual is that it is in essence a Christian work, rather than a pagan one later given a Christian veneer.[105] There are indeed fundamental traits of the text which make such a conclusion easy to draw. Christ is never mentioned because he is treated as not yet having arrived, either to the people concerned or on earth at all; but the Christian god is still very much in charge. The work's pagan heroes believe in a single true deity, who created the whole world and sent a great flood to destroy sinners in it, who ordains whatever happens in it, and whose adversary, who tempts humanity, is the Devil. Bad pagans, in the story, worship the latter and sacrifice to him in heathen shrines, but good pagans do not. They are clearly proto-Christians, just waiting to receive the Christian message.[106] This makes it the harder – indeed at the present time apparently impossible – to determine to what extent the trappings of paganism portrayed in the poem, such as the cremation funerals and the symbolic decorations of armour, were the result of accurately remembered tradition, or imagination, or extrapolation from the observed remains of old burials and hoards, disinterred in Christian times.[107]

Inevitably, the recent vogue for regarding shamanism as the key to the understanding of all ancient religion in northern Europe has affected Anglo-Saxon studies, being given an application to early English poetry by the American scholar Stephen Glosecki.[108] He has taken care to make a more careful than usual study of the phenomenon as portrayed in anthropology, and an accordingly more precise definition of what a shaman is. His shaman is a specialist practitioner who inhabits a natural world which teems with spirits, and works with some of those spirits as allies and helpers. This person communicates with those spirits by entering a trance which allows her or his spirit to go forth into other dimensions and work there to help other humans, most often by healing them. Entry into this practice is secured by training and initiation, a process which often involves vivid and traumatic spiritual experiences. Such a definition certainly accords well with the 'classic' shamanism of Siberia and the adjoining regions of Europe and Asia, which supplied the Western world with the word 'shaman' and the original set of characteristics attached to it. Glosecki finds possible references to all aspects of his defining traits in different passages of Anglo-Saxon poetry and images from artwork of the period. The essential problem with his interpretations is that they cannot be proved and all are doubtful, leaving readers to find more or less plausibility in them. Classic shamanism of the Siberian kind certainly existed in Europe, and indeed across much of ancient Scandinavia, among the Sámi or Lapps. It also appears in Old Norse literature, plainly identified with the Sámi, but with certain traits of it taken up by the Norse themselves to produce a hybrid kind of magical tradition.[109] What is so striking about Anglo-Saxon literature, in this respect, is its total lack of the portraits of shamanic workings of the classical sort, or of practices clearly related to or derived from them, which appear so plainly in the Norse texts. This is why Glosecki had to resort to finding oblique references in passages and images which could easily bear very different meanings. It was an enterprise which was probably worth undertaking, but seems inevitably to have an inconclusive end.

One further kind of textual evidence needs to be considered: that of the runes, the script used by early medieval Germanic and Scandinavian peoples. Its symbols were long thought by scholars to have possessed intrinsically magical qualities, but recent authors have been dismissive of this idea. Christine Fell has denied that there was any native English runic magical tradition, while R. I. Page has called the idea of runes as a magical script 'outdated and nonsensical'. On the other hand, Page allows that the signs could be used for magic, and Fell that Scandinavians, at least, did so use them. Page also leaves open the question of whether people who understood the script, 'rune-masters', had a special status in society. Both Fell and C. J. Arnold have emphasized that both pagans and Christians used the script, and so it had no special association with the older religions, while Arnold notes that the signs are found on different sorts of Anglo-Saxon grave good but without any context that would allow their significance there to be understood now. They may or may not refer to specific deities, as said above, and some were put on to the objects concerned when they were made, so may have had no relevance to the grave.[110] While all this seems to put paid to the notion of an inherently numinous, definitively pagan, script, an association between runes and supernatural qualities and purposes in England, at particular times and for particular purposes, has not been eradicated from the realm of possibility. After all, the late Anglo-Saxon churchman Aelfric condemned things done 'by means of wizardry or runes', though admittedly he was doing so after the arrival of a wave of Scandinavian immigrants.[111]

Anglo-Saxon Paganisms: The Material Evidence

The main material evidence for the spiritual beliefs of the early English consists of burials, which are very abundant: indeed, almost 1,200 pagan Anglo-Saxon cemeteries have so far been discovered.[112] They lie beneath fields and copses in many parts of eastern England, their presence or former presence sometimes betrayed by low hummocks in the grass or leaf mould. Almost 26,000 Anglo-Saxon graves have now been excavated, compared with a handful of settlements, and so we know much more about the early English in death than in life. On the whole, cremation was the preferred mode of burial, and it was more prevalent in the 'Anglian' areas of the East Midlands and East Anglia, while inhumation, of whole bodies, was more common further south in the 'Saxon' regions. Another overall trend is that the poor tended to be cremated and the rich inhumed. Both modes are, however, found almost everywhere and at all social levels, and often together in the same cemetery, and the only really safe generalization is that the pagan English liked to put their dead into the earth, and often with goods. A large minority of inhumations and about half of all cremations were accompanied by the latter, making goods far more common with burials than they had been either in the Iron Age or among the Roman Britons. This represented, in effect, a serious loss of useful possessions by a relatively impoverished agrarian society. The Anglo-Saxons were clearly more inclined than previous societies in Britain to believe that their dead should be equipped for the next world, or that their possessions were owed to them, or that gifts should be made to them or to the deities who were taking them into care: none the less, burials with goods were still a privileged group overall.

Cremations were generally interred in urns, which tended to get larger and better decorated according to the age and riches of the person inside.[113] A very wide range of objects was put with them, including crystal or glass beads, combs, shears, brooches, tweezers and razors. These were often intimate articles, provided perhaps to make the deceased look good in the afterlife, or perhaps because their close association with their previous owner would induce the latter to haunt anybody to whom they were passed on; or perhaps, again, because they had been used by mourners to transform their appearance for the funeral rites. The fact that miniature models of the goods were sometimes provided could argue that the first of those explanations was more important, or that they had a high symbolic value. Women were burned with personal ornaments; by contrast, knives and weapons were rarely put with cremations, but animal parts and whole carcasses were common, burned on the pyre as foodstuffs, companions, totems, symbolic beings related to aspects of cosmology, or offerings to powerful protective beings. About 80 per cent of the urns were decorated, with a very complex iconography: like tombstones, they said things about the deceased. One very common symbol used was the *wyrm*, a serpentine form which may have stood for a snake or a dragon. This could have functioned as a personal protector: here, after all, may be the origin of Aldhelm's 'foul snake'. The swastika was almost as popular, perhaps a symbol of fire or of Thunor. There were many more, and an understanding of their significance would be a little easier if we knew who chose them; whether they were potters' brand-marks, or personal symbols of the dead, or chosen by

87 An Anglo-Saxon cemetery under a copse on the hill above Caistor St Edmund, Norfolk. The hummocks at the foot of the trees, made by excavation, mark the site of the graves.

88 Anglo-Saxon cremation urns from a
cemetery at Sancton, Yorkshire, showing
the swastika motif: redrawn from the
original illustrations made by J. N. L.
Myres.

(a)

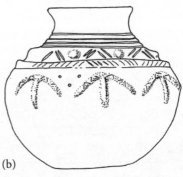

(b)

89 More Anglo-Saxon cremation urns. (a) Another from Sancton bears both the swastika
and the 'T' designs, perhaps indicating the gods Thunor and Tiw or thunder and lightning
(and so divine fire). Redrawn from another of J. N. L. Myres's illustrations.
(b) One from the Spong Hill cemetery, Norfolk, has raised 'T' designs. Redrawn after C. M.
Hills and K. Penn.

mourners, like flowers at present-day funerals. It is even possible that cinerary urns were viewed as dedicatory vessels in which the dead were offered up, often with additional gifts, to deities or ancestors: or rather, parts of the dead, because as before only a portion of the bones was recovered from the pyre.

Almost six thousand inhumations are well recorded. Infants – relatively rare in cemeteries but still more common than in those of earlier periods – tended to be interred with an unusual orientation, stones placed over the bodies, or amulets. All these measures signal anxiety, perhaps because the babies concerned had died suddenly and mysteriously. Children were often buried crouching, like foetuses, and were quite commonly given adult weapons or jewellery, either as marks of their families' rank or because they were expected to keep on growing in the next life. Adults tended to be buried fully clothed and on their backs, either west to east with heads to west, or north to south. Almost half of all adult men had weapons, above all spears and shields, and often vessels for food or drink were laid with them as well. In several cemeteries those with weapons tended to be taller than others, although of all ages and sometimes crippled, and only as well nourished as the other burials; so weaponry was the sign of a special social group rather than of warriors as such. Likewise, women commonly had jewellery, but many did not, and some women had weapons while some men had ornaments of the kind found with women. All this may point to a genuine, if not standard, conception of a world after death. Grave goods were extremely varied. There were fewer animals than with cremations, but still plenty, and as with cremated bodies these were mostly of edible livestock but also of dogs and horses: indeed, the latter were more common in graves than they could possibly have been in the economy. Other frequently deposited items were amulets, especially with women; most often cowrie shells, horses' teeth and boars' tusks. The first and last of those might have been vaginal and lunar symbols respectively. Beads – made from crystal, amber, amethyst or quartz – could also have been amuletic. There was no single 'image of death' in an Anglo-Saxon inhumation, and – just as with many earlier kinds of monument – the process of making a grave may have been more important than its final form. That process, in each case, seems to have been very much the result of a set of individual choices, or those of small groups, or of specialists in those groups – perhaps priests or cunning women – drawing upon a set of relatively localized and dynamically developing ideas. The burial that resulted would, of course, have been merely the last act in a long sequence of funeral rites which are completely lost to us.

Just as in Romano-British cemeteries, certain burials have impressed some modern scholars as sinister. About a quarter of all inhumations were imposed on others, which in most cases may have been a gesture of affection and continued unity in death. In nine cases, well scattered across eastern England, high-status burials – male or female – were accompanied by a lower-status

person put unceremoniously over or under them. They may have been servants, who had died around the same time and were sent to carry on their
service in the next life, but there are a few instances where volition is in doubt.
At Welbeck Hill in Lincolnshire, a beheaded woman was laid over an important old man, while at Portway in Hampshire a man had been laid over a
woman put into the grave with bound wrists; and three similar pairings are
known. In four cases suggestions have even been made that people (all female)
were buried alive, but other explanations are possible for the disarrangement of
the bodies concerned.[114] At another Hampshire site, Worthy Park, a girl had
been thrown into a grave face-down with her wrists and heels apparently
bound. Most of the bodies accompanying burials of higher status were put in
face-down, and this is generally so rare in Anglo-Saxon cemeteries that it was
probably deliberate in many cases. There is no continuation of it from Roman
Britain, as it appears in English graves only in the late sixth century. It may have
been a rite intended to ensure that the spirit of the person remained at the place
and guarded it; whatever the reason, prone burials were given grave goods in
the same measure as the ordinary kind, so the position was not necessarily a
disgrace; and they are almost all found in normal burial grounds. As in Roman
times, also, some bodies were decapitated. In a few cases, such as the mass
grave with fifty headless corpses near Thetford in the Norfolk Breckland, this
is almost certainly the result of a massacre. When such burials are scattered
around cemeteries – fifty-four examples of which are known, most male – they
may have been victims of war or of execution, or disabled to prevent their
ghosts from walking. Inevitably, the spectre of human sacrifice hovers over
some. The Roman historian Tacitus stressed that the tribes of Germany in
general, including the ancestors of the English, were very fond of this custom,
and a fifth-century Roman author from Gaul, Sidonius, asserted that the
Saxons drowned or crucified a slave, chosen by lot, as an offering before going
on a raid. Once again, it is impossible to know what level of distortion or
misunderstanding is present in these accounts. It is notable that not a single
source mentions the sacrifice of humans in Anglo-Saxon England, even those
produced by Christians with the most inveterate hostility to paganism.[115]

It seems likely, from the regularity with which graves were laid out in the cemeteries, that they were marked. In some cases, traces of these markers have been
found, in the form of wooden posts, and of fences and ditches round the site; which
suggests not merely that the layout was kept regular but that some kind of veneration of the dead continued after the burial. Most cemeteries had fewer than a
hundred burials, but fifty of them were larger, and that at Spong Hill on the clay
plateau of central Norfolk had over two thousand. By contrast, there are virtually
no Anglo-Saxon graves in the later counties of Northumberland and Durham,
leaving modern commentators wondering if the first English there did not bury

90 Drawing and reconstruction of the possible 'live' burial of a woman at Sewerby, Yorkshire, after S. M. Hirst.

their dead, but exposed them or scattered their ashes. In their German homeland, the Anglo-Saxons sometimes raised mounds over their dead, but these only appear in England from the late sixth century. They may have been copied from prehistoric barrows – which the Anglo-Saxons indeed often reused as burial places – or used as markers to claim land, or monuments to flaunt an adherence to paganism in the face of Christian challenge. They seem to have been a matter for individual taste – there were four at Spong Hill, for example – and they do not always cover especially wealthy graves. Complete cemeteries of barrow burials, sometimes with impressive mounds, are also known: and huge solitary mounds were constructed as well, often standing prominently in high places with wide views. The problem of cultural influences, in this respect as in others, stems from the fact that the English of the sixth and seventh centuries were very adaptable and culturally dynamic people with horizons extending all over the Scandinavian and German world, links stretching as far as the Mediterranean and ideas taken from the native British and the sight of Roman and prehistoric monuments in the lands which they settled. The goods at Spong Hill alone show influences from Norway, Denmark, Sweden and Germany, while about a quarter of all known Anglo-Saxon burial sites were associated with some form of prehistoric or Roman monument: apparently the early English often liked to lodge their dead in some sense of ancestral continuity with the land, even if the ancestors were not literally their own. There is a pronounced tendency for funerals and graves to become more ornate towards the end of the pagan period as Anglo-Saxon society grew more sophisticated and its kingdoms more powerful: the possible appearance of temples also fits this pattern.

The most remarkable of all the cemeteries are those which probably belonged to the rulers of East Anglia, at Snape and Sutton Hoo near the Suffolk coast. They seem to have begun with cremations in bronze bowls or inhumations in coffins, and barrows were increasingly raised over burials. Then interments with horses were added at Sutton Hoo, and finally (in this conjectural sequence) the bodies were laid in boats or ships, two at Snape and two at Sutton Hoo.[116] The size of the vessels was not standard, one at Snape being 50 feet (over 15 metres) long and the other a mere dinghy. At Sutton Hoo a 65-foot ship was put over a timber chamber, while a 90-foot one in a different mound became the chamber itself, containing the famous treasure of bowls, spoons, weapons, armour and regalia, found in 1939 and now displayed in the British Museum. One item, the helmet with pointed face mask, has become iconic, being the defining face of the Dark Ages for many artists and designers. The ship, the largest known from northern Europe before the Viking era, would have needed forty oars, and it is perhaps notable that the treasure included a bag of thirty-seven coins and three gold pieces, as if to pay a full complement of ghostly rowers. Two elements of the cemetery – cremations under mounds

91 The huge Anglo-Saxon barrow at Taplow, in the Thames Valley in Buckinghamshire, set among the tombs of a now-demolished church which seems to have had an Anglo-Saxon predecessor. The scoop taken out of the mound by the Victorian excavators is clearly visible, a project which yielded a rich treasure of grave goods, from a classic 'warrior' grave of the period. The position of the church nearby suggests either that it was deemed fitting to build a Christian holy place near the resting place of a famous leader, or else (just possibly) that, despite the grave goods and mound, the man laid there was actually a Christian convert, who had been buried with traditional trappings but in consecrated ground and with Christian rites.

and ship burials – were not traditional in Anglo-Saxon England but recent innovations. This was a new and flamboyant manifestation of paganism, probably produced by a newly appeared kingdom.[117]

The excavation was sponsored by the landowner Edith May Pretty, and the story of her decision to do so is one which combines romance, tragedy and (possibly) the supernatural. She and her husband, Colonel Pretty, had fallen in love when she was eighteen, but her parents had forbidden the match, because although both families had made their money from manufacturing, his had turned out less prestigious goods than hers (gasometers instead of corsets). They waited patiently until her mother and father had both died, and then wed, only for Colonel Pretty to perish himself, suddenly, a few years later. His heartbroken widow took up spiritualism in the hope of making contact with him, only to be advised (it is said) by one medium to dig up the ancient mounds that rose from the heath, studded with bracken, birch and gorse, and purple with heather in late summer, on her estate. She duly hired an experienced archaeologist from the Ipswich Museum, who found some looted Anglo-Saxon burials, with a few objects still remaining. A second season of work was under-taken (with further encouragement from the medium), and the ship burial and its treasure were discovered. This immediately resulted in the substitution of a more highly trained and celebrated archaeologist, Charles Phillips of Cambridge University, for the local one, Basil Brown, who had made the find. Tension swiftly erupted between the two, and worsened when Edith Pretty took Brown's side. None the less, the work was completed, to an excellent standard for the time, and an inquest held at Sutton village hall, in classic local English fashion, duly declared the finds, which included 8,000 gems, to be the property of Mrs Pretty. She gallantly donated all to the nation, just in time for them to spend the Second World War hidden in a London Underground station as bombs rained on the city above. The war's end allowed them to take their place at the British Museum, where fifteen years of patient study and reconstruction by a team led by Rupert Bruce-Mitford revealed the true extent of their number and nature.[118]

As important as the original excavation, for our understanding of the site, are the further investigations of the cemetery conducted by Martin Carver between 1983 and 1992. He found more high-status burials, and established the likely site sequence narrated above. He also discovered that the barrows were ringed by other bodies, half of which showed clear signs of violent death, having been beheaded or hanged. This initially raised again the possibility of sacrificial rites, conducted as a feature of the funerals (and perhaps providing the oarsmen for the ship of the dead), but subsequent dating of the remains put them into the Christian Anglo-Saxon period, between the eighth and eleventh centuries. They remain deeply significant, but probably in a different context: that the deserted pagan burial mounds were made a place for the execution of criminals, who were thus removed from the community to a place presumably associated by then with ghosts and devils. Characteristically of the early English, the grave goods have cultural associations extending from Scandinavia to the Mediterranean, and the identity of the warrior buried in the ship remains uncertain, as is his faith. The goods in it included Christian baptismal spoons, which could suggest that the owner had been Redwald, the most powerful of all East Anglian kings and one noted by Bede as having honoured Christ and pagan deities in the same temple. This would accord well with the Christian objects laid in a flamboyantly pagan burial context; but they may have been looted from a Christian owner by one of the dead man's ancestors, or those of a friend who presented them to him.[119] The Sutton Hoo cemetery is now in the hands of the National Trust, which has built an excellent visitor centre and roped off the mounds, access now being permitted only by the purchase of one of the limited places on guided tours. This arrangement protects the site and does justice to it, and it is an unworthy emotion that makes the present writer remember fondly his boyhood image of the place, as a flock of low tumuli, deserted upon the misty heath.

Other forms of material evidence for the religious activities of the early English are not merely eclipsed by the burial evidence but genuinely rare in comparison. It is clear, for example, that they preferred to put goods into graves than into pits by themselves, as ritual deposits. The most famous collection of Anglo-Saxon metalwork yet found in a single location is the 'Staffordshire Hoard' discovered in a field near Ogley Hay in the southern part of the county, by a private treasure hunter in 2009. It consisted of more than 3,490 individual pieces, most from artefacts related to war – above all sword hilts – which seem to date to between the sixth and eighth centuries. It may have been interred as an act of ritual, at a place which was regarded as sacred, or the owner may have intended to return and retrieve it, and failed; the span of presumed dates for the objects extends far enough into the Christian period to make the former possibility rather less likely than the latter. The manner in which the objects were recovered has left experts uncertain of whether they were buried hurriedly, placed in a grave or dropped on the surface of the ground; and so we lack a proper context for them.[120] Likewise, Anglo-Saxon metalwork is sometimes found in rivers – spearheads have been dredged from the Thames and three of its tributaries – but there has been relatively less inclination to emphasize the possibility that it was ritually deposited than when dealing with wetland finds from earlier periods. None has yet been located in lakes or pools.[121]

There is a little more mileage in studying the imagery of early English art, mostly as displayed on metal artefacts. A dancing nude warrior with a horned helmet on a famous belt buckle from a cemetery at Finglesham, near the eastern coast of Kent, might be a votary of Woden (or might not be).[122] Woden himself may appear in a male head wearing a large headpiece, and with a bird on either

92 'Finglesham Man', the dancing nude warrior with a helmet topped by two beaked heads, on a buckle found in a late sixth-century grave in East Kent. The same figure is common on Swedish helmets of the seventh century. The beaked heads could be those of eagles, and eagles and a spear were associated with the Scandinavian god Odin: so the warrior in these images could be a votary of that god. On the other hand, he could simply be performing a victory dance, and there is in any case no guarantee, if the connection with Odin is correct, that it made the journey to Kent, or can be linked to the equivalent Anglo-Saxon deity Woden.

93 The most famous of the Anglo-Saxon boar images, which may have conferred supernatural power on the warrior who donned them: found on a helmet in a grave at Benty Grange, Derbyshire.

94 A motif on the metal fittings of a purse found among the Sutton Hoo treasure. It could display the Scandinavian god Odin, between his attendant wolves, or the equivalent English god Woden, if he shared the same mythology; or a solar god being swallowed by celestial monsters; or a man attacked by wolves or similar creatures; or a shaman in trance, with servitor animal spirits; or a god or spirit who controlled animals; or none of the above. The range of choice is typical for such images.

side, on a brooch from an early sixth-century woman's grave on Chessell Down in the Isle of Wight: if Woden were similar to the Norse Odin, then the headpiece could be a slouched hat and the birds attendant ravens.[123] Shields were commonly ornamented with animal shapes too small to have been seen by others as a badge of the wearer's identity, and featuring open-jawed monstrous beasts. These might well have invested the objects on which they were mounted with spiritual protection.[124] Aleks Pluskowski has noted the central part that animals in general play in Anglo-Saxon art, while animal elements commonly appeared in personal names and (as said) the bodies of beasts were incorporated into mortuary rites. They decorate both weaponry and female jewellery, and may have played the same symbolic and protective role on both. There is very little evidence for active veneration of them as divine, except perhaps for Aldhelm's snake and stag, but they seem to have played a key part in the conceptualization of society and the cosmos. The desirable qualities which some seemed to possess – especially powerful wild beasts such as bears, wolves, boars, stags and eagles – were apparently regarded as being susceptible to access and use by humans; and it is possible that they were used symbolically to facilitate a connection with the supernatural. Among domestic creatures, the horse stands out for its importance in imagery and ritual, equated (unlike, for example, the dog) with high social and political status. Particular species may have been connected with particular deities.[125] All this, however, lacks absolute proof, though it has a strong probability. Overall, it remains true that most of the surviving evidence of Anglo-Saxon religious beliefs and customs surrounds dead human beings, rather than focusing on the living world, the simple result of the survival of so many cemeteries.

The Christianization of the English

In 597 a Christian mission was launched from Rome, at the personal behest of Pope Gregory the Great, to reclaim for his religion the former inhabitants of the Roman province of Britain by converting the English to Christianity and persuading the remnants of the native British to bring their own varieties of the faith into conformity with his own. Both aims were achieved, though the former, which is the business of the present book, much more swiftly than the latter. It was indeed formally completed in 686, so that the whole process took up the space of just one, long, human lifetime. The records of it effectively represent the restoration of history to southern Britain, providing as they do a more or less continuous narrative in which firmly attested leaders operate and have relationships with each other. Those records are, however, as badly defective as a portrait of the manner in which conversion was achieved as they are as a source for the religions which it supplanted. Very few are contemporary with the process, and those are mainly letters from popes, who were physically remote from it and so not directly engaged. Most of the rest consist of histories and saints' lives produced by monks writing at a remove of one to three generations from the events they were describing, and not much interested in how their compatriots actually became Christian. They regarded the superiority of their own religion as self-evident, and reported that it was imparted to heathens by preaching and by the working of miracles by saints, the deeds (and physical relics) of whom lent prestige and authority to the religious houses in which the literature concerned was written.

Most of the representations of ordinary English people caught up in the triumph of Christianity which appear in the works of authors like Bede are set in the period that succeeded conversion, one of uneasy adjustment to the new religion. For example, Bede portrays a crowd of peasants above the mouth of the Tyne in about the year 650, almost two decades after the final imposition of the faith upon their kingdom, watching rafts bearing monks from South Shields being swept out to sea by a gale. They jeer at the helpless men for disdaining the lives of ordinary folk and doing away with the old worship, so that 'now nobody knows what to do'. The point of the anecdote was that the future Saint Cuthbert was at hand and his prayers changed the wind, impressing the crowd: it was told by a man who had been in that crowd to a monk who passed on the story to Bede. Another episode in Cuthbert's life came when he had joined a monastery himself, at Melrose in the Tweed Valley of southern Scotland. Plague struck the district, and many who had been baptized abandoned their new faith and 'fled to idols' with amulets and incantations to ward off the disease. Cuthbert had to go out into the hills to preach them back into belief. Bede knew at least one man who had been at Melrose Abbey at the time and would have been an eyewitness.[126] These are still tales recorded at second and third hand, but the cultural setting which they portray, of a resentful and confused local populace, still unsteady in its recently acquired religion, is not wholly creditable to Christianity and has a ring of truth about it. They also have a recorded chain of transmission, instead of arising from an amorphous mass of pious tradition as so many of the stories of the conversion period itself do.

When all the necessary admissions have been made about the deficiencies of the source material, the outlines of the process of Christianization, and the reasons for its success, are still pretty clear. They boil down to three factors. The first was that the pagan English were almost surrounded by Christians, in the shape of the powerful and influential new kingdom of the Franks to the south and east, the native British and Irish to the west and north, and the Scots of Argyll to the north. In effect, they were taken in a pincer, by a missionary effort launched almost simultaneously from Rome, with the assistance of Continental kings and churches, and from Ireland.[127] It was the Irish who proved the more important, as, operating outwards from their great British base on Iona, they secured the conversion of Northumbria, the northern English kingdom that

became the dominant force in seventh-century British politics. They also established important centres for evangelism as far south as the Suffolk and Sussex
coasts and the upper Thames Valley. The Roman mission, however, never lost its
grip on its original bridgehead in East Kent, even though it suffered two periods
of major reverses and in the first of these, in 616, was reduced to a nucleus at
Canterbury, bereft of royal support. Nevertheless, it hung on, and followed each
spate of losses with a new campaign of evangelism which made up the former
ground and added more, until by the late seventh century it had become the
leading force in British Christianity. Ambitious and devout churchmen were
constantly attracted from the Continent to the work of reclaiming Britain,
coming not just from Rome itself but from the Frankish and Burgundian kingdoms and with the support of the churches there. There is a growing tendency
among scholars to believe that the native British may also have exerted influence
on the Anglo-Saxons, and induced some of them to take on Christianity, in parts
of the West Country and West Midlands. Certainly pagan burials seem to be rare
or absent there, before any external Christian campaign could have reached these
areas, while some cults of British saints continued.[128] The English were thus
subjected to a sustained and determined missionary effort, from most points of
the compass. It also mattered greatly that the faith thus preached to them had
already been adopted by the most powerful, sophisticated and culturally and
technologically advanced states in Europe, to which rulers who accepted it could
much more easily be linked in trade, diplomacy and alliance.

The second factor in Christian success was the pivotal position of the
monarch in the various kingdoms into which the English were forming by the
end of the sixth century. As was the case all over northern Europe, the initial
effort of conversion was always aimed straight at the king, who would then place
the full force of his authority and patronage at the service of his new religion. In
return, Christianity awarded supportive monarchs a consecration and reinforce-
ment of their power over their subjects which it had by now long been accustomed to bestow upon those of the Mediterranean world. The allegiance of the
king was automatically followed by mass baptisms among his people, as native
paganisms possessed no alternative sources of authority.[129] The reception of the
original Roman mission in Kent in 597 was ensured by the fact that the reigning
ruler, Æthelberht, already had a Christian wife, a Frank, who was practising her
religion freely with a bishop as her chaplain. It was another stroke of luck, or act
of providence, that Aethelberht was also the most respected English monarch of
the time, and followed his own conversion by imposing conversion on his
nephew, who held the client state of Essex. He married a daughter to the new
king of Northumbria, on condition that she could take Christianity with her, and
she duly provided the conduit for the conversion of her husband in turn. Upon
his death in battle, this mission was endangered, but rescued by the rapid rise of

another Northumbrian monarch who had spent his exile on Iona and invited in the Irish from there. The continuing expansion of Northumbrian power enabled the imposition of the faith of Christ on the large Midland realm of Mercia, and on Wessex, East Anglia and Essex, which all became client states. The fact that Sussex and the Isle of Wight were the last kingdoms in England to convert was simply due to the fact that they were small and isolated, and outside the main currents of English royal power politics, rather than the result of any special propensity to resistance on their part. Sussex was eventually taken under the wing of Mercia, the monarchs of which had begun to increase their own influence at the expense of that of Northumbria and Wessex. The Mercian king had his Sussex neighbour baptized and offered him two provinces of Wessex if he commenced a missionary effort in his own kingdom, starting with his nobility. The grateful client immediately obliged, and met with no difficulty. The fate of Wight was more violent, because it was conquered by a usurping king of Wessex, anxious to reassert himself in the face of Mercian ambition. Christian priests followed his victorious army, and he graciously allowed the last two princes of the native royal house of Wight to be baptized before he had them killed.[130]

These 'external' considerations were both of major importance in accounting for Christian success, but so was a third: that, unlike Christianity, native English forms of religion were not missionary and militant faiths. To put it another way, pagans simply did not take religion as seriously as Christians did, because they did not regard it as embodying divine law or carrying a choice of salvation or damnation as a consequence. The monks who wrote the histories and saints' lives were not surprised at the apparent ease with which Anglo-Saxons embraced allegiance to Christ, but were puzzled and dismayed by the equally insouciant manner with which they then dumped it when kings and circumstances changed. Most English kingdoms reverted to paganism when the original royal convert died, and the work of redemption had to begin anew. Æthelberht's heir in Kent rejected Christianity because his bishop would not let him marry his father's widow, while the sons of the first Christian sovereign of Essex did so because their bishop would not admit them to communion before they were baptized. Redwald of East Anglia, as described, is said cheerfully to have installed altars to Christ and to pagan deities in his temple, under the impression that this took care of every problem. Essex fell away twice, the second occasion, as late as 665, being precipitated by the same plague epidemic which had shaken the faith of the people of the Tweed Valley. One of the East Saxon kings, with many of his subjects, turned back then to older deities for aid, before he was reclaimed for Christ by an eloquent bishop sent by the pious (and powerful) ruler of Mercia.[131] Furthermore, whether they adopted or discarded Christianity, the pagan English never seem to have regarded it as an evil religion. By this period, orthodox Christians routinely expected the triumph of their faith to be accompanied by the suppression of paganism, but pagans had no similar concerns. Before becoming Christian, the rulers of Sussex had allowed or ignored the establishment of a community of Irish monks on their coast at Bosham. The leader of the original mission sent by Gregory to Kent crossed Britain six years after his arrival, to confer with British bishops in the Severn Valley, and none of the sovereigns of the pagan kingdoms which he traversed seems to have been troubled by his presence. Penda, the last pagan king of Mercia, was similarly unconcerned when his own son and heir converted to Christianity to marry a daughter of the king of Northumbria, and he allowed the priests brought in by his son to preach freely.[132]

It is therefore not surprising that the story of the Christianization of the English, like that of the whole of the British Isles, contains no definite instance of a missionary being put to death by pagans for his religion. In default of any, Christian writers stretched the category of martyrdom to cover especially zealous convert kings who died in battle against pagan opponents, but the exercise is not a convincing one, even on the evidence of the writers themselves. Bede made a particular effort to demonize Penda, who killed five Christian kings, as an enemy of true religion, but it is clear from the context that Penda was merely conducting his share of the brutal power politics of seventh-century English state-building. His allies were generally as Christian as his opponents. When he finally died in battle against the Northumbrians in 655, Bede hailed this as a deliverance 'from the hostile attacks of the heathen'. However, Penda was accompanied on his last campaign by the estranged son of the Northumbrian monarch who defeated him, and by the king of East Anglia, both of them followers of Christ. The king of Wessex who conquered Wight and sent in Christian missionaries to legitimize his act in the eyes of his neighbours was himself still personally a pagan when he did these things, and was not baptized for a few more years.[133] The traditional religious tolerance of the Anglo-Saxons took some time to erode even after conversion. Pope Gregory stated in his letters that he expected a Christian king to terminate pagan worship among his subjects as part of the transformation consequent on baptism, destroying images of the old deities and altars to them. Not for almost half a century after the arrival of his mission in Kent, however, did a ruler of that kingdom order this step, and with it the imposition of Christian feasts and fasts upon all of his people; and he was the first English king to do so, although such a repressive programme had become routine by the end of the seventh century.[134] It seems that the more aggressive, determined and monopolistic religion had the edge over its rivals, simply because it cared more about winning, and demanded absolute victory. This relationship is a classic contrast between examples of what theorists of religious studies currently term 'indigenous' and 'world' religions. The former are generally tribal, territorial and particular, non-proselytizing, folk-orientated, and dependent on mythology and customary law rather than literary texts.[135] The latter are characterized by systematic theology embodied in writing, and by exclusivity, proselytizing and universalism.[136] When the two collide, the result is usually the same as that achieved in Anglo-Saxon England.

The framework of the conversion process can thus be reconstructed with a fair degree of probable accuracy in modern times. What is lost, and must be left to individual or group judgement, is how far the different factors in it combined in the case of particular people, states and situations.

The Viking Incursion

Only about a century after each part of the British Isles had formally embraced Christianity, the new religion faced a fresh challenge, in the form of pagan raiders, who then often became settlers, from Norway and Denmark. In their initial form, as plunderers and slavers, they bore the name of Viking, which has been given to them by history. They represented a brief, if dramatic, interruption to the progress of the faith of Christ, for they appeared at the end of the eighth century, made an increasingly serious impact on the archipelago in the course of the ninth, and were already starting to convert to Christianity by the end of that period. By the late tenth century, most of those settled in the British Isles had made the transition and their Scandinavian homelands had begun to do so, Denmark converting in the 960s and Norway between 995 and 1030. None the less, during their brief period of operation in the British islands as pagans, they were able to make a significant cultural impact and add another layer of pagan tradition to the already rich historic and prehistoric accumulation. This impact was felt especially in the Northern and Western Isles of Scotland, and adjacent parts of the mainland, and in the far north of England and in Yorkshire, the East Midlands and East Anglia.

In recent decades there have been differences of opinion with regard to the amount of damage that the first Viking incursions did to British Christianity; and these have in turn been part of a wider debate over the extent of their destructive impact.[137] It was instigated from the 1960s onwards, pre-eminently by Peter Sawyer but also by other scholars who believed that this impact had been much exaggerated by monastic authors appalled by the paganism of the newcomers. Historians of this school emphasized instead the positive contributions the Scandinavians made to the lands in which they settled, by founding towns, establishing new trade routes and returning accumulated wealth to circulation. In the religious sphere it stressed the rapidity with which they converted to Christianity and the continuity or swift re-establishment of ecclesiastical organization in regions which they took over. This was the more remarkable in the absence of any recorded missionary effort to convert them:

but then written evidence for the process of their conversion, especially in England, is very scarce in any case. It seems that most of the churches in English regions occupied by Danish rulers survived, perhaps because the new lords wanted to keep their Christian subjects tractable. Those lords also, however, showed an enthusiasm for adopting the trappings of the wealthier and more respected English rulers, such as coinage and literacy. The support of churchmen was another of those, and helped to make the newcomers look royal in English eyes. In the Scottish islands there are possible church sites which date from the period in which pagan Norse rulers held control, and an apparent reference to a bishop resident in Orkney. Even in their earliest phases of raiding, there is no sign that Vikings regarded themselves as waging a holy war on Christianity.

On the other hand, the amount of harm done was also considerable. Most dioceses in parts of England taken by Scandinavians vanished at least temporarily, and no activity by higher churchmen is apparent in most of them between 880 and 920. The churches that survived there usually did so with less wealth and status, and an apparent loss of records and books, with an accompanying decline in literacy. Great British Christian centres such as Iona and its English colony on Lindisfarne were relocated to the mainland, and the original sites only reoccupied much later, while other notable monasteries, such as that of Portmahomack, were badly damaged, and yet others, including Bede's own house of Jarrow, were abandoned permanently. It is still possible to make a case that the behaviour of the Vikings was not in itself more atrocious than that of other early medieval northern Europeans, but it is one which fails to take into account the fact that they provoked more horror among Christians because they ignored the usual conventions of warfare. They were strangers from distant places, not familiar local enemies, and attacked from the sea, turning monasteries which had hitherto enjoyed the relative safety of sites on islands and peninsulas into easy targets. They did not merely loot churches frequently and without inhibition, but destroyed them, and killed or enslaved their clergy.

As with all the early historical pagans of Britain, the most abundant evidence of Viking ritual and religious belief is provided by graves. As before, these are distinguished as pagan by the slightly unreliable indicator of the burial of weapons and body ornaments with the dead. Scotland has most, a current total of around 130, and the largest number of those is in the Orkney Islands, by all signs the region of the British Isles most heavily settled by Scandinavians. Scattered graves have been found in the Shetlands and in Caithness, and on most of the Western Isles and a few of the western peninsulas of the Highlands. Orkney has several cemeteries, and three more are known in the Hebrides. Virtually all the burials are inhumations, with one certain cremation, of a richly furnished woman on the isle of Arran. As cremation was the standard rite in the settlers' homeland of Norway, they probably copied the fashion for unburnt burial from the Christian British among whom they took up residence; but they did not often use Christian cemeteries. The position and orientation of bodies varied, and graves were likewise sometimes given low mounds or put into older barrows. Bodies were occasionally interred in boats, which might have been regarded as large coffins, or symbols of the dead person's power or occupation in life, or as modes of transport to the next life. Grave goods may have been everyday objects or chosen specially for the burial rite, and it is hard to distinguish any with specific cultic associations, though one woman in Orkney had a hammer pendant, often taken as a symbol of the Scandinavian thunder god, Thor. A few horses and dogs were included in graves. The timescale for all these finds is a brief one, reckoned at present to be most probably between 850 and 950.[138]

England has only twenty-five known Viking burial sites, most of solitary graves. The majority are in the northern counties but they are scattered as far south as Berkshire and Suffolk. This is an oddly low number, given the density of settlement in those regions and the East Midlands and East Anglia suggested by the number of Scandinavian place names. It also compares strangely with the tens of thousands of known pagan Anglo-Saxon graves. A few Viking weapons found in northern English churchyards probably came from pagan burials. This scant record has been one reason for an assumption that the newcomers quickly converted, although to a more secular form of Christianity less focused on monasticism: at the very least, it is apparent that the Vikings who settled in England did not much need ritual displays of difference from the native population. In recent years three of the twenty-five sites have overshadowed the rest. A cemetery was found in 2009 by treasure hunters, at Cumwhitton in the Eden Valley of Cumbria, near Carlisle. It had a range of weapons, dress ornaments and accessories, the largest object found being a needlework box.[139] Most attention, however, has been drawn to the Anglo-Saxon monastery at Repton on the River Trent, which was the burial place of Mercian kings. In the winter of 873–4 it became the base of a large army of Viking invaders, who left a number of graves. Some were placed at the end of the church, and included the grave of a man who had been killed by a slicing blow through the artery of one thigh. He was laid with a silver hammer amulet, a sword, a knife, a key, a boar's tusk and a jackdaw bone. The royal Mercian mausoleum, however, had been converted into a mass grave, in which disarticulated bones from at least 249 individuals had been interred around the burial of a single high-ranking man. To the east, at Ingleby, is the only known Scandinavian cremation cemetery in the British Isles, of around sixty mounds, many of which covered the bones of men and women who had been burned with weapons and jewels, along with cattle, sheep, dogs and pigs. Some of the animals were complete, as if companions or sacrifices, and others were disjointed, as if for food. Only a third of the bodies were burned on the spot, the rest being represented by small quantities of bone cremated elsewhere.[140]

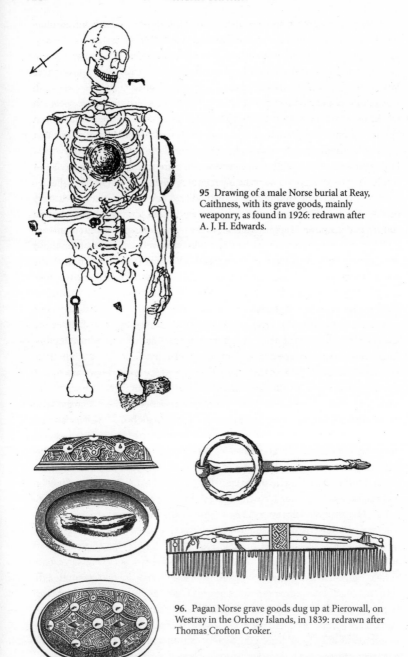

95 Drawing of a male Norse burial at Reay, Caithness, with its grave goods, mainly weaponry, as found in 1926: redrawn after A. J. H. Edwards.

96. Pagan Norse grave goods dug up at Pierowall, on Westray in the Orkney Islands, in 1839: redrawn after Thomas Crofton Croker.

How are the graves in and near Repton to be interpreted? There is no absolute proof that those at Ingleby were left by the army of 873–4, but there is no other credible context for them. It could be that they were those of the Vikings who did not want to make any compromises with the local Christians, unlike those interred at the church. Instead these Vikings consigned their comrades and womenfolk to a starkly pagan and Scandinavian burial rite, the flames of which would have dramatically illuminated the skyline above the Trent. The token burials of bone could have been those of warriors who had fallen on campaign and had portions of their remains brought carefully to this war cemetery for a proper funeral. It is doubtful, however, whether the burials at the church can confidently be interpreted as those of members of the army who felt a greater affinity with the English and with Christianity. They might equally well have represented the deliberate intrusion and imposition of an alien and hostile culture, to desecrate and appropriate one of the most sacred places of a conquered kingdom. Many (at least) of the bones in the mass grave seem to have been those of long-dead English monks and kings, disinterred and thrown into a heap when a defensive ditch was dug around the Viking camp. The warlord buried at their centre might have wanted to lie in the midst of Christian holy men, but might equally have been laid in the midst of the former spiritual and royal leaders of vanquished enemies, piled around him as trophies. The best candidate for his identity remains the fearsome Viking chief Ivar the Boneless, who died at Repton: the grave itself was removed in the nineteenth century. Certainly, the burials at Repton and Ingleby show between them the range of preferences for ritual found even within one pagan Viking host. Whichever the explanation for them, the cremation cemetery was soon disused, but some of the graves in and around the church which had Scandinavian goods date from a generation or so later, so that the site had seemingly remained a burial place for high-ranking Danish settlers.

The Isle of Man has the greatest single concentration of Viking remains in the British Isles, having been the centre of an independent Scandinavian kingdom which lasted until the thirteenth century. This claim is true of burials as in other respects, as Man has over forty in an area of just 232 square miles (some 380 square kilometres).[141] Three sites in particular have produced remarkable discoveries. One is at Peel, the best harbour on the west coast, where an existing Christian cemetery received eight graves with goods datable to the early tenth century, the richest being that of a woman, the 'Lady of Peel'. Her accompanying objects included a splendid necklace, of beads from all over the Viking world, a pestle and mortar, and an iron roasting spit, while bunches of herbs were placed in the grave. As her goods were not generally of Scandinavian kind, she might be taken for a native Manxwoman who had married a pagan Viking, or a descendant of Viking settlers who had adopted locally available possessions. The spit seems too heavy to have functioned as a staff: if this were not the case, she might be associated with a category of Scandinavian prophetesses and wise women to whom a staff was a sign of office and power. The herbs and the mortar (possibly for grinding potions) might also hint at such a role. These part-pagan graves in an otherwise Christian cemetery suggest a society of mixed ethnicity following the Viking conquest, tolerant of different religions. At Balladoole, on a hill overlooking the south coast, another Christian graveyard had been utilized, but this time for one of the island's two Norse ship burials, which had been deliberately dug through existing graves in the centre. This may have been an act intended to plant the newcomer, a well-dressed adult male, in the holy ground of the native religion which was the resting place of previous local lords, but it also resembles one of desecration and humili-ation. Then again, the preceding cemetery may have been irrelevant, and the mourners just determined to make the grave on a convenient hill overlooking the sea. With him were bones from another person, probably female, and over him had been laid burnt remains of horse, ox, pig, sheep or goat, dog and cat. There were no weapons, his goods but tools, a cauldron and horse harness. At Ballateare on the north-western coast, a young man had been buried in a wooden coffin or chamber, surrounded by weapons, including a sword which had been deliberately broken and a spear and shield which may also have been damaged for burial (or in battle). His grave was covered with the cremated bones of a similar range of animals, and the body of a young woman who had been thrown carelessly on to it. A mound was then piled over the lot, topped with sods of earth from a different district which was perhaps the dead man's original land. Both these last two sites were excavated, and the richness of Manx Viking archaeology revealed, by a first-rate German archaeologist, Gerhard Bersu, who had been interned on the island during the Second World War as an enemy alien, and found this employment during his confinement. He dug with a spoon because the rules of internment forbade him better tools which might be employed as weapons.

One habit the Vikings sometimes adopted, which had not belonged to the pagan English, was the making of monumental sculpture. It was influenced by the Christian taste for carved stone crosses and tombs, both of which were accepted with gusto by Scandinavian settlers in some areas. In Britain, such places are found mainly in northern England and southern Scotland, with Man, again, having the most unusual concentration of crosses for its size.[142] Cumbria and Yorkshire between them have over 600 monuments which were erected either by Viking settlers or by Anglo-Saxons copying Scandinavian styles. Modern scholars have often been especially interested in the motifs taken from pagan Scandinavian mythology which feature on a few slabs, and their implications for the process of Christianization. Their assessments of those implications, unsurprisingly, have been varied. To some, the deployment of such scenes argues for a period in which Christian and pagan beliefs were tolerated together and given equal honours: hence Christ's Crucifixion was shown in parallel with the destruction of most of the Norse pagan deities in the great conflict of Ragnarök, and Sigurd, the Scandinavian dragon-slayer, with saints celebrated for vanquishing evil beings, such as Michael. To others, they represent a Christian appropriation of the pagan stories, so that it is actually the Crucifixion that brings about Ragnarök, and Sigurd is enlisted as a Christian hero. Such speculations are made easier by the damage inflicted on many of the slabs concerned by time and humanity: few now survive with their decorative scheme intact, and the fragments that remain can be reconstructed in different ways. The reconstructions are commonly made according to a pagan mythology which is recorded only in Scandinavia, and there in much later texts compiled by Christians, when details of it may have altered.

To take the Manx case, only one scene from the island's many crosses, a piece from the church at Andreas in the far north, certainly portrays a deity. It has a scene of the god Odin, accompanied by his trademark spear and raven and with his foot in the jaws of the demonic wolf Fenrik, who devours him at Ragnarök. This is balanced by a Christian hero on the other side, holding book and cross. Less than half of the original decorative programme of the slab survives, making it even more difficult to tell whether the evangelist represents a complement to the god or his replacement and negation. It is possible that some of the other Manx crosses carry images of pagan deities, but experts have become much less confident in identifying these in British contexts than they were in the early twentieth century, because all of the figures concerned could have alternative meanings. One such specialist speaks entertainingly of the salutary lesson provided by one carving from Aspatria near the Cumbrian coast, 'which early scholars saw as a pagan phallic image, only to discover that when reversed the fragment revealed a Christian figure with arms raised in prayer: his worn head had been mistaken for quite a different part of his anatomy'.[143] There is now apparently universal agreement that none of them, in Britain or Man, are pagan, as they all occur in Christian contexts, but their meaning there can (as said) be located in a great range of possibilities. These arguments can be broadened to take in portable ornaments, such as the hammer-pendants and amulets often taken to represent Thor. Three are known from Britain and its smaller islands, of which two have been mentioned, but 121 from Scandinavia. Academic debate in the latter's nations has not resolved the question of whether they were an independent pagan symbol, a pagan answer to the cross, or just a local adaptation of the Christian cross itself. It may have been each of those in specific places.[144]

No Viking temple or shrine has been found in the British Isles, and the Norse word *hof* which could signify one, occurs as a place name only on Shetland, the most northerly of all.[145] This is not surprising, if the religion of the pagan settlers was conducted mostly in the home and at natural places, and such a conclusion is strongly suggested by the directives issued by Wulfstan,

97 The fragment of carved Viking cross at Andreas on the Isle of Man, still preserved at the church, which probably shows the god Odin being devoured by a demonic wolf at Ragnarök.

archbishop of York, in the aftermath of the official conversion of the Vikings in northern England to Christianity. He does not mention temples, but speaks instead of rites around wells, springs, rocks and trees, especially the elder.[146] As water best preserves the offerings left by such activities, wetlands have provided most of the evidence for them. Deposits of prehistoric and early historic metalwork are relatively common in Scandinavian waters, and one of the peak periods for deposition there was the Viking era.[147] By 1965 a total of thirty-four Viking swords had been found in English rivers, and the scarcity of other kinds of hardware of the period in the same waters suggests that these were deliberately left there and not casual losses. Another sword was placed underneath a jetty or bridge abutment on the River Hull in East Yorkshire, with cattle, horses, dogs and tools: apparently a classic dedication deposit.[148]

The pagan Vikings have been charged with the practice of human sacrifice, and this is supported by an apparent chain of evidence extending the length of Europe. On the River Volga, at its eastern extreme, the Arab traveller Ibn Fadlan himself witnessed, and reported in detail, the killing of a slave girl at the funeral of a chief of the 'Rus' people, as an intrinsic part of the rites. The medieval Christian writer Adam of Bremen wrote a description of a temple at Uppsala in Sweden, at which both humans and animals were offered, and their corpses hung from trees. Bodies which had suffered violent death are occasionally found in Scandinavian graves, placed as apparent companions for higher-status individuals who had been laid there first. A classic example of this phenomenon is recorded on the Isle of Man, where the woman put over the grave at Ballateare had suffered a fatal sword blow which had sheared away part of her skull. All this grim data may give a cumulative impression that in the case of Scandinavian warriors, at least, this most fearsome of rites is plainly proven; but each piece of it is susceptible to challenge. The 'Rus' of Ibn Fadlan were probably Scandinavians, but may have been natives of the Volga basin instead. Archaeology has so far failed to reveal Adam of Bremen's temple, and the quality of his testimony, which was certainly second-hand, has been called into question. The bodies with suspicious features in Scandinavian graves could have been slaves or retainers of the people with whom they were buried, who had died in the same violent event, or criminals who had murdered those people and were executed and thrown into the graves in revenge. These same considerations account for the woman at Ballateare, who could have been a victim of the raid in which the high-status man interred there received a death wound, and a favourite possession or companion of his during life. None of these alternative explanations may be correct, and human sacrifice may indeed account for all or most of these cases; but there is no certainty.[149]

Perhaps most telling is the fact that the British and Irish Christians who expressed such horror at the conduct of the Vikings in general never once charged them with this particular form of atrocity. Instead, the act of ritualized violence with which the Scandinavian invaders became associated was that of the 'Blood Eagle', which features in four stories, dating from the twelfth to the fourteenth centuries, as a horrific means by which a captured enemy leader could be put to death. He was laid on his face, his back cut open, and his ribs and lungs drawn out to resemble the wings of a bird. This was accepted as historical fact until 1984, when Roberta Frank suggested that three of the four accounts actually derived from just one, in the *Orkneyinga Saga*, a twelfth-century work. It described how the ninth-century Viking Torf-Einar killed a rival for his chieftainship over Orkney, in this manner, and Frank thought that the account in the saga was based on a misunderstanding of a poem which had celebrated the event, and which was incorporated into the saga version and merely told of the dead man being torn by eagles, as carrion, on the battlefield.[150] This led to a debate between Frank and Bjarni Einarsson over whether the poem could indeed bear that interpretation, which has ended with other scholars being convinced by one or the other. It seems that nobody can be sure now if the rite was ever enacted in reality even if it was represented as having been so in the poem; and this situation may make a fitting summation of our knowledge of many aspects of Viking religion as practised in the British Isles.[151]

The Nature of Conversion

In the course of the twentieth century, anthropologists and sociologists of religion developed various models and characterizations of the nature of conversion, many of them based on the observation of Christian evangelism in colonial and post-colonial societies. Some emphasized it as a sociological process, others as a psychological one, and yet others as one of cross-cultural communication.[152] One strand of thought in this body of research has particular relevance to early historic Britain: that conversion is generally best understood as a multi-stage process rather than an event. A theorist in this tradition, when looking at modern India, summed up the stages as mass acceptance of the new religion, followed by personal education of the converts in its beliefs and traditions, and finally by the generation of leaders among the native population eager to administer, enforce and promote it.[153] Another, concerned with the specific case of medieval Europe, produced a different tripartite sequence: of social and collective conversion, followed by changes in external individual behaviour, followed by some in internal individual behaviour. Yet another writer, with the same time and place in mind, suggested that once the rulers and nobility accepted Christianity, the young were made the next target, and finally preaching was provided for as much of the adult population as possible.[154] Lesley Abrams has rightly reminded us that religion in the early Middle Ages was more an element of group identity than personal concern or individual choice, enthusiasm with conduct as much as belief, and an aspect of authority and allegiance rather than spiritual conviction.[155] None the less, individual choices and spiritual convictions must have counted, otherwise it is difficult to explain why some people entered monasteries and some did not, and some apostatized from Christianity in changing times and others did not. The real problem is, as indicated above, that the sources available for the early medieval British Isles are not good enough for us to be able to portray any models of conversion experience in action. We can presume that all or most of them operated, without being able to demonstrate this in detail.

The evidence is, however, adequate enough to fit a simpler formula, also articulated by Lesley Abrams, which distinguishes between the formal process of conversion and the deeper and more transformative one of Christianization which followed.[156] It has already been noted that some English kings rejected the new religion when they found that it made social or ritual demands on them to which they were not prepared to submit. The combination of material and textual sources does allow at least a discussion of ways in which the change of religious allegiances affected society in early medieval Britain. Such an exercise might begin with the use of sacred sites, and a famous letter written by Pope Gregory to a missionary he was sending to England in the year 601, as a general statement of policy for his followers in that country.[157] He ordered them to purge pagan temples of idols, but if the buildings were sound, to convert them into churches. This directive made a great impression on the modern British, especially in the years around 1900 when dramatic industrialization and urbanization had produced a great yearning for organic and unbroken continuity with a timeless, rural past. It reached its apotheosis in the work of a medical doctor and keen local antiquary, Walter Johnson, who portrayed an English countryside full of ageless landmarks, in which virtually every parish church stood upon a former pagan shrine.[158] This belief lingered through the twentieth century, featuring prominently, for example, in the ley-hunting movement discussed earlier in this book. Two sites in particular were held to exemplify such continuity, both on chalk hills. One was at Knowlton in the Cranborne Chase district of Dorset, where a ruined medieval church sits inside a Neolithic henge monument, the other at Rudston on the Yorkshire Wolds, where England's tallest prehistoric monolith stands in the parish churchyard. There was also some staying power to a story, current since the sixteenth century, that St Paul's Cathedral, in London, was built on the site of a Roman temple to Diana or Jupiter.

The true picture is much more complicated. The English parish system was commenced in the tenth and eleventh centuries, long after the conversion period (and was not complete until the fourteenth), and so there could have been no straightforward transformation of shrines into parish churches.[159] Archaeology has failed to support the story of the Roman temple under St Paul's, which seems to have originated in a tale put about by the twelfth-century pseudo-historian Geoffrey of Monmouth.[160] As Richard Morris has pointed out, the building at Knowlton is not a parish church but a later medieval chapel, in a landscape studded with older churches which are not inside henges. This makes it even more likely that the prehistoric monument was just adopted as a ready-made churchyard; especially since there were at least two, and possibly three, other henges around it, which the local people thought nothing of levelling in order to exploit the land for farming. Rudston, according to the name, was a rood-stone, one used as a shaft on which to mount a cross as a station for preaching before the church was built.[161] There is no evidence that the pillar concerned was thought to have any inherent sanctity, as opposed to being a convenient existing mount for a cross head. There seems, in fact, to be surprisingly little evidence that the medieval British regarded megalithic monuments as invested with much spiritual significance, positive or negative. What was formerly regarded as a deliberate campaign of burial of stones at Avebury in the early fourteenth century, inspired by Christian hostility, has recently been shown to have been a casual process spanning centuries, which could be accounted for purely as resulting from the practical motives of removing megaliths that had become obstructions to property owners.[162] There does not

98 The medieval chapel at Knowlton, Dorset, set within the survivor of a group of Neolithic henges.

appear to be a single proven case of the deliberate destruction of a prehistoric monument, because it was associated with paganism, in the whole of medieval Britain.[163] Almost needless to say, no Anglo-Saxon temple has been found underneath any medieval church, because (as discussed above) none has been securely identified anywhere, and some scholars doubt that the early English ever had them. Jeremy Harte has proposed that Pope Gregory expected England to be like his own Italy, a land still dominated by cities with impressive stone buildings, rather than one in which the towns were largely ruinous and depopulated, as was the British reality. He seems to have thought that Anglo-Saxon temples would be like the Roman kind, which they clearly were not.[164]

The wider question of whether medieval British churches overlay older structures is, however, far more complex, not least because the experts draw different conclusions. At one extreme was Leslie Grinsell, who could find only twelve cases in which medieval churches or chapels definitely lay over or beside pre-Christian monuments of any period, in the whole of Britain.[165] At the other was Stephen Yeates, who stated that most (50 to 65 per cent) of the churches established in Gloucestershire, Herefordshire, Worcestershire and parts of neighbouring counties between the sixth and eighth centuries were on sites of Iron Age or Romano-British activity. However, he did not provide the evidence in detail, and stated that some of it was 'fragmentary', 'minimal', or 'not yet ascertained'. He does not give one proven example of a church built on a pagan temple. [166] Experts apparently disagreed over the matter in the same volume of essays: in one such, John Blair declared that 'many' English churches overlie prehistoric or Roman sites, and Nancy Edwards that there is insufficient work to determine whether this statement is true. Blair did add that there is not much evidence of actual continuity of use of places between the pagan and Christian periods, but some of a later medieval interest in putting churches at sites which showed evidence of ancient occupation.[167] The sum total of all these different statements is that there is at present no solid proof that Gregory's directive was put into action, or indeed that it was relevant to the English scene, or that any other Christian missionaries in early medieval Britain had a similar policy to that recommended by the Pope. As seen, a few Romano-British or post-Roman churches do seem to have been built on the site of temples, but they did not last. There does, as John Blair pointed out, seem to have been a later medieval Christian interest in places which showed traces of ancient activity, but whether these were identified as pagan, or had taken a new place in Christian legend, is at present impossible to say.

At first sight it is much easier to be certain about the impact of the new religion on funerary customs.[168] Between 600 and 800 cremation vanished, as did grave goods save for high-ranking churchmen who were sometimes interred with symbols of their office. Burial took on an increasingly uniform style, of interment extended on the back, and orientated to face the east, without ornaments or possessions; and from the tenth century it was customarily in yards around churches, which became the dormitories of Christians awaiting the Last Judgement. Indeed, there was very little continuity of place or of rite, pagan cemeteries usually being abandoned and Christian burial grounds commenced.[169] There are a few complications to this picture. It is now recognized that although Christianity certainly abhorred cremation, no directives have been recovered which forbade grave goods or ordered that bodies be laid out in particular ways. Moreover, the two centuries concerned represented a long transition period, in which various hybrid forms of burial were in use. Initially, if grave goods became rarer, those that remained became richer. An increasing number of 'bed burials', graves of Christian women laid on beds with valuable possessions, has been found in eastern England. At Northfleet on the Thames Estuary a group of graves with warrior equipment was identified in 2003, dated to between 620 and 700. It was probably the resting place of the first generations of Christianized West Kentish kings or nobles. Even for royalty, burial in churches only became common in the early eighth century. The cumulative changes were, as stated, large and unmistakable, but forces in addition to religious change may account for them. For example, inheritance patterns may have altered to make it more customary to pass on personal possessions to heirs, while greater trade developed to recycle them and greater industrial processes to absorb used metalwork. The acquisition of writing would have helped ruling elites to say things about the dead in a more enduring mode than simply leaving objects with them. The use of cremation and of grave goods both becoming scarcer before Christianity arrived among the English, indicating that its adoption was part of a set of allied cultural processes already under way as the Anglo-Saxon settlers took on new ideas and customs from the Continent.

This last point is all important for understanding the impact of the new faith: that it was invariably adopted in the British Isles as one component of an extensive cultural package. Harold Mytum and Nancy Edwards have emphasized that in Ireland it represented one aspect of a transformation of the whole of society, in culture, settlement, agriculture and technology as well as religion, based on new contacts overseas.[170] It was suggested above that among the native British it was effectively part of a second wave of Romanization, which is another way of characterizing the situation in Ireland. Among the English much the same process occurred, the new faith arriving with, or in some places after, a switch of fashion away from Germanic styles of good and towards those of the Mediterranean. It was accompanied by reading and writing, masons and glaziers, new trade routes and – perhaps – new forms of ploughing, lime-production and smelting.[171] What is less clear is the impact that these changes had on non-religious behaviour. Stephanie Hollis has suggested that they reduced the status of women, by making marital union the dominant metaphor for relations between the sexes, with wives inferior to husbands and unlike them as beings. By contrast, she finds in the vernacular heroic literature a primacy of kinship and comradeship, with differences between the sexes downplayed.[172] This idea would work, providing that the heroic literature faithfully reflects social reality. Barbara Yorke, by contrast, has emphasized the absence of hostility to women in the writings of English clerical authors between 600 and 800 and the large number of Christian communities controlled by abbesses, suggesting that in England at least the new religion allowed a greater female role in public life.[173] Marilyn Dunn has pointed out simply that we know so little about the position of women in pagan England that comparisons are largely fruitless.[174]

That problem applies elsewhere in early medieval Britain. High claims were made at times in the twentieth century for the status of women in 'Celtic' society, but rested mainly on their representation in medieval mythological literature, especially Irish. Gilbert Márkus has made a polemical attack on those claims, arguing that when mortal women, as opposed to goddesses, are portrayed in the texts concerned they exist primarily to establish the legitimacy of menfolk. When they do wield power and influence, they are usually portrayed as villain-esses. He suggested that Christianity improved their status, enabling them to dispose freely of property and to enter nunneries, though they remained legally disadvantaged and disparaged as temptresses.[175] Wendy Davies has suggested that all the extant early medieval sources in Celtic languages portray women as subject to men in law and politics, though they had some rights over property. Virginity was considered essential for a woman before her first marriage. The Welsh were notably less enthusiastic about female saints than the Irish, the cults of none being recorded in Wales before the eleventh century. Davies's conclusion was that not enough data exists to allow of any firm conclusion concerning the effect of Christianity on the status of women in countries with Celtic languages.[176]

If the attitude of early Christianity in Britain does not seem to have been especially hostile to women, there is no doubt of its suspicion and dislike of sex, which it sought to confine to monogamous and permanent marriage within strict limits of relationship. Men were required to give up their concubines and sex-slaves, annulment of marriage became extremely difficult, and people could no longer marry their close relatives. Some royal and noble figures found these restrictions irritating, but by the ninth century the Church had apparently won the battle over them among the ruling elite. How much success it had in the rest of society, or in other campaigns such as banning sex on religious holidays, is less certain.[177] If churchmen succeeded in making alpha males more chaste, it did not make them much more peaceful, despite sometimes strenuous efforts to limit war. It is possible that the position of non-combatants became safer, and that the foundation of monasteries to atone for blood guilt by those who had committed homicide inhibited blood feuds. The right of the Church to give sanctuary to fleeing criminals and defeated warriors provided another brake on violence; but all over early medieval Britain, as across Europe, society remained organized around warfare. Christianity's traditional regard for the poor and downtrodden may have had some marginal effect, in that kings were now expected to make gifts to the poor, and it was considered virtuous to free slaves. Slavery and poverty both persisted, however, and there was no discernible change to the structure of society, while all over Britain royal and ecclesiastical power increased together.[178]

In this area of study, as in others in this book, a general framework can be established even though so much of the detail is missing. Martin Carver has pointed to one possible form of this, by reminding us of how many echoes of British prehistory can be found in the cultural forms of the British Middle Ages. The enclosures of monasteries in the north and west of the island echoed promontory forts, while places that used stone-lined graves in the prehistoric period used them in the Christian one. Stone crosses, or pillars with inscribed crosses, might have been inspired by standing stones. The quintessential instruments of the new religion were books, but their decorations were based on Iron Age art, and the cult of saints' relics mirrored the special ritual treatment given to parts of the human body at many times since the Neolithic.[179] All these comparisons suggest ways in which the imported faith could be made to seem more familiar, and there is a parallel exercise to be made, in suggesting that medieval British

Christianity matched paganism in so many structural respects that it provided a readily adopted substitute for it.[180] To say this is not to deny the novelty of the faith of Christ in many key respects. As stressed at the beginning of this chapter, it was in many ways a revolutionary form of religious belief and organization: the point here is that, at a popular level, all this novelty was mediated through forms that made it seem more familiar and acceptable.

There is a reasonably good understanding of medieval British Christianities as a whole, though one which is heavily weighted towards English material.[181] A direct comparison with paganisms is difficult to make because of the lack of evidence for pagan English religious practices. Previous scholars have usually elucidated what evidence does exist by analogy with Continental data.[182] The strategy here is to extend that method by comparing the body of information concerning medieval British religion with that for European paganism as a whole. This is most abundant and well studied in the Greek and Roman worlds, but the authors of the few general works on paganism across ancient Europe have found many characteristics in common between the different regions into which what is known of early Anglo-Saxon religion, as said, fits quite well.[183] When that general framework for pagan religion is compared with the specific features of medieval British Christianities, it becomes apparent that the new religion carried over a series of features from the old.

One of those was polytheism. At first sight this may seem a remarkable claim to make for a system which attached such importance to its worship of a single true god, even one formed of a Trinity. This monotheism was, however, much diluted by the cult of the saints, which represented the most active means of devotion for many, if not most, medieval people. There were hundreds to choose from, ranging from international figures who spanned the Christian world to those who were revered only in a county, district or parish, like Sidwell in Devon, Walstan of Bawburgh in Norfolk or the many patrons of Cornish villages. Just as the deities of Greek and Roman paganism (and perhaps all pagans) had done, the saints of medieval Britain often functioned as patrons and protectors of specific human activities and aspects of the natural environment. As such, people might accord them a permanent personal devotion, but could also approach them for favours in times of need, according to a saint's individual power and speciality. They were concerned with trades, age groups, illnesses, genders, nations, regions, farming processes or animals. Some were more overworked than others: Blaise, for example, was the patron of wool-combers, wax-chandlers, wild beasts and sore throats, and Clement of blacksmiths, anchor-makers, iron-workers and carpenters. Although their cults were concentrated in parish and monastery churches, they could also be attached to natural landmarks, above all wells. Those cults were a steadily developing feature of medieval English Christianity, which was more prominent in the later Anglo-Saxon Church than the early one, and still stronger in the later Middle Ages. None the less, it appeared early and soon attracted a popular as well as an elite following.[184]

It does not seem to have derived from a direct transformation of pagan deities. In no known British case was a representation of a goddess or god reused as a Christian icon, as happened in a few celebrated cases on the Continent such as at Enna in Sicily where the Madonna and Child had been cult statues of Ceres and Proserpina, or the Virgin of Chartres, which was taken from a pagan altar.[185] Nor are there any apparent parallels in Britain to the manner in which Irish divinities such as Brigid and Goibhniu have been thought by scholars, at least in the past, to have been refashioned as saints.[186] The medieval British cult of saints, therefore, was not a Christianization of pagan deities, but a provision of new figures who offered a parallel service. By the end of the Middle Ages, most parish churches contained shrines dedicated to saints who were not their patrons. Many were maintained by guilds of laity who paid a subscription to maintain a priest to pray regularly to that saint to intercede on their behalf, both before and after death. All but the very poorest members of society could afford to belong to these.

A second familiar feature of ancient religion which was reproduced in medieval Christianity was that seasonal festivals were the most important forms of ritual observance. Services were indeed provided each Sunday where there were churches, but not until the Reformation were effective laws passed to compel people to attend them, even though from Anglo-Saxon times most work was forbidden on that day.[187] The events that crowded out churches, and on which most care and expenditure were lavished, were the spectacular feast days positioned at key points of the annual calendar. By the later Middle Ages they included the dawn service on Christmas Day, in a church lit by many candles and decorated with holly and ivy; the blessing of candles at the beginning of February, as part of a liturgy which celebrated the power of light to drive back dark; the consecration of spring foliage on Palm Sunday, and its fashioning into protective crosses; the drama of the Resurrection of Christ on Easter Day, a consecrated host and crucifix normally being brought out of a miniature tomb in which they had been placed and guarded since Good Friday; the Rogation processions to bless the growing crops in May; the parades that celebrated Pentecost, with a white dove released or a model one suspended from the ceiling of the nave to symbolize the Holy Ghost; and the prayers for the dead and the ringing of bells to comfort the congregation at the feasts of All Saints and All Souls that ushered in the dark and dead time of year. For most of the time, the church was regarded as a house of the deity, in which a priest or priests kept regular worship going without the need for a congregation; although the personally devout, and those in need, were of course welcome. This seems to have been very much the pagan pattern.

The Christianization of pagan festivals was a much more regular and frequent occurrence than the Christianization of pagan places and deities, but it was not an automatic and comprehensive one. The solstices certainly became the feasts of the Nativity and of John the Baptist, while the quarter day that opened winter was (from the ninth century onwards) appropriated for All Saints. The greatest of all Christian festivals, Easter, was, however, tied not to any pagan celebration but to the Hebrew Passover, and overshadowed the major pre-Christian feast of May Day so much that the latter was given only two minor apostles. In Ireland, the traditional quarter day which opened spring was indeed allotted to that land's favourite female saint, Brigid. Elsewhere, however, it became prominent in church liturgy only because it almost co-incided with the major Christian celebration of the Purification of the Virgin Mary, which had enabled Christ's salutation as the saviour of Gentiles as well as Jews. What happened in general was that seasonal themes were interwoven at festivals with key messages and passages from the Bible, to express both to maximum effect. It was an appropriation of traditional ways, as much as an adaptation to them.[188] For centuries the English Church maintained a distance, often disapproving, from secular revelry such as May games, summer feasts, the crowning of mock monarchs to preside over seasonal celebration, and collections by ploughmen to open their heaviest season, in January. In the late medieval period, however, it incorporated these as well, by converting them into mechanisms to raise money for the upkeep of religious buildings and rites. Parish officers, at least in the south of Britain, would organize seasonal celebrations, with traditional pastimes and entertainments, to which parishioners paid admission, and the profits were put towards the expenses of their church. In rural communities – and the village was the standard social unit of medieval and early modern Britain – these celebrations became the normal means of raising funds for the repair and improvement of the building and its decorations, and the trappings and commodities of services.[189]

Medieval British Christianity also resembled the older religions in the space that it provided for women. Divine female figures were amply represented by saints, and above all by the Virgin Mary herself, who made an effective queen of heaven. Human women had their own religious houses, and came to feature as celebrated mystics, such as Lady Julian of Norwich. Occasionally they served as churchwardens, and were admitted to most parish guilds on an equal basis with men and sometimes served as officials in them; while many such guilds were reserved exclusively for women. All this had the effect of erecting a thick screen before the apparently unequivocal maleness of the single true deity. A fourth major continuity with the old ways was that the central religious rite was sacrifice: that of the mass, offered up at an altar as the old animal sacrifices had been. The major empowering motivation of paganism, the propitiation of deities with gifts, had been succeeded by one in which the deity offered himself as the sacrificial being; a concept which the evolving doctrine of transubstantiation made vividly real. The lesser sacrifices offered by paganism, of incense and flowers, remained in churches as accessories to ritual. Preaching, a distinctive Christian contribution to the religious mainstream, continued to be popular throughout the Middle Ages, being mostly carried on by friars in the later centuries. It was not, however, essential to the practice of the religion in the way that the consecration and communion of the mass were. In general, parish priests were not expected to preach, and their most important role was to enact regular rites for the good of the community, in the manner of pagan priests and priestesses before them.

In this context, it becomes important to emphasize how much the Protestant Reformation and the Catholic Counter-Reformation had in common, as reform movements directed against medieval Christianity, and especially at its popular manifestations. In many key respects they were utterly different, and bitterly opposed, forms of religion, but both were designed to achieve better control over general religious observance and to impose a greatly enhanced level of education, uniformity and active lay piety. This is where historians of a previous generation, such as the French scholar Jean Delumeau, deserve a fresh consideration, for arguing that the Christianity of the early modern period was significantly different from that of the Middle Ages.[190] It represented a fresh and strenuous attempt to inculcate at a popular level what devout churchmen had always held to be the key tenets of Christianity, and in the process to remove from the practice of religion many elements that perpetuated or resembled pagan forms. The transition was especially intense in Protestant nations of the kind that Scotland, Wales and England became, where it involved the abolition of the mass, the cult of the saints, and the seasonal rituals, and the substitution of a religion based on preaching, compulsory Sunday attendance and a far more male-centred concept of the divine order. One argument of this book, however, is that apparent religious change, incremental or radical, is inherent in the story of Britain from deep prehistory. There are fewer fundamental changes in the form of ceremonial monuments between AD 600 and 1600 than there were in the fourth millennium BC; and if Christianity continued to evolve and alter, in belief and in its physical expressions, throughout its ancient and medieval periods, then the material evidence for ritual, at least, had shown the same or greater mutability throughout the previous four thousand years.

THE LEGACY OF BRITISH PAGANISM

The Pagan Middle Ages: A Question of Definition

THE QUESTION OF how far paganism survived clandestinely in Britain after the conversion to Christianity is one that is now rarely discussed by specialists in medieval history, for two reasons. One of these is the breadth of research needed to give it a satisfactory answer, for it cuts through all three of the conventional divisions of the Middle Ages – early (c. 500–1066), high (1066–1300) and late (1300–1485/1500) – and requires reference to legal records, theological tracts, ecclesiastical decrees, archaeology and religious art and architecture. In all these areas, it demands the assimilation of a large amount of new, and ever-accumulating, material. The second reason for the current neglect is that the answer to the question is now generally assumed to be obvious, and firmly negative. Such an attitude is in large part a reaction against a scholarly tradition which dominated for most of the twentieth century, and has now collapsed. Between the 1880s and 1960s there was a very strong disposition among experts to believe that Christianity represented no more than a veneer over medieval British society, concentrated among the elite and barely penetrating the mass of the population, which continued to adhere, for all practical purposes, to the old religions. It was summed up perhaps most eminently by the great historian of monasticism, Geoffrey Coulton, who claimed that 'in church, the women crowded around Mary, yet they paid homage to the old deities by their nightly fireside, or at the time-honoured haunts, grove or stone or spring'.[1]

Research has only just begun into the impulses that lay behind early twentieth-century British attitudes to the Middle Ages, but some preliminary suggestions might focus on two particular factors.[2] One is the sense of aliena-tion and fear experienced by many educated Europeans between 1880 and 1940, on finding themselves in charge of two new and frightening forms of mass population: the industrial and urban working classes and the subject peoples of colonial territories. A view of civilization as something spread precariously over a populace which is essentially alien to it, disaffected from it, and secretly loyal to more primitive, destructive (and in some ways more exciting) instincts, runs through the literature of the age. The other factor consists of a growing disenchantment with conventional and traditional forms of Christianity. At times this resulted in a desire to dilute them rather than abandon them, by mixing in elements from other religions, including varieties of paganism. At others, the same disenchantment manifested as outright hostility to Christianity. It was clearly satisfying to those possessed by it to see the Middle Ages, traditionally regarded as the greatest epoch of fervent Christian faith, apparently being revealed instead as a time in which most people secretly revered pagan deities. It was furthermore a means by which modern urban intellectuals who rejected religion could mock the ignorance of the rural working class, the natural repository of backwardness and supersti-tion.[3] One aspect of this kind of medievalism should be emphasized here: that the evidence which underpinned it was mainly derived not from a study of medieval records themselves but from other sources: from modern folk customs, from early modern and later written texts, and from the physical remains of medieval buildings. The nature of this evidence will be considered more closely below; for now, it is proposed instead to ask what data does exist that could indicate the presence or disappearance of active paganism in the British Middle Ages.

It may be suggested that there are two principal bodies of evidence, which derive from opposite ends of the period. The first consists of the law codes issued by the Anglo-Saxon (or later the Anglo-Scandinavian) kings, and the contemporary edicts of English church councils. Those from the late seventh century, as Christian kings ended the former toleration of continuing pagan worship among their subjects, certainly forbid the old religious ways compre-hensively. However, none of those from the eighth century does so, and indeed those that attack non-Christian practices – the *Dialogue* of Egbert, archbishop of York, composed around 750, and the third decree of the Council of Clouesho in 747 – are primarily concerned with divination and the use of amulets. In other words, they deal mainly with what might be termed folk superstitions and operative magic rather than an actual religion. Egbert's *Dialogue* does also forbid the worship of idols, but this seems to be in the context of consulting soothsayers, indicating that to resort to divination of the future is itself to worship devils.[4] All this accords with the impression strongly given by a more famous English text of the mid eighth century, Bede's *History*, that paganism was no longer an active and independent force by that time. It is one reinforced as the century continued, by a report by papal legates on England in 786 and a commentary on English affairs by the great expatriate churchman Alcuin in the period around 800. The legates were concerned with pagan influence only in residual customs such as eating horse meat or mutilating horses (the significance of these acts not being explained), tattoos, and divination by casting lots. The latter condemned divination as well, in various forms, plus acts of Christian worship outside churches and the wearing of protective amulets which contained biblical passages or saints' relics. Much of this consisted of the policing of specific types of Christianity which were based on pagan custom.[5] There was a further flurry of prohibitions of pagan worship in northern England in 1000–2, issued by Wulfstan, archbishop of York, as described earlier and aimed at the new influx of Viking settlers. In the early 1020s King Canute reissued these as part of a law code for his whole realm, but after this nothing more is heard of the problem.[6] This would accord with the impression given by all the other sources, of a relatively swift and easy absorption of the Scandinavian newcomers into Christendom.

The body of evidence from the other end of the period consists of the records of secular and church courts, which in England are relatively plentiful for the fifteenth and sixteenth centuries, and deal routinely with matters of religious heterodoxy as well as all manner of other criminal and moral offences. They certainly reveal a persistent condemnation of the established Church, covering most of its core doctrines and institutions. Although expressed by a small minority of the population, concentrated in certain central and southern districts, it was determined and enduring. Historians have adopted for those who articulated it the contemporary abusive term of 'Lollards'. These were, however, not pagans but the direct opposite: very devout Christians who happened to disagree profoundly with the interpretation of Christianity made by medieval Catholicism. In addition the same records contain an equally persistent number of cases of individuals who mocked aspects of Christian piety. They were even fewer than the Lollards, belonged to no continuous and articulated rival tradition, and did not argue for any alternative system of religion: they were either mocking the pious or else expressing scepticism regarding the value of any religious faith. What the court records also embody very strongly is the sense that unorthodox religious or moral beliefs held by individuals threatened the whole community to which they belonged, by rupturing its solidarity and tempting divine wrath upon all. It was therefore the duty of ordinary people to spy on their neighbours, or remember conversations with them at social events, and report any suspicious words or actions in order to maintain communal safety and health.[7] A typical and humdrum example of this effect at work would be the case of Margery Northoll, a young widow who was sued for breach of promise at Bristol in 1539. There were witnesses to testify to all of the key words and actions of Margery and her jilted fiancé at each of the three successive stages of their courtship, even when they had made efforts to be alone.[8] It is difficult to imagine how, in such a world, a persisting pagan religion could go completely unreported. The nearest to any expression of one in the whole of this great mass of material is the case of two Hertfordshire men who were accused of declaring that there were no gods but the sun and moon. They were, however, not suggesting that these should be worshipped but – if the charges were true at all – fall into the category of those who cast doubt on the efficacy of religious belief in general.[9]

Such records are much fewer for the other parts of medieval Britain and the Isle of Man, but there are some equivalents, even if a slightly later period needs to be drawn into the picture to provide some of them. Law codes exist for Wales from the tenth century onwards, and show no greater evidence of the surviving practice of pagan religion.[10] Nor is it mentioned in the description of his country in the twelfth century by Gerald of Wales, who notes several curious and aberrant Christian religious customs there.[11] The lack of material comparable to the medieval English legal records is remedied from the sixteenth century by very good equivalents, for all but the north-west of the country, featuring both criminal and civil trials; from which, again, self-conscious paganism is missing.[12] The same is true of the Manx legal archive, which has a complete run of criminal cases from the late sixteenth century, and of church court hearings from the late seventeenth, which do contain much information on magical practices and fairy lore.[13] No Scottish historian seems yet to have detected references to surviving paganism in the laws issued since the union of that kingdom in the ninth century. The role played by the church courts in England is taken in Scotland from the late sixteenth century by the records of the kirk sessions and presbytery meetings of the newly established Protestant national Church. These are a profitable hunting-ground for historians of popular religion, and especially for those aspects of it of which reformed orthodoxy disapproved; but for the Lowlands there is apparently nothing in them concerning anybody who practised paganism as a rival system to Christianity.[14]

The Highlands are slightly different, because of two tantalizing entries. One is a condemnation made in 1656 by the presbytery (the regional church board of government) meeting at Applecross, the place on the north-west coast where Maelrubha had founded his monastery in the seventh century: a monastery which had been abolished, along with the saints' shrines and cult, at the Reformation. It condemned a group of Highlanders for sacrificing a bull, walking sunwise around chapels left ruined by the reformers, and trying to learn the future by inserting their heads into a hole in a stone on Maelrubha's feast. Divination was always a contentious area for rigorous churchmen, as it was often believed to indicate a lack of submission to the divine will. Perambulating holy places sunwise was part of Gaelic Catholic tradition, and certainly a custom inherited from prehistory (for which see Chapter 4 above) though firmly Christianized. The charge of animal sacrifice is of course the most interesting one, and it was repeated by the neighbouring presbytery of Dingwall in 1678, when it accused a family of Mackenzies of sacrificing a bull at a formerly famous healing shrine dedicated to Maelrubha. The object of this act was to restore the health of the grandmother of the family; the presbytery denied that it was offered to the actual saint and declared that instead it was intended for a 'St Mourie' or even 'a god Mourie'. Its members were apparently unaware that Mourie was one of the local forms into which Maelrubha's name had become corrupted.[15] It is possible that both records testify that in these mountains of Wester Ross the fact that Christian saints performed similar roles to those of the old deities had resulted in animals being sacrificed to the former as they had been to the latter. On the other hand, cattle were the major currency of the district, and the animals could have been offered merely as gifts to a shrine in exchange for saintly favour, in a wholly orthodox medieval Christian manner (but one still anathema to Protestants). What is entirely lacking, in both cases, is testimony from the people who carried out the acts concerned, providing a reason for them; and as a result we can never be sure how accurate the charges were. There was certainly a clash between medieval and reformed Christianities involved in both, but the true significance of it is probably beyond recovery.

From the centuries between the early law codes and the later legal records emerge just three incidents which could be interpreted as evidence for pagan cults in Britain. The first occurred at the Scottish seaport of Inverkeithing, at Easter 1282, when the priest allegedly gathered small girls from the neighbouring villages and made them dance around a statue of Bacchus with him, while he carried a wooden image of the male genitals and urged them to indecent actions and language. When some of his parishioners objected, he just became more obscene, and his critics seem to have been too cowed by his authority to make a complaint. At the following Easter – the next occasion on which he would have encountered his parishioners en masse – the report went that he did not repeat this stunt but tried another: when people gathered at his church to do penance, he got some to prick the others with goads. The burgesses of the town then turned upon him in outrage, but he refused to listen to them and was knifed to death that night. The chronicler who recorded this episode stated specifically that the priest was 'reviving' pagan worship rather than carrying on established tradition, and regarded it as a shocking, and unique, event. If the facts were as they are stated – and we cannot test the accuracy of any – then the clergyman concerned looks like an isolated lunatic.[16] So does the protagonist of the second incident, at Bexley in north-west Kent in 1313. There one Stephen le Pope made images of pagan gods and set them up and worshipped them in his garden; his next act, however, was to murder his maidservant.[17]

The last example is the only one to involve an actual cult, of a sort: at Frithelstock Priory in the Torridge Valley of North Devon in 1351. There the monks established a chapel near the monastery with an image in it which was supposed to represent the Virgin Mary but which the bishop of Exeter at the time thought more resembled 'proud and disobedient Eve or unchaste Diana'. He ordered the building and its contents to be destroyed. Nicholas Orme has considered this case in detail and concluded that the real source of the prelate's wrath was that the chapel had been built without his permission, and was used as a source of income for the monks. They did so by attracting pilgrims to it and offering to tell their futures: this was of course divination, that old area of temptation, and moreover people were supposed to go on pilgrimage to pray for healing and remission from sins, not to predict their destinies. It may be that the bishop's fulmination against the image was inspired by the fact that fortune in love was one of the particular services provided by the divination racket; in addition he clearly thought that monks should not be worshipping the Virgin outside their own priory at all.[18] He was certainly exceptional in that his energy, severity and intolerance generated a thick register of interventions, of which this was but one. Yet again, the episode cannot be taken as evidence for a surviving pagan religion.

It may therefore be concluded that the paganisms of early historic Britain died out soon after forms of Christianity were accepted as the official religion of its component states, without leaving any lingering resistance movement or organized tradition of continued allegiance to the old deities in opposition to that to Christ. Historians of the Middle Ages who have read through the last few pages may well wonder why such a conclusion needed to be reached afresh at all: they may well have had the impression of watching an examination of an obviously dead and decomposing corpse, with the intention of checking anew for any signs of life. What needs to be appreciated is that the concept of a surviving medieval and early modern paganism in Britain, in the sense stated above, is not only very much still present in some areas of popular culture, but – as will be seen below – is sometimes still expressed by practitioners of allied scholarly disciplines. Furthermore, there is another sense in which pagan survival, or more properly survivals, can quite legitimately and successfully be traced through the Middle Ages and beyond. This is the sense which inspired the title chosen for a collection of essays edited by Ludo Milis in 1991, *De heidense Middeleeuwen*, and translated into English in 1998 as *The Pagan Middle Ages*. Milis and his colleagues could find no trace of an active and self-conscious paganism surviving in Europe after conversion to the Christian faith had taken place: in particular, they could not find any continuing allegiance to the old deities in preference to Christ. What concerned them instead was the large number of pagan rites, usages, ideas and festivals which were absorbed into forms of Christianity, or into popular superstition (with an ill-defined line between the two). They found that medieval people preserved aspects of the old religions which fulfilled functions for which Christianity did not cater or with which it was not concerned. Those functions often consisted of active solutions to specific earthly problems, such as spells, charms and other magical remedies, which continued to exist in parallel with official Christian doctrine, sometimes condemned by the leaders of Church and state, but more often tolerated.[19]

Over the past forty years, this aspect of medieval culture has received a growing amount of attention, although more from Continental than British scholars. The earlier results of this prompted John van Engen to ask again whether the Middle Ages had been 'a flourishing epoch of Catholic Christianity or a millennium of Indo-European folklore?' His answer was that they had not been a golden age of Christian piety, but that their culture was still a Christian one, even deep in the countryside. He also noted that one of the common factors in this earlier research was the belief that Christianization was most profound in the upper ranks of society, and that it was popular religion that showed the largest number of pagan trace-elements.[20] Van Engen himself had doubts about this, and it is a concept which will be challenged here. The main thrust of the argument against it is not that ordinary rural people were more piously Christian than has been thought, though that is indeed true and has been well made for Britain by some of the works that have underpinned earlier passages of the present book, such as those of Eamon Duffy. It is that surviving elements of paganism could be found at every level of society.[21]

It is easy to perceive that the faith of Christ had to take on physical trappings from the world of paganism: after all, it emerged into that world as a set of sacred writings with a rapidly developing theology and body of ceremony attached. To develop as a public religion, it took over from pagans its forms of sacred buildings and the use of clerical costume, altars, incense, music, veils and cloths, and decorative foliage, as well as the seasonal festivals considered earlier. However, it transformed these, and poured into them the radically new form of religious thought and behaviour discussed above. For that reason, a consideration of pagan survivals is better directed to aspects of the ancient inheritance which were less completely assimilated into the new faith. Four categories of those were identified as especially significant in a predecessor to the present work: learned ceremonial magic; popular magic or 'cunning' craft; popular rites, especially at seasonal festivals; and the general love affair that the Christian centuries carried on with the art and literature of the pre-Christian world.[22] What follows here is a consideration of the way in which those categories have overlapped and interrelated, which also provides an opportunity to distinguish what may be termed clear instances of survivals from those which are now doubtful or disproved.

Church Images

It was the Egyptologist, and prominent member of the Folklore Society, Margaret Murray, who in 1934 drew attention to the figures carved in British churches as evidence for an active surviving paganism in the Middle Ages. In particular, she focused on the occasional representations of naked women with spread legs, which had become known to scholars by the Irish folk nickname of sheela na gigs. These she interpreted as icons of fertility goddesses, installed in Christian buildings because their cults remained so strong among ordinary people.[23] It was almost certainly her example which inspired another member of the society, Lady Raglan, to propose a similar purpose for the much more common medieval church decorations of foliate heads, surrounded by and disgorging leaves. She conflated these with the vegetation-clad figure from English May processions, called the Jack in the Green, to suggest that they represented enduring reverence for a pagan fertility god. To this entity she gave the term, taken from a common pub sign showing a forester, of the Green Man.[24] These interpretations of the two types of figure continued to be proposed all through the middle years of the century. In 1973 the pioneering scholar of Iron Age and Romano-British religion, Anne Ross, contributed an essay which restated the view of the sheela na gig as proof of the living cult of a pagan goddess.[25] Two years later, she and Ronald Sheridan not merely repeated as fact the idea that medieval grotesque art represented enduring pagan deities but added further kinds of image to the list and accused academic scholars of 'almost a conspiracy of silence' in refusing to integrate this truth into general histories of the period.[26] There was, of course, no such conspiracy, but a lack of focused and sustained research. In its absence, popular culture readily absorbed the concepts published by the writers cited above, especially Anne Ross. The sheela na gig became a potent symbol for feminist artists in the 1980s and the Green Man an icon of the environmental movement. As such, both turned into important and dynamic modern images.[27]

99 A sample of Green Men:
(a) in the parish church at Sutton Benger, Wiltshire
(b) in the parish church at Sampford Courtenay, Devon
(c) in Ely Cathedral
(d) in the parish church at Spreyton, Devon

It was only in the 1970s that sustained scholarly investigation of the pagan interpretation of medieval church images commenced, and the interpretation rapidly collapsed. Lady Raglan's composite figure of the Green Man was dismantled component by component. In 1979 Roy Judge proved that the Jack in the Green had no connection with the church decorations, but had evolved out of a London chimney sweeps' dance in the late eighteenth century.[28] From 1978 onwards, Kathleen Basford, Rita Wood, Mercia MacDermott and Richard Hayman showed between them that nobody associated the foliate heads in medieval churches with paganism before the twentieth century. They appeared mainly in buildings commissioned by members of the elite, rather than those in which common people had influence, and were especially popular in the later rather than the earlier Middle Ages. There are few ancient precedents for them, and these show leafy faces, rather than faces gushing foliage from mouth and nostrils in the medieval manner. The first appearance of this form was in fact in manuscripts produced in tenth-century monasteries, from which it spread to churches in the twelfth century; and it is possible that the ultimate source for it lay in India, from which it was transmitted to European culture through the Arab world.[29] Between 1977 and 1986, Jörgen Andersen, Anthony Weir and James Jerman similarly reviewed the sheela na gig, revealing that this image appeared in eleventh-century France and Spain as part of a new repertoire of decoration associated with the evolving style of art and architecture called Romanesque. From there it spread quite rapidly to England, where its popularity peaked in the twelfth and thirteenth centuries, and then to Ireland and Scotland. In England it did not enjoy the continued and increasing interest that the foliate heads received in the late medieval period. Its purpose, taken in context with the other forms in the repertoire, seems to have been to warn against the horrors and temptations of carnal lust, for which the repulsive nature of the image, and its focus on often enlarged and distended female genitalia, would be appropriate.[30] The most famous sheela na gig in Britain is probably now that in Kilpeck church, on the central plain of Herefordshire: it was indeed the type specimen used by Margaret Murray to underpin her original theory. Now, however, the church is known to have been built and decorated at the behest of a recently arrived Norman lord, a courtier and royal official who imported masons working in the new Romanesque style.[31]

When all this recent work is reviewed, it remains true that there are some rather large loose ends still lying around in it. Brandon Centerwall has drawn attention to the existence of figures actually called Green Men who appeared in Tudor and Stuart pageants and entertainments, as leaf-covered men carrying clubs. They also feature on sixteenth-century wooden fittings in one church and one cathedral. Their association seems to be with drunkenness, mirroring the traditional use of a branch or bush as a sign for the sale of alcohol, but how they relate to the foliate heads, if at all, we do not yet know.[32] Moreover, we still do not really know what the foliate heads themselves signified. One way to discover the answer may be to examine late medieval English sermons and devotional works systematically to uncover possible references to the motif, but there is no sign as yet that this enterprise will uncover any. A more general enterprise, of seeking meanings for leaves and greenery in medieval religious symbolism, yields too broad a result, for to some commentators in the period they equated with the entanglements of sin, and especially lust, and for others

a

b

c

100 The Sheela na gig:

(a) A typical specimen, from the parish church at Eastnor, Essex, showing all the usual characteristics of physical ugliness and the absence of distinguishing features other than the display of the huge vulva.

(b) A more unusual example, from the parish church of Whittlesford, Cambridgeshire, which acts as a coping stone to a twelfth-century window on the front of the tower, with which it is contemporary. The style of the female figure herself is normal, but with her is a rarity, a male companion, approaching her in a state of sexual excitement. It was concealed by whitewash for centuries, and uncovered in the late nineteenth century.

(c) The largest example surviving in Britain, on the exterior of the church at Oaksey, in the upper Thames Valley at the far north of Wiltshire.

with the special trees of the Garden of Eden, and for yet others with self-sacrificing love, salvation, immortality or resurrection, while foliage sprouting from faces could suggest decaying corpses and the consequences of sin or the mutability of life.[33] It may be that the best way of understanding the motif is to look at it in specific contexts. At Kilpeck, for example, Richard Hayman has noted that foliage generally represents the snares of Satan, entangling and distracting the humans portrayed with it.[34] Sally Mittuch observes that leaves dominate the eastern walk of the cloister at Norwich Cathedral in a pattern which suggests the journey of the soul after death, through a forest towards salvation; in which case the Green Men in the scheme would be lost souls.[35]

As for the sheela, it has always been noted that this figure enjoyed a greater popularity in Ireland than in Britain and was made there for longer, into the later Middle Ages. The Irish examples, moreover, were increasingly placed in positions which the human eye could not see, and on secular buildings such as castles rather than churches, especially in Gaelic areas. They may be linked in such contexts to a tradition recorded in much later Irish folklore, by a German traveller in the 1840s, that misfortune (in general) could be averted by the display of a woman's genitals.[36] Here there might be a direct relevance to surviving ideas from ancient paganism, which could be associated with goddesses, as a few scholars have indeed suggested in recent years.[37] In other words, in this specific case, Margaret Murray and Anne Ross may have been correct, and especially the latter, who drew most of her material from Ireland. It is also possible that the image itself derives ultimately from pagan Egyptian prototypes, though this is unproved and the Christian use of it was quite different.[38] None of these reflections does anything to rescue the use of medieval church carvings as evidence for a continuing and active paganism in medieval Britain.

Labyrinths and Giants

Rocky Valley is one of those narrow defiles that run inland from the north Cornish coast, with the craggy flanks which gave it its name but also lush vegetation especially rich in spring flowers. In this it is typical of the small valleys of the district. What gives it distinction is that on one of its rock faces is carved a pair of labyrinths, of the 'classic' ancient kind with a single track running in successive loops to the centre and then out again. Fixed to the rock beside them is a notice of green and white metal, installed in the mid twentieth century, declaring that they probably date from the Early Bronze Age. For many this sign has become evidence in its own right, that labyrinths were carved in British prehistory; and this might be the actual truth. On the other hand, nobody seems to have noticed the carvings until 1948, and the idea that they are ancient was propagated by a national newspaper, the *Illustrated London News*. It is a little worrying that Cornwall has abounded with scholars interested in its monuments for about three hundred years, and not one seems to have come across the Rocky Valley labyrinths before the 1940s. It is impossible to date them from their degree of weathering, though the slight apparent degree of this, when they were incised in soft shale rock, might argue that they are relatively recent.[39] They are certainly the only examples of this motif being carved on a rock face in Britain: the abundant incised symbols of the British Neolithic and Bronze Age include many concentric circles and spirals, but not a single labyrinth.

This case sums up the problem of British labyrinths in general.[40] The symbol is certainly ancient, being known both in Syria and Greece by the thirteenth century BC. By the beginning of history it had a strong association, in legend, with dancing, and also with the hero Theseus, who was said to have slain the Minotaur, a human-eating monster with a man's body and a bull's head, inside a labyrinth. This association does not entirely make sense, because the Minotaur was kept in a maze, a bewildering complex of many pathways, most of which led to dead ends, and not in a unicursal labyrinth; but none the less it stuck. By about 600 BC the motif had reached Italy and it became popular with the Romans: examples found in Sardinia, Spanish Galicia and the Italian Alps may all be prehistoric, but may equally well have been carved in Roman times. The labyrinth is also a great modern symbol, which burgeoned in popularity during the late twentieth century, especially in America. On both sides of the Atlantic, clubs, magazines and networks of enthusiasts have been dedicated to making and discussing them, and modern labyrinths, in Britain as else-where, are now important symbols, religious monuments (Christian and non-Christian), and works of art. Built into much of this movement is a belief, or assumption, that the symbol concerned was known and used in northern as well as southern Europe in prehistory.[41] That belief may be correct: but thus far it is unproven.

The Romans certainly carried the image to many parts of their empire, taking it as far north as the Danube Valley and Gaul, but there is as yet no sign that they brought it to Britain. From Roman culture it was taken into Christian churches, including eventually the great French Gothic cathedrals, and into medieval illuminated manuscripts. Its meaning in Christian contexts is not entirely certain: at times it is explicitly attached to the Theseus legend, having pictures of the Minotaur inside, while at others it is described as representing the winding path of life, and at yet others worshippers used to walk it, when it was set into a pavement, for penitential purposes, reciting prayers to expiate feelings of sin or guilt. It seems as if the legend started the use of the design, as one associated with the slaying of evil, and that it was later given other mean-ings and uses. In addition, it is recorded in nineteenth-century British folklore, as a magical shape chalked on doorways so that evil spirits, trying to enter, would be confused and deterred. A famous group of labyrinths, numbering hundreds and laid out in stones, survives in Scandinavia around the Gulf of Bothnia, and especially in Sweden. In their design, they match those in late medieval Swedish church frescoes, which sometimes show girls dancing inside them, but there is no proof of when they themselves were made, or for what purpose. There is one carved upon a prehistoric standing stone in the Wicklow Mountains of Ireland; but there is no certainty that the carving is of the same date as the erection of the stone, and indeed it was first noticed in 1908. As the monolith stands alongside what became a medieval pilgrimage route, the design may have been added to it by Christians.

In Britain, labyrinths are represented mostly by a group constructed of turf on village greens or on hillsides near towns. These are uniquely English (with an isolated one of stones in the Isles of Scilly), and ten survive out of a known previous total of thirty-nine, the most famous and popular being at the market town of Saffron Walden in the north-west Essex farmlands. They were certainly made from the late Middle Ages to the eighteenth century, when their construction by both gentry and common folk is well recorded. The earliest actual reference to one is in Geoffrey Chaucer's poem 'The Legend of Ariadne', in the late fourteenth century. Unfortunately, none can yet be dated from the surviving structure itself, so the tradition of producing them could have commenced in prehistory or at any time thereafter up to Chaucer's own. Their use by Tudor times is documented: they were the setting for sports and dances as part of summer games, as Shakespeare indicated when he wrote of 'quaint mazes in the wanton green'. Fairly often, in Britain as in Scandinavia, they were known as 'Troy Towns', a reference to Virgil's ancient Roman poem the *Aeneid*, which remained a favourite piece of literature during the Middle Ages. There a turf or stone labyrinth was used for what was called 'the Game of Troy' in which young men rode round on horseback, turning their steeds skilfully around it. By Virgil's time it was long established as a favourite pastime of aristocratic Roman youth. The vagueness of all this can be put down to the lack of sustained and professional scholarly study of these monuments, because of disciplinary traditions: historians have tended to assume that they come down from prehistory, while archaeologists do not find them on any British site which can be dated before the late Middle Ages, and so ignore them. Only one British formation that has been interpreted as a labyrinth has been systematically investigated by archaeology, and it was never recognized as one until the mid twentieth century and never firmly accepted as such by either historians or archaeologists. It is also now the most famous among British and American pagans and New Agers: the spiral labyrinth on the dramatic conical hill in Somerset known as Glastonbury Tor.

It was the great novelist and ritual magician Violet Firth, who wrote under the name Dion Fortune, who first drew attention to the terraces on the Tor, which had hitherto been presumed to have been medieval field systems. In the 1930s, she had a vision in which they became a sacred processional way made by refugees from Atlantis. This was brought down to earth by a former colonial from Ceylon called Geoffrey Russell. In 1969 he suggested that the terraces were a giant labyrinth, which he first thought was medieval, but later believed were more likely to have been prehistoric. Geoffrey Ashe, the eminent writer on Glastonbury, accepted the terraces as a huge, and hitherto unsuspected, ancient monument, and Philip Rahtz, a distinguished archaeologist, put on record that he thought this possible. The Tor was promptly adopted as one of the main sacred monuments of the rapidly growing community of people who had

moved into the town dedicated to the practice of 'alternative' forms of spirituality.[42] Archaeologists in general ignored it, as there was no known prehistoric
structure which resembled it in the whole of Europe, though the excavations at
Silbury Hill, undertaken in the 2000s, threw up the idea that Silbury might have
been built with a spiral walkway ascending it. No examination was therefore
made to test the reality of the Tor labyrinth until 2004, when the National Trust,
which has custody of the hill, needed to renew the paths and gateways upon it,
and invited Glastonbury's resident archaeologists, Nancy and Charles
Hollinrake, to make a proper survey of the terraces. They found that these were
indeed human-made but had until recent times been discontinuous, not one
circuit of them having linked up to make a pathway. They seem instead to have
been medieval field systems, as had traditionally been supposed, similar to
others surviving in that part of Somerset and probably made during the thirteenth century, when a rapidly expanding population was creating acute land
hunger, and Glastonbury Abbey was engaged in ambitious building and
drainage projects. No proper excavation was undertaken to confirm this date,
but fragments of medieval pottery were found in one terrace.[43] The labyrinth on
the Tor does not, therefore, seem to be an ancient sacred structure, but it is
certainly now a modern one, converted into a huge open-air temple in the late
twentieth century and consecrated by the feet of thousands of devotees. As such
it performs a religious function extremely well, and deserves the respect that is
accorded to any site of which that is true, old or not.

101 Glastonbury Tor labyrinth, visible as concentric terraces on the side of the steep,
conical hill.

All this uncertainty over the age and nature of British labyrinths relates directly to the question of pagan survivals. If medieval British people who danced or played games in the turf structures were using monuments which had been established in their land in prehistory, and perhaps doing so in similar ways, then this is site continuity of the classic sort. If, on the other hand, the turf structures were translations, into secular use, of an image found in churches, and brought to Britain by a Christianity which had appropriated them from an ancient Mediterranean legend, then it is not. The same sort of consideration applies, with equal intensity, to carved figures on chalk hillsides. One of these, the Uffington White Horse, has (as said) now been firmly proved to be prehistoric. The other white horses which decorate Wessex scarps, and a few other motifs found on southern English downs, are as certainly modern, though precise dates for the creation of two-thirds of the horses are lacking and one or two were made from older figures (though we do not know how old).[44] It is in the gap between the definitely prehistoric and the definitely modern that those which have most relevance to the question of pagan survivals reside.

Two in particular have attracted attention in this respect, because they are the two human hill figures which have been thought to represent possible pagan deities. One, the Long Man, occupies a hillside of the South Downs above the village of Wilmington in Sussex, and its name is well earned by its height, of 231 feet (or over 70 metres). Its masculinity is less certain, for it is a mere outline, with no positive indications of sex, and its main distinguishing feature is that it holds a line, possibly representing a stave, wand or edge of a door, in each hand. It has, however, been significantly altered by successive 'restorations', and the details of its original form are uncertain. Far more robustly delineated is the Cerne Giant, on a slope above the small town of Cerne Abbas in the north Dorset hills. He is 180 feet (55 metres) tall and unquestionably male, with a complete set of genitals including a 30 ft erect penis, though this has been elongated in relatively recent times by engulfing the navel. He brandishes a club, and once had a skin draped over the other shoulder with some kind of head attached; which makes it probable – though not certain – that he represents the classical hero Hercules.

For most of the modern period, scholars considered it most likely that the Cerne Giant was ancient, and the Long Man ancient or early Anglo-Saxon.[45] This possibility has an obvious bearing on the question of pagan survivals, because if both were indeed originally images of pagan deities, their preservation through the Middle Ages argues that some reverence for those still persisted in their localities. The stakes are raised in the matter by the fact that both lay on or close to major medieval highways and both were directly above important monasteries, Cerne Abbey and Wilmington Priory, so that the monks would either have had to collaborate in their continued existence or

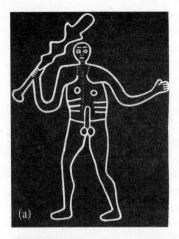 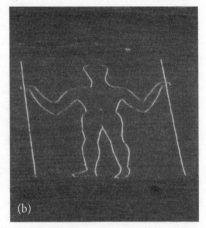

102 The two surviving hillside giants:
(a) The Cerne Abbas one, as mapped out by Sir Flinders Petrie's survey in 1926: on the ground (as viewed across the valley) the figure is foreshortened.
(b) The Long Man of Wilmington, photographed from the floor of the valley below, and so (in contrast to his Cerne Abbas fellow) showing the foreshortening effect resulting from an actual, terrestrial, view.

been repeatedly thwarted in attempts to eradicate them by the devotion of local people. Since the 1990s, doubt has increased as to whether either existed before the early modern period, and the two have become a contrasting pair, in a somewhat frustrating way. The Long Man now seems to have a scientifically determined date, but no known context for construction, while the Giant seems to have a good context for construction, but no proven date.[46] In 2003 a television production jointly sponsored by the Open University and the BBC2 television channel put up the money for an excavation on the hillside below the Long Man. This showed that a great deal of activity had taken place there in the early modern period, with a particular concentration in the mid sixteenth century, and very little before then. It strongly suggested that the figure was first made then, without absolutely proving the fact. No investigation of the history of the district has since been carried out with a view to determining any possible candidates for those who would have sponsored the work. If the Long Man is indeed Tudor or Stuart, then the most likely identity for such a figure is Christ opening the doors of salvation; but this is mere speculation.

Nobody is ever likely to identify the Cerne Giant as Christ, but he may be Oliver Cromwell. The first certain reference to his existence is in 1694, and there are none before then, despite the survival of a relatively large number of Tudor and early Stuart travellers' accounts which describe the area, and an unusually rich set of estate records for Cerne Abbas dating between the thirteenth and early seventeenth centuries, including a particularly detailed survey of 1617. Joseph Bettey has made a case that the figure was cut in the 1650s on the orders of the local landowner, an embittered former politician called Denzil Holles, to satirize Cromwell, then the ruler of the nation and known to some admirers as the British Hercules. Indeed, in the following century the steward of the manor told a Georgian scholar that it was 'cut out in Lord Holles's time'. All this is highly suggestive, though no objective tests for dating have yet been carried out on or near the Giant himself. The present state of knowledge and opinion only makes it impossible to use the two great hill figures as certain evidence for a surviving loyalty to paganism in the English Middle Ages. What they should do, instead, pending a proper and direct dating of both, is redirect attention to the place of giants in the late medieval and early modern English imagination. The most common form of hill figure recorded in Tudor and Stuart England was not a horse but a huge human, lost specimens of which existed at Oxford, Cambridge and Plymouth. By treating these hillside carvings as relics of a prehistoric past, historians have effectively neglected them, even though it is clear from what is already known that giants in general were major figures in early modern English culture. They were part of folklore, mythology, religious tradition and national epic, and featured prominently in municipal and guild processions. It is time that we reunited the material and literary evidence to give them a proper history at last.

Trees and Waters

A theme that is emerging from this chapter is the manner in which an association of certain kinds of material evidence with pagan survivals has served to delay the proper investigation and understanding of them. That theme is sustained in the case of natural features in the landscape. The point has already been made that the prehistoric British almost certainly, and the Romano-British, Anglo-Saxons and Scandinavian settlers in Britain quite certainly, attached a religious significance to particular trees. What seems to have happened subsequently is that this pattern continued, but not by direct transference: rather, in this respect as in others, Christianity established a parallel belief system. Medieval literature identified the sweet apple as the tree, and its fruit, as the most numinous of all, especially associated with paradises and enchanted lands. Chris Lovegrove, however, has argued that both this association and indeed the cultivation of apple orchards themselves were medieval phenomena, not known in ancient Britain.[47] The history of the yew is more complex. Modern authors had always recognized its special association with churchyards and the precincts of abbeys, and during the twentieth century, if not before, an assumption grew up that this must derive from a proportionate sanctity in pre-Christian times.[48] This received a new impetus from the 1980s onwards as a result of the work of a visionary, Allen Meredith, who had experienced dreams which convinced him of the great age of yew trees and their powers of wisdom and healing. These launched him into a long and praiseworthy programme of recording data on them, especially their measurements. He convinced nationally eminent figures such as Alan Mitchell of the Tree Register and the media botanist David Bellamy that a method could be constructed for calculating the age of individual trees from their growth rates, which indicated that some yews were much older than had been thought. The oldest, in fact, had been alive for millennia.[49] By the mid 1990s his ideas were coming close to being accepted as at least a popular orthodoxy, and inspired further works upon the ancient sacred significance of the tree.[50] At the least, it now seemed to many people that yews had been especially venerated in pre-Christian times, and that their presence in Christian churchyards was a strong indication, if not proof, that those sites had been foci for religious activity for thousands of years on end: living proof of continuity of sacred place between different religions. David Bellamy, indeed, took to issuing certificates of age for old yews, to be hung in churches next to them, and 130 of these make the tree concerned older than the establishment of Christianity.

In 1996 Jeremy Harte took a look at the evidence for such suppositions.[51] He pointed out that as the rate of growth of the species is uneven, there is no foolproof method for the calculation of the age of any of its specimens. This throws the historian back on archaeology and historical texts as sources for the matter. The latter show that ancient Mediterranean cultures regarded evergreens as trees of mourning, planted in cemeteries as symbols of continuing life and hope for an existence after death. As such, Christianity, emerging from those cultures into northern Europe, brought the same belief, and focused it especially on the yew as the single evergreen which grows to impressive size and flourishes in those latitudes below the conifer belt. There is absolutely no doubt of its association with Christian churchyards in the British Isles from an early date, attested both by written records and material remains: the name Iona, indeed, is probably derived from 'yew island'. What is much more difficult to prove is a connection with ancient paganism. Early Irish law codes define the sweet apple and the hazel as sacred trees, but not the yew. Plenty of yew trees grow over ancient remains, but there does not seem to be a single case of ancient remains being constructed to pass over the roots of a tree.[52] Subsequent research has done nothing to add to or subtract from Jeremy Harte's case, despite the most painstaking efforts.[53] It remains impossible to date yews, and although each decade produces more and better evidence of the importance of the tree to early (and subsequent) forms of Christianity, no special connection between it and paganism has yet been demonstrated. The matter remains open, and the most important effect of the debate may have been to highlight the need of the growing sub-disciplines of landscape archaeology and landscape history to incorporate individual species of trees into investigations more often than has been done hitherto.

The situation is rather similar when dealing with sacred waters. There is of course ample evidence for the importance of these in pre-Christian Britain, while the cult of holy wells, usually associated with individual saints, was a major feature of the Middle Ages. The problem, again, is one of direct connection between one and the other, because there are very few clearly proven cases in Britain of a piece of water which was the centre of ritual behaviour before the conversion to Christianity remaining as one thereafter. The most spectacular of the island's springs, the hot group at Bath which had been the focus of the worship of Sulis Minerva, sum up the uncertainty which generally hangs over the matter. It is true that from 675 onwards the ruins of the Roman city were reoccupied and the first of a series of important Anglo-Saxon monasteries established there. What is harder to determine is whether any religious cult was centred upon the springs themselves during the Middle Ages, as both material and textual evidence for one seem to be missing.[54] Likewise, while the large number of undoubted medieval holy wells embodied an attitude to water which was itself ancient, so far there is evidence that only a very small number were themselves a focus for ritual before a Christian cult developed there. In this as in other respects, the new kind of religion seems mostly to have offered a parallel service to the old in Britain, rather than adapting places, figures and rites directly. Admittedly, systematic research into the matter has only just begun, and has been pioneered, like that into church carvings, yew trees and labyrinths, mainly by good scholars outside the academic mainstream: in the case of the wells, most notably James Rattue and Jeremy Harte.[55]

Just one well, at Low Leyton in Essex, has yielded evidence of pagan votive offerings followed by a medieval cult: and given its (so far) unique nature, its Christianization might have occurred in ignorance of the earlier activity rather than inspired by it. A dozen more English medieval holy wells occur in association with early Anglo-Saxon activity, or Romano-British remains, or suggestive early place names, and so are probable additions to the record of continuity. This is not a large total out of about nine hundred that are known to have attracted reverence in England during the Middle Ages. The distribution is an odd one, with most medieval holy wells in the Midlands and West Yorkshire and fewest in the south and east, especially East Anglia; which is not a map of Celtic culture, population density, pagan place names, or springs in general. Anglo-Saxon churchmen condemned the worship of wells by pagans rather than recommending them for Christian use, and such disapproval continued later into the Middle Ages. It seems to have been largely if not completely ineffectual, for the establishment of new saints' wells went on all through the medieval period, and the particular patrons chosen for them merely reflected the popularity of those saints at the time. The wells had little association with healing, but functioned as shrines or chapels, especially as alternative foci for devotion to sometimes distant parish churches.

Likewise, rivers continued to be used as repositories for what look like ritual deposits, but not generally at the same places or of the same kind as before. The badges worn by pilgrims who had visited saints' shrines, for example, were regarded as objects of inherent sanctity and protective power. As such they were nailed up in homes, or fixed on doorways or put under foundations of houses, cowsheds and beehives to protect them; but they were also placed in wells and at river crossings, presumably to enhance the power of the former to bless, and to make the latter safer.[56] The most remarkable example of ritual continuity of deposition in rivers to date was identified by David Stocker and Paul Everson along the central Witham Valley in Lincolnshire.[57] Here causeways led from ten medieval monasteries towards the river; these were probably first constructed in ancient times, as prehistoric and Romano-British finds are common along the line of them. Deposition continued near most of them all through the Middle Ages, especially of swords, daggers, axe heads and spearheads, which were laid upriver of the causeways or in pools nearby. In three cases the medieval finds outnumbered the prehistoric, and in general those left between the eleventh and fourteenth centuries were more numerous than those of the Anglo-Saxon period. Stocker and Everson remark that as the crossings were controlled by monks, and the deposits peaked with the power and influence of the monasteries, 'clearly, the practice had been Christianized in some way', but there is no textual evidence to tell us how.[58] Pilgrims, religious processions and funeral corteges would all have passed those points, going to or from the religious houses, and it is likely that the placement of objects in water was associated with such events. In particular, the two archaeologists pointed out that the deposition of weapons declined when the custom of hanging military equipment around tombs became fashionable. In that case, it may have been the weaponry of dead lords that was cast into water as their bodies were taken for burial at the monasteries; and so the moment when Excalibur was cast back into the lake may actually have reflected contemporary medieval custom, rather than a memory of prehistoric ritual, or even the finding of ancient swords in watery places.

All told, the cases of trees and waters do suggest a continuing reverence for both on either side of the change of religion; but the evidence for a direct transference of it in specific cases is weaker than has often been supposed.

Medieval Celtic Literature

It was stated in the fourth chapter of this book that medieval Irish and Welsh literature represented two of the four kinds of source which were routinely used in the twentieth century to evaluate the material evidence for ritual in the British Iron Age. The two others, classical Greek and Roman literature and the images and inscriptions from Roman Britain, have now been considered at some length. It is time to look at the medieval Celtic texts, and explain why they were not employed earlier. Those from Ireland are of relatively small importance to the British context, even though they are much more numerous than the Welsh, and many self-consciously portray a pre-Christian society, with a pantheon of deities and a few descriptions of religious or magical rites. Their changing status as historical sources, however, does need some consideration as it has relevance to that of the Welsh equivalents.

Between the mid nineteenth and late twentieth centuries, it was presumed that the medieval texts which portrayed a pagan Ireland had originated in pre-Christian times and been preserved by oral tradition until they were written down after the coming of Christianity. As such, they were thought to have been preserved by an elite of bards whose technical training and social position had, like their tales, survived the process of conversion almost unchanged. In the ringing words of the celebrated mid-twentieth-century scholar of Celtic languages and literatures Kenneth Hurlstone Jackson, they provided 'a window on the Iron Age'.[59] By the 1980s specialists had doubts about this assumption. The medieval Irish epics showed none of the familiar textual features of orally transmitted stories apparent in other early literatures such as the works of Homer. At the same time archaeologists were discovering that the royal seats which featured in the stories certainly existed in pagan times, but not as the residential halls portrayed in the epics. They had instead been complex ceremonial centres, often open to the sky. The medieval authors had either drawn on an oral tradition which preserved a sense of their former importance, but not of their form or purpose, or were inspired to imaginative reconstruction by the sight of their physical remains. The buildings, dress and war gear of the epics were those of the Middle Ages, not the Iron Age, and the animals described in them include some species never found in Ireland and others introduced after the coming of Christianity.[60] Medieval Irish writers were trying to recreate the glories of their pagan and ancient past to produce an epic literature that could rival that of pagan Greece and Rome, which was generally admired throughout Christian Europe. In doing so they drew on a great deal of native tradition, but we have no real idea of how much of this consisted of authentic memories of the prehistoric past, and how much had been invented for lack of such memories.[61]

The cumulative effect of such doubts can be seen in a series of statements from experts in the years following 1990. In 1992 J. P. Mallory summed up an emerging consensus among archaeologists when he declared that 'in general, no matter what games one attempts to play with the data, it is impossible to make a convincing Iron Age date' for the *Táin bo Cuailgne*, traditionally regarded as the most archaic of the Irish epics.[62] Four years later one of the most famous proponents of the old tradition of using medieval literature to reconstruct Iron Age religion, Proinsias MacCana, admitted gallantly that by then experts in Celtic studies were unable to agree upon the extent to which that literature could be accepted as a reliable index of native religion and mythology.[63] Things moved further over the next decade, so that by 2008 Raimund Karl could state that 'the general consensus' in Celtic studies now seemed to be 'that the Irish heroic tales ... are little more than medieval authors' creative paintings of how they imagined the Irish past to have been, telling us, if anything, more about the early medieval Irish present than about a distant pagan past'.[64] Karl himself added that he completely agreed with this, but suggested that the texts could be used as analogies, some of which might be homologies. In other words, where features of the stories seemed to accord with actual Iron Age remains, they might be taken as possibly accurate representations. The problem is, of course, that there is no way of demonstrating that the apparent similarity is not a coincidence; and Karl himself limited his own exercise to social structures and customs rather than religious behaviour.

Irish literature has sometimes been made directly relevant to the study of Britain, in that some scholars have linked deities found in it to British names, to suggest that they represented the same pan-Celtic deity: examples of this will be considered below. More generally, the same trajectory that has characterized the use of the Irish texts as windows into a pagan past has been matched by that of the Welsh; though the latter were always less amenable to the task than the Irish, and the doubts over their fitness began to be expressed much earlier. For one thing, the surviving body of Welsh medieval writings is much smaller than the Irish, and it makes very little comparable attempt to reconstruct a pagan world. Some of the tales in it, the Four Branches of the Mabinogi, are apparently set in a pre-Christian past, but there is no attempt to portray the religion of that time, save that characters occasionally make pious exclamations which are wholly compatible with Christianity. Instead, the Welsh material has been studied for possible implicit, or even unconscious, references to or survivals from ancient paganism. This process began in the eighteenth century, when the growth of interest in the Druids, as potential spiritual ancestors of all the British peoples, triggered interest in the medieval Welsh texts. After all, the Welsh were ethnically the direct descendants of the native British, and there was a chance that their medieval poems and tales did indeed preserve echoes of Druidic teaching.

Attention focused on two collections of poems, those credited to the legendary bards Taliesin and Myrddin, who entered the Arthurian cycle as the wizard Merlin. Both were believed to date from the sixth century, around or even before the time of the conversion to Christianity, and abounded with obscure passages which might credibly be deciphered as concealing Druidic wisdom. The exercise of decoding this wisdom, commenced in the middle of the Georgian period, took off properly at the opening of the nineteenth century, only to receive a check in its middle decades from Thomas Stephens and David Nash. They pointed out that, from internal references, some of the poems concerned seemed to have been composed as late as the thirteenth century, and that none could be securely dated earlier than the tenth, which made the transmission of Druidic teaching in them much less likely. They proposed also that the texts concerned seemed to have been composed as entertainments, and not as expositions of religious belief.[65]

The debate over those criticisms lasted for almost a hundred years, with the proponents of an earlier date for the poetry more inclined to defend that credited to Taliesin rather than that attributed to Myrddin. It was apparently ended in the mid twentieth century, when Sir Ifor Williams ruled that the only poems in the 'Taliesin' corpus which could have derived from the sixth century, and Taliesin himself, were a dozen which dealt with kings and battles. Those in the 'mystical' category were all later.[66] In recent years there has been a tendency to push the dates of composition for the Welsh literature which has been most often examined for traces of paganism even later, to the twelfth and thirteenth centuries. None of these ascriptions, however, are secure, and some poems have been placed by different scholars at various points between the years 700 and 1130. This renders impossible the work of putting the different texts in a chronological succession, so that the development of characters and motifs can be traced between them. Furthermore, the stories and personalities in them must in at least most cases have been in existence for an entirely unknowable span of time before the extant literary works were created.[67] All this is highly relevant to the fact that from the late nineteenth century onwards authors seeking references to paganism in the literature were preoccupied not so much with finding Druidic teachings in it as with identifying former deities who had been transformed into characters in the stories. Four in particular were highlighted.

The first is Mabon son of Modron, whose name on the surface means 'the son of the mother', but, as the -on suffix is derived from a Celtic one especially associated with deities, seems to signify 'the divine son of the divine mother'. He features in the medieval literature as a great huntsman, and perhaps as a warrior, while his mother bears other sons to another hero. In 1888 one of the great pioneers of Celtic philology, Sir John Rhys, identified Mabon as the god Maponos or Maponus, and Modron as the goddess Matrona, deities attested by inscriptions and reliefs in Roman Britain and Gaul. His argument was based on the linguistically solid derivation of the medieval from the ancient names. This idea was taken up and repeated throughout the twentieth century by a succession of major scholars, one of whom, the American Roger Sherman Loomis, made Modron the original for the character of Morgan la Fee in the Arthurian cycle. The problem is that not a single ancient inscription identifies Maponos as the son of Matrona. The latter was the goddess of the River Marne, in northeastern Gaul, and there is no trace of her in Britain. The triple goddesses known generally as the Matres, discussed earlier in this book, were also sometimes known as the Matronae, but not in Britain, and they never seem to have been associated with the river goddess or Maponos, or indeed with any son. Maponos is recorded both in Britain and Gaul, but though the British references are more numerous they are all in military contexts, while the Gaulish inscriptions, though fewer, are the work of civilians. It is therefore difficult to locate his point of origin. In Britain he was treated as a patron of music and in Gaul as a general protector, but nowhere as a hunter. It seems impossible to prove that the medieval Mabon and Modron originated as the ancient Maponos and Matrona, and the undoubted linguistic connection of the names is a puzzle rather than a means of saying anything useful about either Roman Britain or medieval Wales. Some of the earlier tendency of scholars to give importance to Modron as a great mother goddess derived from the modern wish to believe in such a deity as a universal focus of worship in the ancient world.

The second character is Nudd, who features mainly as the father of two notable heroes, and is significant in modern scholarship because his name is linguistically cognate with those of the Roman-British god Nodens, attested in Lancashire and at Lydney, and Núadu, who appears in Irish medieval literature as king of the supernatural race called the Túatha Dé Danann, generally accepted as former pagan deities. He has also been equated with two other (and separate) characters in the Welsh stories called Lludd, one of whom bore Núadu's epithet of 'silver hand'. It was Sir John Rhys, again, who blended all of these as the same god, and all or most of his attributions were frequently accepted during the twentieth century. It is, however, impossible either to reconstruct with confidence the attributes of Nodens or to prove that his cult was the only or main one at Lydney, and so to use features of the temple there to construct an identity for him as a divinity. It can only be said that he was identified with the Roman Mars, as a general protector-figure, especially in war and farming. None of the associations that can be recovered for him makes any reference to the distinctive features of the medieval legend of Núadu, while the latter bears no more than a superficial resemblance to that of either Lludd. The epithet 'silver hand' could simply have been transferred from Irish to Welsh storytelling during the Middle Ages. Núadu and Nud were fairly common personal names in early medieval Ireland and Wales, respectively, but what connection this has to the fictional characters, and how they do relate to each other, seem at present to be questions beyond convincing resolution.

The Welsh literature contains various characters named Lleu, Llwch, Lloch or Lluch, of whom by far the most important is Lleu Llaw Gyffes, Lleu of the Skilful Hand, a handsome prince in the Fourth Branch of the Mabinogi who suffers various tribulations before becoming ruler of Gwynedd, north-west Wales. It was (of course) Rhys who deified him, drawing on the work of an equally eminent Frenchman, Henri d'Arbois de Jubainville, published in 1884. This linked together four hitherto separate people and places: Lug(h), who was leader of the Túatha Dé Danann after Núadu in the Irish epics; an unnamed god whom Julius Caesar had said was the most popular in Gaul and equated with the Roman Mercury; a set of deities called Lugoves, found in Roman-period inscriptions from Spain to Switzerland; and the ancient name for the Gaulish city of Lyons, 'Lugudunum'. De Jubainville argued that all testified to the existence of a major ancient deity called Lugus, who was venerated across the whole cultural world which scholars at that time were starting to characterize as Celtic. Other authors swiftly took up this idea and began finding Lugus behind other Roman towns with names commencing in 'Lug-' or 'Luc-', from Britain to Germany, and in the other Welsh characters with similar names to Lleu. This process continued through the first two-thirds of the twentieth century; and indeed, the belief in a pan-Celtic god called Lugus became one of the props of the concept of a pan-Celtic family of peoples, and culture, in the ancient world.

From the 1990s questions began to be raised, in passing, about aspects of this construct. In 1996, for example, Bernhard Maier attacked the equation of Caesar's 'Gaulish Mercury' with Lugus, and pointed out that the place names associated with the latter need have no connection with him and that two-thirds are only attested in the Middle Ages. In fact the problem is worse than that, because behind the place names could lie a variety of words commencing in 'lug', 'leu', 'lou' or 'luk' in early Celtic languages, signifying a raven, a dark place, an oath or vow, or light, bright or shining. Ravens almost certainly gave Lugudunum, alias Lyons, its name, because the ancient symbol of the town was a raven or crow. There is not a single definite dedication to a god Lugus across the whole of his presumed range. Instead there are those to the 'Lugoves', a plural form which gives no indication whatever of the nature of the deities concerned, or even of their sex: it was goddesses, and not gods, who were most often found in multiples in the ancient world. In addition, Galicia and Provence have inscriptions to the 'Lucubes', who were probably male and may have been the same figures. So, the bonding of all these shadowy deities, the place names and the medieval Lugh and Lleu into a single mighty god is still possible, but now seems only one option among a number of choices. The only certainty is the cognate relationship between the names Lugh and Lleu, and the still more telling fact that the Irish god and the Welsh prince bear the same epithet, of 'Skilful Hand', even though they are utterly different as characters. The epithet, however, could have crossed the Irish Sea in the Middle Ages, while the name could have done so in the early first millennium, before sound-changes separated the linguistic forms.

Finally there is the figure of Rhiannon, perhaps the most famous female character in the whole of medieval Welsh literature, who features in three of the Four Branches of the Mabinogi. She comes from a supernatural otherworld, riding a white horse which cannot be overtaken by any mortal steed, and marries the human prince of Dyfed. As his wife, she suffers an unjust accusation, for which she is punished by being forced to carry strangers into her court upon her back. Her innocence is proved by an outsider, Teyrnon, and she is reinstated, only to suffer a further indignity at the hands of an enchanter, being forced to wear the collars of asses, before being rescued from this humiliation in turn. It was Sir John Rhys once again, in the 1880s, who started the work of turning her into a pagan goddess, seconded in the years around 1900 by Sir Edward Anwyl, who argued that the names Rhiannon and Teyrnon could have derived from a pair of reconstructed Celtic originals, *Rígantona and *Tigernonos, signifying respectively 'Great (or Divine) Queen' and 'Great (or Divine) Lord' (the asterisks customarily indicate hypothetical words reconstructed by modern philologists): once more the concept of an ancient Great Mother Goddess was an explicit influence in his thought. These ideas were accepted and augmented for the next hundred years, with an increasing emphasis on Rhiannon as a horse goddess, being either a British equivalent to the Continental Epona, or even Epona herself. In the 1970s she was blended with concepts taken from medieval Irish legend to turn her into a goddess of sovereignty as well.

In the past few decades a few cautionary notes have been sounded concerning this whole construct. It has been pointed out that there is absolutely no ancient evidence for a cult of *Rígantona and *Tigernonos, and that all that Rhiannon and Epona have in common is a horse. Jessica Hemming has emphasized that magical steeds which move at uncanny paces are found elsewhere in medieval literature, and just indicate the general deceptiveness of enchanted realms. She has also proved that Rhiannon's punishment, of being ridden, was both a motif in international folk tales and an actual penalty in medieval Europe. Andrew Welsh has analysed the motifs in the Four Branches, and found that none of those in the stories which feature Rhiannon are distinctively 'Celtic', all occurring internationally. These insights can be extended. The whole concept of a 'sovereignty goddess' is based ultimately on Irish tales composed after the year 1000, originally to bolster the claims of a single dynasty: there was not a single kingdom in the whole of ancient Europe and the Near East in which a ruler is actually recorded as commencing his reign by a rite of marriage to a goddess. There is no trace of a widespread cult of Epona in Britain, which could have left a lingering popular memory, as discussed earlier, and no solid evidence for a native British horse goddess. The divine origin of Rhiannon, therefore, is unproven, as is that of the other characters considered above. Readers are free to decide for themselves where they wish to stand, on a spectrum of response stretching from a continued acceptance of such an origin for some or all of these figures (but now as just one possible interpretation of the evidence) to abandonment of it as a waste of time and a preference to concentrate instead on an understanding of what the texts concerned would have meant to their medieval audiences.[68]

A similar conclusion can be proposed for the figure of Ceridwen, though her scholarly trajectory has been somewhat different. She features, as 'Ceridfen', 'Ceritven', 'Kerritven', 'Kyrridven' or 'Kerritwen', in some of the 'mystical' poems accredited to the great legendary bard Taliesin, as a muse who confers the gift of inspiration upon Welsh bards: these texts have the language and diction of twelfth- and thirteenth-century court poets, although it is possible that they incorporated some older material.[69] Her role as giver of inspiration seems to derive from her part in the story of the birth (or rebirth) of Taliesin, who had been her servant. As a mighty enchantress, she had brewed a cauldron containing a potion which conferred great wisdom and magical and creative ability, from which he had accidentally drunk and gained the full benefit. She had then pursued him in a series of different animal shapes before eating him, only to become pregnant with him and give him back to the world with the same remarkable powers. She is one of the great characters of world literature, along with Lleu and Rhiannon, and deserves to move and inspire the imagination to this day, and for very many to come. Although full versions of this story exist only in sixteenth-century texts, it was certainly known much earlier, in the time of the poets who hailed Ceridwen as a muse or before. Some of the characters in it, with the relationships they have there, are named in the Welsh Triads, devices to aid poets to remember and classify aspects of tales which had been put together by 1200. Moreover, for the rest of the Middle Ages Welsh bards referred to episodes from the story.[70]

Nobody seems to have thought that Ceridwen had been a modern goddess until the beginning of the nineteenth century, when a clergyman called Edward Davies joined a contemporary trend, among devout Christians, of attempting to defend the literal truth of the Book of Genesis against the questions that had begun to be raised about it by the developing sciences of geology and palaeontology. One of the favourite devices of this school was to find apparent references to Noah's Flood in the mythologies of different nations, and Davies applied it to a reconstruction of ancient British religion. His material for this was drawn from medieval Welsh literature, and especially from the 'mystical' poems credited to Taliesin. One of his most influential conclusions was that Ceridwen had been the presiding goddess of Britain, the Great Mother of all creation, whose body had represented the earth. This was an early appearance of the need to conceive of a single Great Goddess, related to motherhood and the natural world, in the nineteenth-century imagination. As part of it, Davies transformed the name of the character from the medieval story and poems into its enduring modern form, 'Ceridwen', which carried connotations of beauty and adoration.[71] His idea was repeated as 'generally considered' to be fact in Lady Charlotte Guest's English translation of the main medieval Welsh prose tales, *The Mabinogion*, in 1849.[72] This carried it to a vast audience, far into the twentieth century, being taken up by famous creative writers such as Robert Graves and becoming a significant part of modern popular culture.

Among scholars of Welsh literature, however, the idea of Ceridwen as the Great Mother fared rather less well, as Davies's reputation for scholarship crashed in the mid Victorian period, when critics such as Thomas Stephens and David Nash challenged not only the conclusions that he had drawn from his sources but his ability to read Middle Welsh.[73] As a result, the late Victorian enthusiasm for finding pagan deities behind characters in the medieval literature tended to pass Ceridwen by, and in the mid twentieth century one of that age's leading Welsh scholars, Sir Ifor Williams, had no time for the idea that she had been a goddess. He derived her from the character in the Taliesin story, and argued that her original name had been 'Cyrridfen', meaning 'crooked woman', which would suit the nature of the sorceress whom that character represents. These suggestions were accepted by other famed experts in the literature concerned, such as Rachel Bromwich.[74]

On the other hand, a few archaeologists continued to represent the popular view, in detachment from that of literary specialists. In 1967 Anne Ross suggested that pagan goddesses 'seem' to lurk behind the enchantresses of medieval Welsh fiction, including Ceridwen.[75] The latter disappeared from prominent books on Iron Age and Romano-British deities in the 1980s, such as those of Graham Webster and Miranda Aldhouse-Green.[76] None the less, in 1995 the latter scholar declared, without arguing the case, that Ceridwen had been 'almost certainly a goddess'.[77] At first sight that statement, and one made by the present author four years earlier (with an argument), that 'she fairly clearly was not' a pre-Christian deity, may appear to be polar opposites.[78] In fact they occupy different points in the same category, of acknowledgement that the matter is doubtful. There is therefore every potential for people who wish to see Ceridwen as a deity as a matter of personal choice to continue to do so. What is certain is that to do so is wholly to make a back-projection from medieval literature, and that there would not be such a propensity to make it now were it not for a Christian fundamentalist from the Regency period, Edward Davies.

Other characters from the Welsh poems and stories can be submitted to the same process, and have been (as the reference to Anne Ross has indicated), although not to the same degree as those discussed above, and with equal indeterminacy. That process can also be applied to physical objects. Miranda Aldhouse-Green has made a fine study of the place of cauldrons in the Welsh and Irish literature, where they are repeatedly associated with death and regeneration. She has plausibly suggested that they had the same associations in pre-Christian times.[79] The problem is that cauldrons were prestige objects in the early Middle Ages as well as in prehistory, and that their connotations in medieval myth and legend may not have been the same as those in the earlier period. A major scholarly industry was developed to detect possible traces of paganism in the medieval Arthurian legend, which grew ultimately out of Welsh tradition. Edward Davies, again, got things started by declaring that Arthur himself had been a sun god, and between the mid nineteenth and the mid twentieth centuries first-rank academic authors on both sides of the Atlantic, such as Sir John Rhys and Roger Sherman Loomis, devoted much energy to finding other such connections. So did writers from outside the university system, or on the fringe of it, such as Alfred Nutt and Jessie Weston.[80] In the later twentieth century, this activity waned sharply in professional Arthurian scholarship, although it has persisted outside that.[81] The problem is that the motifs, characters and actions which have been identified as deriving from pre-Christian religion were collected as isolated details from all over the body of medieval Arthurian literature, and frequently from the late medieval romances, in various nations and languages. They are not more numerous in the earlier texts – indeed, the reverse is usually true – and are not found in certain traditions as a coherent body which can be shown as developing into more Christian forms, or disappearing, as the medieval period wears on.

By now it is plain that any attempt to find pagan survivals in the characters and motifs of medieval Welsh literature is fraught with problems, in a way that was not apparent for most of the nineteenth and twentieth centuries. Stepping back from the detail, however, it immediately becomes apparent that much of it, and that of medieval Ireland, contains a major element which could well be a bequest from a pre-Christian age. This is the presence of a supernatural otherworld, populated by beings similar to humans but with magical powers and eternal youth, which regularly interacts with the human one to which it acts as a parallel realm. In Ireland this was, in one of its manifestations, the home of the Túatha Dé Danann, while in Wales it was commonly called Annwn or Annwfn. It becomes slightly more assimilated to Christian cosmology as time goes on: in the fourteenth-century poems of Dafydd ap Gwilym it is much more clearly an underworld, with demonic overtones, than it is in the (almost certainly) twelfth-century Four Branches of the Mabinogi, where it seems to exist in a neighbouring dimension. None the less, as a realm (apparently) separate from the terrestrial one, which is neither heaven nor hell and is populated by superhumans who are not definitively good or evil, it has no place in Christian teaching. Its prominence in wonder-tales and romances, in which magic and the supernatural are major themes, could indicate how tight a hold it kept on the medieval imagination; though it could also represent how free the medieval imagination itself was, when writing fiction, of the hold of any tradition including mainstream Christian belief. It could represent one of the most important survivals from the old religions to the world of the new, never theologically assimilated but apparently accepted without strain as long as the stories that involved it conformed to Christian values or were set in vaguely pre-Christian times; but that is unproven.[82]

Seasonal Customs

The manner in which Christianity appropriated and adapted pagan festivals has been discussed in the previous chapter. Alongside this process went another, whereby particular religious customs and rites which had accompanied the old festivals continued, in the same or in mutated forms, as popular customs at the same seasons.[83] During the late nineteenth century British scholars took up the idea, developed by German colleagues, that traditional forms of festivity recorded among the modern populace – especially in the countryside – often functioned as living fossils, preserving the memory of ancient ritual. This theory further proposed that the study of them could provide insights into ancient culture, and allow the reconstruction of religious beliefs and practices in periods from which no written evidence survived. It depended on two assumptions which were characteristic of the mindset of much of the educated elite of the age. The first was that common people, and especially rural people, were essentially incapable of independent thought and innovation, and so mechanically repeated actions and beliefs handed down to them from much earlier periods; even if they had lost all understanding of the true meaning of them. The second was discussed earlier: the characterization of the ordinary folk of the Middle Ages, and beyond, as having a religious culture to which Christianity had given a mere veneer, and which depended in large part on a continuation of pagan rites and habits of mind.

In the early twentieth century, the 'survivals' theory of folklore fell out of favour among professional scholars, partly because it had proved to rest on too many dubious assumptions and partly because it tumbled into a gap between the emerging disciplines of history and anthropology. This only released it, however, to flourish as an article of faith among enthusiastic amateurs. It probably reached its apogee in the 1930s, when, for example, a president of Britain's Folklore Society, S. H. Hooke, could suggest to its members that pancake-tossing had been a rite to make crops grow, that Shrove Tuesday football matches had begun as ritual struggles representing the contest of dark and light, and that Mother's Day was a relic of the worship of the ancient Earth Mother. With slightly less exuberance, and fewer additions to the canon of belief, it continued to dominate popular attitudes to seasonal customs well into the second half of the century. This situation was made possible by a dearth of interest in the subject among historians, but from the 1980s that situation began to change, and produced a major re-evaluation of the subject, based on solid primary research.

This resulted in a dramatic re-evaluation of attitudes to some of the most famous British calendar customs. The Mummers' Play and Sword Dance, for example, which Edwardian scholars had declared to have been survivals of prehistoric ritual dramas based on themes of death and resurrection, proved to have developed in the eighteenth century, and peaked in popularity during the early nineteenth. The morris dance, assumed by the same school of scholarship to have been an ancient fertility rite, was documented as appearing in the royal and noble courts of late medieval Europe and filtering out from the English one to become a popular craze in the sixteenth century, breaking into regional traditions after that. The seasonal animal disguises found in different parts of Britain at specific times of year, assumed around 1900 to have derived from tribal totems, turned out on documentation to have been local adaptations, made between 1750 and 1850, of the traditional hobby-horse dance, which had itself apparently begun as a professional entertainment in the Middle Ages. All these revelations were accompanied by a realization that traditional popular culture was much more dynamic, porous, imaginative, creative, adaptable and prone to periods of change and renewal, than had formerly been assumed by scholars; the Victorian and Edwardian attitude to it was fundamentally mistaken as well as deeply condescending. There were particular periods which were especially notable for large-scale makeovers of seasonal celebration in Britain, of which the late Middle Ages formed one and the Georgian and Victorian eras another. To judge from the regular changes of form for ritual monuments in prehistory, it is very likely that equivalent adjustments of seasonal ritual also occurred then.

Having said this, it must be emphasized that some calendar customs do pass the test of proper research as having a direct transmission from ancient times, and that the list of pagan survivals has been winnowed and not erased. Christmas presents derive directly from the ancient making of gifts at midwinter, to open the New Year, and the decking of homes and holy places with greenery at festivals, notably with holly and ivy at midwinter and birch and flowers at midsummer, is also found as history begins. The making of sacred fires at the opening of summer and at its solstice, to bless and protect people and their livestock from the dangers of the season, is recorded in late antique or early medieval texts. The medieval Christian Rogation processions, to bless fields in the time of growing crops, were successors to pagan rites of benediction. It is also very likely that other customs are ancient, although only recorded later. The wide distribution of may-poles across areas of Europe which had an agrarian economy, and so were dependent on the flourishing of greenery, ties in with a general celebration of foliage and flowers at this time, as they were fastened on the poles. Hence, although they are not mentioned before the high Middle Ages, they are probably older, and are certainly part of the broader ancient tradition of festive greenery and blooms. Likewise, the proven ancient provenance of gifts at the winter solstice is part of a larger pattern of blessing rites which opened the New Year for many European peoples as the daylight began to lengthen again. This means that the southern English custom of wassailing, of singing to livestock, grain fields or orchards soon after midwinter to encourage them to be productive in the coming year, may well be very old even if it is not recorded until the sixteenth century.

This last consideration touches on another, which has already been present in the discussion of Welsh literature: that the continuities become easier to identify when a larger view is taken. Thus, the precise dances and plays performed around midwinter in Victoria's reign may not have been ancient, but dances and plays of some kind had been performed at that season since history began, and undoubtedly long before. They are part of the enduring character of that festival as a time of feasting, entertainment, fellowship, charity, rest from work and reversals or suspensions of normal systems of authority. The Christmas tree may be a Victorian importation of an early modern German custom, but it is merely the latest expression of a the older tradition of decking homes with greenery at midwinter. Likewise, the opening of summer and its solstice have been marked by open-air revelry all over Europe since records begin, and the conclusion of harvests, of the different products of farming, by equivalent celebrations in farmhouses or the halls of landowners. Whatever the precise content of the rites, the opening of winter has always been a time for meetings and feasts as members of a community return from their summer occupations and draw together for the winter; often with divination rites to predict who was likely to survive that dreaded season and other activities to mock or honour the powers of darkness, cold and death. Occasionally, also, a particular custom will echo one that is clearly ancient, even if it is not so itself. The Victorian summer and autumn tradition of well-dressing in the north Midlands is a modern equivalent of the very old one of paying respects to sacred springs. The Horn Dance at Abbots Bromley in Staffordshire's Forest of Needwood may be a seventeenth-century adaptation of a routine hobby-horse dance, using imported (and much older) reindeer antlers. None the less, the records of early medieval Continental churchmen are full of denunciations of the custom of donning the hides and horns or antlers of animals at midwinter; so the Abbots Bromley dance is an echo of something ancient even though it is probably not a survival of it.

The relationship between calendar customs and changing religions is therefore a complex one, which needs to be considered on a case-by-case basis, with collation of both the available records and the broader contexts. The former tendency to assume that virtually all traditional British seasonal rites were survivors of paganism was clearly misplaced, but blanket dismissal of pagan ingredients in them would be even more erroneous. Broad themes of seasonal festivity often have more staying power than individual customs, though even some of those can be proved to have survived for millennia; and the process of conscious and unconscious replication and recreation of the ancient adds a further dimension of complexity to the subject.

Witches and Fairies

The greatest apparent proof cited by those who believed in the continued existence of an organized and self-conscious British pagan religion throughout the Middle Ages lay in the early modern records of trials for witchcraft. In the nineteenth century first German and then French authors argued that the people tried for that offence had been practitioners of a surviving ancient religion, and all that divided those authors was that reactionaries portrayed that religion as disgusting, and applauded its persecutors, and radicals declared it to have been admirable, and excoriated those who prosecuted it as enemies of liberty, feminism and a love of the natural world. The British came comparatively late to this idea, but took it up with gusto, and the best-known and most persistent exponent of it in the twentieth century was Margaret Murray. In a series of books between 1921 and 1954 she drew selectively upon the records of trials and the writings of demonologists to construct a portrait of a witch religion, descended from remote antiquity, which covered Western Europe and was comprehensively crushed by persecution between the fifteenth and seventeenth centuries. To do so, she made heavy use of British, and especially Scottish, material. By the middle of the century, her view had become something of a scholarly orthodoxy, repeated in textbooks on medieval and early modern history written by distinguished historians who were not themselves experts in witchcraft; of whom, indeed, Europe in general had few at this period. It itself, it seemed to prove the existence of a robust and flourishing medieval paganism, organized into a popular counter-religion which presented a credible, deliberate and successful alternative to Christianity. From the 1970s, however, sustained and careful research into early modern beliefs in witchcraft and trials for it commenced, which gradually covered every part of Europe. It left no possibility that such a religion had existed.[84]

Nevertheless, in a microcosm of changing attitudes to the 'pagan Middle Ages' as a whole, the disappearance of this scholarly error has opened the way for a much more profitable investigation of the manner in which ancient beliefs contributed to the construction of the early modern stereotype of the witch and provided contexts for the trials. There has been no division in this enterprise between historians who have most explicitly condemned the concept of witchcraft as an organized pagan religion and those who have engaged in this alternative, and subsequent, enterprise: they have indeed generally been the same people. Carlo Ginzburg, who has been associated more than anybody else with the project of recovering pre-Christian traditions from early modern trials for witchcraft, declared that a polemic which termed Margaret Murray's work 'amateurish, absurd, bereft of any scientific merit' was 'justified'. He emphasized that the trial records 'simply document myths and not rituals'.[85] Norman Cohn, who was one of the British historians most commonly associated with the attack on the credibility of the Murray thesis, was also the one who stressed most enthusiastically the roots of medieval and early modern witchcraft beliefs in ancient traditions.[86] The Continental scholar who devoted most care to showing how the kinds of trial records used by Murray to document an actual religion were the product of pure fantasy, Gustav Henningsen, was also among the most notable in uncovering old folk beliefs behind images of witchcraft.[87] The present author, who has charted the history of the theory that witchcraft had been a pagan religion, declared in his very first treatment of the issue that the 'vivid medieval realm of the imagination' which produced images of witchcraft drew on ancient, and indeed some worldwide, modes of thought, and 'urgently requires further investigation'.[88]

No concerted effort has, however, been made to that end, and instead something of a cleavage has tended to open between anglophone and Continental schools of witchcraft scholarship. British and American historians have excelled in applying insights from criminology, sociology, psychology, literary studies and cultural studies, and made notable contributions to an understanding of the ideology of early modern witchcraft prosecutions, and of their relation to gender and social class, and to the weakness or strength of state systems.[89] They have been much less inclined to pay attention to parallels from world anthropology or to the question of ancient origins. By contrast, some Continental European colleagues have been very willing to do both, and again achieved excellent results.[90] They have tended, however, to look to broad models of spiritual tradition and behaviour, and especially to that of an archaic shamanism which is sometimes employed as an umbrella concept. It is certainly important to discuss what traditional human societies have in common, and shamanism provides a convenient term for direct contacts with spirits by human specialists in other than normal consciousness. The danger is that an umbrella can all too easily, in this context, turn into a dustbin. Every human society until the eighteenth century believed that it was surrounded and permeated by a spirit world with which it had to deal: it is productive to explore the different ways in which they responded to that universal belief. There is a considerable difference between people who went into trance in the course of a dramatic public performance in order to carry out acts of healing and divination; people who dreamed of going forth from their bodies while asleep to do battle with evil spirits or the spirits of evil humans; people who believed that they were swept up while asleep by spectral cavalcades (or that they were seeing such cavalcades pass by); and people who believed that good spirits visited them by night and made them gifts. All these were distinctive European traditions, rooted in pre-Christian cultures and identified with particular regions, and to sweep them together into the category of 'shamanism' conceals as much as it reveals. It also deprives us of a chance to explain differences in the historic record, whereby some areas of Europe had witch trials and others had not, some tried a majority of women and some of men, and the actions credited to witches took different forms in different places.

The general picture is now clear. In ancient times most societies in Europe and the Near East feared witchcraft, defined as the assumed ability of some human beings to do deliberate injury to others by magical means.[91] They had this in common with most human societies in the world, though by no means all. Ancient witch-hunts could be on a very large scale: if we can trust information provided by the Roman historian Livy, 3,000 people were executed in one wave of trials in Italy (most in Rome itself) during the second century BC and 2,000 more in another, body counts which match or surpass any achieved in single witch-hunts in Christian Europe.[92] The influence of ancient ideas and procedures on early modern European constructions of witchcraft was profound. The materials attributed by Shakespeare to his witches' potion echo those used by witches in the works of the Roman poet Horace, while when Shakespeare's contemporary Ben Jonson wrote an antimasque about witches as a preface to his *Masque of Queenes*, he filled his published text of it with references to Greek and Roman sources.[93] The popular tradition that witches would float if thrown into water, and that this test could be used to detect them, was first given known legal expression in the law code of the Babylonian king Hammurabi in the early second millennium BC.[94] A belief in the threat posed by witchcraft, and a stock of images of it and responses to it, was one of the main bequests of the pagan ancient world to the medieval and early modern Christian one.

There was actually no intrinsic necessity for any form of Christianity to become closely associated with the prosecution of witchcraft. It makes little appearance in the New Testament, where demonic possession, relieved by exorcism, is prominent instead. Christ said nothing about witches, and nor did any of his immediate apostles, and while St Paul did condemn magic, using a term that could be translated as witchcraft, he did so as a sin on a level with anger and lechery, rather than as a lethal crime (Galatians 5:20). A dislike of various forms of magic is patent in the Old Testament, along with one famous injunction to put witches to death (Exodus 22:18); but this was the Mosaic Code, which Christ's coming could be said to have abrogated. It was, rather, their own embedment in general late Roman culture which caused Romanized forms of Christianity to accept legal sanctions against many forms of magic, justified theologically by a new doctrine that any act which disposed of apparently supernatural power outside the mediation of a church had of necessity to involve the aid of a demon. However, the passage from the old to the new forms of religion did not produce any apparent increase in trials for witchcraft, and in northern Europe it even suppressed executions for certain types of imagined magical activity, such as of women who were believed to fly around by night and prey on the life force of human beings.[95] For most of the Middle Ages, the use of magic was punished as a criminal act when it was thought to have resulted in actual injury or been used to influence political events, but the number of executions resulting was relatively small, and scattered through space and time.[96]

In the early fifteenth century, however, some theologians and magistrates began to reconstruct witchcraft as an organized religion of devotion to the Christian Devil, who granted witches the ability to work magic through the activities of demons. Those who made this leap of the imagination were conscious of the fact that they were breaking with tradition, and characterized the satanic cult they were describing as a new and terrifying menace to Christianity. In doing so, they took a step unique among world beliefs in witchcraft, of associating it with a particular kind of religion, deliberately pitted against the true and orthodox one by the cosmic power of evil. Such a development was made possible only by the stark dualism of Christian theology, but even so the only Christian Churches in which it was accepted were the Roman Catholic one of late medieval western and central Europe and the Protestant successors into which it splintered at the Reformation. It was also slow to take hold, the resulting trials of suspects being mainly confined to a corridor between the Netherlands and northern Italy for a hundred and fifty years. Only with the struggle between Protestant and Catholic did the pitch of religious anger, terror and suspicion in Europe spread to the point at which persecution of alleged witches became widespread and intense. None the less, criticism of witch trials always persisted, and the great majority of executions occurred in one long lifetime, between 1560 and 1630, after which the readiness to persecute waned, though it had late flare-ups on the European periphery from New England to Scandinavia and Poland. In many ways it was a brief experiment in ways of dealing with misfortune, which was abandoned largely because it did not produce good results: communities which executed people for witchcraft did not appear to fare any better or to be especially favoured by their deity. Decisive evidence of the satanic conspiracy was always elusive, and tolerance of presumed witches grew with that of other kinds of Christian, and of Jews, as part of a general rejection of murderous religious persecution.[97]

Historians are now agreed that there is no reason to believe in any kind of organized witch religion, pagan or satanic, behind the European witch trials. It is quite likely that some people did curse their neighbours, and quite possible – though the nature of the evidence makes proof elusive – that a few of these imagined that they had made a pact with the Devil in order to do so. That is, however, a very different phenomenon, and there is no solid evidence that any people in early modern Europe actually gathered to worship Satan or any other non-Christian being, in preference to the Christian God, let alone with formalized and prescribed rites. What is very clear instead is that popular traditions concerning the nature of the supernatural, which had survived from pre-Christian times, played a part both in forming the stereotype of the demonic witch and in determining the nature and incidence of trials. The most celebrated, and extreme, example of this effect was discovered by Carlo Ginzburg in the Friuli district of north-eastern Italy, in the form of belief in individuals collectively known as the *benandanti*. These were people distinguished by being born with a caul, which was thought to give them the power to send forth their spirits by night to do battle with local witches who threatened the fertility of the fields. This tradition represented one corner of a belief in dream warriors, whose spirits went forth by night to defend their communities in similar fashion, found all over the Balkans and northwards as far as Hungary. In Friuli, however, those who thought themselves to be *benandanti* fell in the years around 1600 into the hands of Catholic inquisitors seeking witches who, convinced that these benign Christian spirit-voyagers were witches themselves, suppressed them.[98]

As said, the *benandanti* were a most unusual case, of something like a pre-Christian cult (or one that can reasonably be presumed to have been one)

surviving into early modern times, although thoroughly assimilated to
Christianity until the inquisitors decided otherwise. Historians of Britain have
been especially hard put to find anything remotely comparable, not least
because people accused of witchcraft in England and Wales were almost never
presumed to have engaged in communal acts of devil worship. Only in Scotland
were such acts often recorded in confessions, and it was from there that
Margaret Murray drew most of her British evidence for a pagan religion, from
accounts which have subsequently been rejected as fantasy or as reports of
innocent popular revels that were interpreted as satanic by prosecutors.[99]
Emma Wilby and Julian Goodare have both recently applied Carlo Ginzburg's
model of shamanic cults surviving in Christianized form to the Scottish material. Theirs is a fascinating line of enquiry, which thoroughly deserves to be
followed, but thus far the former's use of comparisons with the practices
of figures called shamans by scholars in other continents has yielded only
speculative possibilities.[100] The latter may have detected a Scottish tradition
of communication with spirits similar to that of the *benandanti*, but thus far
its existence is not firmly proven.[101] In a context concerned with pagan
survivals, it is worth pointing out that in neither case is there any indication
that the people concerned regarded themselves as pagans, or could now be
regarded as such.

Once again, however, when a broader view is taken, the element of pagan
tradition assumes major importance. This may be illustrated by the incidence
and nature of prosecution. In this respect, the north-eastern Atlantic islands
may be divided into three sharply delineated zones.[102] One is represented by
England, Lowland Scotland, Scandinavian Scotland (Caithness and the
Northern Isles, the areas of major Viking settlement), frontier areas of the
Highlands where mainstream, Lowland, Scottish cultural influence was strong,
the English settlements in Ireland, and the Channel Islands (culturally part of
Normandy, and so of France). This had in common with most of northern
Europe a strong popular fear of witchcraft, resulting in a large number of trials,
the great majority of which were of women, and – where systems of justice
responded most directly to local opinion – a high rate of execution. The second
zone consists of Iceland, which also produced a high level of witch-hunting,
relative to the size of the population, but where almost all the victims – over
90 per cent – were men. It had this male preponderance in common with some
other northern societies, such as those of the Baltic peoples, the Sámi or Lapps,
(initially) the Finns, and the Russians. The third comprises the areas of the
British Isles where a Celtic language, and associated culture, predominated:
most of the Scottish Highlands and Hebrides, the Isle of Man, Wales, and those
areas of Ireland where the native population remained in the majority. Here
there were few trials and fewer executions, and anxiety concerning witchcraft

seems to have been less than elsewhere. These three differing areas were not separated by religious allegiances, and their social and political structures, and gender relationships, were too similar to explain the apparent discrepancy between them.

One way of providing an explanation consists of examining contrasting cultural traditions, rooted in the ancient world, of destructive magic. Iceland lay on the edge of a cultural province in which male magicians were most feared and respected and operated a dramatic public rite technique in which they would go into a trance and work with a spirit world for the good of clients and their own communities and the detriment of foes. This is shamanism of the classical sort, as found around the Arctic zone of the globe and across Siberia and neighbouring regions, and its presence in Iceland – in a hybrid and diluted form – is attested by the island's famous medieval sagas. The Celtic cultures of medieval and early modern Europe seem to have possessed three characteristics, displayed in medieval literature, early modern court records and later folklore collections, which mitigated the impulse to prosecute witch-craft. The first was a belief in the legitimacy of cursing, if done openly and in response to genuine wrong; the second an acceptance that some people could inflict magical harm involuntarily and unconsciously, by possession of an 'evil eye'; and the third a greater than usual fear, for Europeans, of land spirits, called fairies, elves or by various Celtic names. These spirits were commonly regarded as inflicting the kinds of misfortune on humans which elsewhere were more frequently blamed on witches. The rest of the British Isles conformed to a mainstream European tradition, which greatly feared the harm that evil humans might inflict on others by using magic, and had a special wariness of and respect for the natural magical powers thought to be inherent in women.

The mention of fairies and elves introduces another component into the category of pagan survivals, allied to the concept of parallel worlds already discussed in the form of the Welsh Annwn. Throughout the Middle Ages, and long after, popular tradition all over Britain teemed with rural spirits which had no obvious place in Christianity. Some were associated with particular bodies of water, as ancient goddesses such as Sulis, Coventina and Verbeia had been. The later folkloric water beings, however, like Peg Powler and Jenny Greenteeth in northern England and the Scottish kelpie or *each uisge* (water horse), tended to be much more menacing than their divine predecessors: beings to be avoided or destroyed rather than propitiated or befriended. Only in Wales was there a widespread lingering belief in the presence of lake-people who took human form, might mate with humans and could provide benefits to them. Another category of beings were household spirits, which might help or hinder and went by names such as hobgoblin in England, brownie in Lowland Scotland, *bwca* in Wales and *bodachan sabhaill* in the Scottish Highlands.

There were also the fairies or elves proper, known in Wales as the *Tylwyth Teg*, in the Northern Isles as trows, and in Gaelic regions by various names with the prefix *sí*. These tended to live underground and in a communal society with its own royal court and ruler, usually a nameless queen. They raided and molested humans, but also sometimes gave benefits, though these tended to be illusory or transitory, and for people to deal with such beings was regarded as disreputable as well as dangerous.

The water spirits and household spirits had clear parallels all over pagan Europe, including the Mediterranean, but the fairy society, existing in a parallel world to the human, was strictly a northern tradition, its members being neither personifications of nature nor deities. None of these beings, however, had any agreed place in Christian tradition. When medieval and early modern people tried to find one for them, two suggestions were generally made. One was that they were fallen angels, whose sins had been less than those consigned to hell and so who haunted the terrestrial world or its boundaries; the other that they were the ghosts of human beings who had possessed uncanny traits in life or met with mysterious kinds of death. After the Reformation, evangelical Protestant orthodoxy maintained that they were devils of a wholly straightforward kind, and so individuals who claimed to have dealings with them, or were thought to do so, could end up on a charge of witchcraft, according to the new satanic model. On the whole, however, popular opinion maintained stubbornly that they were neither angels nor demons, of any sort, but an altogether different order of supernatural being which was not recorded in Christian theology; and this was the tradition which has endured into modern times. They were a survival from pagan belief which the new religion had found more or less indigestible, but which gave it little trouble in practice because few if any people attempted to worship fairies so they did not tangle with issues of allegiance or salvation.[103]

As so often when dealing with the subject of survivals, specific case studies, of especially notable and famed examples, can prove more problematic than the broad picture. On the island of Lewis, in the Outer Hebrides, men in the late seventeenth century knelt down at the edge of the waves at Hallowe'en and recited the Lord's Prayer. One then waded waist-deep into the sea, poured out a bowl of ale, and asked a being called Shoney for a good growth of seaweed (for manure) in the coming year. They then went back to a particular chapel, dedicated to St Malvey, and sat there in silence for a while before making merry in the fields.[104] The custom was found elsewhere in the Western Isles, for example on Iona where it was recorded until the late eighteenth century, while it lingered on Lewis until the nineteenth.[105] At first sight it seems a perfect survival of a pagan rite to a marine deity, preserved in a Christianized context; a supposition which is strengthened by the facts that Protestant ministers on

Lewis campaigned to suppress it in the 1670s and that the nineteenth-century version of it actually addresses the being concerned as 'God of the Sea'. The difficulties start with the name, because 'Shoney' is simply a Gaelic version of the English and Lowland Scots 'Johnnie', and it seems odd to find a native deity addressed as such. This raises the possibility that the ceremony was originally directed to one of the saints called John, whose cult, suppressed at the Reformation, would have irritated Scottish Protestant clergy as much as a pagan one. The direct mode of address as a 'god', recorded later, is in a text provided by the folklore collector Alexander Carmichael, who has been suspected of polishing up the material that he gathered.[106] None of these doubts eradicates the ancient quality of the act, of pouring a libation into the sea with a spoken prayer requesting a service, but it may possibly be a relic of a medieval Christian rite, transplanted to the shore when the traditional saints' cults were abolished.

A different case study, that of the English figure of Herne the Hunter, is in many ways more straightforward, though also ultimately inconclusive: what is known of it has been teased out by Jeremy Harte.[107] Herne first appears in Shakespeare's play *The Merry Wives of Windsor* (Act IV), as a royal gamekeeper who, presumably because of a curse or his own evil nature, became doomed after death to haunt the forest in winter. His ghost wore large horns or antlers, shook a chain to terrify humans, and had the power to afflict cattle with disease and death. It is not known, and probably never will be, whether Shakespeare invented the whole story himself, as a useful plot device – for so it proves – or adopted an existing Windsor legend. Local folklore elaborated on it in the eighteenth and nineteenth centuries, as it became a part of the tourist trade of the district, to account (for example) for the keeper's untimely death. The decisive change in Herne's fortunes came in 1843, when the most popular historical novelist in early Victorian England, Harrison Ainsworth, included it in a story entitled *Windsor Castle*. Ainsworth drew on the account of the German tradition of the Wild Hunt, a nocturnal procession of ghostly riders, to turn Herne into the English leader of such a cavalcade, put into that position as a result of a pact with Satan. This new personification duly entered local lore as well as literary tradition, and Herne's hunt was heard and seen around Windsor. It was Margaret Murray who finally transformed him into a pagan god, the English equivalent to the Gaulish Cernunnos, drawing upon Ainsworth's portrait of him as her source material. As such, he has played a prominent part in the modern imagination, whether as a divine and benevolent leader of the Wild Hunt in the children's fiction of Susan Cooper from the 1970s or as the presiding deity of the forest in a popular television series of the 1980s.[108] Like Ceridwen, therefore, he is essentially a literary figure whom modernity has back-projected into the pagan past. Equally, it is possible both to argue that this back-projection cannot positively be disproved and that literary creations can have a spiritual life of their own, or even 'channel' the hitherto unsuspected presence of actual divine powers.[109] As in her case, however, it is possible to remark instead upon the weight with which the hand of the nineteenth century has lain upon the imagination of the twentieth, and beyond. Herne's status as pagan god, at any rate, is very doubtful.

Such specific considerations should not be permitted to detract from the significance of the broader picture, that both a fear of witchcraft and a belief in a parallel world of fairies and related spirits were clear legacies of a world older than Christianity. People who hung up charms or carried out rites against the spells of witches or fairies, or left out gifts of food and drink to propitiate the latter, were genuinely acting out belief systems which had survived from prehistory. It is indeed in these wider systems of thought that the most potent relics of paganism can be found. It may be opportune here to return for a last time to the Old English poem *Beowulf*. In the preceding chapter it was suggested that this was a work by a Christian writer, imagining a lost world of paganism, rather than either a pagan work which had been given a Christian gloss or a Christian one which preserved a vivid memory of pagan rites. Even so, in its social and cultural attitudes, it very successfully transmitted a set of ancient northern values which were at odds with the teachings of Christianity. These included an absolute obligation, amounting to a test of honour, to exact vengeance or demand compensation for wrongs done to oneself or to kin or friends; a love of material objects, as beautiful creations which almost possessed personalities of their own and which gave moral value to their possessors and proved their inherent worthiness; and a deep suspicion of the natural world as a wild and dangerous place, rather than of the human one as a place of corruption and moral danger. In these senses, the new religion did indeed form a veneer over old habits of mind, even while it successfully displaced the former deities as a focus for religious loyalties.

Protective Magic

For much of the twentieth century, scholars who wanted to believe that medieval British Christianity was spread thinly over a still substantially pagan popular culture found further supporting evidence in charms. These were written prayers and spells, intended to be spoken or worn on the person, which were thought to have power to counteract specific ailments and misfortunes.[110] In recent years they have continued to attract the attention of researchers, but there has been something of a reaction against an emphasis on the pagan elements in them. Karen Jolly has pointed instead to the essentially Christian nature of the whole body of surviving texts, into which some pagan ingredients had been successfully assimilated. She concluded that 'these so-called magic or pagan elements represent areligious folklore, transferable from one religious tradition to another', and that they 'should not suggest a lesser understanding of Christian truth or a degradation of Christianity by the influence of paganism'.[111] A subsequent collection of essays on charms stressed that they formed part of popular Christian culture, and that in many cases Latin texts produced by monks preceded corresponding versions in vernacular languages. It concluded that to focus on the tiny number of early charms that show pagan features is to ignore and distort mainstream Western European tradition, and noted that those few early charms were themselves preserved by monks.[112] In view of these changing attitudes, the obvious next step is to consider that 'tiny number' of British texts with pagan features, and see what can be said about them here.

One of the most famous is the 'Lay of the Nine Twigs of Woden', from the late Old English commonplace book known as the *Lacnunga*.[113] Concerned with the healing and protective power of herbs, it describes how 'Woden' took 'nine glory-twigs' to destroy a poisonous snake. Later it explicitly evokes the power of Christ, and in between speaks of two herbs as being created by 'the wise Lord holy in heaven when He hung'. That 'Lord' is probably Jesus, but there is an outside chance that it is Woden, *if* he resembled the Norse Odin in the latter's mythology of hanging nine days from a tree to gain wisdom. On the other hand, there is no explicit indication that Woden himself is treated here as a god, as opposed to being a human magician, and long before the time of the *Lacnunga* he had been brought into Christian English tradition as a mortal man, a descendant of Noah who appears in royal genealogies. The truth is that we do not really understand his role in the charm, which itself appears to be garbled in its recorded form. The same is true of Woden's appearance in another, in which he is actually portrayed as speaking, to cure wrenched body parts: he may be featuring as a god, magician or physician. The same text also mentions 'Baldur': this could be the Norse god of that name, or may be an Anglo-Saxon word for a leader.[114] Similar problems attend a runic charm surviving in a manuscript compiled at Canterbury Cathedral in the 1070s, which calls on Thor to stop blood poisoning. It is accompanied by five others, which invoke the Christian God and saints against different physical ills. The literary scholar who called attention to it, John Frankis, suggested that the monk who copied it did not understand its pagan nature, a possibility strengthened by the fact that he certainly could not handle all of its language, rendering some into mumbo-jumbo.[115] What we do not understand is whether those from whom he obtained it understood it any better: as the god is Thor and not the English Thunor, it would have been gained from Scandinavians, settled in or visiting England.

Another example, as well known as the 'Lay of the Nine Twigs', is the 'Field Blessing Ceremony' or 'Aecerbot', known from a single manuscript of the late tenth or early eleventh century.[116] It is soaked in Christian language and imagery, quoting passages of liturgy and mentioning the Trinity (both together and in its component parts), the Virgin Mary and the four Evangelists. It also, however, calls on 'Erce, Erce, Erce, earth's mother' as the indwelling spirit of the soil that is to be fertilized. The word 'Erce' is not recorded in any other source, and has no discernible meaning in Anglo-Saxon, so that it may be a genuine pagan deity-name or a corruption of the Latin *ecce*, meaning 'behold'. The text embodies a clear theology, whereby the Christian God, who is the object of most of its devotion, grants fertility to the soil, as part of his general remit as ruler of the universe and its creator. Though personified as a 'mother', it is shown as a passive entity, entirely in his power. What is less clear is whether this maternal being is a specific former goddess or an abstraction imagined for the purposes of the rite. There is at least no doubt of the pagan provenance of another field-blessing charm recorded in medieval English literature, the Latin poem 'Praecatio terrae matris'. It is found in several Continental manuscripts dating from the sixth century onwards, and one English one from the eleventh or twelfth century. In its earliest manuscript appearance it is glossed as 'the beginning of the prayer to earth employed by the pagans of old when they wished to collect herbs', and indeed it features in works devoted to herbal medicine, with a Christian prayer appended to it. Whether it was originally a charm may be doubted, for it is a very polished literary work in praise of 'Earth, Divine Goddess, Mother Nature', produced by a talented and sophisticated writer towards the end of the Roman Empire.[117] As such, it is excellent evidence for the incorporation of pagan material into later Christian works, and for the integration of England into mainstream medieval intellectual culture, but not for any surviving paganism in Britain.

The sense that the appearance of figures such as Woden and Thor in charms is a vestigial remnant of their old character as deities, as opposed to a sign of a continuing veneration of them, is enhanced by the lack of an enduring tradition that embodies them: after the eleventh century, they no longer feature in charms and nor does 'Erce' or 'Mother Nature'. Instead, when such texts have a religious character (which they often do), it is wholly Christian, though often of a rather conservative kind: many dating from the period after 1700 call on saints and the Virgin Mary in a medieval manner officially condemned at the Reformation.[118] Once again, however, a broader view of the question reveals deeper continuities, which have been less apparent because of the very success with which they were integrated with Christianity. The very notion that spoken words could tap into hidden powers within the world, to obtain physical results, was pre-Christian, even if it could easily be accepted that the Christian

God had placed those powers there. Medieval herb-lore retained both ancient learned concepts of antithetical properties in nature, found in pagan authors, and ancient popular traditions of the magical associations of plants, and their connection to good and evil spirits and the influence of the moon.[119] Charms were commonly used by specialists who had inherited an inherent, and uncanny, power to wield them, and also formed part of the much broader repertoire of remedies deployed – usually for a fee – by those people known in English as 'cunning folk' or 'wise folk' and by many other names up and down Britain. These used magic as the solution for a host of problems and ailments – of which the removal of bewitchment was perhaps the most important – brought to them by the inhabitants of their locality. They have been recorded in Britain from the first appearance of legal records until the twentieth century, have equivalents in every inhabited Continent of the world, and posed theological and practical difficulties for conscientious or intolerant clergy from Anglo-Saxon times onwards. Not a single one between the conversion period and the twentieth century has been shown to have been a pagan, their recorded beliefs spanning the spectrum of those found in the surrounding Christian society; but their very existence, as an independent source of apparently supernatural power to the clergy, represented an intermittent, but persisting, source of concern for churches.[120]

Narrowing the focus of analysis to Anglo-Saxon charms once more, it can readily be seen that they commonly embody four concepts which certainly derive from pre-Christian Germanic tradition.[121] These were the beliefs in an invisible form of magical attack called 'flying venom' (actually not a bad metaphor for airborne infection); in elves as the cause of many sorts of ailment; in the magical properties of the number nine; and in the wyrm or worm as a malevolent and dangerous form of beast, equating to a form of super-serpent. Less often, they mention other kinds of being from pagan Germanic mythology, such as 'ladies who could free or fetter warriors'.[122] Karen Jolly is certainly right to remind us that 'although it may be of interest to the modern scholar to trace the pagan, Anglo-Saxon, and Christian elements of these remedies, we need to recognize that the remedies existed in their own time as integrated wholes, without any self-consciousness of a conflict of traditions or beliefs.'[123] It may be noted here, as her work and that of her predecessors show, that Greek, Roman and Arabic elements also form part of that integrated whole of early English magical medicine. All that may be worth adding, in the present context, is how significant a contribution the pagan elements – classical Mediterranean and Germanic together – made to that combination, however Christianized it was.

Slightly different problems and reflections attend another form of protective magic: objects and marks placed within buildings and other structures to house the living and dead. This is a field hitherto almost wholly ignored by mainstream historians of the medieval and early modern periods, because the evidence concerned is almost entirely material. This leads to a double neglect, because if magic in general has only relatively recently begun to receive the attention of such historians, the same is even more true of material culture in general.[124] Anthropologists and folklorists were, by contrast, very interested in material objects during the nineteenth and early twentieth centuries, but subsequently they too turned away from them.[125] In recent years important pioneering work, carried out by scholars either outside or on the fringe of the academic system, has revealed the impressive scale of the relevant data. It was an archaeologist attached to the Museum of London, Ralph Merrifield, who first drew attention systematically to it in the 1980s, and made a convincing argument that it represented a direct continuity of the ancient practice of making ritual deposits to consecrate, honour and protect places and bodies. Coins were still put with corpses in nineteenth-century Cambridgeshire and Lincolnshire. Animal bones, especially skulls and lower jaws, have occasionally been found under medieval doorways and building foundations, and so have pots.[126] Brian Hoggard has recently made a survey of objects ritually deposited in concealed places around buildings, from 650 museums and archaeological collections, which must be a mere fraction of those discovered in the past couple of hundred years, as most would have been discarded with repugnance or indifference. Unlike most archaeology, this is a kind which depends on chance finds.[127] The objects were usually put into walls, roofs, floors, hearths and entrances and exits: the spiritually significant and vulnerable 'liminal' points. Most spectacular are 'witch bottles', glass or pottery containers stocked with human urine and metal pins or nails: 200 are recorded from England. More common are shoes, most of them well worn so that they had taken on the shape of the wearer's foot: Northampton Museum alone has 1,500 of these. Over a hundred dried cats are recorded, which is significant, as anecdotal evidence among builders suggests that they are usually thrown away when found, and probably over a thousand have been discarded in this manner. Charms are also found, of the kind obtained from cunning folk, and so are horses' skulls: more rarely, dolls, rats, toads, pipes, knives, coins and garments. Other researchers have recently made particular studies of certain classes of these objects.

Of the whole stock of them, the witch bottles are least mysterious because they have a text to explain them, written in 1651 by Joseph Blagrave, who stated that they represented the bladder of a witch, and were used as counter-magic by people who believed themselves to be bewitched. If the bottle were heated, the witch who had cast the curse was believed to suffer pain, and if this did not apparently work, concealment of the container would lead to her or his slow decay instead. Other than having a linkage to the ancient fear of witchcraft,

103 A carved wooden shoe, found inside the roof of a seventeenth-century cottage at Wrington, north Somerset, photographed by the owner, Tom Henry, in 2011. It is a common experience to find old shoes of the functional, leather, variety concealed in buildings between the later Middle Ages and nineteenth century, apparently as protective charms. A wooden one is, however, unusual, and the name engraved upon it, 'Anvers', which seems to refer to the city of Antwerp, is another puzzle.

they are the least relevant to pagan survivals, because their distribution suggests that they spread from the south-east of England, from the sixteenth century onwards.[128] Shoes are, by contrast, attested in firmly dated contexts from the year 1308 onwards, though their deposition apparently increased in popularity in the eighteenth and nineteenth centuries, and indeed builders often seem routinely to have engaged in it.[129] Here again we have a textual reference, from a Victorian historian who commented on the 'many who nail up an old shoe in our vessels and houses, though not liking to own our belief, yet consider it would be a pity to receive harm from neglecting so easy a precaution'.[130] This proves its purpose as a general protective act, as the shoe is the kind of garment which best retains the shape, and so the essence and power, of the wearer. Here there certainly is a connection with ancient ritual practice, because shoes were found as foundation deposits in the Roman Empire, including Britain, mostly in pits and wells.[131]

The cats also apparently had a function as guardians, perhaps specifically against vermin, though here we lack literary evidence, and some may have been foundation sacrifices of the ancient sort, while the vermin concerned may have been 'spiritual' as well as literal.[132] It seems that, for some reason, they had taken the place that dogs had in earlier ritual deposits; and indeed, dogs seem to disappear from such contexts around the time that cats appear in them. Horses, however, did continue to feature as of old, their skulls being found in walls and under flagstones and floorboards.[133] Between 1500 and 1700 garments were often put into junctures between old and new parts of buildings, or doorways, and knotted, as if ritually to terminate their function as clothing.[134] This whole repertoire of deposited objects travelled out silently across the English-speaking world; an excellent doctoral thesis has found them to be widespread in colonial Australia.[135] Such acts of symbolic magic are more or less timeless, making the transition to Christian culture with ease because they were so private and were apparently directed against hostile spiritual powers which could translate easily into new theologies. None the less, they form the latest episode in a ritual tradition of deposition which in Britain reaches back as far as the Mesolithic.

The solid objects hidden in buildings appear to be related to ritual marks placed upon them from the sixteenth century onwards, a custom to which there seem to be no textual references at all, and the systematic study of which has been pioneered by Timothy Easton and followed up by Brian Hoggard, again, and others.[136] The most common are a conjoined pair of V-signs, sometimes multiplied, and a circle with petals inside it, but there are also crosses, circles, P-shapes and other conjoined letters, notably AMR. In the Mendips they were also placed in caves, perhaps to bless those descending into these places, or to pen in forces that dwelt in the depths or had been exorcized to them. They were also possibly carved on to ships and certainly on to personal utensils.[137] They are found throughout England and Wales, and in English settlements in Australia and America: there seem at present to be no Scottish data. The significance of any of them is at present unknown: it has been suggested that the overlapping Vs and AMR represent the Virgin Mary, signifying 'Virgin of Virgins' and 'Ave Maria Regina', though why this symbol of late medieval Catholic devotion should have been especially popular in Protestant homes and churches in early modern East Anglia and the West Country, is baffling. Parallel to etched marks are burn marks, found at entrances and apertures and in walls in buildings of all kinds between the sixteenth and the nineteenth centuries. A single piece of oral testimony held that these provided protection against fire, and a study of them in East Anglia has suggested that they took the place of prayers to saints after the Reformation.[138] A third kind of symbol in this category are symbols scorched on to ceilings by candles, which seem to be seventeenth-century. Again, there is a set repertoire of signs.[139]

All this would seem of interest only to historians of post-Reformation culture – though it should be of a great deal of interest to them – as, though the concept of protective signs is ancient, the symbols used in this case do not seem to be. What is of possible significance to anyone concerned with pagan survivals is the existence of certain equivalent markings on external structures. A succession of bridges was built to carry existing roads over the main railway line between Manchester and Crewe, laid down in 1840. Each has carvings in the coping stones of the arch, on the keystone and on those at the ends, all the points which took most of the strain of the construction. They represent a standard repertoire on each, consisting of erect penises and the prints of shoe soles and hands, with the occasional interlocking Vs, known from house interiors and caves as protective markings. The shoes are of a design with square toes, obsolete by the early Victorian period, which would suggest that the sign was by then inherited and traditional.[140] The importance of shoes in protection of buildings has already been emphasized, as has their equivalent role in the Roman world, where the erect phallus was a common motif carved on stone structures to encourage them to stand up strongly, as well as functioning as a protective symbol in other contexts.[141] The nineteenth-century builders were therefore blessing their work with a set of signs that have unmistakable ancient parallels, and one of which has a continuous magical use – though one only recently recognized – since the high Middle Ages. Whether the apparent gap in the employment of the shoe as a symbol during the earlier medieval period can be filled, whether the phallus is found on medieval and early modern structures as well, and whether the same set of signs can be recognized on other Victorian works, are all questions that remain to be answered. None the less, whether as a case of survival, revival or parallel development, there is some sort of connection to be made.

In the 1960s, Anne Ross drew attention to a set of carved stone heads found at various locations in the British Isles, interpreting them as Iron Age in date, and as evidence for the cult of the head as a part of pagan 'Celtic' religion. A museum curator, Sidney Jackson, published an argument that they were an important part of Britain's historical and folk heritage.[142] Despite this, archaeologists lost interest in them, largely because they did not seem to belong to datable ancient contexts. In the 1990s a study of them was carried out by a freelance illustrator, John Billingsley, who discovered that the majority that could be dated were seventeenth-century, and that what had been identified as 'Celtic' features in them because of their apparent resemblance to faces in Iron Age art – a flat, pear-shaped face, lentoid eyes and oval mouth – were an early modern tradition. None the less, he emphasized that this represented one stage in a long history and prehistory of stylized heads in British, and indeed in European, art and architecture. Favourite points for their erection in the Tudor and Stuart periods were wells, bridges, gates, doors, windows and gable ends, all places of entry and boundary. They therefore seemed to have a quasi-ritual purpose beyond mere decoration, centring on functions of protection and guardianship. They were especially common in West Yorkshire, where they were made into the nineteenth century.[143] Billingsley, however, acknowledged that they could also have been objects of humour and entertainment. Many (across the British Isles) had a hole in the mouth perfectly suited to hold a clay pipe, which could then be knocked off by people competing to throw balls at it: an explanation which suits both the battered appearance of some heads and anecdotal evidence.[144] Even taking this into account, he could still argue that the frequency with which severed heads are credited with magical and mystical properties in folklore, coupled with the positioning of the early modern specimens when first erected, sustains the theory that they originally had a protective function. The accumulating body of evidence for other symbols and objects in early modern Britain with just that apparent purpose, summarized above, may stand in further support of his interpretation. There is no evidence at all that they were regarded as having any connection with pagan deities, but the very idea that a material object could be invested with inherent spiritual power, not instilled into it by ecclesiastical benediction, was itself an inheritance from a pre-Christian world.

A possible final example of such an inheritance, which may fit into the category of protective magic, is a case of what could be a survival of the ancient tradition of ritual deposits in the earth. Between 2001 and 2008 a total of thirty-five pits in a valley site in west Cornwall were excavated and revealed to contain swan pelts, magpies, eggs of a variety of birds, birds' claws, quartz pebbles, human hair, fingernails and part of an iron cauldron. Each pit had been carefully lined with a swan pelt. The swan skins have been dated to around 1640, and the construction and stocking of the pits would have involved a significant number of people over an extended period, presumably from the neighbouring hamlet of Saveock Water whose inhabitants worked at a local mill. A stone-lined spring there also proved to have been given seventeenth-century deposits, including 128 strips of cloth from dresses as well as pins, shoe parts, cherry stones and nail clippings, before being filled in. Another pit subsequently found, dated to the eighteenth century and containing eggs and the remains of a cat; and another, with parts of a dog and pig, were dated to the 1950s. In an extensive and international publicity campaign in the mass media, the leader of the excavations interpreted the discoveries as evidence for a pagan fertility rite carried on by witches. She added that such an activity would have been extremely dangerous in the period concerned, as any pagan worship was classified as witchcraft and the perpetrators would have been burned at the stake. She suggested that the later pit deposits were evidence that the cult had continued in secret until the present day.[145]

Despite all the attention drawn to them, no proper publication of the excavations has apparently yet been attempted, and so it is difficult to make an independent assessment of their implications. On the face of things, the seventeenth-century pits, at least, do look as if they may well be sites of ritual deposition, but the interpretation offered by the excavator may be questioned. If any professional colleague has begun to wonder why the lack of evidence for the survival of active paganism in Britain after the early Middle Ages should have been so laboured in these pages, and the lack of any connection of such a religion associated with witchcraft, such public statements may serve as justification enough. Leaving aside this larger issue, and the minor point that people convicted of witchcraft in the early modern English realm were not burned but hanged, the perpetrators of these probable rites would only have been in mortal danger if their actions fell into two categories. The first was intentionally to invoke spirits to assist their work, and the second was to direct the latter maliciously towards the injury of other human beings or their possessions.[146] Most other acts of operative magic would have been safe in practice, even if offered for sale to the public, which is why cunning folk could flourish in large numbers throughout the period and until the nineteenth century. The Cornish pits could have been the setting for any of a wide range of practices intended to secure protection or good fortune, for which the other evidence considered above provides an ample context, even while evidence of a surviving pagan witch religion is missing. Such carefully positioned objects and markings testify to a flourishing world of early modern folk magic, much of which was based on the pagan past or even continued acts or images from it, which has hitherto fallen between the disciplines of history, archaeology and folklore studies, and so been largely neglected by all.

Deities

Of all the channels through which pagan ideas and images flowed into Christian culture, by far the most important and effective consisted of the literature, art and orally transmitted stories which depicted the nature and deeds of deities. Pre-eminent in this body of tradition was the classical heritage of Greece and Rome, which made the Olympian deities increasingly familiar and beloved figures in Christian Europe as knowledge of the relevant texts and works of art permeated slowly through society. The immense respect felt by Christian Europeans for the classical Mediterranean heritage helped to provoke northern peoples such as the medieval Irish and Icelanders, in turn, to create a literature which featured their own native deities and the myths which had been told about them. By such means, pagan goddesses and gods who, in strict early theology, had to be regarded as demons came to be treated with affection and admiration by many Christians of differing denominations and degrees of piety; even though they were religiously neutered by being seen as figures of allegory or of fiction.

The concern here is with cases in which medieval authors went further, to try to find a place within a Christian cosmos for older deities who could be accepted and honoured as genuinely potent entities. These authors belonged to a scholarly elite, and virtually all of them were based outside Britain, but their works were known in it as an aspect of its position as part of the international and supranational world of Latin scholasticism.[147] Most of the key antique texts on which members of that world depended for their concept of the universe – above all Aristotle and Plato – taught them that the heavenly bodies were animate beings. A ferocious fourth-century Christian opponent of paganism, Julius Firmicus, could still try to salvage the planets, bearing their pagan names, as deities who served the supreme god. Augustine of Hippo, most influential of all the Church Fathers, wondered if they might indeed be divine beings, of the order of angels. These texts were reconsidered in that great burgeoning of high medieval culture often called the Twelfth-Century Renaissance. It was then that William of Conches suggested that the true God had given to the planetary deities (with their pagan names) the forming of mortal bodies and responsibility for particular qualities of and influences upon human life. Bernard Silvester then called the planets 'gods who serve God in person', and who had been empowered by that god to control the natural world. Similar ideas were articulated by authors in the thirteenth century, and the ancient tradition of ritual magic, perpetuated into the Middle Ages, provided those who dared with an opportunity to work actively with the planetary deities to attract, enhance and so control their assumed effects on matter and destiny. Thirteenth-century scholars such as Albertus Magnus and Roger Bacon came close to giving respectability to that work, and although discussion of it waned in the fourteenth century, texts that provided its rites and objects which enabled the enactment of them continued to be produced.

These ideas came into intellectual prominence again dramatically as part of the Florentine Renaissance in the work of such major figures as Marsilio Ficino and Giovanni Pico della Mirandola. Ficino supplied hymns to invoke the celestial power of Mercury, Apollo and Venus, modelled on the ancient Orphic hymns, while himself entering the Roman Catholic Church as a priest. Pico went further, to argue again for the propriety of investing material objects ritually with the blessings of the planetary deities, and though he was condemned for this by one pope, he was then absolved by another. Even his most determined literary opponent, the Spanish bishop Pedro Garcia, conceded that the one true god had entrusted the planets to good spirits which controlled earthly phenomena. Italian intellectuals continued to express this belief, and sometimes to enact rites to draw upon the powers of the spirits concerned, into the seventeenth century. The same ideas were taken north in the early sixteenth, and given their most famous expression there by the German Cornelius Agrippa von Nettesheim, who preached in full measure both the existence of the planetary deities and the benefits of obtaining their blessings, for those aspects of life especially entrusted to them. He specified the details of the rituals which enabled this achievement, and his survey of Renaissance magic became the standard work on the subject, though never respectable, for British as well as Continental readers. Indeed, it formed a regular component of the libraries of British cunning folk for the next two centuries.[148]

If the planets represented one means by which European intellectuals found a place for pagan deities in the Christian cosmos, an allegorical figure of Nature or of Earth was another. Here the process was somewhat different, because such a figure had not been a centre for important pagan cults as the goddesses and gods identified with the planets had been. Ancient paganism had been notably lacking in veneration of a single maternal Great Goddess who represented the entire natural world and was identified with the earth in particular. In ancient Egypt the earth was male.[149] Asia Minor had Great Goddesses who protected kingdoms and peoples, and sometimes gave fertility, but they were particular to specific regions: nor were they interchangeable, because they had different attributes.[150] The Sumerians, and then the Babylonians, of Mesopotamia, had at first sight a convincing goddess of Mother Earth, Ninhursaga or Ninhursag, who represented the earth, married the paramount sky god and cared for the wombs of all creatures. On closer inspection, however, she turns out specifically to be the indwelling power of the desert and mountain lands that ringed Mesopotamia, where the rain shed by her fertilizing husband was needed, and its results spectacular. The Mesopotamian landscape itself was in the charge of different deities, its great rivers belonging to the god Enki, the wetlands in its southern region to the goddess Ningal, and so on.[151] The single possible case of a northern earth goddess is Nerthus, mentioned in just one source, by the Roman historian Tacitus, as being the main deity of a group of German tribes, who regarded her as Mother Earth. The problem here has always been that linguistically what Tacitus says does not work, as 'Nerthus' is not a female name, which of course casts into doubt the accuracy of the rest of his information. Some scholars have tried to get round the difficulty by turning the deity concerned into an earth god, but the matter will probably never be resolved.[152]

The Greeks and Romans had no difficulty in imagining a goddess who represented the earth as a whole: she features in works spanning about a millennium and including authors as disparate as Sophocles, Plato, Lucian, Ocellus, Proclus, Hesiod and the authors of the Homeric and Orphic hymns.[153] Such a figure came sometimes to overlap with a goddess personifying Nature, who appears in such Roman works as those of Pliny, Firmicus Maternus, Claudian, Macrobius and Damascius, and in the Graeco-Egyptian Hermetic Texts: as that list of names indicates, this deity featured much more prominently towards the end of the ancient world.[154] What all these sources have in common is that they are works of literature. It is very striking that such a prominent presence for these goddesses (or this sort of goddess) in poems, novels and works of philosophy and science was not matched by any major public cult manifested in inscriptions, temples and votive offerings.[155] Gaia or Ge, the earth goddess of Greece, played a vital part in the best-known creation myth, but functioned in practice as a minor deity.[156] Rome had a more important goddess of earth, Tellus, yet one with a very specific role, to quicken the fertilizing power of the cultivated soil. In worship, she was paired with the grain goddess Ceres (and the latter's shadowy husband Cerus) on equal terms, and both were accompanied by twelve lesser figures with special responsibilities for different aspects of the farming cycle.[157] The Romans could conceive of a grander earth goddess, with a more comprehensive remit, Terra Mater, or Mother Earth, but she figured in actual cult even less frequently than Gaia. Augustus included her near the end of a long list of deities to receive sacrifices at a cycle of games, and here there was a conscious philosophical tinge to the innovation: she was accompanied by the Fates and the goddesses of childbirth, to show that both these forces guard the world's fertility.[158] The reason for this discrepancy between literature and cult practice in both cultures seems to have been twofold: that ancient religion tended to be localized, to particular regions, cities and peoples, and also practical, in that deities were invoked because of the specific activities in which they specialized. Only in sophisticated private and initiatory cults of the sort that appeared towards the end of the ancient world, most certainly that of Isis as portrayed by Lucius Apuleius in his *Metamorphoses*, does a paramount goddess feature at the centre of the cosmos who represents all other goddesses within her and is identified specifically with the whole natural world.

It seems to have been this twofold aspect of Mother Earth or Mother Nature – of prominence as a symbolic or allegorical figure in literature without much actual worship which could taint her with demonic associations – which recommended her to some medieval Christians. This probably explains the inclusion of the poem 'Praecatio terrae matris' to her in herbals, as described earlier. Another charm discussed above, the 'Aecerbot', took things a stage further, by giving this entity a place in the Christian cosmos, providing fertility in cultivable soil at the behest, and under the control, of the one true god. This pair of texts has a place alongside others in the early Middle Ages which continue to speak of Nature as an allegorical figure, though without the element of prayer and invocation which these two sources bestow on Mother Earth.[159] These works provide a link between antiquity and the twelfth century, when the figure of Nature featured prominently in the work of the French intellectuals Bernard Silvester, who has already been mentioned as an exponent of the existence of planetary deities, and Alan of Lille.[160] The former made of her a deity sprung from the Christian god and given the task of calling matter into being and then acting as the engendering force of fertility and procreation. The latter called her the agent of that god in earthly affairs and maker of humans. These were poetic romances rather than works of theology, and did not recommend any active worship of their goddess; but they presented her as a powerful and benevolent symbolic entity, a divine female with delegated powers over the world who had no place in biblical tradition. As such she was taken up by vernacular poetry from the fourteenth century, featuring in that of such prominent English writers as Geoffrey Chaucer and Edmund Spenser.

The concept of a goddess operating as a great mediatrix between the Christian god and the material world was also expounded in a celestial form, by early modern scholars interested in the Hermetic tradition of mysticism which derived ultimately from ancient Egypt or seeking to reveal divine truths concealed in the remains of ancient civilizations. They include an English occultist, Robert Fludd, and a Continental Jesuit intellectual, who had great influence in Britain, Athanasius Kircher. Both came up with an image of the Platonic World Soul as a nude female, identified with the moon and crowned with stars, and linking heaven and earth, and God and humanity.[161] Once again, literary tradition retained some sense of the divine feminine, quite distinct from and greater than female saints, even including the Virgin Mary, as the immediate power responsible for earthly existence. This chain of images, stretching from the end of the ancient world to the beginning of the modern, prepared the way for that tremendous burgeoning of interest in, and feeling for, a mighty goddess figure, represented by the natural world and the night sky, who was to have such a claim on the nineteenth- and twentieth-century imagination. The concept of the prehistoric Great Goddess was one consequence of this development, but the impact of the same figure on poetry and fictional prose was as profound.[162]

In making these suggestions, no pretence is offered that the veneration of planetary deities, or the devotion paid to Nature or the female World Soul, ever represented more than a supplement to mainstream types of medieval and early modern Christianity, taken up by an elite of intellectuals and creative authors. This argument comes close, indeed, to an ironic reversal of the former impression of medieval British religion as remaining essentially pagan, while having acquired a thin veneer of Christianity among the elites: we see here a thin elite veneer of paganism over essentially Christian societies. None of the people who advocated such ideas adopted a pagan faith in preference to the faith of Christ, and there is no sign that such ideas filtered down to lower social levels: the cunning folk who read Agrippa and his kind seem to have done so to get practical results, none ever being recorded as having actual pagan beliefs or making much of the old deities.[163] The interest in salvaging room for ancient and non-biblical divinities in a Christian framework pales into insignificance beside the evidence of mass devotion, at all social levels, to the Trinity and the saints. Even so, its very existence has a significance of its own, as one more example of the way in which surviving elements of the old religions could be incorporated into Christian cultures during the Middle Ages and beyond.

From the end of the eighteenth century onwards, that blending of elements began to separate at last, under the impact of a growing importance of ancient literature in the education of more members of society – ensuring a greater knowledge of the Greek and Roman deities in particular – and of a slowly weakening grip of Christianity on the allegiance of the British. There were, in the main, four different responses to these developments. One was to mount a more strenuous assertion of the superiority of Christianity over all other religions, and characterize paganism more fiercely as a religion of backwardness, ignorance and blood thirst. The second was to attempt new reconciliations of the two, with a larger role for the ancient religions and greater appreciation of their positive qualities, as a balance and supplement to the different virtues of the religion of Christ. The third was to reject all forms of religion in favour of atheism, agnosticism and rationalism, which could be accompanied by an emphasis on the follies of all religious faith or by a more subtle disparagement of Christianity, by asserting that it never attracted the loyalty of the bulk of the populace, who retained much of an unthinking, primitive and not very admirable paganism. The fourth response was to reject the Christian faith, while turning to the old religions as a replacement; a development which had begun by the late Georgian period in Britain and slowly produced a complex of modern religious traditions based on ancient ideas and images. All of these were modern developments: but they would hardly have been possible without the manner in which those ideas and images had remained lodged in Christian culture, in so many different ways, for one and a half millennia.

CONCLUSION

⟦⟨≡⟩⟩⟨≡⟩⟩

THIS BOOK WAS prefaced with four questions. Two – those of how much changing cultural patterns have influenced scholarly constructions of ancient paganisms, and the extent to which a wide-ranging study has enabled useful comparisons to be made between different periods – should have been self-evidently answered in the body of it; though the answers gained will vary to some extent from reader to reader. The overall argument is that both propositions are true to a considerable degree, and repeated attempts have been made in the text to illustrate this truth. The first two questions – whether it is possible to have an archaeology or a history of ancient British religions, and where the limits of relativism lie in the interpretation of data – require more extended discussion.

A good starting point for that is a celebration of the sheer richness of the heritage that British paganisms have bequeathed to the present. The sequence that begins at Paviland and ends with the Viking graves provides an astonishing number and variety of monuments, images, artefacts and (eventually) inscriptions, reflecting an equally remarkable range of cultures. This heterogeneity prevents any collective sense of a British paganism. Inhabitants of any of the modern nations that make up Scandinavia, the Baltic states, Russia, Ireland and most of the Mediterranean (to take a few examples) have no difficulty in identifying their pagan heritage. In each case it is embodied in a specific literature, art and archaeology, centred on a particular pantheon of deities. In Britain the material and written evidence from the historic period represent native Iron Age, Roman, Anglo-Saxon and Scandinavian religious traditions, together with many more drawn from the other provinces of the Roman Empire. Beyond those stretch at least five ages of prehistory, in each of which ritual was expressed through very different practices and use of sacred space, which often left a permanent testimony on and in the land in the form of striking carved designs, graves and monuments. The relics of Britain's pagan past offer a powerful challenge and stimulus to the modern imagination, which have been and are expressed in literature, art, music and a definition of personal and collective spirituality (either around or against what these relics seem to embody). Some of them are furthermore major foci of the tourist trade, for both domestic and foreign customers: a trade which forms an increasingly important part of the British economy.

They also have in common, as has been repeatedly emphasized throughout this book, an ability to defy full understanding and confident interpretation, possessed in varying degrees but in some measure uniting all. One logical response to this trait is to encourage, as the book has done, a multiplicity of interpretation, in which different people, and groups of them, reconstruct the pagan past subjectively, according to their own instincts and desires, within the limits of the available evidence. The result of this process is a multiplicity of such pasts, forming a portion of different stories of Britain, suited to a multi-ethnic, multi-faith society in which individual choice is paramount: and in which Britain is not defined as a people, or a culture, or a nation (or collection of them) but simply as a land, with historic and prehistoric resources which are open to those whose families have been here for fourteen thousand years and those whose families have been here for four. Professional groupings still play a vital and indispensable role in this process, in providing the data and setting out its bounds. Archaeologists recover the material evidence, date it, and identify the different portions of it. Heritage managers and curators protect sites and objects, display them to the public and provide the known information on them. Historians act, likewise, as the national experts in locating, understanding and translating written texts, and explaining what they seem to say. All should then be prepared to stand back and let the public dream its own dreams, make its own uses, and tell its own tales. This scheme can be applied to more or less the whole of history and prehistory, but, for reasons that this book should have made clear, it is especially relevant to the subject of ancient British paganisms, where the very nature of the phenomenon, let alone an understanding of its details, is largely unfixed until the coming of history and has only some fixed points after then.

This certainly does not mean an absolute relativism, for nothing that fails to fit the evidence can be admissible save as a private fantasy. It is not possible, for example, to argue convincingly that Stonehenge was built by extraterrestrial aliens, Mycenaeans or Egyptians, or dates from any period other than the third millennium BC. It is equally impossible to declare credibly that it was a factory or a royal dwelling, or anything other than a ceremonial site. It is now equally at odds with the evidence to publish the view that Early Neolithic Britain did not know anything resembling warfare, or that any active pagan religion survived anywhere in the island, in opposition to Christianity, throughout the Middle Ages, let alone longer. Much else, however, regarding the nature of prehistoric British society and religion, and the manner in which ancient paganism blended with medieval and early modern pagan culture, remains entirely open to personal choice. These points have been signalled throughout the book, together with reasons why people – especially learned and expert people – have made differing and altering choices at previous stages of modernity. Those involved in education in recent decades have become used to the concept of pupil-centred learning; perhaps we can similarly accustom ourselves to that of public-centred appreciation, as part of the preparation of the inhabitants of Britain to play their part fully as citizens of a democracy (or, with greater constitutional accuracy, as subjects of a monarchy now rooted in democratic processes). In view of what has been said here of the nature of our times, such a course may seem logical, natural and simple.

In reality, it is likely to prove to be none of those things, because it runs counter to several powerful and persisting traditions, deeply rooted in modern culture. The first of these is the prevalent feeling that professional experts are paid to solve problems and find answers; and this has become if anything more acute in times of greater competition for research funding and a new and heavy stress on the need for those who hold university posts to justify their salaries with results, which are commonly held to mean permanent solutions and discoveries. The second is the love affair of modernity with progress, that expectation that each generation should have greater knowledge than the one before, resulting from better means of acquiring it, and (to echo Leonardo da Vinci, whose generation saw the birth of this ideology) that pupils who do not surpass their teacher betray their teacher. The third is the sense that any community is held together by a common identity, which is fashioned with particular strength if it includes a common collective story accounting for and celebrating that identity. In a period when our actual society is becoming so internally diverse, an impulse to recover such an identity, resting on such a story, is likely to become all the stronger. In this sense, the lineage of modern historians and prehistorians stretches back to ancient bards, who told tales which inculcated the meaning of what it was to be a member of their tribe or clan or kingdom.

Finally, such a course runs counter to one of the oldest and most potent of literary forms, the quest romance, which forms alike the basis for the oldest piece of fully formed literature to survive in the world, the Epic of Gilgamesh, and one of the two oldest to survive in Europe, Homer's *Odyssey*. This form works especially well for historical and archaeological scholarship, which can turn a process of research into just such a romance, in which the adventures along the way are those in which the evidence is recovered and assembled, and the Grail or Golden Fleece is won when another portion of the past is fully recovered or (even better) a famous puzzle about it is – allegedly – solved for good. It is particularly suited to the medium of television or radio, or the newspaper or magazine serial ('The Quest for Arthur', 'In Search of the Trojan War', 'On the Trail of Ancient Mysteries' . . .). By contrast, a proposal for a programme or serial on a historical or archaeological subject which tells the viewers or readers what is known and what the options are, and then invites them to choose between them, is unlikely to get commissioned.

It is possible to present counter-arguments to all these observations. Professional experts who educate and empower the public, and help it to reach informed decisions of its own, are serving their country and society as valuably as those who hand it solutions: history and archaeology are simply not like medicine or engineering in this respect. Moreover, if the evidence does not admit of confident solutions, then such a course is also the more honourable and helpful one. It is, furthermore, compatible with a faith in progress, because it is straightforwardly true that archaeological data increases with each generation as more sites are studied, and understanding of it increases with improvements in technology to aid analysis. History is less fortunate in an accretion of new material, at least when concerned with the ancient and medieval worlds, though new documents are still found or reconstructed, and those that are known are constantly better collated and related. Nevertheless, its ability to reinterpret evidence by asking new questions and putting it into broader and better understood contexts, remains invaluable. A common national story intended to generate a common national identity in a period of diversity and change carries the considerable danger of alienating those members of society who cannot instinctually identify with it. It may be wiser to emphasize that the land and its heritage are held in common, for people to understand in different ways, but with an equal affection and a mutual tolerance. Finally, the process of research remains a quest romance, even if the conclusion consists of drawing back a veil on a new scene, which those invited to observe can populate with their own characters and meanings (always within the bounds of the evidence), as a series of quests of their own.

In the final analysis, however, a proposal of such a way of treating the evidence for pagan Britain is made not because the author believes it is the most ethical in social or political terms, but because it is the most honest in those of scholarship. To admit how much we cannot certainly know, and then to turn that into an opportunity and a strength, rather than an embarrassment or a handicap, is simply to make the best possible use of a common resource. It makes the point that, where the past is concerned, what is open-ended, subjective, multivalent and individual can be as valuable as that which is fixed and certain.

NOTES

A Note on Referencing

In setting out these endnotes, a compromise has been made between providing the fullest possible source references and pressing the bounds of a generous but still strict word limit. The following conventions have therefore been observed. Instead of a bibliography, full publication details have been given of each work cited, afresh, in the notes to each chapter, so that they should be relatively easy to trace. For works published before 1950, only the place of publication is given, but for those after that year – the great majority – the publisher is named as well. Subtitles to works are omitted unless the titles give absolutely no indication of the nature of what the text contains. As this book is intended for a broad readership in addition to a specialist one, and to encourage such readers to follow up any interests which it may provoke, reference is often to the most accessible form of publication in which information appears. In many cases, the author has read the detailed excavation reports on which a particular case study is based, but has chosen instead to cite a more popularly accessible work in which the conclusions are provided, as long as full references to the detailed reports are furnished in the text, and the data presented is adequate. When the sources involved are ancient or medieval texts, references are to the original chapter or section of a work, so that readers may locate them in any modern edition.

1 The Palaeolithic and Mesolithic: How Ritual Came to Britain

1. In the 1990s the span of time involved was thought to be half a million years. During the 2000s it was pushed back to 750,000, and in 2010 discoveries near Happisburgh, Norfolk, were made in strata between 840,000 and 950,000 years old: Ian Sample, 'Early Man', *The Guardian*, 8 July 2010, 2–3. It is entirely possible that the million-year mark will soon be passed.
2. The name was coined by Bryony Coles in 1998. The best recent summary of research upon this drowned region is Vince Gaffrey *et al.*, *Europe's Lost World*, London, Council for British Archaeology, 2009.
3. For recent views of the debate, see Steven Mithen, *The Prehistory of the Mind*, London, Thames and Hudson, 1996; Nicholas Barton, *English Heritage Book of Stone Age Britain*, London, Batsford, 1997, 91–5; Ian Tattersall and Jeffrey H. Schwartz, *Extinct Humans*, Boulder, CO, Westview, 2000, 215–47: Brian Hayden, *Shamans, Sorcerers and Saints*, Washington DC, Smithsonian, 2003, 88–166; Francesco D'Errico, 'Archaeological Evidence for the Emergence of Language, Symbolism and Music', *World Archaeology*, 17 (2003), 1–70; Timothy Insoll, *Archaeology, Ritual, Religion*, London, Routledge, 2004, 24–7; Chris Stringer,

Homo Britannicus, London, Allen Lane, 2006, 190–1; Steven Mithen, 'Searching for the Origins of Language', *British Archaeology*, 93 (2007), 16–19; Alice Roberts, *The Incredible Human Journey*, London, Bloomsbury, 2009, 233–44; and Colin Renfrew and Iain Morley (eds), *Becoming Human*, Cambridge, Cambridge University Press, 2009; Brian Hayden, 'Neandertal Social Structure?', *Oxford Journal of Archaeology*, 31 (2012), 1–26.

4. Clive Gamble, 'The Social Context for European Palaeolithic Art', *Proceedings of the Prehistoric Society*, 57 (1991), 3–15; Roberts, *The Incredible Human Journey*, 264–73; Paul Mellars, 'Cognition and Climate', in Renfrew and Morley (eds), *Becoming Human*, 212–31.

5. It was coined by Christopher Stringer and Paul Mellars, in *The Human Revolution*, Edinburgh, Edinburgh University Press, 1989. For subsequent considerations, see Colin Renfrew, *Prehistory*, London, Weidenfeld & Nicolson, 2007, 79–100; and Clive Gamble, *Origins and Revolutions*, Cambridge, Cambridge University Press, 2007, 33–58.

6. There is an excellent portrait of Buckland in Deborah Cadbury, *The Dinosaur Hunters*, London, Fourth Estate, 2000. For his specific connection with Paviland, see Stephen Aldhouse-Green's report, cited in n. 7; Marianne Sommer, ' "An Amusing Account of a Cave in Wales" ', *British Journal for the History of Science*, 37 (2004), 53–74; and Russell Weston, 'John Traherne, FSA and William Buckland's "Red Lady" ', *Antiquaries Journal*, 88 (2008), 347–64.

7. Stephen Aldhouse-Green, *Paviland Cave and the 'Red Lady'*, Bristol, Western Academic and Specialist Press, 2000.

8. R. M. Jacobi *et al.*, 'Radiocarbon Chronology for the Early Gravettian of Northern Europe', *Antiquity*, 84 (2010), 37.

9. Paul Pettitt, *The Palaeolithic Origins of Human Burial*, London, Routledge, 2011, 139–214.

10. Paul Pettitt, 'The British Upper Palaeolithic', in Joshua Pollard (ed.), *Prehistoric Britain*, Oxford, Blackwell, 2008, 27–8.

11. William Buckland, *Reliquiae Diluvianae*, London, 1823, 82.

12. Leslie Armstrong, quoted in Paul Bahn and Paul Pettitt, *Britain's Oldest Art*, London, English Heritage, 2009, 14.

13. What follows is based on Paul Pettitt *et al.* (eds), *Palaeolithic Cave Art at Creswell Crags in European Context*, Oxford, Oxford University Press, 2007; and Bahn and Pettitt, *Britain's Oldest Art*, supplemented by information gained on visits to the site in 2005 and 2012.

14. I attended a debate over the markings, held on the spot, between various specialists on 17 October 2010.

15. George Nash *et al.*, 'Marks of Sanctity?', *Time and Mind*, 4 (2011), 149–54; Matthew Symonds, 'Rethinking Rock Art', *Current Archaeology*, 270 (2012), 7.

16. The data was summarized in Ruth Charles, 'Incised Ivory Fragments and other Late Palaeolithic Finds from Gough's Cave', *Proceedings of the University of Bristol Spelaeological Society*, 18.3 (1989), 400–8. The existing interpretations were summed up in Barton, *English Heritage Book of Stone Age Britain*, 118–22; since then see Larry Barham *et al.*, *In Search of Cheddar Man*, Stroud, Tempus, 1999, 79–82; Pettitt, 'The British Upper Palaeolithic', 47.

17. Frances Lynch *et al.*, *Prehistoric Wales*, Stroud, Sutton, 2000, 21; Paul Pettitt and Paul Bahn, 'Rock Art and Art Mobilier of the British Upper Palaeolithic', in Aron Mazel *et al.* (eds), *Art as Metaphor*, Oxford, Archaeopress, 2007, 13.

18. A. P. Currant *et al.*, 'Excavations at Gough's Cave, Somerset 1986–7', *Antiquity*, 63 (1989), 131–6; Jill Cook, 'Preliminary Report on Marked Human Bones from the 1986–1987 Excavations at Gough's Cave, Somerset, England', in R. N. E. Barton *et al.* (eds), *The Late Glacial in North-West Europe*, London, Council for British Archaeology, 1991, 160–8.

19. For the differing views, see Barton, *English Heritage Book of Stone Age Britain*, 118–22; Ruth Charles, 'Creswell, Cheddar and Paviland', *Current Archaeology*, 160 (1998), 131–5; Barham *et al.*, *In Search of Cheddar Man*, 75–82; Timothy Taylor, *The Buried Soul*, London, Fourth Estate, 2002, 79–80; Francis Pryor, *Britain BC*, London, HarperCollins, 2003, 60–5; Stringer, *Homo Britannicus*, 204–18; Roger Jacobi, 'The Late Upper Palaeolithic Collection from Gough's Cave, Cheddar, Somerset, and Human Use of the Cave', *Proceedings of the Prehistoric Society*, 70 (2004), 1–92; Nicholas Barton, 'The Lateglacial or Latest Palaeolithic Occupation of Britain', in John Hunter and Ian Ralston (eds), *The Archaeology of Britain*, London, Routledge, 2nd edition, 2009, 35–7; Timothy Darvill, *Prehistoric Britain*, London, Routledge, 2nd edition, 2010, 50.

20. British Museum of Natural History, Press Release 16 February 2011.

21. Jacobi, 'The Late Upper Palaeolithic Collection from Gough's Cave', 89–92; Pettitt, 'The British Upper Palaeolithic', 40–1.

22. Pettitt, *Palaeolithic Origins of Human Burial*, 215–60.

23. The exhibit is catalogued as A6473, and I viewed it in 2010. It was recently discussed in 'Cannibalism in Prehistoric Devon', *Current Archaeology*, 235 (2009), 6, where Roger Jacobi and Rick Schulting agreed that the defleshing was part of a funeral rite.

24. Hugh Cornwell, pers. comm. 17 October 2010. I am very grateful to Mr Cornwell for his generous hospitality as manager of the caves and museum.

25. Andrew Chamberlain, 'A Review of the Archaeological Caves of the Creswell Region', in Bahn and Pettitt, *Britain's Oldest Art*, 39.

26. This paragraph is based on a composite of John E. Pfeiffer, *The Creative Explosion* (New York, Harper & Row, 1982); Barton, *English Heritage Book of Stone Age Britain*; and Stringer, *Homo Britannicus*.

27. The comprehensive British refutation of the hunting and fertility concepts is in Peter Ucko and Andrée Rosenfeld, *Palaeolithic Cave Art*, London, Weidenfeld & Nicolson, 1967. See also Paul Bahn, 'Where's the Beef? The Myth of Hunting Magic in Palaeolithic Art', in Paul Bahn and Andree Rosenfeld (eds), *Rock Art and Prehistory*, Oxford, Oxbow, 1991, 1–13.

28. His great primary work was *Préhistoire de l'art occidental*, Paris, Editions de l'art Mazenod, 1965. For discussions of the rise and fall of his ideas, see Richard Bradley, *Image and Audience: Rethinking Prehistoric Art*, Oxford, Oxford University Press, 2009, 26–40; and Jean Clottes and David Lewis-Williams, *The Shamans of Prehistory*, New York, Abrams, 1998, 73.

29. Full references are provided in Ronald Hutton, *Shamans*, London, Hambledon and London, 2001, 131, 186–7.

30. The initial article was David Lewis-Williams and Thomas Dowson, 'The Signs of All Times', *Current Anthropology*, 29 (1988), 201–45; the book is Clottes and Lewis-Williams, *The Shamans of Prehistory*.

31. Robert G. Bednarik, 'European Palaeolithic Art – Typical or Exceptional?', *Oxford Journal of Archaeology*, 12 (1993), 1–8.

32. The debate up to the end of the 1990s was given a useful overview by Robert Layton, 'Shamanism, Totemism and Rock Art', *Cambridge Archaeological Journal*, 10 (2000), 169–86. Important contributions since then include David Lewis- Williams, 'Putting the Record Straight', *Antiquity*, 77 (2003), 165–70, and *The Mind in the Cave*, London, Thames and Hudson, 2002; Christopher Chippindale, 'Visionary Experience and the Archaeology of Rock Art', *Cambridge Archaeological Journal*, 13 (2003), 129–32; Patricia Helveston *et al.*, 'Testing The "Three Stages of Trance" Model', *Cambridge Archaeological Journal*, 13 (2003), 213–24; the discussion by four experts of Lewis-Williams, *The Mind in the Cave*, in *Cambridge Archaeological Journal*, 13 (2003), 263–79; Hayden, *Shamans, Sorcerers and Saints*, 142–51; Thomas A. Dowson, 'Debating Shamanism in Southern African Rock Art', *South African Archaeological Bulletin*, 62 (2007), 49–61, and 'Re-animating Hunter-gatherer Rock-art Research', *Cambridge Archaeological Journal*, 19 (2007), 378–87; Georges Sauvet *et al.*, 'Thinking with Animals in Upper Palaeolithic Rock Art', *Cambridge Archaeological Journal*, 19 (2009), 319–36; Homayun Sidky, 'On the Antiquity of Shamanism and its Role in Human Religiosity', *Method and Theory in the Study of Religion*, 22 (2010), 68–92; David S. Whitley, *Cave Paintings and the Human Spirit*, New York, Prometheus, 2009.

33. Clottes and Lewis-Williams, *The Shamans of Prehistory*, 59.

34. Randall White, *Prehistoric Art*, New York, Abrams, 2003, 121–2; Miranda and Stephen Aldhouse-Green, *The Quest for the Shaman*, London, Thames and Hudson, 2005, 64–5.

35. White, *Prehistoric Art*, 20–1.

36. One of the first statements of this approach was Margaret Conkey, 'Beyond Art and between the Caves', in Margaret Conkey *et al.* (eds), *Beyond Art*, San Francisco, California Academy of Sciences, 1997, 343–68.

37. For this see Michel Lorblanchet, *Art Parietal*, Paris, Rouergue, 2010.

38. For interpretations up to the end of the 1980s, see Ronald Hutton, *The Pagan Religions of the Ancient British Isles*, Oxford, Blackwell, 1991, 3–6. Those since are rounded up and discussed in Paul B. Pettitt, 'The Living Dead and the Dead Living', in Rebecca Gowland and Christopher Knüsel (eds), *Social Archaeology of Funerary Remains*, Oxford, Oxbow, 2006, 300–6.

39. Hutton, *Pagan Religions*, 10, and sources given there.
40. Ibid.
41. I discussed this problem in Ronald Hutton, *Witches, Druids and King Arthur: Studies in Paganism, Myth and Magic*, London, Hambledon and London, 2003, 33–5, where I misled some readers into thinking that by pointing out that certain features cannot be seen from the floor I was suggesting that none of these existed. What I was proposing is that they should not be presumed to exist unless established by further careful examination: and the problem is that none of the people to whom I have spoken personally who has indeed examined the figure at close quarters (which I have not) has been able to agree completely on how many of the body parts shown by Breuil are actually there.
42. Ann Sieveking, *Engraved Magdalenian Plaquettes*, London, British Archaeological Reports, 1987.
43. Steven Mithen, 'To Hunt or to Paint', *Man*, 23 (1988), 671–95; Paul G. Bahn, *The Cambridge Illustrated History of Prehistoric Art*, Cambridge, Cambridge University Press, 1998, 174.
44. Bahn and Pettitt, *Britain's Oldest Art*, 43–86.
45. Bahn, *The Cambridge Illustrated History of Prehistoric Art*, 177.
46. Jean Clottes, 'Recent Studies on Palaeolithic Art', *Cambridge Archaeological Journal*, 6 (1996), 179–89.
47. Michel Lorblanchet, 'From Man to Animal and Sign in Palaeolithic Art', in Howard Murphy (ed.), *Animals into Art*, London, Unwin Hyman, 1989, 109–43.
48. Ibid.; Jean Clottes, 'The Identification of Human and Animal Figures in European Palaeolithic Art', in Murphy (ed.), *Animals into Art*, 21–56.
49. Sieveking, *Engraved Magdalenian Plaquettes*, passim; Rosemary Powers, 'The Human Form in Palaeolithic Art', *Modern Geology*, 19 (1994), 109–346.
50. Lorblanchet, 'From Man to Animal', passim.
51. On this see Paul Bahn's comments on p. 248 of the debate over the figurines in *Current Anthropology*, 37 (1996); and in 'The "Dead Wood" Stage of Prehistoric Art Studies', in Michel Lorblanchet and Paul G. Bahn (eds), *Rock Art Studies* Oxford, Oxbow, 1993, 51–9.
52. Margherita Mussi *et al.*, 'Echoes from the Mammoth Steppe', in Wil Roebroeks *et al.* (eds), *Hunters of the Golden Age*, Leiden, University of Leiden Press, 2000, 105–24.
53. Aldhouse-Green and Aldhouse-Green, *The Quest for the Shaman*, 45–6.
54. The best overall discussion of this subject is probably in Bahn, *The Cambridge Illustrated History of Prehistoric Art*, 71–81.
55. A beginning has been made by Karl Schleiser, *The Wolves of Heaven: Cheyenne Shamanism, Ceremonies and Prehistoric Origins*, Norman, OK, University of Oklahoma Press, 1987; and Ake Hultkranz, ' A New Look at the World Pillar in Arctic and Sub-Arctic Religions', in Juha Pentikäinen (ed.), *Shamanism and Northern Ecology*, Berlin, Mouton de Gruyer, 1996, esp. p. 43.
56. See particularly Tim Ingold, *The Perception of the Environment*, London, Routledge, 2000.
57. Brian Fagan, *The Long Summer*, London, Granta, 2004, 22–110; Steven Mithen, *After the Ice*, London, Weidenfeld & Nicolson, 2003, 132–57; Barton, 'The Lateglacial or Latest Palaeolithic Occupation of Britain', 25–46; Sebastian Payne, 'What Was the Old Forest Really Like?', *British Archaeology* (November–December 2009), 13.
58. Barton, *English Heritage Book of Stone Age Britain*, 135; Derek Yalden, *The History of British Mammals*, London, Academic Press, 1999, 63–88; Fagan, *The Long Summer*, 68–70; Mithen, *After the Ice*, 138–41; Tom Greeves, 'Dartmoor's Vanishing Archaeology', *British Archaeology* (September–October 2009), 33; Barry Cunliffe, *Europe between the Oceans*, London, Yale University Press, 2009, 69–76; Nicky Milner and Steven Mithen, 'Hunter-Gatherers of the Mesolithic', in Hunter and Ralston (eds), *The Archaeology of Britain*, 53–6; Christopher Smith, 'The Population of Late Upper Palaeolithic and Mesolithic Britain', *Proceedings of the Prehistoric Society*, 58 (1992), 37–40.
59. Clark's classic report is J. G. D. Clark, *Excavations at Star Carr*, Cambridge, Cambridge University Press, 1954. For recent discussions, see Richard Chatterton, 'Ritual' in Chantal Conneller and Graeme Warren (eds), *Mesolithic Britain and Ireland: New Approaches*, Stroud, Tempus, 2006, 101–20; Mithen, *After the Ice*, 134–8; Darvill, *Prehistoric Britain*, 61. For the Siberian parallel, see Hutton, *Shamans*, 32.
60. 'Britain's Oldest Cemetery Revealed', *Current Archaeology*, 188 (2003), 327.

61. Graham Mullan, 'Mesolithic Engravings at Cheddar Gorge', *Current Archaeology*, 199 (2005), 333–5; Graham Mullan and Linda Wilson, 'Possible Mesolithic Cave Art in Southern England', in Mazel *et al.* (eds), *Art as Metaphor*, 39–48.

62. Barham *et al.*, *In Search of Cheddar Man*, 105–8; Lynch *et al.*, *Prehistoric Wales*, 37–8; Chantal Conneller, 'Death', in Conneller and Warren (eds), *Mesolithic Britain*, 139–64; A. Boycott and L. J. Wilson, 'Contemporary Accounts of the Discovery of Aveline's Hole', *Proceedings of the University of Bristol Spelaeological Society*, 25 (2010), 11–25; R. J. Schulting *et al.*, 'The Mesolithic and Neolithic Human Bone Assemblage from Totty Pot', *Proceedings of the University of Bristol Spelaeological Society*, 25 (2010), 11–25; G. J. Mullan and L. J. Wilson, 'A Possible Mesolithic Engraving in Aveline's Hole', *Proceedings of the University of Bristol Spelaeological Society*, 23 (2004), 75–85; R. J. Schulting *et al.*, '. . . Pursuing a Rabbit in Burrington Combe', *Proceedings of the University of Bristol Spelaeological Society*, 23 (2004), 171–265; A. Boycott and L. Wilson, 'In Further Pursuit of Rabbits', ibid., 25 (2011), 187–232.

63. Pryor, *Britain BC*, 100–1; Chatterton, 'Ritual', 101–20; Conneller, 'Death', 139–64; Joshua Pollard, 'Ancestral Places in the Mesolithic Landscape', *Archaeological Review from Cambridge*, 17.1 (2000), 123–38; Steven Mithen, *To the Islands*, Uig, Two Ravens, 2010, 344–9.

64. Lance and Faith Vatcher, 'Excavation of Three Post Holes in Stonehenge Car Park', *Wiltshire Archaeological and Natural History Magazine*, 68 (1973), 57–63; R. M. J. Cleal *et al.*, *Stonehenge in its Landscape*, London, English Heritage, 1995, 55; Darvill, *Prehistoric Britain*, 64; Frances Healy, 'Hambledon Hill and its Implications', in Rosamund Cleal and Joshua Pollard (eds), *Monuments and Material Culture*, Salisbury, Hobnob, 2004, 16–17. The information about the glacial striations, discovered by the Stonehenge Riverside Project in 2008, is from Joshua Pollard, pers. comm., 12 November 2008.

65. Darvill, *Prehistoric Britain*, pp. 65–73, is especially good on the Mesolithic pits. For the Down Farm one, see Martin Green, *A Landscape Revealed*, Stroud, Tempus, 2000, 27–8, 40–5.

66. Chatterton, 'Ritual', 15–20.

67. Milner and Mithen, 'Hunter-Gatherers of the Mesolithic', 62–3; 'Isle of Man House is One of Britain's First', *British Archaeology* (September–October 2009), 9; Brian Taylor, 'The Little House by the Shore', *British Archaeology* (November–December 2010), 14–17.

68. Chatterton, 'Ritual', 101–10; Pollard, 'Ancestral Places'.

69. Stringer, *Homo Britannicus*, 224–5.

70. Paul Mellars, 'Moonshine over Star Carr', *Antiquity*, 83 (2009), 502–17.

71. Graeme Warren, 'Mesolithic Myths', in Alasdair Whittle and Vicki Cummings (eds), *Going Over: The Mesolithic–Neolithic Transition in North-West Europe*, Oxford, Oxford University Press, 2007, 311–28.

72. Vicki Cummings, *A View from the West: The Neolithic of the Irish Sea Zone*, Oxford, Oxbow, 2009, 7–28.

2 The Earlier Neolithic: A Craze for Monuments

1. John Lubbock, *Pre-Historic Times*, London, 1865.

2. Alasdair Whittle, 'The Neolithic Period', in John Hunter and Ian Ralston (eds), *The Archaeology of Britain*, London, Routledge, 2nd edition, 2009, 81–3; Joshua Pollard, 'The Construction of Prehistoric Britain', in Joshua Pollard (ed.), *Prehistoric Britain*, Oxford, Blackwell, 2008, 1–17.

3. Alasdair Whittle, 'The Coming of Agriculture', in Paul Slack and Ryk Ward (eds), *The Peopling of Britain*, Oxford, Oxford University Press, 2002, 77–109; Barry Cunliffe, *Europe between the Oceans*, London, Yale University Press, 2009, 88–140.

4. On this see particularly Julian Thomas, *Understanding the Neolithic*, London, Routledge, 1999, 14–29; and Ann Tresset and Jean-Denis Vigne, 'Substitution of Species, Techniques and Symbols at the Mesolithic–Neolithic Transition in Western Europe', in Alasdair Whittle and Vicki Cummings (eds), *Going Over: The Mesolithic–Neolithic Transition in North-West Europe*, Oxford, Oxford University Press, 2007, 189–210.

5. Whittle and Cummings (eds), *Going Over*, 141–3.

6. Mike Richards, ' "First Farmers" with No Taste for Grain', *British Archaeology*, 12 (1996), 6–7; John Barnatt, 'Monuments in the Landscape', in Alex Gibson and Derek Simpson (eds), *Essays in Honour of Aubrey Burl*, Stroud, Sutton, 1998, 92–105; Joshua Pollard and Andrew

Reynolds, *Avebury*, Stroud, Tempus, 2002, 30–43; Gordon Noble, 'Islands in the Neolithic', *British Archaeology*, 71 (2003), 20–3; Ian Armit *et al.*, *Neolithic Settlement in Ireland and Western Britain*, Oxford, Oxbow, 2003; Whittle, 'The Coming of Agriculture'; Richard Bradley, *The Prehistory of Britain and Ireland*, Cambridge, Cambridge University Press, 2007, 27–35; Julian Thomas, 'The Mesolithic–Neolithic Transition in Britain', in Pollard (ed.), *Prehistoric Britain*, 67–72; Timothy Darvill, *Prehistoric Britain*, London, 2nd edition, Routledge, 2010, 83–90; Alex Brown, 'Dating the Onset of Cereal Cultivation in Britain and Ireland', *Antiquity*, 81 (2007), 1042–53.

7. Janet Montgomery *et al.*, 'Reconstructing the Lifetime Movements of Ancient People', *Journal of European Archaeology*, 3 (2000), 370–85.

8. M. P. Richards and R. E. M. Hedges, 'A Neolithic Revolution', *Antiquity*, 73 (1999), 891–7; Whittle, 'The Coming of Agriculture'; N. Milner *et al.*, 'Something Fishy in the Neolithic?', *Antiquity*, 78 (2004), 9–22; Fraser Stuart, 'Fishing for Meaning', in Vicki Cummings and Amelia Pannett (eds), *Set in Stone*, Oxford, Oxbow, 2005, 68–80; Julian Richards, 'Mesolithic–Neolithic Transitions in Britain', in Whittle and Cummings (eds), *Going Over*, 423–39.

9. W. Boyd Dawkins, *Early Man in Britain*, London, 1880, 282–343.

10. Jacquetta Hawkes, *Early Britain*, London, 1945, 13.

11. E.g. V. Gordon Childe, *The Prehistory of Scotland*, London, 1935, 22–50; Graham Clark, *Prehistoric England*, 1940, 3rd edition, London, 1945, 6; Jacquetta and Christopher Hawkes, *Prehistoric Britain*, 1943, 2nd edition, Harmondsworth, 1949, 45–6; Stuart Piggott, *The Neolithic Cultures of the British Isles*, Cambridge, Cambridge University Press, 1954, 14–276, passim.

12. Darvill, *Prehistoric Britain*, 122–4.

13. E.g. Thomas, *Understanding the Neolithic*, 15; Marek Zvelebil, 'The Social Context of the Agricultural Transition in Europe', in Colin Renfrew and K. Boyle (eds), *Archaeogenetics*, Cambridge, McDonald Institute, 2000, 57–79; Miles Russell, *Monuments of the British Neolithic*, Stroud, Tempus, 2002, 167–70; Whittle, 'The Coming of Agriculture'.

14. Cunliffe, *Europe between the Oceans*, 88–9; Brian Sykes, *The Seven Daughters of Eve*, 2001, London, Corgi edition, 2002, passim; and *Blood of the Isles*, London, Bantam, 2006, 267–88; Stephen Oppenheimer, *The Origins of the British*, London, Constable and Robinson, 2006, 112–212.

15. Robin McKie, *Face of Britain*, London, Simon & Schuster, 2006, 78–9.

16. Darvill, *Prehistoric Britain*, 79–80; Bradley, *The Prehistory of Britain and Ireland*, 35–7.

17. Mark Lollard *et al.*, 'Radiocarbon Evidence that Migrants Introduced Farming to Britain', *Journal of Archaeological Science*, 37 (2010), 866–70.

18. Alasdair Whittle *et al.*, *Gathering Time*, Oxford, Oxbow, 2011.

19. Chris Scarre, 'Introduction', in Chris Scarre (ed.), *Monuments and Landscape in Atlantic Europe*, London, Routledge, 2002, 2–3.

20. Chris Tilley, 'The Neolithic Sensory Revolution', in Whittle and Cummings (eds), *Going Over*, 329–45.

21. Darvill, *Prehistoric Britain*, 83.

22. Peter Drew and Sue Hamilton, 'Caburn', *Current Archaeology*, 174 (2001), 256–62.

23. This suggestion of a change in attitudes to woods was made by Whittle, 'The Coming of Agriculture', 100.

24. Ian Brown, *Discovering a Welsh Landscape*, Macclesfield, Windgather Press, 2004, 37–9; Marion Dowd, 'The Use of Caves for Funerary and Ritual Purposes in Neolithic Ireland', *Antiquity*, 82 (2008), 305–17; R. J. Schulting *et al.*, 'The Mesolithic and Neolithic Human Bone Assemblage from Totty Pot, Cheddar, Somerset', *Proceedings of the University of Bristol Spelaeological Society*, 25 (2010), 75–95; Stephany Leach, 'Odd One Out? Earlier Neolithic Deposition of Human Remains in Caves and Rock Shelters in the Yorkshire Dales', in Eileen Murphy (ed.), *Deviant Burial in the Archaeological Record*, Oxford, Oxbow, 2008, 35–56.

25. Stephen Adams, 'A Mine of Information', *Heritage Today* (March 2010), 16–18; Russell, *Monuments of the British Neolithic*, 97–112; Pete Topping, 'The South Downs Flint Mines', in Jonathan Cotton and David Field (eds), *Towards a New Stone Age*, York, Council for British Archaeology, 2004, 177–90; Francis Pryor, *Britain BC*, London, HarperCollins, 2003, 154–5.

26. Cunliffe, *Europe between the Oceans*, 150–4.

27. Richard Bradley, *An Archaeology of Natural Places*, London, Routledge, 2000, 85–8; Gabriel Cooney, 'Breaking Stones, Making Places', in Alex Gibson and Derek Simpson (eds), *Essays in Honour of Aubrey Burl*, Stroud, Sutton, 1998, 108–18; Pryor, *Britain BC*, 151–3; Bronwen Price, 'Journeying into Different Realms', in Vicki Cummings and Robert Johnston (eds), *Prehistoric Journeys*, Oxford, Oxbow, 2007, 85–101.

28. Christopher Tilley, *Metaphor and Material Culture*, Oxford, Blackwell, 1999, 36–76; Joshua Pollard, 'The Art of Decay and the Transformation of Substance', in Colin Renfrew *et al.* (eds), *Substance, Memory, Display: Archaeology and Art*, Cambridge, Mcdonald Institute, 2004, 47–62; Christopher Fowler, *The Archaeology of Personhood*, London, Routledge, 2004, 101–29; Ann Woodward, 'Ceramic Technologies and Social Relations', in Pollard (ed.), *Prehistoric Britain*, 288–309.

29. Richard Bradley, 'Monuments and Places', in P. Garwood *et al.* (eds), *Sacred and Profane*, Oxford, Oxford University Press, 1991, 135–40; *Altering the Earth*, Edinburgh, Society of Antiquaries of Scotland, 1993; *The Significance of Monuments*, London, Routledge, 1998.

30. Pollard and Reynolds, *Avebury*, 45.

31. Joshua Pollard, 'Memory, Monuments and Middens in the Neolithic Landscape', in Graham Brown *et al.* (eds), *The Avebury Landscape*, Oxford, Oxbow, 2005, 103–14.

32. His ideas on this theme are especially well articulated in his various contributions to Julian Thomas (ed.), *Place and Memory*, Oxford, Oxbow, 2007.

33. For strong reminders of this, see John Barrett, *Fragments from Antiquity*, Oxford, Blackwell, 1994, 50; Mike Parker Pearson, *The Archaeology of Death and Burial*, Stroud, Sutton, 1999, 83–93; M. J. O'Kelly, 'Neolithic Ireland', in Dáibhí O Cróinín (ed.), *A New History of Ireland*, Oxford, Oxford University Press, 2005, 90.

34. News of this was published in the most popularly accessible form by Alice Roberts, *The Incredible Human Journey*, London, Bloomsbury, 2009, 273–82. I remain very grateful to Dr Roberts for the gift of this book.

35. Chris Scarre *et al.*, 'Megalithic Chronologies', in Göran Burenhult and Suzanne Westergaard (eds), *Stones and Bones: Formal Disposal of the Dead in Atlantic Europe during the Mesolithic-Neolithic Interface*, Oxford, British Archaeological Reports, 2003, 65–111.

36. Jan Albert Bakker, *The Dutch Hunebedden*, Ann Arbor, University of Michigan Press, 1992.

37. For an example of both operating in one area, see Chris Scarre, 'Diverse Inspirations', in Burenhult and Westergaard (eds), *Stones and Bones*, 39–52.

38. The evolution of this idea up to the mid 2000s is discussed in Timothy Darvill, *Long Barrows of the Cotswolds and Surrounding Areas*, Stroud, Tempus, 2004, 67–86.

39. Alasdair Whittle *et al.*, 'Building for the Dead', in Alex Bayliss and Alasdair Whittle (eds), *Histories of the Dead* (Cambridge Archaeological Journal Supplement, 2007), 130–7.

40. The most recent declaration of the 'houses of the dead' theory, as established fact, was probably O'Kelly, 'Neolithic Ireland', 90.

41. This interpretation is found among most experts in the British Neolithic between 1930 and 1960, but especially in the many publications of the most distinguished: Gordon Childe, O. G. S. Crawford, Stuart Piggott and Glyn Daniel.

42. O'Kelly, 'Neolithic Ireland', 90.

43. The most prominent British author to assert this idea in the 1970s was probably Colin Renfrew, whose most influential work on the matter was perhaps 'Megaliths, Territories and Populations', in S. J. de Laet (ed.), *Acculturation and Continuity in Atlantic Europe*, Bruges, De Tempei, 1976, 198–220.

44. James Whitley, 'Too Many Ancestors', *Antiquity*, 76 (2002), 119–26.

45. Alasdair Whittle, *The Archaeology of People*, London, Routledge, 2003, 128–32.

46. Whittle *et al.*, *Gathering Time*, 848–914.

47. See, for example, Frances Lynch *et al.*, *Prehistoric Wales*, Stroud, Sutton, 2000, 121; John Gale, *Prehistoric Dorset*, Stroud, Tempus, 2003, 35; Whittle, *The Archaeology of People*, 130–2.

48. Darvill, *Long Barrows*, 17–18.

49. Ian Kinnes, *Non-Megalithic Long Barrows and Allied Structures in the British Neolithic*, London, British Museum, 1992; David Field, *Earthen Long Barrows*, Stroud, Tempus, 2006.

50. Field, *Earthen Long Barrows*, 132.

51. Miles Russell, *Prehistoric Sussex*, Stroud, Tempus, 2002, 58–9; and *Monuments of the British Neolithic*, 34–65; with details added from Field, *Earthen Long Barrows*, 127–31, 140–3.

52. Gordon Noble, *Neolithic Scotland*, Edinburgh, Edinburgh University Press, 2006, 71–101.

53. Christopher Evans and Ian Hodder, *A Woodland Archaeology: Neolithic Sites at Haddenham*, Cambridge, McDonald Institute, 2006, 67–200.

54. Darvill, *Long Barrows*, 34, discusses Daniel's pivotal work.

55. Ibid., 132–65.

56. Ibid., 132–40.

57. Aubrey Burl, 'By the Light of the Cinerary Moon', in C. N. Ruggles and A. W. R. Whittle (eds), *Astronomy and Society in Britain during the Period 4000–1500 BC*, (Oxford, British Archaeological Reports, 1981), 248–56.

58. John North, *Stonehenge: Neolithic Man and the Cosmos*, London, HarperCollins, 1996, 13–137.

59. E.g. Darvill, *Long Barrows*, 93–5; Field, *Earthen Long Barrows*, 69–70.

60. Bayliss and Whittle (eds), *Histories of the Dead*; Martin Smith and Megan Brickley, 'The Date and Sequence of Use of Neolithic Funerary Monuments', *Oxford Journal of Archaeology*, 25 (2006), 335–55; Don Benson and Alasdair Whittle (eds), *Building Memories: The Neolithic Cotswold Long Barrow at Ascott-under-Wychwood*, Oxford, Oxbow, 2007.

61. Alasdair Whittle and Vicki Cummings, *Places of Special Virtue: Megaliths in the Neolithic Landscapes of Wales*, Oxford, Oxbow, 2004, 24–40.

62. George Nash, *The Architecture of Death: Neolithic Tombs in Wales*, Little Logaston, Logaston Press, 2006, 18–20.

63. Whittle and Cummings, *Places of Special Virtue*, 24–40.

64. Ibid., 69–91; Alasdair Whittle, 'Stones that Float to the Sky', in Vicki Cummings and Chris Fowler (eds), *The Neolithic of the Irish Sea*, Oxford, Oxbow, 2004, 81–90.

65. Colin Richards, 'Labouring with Monuments', in Cummings and Fowler (eds), *The Neolithic of the Irish Sea*, 72–80.

66. Whittle, 'Stones that Float to the Sky'; George Children and George Nash, *Neolithic Sites of Cardiganshire, Carmarthenshire and Pembrokeshire*, Little Logaston, Logaston Press, 1997, 20–1; Steve Burrow, *The Tomb Builders in Wales 4000–3000 BC*, Cardiff, National Museum of Wales, 2006, 26, 112–13.

67. Nash, *The Architecture of Death*, 178–83, 185–6, 191, 194–5, 226–7.

68. Carleton Jones, *Temples of Stone: Exploring the Megaliths of Ireland*, Wilton, Co. Cork, Collins, 2007, 146–7.

69. Christopher Tilley, *A Phenomenology of Landscape*, Oxford, Berg, 1994, 94–109.

70. Andrew Fleming, 'Phenomenology and the Megaliths of Wales', *Oxford Journal of Archaeology* 18 (1999), 119–25; and 'Megaliths and Post-Modernism', *Antiquity*, 79 (2005), 921–32; Lesley McFadyen, 'Temporary Spaces in the Mesolithic and Neolithic', in Pollard (ed.), *Prehistoric Britain*, 121–34; Joanna Brück, 'In the Footsteps of the Ancestors', *Archaeological Review from Cambridge*, 15 (1998), 23–36.

71. Vicki Cummings, 'All Cultural Things', in Scarre (ed.), *Monuments and Landscape*, 107–21; Chris Fowler and Vicki Cummings, 'Places of Transformation', *Journal of the Royal Anthropological Institute*, 9 (2003), 1–20; Vicki Cummings and Alasdair Whittle, 'Tombs with a View', *Antiquity*, 77 (2003), 255–66; Vicki Cummings, 'Connecting the Mountains and the Sea', in Cummings and Fowler (eds), *The Neolithic of the Irish Sea*, 29–36; Vicki Cummings and Chris Fowler, 'The Setting and Form of Manx Chambered Cairns', ibid., 113–22; Vicki Cummings, 'Between Mountains and Sea', *Proceedings of the Prehistoric Society*, 68 (2002), 125–46; Vicki Cummings, *A View from the West: The Neolithic of the Irish Sea Zone*, Oxford, Oxbow, 2009, 122–54.

72. Vicki Cummings, 'Megalithic Journeys', in Cummings and Johnston (eds), *Prehistoric Journeys*, 54–63.

73. Lesley McFadyen, 'Building Technologies, Quick and Slow Architectures and Early Neolithic Long Barrow Sites in Southern Britain', *Archaeological Review from Cambridge*, 21 (2006), 70–81.

74. Francis Pryor, *Farmers in Prehistoric Britain*, Stroud, Tempus, 1998, 50–3; Alastair Oswald, et al., *The Creation of Monuments: Neolithic Causewayed Enclosures in the British Isles* London, English Heritage, 2001; Gale, *Prehistoric Dorset*, 25–7.

75. Darvill, *Prehistoric Britain*, 96–7; Oswald et al., *The Creation of Monuments*, 81–5; Francis Pryor, 'Welland Bank Quarry', *Current Archaeology*, 160 (1998), 139–45.

76. Whittle et·al., *Gathering Time*, 897–8.
77. The latest and most comprehensive study is Alasdair Whittle et al., *The Harmony of Symbols*, Oxford, Oxbow, 1999.
78. Ibid., 356.
79. Roger Mercer, *Hambledon Hill*, Edinburgh, Edinburgh University Press, 1980; Frances Healey, 'Hambledon Hill and its Implications', in Rosamund Cleal and Joshua Pollard (eds), *Monuments and Material Culture*, Salisbury, Hobnob, 2004, 15–38; Roger Mercer and Frances Healey, *Hambledon Hill*, London, English Heritage, 2009; Oliver Harris, 'Emotional and Mnemonic Geographies at Hambledon Hill', *Cambridge Archaeological Journal*, 20 (2010), 357–71.
80. Russell, *Prehistoric Sussex*, 43–51.
81. Pryor, *Farmers in Prehistoric Britain*, 50–67.
82. Michael J. Allen et al., 'Neolithic Causewayed Enclosures and Later Prehistoric Farming', *Proceedings of the Prehistoric Society*, 74 (2008), 235–322.
83. Julian Thomas, *Rethinking the Neolithic*, Cambridge, Cambridge University Press, 1991, 35–6; Alasdair Whittle, *Europe in the Neolithic*, Cambridge, Cambridge University Press, 1996, 266–70; Jan Harding, 'An Architecture of Meaning', in Mark Edmonds and Colin Richards (eds), *Understanding the Neolithic of North-Western Europe*, Glasgow, Cruithne, 1998, 223; Oswald et al., *The Creation of Monuments*, 120–7; Russell, *Monuments of the British Neolithic*, 71–96; Darvill, *Prehistoric Britain*, 97–102; Bradley, *The Prehistory of Britain and Ireland*, 69–76.
84. Alistair Barclay and Jan Harding, 'Introduction' in Barclay and Harding (eds), *Pathways and Ceremonies: The Cursus Monuments of Britain and Ireland*, Oxford, Oxbow, 1999, 1.
85. The first figure is from Darvill, *Prehistoric Britain*, 119, the second from Russell, *Monuments of the British Neolithic*, 115; and Barclay and Harding (eds), 'Introduction', 4.
86. Gale, *Prehistoric Dorset*, 46–7; Roy Loveday, *Inscribed across the Landscape: The Cursus Enigma*, Stroud, Tempus, 2006, 12–25; Darvill, *Prehistoric Britain*, 119–20; Bradley, *The Prehistory of Britain and Ireland*, 68–9; David McOmish, 'Cursus', *British Archaeology* (March 2003), 9–13; Richard Bradley, 'Making Strange', in Andrew Fleming and Richard Hingley (eds), *Prehistoric and Roman Landscapes*, Macclesfield, Windgather, 2007, 33–42.
87. Julian Thomas, 'On the Origins and Development of Cursus Monuments in Britain', *Proceedings of the Prehistoric Society*, 72 (2006), 229–41; Bradley, *The Prehistory of Britain and Ireland*, 65; Russell, *Monuments of the British Neolithic*, 119; Alistair Barclay and Alex Bayliss, 'Cursus Monuments and the Radiocarbon Problem', in Barclay and Harding (eds), *Pathways and Ceremonies*, 11–29; Whittle et al., 'The Domestication of Britain'; Whittle et al., *Gathering Time*, 897–8.
88. I. J. Thorpe, *The Origins of Agriculture in Europe*, London, Routledge, 1996, 165–77; McOmish, 'Cursus'; Russell, *Monuments of the British Neolithic*, 120–1; Loveday, *Inscribed across the Landscape*, 143–61; Bradley, *The Prehistory of Britain and Ireland*, 65–8; Kenneth Brophy, 'Seeing the Cursus as a Symbolic River', *British Archaeology*, 42 (1999), 6–7.
89. Christopher Catling, 'Heathrow's Everyday Landscape', *Current Archaeology*, 256 (2011), 20–7.
90. Kenneth Brophy, 'From Big Houses to Cult Houses', *Proceedings of the Prehistoric Society*, 73 (2007), 75–96; Hilary Murray et al., 'Crathes Warrenfield', *British Archaeology* (July/August 2007), 12–17; Thomas, 'The Mesolithic–Neolithic Transition', 77–9.
91. Noble, *Neolithic Scotland*, 45–70.
92. Suggested by Bradley, *The Prehistory of Britain and Ireland*, 64.
93. Darvill, *Prehistoric Britain*, 106–7, 117–18; Bradley, *The Prehistory of Britain and Ireland*, 47–8.
94. Loveday, *Inscribed across the Landscape*, 88–102; Thomas, 'On the Origins and Development of Cursus Monuments'; Darvill, *Prehistoric Britain*, 118–21.
95. Darvill, *Prehistoric Britain*, 107; Jan Harding, 'Interpreting the Neolithic', *Oxford Journal of Archaeology*, 16 (1997), 279–97; Jan Harding, 'Reconsidering the Neolithic Round Barrows of Eastern Yorkshire', in Paul Frodsham (ed.), *Neolithic Studies in No-Man's Land* (Northern Archaeology special edition, 1996), 167–78.
96. Darvill, *Prehistoric Britain*, 108–9, collates the evidence for both modes of burial.
97. Ibid., 82–3.

98. Jan Harding, 'Pit-Digging, Occupation and Structured Deposition on Rudston Wold, Eastern Yorkshire', *Oxford Journal of Archaeology*, 25 (2006), 109–26.

99. Kirsty Millican, 'Timber Monuments, Landscape and the Environment in the Nith Valley', *Oxford Journal of Archaeology*, 31 (2012), 27–46.

100. Richard Bradley, 'Learning from Places', in Frodsham (ed.), *Neolithic Studies*, 87.

101. Their books were Ronald W. B. Morris, *The Prehistoric Rock Art of Argyll*, Poole, Dolphin, 1977; *The Prehistoric Rock Art of Galloway and the Isle of Man*, Poole, Blandford, 1979; and *The Prehistoric Rock Art of Southern Scotland*, Oxford, British Archaeological Reports, 1981; Stan Beckensall and Tim Laurie, *Prehistoric Rock Art of County Durham, Swaledale and Wensleydale*, Durham, County Durham Books, 1998; Stan Beckensall, *British Prehistoric Rock Art*, Stroud, Tempus, 1999; *Prehistoric Rock Art in Northumberland*, Stroud, Tempus, 2000); *Prehistoric Rock Art in Cumbria*, Stroud, Tempus, 2002; *Circles in Stone*, Stroud, Tempus, 2006.

102. Clive Waddington, 'Putting Rock Art to Use', in Frodsham (ed.), *Neolithic Studies*, 147–77; 'Cup and Ring Marks in Context', *Cambridge Archaeological Journal*, 8 (1998), 29–54; and 'Neolithic Rock Art in the British Isles', in Aron Mazel *et al.* (eds), *Art as Metaphor*, Oxford, Archaeopress, 2007, 49–68; Stan Beckensall. 'British Prehistoric Rock-Art in the Landscape', in George Nash and Christopher Chippindale (eds), *European Landscapes of Rock Art*, London, Routledge, 2002, 39–70; Clive Waddington, 'Rock of Ages', *British Archaeology* (September 2004), 16–17.

103. Stan Beckensall, 'Symbols on Stone', in Frodsham (ed.), *Neolithic Studies*, 139–40.

104. Bradley, 'Learning from Places'; George Nash, 'A Scattering of Images', in Mazel *et al.* (eds), *Art as Metaphor*, 175–95.

105. Bradley, 'Learning from Places'; *Rock Art and the Prehistory of Atlantic Europe*, London, Routledge, 1997, 90–126; and 'Symbols and Signposts', in Colin Renfrew and Ezra Zubrow (eds), *The Ancient Mind*, Cambridge, Cambridge University Press, 1994, 95–106; Waddington, 'Putting Rock Art to Use'; Sara Fairen-Jiménez, 'British Neolithic Rock Art in its Landscape', *Journal of Field Archaeology*, 32 (2007), 283–96; George Nash, Review of four titles in *Antiquaries' Journal*, 91 (2011), 353.

106. A point made by Bradley, *Rock Art*, 5.

107. Andy Jones, 'Between a Rock and a Hard Place', in Vicki Cummings and Amelia Pannett (eds), *Set in Stone*, Oxford, Oxbow, 2005, 107–17.

108. See Morris, *The Prehistoric Rock Art of Galloway*.

109. See especially Bradley, 'Symbols and Signposts'; Paul M. Brown and Graeme Chappell, *Prehistoric Rock Art in the North Yorks Moors*, Stroud, Tempus, 2005, 197–217; Blaze O'Connor, 'Carving Identity', in David A. Barrowclough and Caroline Malone (eds), *Cult in Context*, Oxford, Oxbow, 2007, 183–90; Robert Wallis, 'Re-enchanting Rock Art Landscapes', *Time and Mind*, 2 (2010), 47–70; Kate E. Sharpe, 'Rock-art and Rough Cuts', in Mazel *et al.* (eds), *Art as Metaphor*, 151–73.

110. What follows, down to the 1990s, is argued, with full source references, in two previous publications of mine: 'The Neolithic Great Goddess', *Antiquity*, 71 (1997), 91–9; and 'The Discovery of the Modern Goddess', in Joanne Pearson *et al.* (eds), *Nature Religion Today*, Edinburgh, Edinburgh University Press, 1998, 89–100; and references should be to those except where additional sources are provided below. A digest of these two works appeared in Ronald Hutton, *The Triumph of the Moon: A History of Modern Pagan Witchcraft*, Oxford, Oxford University Press, 1999, 32–43, 278–82.

111. Albrecht Dieterich, *Mutter Erde*, Berlin, 1905.

112. Mircea Eliade, *Occultism, Witchcraft and Cultural Fashions*, Chicago, University of Chicago Press, 1976, 5.

113. Olaf Petterson, *Mother Earth*, Lund, Regiae Societatis Humanorum Litterorum Lundensis, 1965–6.

114. Samuel D. Gill, *Mother Earth*, Chicago, University of Chicago Press, 1987; Tony Swain, 'The Mother Earth Conspiracy', *Numen*, 38 (1991), 3–26.

115. E.g. Monica Sjoo and Barbara Mor, *The Great Cosmic Mother*, San Francisco, Harper & Row, 1987; Sigfrid Lonegren, *Labyrinths*, Glastonbury, Gothic Image, 1991; Cheryl Straffon, *The Earth Goddess*, London, Blandford, 1997; Kathy Jones, *The Ancient British Goddess*, Glastonbury, Ariadne, 1991. I acknowledge that only two of these authors were actually British, the others being Americans and a Swede, but all except Barbara Mor settled in Britain.

116. Lynn Meskell, 'Twin Peaks', in Lucy Goodison and Christine Morris (eds), *Ancient Goddesses* London, British Museum, 1998, 46–62; Ian Hodder, *Catalhöyük*, London, Thames and Hudson, 2006; Steven Mithen, *After the Ice*, London, Weidenfeld & Nicolson, 2003, 88–96; Lynn Meskell *et al.*, 'Figured Lifeworlds and Depositional Practices at Catalhöyük', *Cambridge Archaeological Journal*, 18 (2008), 139–61; Lauren E. Talalay, *Deities, Dolls and Devices* Bloomington, Indiana University Press, 1993; Lynn Meskell, 'Goddesses, Gimbutas and the New Age', *Antiquity*, 69 (1995), 74–86; Naomi Hamilton *et al.*, 'Viewpoint: Can We Interpret Figurines?'; *Cambridge Archaeological Journal*, 6 (1996), 281–307; Lynn Meskell, 'Masquerades and Misrepresentations', *Cambridge Archaeological Journal*, 10 (2000), 370–2; Whittle, *Europe in the Neolithic*, 64–6; Ruth Tringham and Margaret Conkey, 'Rethinking Figurines', in Goodison and Morris (eds), *Ancient Goddesses*, 22–45; John Chapman, 'Understanding Material Cultural Representation', *Kvinner Arkeologi Norge*, 22–3 (1999), 91–6 (I am grateful to the author for the gift of this piece); Lauren Talalay, 'Archaeological Ms.conceptions', in Moira Macdonald and Linda Hurcombe (eds), *Representations of Gender from Prehistory to the Present*, London, Macmillan, 2000, 3–17; Naomi Hamilton, 'Ungendering Archaeology', ibid., 17–30; Douglass W. Bailey, *Balkan Prehistory*, London, Routledge, 2000; and *Prehistoric Figurines*, London, Routledge, 2005; Catherine Perlès, *The Early Neolithic in Greece*, Cambridge, Cambridge University Press, 2001, 256–7; Christine Marangou, 'Figurines and Models', in George A. Papathanassopoulos (ed.), *Neolithic Culture in Greece*, Athens, Nicholas P. Goulandris Foundation, 1996, 146–50; Richard G. Lesure, *Interpreting Ancient Figurines*, Cambridge, Cambridge University Press, 2011; David W. Anthony, 'The Rise and Fall of Old Europe', in David W. Anthony and Jennifer Y. Chi (eds), *The Lost World of Old Europe*, Princeton, NJ, Princeton University Press, 2010, 39–45; Douglass W. Bailey, 'The Figurines of Old Europe', ibid., 113–27; Colin Renfrew, *The Cycladic Spirit*, London, Thames and Hudson, 1993, 95–105; Diane Bolger, 'Figurines, Fertility, and the Emergence of Complex Society in Prehistoric Cyprus', *Current Anthropology*, 37 (1996), 365–73; A. Bernard Knapp and Lynn Meskell, 'Bodies of Evidence on Prehistoric Cyprus', *Cambridge Archaeological Journal*, 7 (1997), 183–204; Nanno Marinatos, *Minoan Religion*, Chapel Hill, University of North Carolina Press, 1993; O.T. P. K. Dickinson, 'Comments on a Popular Model of Minoan Religion', *Oxford Journal of Archaeology*, 13 (1994), 173–84; Lucy Goodison and Christine Morris, 'Beyond the "Great Mother"', in Goodison and Morris (eds), *Ancient Goddesses*, 113–32; James Alexander Gillivray, *Minotaur*, New York, Hill & Wang, 2000; Cathy Gere, 'Restoring Faith', *History Today*, 59 (July 2009), 48–50; Matthew Haysom, 'The Double Axe', *Oxford Journal of Archaeology*, 29 (2010), 35–55; Caroline Malone, 'God or Goddess', in Goodison and Morris (eds), *Ancient Goddesses*, 148–63; Colin Renfrew, 'Ritual and Cult in Malta and Beyond', in Barraclough and Malone (eds), *Cult in Context*, 8–13; Caroline Malone, 'Ritual, Space and Structure', ibid., 23–4; David A. Barrowclough, 'Putting Cult in Context', ibid., 45–53; Anthony Bonanno, 'Rituals of Life and Rituals of Death', in Daniel Cilia (ed.), *Malta before History*, Malta, Miranda, 2004, 271–87; Anthony Pace, 'The Sites', ibid., 82–3; Ann Monsarrat, 'The Deity: God or Goddess?', ibid., 289–305; C. A. T. Malone *et al.*, 'The Landscape of the Island Goddess?', in M. Maaskant-Kleibrink (ed.), *The Landscape of the Goddess*, Groningen, Archaeological Institute, Groningen University, 1995, 1–17; Elizabeth Shee Twohig, 'A "Mother Goddess" in North-West Europe c. 4200–2500', in Goodison and Morris (eds), *Ancient Goddesses*, 164–79; Stephanie Lynn Budin, *Images of Mother and Child from the Bronze Age*, Cambridge, Cambridge University Press, 2011; Katina L. Lillios, *Heraldry for the Dead: Memory, Identity and the Engraved Stone Plaques of Neolithic Iberia*, Austin, University of Texas Press, 2008; Chris Scarre, *Landscapes of Neolithic Brittany*, Oxford, Oxford University Press, 2011, 227–66. I am very grateful to Professor Lillios for corresponding with me on this issue and sending me a manuscript chapter of her book. For the classic critique of the Goddess Movement by two feminist archaeologists, see Margaret Conkey and Ruth Tringham, 'Archaeologies and the Goddess', in Donna C. Stanton and Abigail J. Stewart (eds), *Feminisms in the Academy*, Ann Arbor, University of Michigan Press, 1995, 199–247. I emphasize here that I do not myself make any endorsement of these works, being not sufficiently expert in the archaeology of the lands concerned: I merely recognize their existence. Some of them argue against evidence for goddess worship at all, and some against the worship of a single great and primordial goddess, while others conclude that the data could favour a range of different interpretations. None the less, they

all function as critiques of the earlier straightforward use of the data concerned as proof of an original Great Mother Goddess.

117. Nicole Loraux, 'What is a Goddess?', in Pauline Schmitt Pantel (ed.), *A History of Women in the West. Volume One*, Cambridge, MA, Harvard University Press, 1992, 11–44; Juliette Wood, 'The Concept of the Goddess', in Sandra Billington and Miranda Green (eds), *The Concept of the Goddess*, London, Routledge, 1996, 8–25; Lucy Goodison and Christine Morris, 'Exploring Female Divinity', in Goodison and Morris (eds), *Ancient Goddesses*, 6–21; Joan Goodnick Westenholz, 'Goddesses of the Ancient Near East', ibid., 63–82; Mike Parker Pearson, 'From Ancestor Cult to Divine Religion', *British Archaeology*, 45 (1999), 10–11.

118. Bryony and John Coles, *Sweet Track to Glastonbury*, London, Thames and Hudson, 1986, 81.

119. Clive Jonathan Bond, 'Walking the Track and Believing', in Barrowclough and Malone (eds), *Cult in Context*, 158–66.

120. H. W. F. Saggs, *The Greatness that was Babylon*, London, Sidgwick & Jackson, 1962, 328.

121. In my first work to deal with the subject, *The Pagan Religions of the Ancient British Isles*, Oxford, Blackwell, 1991, I recorded that there was no solid evidence for the Neolithic great goddess, but I also (on p. 40) stated both that it was still possible that her worship had in fact existed and that her modern followers had 'a tremendous power to comfort or inspire'. I still insist both that it remains possible to believe that their goddess was venerated in the Neolithic and that they represent a present-day religion with as much legitimacy as any other. However, a few of her more extreme devotees have attacked me with such fury, simply because I spoke in that book of an absence of solid evidence, that I can no longer personally regard their faith as comforting or inspiring.

122. Lubbock, *Pre-Historic Times*, 336–447; Dawkins, *Early Man in Britain*, 282–343.

123. Charles Grant B. Allen, *Falling in Love: With Other Essays*, London, 1889, 296–7.

124. Edward B. Tylor, *Primitive Culture*, London, 1871.

125. For this, see the many sources listed above, for the interpretation of causewayed enclosures and tomb-shrines.

126. This tradition is summed up, with references, in Laurence H. Keeley, *War before Civilization*, Oxford, Oxford University Press, 1996, 9–22.

127. Ibid., 25–141; Raymond C. Kelly, *Warless Societies and the Origins of War*, Ann Arbor, University of Michigan Press, 2000, 11–161.

128. Kelly, *Warless Societies*, 152–4.

129. Ibid., 148–54.

130. Slavomil Vencl, ' Stone Age Warfare', and John Chapman, 'The Origins of Warfare in the Prehistory of Central and Eastern Europe', in John Carman and Anthony Harding (eds), *Ancient Warfare*, Stroud, Sutton, 1999, 57–72, 101–42; David W. Frayer, 'Offnet: Evidence For a Mesolithic Massacre', Lawrence Keeley, 'Frontier Warfare in the Early Neolithic', and R. Brian Ferguson, 'Violence and War in Prehistory', in Debra L. Martin and David W. Frayer (eds), *Troubled Times: Violence and Warfare in the Past*, Amsterdam, Gordon & Breach, 1997, 181–212, 303–19, 321–55; Mark Golito and Lawrence Keeley, 'Beating Ploughshares back into Swords', *Antiquity*, 8 (2007), 332–43; Bruno Boulestin *et al.*, 'Mass Cannibalism in the Linear Pottery Culture at Herxheim', *Antiquity*, 82 (2008), 968–82.

131. Niall Sharples, *Maiden Castle*, London, Batsford, 1991, 47; Mercer and Healey, *Hambledon Hill*; Martin Smith, 'Bloody Stone Age', *Current Archaeology*, 230 (May 2009), 12–19; Paul Hill and Julie Wileman, *Landscapes of War*, Stroud, Tempus, 2002, 19; R. J. Mercer, 'The Origins of Warfare in the British Isles', in Carman and Harding (eds), *Ancient Warfare*, 143–56.

132. Rick J. Schulting and Michael Wysocki, ' "In this Chambered Tumulus were found Cleft Skulls" ', *Proceedings of the Prehistoric Society*, 71 (2005), 107–38.

133. Mercer, 'The Origins of Warfare', 145–50.

134. Martin Smith and Megan Buckley, 'Boles Barrow', *British Archaeology*, 93 (March–April 2007), 22–7.

135. Editorial, 'The New Radiocarbon Dating Revolution', *Current Archaeology*, 209 (2007), 10–11.

136. Pryor, *Britain BC*, 130; Mercer, 'The Origins of Warfare', 144–8.

137. A point made by Mercer, above.

138. Russell, *Monuments of the British Neolithic*, 68.

139. Schulting and Wysocki, '"In this Chambered Tumulus"'.

3 The Late Neolithic and Early Bronze Age: The Time of the Sacred Circle

1. All points made neatly by Alex Gibson, 'Round in Circles', in Rosamund Cleal and Joshua Pollard (eds), *Monuments and Material Culture*, Salisbury, Hob Nob, 2004, 70.

2. The first date is that of Mike Parker Pearson, 'The Earlier Bronze Age', in John Hunter and Ian Ralston (eds), *The Archaeology of Britain*, London, Routledge, 2009, 103; the second that of Joshua Pollard, 'The Construction of Prehistoric Britain', in Joshua Pollard (ed.), *Prehistoric Britain*, Oxford, Blackwell, 2008, 1–17.

3. For a summary of what was known about these until the end of the 1980s, see Ronald Hutton, *The Pagan Religions of the Ancient British Isles*, Oxford, Blackwell, 1991, 52–62. For updates since then, see Carleton Jones, *Temples of Stone*, Wilton, Co. Cork, Collins, 2007.

4. Michael J. O'Kelly, *Newgrange*, London, Thames and Hudson, 1982; George Eogan, *Knowth and the Passage Tombs of Ireland*, London, Thames and Hudson, 1986; Peter Harbison, *Pre-Christian Ireland*, London, Thames and Hudson, 1988, 56–82.

5. Jeremy Dronfield, 'Subjective Vision and the Source of Irish Megalithic Art', *Antiquity*, 69 (1995), 539–49; Debate over Dronfield thesis, with nine contributors, in *Cambridge Archaeological Journal*, 6 (1996), 39–72; Richard Bradley, 'Decorating the Houses of the Dead', *Cambridge Archaeological Journal*, 11 (2001), 45–67; David Lewis-Williams and David Pearce, *Inside the Neolithic Mind*, London, Thames and Hudson, 2005, 198–249.

6. Richard Bradley, *Image and Audience: Rethinking Prehistoric Art*, Oxford, Oxford University Press, 2009, 51–76.

7. George Nash, 'Light at the End of the Tunnel', in Ann Mazel *et al.* (eds), *Art as Metaphor*, Oxford, Archaeopress, 2007, 123–50; and 'The Symbolic Use of Fire', *Time and Mind*, 1 (2008), 143–5.

8. Frances Lynch, *Prehistoric Anglesey*, Llangefni, Anglesey Antiquarian Society, 1970, 55–65; 'Sensational New Discoveries at Bryn Celli Ddu', *British Archaeology*, 89 (2006), 6; George Nash, 'Graves, Symbols and the Stone Age', *Current Archaeology*, 211 (2007), 25–30.

9. This is at any rate the traditional interpretation of the deposit, but there may be others. Joshua Pollard suggests that it might have been formed of the pellets regurgitated by birds of prey: pers. comm. 30 May 2012.

10. Lynch, *Prehistoric Anglesey*, 34–40; Nash, 'The Symbolic Use of Fire', and 'Light at the End of the Tunnel'; Editorial, 'Anglesey's Neolithic Rock Art', *Current Archaeology*, 250 (2011), 11.

11. Anna Ritchie, *Prehistoric Orkney*, London, Batsford, 1995, 40–84; Patrick Ashmore, *Maes Howe*, Edinburgh, Historic Scotland, 2000; Colin Richards (ed.), *Dwelling among the Monuments*, Oxford, Oxbow, 2005, 126–7; Richard Bradley, 'Incised Motifs in the Passage-Graves at Quoyness and Cuween, Orkney', *Antiquity*, 72 (1998), 387–90; Euan Mackie, 'Maes Howe and the Winter Solstice', *Antiquity*, 71 (1997), 338–59; Richard Bradley *et al.*, 'Discovering Decorated Tombs in Neolithic Orkney', *Current Archaeology*, 161 (1999), 184–7; Anna Ritchie (ed.), *Orkney in its European Context*, Cambridge, McDonald Institute, 2000; Miles Russell, *Monuments of the British Neolithic*, Stroud, Tempus, 2002, 157–60; Caroline Wickham-Jones, *Between the Wind and the Water: World Heritage Orkney*, Macclesfield, Windgather, 2006.

12. Colin Renfrew, *Before Civilization*, London, Jonathan Cape, 1973, 132–41; Vicki Cummings and Amelia Pannett, 'Island Views', in Vicki Cummings and Amelia Pannett (eds), *Set in Stone: New Approaches to Neolithic Monuments in Scotland*, Oxford, Oxbow, 2005, 14–24.

13. John W. Hedges, *Tomb of the Eagles*, London, John Murray, 1984; Barry Cunliffe, *Facing the Ocean*, Oxford, Oxford University Press, 2001, 182; John Barber, 'Death in Orkney', in Anna Ritchie (ed.), *Neolithic Orkney in its European Context*, Cambridge, McDonald Institute, 2000, 185–7; Stuart Reilly, 'Processing the Dead in Neolithic Orkney', *Oxford Journal of Archaeology*, 22 (2003), 133–54; Timothy Taylor, *The Buried Soul*, London, Fourth Estate, 2002, 24–6; Richards (ed.), *Dwelling among the Monuments*, 202.

14. I have very happy memories of sitting on the farmhouse kitchen floor one Sunday morning in 1987, with Ronald Simison's wife Morgan, examining the finds from the site at leisure, and noticing things in the process that would normally have eluded me, such as that some of the pottery had been decorated by incised patterns made by human fingernails, so small that the job must have been given to children. Ronald (and his sheepdog) then showed me round the monument.

15. Joshua Pollard suggests to me from unpublished information that this is indeed proving to be the case: pers. comm., 30 May 2012.

16. Hedges, *Tomb of the Eagles*; John Barber, 'Isbister, Quanterness and the Point of Cott', in John Barrett and I. A. Kinnes (eds), *The Archaeology of Context in the Neolithic and Bronze Age*, Sheffield, Sheffield University Press, 1988, 42–62; Anna Ritchie, *On the Fringe of Neolithic Europe*, Edinburgh, Society of Antiquaries of Scotland, 2009; Anna Ritchie, 'The Use of Human and Faunal Material in Chambered Tombs in Orkney', in Alex Gibson and Alison Sheridan (eds), *From Sickles to Circles*, Stroud, Tempus, 2004, 92–105.

17. Emphasized by Roy Loveday, 'Double-Entrance Henges', in Alex Gibson and Derek Simpson (eds), *Prehistoric Ritual and Religion*, Stroud, Sutton, 1998, 14–31; Timothy Darvill, *Prehistoric Britain*, 2nd edition, London, Routledge, 2010, 163–7; and Gordon Noble, *Neolithic Scotland*, Edinburgh, Edinburgh University Press, 2006, 194–218.

18. Stuart and C. M. Piggott, 'Stone and Earth Circles of Dorset', *Antiquity*, 13 (1939), 138–58; Richard Atkinson *et al.*, *Excavations at Dorchester, Oxon*, Oxford, Ashmolean Museum, 1951, 82.

19. Jan Harding, *Henge Monuments of the British Isles*, Stroud, Tempus, 2003; G. J. Barclay, 'The "Henge" and "Hengiform" in Scotland', in Cummings and Pannett (eds), *Set in Stone*, 81–94.

20. Jan Harding, 'Later Neolithic Ceremonial Centres, Ritual and Pilgrimage', in Ritchie (ed.), *Neolithic Orkney*, 31–46.

21. Alex Gibson, *Stonehenge and Timber Circles*, Stroud, Tempus, 1998.

22. Alex Gibson, 'A Neolithic Enclosure at Hindwell', *Oxford Journal of Archaeology*, 15 (1996), 341–8.

23. Mark Brennand and Maisie Taylor, 'Seahenge', *Current Archaeology*, 167 (2000), 417–24; Mark Brennand and Maisie Taylor, 'The Survey and Excavation of a Bronze Age Timber Circle at Holme-next-the-Sea', *Proceedings of the Prehistoric Society*, 69 (2003), 1–84; Mark Brennand, 'This is Why We Dug Seahenge', *British Archaeology* 78 (2004), 24–9.

24. Aubrey Burl, *The Stone Circles of the British Isles*, New Haven, Yale University Press, 1976; John Barnatt, *Stone Circles of Britain*, Oxford, British Archaeological Reports, 1989, 2 vols.

25. Tom Clare, 'Megalith Size and the Implications for Our Understanding of Contemporary Society', *Oxford Journal of Archaeology*, 29 (2010), 245–52.

26. John Barnatt, 'Monuments in the Landscape', in Gibson and Simpson (eds), *Prehistoric Ritual and Religion*, 92–105; Richard Bradley, *The Past in Prehistoric Societies*, London, Routledge, 2002, 75–7; Peter Herring, 'Stepping on to the Commons: South-Western Stone Rows', in Paul Rainbird (ed.), *Monuments in the Landscape*, Stroud, Tempus, 79–98.

27. Alex Gibson, 'The Timber Circle at Sarn-y-Bryn-Caled', *Antiquity*, 66 (1992), 84–92.

28. Timothy Darvill and Geoffrey Wainwright, 'Stone Circles, Oval Settings and Henges in South-West Wales and Beyond', *Antiquaries' Journal*, 83 (2003), 9–46.

29. Alex Gibson, 'Round in Circles'.

30. Gordon Noble *et al.*, 'Forteviot', *Current Archaeology*, 231 (2009), 12–19.

31. Julian Thomas, 'The Late Neolithic Cultural Repertoire', in Cleal and Pollard (eds), *Monuments and Material Culture*, 98–108; Barclay, 'The "Henge" and "Hengiform" in Scotland'. 81–94.

32. Richard Bradley, *Stages and Screens*, Edinburgh, Society of Antiquaries of Scotland, 2011.

33. Gibson, 'Round in Circles'; Harding, *Henge Monuments*, 10–23, 107–12; Richard Bradley, *The Prehistory of Britain and Ireland*, Cambridge, Cambridge University Press, 2007, 122.

34. Cf. Russell, *Monuments of the British Neolithic*, 131; Gibson, 'Round in Circles'; Parker Pearson, 'The Earlier Bronze Age', 121.

35. Ralph M. Fyfe and Tom Greeves, 'The Date and Context of a Stone Row', *Antiquity*, 82 (2010), 55–70.

36. Richard Bradley, 'Croft Moraig and the Chronology of Stone Circles', *Proceedings of the Prehistoric Society*, 71 (2005), 269–81.

37. These differing views are represented by Miles Russell, *Prehistoric Sussex*, Stroud, Tempus, 2002, 73–9; Bradley, *Prehistory of Britain and Ireland*, 128–30; Gibson, 'Round in Circles'; and Aaron Watson, 'Monuments that Made the World', in Cleal and Pollard (eds), *Monuments and Material Culture*, 83–97.

38. M. Parker Pearson and Ramilisonina, 'Stonehenge for the Ancestors', *Antiquity*, 72 (1998), 308–26; Alasdair Whittle, 'People and the Diverse Past', ibid., 852–5; John C. Barrett and Kathryn J. Fewster, 'Stonehenge', ibid., 847–52; M. Parker Pearson and Ramilisonina, 'Stonehenge for the Ancestors. Part Two', ibid., 855–6.

39. E.g. Bradley, *Prehistory of Britain and Ireland*, 126–7; Noble, *Neolithic Scotland*, 194–218.

40. Richards (ed.), *Dwelling among the Monuments*, 205–27.

41. Roy Loveday, 'Dorchester-on-Thames', in Alistair Barclay and Jan Harding (eds), *Pathways and Ceremonies*, Oxford, Oxbow, 1999, 49–63; John Gale, *Prehistoric Dorset*, Stroud, Tempus, 2003, 48–50; Timothy Darvill, *Long Barrows of the Cotswolds*, Stroud, Tempus, 2004, 173–82; Noble, *Neolithic Scotland*, 139–93.

42. Lynch, *Prehistoric Anglesey*, 55–65.

43. Cole Henley, 'Choreographed Monumentality', in Cummings and Pannett (eds), *Set in Stone*, 95–106.

44. Richards (ed.), *Dwelling among the Monuments*, passim; Colin Renfrew, 'The Auld Hoose Speaks', in Ritchie (ed.), *Neolithic Orkney*, 1–30; Nick Card, 'Neolithic Temples of the Northern Isles', *Current Archaeology*, 241 (2010), 12–19.

45. David Clarke and Patrick Maguire, *Skara Brae*, Edinburgh, Historic Scotland, 2000; Bradley, 'Incised Motifs'; Rosamund Cleal and Ann MacSween (eds), *Grooved Ware in Britain and Ireland*, Oxford, Oxbow, 1999; Russell, *Monuments of the British Neolithic*, 157–60; Richards (ed.), *Dwelling among the Monuments*, 122–204; Wickham-Jones, *Between the Wind and the Water*, 50–75. The news about the paintings at the Ness of Brodgar was published in the November–December 2010 issue of *British Archaeology*, p. 9.

46. The discoveries there were publicized in successive issues of *Salon*, 220 (2009) and 238 (2010), and of *British Archaeology*, July–August and September–October 2010; and *Current Archaeology*, 272 (2012), 8.

47. Richards (ed.), *Dwelling among the Monuments*, 249–59; Wickham-Jones, *Between the Wind and the Water*, 91–5.

48. Hutton, *Pagan Religions*, 64–6, updated by Jones, *Temples of Stone*, 219–23.

49. Frances Lynch *et al.*, *Prehistoric Wales*, Stroud, Sutton, 2000, 122–5.

50. Darvill, *Prehistoric Britain*, 185–7; Trevor Kirk, 'Memory, Tradition and Materiality', in Vicki Cummings and Chris Fowler (eds), *The Neolithic of the Irish Sea*, Oxford, Oxbow, 2004, 233–44.

51. Richard Bradley, *The Good Stones*, Edinburgh, Society of Antiquaries of Scotland, 2000; 'The Land, the Sky and the Scottish Stone Circle', in Chris Scarre (ed.), *Monuments and Landscape in Atlantic Europe*, London, Routledge, 2002, 122–38; and *The Moon and the Bonfire*, Edinburgh, Society of Antiquaries of Scotland, 2005, 99–115.

52. Ronald Hutton, *Blood and Mistletoe: The History of the Druids in Britain*, London, Yale University Press, 2009.

53. Bradley, *The Moon and the Bonfire*, contrasted with Adam Welfare, *Great Crowns of Stone*, ed. Stratford Halliday, Edinburgh, Royal Commission on the Ancient and Historic Monuments of Scotland, 2011.

54. Bradley, 'The Land, the Sky and the Scottish Stone Circle'; and *The Moon and the Bonfire*, passim.

55. Miles Russell, *Prehistoric Sussex*, Stroud, Tempus, 2002, 73–9; David Mullin, 'Evidence of Absence?', in Cummings and Fowler (eds), *The Neolithic of the Irish Sea*, 185–90; Christopher Tilley, *Interpreting Landscapes*, Walnut Creek, CA, Left Hand Press, 2010, 293–347.

56. Richard Bradley, *The Past in Prehistoric Societies*, London, Routledge, 2002, 89–93.

57. Jim Leary and David Field, 'Marden: The Unsung Henge', *Current Archaeology*, 253 (2011), 28–35; Christopher Catling, 'Sweating at Marsden', *Current Archaeology*, 255 (2011), 10.

58. G. J. Wainwright, *Mount Pleasant*, London, Society of Antiquaries, 1979; Mark Gillings *et al.*, *Landscape of the Megaliths*, Oxford, Oxbow, 2008, 208–9.

59. Peter J. Ucko *et al.*, *Avebury Reconsidered*, London, Unwin Hyman, 1990, 248; Gillings *et al.* *Landscape of the Megaliths*, 1–128.

60. Gillings *et al.*, *Landscape of the Megaliths*, 118–69, 202–4; Mark Gillings and Joshua Pollard, 'Non-portable Stone Artefacts and Contexts of Meaning', *World Archaeology*, 31 (1999), 179–93; and *Avebury*, London, Duckworth, 2004, 62–84.

61. Mike Pitts, 'Return to the Sanctuary', *British Archaeology*, 51 (2000), 14–19: Joshua Pollard and Andrew Reynolds, *Avebury*, Stroud, Tempus, 2002, 109.

62. Alasdair Whittle, *Sacred Mound, Holy Rings*, Oxford, Oxbow, 1997, 2, 125–65.

63. Jim Leary and David Field, *The Story of Silbury Hill*, London, English Heritage, 2010, ch. 5.

64. Ibid., ch. 6.

65. The most recent of a succession of books published by Michael Dames on the subject since 1976 is *Silbury: Resolving the Enigma*, Stroud, History Press, 2010.

66. It was based on the alleged discovery in Richard Atkinson's excavations of 1969–70 of flying ants, which occur in England in late July and early August, in the earliest phase of the mound. Leaving aside the problem that the purpose of the final phase may have been very different, the earth with the dead ants may have been put there at any season; moreover, it now seems uncertain that ants were actually found at all. For all this see Jim Leary, 'The Silbury Myth Buster', *British Archaeology*, 110 (2010), 13.

67. David Keys, 'Silbury's Spiritual Past', *BBC History Magazine*, 8.12 (December 2007), 8–9.

68. I tested this theory by using the resources of a television company, Atlantic Productions, at Silbury on 9 June 2006, when a large flag was raised on the summit, and proved to be visible from all the different points concerned in the henge complex. The article that opened up the possibility of the mound as an observatory of heavenly bodies was Paul Devereux, 'Three-Dimensional Aspects of Apparent Relationships between Selected Natural and Artificial Features within the Topography of the Avebury Complex', *Antiquity*, 65 (1991), 894–8.

69. Martyn Barber *et al.*, 'The Brood of Silbury', in Jim Leary *et al.* (eds), *Round Mounds and Monumentality in the British Neolithic and Beyond*, Oxford, Oxbow, 2010, 153–73.

70. The various press reports at the time lacked vital detail, so I am all the more grateful to Jim Leary for supplying the full results of his dig to me directly: pers. comm. 28 June 2011.

71. An oddity here: the vagaries of pre-modern English spelling have left the river as the Kennet and the villages beside it here as West and East Kennett. By some kind of unspoken convention, however, archaeologists, and so heritage managers, have combined the two versions so that the long barrow, the stone avenue and the palisade enclosures are always spelled West Kennet.

72. Geoffrey Wainwright, *Durrington Walls*, Dorking, Society of Antiquaries, 1971.

73. Editorial, 'Before Stonehenge', *Current Archaeology*, 208 (2007), 17–21; Mike Pitts, 'Stonehenge', *British Archaeology*, 102 (2008), 12–17; Maeve Kennedy, 'The Stonehenge Takeaway', *The Guardian*, 21 December 2009, 14. These published reports have been supplemented for me by annual personal communications, throughout the project, from Joshua Pollard, and a visit from Mike Parker Pearson.

74. Aubrey Burl, *Great Stone Circles*, New Haven, Yale University Press, 1999, 91–6; Julian Richards, *Stonehenge: The Story So Far*, Swindon, English Heritage, 2007, 110–12. The results of the 2006 excavation remain unpublished to date, and my information on it derives from Joshua Pollard.

75. A more detailed version of what follows in the next few paragraphs, with full references, may be found in Ronald Hutton, 'The Cultural History of Stonehenge', in Stephen Banfield (ed.), *The Sounds of Stonehenge*, Oxford, British Archaeological Reports, 2009, 43–5.

76. SPACES = Strumble-Preseli Ancient Communities and Environment Study.

77. For comments on the two theories, see Timothy Darvill, *Stonehenge*, Stroud, Tempus, 2006, 141–56; and Richards, *Stonehenge*, 215–30.

78. Bradley, *Prehistory of Britain and Ireland*, 138–41; Anthony Johnson, *Solving Stonehenge*, London, Thames and Hudson, 2008, passim; Richards, *Stonehenge*, 166–77; Mike Parker Pearson *et al.*, 'Who was Buried at Stonehenge?', *Antiquity*, 83 (2009), 23–39; Timothy Darvill and Geoffrey Wainwright, 'Stonehenge Excavations 2008', *Antiquaries Journal*, 89 (2009), 1–20; David Field *et al.*, 'Introducing "Stonehedge"', *British Archaeology*, 111 (2010), 32–54; Darvill, *Stonehenge*, 119–29.

79. Mike Parker Pearson *et al.*, 'Newhenge', *British Archaeology*, 110 (2010), 14–19 Field *et al.*, 'Introducing "Stonehedge"'.

80. Paul Ashbee, 'Stonehenge', *Wiltshire Archaeological and Natural History Magazine*, 91 (1998), 139–43.
81. For a discussion of the date of the fall, see Johnson, *Solving Stonehenge*, 139.
82. C. P. Green, 'The Provenance of Rocks Used in the Construction of Stonehenge', J. D. Scourse, 'Transport of the Stonehenge Bluestones', and O. Williams-Thorpe *et al.*, 'The Stonehenge Bluestones', all in Barry Cunliffe and Colin Renfrew (eds), *Science and Stonehenge*, Oxford, Oxford University Press, 1997, 257–318; Olwen Williams-Thorpe *et al.*, 'Preseli Dolerite Bluestones', *Oxford Journal of Archaeology*, 25 (2006), 29–46; Aubrey Burl, *Stonehenge*, London, Constable and Robinson, 2006, 133–49; Christopher Catling, 'Message in the Stones', *Current Archaeology*, 212 (2007), 12–19; Brian John, *The Bluestone Enigma*, Newport, Greencroft, 2008, passim; Editorial, 'Missing Stonehenge Circle Did Not Come from Preselis', *British Archaeology*, 109 (2009), 7; Timothy Darvill and Geoffrey Wainwright, 'The Stones of Stonehenge', *Current Archaeology*, 252 (2011), 28–35; Richard E. Bevins *et al.*, 'Stonehenge Rhyolitic Bluestone Sources and the Application of Zircon Chemistry', *Journal of Archaeological Science*, 38 (2011), 605–22.
83. Renfrew, *Before Civilization*, 228–34.
84. Mike Parker Pearson, 'Chieftains and Pastoralists in Neolithic and Bronze Age Wessex', in Rainbird (ed.), *Monuments in the Landscape*, 34–53. See also John C. Barrett, *Fragments from Antiquity*, Oxford, Blackwell, 1994, 27–8, and Whittle, *Sacred Mound, Holy Rings*, 139–47.
85. Richards, *Stonehenge*, 188–9; Gibson, 'The Timber Circle at Sarn-y-Bryn-Caled'; Mike Parker Pearson, pers. comm., 7 December 2005.
86. For two late examples (from the 1980s), see Aubrey Burl, *Rites of the Gods*, London, Dent, 1981, 107, 146–7; and David Burnett, *Priestess of Henge*, London, Hamlyn, 1984, 433.
87. Mike Pitts, *Hengeworld*, London, Century, 2000, 37–8; Joshua Pollard, pers. comm., 30 November 2006.
88. Mike Parker Pearson, 'Stonehenge and the Beginning of the British Neolithic', in Andrew Meirion Jones *et al.* (eds), *Image, Memory and Monumentality*, Oxford, Oxbow, 2012, 18–28.
89. A. P. Fitzpatrick *et al.*, *The Amesbury Archer and the Boscombe Bowmen*, Oxford, Oxbow, 2011.
90. John Mortimer, *Forty Years' Researches in British and Saxon Burial Mounds of East Yorkshire*, London, 1905, 23–42; Alex Gibson *et al.*, 'Recent Research at Duggleby Howe', *Archaeological Journal*, 166, 2009, 38–78.
91. A point made by Chris Fowler, *The Archaeology of Personhood*, London, Routledge, 2004, 79–100.
92. Sharon Bishop, 'Tarrant Launceston 15', *English Heritage Research News* (January 2010), 28–9.
93. Frances Peters, 'Bronze Age Barrows', *Oxford Journal of Archaeology*, 18 (1999), 255–64; David Field, 'Bury the Dead in a Sacred Landscape', *British Archaeology*, 42 (1999), 6–7.
94. Sandy Gerrard, *English Heritage Book of Dartmoor*, London, Batsford, 1997, 59–60.
95. Bradley, *The Prehistory of Britain and Ireland*, 158–68; Richard Bradley and Elise Fraser, 'Bronze Age Barrows on the Heathlands of Southern England', *Oxford Journal of Archaeology*, 29 (2010), 15–33; Paul Garwood, ' "Before the Hills in Order Stood" ', in Jonathan Last (ed.), *Beyond the Grave*, Oxford, Oxbow, 2007, 30–52.
96. Darvill, *Prehistoric Britain*, 200–10.
97. Gale, *Prehistoric Dorset*, 77–8.
98. Ian Brown, *Discovering a Welsh Landscape*, Macclesfield, Windgather, 2004, 46–50.
99. Darvill, *Prehistoric Britain*, 203–4; J. R. Turner, 'Ring Cairns, Stone Circles and Related Monuments on Dartmoor', *Devon Archaeological Society Proceedings*, 48 (1990), 27–86.
100. Wickham Jones, *Between the Wind and the Water*, 91–5.
101. Gwilym Hughes, 'Luckington', and Michael Allen and Barbara Applin, 'The Story of the Buckskin Barrow', *Current Archaeology*, 146 (1996), 44–9, 52–6.
102. Parker Pearson, 'The Earlier Bronze Age', 114–19; Bradley, *The Prehistory of Britain and Ireland*, 158–68.
103. For a discussion of it, see Gale, *Prehistoric Dorset*, 78–9.
104. Darvill, *Prehistoric Britain*, 200–3.

105. Peter J. Woodward, *The South Dorset Ridgeway*, Dorchester, Dorset Natural History and Archaeological Society, 1991, 146.

106. Ann Woodward, *British Barrows*, Stroud, Tempus, 2000, 104–16.

107. See ibid.; Francis Pryor, *Britain BC*, London, HarperCollins, 2003, 250–3; Andrew Jones, 'How the Dead Live', in Pollard (ed.), *Prehistoric Britain*, 189–90; Stuart Needham *et al.*, ' "A Noble Group of Barrows" ', *Antiquaries Journal*, 90 (2010), 1–39.

108. Jonathan Last, 'Books of Life', *Oxford Journal of Archaeology*, 17 (1998), 43–54; Woodward, *British Barrows*, 45; Gale, *Prehistoric Dorset*, 81; John Thomas, 'Monuments, Memories and Myths in the Early Bronze Age', *Current Archaeology*, 27 (2008), 153–74.

109. Ann Woodward *et al.*, 'Ritual in Some Early Bronze Age Gravegoods', *Archaeological Journal*, 162 (2005), 31–64.

110. Francis Pryor, *Britain AD*, London, HarperCollins, 2004, 79.

111. Frances Healy and Jan Harding, 'A Thousand and One Things to Do with a Round Barrow', in Last (ed.), *Beyond the Grave*, 53–71.

112. Joanna Brück, 'Early Bronze Age Burial Practices in Scotland and Beyond', in Ian Shepherd and Gordon Barclay (eds), *Scotland in Ancient Europe*, Edinburgh, Society of Antiquaries of Scotland, 2004, 185–8.

113. Robert Johnston, 'Dying, Becoming and Being the Field', in Jan Harding and Robert Johnston (eds), *Northern Pasts*, Oxford, British Archaeological Reports, 2000, 57–70.

114. Cyril Fox, *Life and Death in the Bronze Age*, London, Routledge, 1959, xxvi.

115. Colin Renfrew was the great proponent of this sub-discipline: *Towards an Archaeology of Mind*, Cambridge, Cambridge University Press, 1982; and 'Cognitive Archaeology', *Cambridge Archaeological Journal*, 3 (1993), 248–50.

116. The equivalent ideologues here were Michael Shanks and Ian Hodder, for example in Ian Hodder *et al.* (eds), *Interpreting Archaeology*, London, Routledge, 1995.

117. See, for example, Colin Renfrew, 'Towards a Cognitive Archaeology', in Colin Renfrew and Ezra B. W. Zubrow (eds), *The Ancient Mind*, Cambridge, Cambridge University Press, 1994, 3–12; and K. R. Dark, *Theoretical Archaeology*, London, Duckworth, 1995, 9–23. For a later perspective on the common themes that have emerged, Matthew Johnson, *Archaeological Theory*, Oxford, Wiley-Blackwell, 2nd edition, 2010, 224–7, is succinct.

118. Johnson, *Archaeological Theory*, 219.

119. Colin Renfrew, *The Archaeology of Cult*, London, Thames and Hudson, 1985.

120. Timothy Insoll, *Archaeology, Ritual, Religion*, London, Routledge, 2004, 155.

121. The key texts are John Thurnam, 'On Ancient British Barrows', *Archaeologia*, 42 (1869), 161–244, and 43 (1871), 285–544; and W. Boyd Dawkins, *Early Man in Britain*, London, 1880, 233–497. For the wider scholarly context and detailed reasoning of them, see Ronald Hutton, *Blood and Mistletoe: The History of the Druids in Britain*, London, Yale University Press, 2009, 299–303.

122. For various stages in this model, see Jacquetta Hawkes, *Early Britain*, London, 1945, 18–23; Jacquetta and Christopher Hawkes, *Prehistoric Britain*, Harmondsworth, Penguin, 2nd edition, 1949, 66–71; Stuart Piggott, *The Neolithic Cultures of the British Isles*, Cambridge, Cambridge University Press, 1954, 270; D.L. Clarke, *Beaker Pottery of Great Britain and Ireland*, Cambridge, Cambridge University Press, 1970, 276–80.

123. Stephen Oppenheimer, *The Origins of the British*, London, Constable and Robinson, 2006, 210–370; Brian Sykes, *Blood of the Isles*, London, Bantam, 2006, passim.

124. Darvill, *Prehistoric Britain*, 167–77; Pryor, *Seahenge*, 214–17; Rosamund Cleal, 'The Small Compass of a Grave', in Graham Brown *et al.* (eds), *The Avebury Landscape*, Oxford, Oxbow, 2005, 115–32; Bradley, *Prehistory of Britain and Ireland*, 133–4; Julian Thomas, 'The Return of the Rinyo-Clacton Folk?', *Cambridge Archaeological Journal*, 20 (2010), 1–15; Darvill, *Prehistoric Britain*, 139.

125. Richard Bradley, *The Social Foundations of Prehistoric Britain*, London, Longman, 1984, was perhaps the most celebrated expression of this approach. For a later formulation of it, see Julian Thomas, 'Reading the Body', in P. Garwood *et al.* (eds), *Sacred and Profane*, Oxford, Oxford University Committee for Archaeology, 1991, 33–42.

126. John Barrett, *Fragments from Antiquity*, Oxford, Blackwell, 1994, 27–50, 97–108; Julian Thomas, *Culture and Identity*, London, Routledge, 1996, 180.

127. John Chapman, 'Approaches to Trade and Exchange in Earlier Prehistory', in Andrew Jones (ed.), *Prehistoric Europe*, Chichester, Wiley, 2008, 333–55.

128. Hawkes and Hawkes, *Prehistoric Britain*, 13–14.

129. Barrett, *Fragments from Antiquity*, 27–32.

130. Julian Thomas, *Time, Culture and Identity*, London, Routledge, 1999, 96.

131. Harding, *Henge Monuments*, 112–21.

132. Andrew Jones, 'How the Dead Live', in Pollard (ed.), *Prehistoric Britain*, 177–201.

133. Richard Harrison and Volker Heyd, *The Transformation of Europe in the Third Millennium* BC, Berlin, De Gruyter, 2008.

134. Barry Cunliffe, *Europe between the Oceans*, London, Yale University Press, 2008, 167–227.

135. Darvill, *Prehistoric Britain*, 132–200; Bradley, *The Moon and the Bonfire*, 99–115.

136. This story is told in full in Hutton, *Blood and Mistletoe*, 49–312.

137. See Adam Stout, *Creating Prehistory*, Oxford, Blackwell, 2008, 173–214 for the first proper history of Watkins's career and that of the Straight Track Club.

138. The story of the professionalization of British archaeology, and its implications for amateurs, is told in Hutton, *Blood and Mistletoe*, 387–93.

139. What follows draws partly on ideas first aired in Ronald Hutton, 'Modern Druidry and Earth Mysteries', *Time and Mind*, 2 (2009), 313–32.

140. J. A. D. Wedd, *Skyways and Landmarks*, Hull, Star Fellowship, 1972, passim; Paul Devereux, 'The Earth Remembered', *Ley Hunter*, 96 (1984), 4–7.

141. John Michell, *The Flying Saucer Vision*, London, Sidgwick & Jackson, 1967.

142. John Michell, *The View over Atlantis*, London, Sage, 1969.

143. Ibid., vii, 62–4, 185.

144. Ibid., 64.

145. Janet and Colin Bord, *Mysterious Britain*, London, Garnstone, 1972.

146. Colin Bord, 'The Cosmic Continent', *Gandalf's Garden*, 4 (1969), 4–8.

147. Paul Screeton, *Quicksilver Heritage*, Wellingborough, Thorson's, 1974, 13, 67–73.

148. John Michell incorporated mystical numerology into *The View over Atlantis*, and developed it in *City of Revelation*, London, Abacus, 1973; see also Michael Behrend, *The Landscape Geometry of Southern Britain*, Cambridge, Institute of Geomantic Research, 1976 for an application of geometry to the earth mysteries. The works on dowsing which had most influence on the movement included Guy Underwood, *The Pattern of the Past*, London, Museum Press, 1976; and Tom Graves, *Dowsing*, London, Turnstone, 1976; and *Needles of Stone*, London, Turnstone, 1978. For an application of the earth mysteries approach to archaeological data, see Francis Hitching, *Earth Magic*, London, Cassell, 1976, who made the Beaker People the villains who ended the Neolithic golden age. Nigel Pennick, *The Ancient Science of Geomancy*, London, Thames and Hudson, 1979, united archaeology with divination and various other esoteric traditions.

149. All played out in the successive issues of the *Ley Hunter* between 1970 and 1984.

150. Don Robins, 'The Dragon Project and the Talking Stones', *New Scientist*, 21 October 1982, 6–8; Paul Devereux, five reports in the *Ley Hunter*, 1985–8, entitled 'Radiation at Megalithic Sites', as well as *Earth Lights*, London, Turnstone, 1982; *Earth Lights Revelation*, London, Blandford, 1989; and *Places of Power*, London, Blandford, 1990.

151. This story can be followed through successive issues of the *Ley Hunter*, nos 10 to 14, between August and December 1970.

152. For Glyn Daniel's views concerning the policing of truth, see his *A Short History of Archaeology*, London, Thames and Hudson, 1981. For his application of it, see his editorials in *Antiquity* between 1962 and 1982.

153. Adam Stout, *What's Real and What's Not*, Bath, Runetree, 2006, 15–18.

154. Tom Williamson and Liz Bellamy, *Ley Lines in Question*, Tadworth, World's Work, 1983.

155. Anthony Roberts, 'Contract Killers (Psychic Cripples)', *Shaman*, 4 (1984), 3–4.

156. It has also dispersed quite far in other parts of society among people inclined to mysticism: in 1993 I was at dinner with a marquess, bearing a title established under the Tudors, at his country seat, and he remarked proudly that three leys converged upon his estate.

157. First in Paul Devereux and Robert Forrest, 'Ley Lines in Question Answered', *Ley Hunter*, 97 (1984), 11–24.

158. Nigel Pennick and Paul Devereux, *Lines on the Landscape*, London, Hale, 1989.

159. Among a large array of titles, my personal favourites are *Shamanism and the Mystery Lines*, London, Quantum, 1992; *The New Ley Hunter's Guide*, Glastonbury, Gothic Image, 1994; *The Long Trip: A Prehistory of Psychedelia*, London, Penguin, 1997; *The Illustrated Encyclopedia of Ancient Earth Mysteries*, London, Cassell, 2000; *The Sacred Place*, London, Cassell, 2000; *Stone Age Soundtracks*, London, Vega, 2001; *Haunted Land*, London, Piatkus, 2001; *Mysterious Ancient America*, London, Vega, 2002; *Fairy Paths and Spirit Roads*, London, Chrysalis, 2005.

160. Devereux, 'Three-Dimensional Aspects of Apparent Relationships', as cited above in connection with Silbury.

161. Prudence Jones and Nigel Pennick, *A History of Pagan Europe*, London, Routledge, 1995; A select list of Nigel Pennick's own works would include *The Oracle of Geomancy*, Chieveley, Capall Bann, 1995; *On the Spiritual Arts and Crafts*, Cambridge, Old England House, 2001; *Masterworks*, Wymeswold, Heart of Albion, 2002; *The Three Fates*, Cambridge, Lanfal, 2004; *Makings*, Cambridge, Old England House, 2004; *New Troy Resurgent*, Cambridge, Spiritual Land, 2005; *The Mysteries of St Martin's*, Cambridge, Spiritual Land, 2005.

162. Jeremy Harte, *Explore Fairy Traditions*, Wymeswold, Heart of Albion, 2004; *English Holy Wells*, 3 vols, Wymeswold, Heart of Albion, 2008.

163. Bob Trubshaw, *Explore Folklore*, 2002; *Explore Mythology*, 2003; *Sacred Places*, 2005; and *Horn Dance or Stag Night*, 2007; all published at Wymeswold by Heart of Albion Press. All of the four authors cited in notes 161–3 above have treated me with a generosity far beyond anything that I have deserved, and the fact that I can so readily cite their works has been based partly on the kindness with which they have shared them with me.

164. For comment and context, see Trubshaw, *Sacred Places*, 103.

165. Tom Williamson and Liz Bellamy, 'Our Reasons and Aims', *Shaman*, 4 (1984), 2–3, contextualized by various conversations with Tom between 1996 and the present.

166. One further thought, which may best be inserted here, is that when considering the various leys mapped out by ley-hunters during the 1970s and 1980s, in town and country, it is noticeable that virtually all of them depend on medieval churches for viability. The assumption built into the inclusion of these buildings was, as said, that all could be presumed to have been built over pre-Christian sacred sites. In recent years stress has been laid by architectural historians on the way in which the builders of medieval religious structures incorporated into them principles of mathematics and geometry with a sacred significance: see Thomas Cooke and Peter Kidson, *Salisbury Cathedral*, London, Her Majesty's Stationery Office, 1993, 35–91; Eric Fernie, *The Architecture of Norman England*, Oxford, Oxford University Press, 2000; and Nigel Hiscock, *The Wise Master Builder*, Aldershot, Ashgate, 2000. Is it possible that the same principles may have been applied between as well as within buildings, and that, at least in some towns, churches were built in alignment with each other? If so, ley-hunters may have been the first to notice a hitherto unremarked feature of medieval culture, while setting it in an altogether different conceptual framework.

167. A story that is told in detail in Hutton, *Blood and Mistletoe*, 348–417.

168. Lockyer's work is considered with full references ibid., 314–15, 333, 366, 404.

169. References to substantiate these disproofs are found scattered through the last two-thirds of Hutton, *Blood and Mistletoe*.

170. Chronicled in John Michell, *A Little History of Astro-Archaeology*, London, Thames and Hudson, 1977, 45–7.

171. H. Boyle Somerville, 'Orientation in Prehistoric Monuments in the British Isles', *Archaeologia*, 73 (1924), 193–224 (quotation on p. 193); and 'Orientation', *Antiquity*, 1 (1927), 31–41.

172. Notably Alexander Thom, of whom much more is about to be said, and C. A. ('Peter') Newham.

173. The most celebrated of his early publications had the same title as the book, and appeared in *Nature*, 200 (1963), 306–8. The book was first published in New York by Doubleday: a hardback edition followed in England in 1966 and a Fontana paperback in 1970.

174. F. Hoyle, 'Stonehenge', *Nature*, 211 (1966), 454–6; and 'Speculations on Stonehenge', *Antiquity*, 40 (1966), 262–76.

175. J. C. Atkinson, 'Moonshine on Stonehenge', *Antiquity*, 40 (1966), 212–16; and 'Hoyle on Stonehenge', *Antiquity*, 41 (1967), 92–5; see also Jacquetta Hawkes, 'God in the Machine', *Antiquity*, 41 (1967), 174–80.

176. Biographical sketches of Thom, with a bibliography of his works, are provided by his son Archie Thom, 'A Personal Note about my Late Father', in C. L. N. Ruggles (ed.), *Records in Stone*, Cambridge, Cambridge University Press, 1988, 3–13; and Hans Metz, 'A Personal Appreciation of Professor Alexander Thom', in the same volume, pp. 14–30. Archie Thom later published a biography, *Walking in All of the Squares* (Argyll Publishing, 1995), and there are further valuable details in Robin Heath, *Alexander Thom*, St Domaels, Bluestone, 2007, 1–24.

177. The best-known of these were *Megalithic Sites in Britain*, Oxford, Oxford University Press, 1967; *Megalithic Lunar Observatories*, Oxford, Oxford University Press, 1971; and (with Archibald S. Thom), *Megalithic Remains in Britain and Brittany*, Oxford, Oxford University Press, 1978. Hawkins had cited him in *Stonehenge Decoded*, New York, Doubleday, 1965, 151–8.

178. E.g. Michell, *The View over Atlantis*, passim; Screeton, *Quicksilver Heritage*, 22–6; Hitching, *Earth Magic*, 1–24; Pennick, *The Ancient Science of Geomancy*, 31–4.

179. Ronald Hutton, 'Modern Pagan Festivals', *Folklore*, 119 (2008), 251–73.

180. J. N. Lockyer, *Stonehenge and Other British Stone Monuments Astronomically Considered*, London, 1906, passim. I have talked extensively about the adoption of the Wiccan calendar with Fred Lamond, an eyewitness of the process.

181. Thom, *Megalithic Lunar Observatories*, 9.

182. Richard Atkinson, 'Megalithic Astronomy', *Journal of the History of Astronomy*, 6 (1975), 51.

183. Michell, *A Little History of Astro-Archaeology*, 85.

184. Alexander Thom, Archibald S. Thom and Aubrey Burl, *Megalithic Rings*, Oxford, British Archaeological Reports, 1980.

185. Aubrey Burl, 'Science or Symbolism', *Antiquity*, 54 (1980), 191–200; C. L. N. Ruggles and A. W. R. Whittle (eds), *Astronomy and Society in Britain during the Period 4000–1500 BC*, Oxford, British Archaeological Reports, 1981; Douglas C. Heggie, *Megalithic Science*, London, Thames and Hudson, 1981; Douglas C. Heggie (ed.), *Archaeoastronomy in the Old World*, Cambridge, Cambridge University Press, 1982; C. L. N. Ruggles, *Megalithic Astronomy*, Oxford, British Archaeological Reports, 1984; John Barnatt and Gordon Moir, 'Stone Circles and Megalithic Mathematics', *Proceedings of the Prehistoric Society*, 50 (1984), 197–216.

186. Clive Ruggles, 'The Stone Alignments of Argyll and Mull', in Ruggles (ed.), *Records of Stone*, 232–50.

187. Especially his large book *Astronomy in Prehistoric Britain and Ireland*, London, Yale University Press, 1999.

188. John North, *Stonehenge*, London, HarperCollins, 1996.

189. Clive Ruggles, 'Astronomy and Stonehenge', in Barry Cunliffe and Colin Renfrew (eds), *Science and Stonehenge*, Oxford, Oxford University Press, 1997, 203–29.

190. Julian Richards, *Stonehenge: The Story So Far*, London, English Heritage, 2007, 217–19.

191. Julian Richards, *Stonehenge*, London, English Heritage, 2005, 17.

192. Clive Ruggles *et al.*, *Stonehenge and Ancient Astronomy*, London, Royal Astronomical Society, 2009.

193. Ibid., 6–11; Clive Ruggles, 'Astronomy, Cosmology, Monuments and the Landscape in Prehistoric Ireland', in Clive Ruggles *et al.* (eds), *Astronomy, Cosmology and Landscape*, Bognor Regis, Ocarina, 2001, 51–2.

194. Ruggles, 'Astronomy, Cosmology, Monuments'.

195. Ruggles, *Astronomy in Prehistoric Britain*, 128. In justice to him, even the interpreters of the site failed to find any astronomical correlations for eleven of the twenty-four posts, including the one in the centre of the entrance, and those suggested for the others covered such a range that the possibility of coincidence was high: Fachtna McAvoy, 'The Development of a Neolithic Monument Complex at Godmanchester', in Mike Dawson (ed.), *Prehistoric, Roman and Post-Roman Landscapes of the Great Ouse Valley*, London, Council for British Archaeology, 2000, 51–6.

196. E.g. A. S. Thom *et al.*, 'The Bush Barrow Gold Lozenge', *Antiquity*, 62 (1988), 108–19; and Euan McKie, 'Maeshowe and the Winter Solstice', *Antiquity*, 74 (2000), 62–74; and 'The Structure and Skills of British Neolithic Society', *Antiquity*, 76 (2002), 666–8; John Oswin, 'Stones and Solstices on Scotland's Remotest Island', *Current Archaeology*, 227 (2009), 30–7.

197. The main example is Lionel Sims, author of, among other essays, 'The Solarization of the Moon', *Cambridge Archaeological Journal*, 16 (2006), 191–207; 'Entering, and Returning, from the Underworld', *Journal of the Royal Anthropological Society*, 15 (2009), 386–409; and 'Coves, Cosmology and Cultural Astronomy', in Nicholas Campion (ed.), *Cosmologies*, Lampeter, Sophia Centre Press, 2010, 4–28.

198. Robin Heath, *Sun, Moon and Stonehenge*, Cardigan, Bluestone, 1998; *Sun, Moon and Earth*, Presteigne, Wooden Books, 1999; *Stonehenge*, Presteigne, Wooden Books, 2002; *The Moon and Ancient Calendars*, St Dogmaels, Bluestone, 2009; *www.skyscript.co.uk*.

199. Heath, *Sun, Moon and Stonehenge*, xiii.

200. Ibid., 138.

201. Heath, *Alexander Thom*. My efforts to obtain this text illustrate well the difficulties experienced by mainstream scholars in trying to engage with such alternative viewpoints. It did not exist in the nearest copyright library to me, at Oxford, and when I put in an order through the inter-library loan system, I was informed that no copy was held in any institution in the nation which was able to lend it. A confined copy existed in the British Library in London, and there was one in a branch library at the opposite end of Somerset; but the easiest way to obtain the book was to locate and purchase it on the internet. I found it worth the effort and expense, but many mainstream scholars might not think so, given the peripheral status which the subject is now commonly perceived to have. There is also a further disincentive to them to take any notice of counter-cultural writers: that to do so is to be attacked by such writers in a direct and personal fashion, while to ignore them is only to invite denunciation in general and anonymous terms.

202. *Woodhenge Embryology*, privately published, 2008; *Alexander Thom's Megalithic Yard*, privately published, 2009; *www.definitivestonehenge.com*. In this case there was no problem in obtaining his works, because he sent copies to various scholars, including me, and I am accordingly grateful to him.

203. Anthony Murphy and Richard Moore, *Island of the Setting Sun*, Dublin, Liffey Press, 2006. This would have passed me by completely had I not met Mr Murphy at a conference of earth mysteries researchers at which we were both invited to speak. I found him as charming in person as in print.

204. It may be noted that relations between mainstream and unorthodox ideas about prehistory have been just as strained in Ireland as in Britain: see the bitter remarks of the archaeologist Muirus O'Sullivan, *Megalithic Art in Ireland*, Dublin, Town House and Country House, 1993, 26.

205. Nicholas R. Mann, *Avebury Cosmos*, Winchester, O-Books, 2011. I was sent this title by the author, and thank him for it.

206. Pryor, *Britain BC*, 224.

207. Timothy Darvill, 'Billtown, Isle of Man', *Current Archaeology*, 150 (1996), 233.

208. Christopher Tilley, 'The Power of Rocks', *World Archaeology*, 28 (1996), 161–76.

209. Frances Lynch, 'Colour in Prehistoric Architecture', in Alex Gibson and Derek Simpson (eds), *Prehistoric Ritual and Religion*, Stroud, Sutton, 1998, 62–7; David Trevarthen, 'Illuminating the Monuments', *Cambridge Archaeological Journal*, 10 (2000), 295–315.

210. Vicki Cummings, 'Experiencing Texture and Transformation in the British Neolithic', *Oxford Journal of Archaeology*, 21 (2002), 249–61.

211. Aaron Watson and David Keating, 'The Architecture of Sound in Neolithic Orkney', in Ritchie (ed.), *Neolithic Orkney*, 259–63; and *www.monumental.uk.com/site/research*, accessed 25 November 2010. See also Tom Graves and Liz Poraj-Wilczynnska, ' "Spirit of Place" as Process', *Time and Mind*, 2 (2009), 153–66.

212. Joshua Pollard, 'Some Notes on an Acoustic Archaeology', in Stephen Banfield (ed.), *The Sounds of Stonehenge* Oxford, British Archaeological Reports, 2009, 1–3.

213. Timothy Darvill, 'White on Blonde: Quartz Pebbles and the Use of Quartz at Neolithic Monuments in the Isle of Man and Beyond', in Andrew Jones and Gavin MacGregor (eds), *Colouring the Past*, Oxford, Berg, 2002, 73–91.

214. Ffion Reynolds, 'Regenerating Substances', *Time and Mind*, 2 (2009), 153–66.

215. Vicki Cummings, *A View from the West: The Neolithic of the Irish Sea Zone*, Oxford, Oxbow, 2009, 110–14.

216. Andrew Sherratt, 'Sacred and Profane Substances', in Paul Garwood *et al.* (eds), *Sacred and Profane*, Oxford, Oxford University Committee for Archaeology, 1991, 50–64; Devereux, *The Long Trip*.

217. Woodward, *British Barrows*, 113–14.

218. D. J. Long *et al.*, 'The Use of Henbane (Hyoscyamus niger L.) as a Hallucinogen at Neolithic "Ritual" Sites', *Antiquity*, 74 (2000), 49–53.

219. For the importance of this in human societies across the world, see Patrick E. McGovern, *Uncorking the Past*, Berkeley, University of California Press, 2009.

220. Libations feature constantly in accounts of the European paganisms best attested from contemporary sources, those of Greece and Rome.

221. E.g. Christopher Chippindale *et al.*, *Who Owns Stonehenge?*, London, Batsford, 1990; Barbara Bender *et al.*, *Stonehenge: Making Space*, Oxford, Berg, 1998; Timothy Darvill *et al.*, *The Cerne Giant*, Oxford, Oxbow, 1999, 125–60; Robert Wallis and Kenneth Lymer (eds), *A Permeability of Boundaries?*, Oxford, British Archaeological Reports, 2001.

222. Mainly Robert Wallis and Jenny Blain: Robert Wallis, *Shamans and Neo-Shamans*, London, Routledge, 2003; Jenny Blain and Robert Wallis, *Sacred Sites: Contested Rites/Rights*, Brighton, Sussex Academic Press, 2007; and many essays written jointly or separately.

223. Bradley, *Prehistory of Britain and Ireland*, 178–81. Joshua Pollard's dates are almost the same: 2200–1500, 1500–1200 and 1200–800 BC respectively, which preserves the watershed at 1500: Pollard, 'The Construction of Prehistoric Britain', 1–17. Mike Parker Pearson, 'The Earlier Bronze Age', divides the Bronze Age simply into Early (2500–1400) and Late (1400–750), but that amounts to virtually the same argument.

224. Bradley, *Prehistory of Britain and Ireland*, 187–202; Ritchie, *Prehistoric Orkney*, 87–9; Gale, *Prehistoric Dorset*, 83–93; David Field, 'Place and Memory in Bronze Age Wessex', in Joanna Brück (ed.), *Bronze Age Landscapes*, Oxford, Oxbow, 2001, 57–64; Darvill, *Prehistoric Britain*, 210–24; plus many of the works on ceremonial monuments cited earlier in this chapter.

225. Hutton, *Pagan Religions*, 135–7, which cites all sources including Bradley.

226. Ibid., 134; Darvill, *Prehistoric Britain*, 238–9; Derek Yalden, *The History of British Mammals*, London, Academic Press, 1999, 89–116.

227. This argument is made with special clarity by Pryor, *Britain BC*, 262.

228. Rachel Pope, 'Roundhouses', *Current Archaeology*, 222 (2008), 14–21.

229. Barbara Bender *et al.*, *Stone Worlds*, Walnut Creek, CA, Left Coast Press, 2007, 127–86.

230. Bradley, *Prehistory of Britain and Ireland*, 187–202.

4 Late Prehistory: Earthworks, Pits and Bones

1. Alasdair Whittle, Frances Healey and Alex Bayliss, 'The Domestication of Britain', *British Archaeology*, 119 (2011), 21.

2. Though Sir Barry Cunliffe reminds me that the lost book of the Greek traveller Pytheas, who long predated Caesar, and of which fragments are preserved in the works of later ancient authors, contained geographical information on Britain: pers. comm., 1 February 2012.

3. Richard Bradley, *The Prehistory of Britain and Ireland*, Cambridge, Cambridge University Press, 2007, 276.

4. A point emphasized by Barbara S. Ottaway and Ben Roberts, 'The Emergence of Metalworking', in Andrew Jones (ed.), *Prehistoric Europe*, Chichester, Wiley, 2008, 193–225.

5. The dates are recorded as standard by Joshua Pollard, 'The Construction of Prehistoric Britain', in Joshua Pollard (ed.), *Prehistoric Britain*, Oxford, Blackwell, 2008, 1–17.

6. Timothy Champion, 'The Later Bronze Age', in John Hunter and Ian Ralston (eds), *The Archaeology of Britain*, London, Routledge, 2nd edition, 2009, 127.

7. Barry Cunliffe, *Europe between the Oceans*, London, Yale University Press, 2008, 230–4, 254–69.

8. Jasper Copping, 'Bronze Age Wreck Yields its Secrets', *Sunday Telegraph*, 14 February 2010, 10.

9. Francis Pryor, *Britain BC*, London, HarperCollins, 2003, 300.

10. Bradley, *Prehistory of Britain and Ireland*, 202–22; Champion, 'The Later Bronze Age', 131–7; Timothy Darvill, *Prehistoric Britain*, London, Routledge, 2nd edition, 2010, 225–39; David Miles, *The Tribes of Britain*, London, Weidenfeld & Nicolson, 2005, 99–100.

11. Pryor, *Britain BC*, 313; Darvill, *Prehistoric Britain*, 240–3; Champion, 'The Later Bronze Age', 144–5.
12. John Gale, *Prehistoric Dorset*, Stroud, Tempus, 2003, 98; Stuart Needham, '800 BC, The Great Divide', in Colin Haselgrove and Rachel Pope (eds), *The Earlier Iron Age in Britain and the Near Continent*, Oxford, Oxbow, 2007, 39–63.
13. Mark Collard *et al.*, 'Ironworking in the Bronze Age?', *Proceedings of the Prehistoric Society*, 72 (2006), 367–421; Stuart Needham, 'Chronology and Periodisation in the British Bronze Age', *Acta Archaeologia*, 67 (1996), 137; W. H. Manning, 'Ironwork Hoards in Iron Age and Roman Britain', *Britannia*, 3 (1972), 224–50.
14. Bradley, *Prehistory of Britain and Ireland*, 230–5; Cunliffe, *Europe between the Oceans*, 299–316; Needham, '800 BC'; Colin Haselgrove and Rachel Pope, 'Characterising the Earlier Iron Age', in Haselgrove and Pope (ed.), *The Earlier Iron Age*, 1–23.
15. Darvill, *Prehistoric Britain*, 244–6; Martin Bell, 'Environment in the First Millennium BC', in T. C. Champion and J. R. Collis (eds), *The Iron Age in Britain and Ireland*, Sheffield, J. R. Collis, 1996, 5–16; Colin Haselgrove, 'The Iron Age', in Hunter and Ralston (eds), *Archaeology of Britain*, 149–74.
16. Derek Yalden, *The History of British Mammals*, London, Academic Press, 1999, 122–8.
17. Haselgrove, 'The Iron Age'.
18. Richard Bradley and David Yates, 'After "Celtic" Fields', in Haselgrove and Pope (eds), *The Earlier Iron Age*, 94–102; Colin Haselgrove, 'Social Organisation in Iron Age Wessex', in A. P. Fitzpatrick and Elaine L. Morris (eds), *The Iron Age in Wessex*, Salisbury, Trust for Wessex Archaeology, 1994, 1–3; Pryor, *Britain BC*, 341.
19. Darvill, *Prehistoric Britain*, 246–77.
20. Pollard, 'Construction of Prehistoric Britain'; Gale, *Prehistoric Dorset*, 107; Bradley, *Prehistory of Britain and Ireland*, 236–40.
21. Bradley, *Prehistory of Britain and Ireland*, 234–5; Haselgrove, 'The Iron Age', 150.
22. Haselgrove, 'The Iron Age', 168–70; Darvill, *Prehistoric Britain*, 302–25; J. D. Hill, 'The Dynamics of Social Change in Later Iron Age Eastern and South-Eastern England *c.* 300 BC–AD 43', in Colin Haselgrove and Tom Moore (eds), *The Later Iron Age in Britain and Beyond*, Oxford, Oxbow, 2007, 16–40.
23. For this see Ronald Hutton, *Blood and Mistletoe: The History of the Druids in Britain*, London, Yale University Press, 2009, 301–3, 337–41.
24. Jacquetta Hawkes, *Early Britain*, London, 1945, 25–31.
25. This process of composition is extensively analysed and deconstructed in several of the revisionist studies cited below.
26. As such, it achieved its last great flowering (to date), in the many works of Miranda Green (subsequently Aldhouse-Green), published in the 1980s and early 1990s.
27. Nick Merriman, 'Value and Motivation in Prehistory', in Ian Hodder (ed.), *The Archaeology of Contextual Meanings*, Cambridge, Cambridge University Press, 1987, 111–16; J. D. Hill, 'Rethinking the Iron Age', *Scottish Archaeological Review*, 6 (1989), 16–24.
28. John Collis, 'The Origin and Spread of the Celts', *Studia Celtica*, 30 (1996), 17–34; 'Celtic Myths', *Antiquity*, 71 (1997), 195–201; *The Celts*, Stroud, Tempus, 2003; 'The Celts as Grand Narratives', in Andrew Jones (ed.), *Prehistoric Europe*, Chichester, Wiley, 2008, 35–53 and ' "Reconstructing Iron Age Society" Revisited', in Tom Moore and Xosé-Lois Armada (eds), *Atlantic Europe in the First Millennium BC*, Oxford, Oxford University Press, 2011, 223–41; Simon James, 'Celts, Politics and Motivation in Archaeology', *Antiquity*, 72 (1998), 200–9; and *The Atlantic Celts*, London, British Museum, 1999.
29. Ruth and Vincent Megaw, 'Ancient Celts and Modern Ethnicity', *Antiquity*, 70 (1996), 175–81; 'Do the Ancient Celts Still Live?', *Studia Celtica*, 31 (1997), 107–24; 'The Mechanism of (Celtic) Dreams', *Antiquity*, 72 (1998), 432–5; 'Review of John Collis, *The Celts*', *Antiquity*, 78 (2004), 733–5.
30. E.g. Gillian Carr and Simon Stoddart, 'Whither Celts?', in Carr and Stoddart (eds), *The Celts*, Stroud, Tempus, 2002), 327–31; Miles Russell, *Prehistoric Sussex*, Stroud, Tempus, 2002, 111; Edward James, *Britain in the First Millennium*, London, Arnold, 2001, 21–2; Ian Brown, *Discovering a Welsh Landscape*, Macclesfield, Windgather, 2004, 59–64; Pryor, *Britain BC*, 465; D. W. Harding, *The Iron Age in Northern Britain*, London, Routledge, 2004, 18–20; Richard Bradley, *Image and Audience*, Oxford, Oxford University Press, 2009, 13; Andrew P.

Fitzpatrick, '"Celtic" Iron Age Europe', in Paul Graves-Brown *et al.* (eds), *Cultural Identity and Archaeology*, London, Routledge, 1996, 238–51. The last of these should be termed not so much a reaction to the revisionist case as part of it, coming as it did near the beginning of the debate.

31. Ellen C. Røyrvik, 'Western Celts?', in Barry Cunliffe and John T. Koch (eds), *Celtic from the West*, Oxford, Oxbow, 2010, 83–106; Brian P. McEvoy and Daniel G. Bradley, 'Irish Genetics and Celts', ibid., 107–20; Stephen Oppenheimer, 'A Reanalysis of Multiple Prehistoric Immigrations to Britain and Ireland Aimed at Identifying the Celtic Contributions', ibid., 121–35.

32. The German was Bernhard Maier, *The Celts*, Edinburgh, Edinburgh University Press, 2003 (the German edition appeared in 2000). In Ireland, for example, an archaeologist, John Waddell, *The Prehistoric Archaeology of Ireland*, Galway, Galway University Press, 1998, 288–9, accepted revisionism, but four years later a distinguished expert in folklore and medieval literature, Dáithí Ó hÓgáin, *The Celts*, Wilton, Co. Cork, 2002, could restate the traditional picture as if it had never been questioned.

33. Patrick Sims-Williams, 'Celtomania and Celtoscepticism', *Cambrian Medieval Celtic Studies*, 36 (1998), 1–35.

34. Barry Cunliffe, *Facing the Ocean*, Oxford, Oxford University Press, 2001, 294–6; *The Celts*, Oxford, Oxford University Press, 2003; *Europe between the Oceans*, 354–62; 'A Race Apart: Insularity and Connectivity', *Proceedings of the Prehistoric Society*, 75 (2009), 55–64; John T. Koch, 'Mapping Celticity, Mapping Celticization', in Chris Gosden *et al.* (eds), *Communities and Connections*, Oxford, Oxford University Press, 2007, 263–86; Barry Cunliffe and John T. Koch, 'Introduction', in Cunliffe and Koch (eds), *Celtic from the West*, 1–10; quotation on p. 6.

35. At the time of writing, responses are only just beginning, and it may be noted that in their own volume one of the contributors took issue with them (but also with the revisionists): Raimund Karl, 'The Celts from Everywhere and Nowhere', in Cunliffe and Koch (eds), *Celtic from the West*, 39–63. It should perhaps be emphasized that no intervention in this debate is made here, nor any judgement pronounced upon it other than of interest.

36. Grahame Clark 'The Invasion Hypothesis in British Prehistory', *Antiquity*, 40 (1966), 172–89; quotation on p. 186. The most recent citation of its importance seems to have been in Cunliffe, 'A Race Apart', 55.

37. Julius Caesar, *De bello gallico*, V.12.

38. Haselgrove, 'The Iron Age', 169–71.

39. This story is the major theme of Ronald Hutton, *The Druids*, Hambledon, Continuum, 2007, and *Blood and Mistletoe*.

40. For an analysis of each, see Hutton, *Blood and Mistletoe*, 1–22.

41. Tacitus, *Annals*, XIV. 28–30.

42. Hutton, *The Druids*, 2–6; and *Blood and Mistletoe*, 12–14.

43. Hutton, *Blood and Mistletoe*, 30–48.

44. Ibid., 23–30.

45. Philip Crummy *et al.*, *Stanway*, London, Society for the Promotion of Roman Studies, 250, 444–5. (Though it may be noted that the different contributors promoted the Druidic interpretation with varying degrees of enthusiasm, it was given the most attention.) When the report was summarized in the magazine *British Archaeology* in the March–April issue of 2008 (pp. 28–33), this reading of the burial was also given most prominence, provoking the cover headline 'The Druid Who Saw The Romans Invade UK'.

46. E.g. Sean B. Dunham, 'Caesar's Perception of Gallic Social Structures', in Bettina Arnold and D. Blair Gibson (eds), *Celtic Chiefdom, Celtic State*, Cambridge, Cambridge University Press, 1995, 114–15; Maier, *The Celts*, 65–6; Jane Webster, 'The Just War', in *TRAC 94: Proceedings of the Fourth Annual Theoretical Roman Archaeology Conference*, Oxford, Oxbow, 1994, 6–7; E. W. Black, 'The First-Century Historians of Roman Britain', *Oxford Archaeological Journal*, 20 (2001), 415–28; David Braund, *Ruling Roman Britain*, London, Routledge, 1996, passim; Holly Haynes, *The History of Make-Believe*, Berkeley, University of California Press, 2003; Mary Beagon, *Roman Nature: The Thought of Pliny the Elder*, Oxford, Oxford University Press, 1992; and see the analyses in Hutton, *Blood and Mistletoe*, 1–22.

47. Its inception is not likely to be furthered by a tendency among a few authors to misunderstand my own views on the matter. Nick Thorpe, in a review of Miranda Aldhouse-Green, *Caesar's Druids*, London, Yale University Press, 2010, published in *British Archaeology*, 114 (2010), 54, declares that I have suggested that 'we should scrap the Druids from Iron Age archaeology'. On p. 266 of the book under review by him, Miranda Aldhouse-Green states that I view Druids as 'creations of fictive writing' and 'fabrication'. Neither statement can be found among the hundreds of thousands of words that I have published on the subject: rather, I have always written, as here, that archaeologists should reach their own conclusions on the matter, taking more fully into account the problems now perceived in the details of how ancient authors portrayed Druids. Dr Thorpe provided no source for his assertion. Professor Aldhouse-Green footnoted her statement to an oral presentation that I gave at a Prehistoric Society event in 2008, which she plainly misheard. She goes on (p. 299) to liken an attempt to exclude Druids from a discussion of the Iron Age to Holocaust denial: a demonstration of how emotive the subject has become to some traditionally minded scholars.

48. These would include most of those whose work is cited in reference to forthcoming sections of this chapter.

49. Barry Cunliffe, *Druids: A Very Short Introduction*, Oxford, Oxford University Press, 2010, 50–84.

50. Aldhouse-Green, *Caesar's Druids*.

51. This is argued, with full source-references, in Hutton, *Blood and Mistletoe*, 32–4.

52. See Ronald Hutton, *Shamans*, London, Hambledon and London, 2001. Closer to home, the collection of essays edited by Mary Beard and John North, *Pagan Priests*, London, Duckworth, 1990, repeatedly makes the point that modern historians have imposed the blanket term 'priest' on a very wide range of religious functionaries in the ancient Near East and Mediterranean basin, in a manner which conceals the great variety and difference of function which these people fulfilled.

53. Hutton, *Blood and Mistletoe*, 32–8.

54. Andrew Fitzpatrick, 'Druids: Towards an Archaeology', in Gosden *et al.* (eds), *Communities and Connections*, 302–6.

55. This is the main theme of Hutton, *The Druids*, and *Blood and Mistletoe*.

56. Hutton, *Blood and Mistletoe*, is designed to prove this point, and pp. 22–30 are devoted to its manifestation among academic authors in the late twentieth century.

57. The derivation of the name is discussed in Ian Brown, *Beacons in the Landscape*, Oxford, Oxbow, 2009, 2–13.

58. Ibid.; A. H. A. Hogg, *British Hill Forts: An Index*, Oxford, Hillfort Study Group, 1979.

59. The most recent survey volume published by Sir Barry is *Danebury Hillfort*, Stroud, Tempus, 2003. The opinion regarding the pre-eminence of the project was suggested by John Collis, in a review of Sir Barry's first such volume, in the *Proceedings of the Prehistory Society*, 51 (1985), 348–9.

60. Niall M. Sharples, *English Heritage Book of Maiden Castle*, London, Batsford, 1991, 70–131; Francis Pryor, *Britain AD*, London, HarperCollins, 2004, 63; Bradley, *The Prehistory of Britain and Ireland*, 202–22, 240–52; Barry Cunliffe, 'Understanding Hillforts', in Andrew Payne (ed.), *The Wessex Hillforts Project*, London, English Heritage, 2006, 151–62.

61. Collis, review of Cunliffe, *Danebury*; Mark Bowden and Dave McOmish, 'The Required Barrier', *Scottish Archaeological Review*, 4 (1987), 84–97; and 'Little Boxes: More about Hillforts', ibid., 6 (1989), 12–16; Richard Hingley, 'Boundaries Surrounding Iron Age and Romano-British Settlements', ibid., 7 (1990), 96–103; J. D. Hill, 'How Should We Understand Iron Age Societies and Hillforts?' in J. D. Hill and C. G. Cumberpatch (eds), *Different Iron Ages*, Oxford, British Archaeological Reports, 1995, 45–60; Miles Russell, *Prehistoric Sussex*, Stroud, Tempus, 2002, 115–24.

62. Cunliffe, *Facing the Ocean*, 350.

63. John Collis, 'Hill-forts, Enclosures and Boundaries', in Chapman and Collis (eds), *The Iron Age in Britain and Ireland*, 87–94; J. D. Hill, 'Hill-forts and the Iron Age of Wessex', ibid., 95–116; Gale, *Prehistoric Dorset*, 108–19; David McOmish *et al.*, *The Field Archaeology of the Salisbury Plain Training Area*, Swindon, English Heritage, 2002, 155; Harding, *The Iron Age in Northern Britain*, 90–3; Paul Frodsham and Colm O'Brien (eds), *Yeavering*, Stroud,

Tempus, 2005, 42; Barry Cunliffe 'Understanding Hillforts'; Robert Van de Noort and Henry Chapman, 'Excavating Sutton Common', *British Archaeology*, 96 (2007), 35–9; Bradley, *Prehistory of Britain and Ireland*, 250–2; Gary Lock, 'Wessex Hillforts after Danebury', in Gosden *et al.* (eds), *Communities and Connections*, 341–55; Ian Armit, 'Hillforts at War', *Proceedings of the Prehistoric Society*, 73 (2007), 25–37; Darvill, *Prehistoric Britain*, 244–71; Brown, *Beacons in the Landscape*, 183–237.

64. Brown, *Beacons in the Landscape*, 214–23.

65. Martin Jones, 'A Feast of Beltain?', in Gosden *et al.* (ed.), *Communities and Connections*, 142–53.

66. Hill, 'How Should We Understand Iron Age Societies and Hillforts?'.

67. Niall Sharples, *Social Relations in Later Prehistory*, Oxford, Oxford University Press, 2010.

68. Richard Bradley, *The Passage of Arms*, Cambridge, Cambridge University Press, 1990; Christopher J. Scurfield, 'Bronze Age Metalwork from the River Trent in Nottinghamshire', *Transactions of the Thoroton Society of Nottinghamshire*, 101 (1997), 29–57; Bryan Walters, *The Archaeology of Ancient Dean and the Wye Valley*, Cheltenham, Thornhill, 1992, 42–3; G. A. Wait, *Ritual and Religion in Iron Age Britain*, Oxford, British Archaeological Reports, 1985, 15–50; Tim Mallin, 'Place and Space in the Cambridgeshire Bronze Age', in Joanna Brück (ed.), *Bronze Age Landscapes*, Oxford, Oxbow, 2001, 9–22; David T. Yates, 'Bronze Age Field Systems in the Thames Valley', *Oxford Journal of Archaeology*, 18 (1999), 157–70; and 'Bronze Age Agricultural Intensification in the Thames Valley and Estuary', in Brück (ed.), *Bronze Age Landscapes*, 65–82; David Yates and Richard Bradley, 'Still Water, Hidden Depths', *Antiquity*, 324 (2010), 405–15.

69. Cyril Fox, *A Find of the Early Iron Age from Llyn Cerrig Bach, Anglesey*, Cardiff, 1945; Philip Macdonald, *Llyn Cerrig Bach*, Cardiff, University of Wales Press, 2007. The story of how the hoard was found is well retold in Chris Catling, 'The Riddle of the Lake', *Current Archaeology*, 273 (2012), 26–33.

70. Francis Pryor, *English Heritage Book of Flag Fen*, London, Batsford, 1991; Richard Bradley, *An Archaeology of Natural Places*, London, Routledge, 2000, 51–3; Pryor, *Britain BC*, 275.

71. Colin Pendleton, 'Firstly, Let's Get Rid of Ritual', in Brück (ed.), *Bronze Age Landscapes*, 170–8.

72. Richard Bradley, 'The Interpretation of Later Bronze Age Metalwork from British Rivers', *International Journal of Nautical Archaeology*, 8 (1979), 3–6; Margaret Ehrenburg, 'The Occurrence of Bronze Age Metalwork in the Thames', *Transactions of the London and Middlesex Archaeological Society*, 31 (1980), 1–15; ; Richard Bradley and Ken Gordon, 'Human Skulls from the River Thames', *Antiquity*, 62 (1988), 503–9; Bradley, *Image and Audience*, 20.

73. This idea was proposed by Colin Burgess in the mid 1970s: 'The Bronze Age', in Colin Renfrew (ed.), *British Prehistory*, London, Duckworth, 1974, 195–7, 311.

74. Strabo, *Geographia*, IV.1.13.

75. This explanation is suggested in Scurfield, 'Bronze Age Metalwork from the River Trent', along with that of the deposition of goods to accompany burials in water.

76. Jill York, 'The Life Cycle of Bronze Age Metalwork from the Thames', *Oxford Journal of Archaeology* 21 (2002), 77–92, embraces most of the explanations provided above, and a further one: that shining bronze objects sinking into water may have symbolized the setting sun.

77. Frances Lynch *et al.*, *Prehistoric Wales*, Stroud, Sutton, 2000, 183–4.

78. Pryor, *Britain BC*, 275.

79. Ibid., 287.

80. Richard Bradley, *Ritual and Domestic Life in Prehistoric Europe*, London, Routledge, 2005, 145–64.

81. Richard Hingley, 'Iron, Ironworking and Regeneration', in Adam Gwilt and Colin Haselgrove (eds), *Reconstructing Iron Age Societies*, Oxford, Oxbow, 1997, 9–18.

82. Pryor, *Britain BC*, 264, 287.

83. David Yates and Richard Bradley, 'The Siting of Metalwork Hoards in the Bronze Age of South-East England', *Antiquaries' Journal*, 90 (2010), 41–72.

84. Fraser Hunter, 'Iron Age Hoarding in Scotland and Northern England', in Gwilt and Haselgrove (eds), *Reconstructing Iron Age Societies*, 108–33.

85. This as yet unpublished excavation by Steven Birch is summarized in Aldhouse-Green, *Caesar's Druids*, 199: the discovery of the lyre bridge was announced in *Salon* (27 May 2012), n.p.

86. Brown, *Beacons in the Landscape*, 140–4; James Morris, 'Associated Bone Groups', in Oliver Davis *et al.* (eds), *Changing Perspectives on the First Millennium BC*, Oxford, Oxbow, 2008, 83–98.

87. Barry Cunliffe, 'Pits, Preconceptions and Preoccupations in the British Iron Age', *Oxford Journal of Archaeology*, 11 (1992), 69–85; Brown, *Beacons in the Landscape*, 145–8.

88. D. Searjeantson and J. Morris, 'Ravens and Crows in Iron Age and Roman Britain', *Oxford Journal of Archaeology*, 30 (2011), 85–107.

89. Brown, *Beacons in the Landscape*, 145–8.

90. David McOmish. 'East Chisenbury: Ritual and Rubbish at the British Bronze Age–Iron Age Transition', *Antiquity*, 70 (1996), 68–76.

91. J. D. Hill, *Ritual and Rubbish in the Iron Age of Wessex*, Oxford, British Archaeological Reports, 1995: quotation on p. 126.

92. Hill, 'Hill-forts and the Iron Age of Wessex', 109–12.

93. Richard Hingley, 'The Deposition of Iron Objects in Britain during the Later Prehistoric and Roman Periods', *Britannia*, 34 (2003), 81–95.

94. Matt Brudenell and Anwen Cooper, 'Post-Middenism', *Oxford Journal of Archaeology*, 27 (2008), 15–36.

95. James Morris, 'Associated Bone Groups', in Oliver Davis *et al.* (eds), *Changing Perspectives on the First Millennium BC*, Oxford, Oxbow, 83–98; the quotation is the subtitle of the essay.

96. This was suggested by Richard Bradley, *The Social Foundations of Prehistoric Britain*, London, Longman, 1984, 163; and still upheld by Pryor, *Britain BC*, 287.

97. The theory was tested experimentally at Moseley Moss, Birmingham, when a particular set of modern Druids, who regularly operated sweat lodges as part of their spiritual practice, conducted one in the presence of archaeologists, and produced a perfect replica of material from a burnt mound: the present author received a personal report on the event by a participant, Mark Graham. For published works which interpret the mounds as the remains of such lodges, or saunas, see Laurence Barfield and Mike Hodder, 'Burnt Mounds as Saunas, and the Prehistory of Bathing', *Antiquity*, 61 (1987), 370–9; and Bradley, *The Prehistory of Britain and Ireland*, 215–16.

98. Mike Pitts, 'Welsh Find May Be Key to Mysterious Mounds', *British Archaeology*, 105 (2009), 6; and 'Burnt Mound Theory Tested to Perfection', ibid., 110 (2010), 6.

99. Brendon Wilkins, 'Past Orders', *Current Archaeology*, 256 (2011), 28–35.

100. Miranda Aldhouse-Green provides a beautiful reconstruction of this scenario: *Caesar's Druids*, 199.

101. Simon Denison, 'Burial in Water "Normal Rite" for 1000 Years', *British Archaeology*, 53 (2000), 4.

102. Bradley, *The Prehistory of Britain and Ireland*, 211–14.

103. Joanna Brück, 'A Place for the Dead', *Proceedings of the Prehistoric Society*, 61 (1995), 245–77; 'Body Metaphors and Technologies of Transformation in the English Middle and Late Bronze Age' in Brück (ed.), *Bronze Age Landscapes*, 149–60; and 'Fragmentation, Personhood and the Social Construction of Technology in Middle and Late Bronze Age Britain', *Cambridge Archaeological Journal*, 16 (2006), 297–315.

104. For this see Brown, *Beacons in the Landscape*, 154–7.

105. Strabo, *Geographia*, IV.4.5.

106. Ian Armit has usefully drawn attention to the possible parallels between the use and burial of bits of human body in Iron Age Britain and the employment of 'medicine bundles' in native America and the employment of human and animal parts as 'muti' magic in modern southern Africa: *Headhunting and the Body in Iron Age Europe*, Cambridge, Cambridge University Press, 2012, 204–21.

107. Mike Parker Pearson *et al.*, 'Evidence for Mummification in Bronze Age Britain', *Antiquity*, 79 (2005), 529–46.

108. Carly Hilts, 'Jigsaw Mummies', *Current Archaeology*, 265 (2012), 42–3.

109. Ian Armit and Victoria Ginn, 'Beyond the Grave', *Proceedings of the Prehistoric Society*, 73 (2007), 75–96; Fiona Tucker and Ian Armit, 'Living with Death in the Iron Age', *British*

Archaeology, 112 (2010), 42–7; Jacqui Mulville *et al.*, 'Quarters, Arcs and Squares', in Jane Downes and Anna Ritchie (eds), *Sea Change: Orkney and Northern Europe in the Later Iron Age 300–800*, Balgavies, Pinkfoot Press, 2003, 20–34.

110. Armit, *Headhunting and the Body*, 120–7.

111. Sharples, *English Heritage Book of Maiden Castle*, 118–19; and *Social Relations in Later Prehistory*, 287–309; Barry Cunliffe and Cynthia Poole, *Danebury: Volume Five*, London, Council for British Archaeology, 1991, 418–25; Ann Woodward, *English Heritage Book of Shrines and Sacrifice*, London, Batsford, 1992, 81–2; Brown, *Beacons in the Landscape*, 145–6, 154–7.

112. Mike Lally, 'Bodies of Difference in Central Southern England', in Oliver Davis *et al.* (eds), *Changing Perspectives on the First Millennium BC*, Oxford, Oxbow, 2006, 119–38; Richard Madgwick, 'Patterns in the Modification of Animal and Human Bones in Iron Age Wessex', ibid., 99–118; Gillian Carr and Christopher Knüsel, 'The Ritual Framework of Excarnation by Exposure as the Mortuary Practice of the Early and Middle Iron Ages of Central Southern Britain', in Gwilt and Haselgrove (eds), *Reconstructing Iron Age Societies*, 167–73.

113. Barry Cunliffe and Cynthia Poole (eds), *The Danebury Environs Porgramme: Volume 2, Part 3*, Oxford, Institute of Archaeology, 2000.

114. Gill Hey *et al.*, 'Iron Age Inhumation Burials at Yarnton, Oxfordshire', *Antiquity*, 73 (1999), 551–62; Barry Cunliffe, *Iron Age Communities in Britain*, London, Routledge, 4th edition, 2005, 552. Sir Barry has suggested to me that some of the tied-up bodies may have been exhibited before eventual burial, after being exposed and dried out, which would make them perfect parallels for the 'mummies' from the Hebrides: pers. comm., 1 February 2012.

115. Rowan Whimster, *Burial Practices in Iron Age Britain*, Oxford, British Archaeological Reports, 1981, 75–105; J. D. Hill, 'A New Cart/Chariot Burial from Wetwang, East Yorkshire', *PAST*, 38 (2001), 2–3; I. M. Stead, *Iron Age Cemeteries in East Yorkshire*, London, English Heritage, 1991; Angela Boyle, 'Riding into History', *British Archaeology*, 76 (2004), 22–7; Andrew Selkirk, 'Chariot Burials', *Current Archaeology*, 200 (2005), 386–9; Harding, *The Iron Age in Northern Britain*, 35–7; Mike Parker Pearson, 'Food, Sex and Death', *Cambridge Archaeological Journal*, 9 (1999), 43–69; Mandy Jay *et al.*, 'Chariot and Context', *Oxford Journal of Archaeology*, 31 (2012), 161–89.

116. Whimster, *Burial Practices*, passim; Sharples, *English Heritage Book of Maiden Castle*, 118–20; Gale, *Prehistoric Dorset*, 133; Darvill, *Prehistoric Britain*, 310–18; A. P. Fitzpatrick *et al.*, *Archaeological Investigations on the Route of the A27 Westhampnett Bypass*, Salisbury, Wessex Archaeology, 1997; Ralph Merrifield, *The Archaeology of Ritual and Magic*, London, Batsford, 1987, 65–6.

117. Miranda Green, *The Gods of the Celts*, Gloucester, Sutton, 1986, 129–30; Philip Crummy, 'Aristocratic Graves at Colchester', *Current Archaeology*, 132 (1993), 492–4.

118. Martin Millett, *The Romanization of Britain*, Cambridge, Cambridge University Press, 1990, 9–39.

119. Harding, *The Iron Age in Northern Britain*, 79–81, 195–6.

120. The discussion that follows is a condensed and amended form of those found in Hutton, *The Druids*, 93–100; and *Blood and Mistletoe*, 17–18, 24–5, 40–1, 413–16.

121. They are discussed in detail in *Blood and Mistletoe*, 1–17.

122. J. Rives, 'Human Sacrifice among Pagans and Christians', *Journal of Roman Studies*, 85 (1995), 64–85.

123. Lautaro Roig Lanzillotta, 'The Early Christians and Human Sacrifice', in Jan N. Bremmer (ed.), *The Strange World of Human Sacrifice*, Louvain, Peeters, 2007, 81–102.

124. Jacqueline Borsje, 'Human Sacrifice in Medieval Irish Literature', ibid., 31–54.

125. This is one of the themes of Hutton, *Blood and Mistletoe*.

126. Perhaps pre-eminently Miranda Aldhouse-Green, 'Humans as Ritual Victims in the Later Prehistory of Western Europe', *Oxford Journal of Archaeology*, 17 (1998), 169–90; and *Dying for the Gods*, Stroud, Tempus, 2001; Hill, *Ritual and Rubbish*, passim; and Sir Barry Cunliffe, in the works cited in n. 129.

127. Previous thoughts of mine on this subject have been summarized in *The Druids*, 130–3, 225; *Blood and Mistletoe*, 27–8; and 'Why Does Lindow Man Matter?', *Time and Mind*, 4 (2011), 135–48. What follows represents a summary and updating.

128. All these analyses and suggestions are found in the report of the team engaged by the British Museum to investigate the body: Ian Stead (ed.), *Lindow Man*, London, British Museum, 1986.

129. E.g. Barry Cunliffe, *Iron Age Communities in Britain*, London, Routledge, 1991, 518; *English Heritage Book of Iron Age Britain*, London, Batsford, 1995, 100; and *The Ancient Celts*, Oxford, Oxford University Press, 1997, 192; Miranda (Aldhouse-) Green, *The Gods of the Celts*, London, Batsford, 1986, 128; *Exploring the World of the Druids*, London, Thames and Hudson, 1997, 53; and *Dying for the Gods*, 196, 201; Merrifield, *The Archaeology of Ritual and Magic*, 24; Jane Webster, 'Sanctuaries and Sacred Places', in Miranda Green (ed.), *The Celtic World*, London, Routledge, 1995, 445–64; Mike Parker Pearson, *The Archaeology of Death and Burial*, Stroud, Tempus, 1999, 70–1; Timothy Taylor, *The Buried Soul*, London, Fourth Estate, 2002, 145–69. I cheerfully own up to incorporating this view of Lindow Man, as the prevailing orthodoxy, in *The Pagan Religions of the Ancient British Isles*, Oxford, Blackwell, 1991, 194.

130. E.g. Beth Coombe Harris, *In the Grip of the Druids*, Southampton, Mayflower, 1999 (see the preface to this reprint of a 1930s evangelical novel); Jonathan Jones, article in the *Guardian*, 21 June 2007, archived at http://www.guardian.co.uk/g2/story/0,2107640,00.html.

131. P. V. Glob, *The Bog People*, Ithaca, NY, Cornell University Press, 1969.

132. The source is Tacitus, *Germania*, 40, the famous passage in which he states that seven peoples in the Jutland Peninsula and adjoining areas around its base worshipped an earth goddess called Nerthus, whose sacred chariot was drawn around the region at festivals and then washed in a lake by slaves who were drowned immediately after. The passage – whatever its truth – does not say that the bodies of the slaves were then deposited in water, whereas there is another section of the same work (117) in which Tacitus says that the Germans in general punished those convicted of what they considered to be deeds of shame (cowardice, laziness and sodomy) by pressing them down into bogs with hurdles. This would make a good fit with the wide distribution of the bog bodies and the violence and apparent contempt with which some were treated; but, again, we have no test of the reliability of his information. Likewise, Adam of Bremen, about a millennium later, describing how a pagan mob in Sweden murdered a Christian missionary for destroying an image of Thor, records how they then mutilated the body and threw it into a bog: *History of the Archbishops of Hamburg-Bremen*, II.62.97. Adam is no more reliable a witness than Tacitus, but the tradition of using wetlands as a repository for hated criminals is worthy of notice as present in both texts.

133. For an extreme sceptical view of the Continental evidence, see C. S. Briggs, 'Did They Fall or Were They Pushed?', in R. C. Turner and R. G. Scaife (eds), *Bog Bodies*, London, British Museum, 1995, 168–82. Hilda Ellis Davidson has agreed with the German scholar Karl Struve that there are no accompanying signs of ritual with the Continental bodies, such as animal bones or fires, which makes the hypothesis of sacrifice less likely and that of execution more so: 'Human Sacrifice in the Late Pagan Period', in M. O. H. Carver (ed.), *The Age of Sutton Hoo*, Woodbridge, Boydell, 1992, 333.

134. This statistic is discussed in R. M. J. Isser, 'Thinking the Unthinkable', in Karen Meadows *et al.* (eds), *TRAC 96*, Oxford, Oxbow, 1997, 91–100.

135. The local archaeologist who was the first expert on the scene of discovery, Rick Turner, recalled later that he reread Glob as soon as he identified the body as probably ancient: 'Finding Lindow Man', *British Archaeology*, 107 (2009), 18–22. Karin Sanders has termed Glob's book 'a sort of archaeo-literature. . .loaded with all the appurtenances. . .that facilitate cross-fertilization between disciplines dedicated to fact. . .and those committed to fiction': *Bodies in the Bog and the Archaeological Imagination*, Chicago, University of Chicago Press, 2009, 20. Her book shows the profound influence exerted by Glob on creative writers, most notably Seamus Heaney, and artists and sculptors.

136. It may be added here that it might also have been a halter by which he was led or pulled to the bog.

137. Robert Connolly, 'Lindow Man', *Anthropology Today*, 1 (1985), 15–17; and 'The Anatomical Description of Lindow Man', in Stead (ed.), *Lindow Man*, 54–62.

138. The texts are summarized in Anne Ross, 'Lindow Man and the Celtic Tradition', in Stead (ed.), *Lindow Man*, 162–9. See Joan Newlon Radner, 'The Significance of the Threefold Death in Celtic Tradition', in Patrick K. Ford (ed.), *Celtic Folklore and Christianity*, Los Angeles, Center for the Study of Comparative Folklore and Mythology, 1983, 180–99.

139. Don Brothwell, *The Bog Man and the Archaeology of People*, London, British Museum, 1986, 96.

140. T. G. Holden, 'The Last Meals of the Lindow Bog Men', and R. G. Scaife, 'Pollen Analysis of the Lindow III Food Residue', in Turner and Scaife (eds), *Bog Bodies*, 76–82, 83–5.

141. J. A. J. Gowlett *et al.*, 'Accelerator Radiocarbon Dating of Ancient Human Remains from Lindow Moss', in Stead (ed.), *Lindow Man*, 22–4; and 'Radiocarbon Accelerator Dating of Ancient Human Remains from Lindow Moss', *Antiquity*, 63 (1989), 71–9; R. L. Otlet *et al.*, 'Report on Radiocarbon Dating of the Lindow Man', in Stead (ed.), *Lindow Man*, 27–30.

142. P. C. Buckland and K. E. Barber, 'Two Views of the Peat Stratigraphy and the Age of the Lindow Bodies'; and R. A. Housley *et al.*, 'Radiocarbon Dating of the Lindow III Bog Body', in Turner and Scaife (eds), *Bog Bodies*, 39–46, 47–62.

143. A. N. Garland, 'Worsley Man, England', in Turner and Scaife (eds), *Bog Bodies*, 104–7.

144. Alison Taylor, 'Burial with the Romans', *British Archaeology*, 69 (2003), 14–19; J. D. Hill, 'Lindow Man's Moustache', *Times Literary Supplement*, 5 March 2004.

145. Darvill, *Prehistoric Britain*, 180; Hilda Ellis Davidson, *The Lost Beliefs of Northern Europe*, London, Routledge, 1993, 98; Briggs, 'Did They Fall or Were They Pushed?', 174–5.

146. *Overkill*, screened on BBC2 on 2 April 1998.

147. I plead guilty to having provoked this, with an article entitled 'How Did Lindow Man Die', published in the *Times Literary Supplement* on 30 January 2004. This drew out J. D. Hill, who was both one of the leading proponents, hitherto, of the interpretation of Iron Age material as evidence for human sacrifice and the curator of the gallery in which Lindow Man was exhibited. His reply, in the same journal on 5 March, made a restatement of the established orthodoxy, to which I replied in turn on 12 March. An article in *The Times* on 22 March quoted Hill as saying that we could never know how Lindow Man had died, which conceded my basic point, but I was misquoted in it as dismissing the interpretation of ritual killing – which I have never done – and calling for the removal of the body from exhibition (a position adopted by a different contributor to the piece), so Dr Hill's statement may have been falsely attributed as well.

148. It included a prominent contribution from J.D. Hill, who now nobly and unequivocally advocated a plurality of interpretation.

149. I was generously invited to deliver the keynote address.

150. Jody Joy, *Lindow Man*, London, British Museum, 2009.

151. Darvill, *Prehistoric Britain*, 324.

152. Bradley, *Ritual and Domestic Life in Prehistoric Europe*, 81–2.

153. Aldhouse-Green, *Caesar's Druids*, 10–11, 72–3; Cunliffe, *Druids*, 36.

154. Aldhouse-Green, *Caesar's Druids*, 73–4, collects the data available by 2009. Eamonn Kelly, Keeper of Antiquities at the National Museum, emphasized the significance of the presence of the bodies close to boundaries, and his interpretation dominated the exhibition, which I visited in 2007. For further information, see Isabella Mulhall, 'The Peat Men from Clonycavan and Oldcroghan', *British Archaeology*, 110 (2010), 34–41.

155. They may also note the apparent paradox that during the sections of this book devoted to the Neolithic, the status of human sacrifice as one plausible interpretation of the data was emphasized in the face of a dominant scholarly tradition which did not do so; whereas when dealing with the Iron Age, the opposite course has been taken. Both approaches are, however, devoted to a consistent end, of opening up as many avenues for the imagination as possible when expert opinion currently inclines to only some.

156. Wait, *Ritual and Religion in Iron Age Britain*, 154–77; Woodward, *The English Heritage Book of Shrines and Sacrifice*, 17, 66; Russell, *Prehistoric Sussex*, 34–8; Frank Hargrave, 'The Hallaton Treasure', *Current Archaeology*, 235 (2009), 36–41; Colin Haselgrove, 'The Iron Age', in Hunter and Ralston (eds), *The Archaeology of Britain*, 160–1.

157. Peter Harbison, *Pre-Christian Ireland*, London, Thames and Hudson, 1988, 155–92; Chris Lynn, 'Navan Fort', *Current Archaeology*, 134 (1993), 44–9; Conor Newman, 'Reflections on the Making of a "Royal" Site in Early Ireland', *World Archaeology*, 30 (1998), 127–41; Edel Bhreathnach (ed.), *The Kingship and Landscape of Tara*, Dublin, Four Courts, 2005; Richard Bradley, *The Past in Prehistoric Societies*, London, Routledge, 2002, 141–6.

158. See the discussion in Hutton, *Blood and Mistletoe*, 24–5, and sources there.

159. Christopher Evans and Mark Knight, 'The "Community of Builders": The Barleycroft Post Alignments', in Brück (ed.), *Bronze Age Landscapes*, 83–98.

160. Mark Collard et al., 'Ironworking in the Bronze Age?', Proceedings of the Prehistoric Society, 72 (2006), 367–421.

161. Naomi Field and Mike Parker Pearson, Fiskerton, Oxford, Oxbow, 2004.

162. Richard Warner, 'Irish Souterrains', Archaeologia Atlantica, 3 (1980), 81–100; Mark Clinton, The Souterrains of Ireland, Dublin, Wordwell, 2003.

163. Such as Warner, 'Irish Souterrains'; and Darvill, Prehistoric Britain, 318–25.

164. Warner, 'Irish Souterrains', 95–100.

165. T. E. Wainwright, The Souterrains of Southern Pictland, London, Routledge, 1963; Gordon Barclay, 'Newmill and the Souterrains of Southern Pictland', Proceedings of the Society of Antiquaries of Scotland, 110 (1980), 206; Lloyd and Jennifer Laing, Celtic Britain and Ireland, Dublin, Irish Academic Press, 1990, 127–31; Ian Armit, 'The Abandonment of Souterrains', ibid., 129 (1997), 577–96; Harding, The Iron Age in Northern Britain, 196–9; Hazel Moore and Graeme Wilson, 'The Langskaill Souterrain', Current Archaeology, 199 (2005), 333–5; Mairi H. Davies, 'Dominated by Unenclosed Settlement? The Later Iron Age in Eastern Scotland North of the Firth of Forth', in Haselgrove and Moore (eds), The Later Iron Age in Britain and Beyond, 275–8; Nick Cord and Jane Downes, 'Mine Howe', in Jane Downes and Anna Ritchie (eds), Sea Change: Orkney and Northern Europe in the Later Iron Age, Balgavies, Pinkfoot Press, 2003, 11–19.

166. Evelyn Clark, Cornish Fogous, London, Methuen, 1961; Patricia Christie, 'Cornish Souterrains in the Light of Recent Research', Bulletin of the Institute of Archaeology, 16 (1979), 187–213; Charles Thomas, 'Souterrains in the Sea Province', in Charles Thomas (ed.), The Iron Age in the Irish Sea Province, London, Council for British Archaeology, 1972, 75–8.

167. Rachel Maclean, 'The Fogou', Cornish Archaeology, 31 (1992), 41–64.

168. Ian M. Cooke, Mother and Sun: The Cornish Fogou, Penzance, Men an Tol Studio, 1993. His precise explanation for the structures was that they embodied a mating of the sun with the Earth Goddess. This concept of prehistoric religion goes back to the eighteenth century (as is discussed, with its subsequent history, in Hutton, Blood and Mistletoe, 277–8), but was given a new lease of life in the 1980s by the Goddess Movement. While I have no inherent dislike of the idea, such simple dualisms of mighty cosmological figures do seem to be missing from the luxuriant polytheism of Iron Age British religion when it emerges into history with the arrival of the Romans (for which see below). I was, as far as I know, the first 'orthodox' scholar to take notice of Mr Cooke's ideas, as published in an earlier book of his, when I wrote Pagan Religions of the Ancient British Isles (pp. 131, 168–70). There I anticipated Rachel Maclean's argument, by suggesting that fogous were probably refuges, while acknowledging that there was no certainty with regard to their function. My reward was to be singled out by Mr Cooke for bitter attack in his subsequent book, seconded in letters from others in his local counter-cultural community. This fits the pattern, noted when discussing archaeoastronomy, that an academic author who simply ignores the writings of non-academic writers driven by powerful ideological impulses, almost invariably gets better treated by those writers than one who regards them as making a case worth addressing.

169. In Cornish Archaeology, 33 (1994), 247–50.

170. Cunliffe, Facing the Ocean, 350.

171. A. P. Fitzpatrick et al., 'An Early Iron Age Settlement at Dunston Park, Thatcham', in Ian Barnes et al., Early Settlement in Berkshire, Salisbury, Wessex Archaeology, 1995, 65–92; A. P. Fitzpatrick, 'Everyday Life in Iron Age Wessex', in Gwilt and Haselgrove (eds), Reconstructing Iron Age Societies, 73–86. The significance of the orientation of roundhouses was first suggested by Wait, in Ritual and Religion in Iron Age Britain.

172. Parker Pearson, 'Food, Sex and Death'.

173. By Sir Barry Cunliffe in a note at the end of Parker Pearson's article, above.

174. Pryor, Britain BC, 328–30.

175. Leo Webley, 'Using and Abandoning Roudhouses', Oxford Journal of Archaeology, 26 (2007), 127–44.

176. Rachel Pope, 'Roundhouses', Current Archaeology, 222 (2008), 14–21.

177. Alistair Oswald, 'A Doorway on the Past', in Gwilt and Haselgrove (eds), Reconstructing Iron Age Societies, 87–95.

178. Rachel Pope, 'Ritual and the Roundhouse', in Haselgrove and Pope (eds), *The Earlier Iron Age in Britain and the Near Continent*, 204–28.

179. Ann Woodward and Gwilym Hughes, 'Deposits and Doorways', in Haselgrove and Pope (eds), *The Earlier Iron Age in Britain and the Near Continent*, 185–203.

180. These sources are discussed in Hutton, *Blood and Mistletoe*, 8–17. The modern interpretation of them is the theme of most of the rest of the book.

181. A point well made by Miranda Aldhouse-Green, *Seeing the Wood for the Trees*, Aberystwyth, Centre for Advanced Welsh and Celtic Studies, 2000, 3–10.

182. This was confirmed for me by a visit to the Roman Baths Museum, with this question in mind, on 12 December 2011, and I am very grateful to the staff for assisting me, and admitting me to all the collections, on that occasion.

183. Webster, 'Sanctuaries and Sacred Places'.

184. Andy M. Jones, 'Misplaced Monuments?', *Oxford Journal of Archaeology*, 29 (2010), 203–28.

185. Richard Bradley, 'From Ritual to Romance', in Graeme Guilbert (ed.), *Hill-Fort Studies*, Leicester, Leicester University Press, 1981, 20–7; and *The Past in Prehistoric Societies*, 141–6.

186. Mark Gillings and Joshua Pollard, *Avebury*, London, Duckworth, 2004, 85–8; Rosamund M. J. Cleal *et al.*, *Stonehenge in its Landscape*, London, English Heritage, 1995, 360–5, 337–42.

187. Richard Hingley, 'Esoteric Knowledge?', *Proceedings of the Prehistoric Society*, 75 (2009), 143–65; 'Ancestors and Identity in the Later Prehistory of Atlantic Scotland', *World Archaeology*, 28 (1996), 231–43.

188. Tim Mallin, 'Place and Space in the Cambridgeshire Bronze Age', in Brück (ed.), *Bronze Age Landscapes*, 9–22.

189. Bradley, *The Past in Prehistoric Societies*, 136–41.

190. John C. Barrett, 'The Mythical Landscapes of the British Iron Age', in Wendy Ashmore and A. Bernard Knapp (eds), *Archaeologies of Landscape*, Oxford, Blackwell, 1999, 253–68.

191. The history of it is told, with reference to specific cases, in Ronald Hutton, 'Medieval Welsh Literature and Pre-Christian Deities', *Cambrian Medieval Celtic Studies*, 61 (2011), 57–85.

192. Published in London by Routledge & Kegan Paul.

193. In a chain of publications extending from *The Gods of the Celts*, cited above, to *Celtic Goddesses*, London, British Museum, 1995.

194. David Miles *et al. Uffington White Horse and its Landscape*, Oxford, Oxford Archaeology, 2003, 61–78.

195. R. D. Van Arsdell, *Celtic Coinage of Britain*, London, Spink, 1989; Peter Gelling and Hilda Ellis Davidson, *The Chariot of the Sun*, London, Dent, 1969.

196. Alistair Moffat, *The Wall: Rome's Greatest Frontier*, Edinburgh, Birlinn, 2008, 46, makes the point that some Iron Age tribes in the north of Scotland had names, recorded by Greek and Roman geographers, which echoed those of animals: thus, the Carvetii translate as the Deer People, the Lugi as the Raven People, the Epidii as the Horse People and the Venicones as the Hound People. What is not clear from this is whether they had spiritual connections with the beasts concerned, perhaps even akin to a belief in them as totemic ancestors, or whether the animals simply functioned as emblems, as the unicorn was later to be for Scotland.

197. Van Arsdell, *Celtic Coinage of Britain*; Koch, 'Mapping Celticity', 280; Justin Claxton, 'A Victory for Common Sense', in Robert Wallis and Kenneth Lymer (eds), *A Permeability of Boundaries?*, Oxford, British Archaeological Reports, 2001, 85–92.

198. John Creighton, 'Visions of Power', *Britannia*, 26 (1995), 285–301.

199. A fogou at Boleigh in the Lamorna Valley of west Cornwall has a carving at the entrance which Evelyn Clark interpreted as depicting an Iron Age god. Maclean, 'The Fogou', discussed this interpretation at length and found nothing to indicate the age or nature of the marking, which she found too weathered for any decisive conclusions to be drawn on the matter. I agree with her, having visited the site in 1984.

200. Bryony Coles has studied these finds as a group, in 'Wood Species for Wooden Figures', in Alex Gibson and Derek Simpson (eds), *Prehistoric Ritual and Religion*, Stroud, Sutton, 1998, 163–73. She has ingeniously suggested that the oak figure from Kingsteignton might have been the god Thor, and the one from Roos Carr, which seems to lack one eye, Odin. Neither of these Norse deities, however, seems to be reflected in the many native god-forms revealed by the Roman occupation of Britain. Further details of the figurines can be found in Aubrey

Burl, *Rites of the Gods*, London, Dent, 1981, 213, 226–7, and sources cited there. Miranda Aldhouse-Green has suggested that the Ballachulish image may have been a substitute for a human sacrifice: *Dying for the Gods*, 121.

201. News release, 'Garton Slack Figurines', *Current Archaeology*, 17 (1969), 170; Melanie Giles, 'Good Fences Make Good Neighbours?', in Haselgrove and Moore (eds), *The Later Iron Age in Britain and Beyond*, 235–49.

202. Anne Ross, *Pagan Celtic Britain*, Cardinal Edition, London, 1974, 94–171: the idea seems to have featured first as a motif in P. F. Jacobsthal, *Early Celtic Art*, Oxford, Oxford University Press, 1944.

203. Sarah Ralph, 'Broken Pots and Severed Heads', in David Barrowclough and Caroline Malone (eds), *Cult in Context*, Oxford, Oxbow, 2007, 305–1; Armit, *Headhunting and the Body*, passim.

204. Jody Joy, *Iron Age Mirrors*, Oxford, Archaeopress, 2010.

205. Miranda Aldhouse-Green, 'Images in Opposition', *Antiquity*, 71 (1997), 810–30; 'Vessels of Death', *Antiquaries' Journal*, 78 (1998), 63–84; 'Back to the Future', in Amy Gazin-Schwartz and Cornelius J. Holthorf (eds), *Archaeology and Folklore*, London, Routledge, 1999, 48–66; 'Cosmovision and Metaphor', *European Journal of Archaeology*, 4 (2001), 209–32; *An Archaeology of Images*, London, Routledge, 2004 (quotation from p. 2); 'Gender-bending Images', in Wallis and Lymer (eds), *A Permeability of Boundaries*, 19–29. The same author has herself proposed shamanism as the explanation for the kind of imagery discussed here, which is a perfectly legitimate interpretation though I am myself less happy with it because of the lack, in her work as in that of many others, of a rigorous definition of the term against which data can be tested: her main work on the subject was co-authored with Stephen Aldhouse-Green: *The Quest for the Shaman*, London, Thames and Hudson, 2005. I also have reservations about the methodology employed, of assembling a long and diffuse checklist of possible indicators of shamanic activity, and applying it to a range of evidence drawn from a wide area, which could all be explained in other ways. The same unease regarding methodology attaches for me to her work on Druids, in the recent *Caesar's Druids* and the earlier *Exploring the World of the Druids*, London, Thames and Hudson, 1998. I have, however, hinted at these differences above, and discussed them before in *Blood and Mistletoe*, 412–16, and my concern here is to celebrate the many aspects of her work which I find admirable and inspiring.

206. Good general surveys of paganism across the Continent are Prudence Jones and Nigel Pennick, *A History of Pagan Europe*, London, Routledge, 1995; and Kenneth Dowden, *European Paganism*, London, Routledge, 2000.

207. What follows is based on Ronald Hutton, *The Stations of the Sun: A History of the Ritual Year in Britain*, Oxford, Oxford University Press, 1996.

208. It is much less certain that there were equivalent celebrations at the equinoxes to match those at the solstices: this is considered in my book above, and for the astronomical evidence, see Clive Ruggles, *Astronomy in Prehistoric Britain and Ireland*, London, Yale University Press, 1999, passim; his views are summarized in his 'Astronomy and Stonehenge', in Barry Cunliffe and Colin Renfrew (eds), *Science and Stonehenge*, Oxford, Oxford University Press, 1997, 203–29.

209. Athenaeus, *Deipnosophistae*, IV.152D. Sir Barry Cunliffe reminds me that the right side may also have possessed a powerful symbolic significance simply because most people are right-handed: pers. comm., 1 February 2012.

210. The texts are cited and analysed in Hutton, *Blood and Mistletoe*, 18–21.

5 The Roman Impact: Temples, Statues and Inscriptions

1. The classic study of this phenomenon in the nineteenth century is Richard Hingley, *Roman Officers and English Gentlemen*, London, Routledge, 2000; to which can be added Mark Bradley, 'Tacitus's "Agricola" and the Conquest of Britain', in Mark Bradley (ed.), *Classics and Imperialism in the British Empire*, Oxford, Oxford University Press, 2010, 123–57. I have made some contribution to its twentieth-century manifestation in 'The Post-Christian Arthur', *Arthurian Literature*, 26 (2009), 149–70; and 'Druids in Recent British Fiction', in Marion Gibson *et al.* (eds), *Mysticism, Myth and Celtic Nationalism*, forthcoming from Routledge.

2. This pattern is examined in my pair of essays cited above.

3. Francis Pryor, *Britain BC*, London, HarperCollins, 2003, 429–39.

4. E.g. Stuart Laycock, *Britannia: The Failed State*, Stroud, Tempus, 2008; Miles Russell and Stuart Laycock, *UnRoman Britain*, Stroud, History Press, 2010; and Neil Faulkner, *The Decline and Fall of Roman Britain*, Stroud, Tempus, 2000.

5. J. D. Hill, 'Romanization, Gender and Class', in Simon James and Martin Millett (eds), *Britons and Romans*, London, Council for British Archaeology, 2001, 12–18; John Creighton, *Britannia*, London, Routledge, 2006, passim; David Mattingley, *An Imperial Possession*, London, Allen Lane, 2006, 520–8; Many of these ideas were presaged in Martin Millett, *The Romanization of Britain*, Cambridge, Cambridge University Press, 1990, 1–8.

6. Simon James, 'Soldiers and Civilians', in James and Millett (eds), *Britons and Romans*, 77–89.

7. Guy de la Bédoyère, *Eagles over Britannia*, Stroud, Tempus, 2001, 11–19.

8. Millett, *The Romanization of Britain*, 65–180; Edward James, *Britain in the First Millennium*, London, Arnold, 2001, 22–56; Petra Dark, *The Environment of Britain in the First Millennium*, London, Duckworth, 2000, 128–9; Timothy Darvill, *Prehistoric Britain*, London, 2nd edition, Routledge, 2010, 331–2; David Miles, *The Tribes of Britain*, London, Weidenfeld & Nicolson, 2005, 153–4; Mattingley, *An Imperial Possession*, 520–8; Robin Fleming, *Britain after Rome*, London, Allen Lane, 2010, 1–6.

9. Fleming, *Britain after Rome*, 6–17; Millett, *The Romanization of Britain*, 125–211; Mattingley, *An Imperial Possession*, 1–213, 316–519.

10. The account of it that follows is based on H. J. Rose, *Ancient Roman Religion*, London, 1948; Mary Beard *et al.*, *Religions of Rome: Volume One*, Cambridge, Cambridge University Press, 1998; John Scheid, *An Introduction to Roman Religion*, Edinburgh, Edinburgh University Press, 2003; Clifford Ando (ed.), *Roman Religion*, Edinburgh, Edinburgh University Press, 2003; Valerie M. Warrior, *Roman Religion*, Cambridge, Cambridge University Press, 2006; Jörg Rupke, *Religion of the Romans*, trans. and ed. Richard Gordon, Cambridge, Polity Press, 2007; Clifford Ando, *The Matter of the Gods*, Berkeley, University of California Press, 2008.

11. Again, easy overviews are provided by Prudence Jones and Nigel Pennick, *A History of Pagan Europe*, London, Routledge, 1995; and Ken Dowden, *European Paganism*, London, Routledge, 2000.

12. Guy de la Bédoyère, *Gods with Thunderbolts*, Stroud, Tempus, 2002, 32–9.

13. Guy de la Bédoyère, *Roman Britain*, London, Thames and Hudson, 2006, 228–32; quotation on p. 229; see also Simon Esmonde Cleary, 'Roman Britain', in John Hunter and Ian Ralston (eds), *The Archaeology of Britain*, London, Routledge, 2nd edition, 2009, 212–15.

14. Miranda (Aldhouse-) Green, *The Gods of the Celts*, Gloucester, Sutton, 1986; Graham Webster, *The British Celts and their Gods under Rome*, London, Batsford, 1986; Guy de la Bédoyère, *English Heritage Book of Roman Villas and the Countryside*, London, Batsford, 1993, 102; Martin Henig, *Religion in Roman Britain*, London, Batsford, 1984; Joan P. Alcock, 'The Concept of Genius in Roman Britain', in Martin Henig and Anthony King (eds), *Pagan Gods and Shrines of the Roman Empire*, Oxford, Oxford University Committee for Archaeology, 1986, 113–34.

15. Miranda (Aldhouse-) Green, *The Religions of Civilian Roman Britain*, Oxford, British Archaeological Reports, 1976, 67–71; Henig, *Religion in Roman Britain*, chs 4–5; Ann Woodward, *English Heritage Book of Shrines and Sacrifice*, London, Batsford, 1992, 58; J. Bagnall Smith, 'Votive Objects and Objects of Votive Significance from Great Walsingham, Norfolk', *Britannia*, 30 (1999), 21–56; Christopher J. Arnold and Jeffrey L. Davies, *Roman and Early Medieval Wales*, Stroud, Sutton, 2000, 127–8.

16. Henig, *Religion in Roman Britain*, ch. 4; David Rudling, 'Roman-Period Temples, Shrines and Religion in Sussex', in David Rudling (ed.), *Ritual Landscapes of Roman Southeast Britain*, Oxford, Oxbow, 2008, 95–137.

17. For what follows, see Henig, *Religion in Roman Britain*, 97–109, updated by Matthew Symonds, 'New Light on Mithraic Scotland', *Current Archaeology*, 256 (2011), 6; John Shepherd, *The Temple of Mithras, London*, London, English Heritage, 1998; and Roger Ling, 'Mosaics in Roman Britain', *Britannia*, 28 (1997), 275.

18. Henig, *Religion in Roman Britain*, 136–7.

19. Green, *The Gods of the Celts*, ch. 3; and *Celtic Goddesses*, London, British Museum, 1995, 106–11; Webster, *The British Celts and their Gods under Rome*, 63–6. The basic study remains F. Haverfield, 'The Mother Goddesses', *Archaeologia Aeliana*, 15 (1892), 314–36.

20. Green, *The Gods of the Celts*, 87–91; Webster, *The British Celts and their Gods under Rome*, 66–70.

21. Green, *The Gods of the Celts*, 95–7; Webster, *The British Celts and their Gods under Rome*, 59–60. It should be noted that no British relief of this goddess actually identifies her as Rosmerta, though her iconography, and pairing with Mercury, is the same as the Gaulish deity of that name. Stephen Yeates has suggested that she was a native goddess of the Dobunni with similar attributes: *Religion, Community and Territories*, Oxford, British Archaeological Reports, 2006, 87. Her icons are in the City Museum, Gloucester, the Corinium Museum at Cirencester, and the Roman Baths Museum at Bath.

22. Discussed in Green, *The Gods of the Celts*, 94–5; the Museum of London has some especially fine specimens, but they are also found in a number of provincial collections, such as those of the Verulamium Museum at St Albans and the Corinium Museum, Cirencester.

23. Adam Daubney, 'Lord of the Rings', *Current Archaeology*, 254 (2011), 36–9.

24. Proinsias MacCana, *Celtic Mythology*, London, Hamlyn, 1970, 32.

25. Green, *The Gods of the Celts*, 95.

26. The classic modern study in English is Phyllis Fray Bober, 'Cernunnos', *American Journal of Archaeology*, 55 (1951), 13–51.

27. These doubts were summed up by F. Le Roux, 'Cernunnos', *Ogam*, 25 (1953), 324–9.

28. Margaret Murray, *The God of the Witches*, 1931: I have used the Oxford University Press reprint of 1970, where Cernunnos is discussed on p. 29.

29. It is in the Corinium Museum at Cirencester.

30. The classic catalogue of material relating to her is René Magnen and Émile Thevenot, *Épona*, Bordeaux, Delmas, 1956; for updates, see Claude Sterckx, *Éléments de cosmogonie celtique*, Brussels, University of Brussels, 1986, 9–54; and Katherine M. Lindoff, 'Epona: A Celt Among the Romans', *Latomus*, 38 (1979), 817–37.

31. *The Roman Inscriptions of Britain*, ed. R. G. Collingwood and R. P. Wright, Oxford, Oxford University Press, 1965, nos 1777 and 2177; Anne Ross, *Pagan Celtic Britain*, London, Sphere Books reprint, 1974, 286–7; M. R. Hull, 'An Epona Sculpture in the Colchester and Essex Museum', *Transactions of the Essex Archaeological Society*, 19 (1930), 198–9; Martin Biddle, 'Excavations at Winchester, 1971', *Antiquaries' Journal*, 55 (1977), 299 and 335–6.

32. Webster, *The British Celts and their Gods under Rome*, 55, 73–9; See also Green, *The Gods of the Celts*, 103–9; and Henig, *Religion in Roman Britain*, 47–8. The statue of the Tyne god is in the museum kept by English Heritage at the Chesters Roman fort.

33. Green *The Gods of the Celts*, 148–50.

34. Ibid., 103–9.

35. The figures concerned are kept, respectively, in the Newport, Corinium and Gloucester Museums, and that maintained by the National Trust at Chedworth Roman Villa.

36. It was Anne Ross who first comprehensively drew attention to this category of deity in Britain: *Pagan Celtic Britain*, 172–220.

37. Dio Cassius, *Roman History*, LXII.1–7.

38. Jane Webster, 'Interpretatio', *Britannia*, 26 (1995), 153–62; 'Translation and Subjection', in J. D. Hill and C. G. Cumberpatch (eds), *Different Iron Ages*, Oxford, British Archaeological Reports, 1995, 175–83; and 'Necessary Comparisons', *World Archaeology*, 28 (1997), 324–37; Amy L. Zoll, 'Patterns of Worship in Roman Britain', in Sally Cottam *et al.* (eds), *TRAC 94*, Oxford, Oxbow, 1994, 32–40; and see Mattingley, *An Imperial Possession*, 214–19.

39. Green, *The Gods of the Celts*, ch. 2, collated the evidence.

40. Edward James, *Britain in the First Millennium*, London, Arnold, 2001, 68; Green, *Celtic Goddesses*, 99–102; Lindsay Allason-Jones, 'Coventina's Well', in Sandra Billington and Miranda Green (eds), *The Concept of the Goddess*, London, Routledge, 1996, 107–19.

41. The inscriptions are cited, with full source references, in Ronald Hutton, 'Medieval Welsh Literature and Pre-Christian Deities', *Cambrian Medieval Celtic Studies*, 61 (2011), 57–85.

42. Jane Webster has gone so far as to assert that Brigantia was the creation of a single emperor who visited Britain in the early third century, Septimius Severus: see her 'Translation and Subjection', 182–3.

43. De la Bédoyère, *Gods with Thunderbolts*, 69–71.
44. Warwick Rodwell (ed.), *Temples, Churches and Religion: Recent Research in Roman Britain*, Oxford, British Archaeological Reports, 1980; updated by David Bird, *Roman Surrey*, Stroud, Tempus, 2004, 147–51. Hallaton in Leicestershire is an example of an Iron Age shrine which was abandoned when the Romans arrived, but the site of this open-air sanctuary continued to receive deposits of metalwork until near the end of imperial rule: Frank Hargrave, 'The Hallaton Treasure', *Current Archaeology*, 236 (2009), 36–41.
45. The finds from which are kept in the museum maintained by English Heritage on the site.
46. W. J. Wedlake, *Excavations of the Shrine of Apollo at Nettleton, Wiltshire*, London, Society of Antiquaries, 1982.
47. Ann Woodward, *The Uley Shrines*, London, English Heritage, 1993.
48. Collingwood and Wright (eds), *Roman Inscriptions of Britain*, nos 616 and 617.
49. R. E. M. Wheeler and T. V. Wheeler, *Report on the Excavation of the Prehistoric, Roman and Post-Roman Site in Lydney Park, Gloucestershire*, Oxford, 1932.
50. Roger Leech, 'Religion and Burials in South Somerset and North Dorset', in Rodwell (ed.), *Temples, Churches and Religion*, 332–3.
51. De la Bédoyère, *Gods with Thunderbolts*, 124.
52. The items are listed, and the attributions made, in Henig, *Religion in Roman Britain*, 130–42; see also Miranda Aldhouse-Green, *Caesar's Druids*, London, Yale University Press, 2010, 154–65; and Bird, *Roman Surrey*, 164–7.
53. Christopher J. Arnold and Jeffrey L. Davies, *Roman and Early Medieval Wales*, Stroud, Sutton, 2000, 126; Chris Catling, 'The Riddle of the Lake', *Current Archaeology*, 273 (2012), 26–33.
54. Ralph Merrifield, *The Archaeology of Religion and Magic*, London, Batsford, 1987, 26–30.
55. Philippa Walton, 'Roman Votives from the Water of the Tees', *Current Archaeology*, 221 (2008), 36–41.
56. The original excavation report is in *Abstracts of the Proceedings of the Ashmolean Society*, 2 (1843–53), 55.
57. 'By the Rev. C. R. Manning', *Archaeological Journal*, 32 (1875), 108–9, and 46 (1889), 352.
58. Pliny, *Historia naturalis*, XXII.2
59. Lindsay Allason-Jones and Bruce McKay, *Coventina's Well*, Chesters, Trustees of the Clayton Collection, 1985; Allason-Jones, 'Coventina's Well'.
60. Walton, 'Roman Votives from the Water of the Tees'.
61. Data collected by Merrifield, *The Archaeology of Ritual and Magic*, 45–8.
62. The great pioneering work into these, which established their nature and importance, was Anne Ross, 'Shafts, Pits, Wells', in J. M. Coles and D. D. A. Simpson (eds), *Studies in Ancient Europe*, Leicester, Leicester University Press, 1968, 255–85.
63. There is a general survey of the evidence here by Ernest Black, 'Pagan Religion in Rural South-East Britain', in Rudling (ed.), *Ritual Landscapes of Roman Southeast Britain*, 1–26.
64. Anthony King, 'Animal Remains from Temples in Roman Britain', *Britannia*, 34 (2005), 329–69.
65. Maria Medlycott, *The Roman Town of Great Chesterford*, Norwich, East Anglian Archaeology, 2011.
66. Michael Fulford, 'Links with the Past', *Britannia*, 32 (2001), 199–218.
67. Bryn Walters, 'Roman Villas in Britain', *Current Archaeology*, 229 (2009), 30–5.
68. Eleanor Scott, 'Animal and Infant Burials in Romano-British Villas', in Paul Garwood *et al.* (eds), *Sacred and Profane*, Oxford, Oxford University Committee for Archaeology Monographs, 1991, 115–21.
69. Merrifield, *The Archaeology of Ritual and Magic*, 37–44.
70. De la Bédoyère, *Gods with Thunderbolts*, 39–42.
71. Merrifield, *The Archaeology of Ritual and Magic*, 32.
72. Martin Millett, 'Treasure: Interpreting Roman Hoards', in Sally Cottam *et al.* (eds), *TRAC 94*, Oxford, Oxbow, 1994, 99–106; H. E. M. Cool, 'The Significance of Snake Jewellery Hoards', *Britannia*, 31 (2000), 29–40; Christopher Catling, 'Britain's Biggest Ever Coin Hoard', *Salon*, 237 (12 July 2010), n.p.; Mike Pitts, 'Frome Hoard May Have Been Sacrifice – and Not Alone', *British Archaeology*, 114 (2010), 9; Sam Moorhead *et al.*, 'Hoarding in Roman Britain', *Current Archaeology*, 218 (2010), 12–15.

73. E.g. Catherine Johns *et al.*, *The Hoxne Late Roman Treasure*, London, British Museum Press, 2010.

74. Mike Pitts, 'Coin Hoard Raises Questions about Roman Hoards', *British Archaeology*, 122 (2012), 6.

75. M. W. C. Hassall and R. S. O. Tomlin, 'Roman Britain in 1983: Inscriptions', *Britannia*, 15 (1984), 337.

76. Henig, *Religion in Roman Britain*, 179–89; De la Bédoyère, *Gods with Thunderbolts*, 127–9.

77. Cool, 'The Significance of Snake Jewellery Hoards', made the point about the iconic significance of money. See also the case of Piercebridge, pp.253, 255 above.

78. Webster, *British Celts and their Gods*, 43–51, 83–98; Anthony Weir and James Jerman, *Images of Lust*, London, Batsford, 1986, 145–6.

79. Collingwood and Wright, *Roman Inscriptions of Britain*, no. 1041.

80. Ibid., no. 1329.

81. Ibid., no. 1791.

82. L. J. F. Keppie, 'Roman Inscriptions from Scotland', *Proceedings of the Society of Antiquaries of Scotland*, 113 (1983), 401.

83. Webster, *British Celts and their Gods*, 54.

84. R. S. O. Tomlin, 'The Curse Tablets', in Barry Cunliffe (ed.), *The Temple of Sulis Minerva at Bath. Volume Two*, Oxford, Oxford University Committee for Archaeology, 1988, 150.

85. Anne Ellison, 'Natives, Romans and Christians on West Hill, Uley', in Rodwell (ed.), *Temples, Churches and Religion*, 327. For the list of sites which had produced curse tablets up to 2006, see Mattingley, *An Imperial Possession*, 458–9.

86. Alison Taylor, *Burial Practice in Early England*, Stroud, Tempus, 2001, 118–20.

87. Roger Leech, 'Religion and Burials in South Somerset and North Dorset', in Rodwell (ed.), *Temples, Churches and Religion*, 337–52; E. W. Black, 'Romano-British Burial Customs and Religious Beliefs in South-East England', *Archaeological Journal*, 143 (1986), 203–32; Ann Woodward, *English Heritage Book of Shrines and Sacrifice*, 89–91; Rosalind Niblett, *The Excavation of a Ceremonial Site at Folly Lane, Verulamium*, London, Society for Roman Studies, 1999; Philip Crummy *et al.*, *Stanway*, London, Society for the Promotion of Roman Studies, 2007; Taylor, *Burial Practice in Early England*, 97–101.

88. Simon Esmonde Cleary, 'Putting the Dead in their Place', in John Pearle *et al.* (eds), *Burial, Society and Context in the Roman World*, Oxford, Oxbow, 2000, 127–42.

89. Jacqueline I. McKinley, 'Phoenix Rising', in ibid., 38–43.

90. Alison Taylor suggests that the spread of inhumation roughly matches that of the mystery religions, which tended to favour preservation of the body: *Burial Practice in Early England*, 110–13.

91. Ibid., 118–20.

92. Joan P. Alcock, 'Classical Religious Belief and Burial Practice in Roman Britain', *Archaeological Journal*, 137 (1980), 50–6; Bruno Barber and David Bowsher, *The Eastern Cemetery of Roman London*, London, Museum of London, 2000; Hilary Cool, 'Pyromania', *British Archaeology*, 80 (2005), 12–19; Elizabeth O'Brien, *Post Roman Britain to Anglo-Saxon England: Burial Practices Reviewed*, Oxford, British Archaeological Reports, 1999.

93. Alcock, 'Classical Religious Belief and Burial Practice in Roman Britain', 56–62; Leech, 'Religion and Burials', 337–49; Merrifield, *The Archaeology of Ritual and Magic*, 65–70; Jake Weekes, 'Classification and Analysis of the Archaeological Contexts for the Reconstruction of Early Romano-British Cremation Funerals', *Britannia*, 39 (2008), 145–60; A. P. Fitzpatrick *et al.*, *Archaeological Investigations on the Route of the A27 Westhampnett Bypass, West Sussex, 1992*, Salisbury, Wessex Archaeology, 1997, 242–86; Sonia Puttock, *Ritual Significance of Personal Ornament in Roman Britain*, Oxford, British Archaeological Reports, 2002.

94. Black, 'Romano-British Burial Customs', 210–11.

95. Ibid., 225–7.

96. M. Harman *et al.*, 'Burials, Bodies and Beheadings in Romano-British and Anglo-Saxon Cemeteries', *Bulletin of the British Museum of Natural History (Geology)*, 35 (1981), 145–88; Merrifield, *The Archaeology of Ritual and Magic*, 71–5; Alison Taylor, 'Aspects of Deviant Burial in Britain', in Eileen M. Murphy (ed.), *Deviant Burial in the Archaeological Record*, Oxford, Oxbow, 2008, 91–114.

97. Harman *et al.*, 'Burials, Bodies and Beheadings'; Caroline Arcini, 'Buried Face Down', *Current Archaeology*, 231 (2009), 30–5; Taylor, 'Aspects of Deviant Burial in Britain'.

98. Miranda (Aldhouse-) Green, *Exploring the World of the Druids*, London, Thames and Hudson, 1998, 98–9.

99. Black, 'Romano-British Burial Customs', 225–7.

100. Merrifield, *The Archaeology of Ritual and Magic*, 67.

101. Ibid., 45–6, 52.

102. Ibid., 37–8, 51; Green, *The Gods of the Celts*, 131; R. M. J. Isserlin, 'Thinking the Unthinkable', in Karen Meadows *et al.* (eds), *TRAC 96*, Oxford, Oxbow, 1997, 91–100.

103. Miranda (Aldhouse-) Green, *Dying for the Gods*, Stroud, Tempus, 2001, 104–7; and *Caesar's Druids*, 76–80, 180–2; Isserlin, 'Thinking the Unthinkable'; Simon Mays and James Steele, 'A Mutilated Human Skull from Roman St Albans', *Antiquity*, 70 (1996), 155–61; Scott, 'Animal and Infant Burials in Romano-British Villas'.

104. (Aldhouse-) Green, *Dying for the Gods*; and *Caesar's Druids*; Isserlin, 'Thinking the Unthinkable'; Alison Taylor, 'Burial with the Romans', *British Archaeology*, 69 (2003), 14–19.

105. De la Bédoyère, *Gods with Thunderbolts*, 107.

106. N. B. Aitchison, 'Roman Wealth, Native Ritual', *World Archaeology*, 20 (1988), 270–83; K. R. Dark, 'Roman-Period Activity at Prehistoric Ritual Monuments in Britain and the Armorican Peninsula', in Eleanor Scott (ed.), *Theoretical Roman Archaeology First Conference Proceedings*, Aldershot, Avebury, 133–46.

107. Howard Williams, 'The Ancient Monument in Romano-British Ritual Practices', in Colin Forcey *et al.* (eds), *TRAC 97: Proceedings of the Sixth Annual Theoretical Roman Archaeology Conference*, Oxford, Oxbow, 1998, 71–86.

108. Richard Hingley, 'Esoteric Knowledge?', *Proceedings of the Prehistoric Society*, 75 (2009), 143–65; Paul Robinson, 'Miniature Socketed Bronze Axes from Wiltshire', *Wiltshire Archaeological and Natural History Magazine*, 88 (1995), 60–8.

109. Ronald Hutton, 'Romano-British Reuse of Prehistoric Ritual Sites', *Britannia*, 42 (2011), 1–22.

110. Christopher Gosden and Gary Lock, 'Prehistoric Histories', *World Archaeology*, 30 (1998), 2–12.

6 The Conversion to Christianity: A Clash of Religions, A Blend of Religions

1. From the nineteenth century, the Latin word *paganus* was commonly believed to signify a country-dweller, and its application to a believer in the older deities to be a consequence of the period in which Christianity had claimed the cities and the old religions had been pushed into the literal backwoods. In 1986 Robin Lane Fox established that there was no solid evidence for this, and suggested that it had meant a civilian instead, one not enrolled in the army of Christ: *Pagans and Christians in the Mediterranean World from the Second Century to the Conversion of Constantine*, London, Viking, 1986, 30–1. Four years later Pierre Chuvin pointed out that the term was used in a religious sense when most city-dwellers were still pagan, and after the usage for a civilian had died out. He proposed that as it derived, undoubtedly, from the word *pagus*, the standard Roman local administrative unit, it signified simply a believer in the local and rooted faiths, in other words the old religions: *A Chronicle of the Last Pagans*, Cambridge, MA, Harvard University Press, 1990, 7–9. This does not seem to have been challenged, and is the interpretation adopted here.

2. Again, this was long thought to signify the countryside, being derived from 'heath'. It was coined, however, in Gothic, where there is no such matching word for a wild place, so the actual origins of 'heathen' seem to be lost: see the *Oxford English Dictionary* on this point.

3. I have retained the conventional honorific titles for Constantine and Theodosius because of their undoubted achievement in stabilizing and reuniting the empire after a period of acute disruption, in the latter's case for the very last time. Likewise Pope Gregory the Great, in a succeeding period, deserves his title for being an outstanding leader and author. In none of these cases is their religious allegiance the determining factor here.

4. W. H. C. Frend, *The Rise of Christianity*, London, Darton, Longman & Todd, 1984, 608–9; and 'Roman Britain, a Failed Promise', in Martin Carver (ed.), *The Cross Goes North*, York, York Medieval Press, 2003, 79–91; Martin Henig, *Religion in Roman Britain*, London,

Batsford, 1984, 13–14; Dorothy Watts, *Christians and Pagans in Roman Britain*, London, Routledge, 1991; and *Religion in Late Roman Britain*, London, Routledge, 1998, passim; K. R. Dark, *Civitas to Kingdom*, Leicester, Leicester University Press, 1994, 34; Martin Millett, *The Romanization of Britain*, Cambridge, Cambridge University Press, 1990, 195–6; Edward James, *Britain in the First Millennium*, London, Arnold, 2001, 78; Michelle P. Brown, *How Christianity Came to Britain*, Oxford, Lion, 2006, 46–7; Barbara Yorke, *The Conversion of Britain*, Harlow, Pearson Longman, 2006, 110; Neil Faulkner, *The Decline and Fall of Roman Britain*, Stroud, Tempus, 2000, 120; David Petts, *Christianity in Roman Britain*, Stroud, Tempus, 2003, 170–2; Malcolm Lambert, *Christians and Pagans*, London, Yale University Press, 2010, 1–43; Kenneth Hylson-Smith, *Christianity in England from Roman Times to the Reformation: Volume One*, London, SCM Press, 1999, 58–64.

5. Bede, *Historia ecclesiastica gentis Anglorum*, I.13; Gildas, *De excidio*, c. 10.

6. Lambert, *Christians and Pagans*, 1–5; Petts, *Christianity in Roman Britain*, 30–5.

7. Petts, *Christianity in Roman Britain*, 38, conducts a particularly careful analysis of the list.

8. Victricius, *De laude sanctorum*, I (edited in *Patrologia Latina* XX, 443–4).

9. Petts, *Christianity in Roman Britain*, 44–5.

10. A point emphasized by Guy de la Bédoyère, *Gods with Thunderbolts*, Stroud, Tempus, 2002, 215–16.

11. Susan Pearce, 'The Hinton St Mary Mosaic Pavement', *Britannia*, 39 (2008), 193–218; Petts, *Christianity in Roman Britain*, 107–15; Brown, *How Christianity Came to Britain*, 41–7.

12. Guy de la Bédoyère, *English Heritage Book of Roman Villas and the Countryside*, London, Batsford, 1993, 114–15; Roger Ling, 'Mosaics in Roman Britain', *Britannia*, 28 (1997), 278; Dominic Perring, 'Gnosticism in Fourth-Century Britain', *Britannia*, 34 (2003), 97–127; Lambert, *Christians and Pagans*, 10–43; Petts, *Christianity in Roman Britain*, 115.

13. Pete Wilson, *Lullingstone Roman Villa*, London, English Heritage, 2009, 6–10.

14. Watts, *Christians and Pagans*, 38–51.

15. Elizabeth O'Brien, *Post-Roman Britain to Anglo-Saxon England: Burial Practices Reviewed*, Oxford, British Archaeological Reports, 1999, passim; Alison Taylor, *Burial Practice in Early England*, Stroud, Tempus, 2001, 125–9; Ann Woodward, *English Heritage Book of Shrines and Sacrifice*, London, Batsford, 1992, 89–97; Bruno Barber and David Bowsher, *The Eastern Cemetery of Roman London*, London, Museum of London, 2000, esp. 322.

16. Watts, *Religion in Late Roman Britain*, 74–95.

17. See David Petts's careful reflections on the former point in *Christianity in Roman Britain*, 139–49; and Christopher Sparey-Green's restatement of the argument that the cemeteries of well-spaced, individual graves with few or no goods are a Christian, or Christian-inspired, phenomenon: 'Where Are the Christians?', in Carver (ed.), *The Cross Goes North*, 93–118.

18. Watts, *Christians and Pagans*, 99–145; Lambert, *Christians and Pagans*, 30–43; Martin Henig, ' "And Did Those Feet in Ancient Times" ', in David Rudling (ed.), *Ritual Landscapes of Roman Southeast Britain*, Oxford, Oxbow, 2008, 191–206; Petts, *Christianity in Roman Britain*, 56–65.

19. Petts, *Christianity in Roman Britain* 118–27.

20. C. F. Mawer, *Evidence for Christianity in Roman Britain: The Small Finds*, Oxford, British Archaeological Reports, 1995.

21. Petts, *Christianity in Roman Britain*, 96–9.

22. Belinda Crerar, 'Contextualising Roman-British Lead Tanks', *Britannia*, 43 (2012), 131–66.

23. Philip Rahtz and Lorna Watts, 'The End of Roman Temples in the West of Britain', in P. J. Casey (ed.), *The End of Roman Britain*, Oxford, British Archaeological Reports, 1980, 183–201; Peter Salway, *The Oxford Illustrated History of Roman Britain*, Oxford, Oxford University Press, 1993, 525–6; Guy de la Bédoyère, *The Golden Age of Roman Britain*, Stroud, Tempus, 1999, 99–109; Philip Rahtz, '150 Years of Somerset Archaeology', in C. J. Webster (ed.), *Somerset Archaeology*, Taunton, Somerset County Council, 2000, 4; K. Hylson-Smith, *Christianity in England from Roman Times to the Reformation*, London, SCM Press, 1999, 61; Ann Woodward and Peter Leach, *The Uley Shrines*, London, English Heritage, 1993, passim; Alex Smith, 'The Fate of Pagan Temples in South-East Britain during the Late and Post-Roman Period', in David Rudling (ed.), *Ritual Landscapes of Roman Southeast Britain*, 171–90; Watts, *Religion in Late Roman Britain*, 18–73.

24. The most succinct recent summary of this process is in Robin Fleming, *Britain after Rome*, London, Allen Lane, 2010, 22–9.

25. Lloyd Laing, 'Segontium and the Post-Roman Occupation of Wales', in Lloyd Laing (ed.), *Studies in Celtic Survival*, Oxford, British Archaeological Reports, 1977, 57–8; Salway, *The Oxford Illustrated History of Roman Britain*, 525.

26. Ralph Merrifield, *The Archaeology of Ritual and Magic*, London, Batsford, 1987, 96–101; Barry Cunliffe, *The City of Bath*, Gloucester, Sutton, 1986, 25.

27. The lead tablets concerned are preserved in the Roman Baths Museum.

28. John Shepherd, *The Temple of Mithras, London*, London, English Heritage, 227–9.

29. Ben Croxford, 'Iconoclasm in Roman Britain', *Britannia*, 34 (2003), 81–95.

30. David Petts, 'How Christian was Late Roman Britain?', *Current Archaeology*, 204 (2006), 648–51.

31. My own reviews of the debate are published in Ronald Hutton, *Witches, Druids and King Arthur*, London, Hambledon and London, 2003, 39–58; and 'The Early Arthur', in Elizabeth Archibald and Ad Putter (eds), *The Cambridge Companion to the Arthurian Legend*, Cambridge, Cambridge University Press, 2009, 21–35.

32. See for example Dark, *Civitas to Kingdom*, 32–63; Christopher A. Snyder, *An Age of Tyrants*, Stroud, Sutton, 1998, 235–6.

33. Wendy Davies, *Wales in the Early Middle Ages*, Leicester, Leicester University Press, 1982, 168; Yorke, *Conversion of Britain*, 28. The earliest Life to deal with a British saint of this period is usually considered to be that of Samson of Dol, which is sometimes used uncritically as an account of a conditions in Wales and Cornwall during the sixth century: the most recent author to do so is Lambert, *Christians and Pagans*, 94–6. It was, however, probably written in Brittany one or two hundred years later: Yorke, *Conversion of Britain*, 11–14.

34. Constantius, *Vita sancti Germani*, c. 14–17.

35. Prosper and Constantius are compared by E. A Thompson, *Saint Germanus of Auxerre and the End of Roman Britain*, Woodbridge, Boydell, 1984, 1–13, who on pp. 15–25 makes the point about the mass baptism being most probably of people already Christian.

36. Patrick, *Confessio*, esp. c. 1, 27, 32 and *Epistola*. For interpretations (along the lines suggested here), see Yorke, *Conversion of Britain*, 111; and Petts, *Christianity in Roman Britain*, 44–5. David Dumville *et al.*, *St Patrick*, Woodbridge, Boydell, 1993, agreed that a later fifth-century date for the saint is the most likely.

37. Gildas, *De excidio Britonum*, esp. IV.2.

38. All points made by Thompson, *Saint Germanus*, 15–25, though he makes a general assumption that the Romano-British countryside had to be more pagan than the towns, which subsequent archaeology has called into question, as noted above.

39. *Historia Brittonum*, c. 56. Since the Second World War, however, writers of novels have manifested a new preoccupation with Arthur as the ruler of a Britain still deeply divided between pagan and Christian, in a long succession of works which provide fascinating insights into the religious cultures of modern Britain and America: see Ronald Hutton, 'The Post-Christian Arthur', *Arthurian Literature*, 26 (2009), 149–70.

40. Source as in n. 23

41. James Gerrard, 'The Temple of Sulis Minerva at Bath and the End of Roman Britain', *Antiquaries' Journal*, 87 (2007), 148–64.

42. Woodward and Leach, *The Uley Shrines*, 71.

43. I summarized what is known of the conversion of the Irish in *The Pagan Religions of the Ancient British Isles*, Oxford, Blackwell, 1991, 262–3.

44. James E. Fraser, *From Caledonia to Pictland*, Edinburgh, Edinburgh University Press, 2009, 36–8, 71; Lambert, *Christians and Pagans*, 103–9; T. O. Clancy, 'The Real St Ninian', *Innes Review*, 22 (2001), 1–28; Edwina Proudfoot, 'The Hollow Hill and the Origins of Christianity in Eastern Scotland', in Barbara E. Crawford (ed.), *Conversion and Christianity in the North Sea World*, St Andrews, Committee for Dark Age Studies, 1998, 57–73; Ian Smith, 'The Archaeology of the Early Christian Church in Scotland and Man AD 400–1200', in John Blair and Carol Pyrah (eds), *Church Archaeology*, York, Council for British Archaeology, 1996, 19–36.

45. P. H. Hill, *Whithorn and St Ninian*, Stroud, Sutton, 1997; and 'Whithorn, Latinus and the Origins of Christianity in Scotland', in Helena Hamerow and Arthur MacGregor (eds), *Image and Power in the Archaeology of Early Medieval Britain*, Oxford, Oxbow, 2001, 23–32. The archaeology of early Christian sites along the Forth–Clyde line provides a frustratingly imprecise chronology for the conversion period. Textual evidence makes it likely that the

local rulers along the Clyde were Christian by the 560s, but the earliest properly datable religious site there is from the early seventh century: Christopher Lowe, *Inchmarnock*, Edinburgh, Society of Antiquaries of Scotland, 2008. An equivalent monastic site on the Isle of May at the mouth of the Firth of Forth commences, in terms of detectable remains, with a cemetery which could have been inaugurated at any point between the fifth and the eighth centuries: Heather F. James and Peter Yeoman, *Excavations at St Ethernan's Monastery, Isle of May, Fife, 1992–7*, Perth, Tayside and Fife Archaeological Committee, 2008.

46. It was long presumed that Argyll was settled from Ireland in the post-Roman period because three early medieval texts said specifically that it was, and because of the close linguistic, social and political links between the two. Ewan Campbell, 'Were the Scots Irish?', *Antiquity*, 75 (2001), 285–92, pointed out, however, that the two areas were completely different in the form both of their settlements and their ornaments, and there was no trace of a British linguistic substratum to Argyll place names; while the texts concerned dated from the eighth to the tenth centuries and probably reflected the political ambitions of the time, rather than any historical reality.

47. Alfred Smyth, *Warlords and Holy Men*, London, Arnold, 1984, 57–72; W. D. H. Sellar, 'Warlords, Holy Men and Matrilineal Succession', *Innes Review*, 36 (1985), 41; Stephen T. Driscoll, 'Picts and Prehistory', *World Archaeology*, 30 (1998), 142–58; Martin Carver, *Portmahomack*, Edinburgh, Edinburgh University Press, 2008, 94; and 'Lost, Found, Repossessed or Argued Away – the Case of the Picts', *Antiquity*, 85 (2011), 1165–83; Meggen Gondek, 'Pictish Symbol Stones: Caught between Prehistory and History', in Aron Mazel *et al.* (eds), *Art as Metaphor*, Oxford, Archaeopress, 2007, 69–89; George and Isabel Henderson, *The Art of the Picts*, New York, Thames and Hudson, 2004, 168–72. The development of Pictish identity is the main theme of Fraser, *From Caledonia to Pictland*.

48. Leslie Alcock, *Kings and Warriors, Craftsmen and Priests in Northern Britain, AD 550–850*, Edinburgh, Society of Antiquaries of Scotland, 2003, 371–6.

49. Henderson and Henderson, *The Art of the Picts*, 168–72. Martin Carver also tells me of the discovery of a site at Rhynie in 2012, where nine Pictish symbol stones seem to be associated with a cult centre which included animal sacrifice, and was therefore pagan: pers. comm., 19 October 2012.

50. The best recent account is in Fraser, *From Caledonia to Pictland*, 94–115; see also Lambert, *Christians and Pagans*, 149–63; and Douglas MacLean, 'Maelrubai, Applecross and the Late Pictish Contribution West of Druimalban', in *The Worm, the Germ and the Thorn*, Balgavies, Pinkfoot, 1997, 173–87.

51. Lambert, *Christians and Pagans*, 161–2.

52. See Fraser, *From Caledonia to Pictland*, 343–4, for the most recent consideration of the problem.

53. Carver, *Portmahomack*, esp. p. 68.

54. Anna Ritchie, 'Paganism among the Picts and the Conversion of Orkney', in Jane Downes and Anna Ritchie (eds), *Sea Change: Orkney and Northern Europe in the Later Iron Age AD 300–800*, Blagavies, Pinkfoot Press, 2003, 3–10.

55. For a recent example of this exercise, by a distinguished historian, see Lambert, *Christians and Pagans*.

56. These are the three modes of Christian administration defined by Martin Carver, especially in 'Why There? Why That? Why Then? The Politics of Early Medieval Monumentality', in Hamerow and MacGregor (eds), *Image and Power*, 1–22.

57. A point emphasized by Fraser, *From Caledonia to Pictland*, 375–9.

58. See especially Patrick Sims-Williams, 'The Settlement of England in Bede and the Chronicle', *Anglo-Saxon England*, 12 (1983), 1–41; and Barbara Yorke, 'Fact or Fiction?', *Anglo-Saxon Studies in Archaeology and History*, 6 (1993), 45–51.

59. A story well told by Sam Lucy, *The Anglo-Saxon Way of Death*, Stroud, Sutton, 2000, 110–13.

60. Ibid., 163–5; N. J. Higham, *The English Conquest*, Manchester, Manchester University Press, 1994, 1–2.

61. These developments are well summarized in Nicholas Higham, *Britain and the Anglo-Saxons*, London, Seaby, 1992, 1–14. For a detailed and triumphant listing of them, see Francis Pryor, *Britain AD*, London, HarperCollins, 2004.

62. Brian Sykes, *Blood of the Isles*, London, Bantam, 2006, 267–88; Stephen Oppenheimer, *The Origins of the British*, London, Constable and Robinson, 2006, 367–82.

63. The development of this interpretation is traced by Helena Hamerow, 'Migration Theory and the Anglo-Saxon "Identity Crisis" ', in John Chapman and Helena Hamerow (eds), *Migrations and Invasions in Archaeological Explanation*, Oxford, British Archaeological Reports, 1997, 33–44; and Nicholas Higham, 'Introduction', in N. J. Higham (ed.), *Britons in Anglo-Saxon England*, Woodbridge, Boydell, 2007, 9–15.

64. The sources for this are in Hamerow and Higham, in the previous note; see also Fleming, *Britain after Rome*, 39–60.

65. See especially Sam Lucy's many publications, above all 'The Early Anglo-Saxon Burial Rite', in Martin Rundkvist (ed.), *Grave Matters*, Oxford, British Archaeological Reports, 1999, 33–40; and *The Anglo-Saxon Way of Death*.

66. The arguments in this paragraph are summarized in Helena Hamerow, 'Migration Theory and the Anglo-Saxon "Identity Crisis" '; and 'Migration Theory and the Migration Period', in Blaise Viner (ed.), *Building on the Past*, London, Royal Archaeological Institute, 1994, 164–77; Catherine Hills, 'Spong Hill and the Adventus Saxonum', in Catherine E. Karkov *et al.* (eds), *Spaces of the Living and the Dead*, Oxford, Oxbow, 1999, 15–26; 'Who Were the East Anglians?' in Julie Gardiner (ed.), *Flatlands and Wetlands*, Norwich, Scole Archaeological Committee for East Anglia, 1993, 14–23; and *Origins of the English*, London, Duckworth, 2003; Sally Crawford, 'Britons, Anglo-Saxons and the Germanic Burial Ritual', in Chapman and Hamerow (eds), *Migrations and Invasions*, 45–72; John T. Baker, *Cultural Transition in the Chilterns and Essex Region, 350 AD to 650 AD*, Hatfield, University of Hertfordshire Press, 2006; Don Henson, *The Origins of the Anglo-Saxons*, Hockwold-cum-Wilton, Anglo-Saxon Books, 2006; Higham (ed.), *Britons in Anglo-Saxon England*, passim; and Heinrich Härke, 'Kings and Warriors', in Paul Slack and Ryk Ward (eds), *The Peopling of Britain*, Oxford, Oxford University Press, 2002, 146–52. These authors find different solutions to the problem posed by the evidence; as is indeed the point of the following paragraph.

67. The great exceptions are in Warwickshire, far west of what ought to have been the initial area of Anglo-Saxon settlement, at Stretton on the Fosse, and (much more famously) Wasperton: see Martin Carver *et al.*, *Wasperton*, Woodbridge, Boydell, 2009.

68. The cultural discontinuity is apparent even in the rare and celebrated cases where continuity is seemingly present between Briton and Anglo-Saxon in the same settlement, as at West Heslerton in Yorkshire and Dorchester in Oxfordshire: Philip Rahtz, 'West Heslerton Seminar', *Antiquity*, 75 (2001), 305–8; and C. M. Hills and T. C. O'Connell, 'New Light on the Anglo-Saxon Succession', *Antiquity*, 83 (2009), 1096–108.

69. See for example, Eddius Stephanus, *Vita sancti Wilfrithi*, c. 17.

70. Oppenheimer, *The Origins of the British*, 404.

71. Higham, *The English Conquest*, 2.

72. This, and a few more of the summary reflections below were presaged in my 'Afterword' to Carver *et al.* (eds), *Signals of Belief in Early England*, 201–6.

73. This traditional compendium is compiled from proportionately traditional books: Brian Branston, *The Lost Gods of England*, London, Thames and Hudson, 1957, chs 6–8; Gale R. Owen, *Rites and Religions of the Anglo-Saxons*, Newton Abbot, Barnes and Noble, 1981, 24–37; David Wilson, *Anglo-Saxon Paganism*, London, Routledge, 1992, ch. 1. More recently Richard North has found further possible references to obscure deities and details of the worship of those known, by conflating what he himself honestly terms 'a far-flung variety of sources': *Heathen Gods in Old English Literature*, Cambridge, Cambridge University Press, 1997: quotation on p. 78. To me he makes many fascinating suggestions, but the linkages involved are a little too daring for certainty.

74. Points made by C. J. Arnold, *An Archaeology of the Early Anglo-Saxon Kingdoms*, London, Routledge, 2nd edition, 1997, 151–2.

75. Audrey Meaney, 'Pagan English Sanctuaries, Place Names and Hundred Meetings Places', *Anglo-Saxon Studies in Archaeology and History*, 8 (1995), 29–42; Hilda Ellis Davidson, *The Lost Beliefs of Northern Europe*, London, Routledge, 1993, 57.

76. Kris Kershaw, *The One-Eyed God*, Washington, DC, Journal of Indo-European Studies, 2000, 1–9.

77. R. I. Page, 'Anglo-Saxon Paganism', in T. Hofstra *et al.* (eds), *Pagans and Christians*, Groningen, Egbert Forsten, 1995, 125–6. The earlier historiography of the issue is discussed by Venetia Newall, *An Egg at Easter*, London, Routledge, 1971, 384–6. More recent contributions include Alby Stone, 'Eostre', *Talking Stick*, 10 (1993), 1–2, and the review of the debate

by Carole Cusack, 'The Goddess Eostre', *Pomegranate*, 9 (2007), 22–9. Hretha is an odd name for an Anglo-Saxon goddess, as the feminine ending in the language is not 'a' but 'e': Audrey Meaney, 'Bede and Anglo-Saxon Paganism', *Parergon*, NS 3 (1985), 7. Meaney was one of the most distinguished of the scholars to argue that Bede's information on Anglo-Saxon paganism should be trusted throughout, and to characterize the only possible other position as one of suggesting that he invented it. This is not necessarily the case. My own stance is to acknowledge that he believed that he had good reason to derive the names of the months from goddesses, but that since we do not know what that reason was, we cannot evaluate its worth.

78. For example in Jens David Baumbach's study of the growth of the worship of the goddess Hera in Archaic Greece, from different local cults: *The Significance of Votive Offerings in Selected Hera Sanctuaries in the Peloponnese, Ionia and Western Greece*, Oxford, Archaeopress, 2004.

79. The poetry in *Kormák's Saga* alone, for example, contains the names of ten goddesses and two gods who are not in the familiar pantheon, but are usually taken by editors to be 'kennings' for those who are.

80. The bulk of what follows in this paragraph is based on Branston, *Lost Gods*, 31–3; Owen, *Rites and Religions*, 41–5; Wilson, *Anglo-Saxon Paganism*, chs 1–2; and Meaney, 'Pagan English Sanctuaries, Place Names and Hundred Meetings Places'.

81. Sarah Semple, 'Defining the OE *Hearg*', *Early Medieval Europe*, 15 (2007), 364–85.

82. See the comment by John Blair, 'Anglo-Saxon Pagan Shrines and their Prototypes', *Anglo-Saxon Studies in Archaeology and History*, 8 (1995), 1.

83. Ibid., 1–28.

84. Sarah Semple, 'In the Open Air', in Carver *et al.* (eds), *Signals of Belief*, 24–33.

85. Suggested by John Hines, 'Religion', in John Hines (ed.), *The Anglo-Saxons from the Migration Period to the Eighth Century*, Woodbridge, Boydell, 1997, 385.

86. On which see Brian Hope-Taylor, *Yeavering*, London, Her Majesty's Stationery Office, 1977, 91–332; John Blair, 'Churches in the Early English Landscape', in Blair and Pyrah (eds), *Church Archaeology*, 8, and Blair, 'Anglo-Saxon Pagan Shrines'.

87. A point made by Richard Morris, *Churches in the Landscape*, London, Dent, 1989, 59.

88. Bede, *Historia ecclesiastica*, II.13, 15.

89. Michael Lapidge and Michael Herren (eds), *Aldhelm: The Prose Works*, Ipswich, Brewer, 1979, 160–1.

90. It may be noted that, over half a millennium before, Tacitus had spoken of the German tribes – including those with whom his fellow Romans had come into direct contact – as having priests: *Germania*, VII, IX, XI, XLIII.

91. Eddius Stephanus, *Vita sancti Wilfrithi*, c. 13.

92. Bertram Colgrave (ed.), *The Earliest Life of Gregory the Great*, Cambridge, Cambridge University Press, 1968, c. 15.

93. Most of this paragraph is based on Branston, *Lost Gods*, ch. 4; and Owen, *Rites and Religions*, 50–60.

94. Meaney, 'Bede and Anglo-Saxon Paganism', 19–21.

95. A. L. Meaney, *Anglo-Saxon Amulets and Curing Stones*, Oxford, British Archaeological Reports, 1981, 249–62; Helen Geake, 'The Control of Burial Practice in Anglo-Saxon England', in Carver (ed.), *The Cross Goes North*, 259–69.

96. *The Earliest Life of Gregory the Great*, c. 16.

97. The most relevant comparisons for this specific case are assembled by Meaney, 'Bede and Anglo-Saxon Paganism', 23–4.

98. North, *Heathen Gods in Old English Literature*, 333–4.

99. S. D. Church, 'Paganism in Conversion-Age Anglo-Saxon England', *History*, 93 (2008), 161–210.

100. D. H. Green, *Language and History in the Early Germanic World*, Cambridge, Cambridge University Press, 1998, 13–20.

101. A selection includes B. J. Timmer, 'Wyrd in Anglo-Saxon Prose and Poetry', *Neophil*, 26 (1940–1), 24–33; G. W. Weber, *Wyrd*, Frankfurt, Frankfurter Beiträge zur Germanistik, 1969; and E. G. Stanley, *The Search for Anglo-Saxon Paganism*, Cambridge, Cambridge University Press, 1975, 92–121.

102. Bede, *De temporum ratione*, c. 15.

103. Page, 'Anglo-Saxon Paganism', 124, following Bosworth-Toller's standard dictionary.

104. On this in a British context, with some comparisons abroad, see Ronald Hutton, *The Stations of the Sun*, Oxford, Oxford University Press, 1996. Meaney, 'Bede and Anglo-Saxon Paganism', 5–6, finds in the 'Mothers' of the Mothers' Night the Matres of the Roman Rhineland, which is entirely possible, if Bede got the derivation of the name right.

105. On this consensus, see J. G. Ogilvy and Donald Baker, *Reading Beowulf*, Norman, University of Oklahoma Press, 1993, 180–1; and Andy Orchard, *A Critical Companion to Beowulf*, Woodbridge, Brewer, 2003, 130–7.

106. All this is my own reading of the work, but fits the consensus in the publications listed below.

107. For comparisons, see Lewis E. Nicolson (ed.), *An Anthology of Beowulf Criticism*, Notre Dame, University of Indiana Press, 1963; Patrick Wormald, 'Bede, "Beowulf" and the Conversion of the Anglo-Saxon Aristocracy', in Robert T. Farrell (ed.), *Bede and Anglo-Saxon England*, Oxford, British Archaeological Reports, 1978, 32–90; Malcolm Godden and Michael Lapidge (eds), *The Cambridge Companion to Old English Literature*, Cambridge, Cambridge University Press, 1991; Roberta Frank, ' "Beowulf" and Sutton Hoo', in Calvin B. Kendall and Peter S. Wells (eds), *Voyage to the Other World*, Minneapolis, University of Minnesota Press, 1992, 47–64; Fred C. Robinson, *The Tomb of Beowulf*, Oxford, Oxford University Press, 1993; Sam Newton, *The Origins of 'Beowulf' and the Pre-Viking Kingdom of East Anglia*, Cambridge, Brewer, 1993; James W. Earl, *Thinking about 'Beowulf'*, Stanford, CA, Stanford University Press, 1994; Peter S. Baker (ed.), *Beowulf*, New York, Garland, 1995; C. E. Fell, 'Paganism in "Beowulf" ', in T. Hofstra *et al.* (eds), *Pagans and Christians*, Groningen, Forsten, 1995, 9–34 Robert E. Bjork and John D. Niles (eds), *A Beowulf Handbook*, Exeter, Exeter University Press, 1997; Christina Rauer, *Beowulf and the Dragon*, Cambridge, Brewer, 2000; Gale R. Owen-Crocker, *The Four Funerals in 'Beowulf'*, Manchester, Manchester University Press, 2000; Geoffrey Russom, 'At the Center of "Beowulf" ', in Stephen O. Glosecki (ed.), *Myth in Early Northwest Europe*, Turnhout, Brepols, 2007, 225–40.

108. In *Shamanism and Old English Poetry*, New York, Garland, 1989. The shamanism hypothesis, with less close definition, hangs over a few of the essays in Carver *et al.* (eds), *Signals of Belief*, especially Alexandra Sanmark, 'Living On': pp. 158–80.

109. That is my reading, as expounded in *Shamans*, London, Hambledon and London, 2001, 129–49; and 'The Global Context of the Scottish Witch-Hunt', in Julian Goodare (ed.), *The Scottish Witch-Hunt in Context*, Manchester, Manchester University Press, 2002, 16–32. For different parallel views, which are still compatible with mine, see Neil Price, *The Viking Way*, Uppsala, Department of Archaeology and Ancient History, 2002; and Clive Tolley, *Shamanism in Norse Myth and Magic*, Helsinki, Academia Scientiarum Fennica, 2 vols, 2009.

110. R. I. Page, *Runes*, London, British Museum, 1987, esp. 11–12; Christine E. Fell, 'Runes and Semantics', in Alfred Bammesberger (ed.), *Old English Runes and their Continental Background*, Heidelberg, Carl Winter, 1991, 195–229; C. J. Arnold, *An Archaeology of the Early Anglo-Saxon Kingdoms*, London, 2nd edition, Routledge, 1997, 151–3.

111. *Ælfric's Catholic Homilies, The Second Series*, ed. M. Godden, London, Early English Texts Society, 1979, 204.

112. Unless otherwise stated, the material in the following discussion of pagan Anglo-Saxon burials is based on Owen, *Rites and Religions*, 61–95; Wilson, *Anglo-Saxon Paganism*, chs 4–5; J. D. Richards, 'Style and Symbol', in Stephen D. Driscoll and Margaret R. Nieke (eds), *Politics and Power in Early Medieval Britain and Ireland*, Edinburgh, Edinburgh University Press, 1988, 145–61; Rosemary Cramp, 'Northumbria', ibid., 72–3; M. Harman *et al.* 'Burials, Bodies and Beheadings in Romano-British and Anglo-Saxon Cemeteries', *Bulletin of the British Museum of Natural History (Geology)*, 35 (1981), 145–88; Sally Crawford, 'Children, Death and the Afterlife', *Anglo-Saxon Studies in Archaeology and History*, 6 (1993), 83–91; Nick Stoodley, 'From the Cradle to the Grave', *World Archaeology*, 31 (2000), 456–72; Arnold, *An Archaeology of the Early Anglo-Saxon Kingdoms*, 156–65; Heinrich Harke, ' "Warrior Graves"?', *Past and Present*, 126 (1990), 22–43; and 'The Circulation of Weapons in Anglo-Saxon Society', in Frans Theuws and Janet L. Nelson (eds), *Rituals of Power from Late Antiquity to*

the Middle Ages, Leiden, Brill, 2000, 377–400; Martin Carver, 'Reflections on the Meanings of Monumental Barrows in Anglo-Saxon England', in Sam Lucy and Andrew Reynolds (eds), *Burial in Early Medieval England and Wales*, London, Society for Medieval Archaeology, 2002, 132–43; Sarah Semple, 'Politics and Princes AD 400–800', *Oxford Journal of Archaeology*, 27 (2008), 407–29; Howard Williams, 'At the Funeral', in Carver *et al.* (eds), *Signals of Belief in Early England*, 67–82; Andrew Reynolds, *Anglo-Saxon Deviant Burial Customs*, Oxford, Oxford University Press, 2009; Pam J. Crabtree, 'The Symbolic Role of Animals in Anglo-Saxon England', in Kathleen Ryan and Pam J. Crabtree (eds), *The Symbolic Role of Animals in Archaeology*, Philadelphia, University of Pennsylvania Press, 1995, 20–6; Alison Taylor, *Burial Practice in Early England*, Stroud, Tempus, 2001, 135–61; Howard Williams, 'Animals, Ashes and Ancestors', in Aleksander Pluskowski (ed.), *Just Skin and Bones?*, Oxford, British Archaeological Reports, 2005, 19–40; *Death and Memory in Early Medieval Britain*, Cambridge, Cambridge University Press, 2006; and 'Transforming Body and Soul', *Anglo-Saxon Studies in Archaeology and History*, 14 (2007), 66–91; Chris Fern, 'Early Anglo-Saxon Horse Burial of the Fifth to Seventh Centuries AD', *Anglo-Saxon Studies in Archaeology and History*,14 (2007), 92–109; Sally Crawford, 'Votive Deposition, Religion and the Anglo-Saxon Furnished Burial Ritual', *World Archaeology*, 36 (2004), 82–102; Christina Lee, *Feasting the Dead*, Woodbridge, Boydell, 2007; Lucy, *The Anglo-Saxon Way of Death*.

113. A point demonstrated especially by J. D. Richards, *The Significance of Form and Decoration of Anglo-Saxon Cremation Urns*, Oxford, British Archaeological Reports, 1987.

114. The most famous case is that at Sewerby where the Yorkshire chalk wolds reach the coast, of an older, grossly contorted, woman put prone over the body of a younger one. Both, however, were given their own goods, and there is no proof that they were buried together or that the people who interred the upper body were aware of the lower. The contortion could have been produced by pre-burial trauma, such as death in a fire, or rigor mortis, or by the collapse of the coffin below; but then again, the woman might still possibly have been buried alive, as a criminal or sacrifice. For reviews of the debate over the case, see Reynolds, *Anglo-Saxon Deviant Burial Customs*, 60–8; Williams, *Death and Memory*, 97–100; and Lucy, *The Anglo-Saxon Way of Death*, 78–9. In that debate, the original proponent of live burial, Susan Hirst, has hit back at critics of that interpretation by accusing them of wanting a 'sanitized' version of the past. Such a charge has sometimes been made against those who have questioned the identification of bodies from British prehistory as victims of human sacrifice, by proponents of that interpretation. Perhaps significantly, I myself do not know of a case in which those who question the hypothesis of sacrifice have accused those who are fond of it of the opposite impulse.

115. A point made most forcefully by Hilda Ellis Davidson, 'Human Sacrifice in the Late Pagan Period in North-Western Europe', in M. O. H. Carver (ed.), *The Age of Sutton Hoo*, Woodbridge, Boydell, 1994, 331–4. See also Marilyn Dunn, *The Christianization of the Anglo-Saxons*, London, Continuum, 2009, 73–4.

116. For the Snape cemetery, see William Filmer Sankey, 'Snape', *Current Archaeology*, 118 (1990), 348–52; for Sutton Hoo, below.

117. A point stressed repeatedly by Martin Carver, especially in 'Boat Burial in Britain', in Ole Crumlin Pederson and B. Munch Thye (eds), *The Ship and Symbol in Prehistoric and Medieval Scandinavia*, Copenhagen, National Museum of Denmark, 1995, 111–24. As he notes, a third cemetery of boat burials seems to have existed at Caister-on-Sea, also in East Anglia, where clench-nails of the kind used in boats were found in twelve graves.

118. Most of this story is in Steven J. Plunkett, *Sutton Hoo*, London, National Trust, 2002, 1–8; and Martin Carver, *Sutton Hoo*, London, British Museum, 1998, 1–14; I have added a few details from the testimony of elderly residents of Sutton and Tranmere during my visits in 1969 and 2010.

119. Martin Carver, *Sutton Hoo*, London, Society of Antiquaries, 2005; Frank, '"Beowulf" and Sutton Hoo'; Tom Williamson, *Sutton Hoo and its Landscape*, Oxford, Oxbow, 2008. Mike Parker Pearson has usefully reminded us that it is not absolutely certain that the elite buried at Sutton Hoo represented East Anglian royalty: but see Helen Geake's reply, 'Three Men and a (Leaky) Boat', *British Archaeology* 112 (2010), 38–41.

120. Lisa Westcott, 'Trophies of Kings', *Current Archaeology*, 21 (2010), 30–5; Stephen Dean *et al.*, 'The "Staffordshire Hoard"', *Antiquaries' Journal*, 90 (2010), 139–52; Leslie Webster, 'The Staffordshire (Ogley) Hoard', *Antiquity*, 85 (2011), 221–9; Martin Carver, 'The Best We Can Do?', ibid., 230–4.

121. John Hines, 'Religion', in John Hines (ed.), *The Anglo-Saxons from the Migration Period to the Eighth Century*, Woodbridge, Boydell, 1997, 380; Julie Lund, 'At the Water's Edge', in Carver *et al.* (eds), *Signals of Belief*, 49–66.

122. The connection with Woden was made because the same figure is common on Swedish helmets of a roughly equivalent date where it has been identified (again not conclusively) as connected to the iconography of the Scandinavian Odin: Sonia Chadwick Hawkes *et al.* 'The Finglesham Man', *Antiquity*, 39 (1965), 17–32. Significantly, the recent publication of the excavation, S. Chadwick Hawkes *et al.* (ed.), *The Anglo-Saxon Cemetery at Finglesham, Kent*, Oxford, Oxford University Press, 2006, 21, 78–81, 263–6, avoids any such speculation, but a confident identification of the image with Woden still appears in some survey books on the period.

123. Chris Catling, 'Finding Meaning in Anglo-Saxon Art', *Current Archaeology*, 267 (2012), 31.

124. Tania Dickinson, 'Symbols of Protection', *Medieval Archaeology*, 49 (2005), 109–64.

125. Aleks Pluskowski, 'Animal Magic', and Chris Fern, 'Horses in Mind', in Carver *et al.* (eds), *Signals of Belief*, 103–57.

126. Bede, *Vita sancti Cuthberti*, c. 3, 9.

127. What follows is based essentially on Bede, *Historia ecclesiastica*, I–IV, reinforced by details from the saints' Lives cited in notes above, and entries in the *Anglo-Saxon Chronicle*. Extended recent retellings of the story, with differing emphases, may be found in Lambert, *Christians and Pagans*, 164–276; and Marilyn Dunn, *The Christianization of the Anglo-Saxons c. 597 to c. 700*, London, Continuum, 2009, 48–56, 101–34.

128. John Blair, *The Church in Anglo-Saxon Society*, Oxford, Oxford University Press, 2005, 10–34; Yorke, *The Conversion of Britain*, 118–21.

129. This is the major theme of Carole M. Cusack, *Conversion among the Germanic Peoples*, London, Cassell, 1998.

130. Bede, *Historia ecclesiastica*, I–IV. Nicholas Higham, *The Convert Kings*, Manchester, Manchester University Press, 1997, enumerated in detail the political benefits that kings obtained from Christianity, and the practical considerations which propelled the conversion of each kingdom. Damian Tyler provided a useful balance by pointing out that Christianity would have carried some disadvantages for rulers as well, in limitations on their freedom of action and alienation of land to churches, but these must have been outweighed by the advantages, or more would have rejected the new faith: 'Reluctant Kings and Christian Conversion in Seventh-Century England', *History*, 92 (2007), 144–61.

131. Bede, *Historia ecclesiastica*, II.5, 15, III.30.

132. Ibid., II.2, III.21, IV.13

133. Ibid., II.20, III.9, 18, 24, IV.13.

134. Ibid., I.32, III. 8.

135. For a good collection of work built around this concept, see Graham Harvey (ed.), *Indigenous Religions*, London, Cassell, 2000.

136. For which see Tomoko Masuzawa, *The Invention of World Religions*, Chicago, University of Chicago Press, 2005.

137. For what follows in the next three paragraphs, see Dawn M. Hadley and Julian D. Richards (eds), *Cultures in Contact*, Turnhout, Brepols, 2000; D. M. Hadley, *The Vikings in England*, Manchester, Manchester University Press, 2006, 28–80, 192–236; James Graham-Campbell *et al.* (eds), *Vikings and the Danelaw*, Oxford, Oxbow, 2001; Sarah Foot, 'Violence against Christians', *Medieval History*, 1 (1991), 3–16; Guy Halsall, 'Playing by Whose Rules?', *Medieval History*, 2 (1992), 1–12; Alfred P. Smyth, 'The Effect of Scandinavian Raiders on the English and Irish Churches', in Brendan Smith (ed.), *Britain and Ireland 900–1300*, Cambridge, Cambridge University Press, 1999, 1–38; James H. Barrett, 'Christian and Pagan Practice during the Conversion of Viking Age Orkney and Shetland', in Carver (ed.), *The Cross Goes North*, 207–26.

138. James Graham-Campbell and Colleen E. Batley, *Vikings in Scotland*, Edinburgh, Edinburgh University Press, 1998, 54–92, 143–54; Héléna Gray *et al.*, 'The Viking Buried at Swordle Bay', *Current Archaeology*, 265 (2012), 28–33.

139. Jacqui Watson, 'Hollow Swords and Needles in a Soil Block', *English Heritage Research News*, (January 2010), 14–16.

140. Julian Richards *et al.*, 'Excavations at the Viking Barrow Cemetery at Heath Wood, Ingleby, Derbyshire', *Antiquaries' Journal*, 84 (2004), 23–116; Julian Richards, 'The Case of the

Missing Vikings', in Lucy and Reynolds (eds), *Burial in Early Medieval England and Wales*, 156–70; D. M. Hadley, 'Burial Practices in Northern England during the Later Anglo-Saxon Period', ibid., 209–28; Hadley, *The Vikings in England*, 237–63; Martin Arnold, *The Vikings*, Lanham, MD, Rowman and Littlefield, 2007, 1–11; Martin Biddle and Birthe Kjolbye-Biddle, 'Repton and the "Great Heathen Army"', in Graham-Campbell *et al.* (eds), *Vikings and the Danelaw*, 45–96; Julian Richards, 'Boundaries and Cult Centres', ibid., 97–104.

141. Marshall Cubbon, 'The Archaeology of the Vikings in the Isle of Man', in Christine Fell *et al.* (eds), *The Vikings in the Isle of Man*, London, Viking Society for Northern Research, 1983, 13–26; David M. Wilson, *The Vikings in the Isle of Man*, Aarhus, Aarhus University Press, 2008, 27–56; Neil S. Price, *The Viking Way*, Uppsala, Department of Archaeology and Ancient History, 2002, 127–61. Further information on the burials, and Bersu, may be gained from the displays in the Manx National Museum.

142. What follows is taken from Julian D. Richards, *English Heritage Book of Viking Age England*, London, Batsford, 1991, ch. 11; Sue Margeson, 'On the Iconography of the Manx Crosses', in Fell *et al.* (eds), *The Vikings in the Isle of Man*, 95–106; Hadley, *The Vikings in England*, 213–36; Richard N. Bailey, *England's Earliest Sculptors*, Toronto, Pontifical Institute of Medieval Studies, 1996, 80–94.

143. Bailey, *England's Earliest Sculptors*, 92.

144. Jön Staecker, 'Thor's Hammer', *Lund Archaeological Review*, 5 (1999), 89–104.

145. Barbara E. Crawford, *Scandinavian Scotland*, Leicester, Leicester University Press, 1987, 198.

146. Dorothy Whitelock *et al.* (eds), *Councils and Synods, with Other Documents Relating to the English Church*, Oxford, Oxford University Press, 1981, i.304–19, 409, 461–3, 489.

147. Lund, 'At the Water's Edge'.

148. Merrifield, *The Archaeology of Ritual and Magic*, 107–8.

149. Gerhard Bersu and David M. Wilson, *Three Viking Graves in the Isle of Man*, London, Society for Medieval Archaeology, 1966, 47–8; Arnold, *The Vikings*, 23–6; Davidson, 'Human Sacrifice in the Late Pagan Period'; Henrik Janson, 'Adam of Bremen and the Conversion of Scandinavia', in Ian N. Wood and Guyda Armstrong (eds), *Christianizing Peoples and Converting Individuals*, Turnhout, Brepols, 2000, 88. Adam of Bremen's original account is in his *Gesta Hammaburgensis ecclesiae pontificum*, IV.26.

150. Roberta Frank, 'Viking Atrocity and Skaldic Verse', *English Historical Review*, 99 (1984), 332–43.

151. The debate took place in four articles published in the journal *Saga-Book* between 1986 and 1989. For differing reactions, see Halsall, 'Playing by Whose Rules?'; and Smyth, 'The Effect of Scandinavian Raiders'.

152. There is a good short summary of these, in a context directly related to the Christianization of early medieval northern Europe, in Cusack, *Conversion among the Germanic Peoples*, 1–29.

153. J. W. Pickett, *Christian Mass Movements in India*, Cincinnati, Abingdon Press, 1933.

154. Milis, 'Introduction', and Martine de Reu, 'The Missionaries', in Milis (ed.), *The Pagan Middle Ages*, 1–10, 13–37.

155. Lesley Abrams, 'Conversion and Assimilation', in Hadley and Richards (eds), *Cultures in Contact*, 135–53.

156. Lesley Abrams, 'The Conversion of the Danelaw', in Graham-Campbell *et al.* (eds), *Vikings and the Danelaw*, 31–2.

157. Bede, *Historia ecclesiastica*, I.29.

158. Walter Johnson, *Folk Memory*, Oxford, 1908; and *By-Ways in British Archaeology*, Cambridge, 1912.

159. Blair, 'Churches in the Early English Landscape', 12.

160. Derek Keene *et al.*, *St Pauls'*, London, Yale University Press, 2004, 2–4.

161. Morris, *Churches in the Landscape*, 72–83.

162. Mark Gillings and Joshua Pollard, *Avebury*, London, Duckworth, 2004, 123–33.

163. Paul Ashbee, 'The Medway Megaliths in Perspective', *Archaeologia Cantiana*, 111 (1993), 63–5, believed that the Neolithic tomb-shrines of Kent were systematically wrecked in the thirteenth century as an act of religious desecration. He also, however, considered that the damage might have been the work of treasure hunters, against whose depredations laws were passed at that time; and this remains an alternative possibility.

164. Jeremy Harte, 'Blót on the Landscape', *Third Stone*, 34 (1999), 23–6.
165. Leslie Grinsell, 'The Christianization of Prehistoric and Other Pagan Sites', *Landscape History*, 8 (1986), 27–37.
166. Stephen James Yeates, *Religion, Community and Territory*, Oxford, British Archaeological Reports, 2006, 71.
167. Blair, 'Churches in the Early English Landscape', and Nancy Edwards, 'Identifying the Archaeology of the Early Church in Wales and Cornwall', in Blair and Pyrah (eds), *Church Archaeology*, 6–12, 53.
168. What follows is based on Andy Boddington, 'Modes of Burial, Settlement and Worship', in Edward Southworth (ed.), *Anglo-Saxon Cemeteries*, Stroud, Sutton, 1991, 177–89; Jack Watkins, 'The Anglo-Saxon Grave Mystery', *Heritage Today* (September 2006), 40–2; Mike Pitts, 'Kent Anglo-Saxon Cemetery Could Be Royal', *British Archaeology*, 100 (2008), 9; Stephen J. Sherlock and Mark Simmons, 'The Last Royal Cult of Street House', ibid., 30–7; Blair, *The Church in Anglo-Saxon Society*, 58–65; Taylor, *Burial Practice in Early England*, 135–9; Yorke, *The Conversion of Britain*, 212–19; Dunn, *The Christianization of the Anglo-Saxons*, 163–78; Helen Geake, 'Burial in Seventh- and Eighth-Century England', in Carver (ed.), *The Age of Sutton Hoo*, Woodbridge, Boydell, 1994, 83–94; and *The Use of Grave Goods in Conversion-Period England*, Oxford, British Archaeological Reports, 1997; Sam Lucy *et al.*, *The Anglo-Saxon Settlement and Cemetery at Bloodmoor Hill, Carlton Colville, Suffolk*, Cambridge, Cambridge Archaeological Unit, 2009; Richard Hoggett, *The Archaeology of the East Anglian Conversion*, Woodbridge, Boydell, 2010; Christopher Scull, *Early Medieval (Late 5th–Early 8th Centuries AD) Cemeteries at Boss Hall and Buttermarket, Ipswich, Suffolk*, Leeds, Society for Medieval Archaeology, 2009; Sam Lucy, *The Early Anglo-Saxon Cemeteries of East Yorkshire: An Analysis and Reinterpretation*, Oxford, J. & E. Hedges, 1998, 102–8; and *The Anglo-Saxon Way of Death*, 183–4.
169. The major exception is Butler's Field, near Lechlade, Gloucestershire: Angela Boyle *et al.*, *The Anglo-Saxon Cemetery at Butler's Field*, Oxford, Oxford Archaeological Unit, 1998.
170. Harold Mytum, *The Origins of Early Christian Ireland*, London, Routledge, 1992; Nancy Edwards, *The Archaeology of Early Medieval Ireland*, London, Batsford, 1990, 1–25.
171. Geake, *The Use of Grave Goods in Conversion-Period England*; Hoggett, *The Archaeology of the East Anglian Conversion*; Scull, *Early Medieval (Late 5th–Early 8th Centuries AD) Cemeteries*; Yorke, *The Conversion of Britain*, 272–4.
172. Stephanie Hollis, *Anglo-Saxon Women and the Church*, Woodbridge, Boydell, 1992.
173. Yorke, *The Conversion of Britain*, 236–44.
174. Dunn, *The Christianization of the Anglo-Saxons*, 135–7.
175. Gilbert Márkus, 'Early Irish Feminism', *New Blackfriars*, 73 (1992), 375–88.
176. Wendy Davies, 'Celtic Women in the Early Middle Ages', in Averil Cameron and Amelie Kuhrt (eds), *Images of Women in Antiquity*, London, Routledge, 1983, 145–67. Six years later, Patrick Ford noted that medieval Irish literature, Roman historians and archaeology alike suggested that women had high status in ancient Gaulish, British and Irish society, but that this did not seem to be reflected in the earliest Irish law codes, and that their position actually seemed to improve in the first few centuries of Christianization: 'Celtic Women', *Viator*, 19 (1988), 417–38.
177. Yorke, *The Conversion of Britain*, 223–8; Dunn, *The Christianization of the Anglo-Saxons*, 137–8.
178. These are the conclusions of Yorke, *The Conversion of Britain*, 228–44.
179. Martin Carver, 'Early Scottish Monasteries and Prehistory', *Scottish Historical Review*, 87 (2009), 332–51. I am very grateful to Professor Carver for the gift of this article.
180. A first draft of this argument appeared as part of Ronald Hutton, 'How Pagan Were Medieval English Peasants?', *Folklore*, 122 (2011), 235–50.
181. E.g. Keith Thomas, *Religion and the Decline of Magic*, London, Weidenfeld & Nicolson, 1971; David Rollason, *Saints and Relics in Anglo-Saxon England*, Oxford, Blackwell, 1989; Eamon Duffy, *The Stripping of the Altars*, London, Yale University Press, 1992; and 'Religious Belief' in Rosemary Horrox and W. Mark Ormerod (eds), *A Social History of England 1200–1500*, Cambridge, Cambridge University Press, 2006, 340–55; Andrew D. Brown, *Popular Piety in Late Medieval England*, Oxford, Oxford University Press, 1995; Richard Davies, 'The Church', in Ralph Griffiths (ed.), *The Fourteenth and Fifteenth Centuries*, Oxford, Oxford University Press, 2003, 87–116; Blair, *The Church in Anglo-Saxon Society*; Ronald Hutton,

The Rise and Fall of Merry England, Oxford, Oxford University Press, 1994; Valerie Flint, 'A Magical Universe', in Horrox and Ormerod (eds), *A Social History of England*, 293–339; Charles Phythian-Adams, 'Ritual Constructions of Society', ibid., 369–82; Richard William Pfaff, *The Liturgy in Medieval England*, Cambridge, Cambridge University Press, 2009; Clive Burgess and Noel Duffy (eds), *The Parish in Medieval England*, Donnington, Tyas, 2006; Ian Cowan, *The Medieval Church in Scotland*, Edinburgh, Scottish Academic Press, 1995; Steve Boardman and Ella Williamson (eds), *The Cult of Saints and of the Virgin Mary in Medieval Scotland*, Woodbridge, Boydell & Brewer, 2010; Peter Yeoman, *Pilgrimage in Medieval Scotland*, London, Batsford, 1999; R. R. Davies, *Conquest, Coexistence and Change: Wales 1063–1415*, Oxford, Oxford University Press, 1987, 202–10.

182. Owen, *Rites and Religions*; Wilson, *Anglo-Saxon Paganism*; Carver *et al.* (ed.), *Signals of Belief*.

183. For Greek and Roman paganism, see Walter Burkert, *Greek Religion*, Oxford, Blackwell, 1985; Robin Lane Fox, *Pagans and Christians*, London, Viking, 1986; Tom Derks, *Gods, Temples and Ritual Practices*, Amsterdam, Amsterdam University Press, 1998; Mary Beard *et al.*, *Religions of Rome*, Cambridge, Cambridge University Press, 1998; Jan D. Bremmer, *Greek Religion*, Oxford, Oxford University Press, 1999; J. A. North, *Roman Religion*, Oxford, Oxford University Press, 2000; Robert Turcan, *The Gods of Ancient Rome*, Edinburgh, Edinburgh University Press, 2000; Clifford Ando (ed.), *Roman Religion*, Edinburgh, Edinburgh University Press, 2003; Valerie Warrior, *Roman Religion*, Cambridge, Cambridge University Press, 2006; James B. Rivers, *Religion in the Roman Empire*, Oxford, Blackwell, 2007; Clifford Ando, *The Matter of the Gods*, Berkeley, University of California Press, 2008; Jon D. Mikalson, *Ancient Greek Religion*, 2nd edition, Chichester, Wiley-Blackwell, 2010; Daniel Odgen (ed.), *A Companion to Greek Religion*, Chichester, Wiley-Blackwell, 2010. The general surveys are Prudence Jones and Nigel Pennick, *A History of Pagan Europe*, London, Routledge, 1995; and Ken Dowden, *European Paganism*, London, Routledge, 2000.

184. For the appearance of saints' cults in England, see Lambert, *Christians and Pagans*, 208–11; and Dunn, *The Christianization of the Anglo-Saxons*, 140–52.

185. Leonard Moss and Stephen C. Cappanari, 'In Quest of the Black Virgin', in James J. Preston (ed.), *Mother Worship*, Chapel Hill, University of North Carolina Press, 1982.

186. The origin of these saints as pagan deities is confidently stated in traditional texts such as Michael J. O'Kelly, 'St Gobnet's House, Ballyvourney', *Journal of the Cork Historical and Archaeological Society*, 57 (1952), 18–40; and Proinsias MacCana, *Celtic Mythology*, London, Hamlyn, 1970, 34–5. Recently there seems to be a tendency to downplay this idea: see Katherine Mckenna, 'Apotheosis and Evanescence', in Joseph Falaky Nagy (ed.), *The Individual in Celtic Literatures*, Dublin, Four Courts, 2001, 74–108; and Dorothy Ann Bray, 'Ireland's Other Apostle', *Cambrian Medieval Celtic Studies*, 59 (2010), 55–70.

187. Yorke, *The Conversion of Britain*, 219–23, discusses Anglo-Saxon legislation regarding Sunday.

188. For this see Hutton, *The Stations of the Sun*.

189. This is one of the main arguments of Hutton, *The Rise and Fall of Merry England*.

190. Jean Delumeau, *Catholicism entre Luther et Voltaire*, Paris, Presses Universitaires de France, 1971. Delumeau described the transition from medieval to early modern forms as being the true Christianization of Europe, but even on his own evidence it was more of a move from one sort of Christianity to another, though one which had fewer parallels with and adoptions from paganism.

7 The Legacy of British Paganism

1. Geoffrey Coulton, *Five Centuries of Religion. Volume One*, Cambridge, Cambridge University Press, 1925, 182–3.

2. Discussed in Ronald Hutton, *The Triumph of the Moon: A History of Modern Pagan Witchcraft*, Oxford, Oxford University Press, 1999, 112–31.

3. See the famous Victorian historian James Anthony Froude, *The Nemesis of Faith*, London, 1849, 20–1 as an early example of this attitude: he comments how the pagan deities long found a refuge in 'the simple minds of simple men' in the countryside, and boasted that Christianity itself, now 'decrepit', was lingering among the same benighted people, in the same way.

4. Commissioners of Public Works (eds), *Ancient Laws and Institutes of England*, London, 1840, passim; John Johnson (ed.), *A Collection of the Laws and Canons of the Church of England*, Oxford, 1850, i.219; Arthur West Haddan and William Stubbs (eds), *Councils and Other Ecclesiastical Documents Relating to Great Britain and Ireland*, Oxford, 1871, iii.189; Henry Gee and John William Hardy (eds), *Documents Illustrative of English Church History*, London, 1896, 41–2. See Audrey Meaney, 'Anglo-Saxon Idolators and Ecclesiasts from Theodore to Alcuin', *Anglo-Saxon Studies in Archaeology and History*, 5 (1992), 103–27, for a commentary on some of these texts. She rejects one, the so-called *Penitential of Egbert*, as evidence for England, being seemingly a Continental compilation misattributed to the archbishop.

5. For a discussion of these sources, see Meaney, 'Anglo-Saxon Idolators and Ecclesiasts', 117–27.

6. Commissioners of Public Works (eds), *Ancient Laws and Institutes of England*, passim; Dorothy Whitelocke *et al.* (eds), *Councils and Synods, with Other Documents Relating to the English Church*, i.304–19, 409–89.

7. A. G. Dickens, *Lollards and Protestants in the Diocese of York 1509–1558*, Oxford, Oxford University Press, 1959; John A. F. Thompson, *The Later Lollards*, Oxford, Oxford University Press, 1965; Keith Thomas, *Religion and the Decline of Magic*, London, Weidenfeld & Nicolson, 1971, 166–73; Margaret Aston, *Lollards and Reformers*, London, Hambledon, 1984; Anne Hudson, *The Premature Reformation*, Oxford, Oxford University Press, 1988; Richard Rex, *The Lollards*, Basingstoke, Palgrave, 2002; Fiona Somerset *et al.*, *Lollards and their Influence in Late Medieval England*, Woodbridge, Boydell, 2003; Shannon McSheffrey and Norman Tanner (eds), *Lollards of Coventry*, Cambridge, Camden Society 5th series 23 (2003); Judy Anne Ford, *John Mirk's 'Festial'*, Cambridge, Brewer, 2006.

8. Bristol Record Office, D/D/Cd 4, 1535–40. Joseph Bettey first drew my attention to the richness of this ecclesiastical archive.

9. National Archives, KB9, file 40, no. 4.

10. Timothy Lewis (ed.), *The Laws of Howel Dda*, Aberystwyth, National Library of Wales, 1912; Richard Melville (ed.), *The Laws of Hywel Dda*, Liverpool, Liverpool University Press, 1954.

11. Gerald of Wales, *Itinerarium Kambriae*.

12. National Library of Wales, Courts of Great Sessions Records. My information on the content of these is derived from conversations with Richard Suggett, who has made a particular study of them, with special regard to cases concerned with religion and magic.

13. Manx National Heritage Library, Liberi Placitorum, Liberi Scaccarrii, and Consistory Court Book of Presentments. I am personally well acquainted with these sources.

14. For different uses of them in this context, see Margo Todd, *The Culture of Protestantism in Early Modern Scotland*, London, Yale University Press, 2002; and F. Marian McNeill, *The Silver Bough*, 3 vols, Glasgow, Mclellan,1959.

15. Mary Beth, *Healing Threads: Traditional Medicines of the Highlands and Islands*, Edinburgh, Birlinn, 2004, 87, 138–40, puts these references into local cultural context.

16. The record is in the Chronicle of Lanercost, British Library, Cotton MS Claudius D VII, f. 192. There is a Latin edition of the chronicle by Joseph Stevenson published by the Maitland Club in 1839, and an English translation by Sir Herbert Maxwell, published in 1913. The innocent should not be misled by a scurrilous tract entitled *Essay on the Worship of the Generative Powers during the Middle Ages in Western Europe*, published in London in 1865 as an appendix to a new adition of Richard Payne Knight, *A Discourse on the Worship of Priapus*. It was anonymous but was credited at the time to the radical antiquary Thomas Wright, and is an early and extreme example of the modern desire, on which comment was passed above, to see Christianity as a mere veneer over a medieval culture which remained essentially pagan. As such, on pp. 130–1, it recounts the Inverkeithing incident and embellishes it with false details, such as that the priest was pardoned by his bishop for his rites of Bacchus because he insisted that he was carrying on local custom, and that his death occurred in a brawl, with the implication that this was not connected to his interpretation of religion. The same incident was used repeatedly by Margaret Murray, likewise, to support her argument of a continuing paganism through the Middle Ages, and while she did not add any false details to it, she drew one unwarranted inference, and suppressed aspects of the story which told against her interpretation: *The Witch Cult in Western Europe*, Oxford University Press, 1921, 23; and *The God of the Witches*, Sampson Low, 1933, 18. 207. It was

left to Jeffrey Burton Russell, *Witchcraft in the Middle Ages*, Ithaca, NY, Cornell University Press, 1972, 164–5, to provide an accurate version of the record and draw the conclusion that it did not support Murray's argument.

17. W. H. Mandy, 'An Incident at Bexley', *Woolwich and District Antiquarian Society Annual Report and Transactions*, 23 (1920–5), 25–37.

18. Nicholas Orme, 'Bishop Grandisson and Popular Religion', *Transactions of the Devonshire Association*, 124 (1992), 107–18.

19. Ludo Milis, 'Introduction', and 'Conclusion', in Ludo J. R. Milis (ed.), *The Pagan Middle Ages*, Woodbridge, Boydell, 1998, 1–10, 151–6. For an identical view from a scholar of Victorian popular culture, see James Obelkevitch, *Religion and Society in South Lindsey 1825–1875*, Oxford, Oxford University Press, 1976. He routinely uses the term 'paganism' for the non-Christian elements in popular religion, while emphasizing that 'it was not a counter-religion to Christianity; rather, the two coexisted and complemented each other', and that the 'pagan' traditions represented 'not a cosmos to be contemplated or worshipped but a treasury of separate and specific resources to be used and applied in concrete situations' (pp. 280–1).

20. John van Engen, 'The Christian Middle Ages as an Historiographical Problem', *American Historical Review*, 91 (1986), 519–52.

21. This is a view supported by another notable scholar of ancient and medieval religion, R. A. Markus, who attacked the view taken by the school of French historians around Jacques Le Goff, in the 1970s, that if the medieval populace in a given area had a different culture from the elite it could not by definition be Christian: *The End of Ancient Christianity*, Cambridge, Cambridge University Press, 1990, 4–14. At the opposite extreme from Le Goff is now C. S. Watkins, *History and the Supernatural in Medieval England*, Cambridge, Cambridge University Press, 2007, 76–106, who classes together Norman Cohn, Carlo Ginzburg, Jean Delumeau and myself as historians who have argued for a degree of pagan survivals in medieval culture which, even by the definition of ideas and images left over from ancient paganism, he finds unhelpful. He prefers instead to speak of such phenomena as 'non-Christian', or 'magic', but to me such differences are merely personal choices of semantics. I agree entirely with his point that 'pagan' could mean very different things in different periods and that medieval churchmen commonly deployed it to condemn forms of Christianity of which they disapproved.

22. Ronald Hutton, 'The Roots of Modern Paganism', in Charlotte Hardman and Graham Harvey (eds), *Paganism Today*, London, Thorsons, 1996, 3–15.

23. 'Female Fertility Figures', *Journal of the Royal Anthropological Institute*, 64 (1934), 93–100.

24. 'The Green Man in Church Architecture', *Folklore*, 50 (1939), 45–57.

25. 'The Divine Hag of the Pagan Celts', in Venetia Newall (ed.), *The Witch Figure*, London, Routledge, 1973, 139–64.

26. Ronald Sheridan and Anne Ross, *Grotesques and Gargoyles*, Newton Abbot, David & Charles, 1975.

27. Clearly it has been good to see them brought into the public eye in this way, but the process has occasionally been to the detriment of the images themselves: in 2004 the sheela-na-gig in the church at Buncton in West Sussex was destroyed in what was treated as 'an act of Christian protest'. One parishioner condemned the vandalism, but still stated that there was no place for a 'pagan symbol' in a church: Jacqueline Simpson, 'Sheela at Buncton Destroyed', *Folklore Society Newsletter*, 46 (2005), 4–5. On the other hand, the recent relation of the images to female empowerment and goddess worship has inspired some good guides to and gazetteers of them, listed in Rosemary Power's article in n. 37 below.

28. Roy Judge, *The Jack-in-the-Green*, London, Folklore Society, 1979.

29. Kathleen Basford, *The Green Man*, Ipswich, Brewer, 1978; Rita Wood, 'Before the Green Man', *Medieval Life*, 14 (2000), 8–13; Mercia MacDermott, *Explore Green Men*, Wymeswold, Heart of Albion, 2003; Richard Hayman, 'Green Men and the Way of All Flesh', *British Archaeology*, 100 (2008), 12–17; and 'Ballad of the Green Man', *History Today*, 60.4 (2010), 37–44; Alex Woodcock, *Liminal Images*, Oxford, British Archaeological Reports, 2005, 47–63. A mid-twentieth-century extension of the Green Man idea by literary critics had been to identify the Green Knight in the famous fourteenth-century poem *Sir Gawain and the Green Knight* as another appearance of the same fertility deity. This was contested in turn by Bella Millett, 'How Green is the Green Knight', *Nottingham Medieval Studies*, 38 (1994),

138–51; though it is worth noting that even Roger Sherman Loomis, the American literary scholar who had done so much to find pagan origins for motifs in the Arthurian legend, thought any for the Green Knight doubtful: *The Development of Arthurian Romance*, London, Hutchinson, 1963, 9.

30. Jörgen Andersen, *The Witch on the Wall*, Copenhagen, Rosenkilde & Bogger, 1977; Anthony Weir and James Jerman, *Images of Lust*, London, Batsford, 1986.

31. Malcolm Thurlby, *The Herefordshire School of Romanesque Sculpture*, Almeley, Logaston, 1999.

32. Brandon S. Centerwall, 'The Name of the Green Man', *Folklore*, 108 (1997), 25–33.

33. See sources at n. 9.

34. Hayman, 'Green Men and the Way of All Flesh'.

35. Sally Mittuch, 'Medieval Art of Death and Resurrection', *Current Archaeology*, 209 (2007), 34–40.

36. Cited in Andersen, *The Witch on the Wall*, 23.

37. Eamonn Kelly, 'Sheela-na-gigs in the National Museum of Ireland', in Michael Ryan (ed.), *Irish Antiquities*, Bray, Wordwell, 1992, 173–84; Catherine Karkov, 'Sheela-na-gigs and Other Unruly Women', in Collum Hourihane (ed.), *From Ireland Coming*, Princeton, NJ, Princeton University Press, 2001, 313–31. Eamonn Kelly, 'Irish Sheela-na-gigs and Related Figures', in Nicola McDonald (ed.), *Medieval Obscenities*, York, York Medieval Press, 2006, 124–37; Etienne Rynne, 'A Pagan Celtic Background for Sheela-na-gigs', in Helen M. Roe (ed.), *Figures from the Past*, Dublin, Glendale, 1987, 189–204. Rosemary Power has recently made a strong argument for the figures as magical images intended to ward off evil (though against any association with goddesses), working mainly from the Irish evidence: 'Iona's Sheela-na-Gig and its Visual Context', *Folklore*, 123 (2012), 330–54.

38. Kelly, 'Irish Sheela-na-gigs'.

39. Abegael Saward, 'The Rocky Valley Labyrinths', *Caerdroia*, 32 (2001), 21–7.

40. The historical outline provided below is taken from Penelope Reed Doob, *The Idea of the Labyrinth from Classical Antiquity through the Middle Ages*, Ithaca, NY, Cornell University Press, 1990; W. M. S. and Claire Russell, 'English Turf Mazes, Troy and the Labyrinth', *Folklore*, 102 (1991), 77–88; Hermann Kern, *Through the Labyrinth*, Munich, Prestel, English edition, 2000; and Craig Wright, *The Maze and the Warrior*, Cambridge, MA, Harvard University Press, 2001, to which I have added my own comments.

41. For which see Jeff Saward, *The Labyrinth*, Thundersley, Caerdroia, 1990; Sig Lonegren, *Labryinths*, Glastonbury, Gothic Image, 1991; Wright, *The Maze and the Warrior*, 1–5.

42. The story to this point may be found, in detail and with full source references, in Ronald Hutton, *Witches, Druids and King Arthur*, London, Hambledon and London, 2003, 65–79.

43. Charles and Nancy Hollinrake, 'An Archaeological Watching Brief at Glastonbury Tor during the Entrances and Pathways Enhancement', unpublished report kept in Glastonbury Public Library. Nancy Hollinrake telephoned me to ask me in person if I would publicize the existence of this work in a future publication of mine; and I am keeping faith with her here. The *Landscape Mysteries* television series, which dated the Long Man of Wilmington (for whom see later in this section) sponsored a bore for pollen data on the Tor, which provided evidence that the slopes of the hill were thickly forested during the Neolithic and Bronze Age, another piece of information which tells against a prehistoric date for the terraces.

44. The best history of these is still Morris Marples, *White Horses and Other Hill Figures*, London, Country Life Books, 1949.

45. For a good traditional description of both, with a bibliography of works on them until that date, see Paul Newman, *Lost Gods of Albion*, Stroud, Sutton, 1997.

46. For what follows, see Timothy Darvill *et al.*, *The Cerne Giant*, Oxford, Oxbow, 1999, and especially the section edited and contributed to by myself on pp. 69–124; and Martin Bell and Ronald Hutton, 'Not So Long Ago', *British Archaeology*, 77 (2004), 17–21.

47. Chris Lovegrove, 'An Earthly Paradise', *Pendragon*, 29 (2001), 22–26.

48. A classic restatement of this is J. Daryll Evans, *The Churchyard Yews of Gwent*, Pontypool, Archangel, 1988.

49. This story is summarized, with the data, in Anand Chetan and Diana Brueton, *The Sacred Yew*, London, Arkana, 1994.

50. One of the most remarkable of these is Fred Hageneder, *Yew: A History*, Stroud, Sutton, 2007, which, while some of its ideas remain speculative, contains much valuable research.

51. 'How Old *is* that Old Yew?', *At the Edge*, 4 (1996), 1–9.

52. Such a claim has been made for the churchyard yew at Tandridge in Surrey, but Harte found it to be false. He has made a good case that the tree which grew at Fortingall in Perthshire was a major landmark and meeting place before Christianity, but not that it was regarded as sacred then: though this is distinctly possible.

53. I think here of Robert Bevan-Jones, *The Ancient Yew*, Macclesfield, Windgather, 2002.

54. Barry Cunliffe, *The City of Bath*, Gloucester, Sutton, 1986, 44–91.

55. James Rattue, *The Living Stream*, Woodbridge, Boydell, 1995; Jeremy Harte, *English Holy Wells*, Wymeswold, Heart of Albion, 2008. Their findings for England are compatible with the older and (in historical respects) less systematic work for other regions of Britain: M. and L. Quiller-Couch, *Ancient and Holy Wells of Cornwall*, London, 1894; Francis Jones, *The Holy Wells of Wales*, Cardiff, University of Wales Press, 1954; Ruth and Frank Morris, *Scottish Healing Wells*, Sandy, Alethea, 1982.

56. Brian Spencer, *Pilgrim Souvenirs and Secular Badges*, London, Her Majesty's Stationery Office, 1998, 18.

57. David Stocker and Paul Everson, 'The Straight and Narrow Way', in Martin Carver (ed.), *The Cross Goes North*, York, York Medieval Press, 2003, 271–88.

58. Ibid., 281.

59. Kenneth Hurlstone Jackson, *The Oldest Irish Tradition: A Window on the Iron Age*, Cambridge, Cambridge University Press, 1964.

60. Source references for this process may be found in Ronald Hutton, *The Pagan Religions of the Ancient British Isles*, Oxford, Blackwell, 1991, 147–9; with more added from J. P. Mallory, 'The World of Cu Chulainn', in J. P. Mallory (ed.), *Aspects of the Tain*, Belfast, Universities Press, 1992, 147–9.

61. For a concise summary of these conclusions, see ibid.; and Ruari Ó hUiginn, 'The Background and Development of Tain bo Cuailnge', in Mallory (ed.), *Aspects of the Tain*, 32–62.

62. Mallory, 'The World of Cu Chulainn', 153.

63. Proinsias MacCana, 'Mythology and the Oral Tradition', in Miranda J. Green (ed.), *The Celtic World*, London, Routledge, 1995, 779–84.

64. Raimund Karl, 'Random Coincidences', *Proceedings of the Prehistoric Society*, 74 (2008), 69–78.

65. The sources are all listed and discussed in Ronald Hutton, *Blood and Mistletoe: The History of the Druids in Britain*, London, Yale University Press, 2009, 145–82, 241–63.

66. Ibid., 313–14. Even those poems which Williams did allot to the sixth century are now considered by some experts to be much later; but that is not of relevance here.

67. For an extended argument of this section, and the paragraphs that follow, and full source references, see Ronald Hutton, 'Medieval Welsh Literature and Pre-Christian Deities', *Cambrian Medieval Celtic Studies*, 61 (2011), 57–85.

68. Here ends the material developed and referenced fully in the article cited just above.

69. The latest edition and analysis of these is Marged Haycock, *Legendary Poems from the Book of Taliesin*, Aberystwyth, CMCS, 2007.

70. Ibid., 313–19; Rachel Bromwich, *Trioedd Ynys Prydein*, Cardiff, University of Wales Press, 1978, 42, 103, 198, 308, 463–4; Patrick Ford, *Ystoria Taliesin*, Cardiff, University of Wales Press, 1992.

71. This story is told in full, with complete references, in Hutton, *Blood and Mistletoe*, 172–9.

72. The version which I have to hand is the 1906 Dent one: the reference is on p. 429 of that.

73. Hutton, *Blood and Mistletoe*, 259–63.

74. Ifor Williams, *Chwedl Taliesin*, Cardiff, University of Wales Press, 1960, 3–4; Bromwich, *Trioedd Ynys Prydein*, 308–9; Ifor Williams, *Lectures on Early Welsh Poetry*, Dublin, Dublin Institute for Advanced Studies, 1944, 59–65. Williams's derivation of the name is now regarded as unsound, but there seems to be no agreement on an alternative, and the true origins of it may be lost, candidates being 'fevered woman', 'passionate woman', or 'woman with the angular embrace'(!). See Haycock, *Legendary Poems*, 318–19.

75. Anne Ross, *Pagan Celtic Britain*, London, Cardinal edition, 1974, 290.

76. Graham Webster, *The British Celts and their Gods under Rome*, London, Batsford, 1986; Miranda Green, *The Gods of the Celts*, Gloucester, Sutton, 1986.

77. Miranda Green, *Celtic Goddesses*, London, British Museum, 1995, 68–9.

78. Hutton, *Pagan Religions*, 323. I was harsh partly because of my knowledge of the origins of Ceridwen's divine attribution, in Edward Davies, and her absence from the 1980s' works on pagan 'Celtic' religion, and partly because it seemed to me odd that dubious goddesses like Ceridwen should have such a presence in the modern imagination – thanks to old and flawed scholarship – while so many undoubted and striking ancient British goddesses, attested from the archaeological record, were completely missing from it.

79. Miranda J. Green, 'Vessels of Death', *Antiquaries' Journal*, 78 (1998), 63–84.

80. E.g. Edward Davies, *The Mythology and Rites of the British Druids*, London, 1809; John Rhys, *Studies in the Arthurian Legend*, Oxford, 1891; Roger Sherman Loomis, *Celtic Myth and Arthurian Romance*, New York, 1927; Alfred Nutt, *Studies in the Legend of the Holy Grail*, London, 1888; Jessie Laidley Weston, *From Ritual to Romance*, New York, 1925.

81. A notable contributor here has been John Darrah, *The Real Camelot*, London, Thames and Hudson, 1981; and *Paganism in Arthurian Romance*, Woodbridge, Boydell, 1994. Darrah's detection criteria for paganism are 'strange behaviour and an uncanny atmosphere', which will naturally net a large number of likely instances in any literature (*Paganism in Arthurian Romance*, p. 14).

82. I am inclined to think that it is a survival; but Brendan Smith has cautioned me, very properly, that this is only a possibility and I may underestimate the creative power of the medieval mind: pers. comm., 15 October 2012.

83. For all that follows in this section, see Ronald Hutton, *The Stations of the Sun: A History of the Ritual Year in Britain*, Oxford, Oxford University Press, 1996, with some additional material in Hutton, *The Triumph of the Moon*, 112–31.

84. For the telling of this story with full source references, see Hutton, *Triumph of the Moon*, 132–50, 194–201, 272–86, 369–88.

85. Carlo Ginzburg, *Ecstasies: Deciphering the Witches' Sabbath*, London, Penguin, 1990, 8–9.

86. Norman Cohn, *Europe's Inner Demons*, London, Chatto and Heinemann, 1975.

87. Gustav Henningsen, *The Witches' Advocate*, Reno, University of Nevada Press, 1980; 'The Ladies from Outside', in Bengt Ankarloo and Gustav Henningsen (eds), *Early Modern Witchcraft*, Oxford, Oxford University Press, 1980, 191–218; 'The Witches' Flying and the Spanish Inquisitors', *Folklore*, 120 (2009), 57–74.

88. Hutton, *Pagan Religions*, 306–7.

89. Relatively recent outstanding contributions include James Sharpe, *Instruments of Darkness*, London, Hamilton, 1996; Diane Purkiss, *The Witch in History*, London, Routledge, 1996; Stuart Clark, *Thinking with Demons*, Oxford, Oxford University Press, 1997; Lyndal Roper, *Witch Craze*, London, Yale University Press, 2004; Brian Levack, *The Witch-Hunt in Early Modern Europe*, Harlow, Pearson, 3rd edition, 2006; Robin Briggs, *The Witches of Lorraine*, 2007; Julian Goodare *et al.* (eds), *Witchcraft and Belief in Early Modern Scotland*, Basingstoke, Palgrave Macmillan, 2008; Stephen Mitchell, *Witchcraft and Magic in the Nordic Middle Ages*, Philadelphia, University of Pennsylvania Press, 2011.

90. Any representative selection should include Ginzburg, *Ecstasies*; Eva Pocs, *Between the Living and the Dead*, Budapest, Central European University Press, 1998; Wolfgang Behringer, *Shaman of Oberstdorf*, Charlottesville, University of Virginia Press, 1998; Henningsen, 'The Ladies from Outside'; and 'The Witches' Flying and the Spanish Inquisitors'.

91. For easy overviews of ancient attitudes to witchcraft, see the first two volumes of the series *Witchcraft and Magic in Europe*, edited by Bengt Ankarloo and Stuart Clark for the Athlone Press in 1999–2001; and Wolfgang Behringer, *Witches and Witch-Hunts*, Cambridge, Polity Press, 2004, 1–51.

92. Livy, *Ab urbe condita*, VIII.18, XXXIX.41, XL.43.

93. William Shakespeare, *Macbeth*, lines 1526–75; Horace, Epode V and Satire VIII; Ben Jonson, *The Masque of Queenes*, lines 1–35.

94. Marie-Louise Thomsen, 'Witchcraft in Ancient Mesopotamia', in Ankarloo and Clark (eds), *Witchcraft and Magic in Europe. Volume One*, 25–7.

95. Cohn, *Europe's Inner Demons*, 2nd edition, London, Pimlico, 1993, 162–66.

96. Ibid.; Richard Kieckhefer, *Magic in the Middle Ages*, Cambridge, Cambridge University Press, 1989; Behringer, *Witches and Witch-Hunts*, 47–57. It should perhaps be emphasized that a comparatively low total of executions, in relation to what came before or after, could still produce some large local figures.

97. For general overviews, see Levack, *The Witch-Hunt*; Behringer, *Witches and Witch-Hunts*; and Geoffrey Scarre and John Callow, *Witchcraft and Magic in Sixteenth- and Seventeenth-Century Europe*, Basingstoke, Palgrave, 2001.

98. Carlo Ginzburg, *The Night Battles*, London, Routledge, 1983.

99. The best recent accounts of the Scottish witch trials are Julian Goodare (ed.), *The Scottish Witch-Hunt in Context*, Manchester, Manchester University Press, 2002; and 'The Aberdeenshire Witchcraft Panic of 1597', *Northern History*, 21 (2001), 17–38; Stuart Macdonald, *The Witches of Fife*, East Linton, Tuckwell, 2002; P. G. Maxwell-Stuart, *An Abundance of Witches*, Stroud, Tempus, 2005; Goodare *et al.* (eds), *Witchcraft and Belief in Early Modern Scotland*; Brian Levack, *Witch-Hunting in Scotland*, London, Routledge, 2008.

100. Emma Wilby, *Cunning Folk and Familiar Spirits*, Brighton, Sussex Academic Press, 2005; and *The Visions of Isobel Gowdie*, Brighton, Sussex Academic Press, 2010. I would emphasize that, the question of the shamanic component aside, these works do bring us closer than others to understanding the possible thought-worlds of people accused of witchcraft in early modern Britain; and the shamanic comparison is itself well worth making.

101. Julian Goodare, 'The Cult of the Seely Wights in Scotland', *Folklore*, 123 (2012), 198–212.

102. For what follows, see Ronald Hutton, 'The Global Context of the Scottish Witch-Hunt', in Goodare (ed.), *The Scottish Witch-Hunt in Context*, 16–32; and 'Witch-Hunting in Celtic Societies', *Past and Present*, 212 (2012), 43–71.

103. Key works on the subject in Britain include Minor White Latham, *The Elizabethan Fairies*, New York, Columbia University Press, 1930; Katharine Briggs, *The Anatomy of Puck*, London, Routledge, 1959; and *The Fairies in Tradition and Literature*, London, Routledge, 1967; Diane Purkiss, *Troublesome Things*, London, Allen Lane, 2000; Lizanne Henderson and Edward J. Cowan, *Scottish Fairy Belief*, East Linton, Tuckwell, 2001; and Jeremy Harte, *Explore Fairy Traditions*, Loughborough, Heart of Albion Press, 2004. Robert Bartlett, *England under the Norman and Angevin Kings*, Oxford, Oxford University Press, 2000, 686–92, presents an excellent brief summary of the relationship between high medieval English thought and these beings.

104. Martin Martin, *A Description of the Western Islands of Scotland*, London, 1703, 28–9.

105. Alexander Carmichael, *Carmina Gadelica*, Edinburgh, 1900, i.163.

106. The controversy and its conclusion are well summarized in John MacInnes's preface to the Floris edition of *Carmina Gadelica*, Edinburgh, 1992.

107. Jeremy Harte, 'Herne the Hunter', *At the Edge*, 3 (1996), 27–33.

108. Susan Cooper, *The Dark is Rising*, Chatto & Windus, 1975; Goldcrest Productions, *Robin of Sherwood* (1983–5).

109. Certainly this is true in practice: witness, for example, the cults now built around the super-humans in the novels of H. P. Lovecraft.

110. Especially notable among such scholars were Godfrid Storms, *Anglo-Saxon Magic*, Halle, 1948; and J. H. G. Grattan and Charles Singer, *Anglo-Saxon Magic and Medicine*, Oxford, Oxford University Press, 1952.

111. Karen Louise Jolly, *Popular Religion in Late Anglo-Saxon England*, Chapel Hill, University of North Carolina Press, 1996, 122, 140.

112. Jonathan Roper (ed.), *Charms and Charming in Europe*, Basingstoke, Palgrave, 2004.

113. Translations can be found in Jolly, *Popular Religion*, 125–7; Bill Griffiths, *Aspects of Anglo-Saxon Magic*, Hockwold-cum-Wilton, Anglo-Saxon Books, revised edition, 2003, 180–5; and Grattan and Singer, *Anglo-Saxon Magic*, 152–4.

114. Griffiths, *Aspects of Anglo-Saxon Magic*, 174.

115. John Frankis, 'Sidelights on Post-Conquest Canterbury', *Nottingham Medieval Studies*, 22 (2000), 1–27.

116. British Library Cotton MS Caligula A7, fos 176a-178a. Translations are in Storms, *Anglo-Saxon Magic*, 172–87; Jolly, *Popular Religion*, 6–8; Griffiths, *Aspects of Anglo-Saxon Magic*, 175–9; Grattan and Singer, *Anglo-Saxon Magic*, 62–3.

117. Grattan and Singer, *Anglo-Saxon Magic*, 45–6; A. D. Nock, 'Some Latin Spells', *Folklore*, 36 (1925), 93–6; J. Wight Duff and Arnold M. Duff (eds), *Minor Latin Poets*, Cambridge, MA, 1934, 339–50, where it is anthologized as a literary work as it deserves.

118. Roper (ed.), *Charms and Charming*; Hutton, *Triumph of the Moon*, 84–111; Owen Davies, 'Charmers and Charming in England and Wales from the Eighteenth to the Twentieth Century', *Folklore*, 109 (1998), 41–52; and sources cited in those.

119. For this see especially Veronique Charon, 'The Knowledge of Herbs', in Milis (ed.), *The Pagan Middle Ages*, 109–28.

120. The best overall survey is Owen Davies, *Cunning Folk*, London, Hambledon and London, 2003; see also Hutton *Triumph of the Moon*, 84–111.

121. Identified, with the drawing of different implications, by Grattan and Singer, *Anglo-Saxon Magic*; and Jolly, *Popular Religion*.

122. Griffiths, *Aspects of Anglo-Saxon Magic*, 173.

123. Jolly, *Popular Religion*, 170.

124. See the strictures of Karen Harvey in her introduction to her edition of essays, *History and Material Culture*, London, Routledge, 2009, 1.

125. This is a theme of Chris Gosden and Frances Larson, *Knowing Things*, Oxford, Oxford University Press, 2007.

126. Ralph Merrifield, *The Archaeology of Ritual and Magic*, London, Batsford, 1987, 118–29.

127. Brian Hoggard, 'The Archaeology of Counter-Witchcraft and Popular Magic', in Owen Davies and Willem de Blecourt (eds), *Beyond the Witch Trials*, Manchester, Manchester University Press, 2004, 167–86; and his website, www.apotropaios.co.uk.

128. Sources as in previous note.

129. June Swann, 'Shoes Concealed in Buildings', *Costume*, 30 (1996), 56–69.

130. George Roberts, *The Social History of the People of the Southern Counties of England in Past Centuries*, London, 1856, 530.

131. Carol van Driel-Murray, 'And did those Feet in Ancient Time . . . Feet and Shoes as a Material Projection of the Self', in Patricia Baker *et al.* (eds), *TRAC 98*, Oxford, Oxbow, 1999, 131–40.

132. Brian Hoggard's Apotropaios site; Margaret M. Howard, 'Dried Cats', *Man*, 61 (1951), 148–51. Howard mentions a possible textual parallel, of the case of some workmen on a cottage at Falmouth in 1890, who said that their construction needed the sacrifice of 'a virgin hare trapped by a virgin boy' to the 'outside gods'. This is tantalizing, but hares are not recorded in buildings, the incident was not reported until the mid twentieth century and so is doubtful, and, if it occurred, the men might have been joking.

133. Merrifield, *The Archaeology of Ritual and Magic*, 118–29; Hoggard, 'The Archaeology of Counter-Witchcraft'.

134. Giorgio Riello, 'Things that Shape History', in Harvey (ed.), *History and Material Culture*, 24–46; Dinah Eastop, 'Garments Deliberately Concealed in Buildings', in Robert Wallis and Kenneth Lymer (eds), *A Permeability of Boundaries?*, Oxford, British Archaeological Reports, 2001, 179–83; *www.concealedgarments.org/publications* (the Deliberately Concealed Garments Project).

135. Ian Joseph Evans, 'Touching Magic', University of Newcastle, Australia, PhD thesis, 2011. It is noted in this thesis, and needs to be stated here, that the ritual concealment of objects in buildings is also found in Continental Europe: it is a ubiquitous inheritance from the ancient world.

136. Hoggard, 'The Archaeology of Counter-Witchcraft'; and the Apotropaios site; C. J. Binding and L. J. Wilson, 'Ritual Protection Marks in Goatchurch Cavern', *Proceedings of the University of Bristol Spelaeological Society*, 23 (2004), 119–33; 'Ritual Protection Marks in Wookey Hole and Long Hole, Somerset', forthcoming in *Proceedings of the University of Bristol Spelaeological Society*; Timothy Easton, 'Apotropaic Marks Scribed and Scratched in Barns and Houses', *Suffolk Institute of Archaeology and History Newsletter*, 27 (1988), 7–8; 'Scribed and Painted Symbols', in Paul Oliver (ed.), *The Encyclopedia of Vernacular Architecture of the World. Volume One*, Cambridge, Cambridge University Press, 1998, 533–4; 'Ritual Marks on Historic Timber', *Third Stone*, 38 (2000), 11–17; Evans, 'Touching Magic'.

137. The conjoined Vs are present on a wooden bowl found in the *Mary Rose*, which sank in 1545, and I was informed by its curator that they are also present on at least one timber of the ship itself, constructed between 1509 and 1511: Mary Rose Museum, Portsmouth.

138. Virginia Lloyd *et al.*, 'Burn Marks as Evidence of Apotropaic Practices in Houses, Farm Buildings and Churches in Post-Medieval East Anglia', in Wallis and Lymer (eds), *A Permeability of Boundaries*, 57–70.

139. Timothy Easton, 'Candle Powers', *Cornerstone*, 32 (2011), 56–60.

140. I was shown these markings in August 2007 by my friend, the novelist Alan Garner, as part of his remarkable knowledge of the folkways of his native north-eastern Cheshire. It is of a piece with this that Alan also pointed out the significance of the style of the shoes.

141. The information for the British context is summarized in Hutton, *Pagan Religions*, 241–2.

142. An argument made above all in Anne Ross, *Pagan Celtic Britain*, London, Routledge 1967, pp. 91–174 in the Cardinal edition of 1974. See also Sidney Jackson, *Celtic and Other Stone Heads*, privately published, 1975.

143. John Billingsley, *Stony Gaze*, Chieveley, Capall Bann, 1998.

144. In 1996–7 an elderly man in Anglesey created a stir in the Welsh mass media by claiming to be a member of a pagan cult on the island, which had survived from ancient times and was focused on stone heads, one of which was in the island museum. This turns out to be a classic example of the seventeenth-century type identified by Billingsley, complete with the hole that a clay pipe fits. This makes it all the more likely that the cult – if it ever existed – was a revival rather than a survival, but no evidence was ever produced for its existence, though the man claimed it to have been over a thousand strong, and he now seems to have disappeared.

145. Simon de Bruxelles, 'Mysterious Pits Shed Lights on Forgotten Witches of the West', *The Times*, 10 March 2008; Kate Ravilious, 'Witches of Cornwall', *Archaeology*, 61 (2008), at *www.archaeology.org/0811/etc/witches.html*, accessed 4 November 2011.

146. The details of English laws against witchcraft have been readily available since the pioneering work of L'Estrange Ewen in the 1920s and 1930s, followed by that of Alan Macfarlane in 1970. Recently, excellent surveys of the subject have been provided by James Sharpe: *Instruments of Darkness*; and *Witchcraft in Early Modern England*, Harlow, Longman, 2001.

147. What follows is based on Ronald Hutton, *Witches, Druids and King Arthur*, 137–92; and 'Astral Magic', in Nicholas Campion *et al.* (eds), *Astrology and the Academy*, Bristol, Cinnabar Books, 2004, 10–24; where full references may be found.

148. Hutton, *Triumph of the Moon*, 90–5.

149. A point first emphasized in this context by Peter Ucko, *Anthropomorphic Figurines of Predynastic Egypt and Neolithic Crete*, London, Royal Anthropological Institute, 1968, 411.

150. For example, Hecate in Lycia, Ephesian Artemis in Lydia, and Cybele in Phrygia. It was Sir James Frazer who popularized the idea that all these deities should be fused (with others) into 'a great Mother Goddess, the personification of all the reproductive energies of nature', an exemplar of the Edwardian belief in the former universal existence of such a figure: *Adonis, Attis, Osiris*, London, 1907, 34–6.

151. Thorkild Jacobsen, *The Treasures of Darkness*, New Haven, Yale University Press, 1976, passim. This was the book which laid down the prevailing interpretation of the evolution of Mesopotamian religion as well as being an excellent introduction to it.

152. Richard North, *Heathen Gods in Old English Literature*, Cambridge, Cambridge University Press, 1997, 44–77, contains the most recent discussion of it. Hilda Ellis Davidson has found hints in the medieval Scandinavian literary texts of a 'supreme and powerful goddess' as well as the multiplicity of local counterparts, but concludes that these are 'vague and suggestive merely' (and does not link them to the earth): *The Lost Beliefs of Northern Europe*, London, Routledge, 1993, 108–11.

153. The first five of those were cited by Ucko, *Anthropomorphic Figurines*, 410. I have added the others.

154. Brian Stock, *Myth and Science in the Twelfth Century*, Princeton, NJ, Princeton University Press, 1972, 44–102; Hutton, *Witches, Druids and King Arthur*, 96–7.

155. This discrepancy was noted by Ucko, *Anthropomorphic Figurines*, 410. Likewise, Nicole Loraux noted that the Greeks did sometimes speak of 'The Mother' and more rarely identified her with the earth, but could not agree on whether she was one goddess or several, and Greek or Asiatic. Loraux adds that 'in short, nothing is certain', and that modern scholars have made the matter much worse; presumably a reference to the modern belief in a universal ancient Mother Goddess: 'What is a Goddess', in Pauline Schmitt Pantel (ed.), *A History of Women in the West: Volume One*, Cambridge, MA, Harvard University Press, 1992, 11–44. Sue Blundell has emphasized that over half of the goddesses most worshipped in ancient Greece were virgins, and that these included most of those helpful to humanity: Sue Blundell, *Women in Ancient Greece*, London, British Museum, 1995, 25–46.

156. The belief that she was a more important one, which still features at times in popular handbooks and encyclopaedias of ancient mythology or religion, is based mainly on Lewis Richard Farnell, *The Cults of the Greek States*, Oxford, Oxford University Press, 1907, iii.1–28. Influenced by the prevailing scholarly belief in a universal prehistoric mother goddess, he argued for her former supremacy from the literary texts and from conjectural reconstructions of inscriptions and attributions of statues. He still ended up concluding (on p. 28) that 'this cult has scarcely a point of contact with the more advanced life of the [Greek] race . . . it seems that she must disguise herself under other names'. Walter Burkert, *Greek Religion*, Cambridge, MA, Harvard University Press, 1985, 175, was more forthright, pointing out her large place in the literature of 'speculation' while adding that 'in customary religion the role of Gaia is exceedingly modest', confined mainly to the pouring of libations. Jennifer Larson, 'A Land Full of Gods', in Daniel Ogden (ed.), *A Companion to Greek Religion*, Chichester, Wiley-Blackwell, 2010, 67, considers her role in city states and finds it 'widespread yet never prominent', consisting of a statue or place for offerings in a few sanctuaries of her son or grandson Zeus, and an annual offering in two local religious calendars.

157. H. J. Rose, *Ancient Roman Religion*, London, 1948, 25.

158. Mary Beard *et al.*, *Religions of Rome*, Cambridge, Cambridge University Press, 1998, i.203, ii.142.

159. George D. Economou, *The Goddess Natura in Medieval Literature*, Cambridge, MA, Harvard University Press, 1972, 28–52.

160. What follows in this paragraph is based on Hutton, *Witches, Druids and King Arthur*, 96–7, 166–85. A parallel process to the enlargement of the role of Mother Earth and Mother Nature in Christian medieval thought is that of how Pan, a relatively minor Greek god (though one with important local cults), was given a greater prominence in medieval Christian writings because of two accidents: a story, recorded by Plutarch, that he had died (which was held to be the direct result of the Crucifixion), and the fact that his name was misinterpreted, because of a philological coincidence as meaning 'everything': Patricia Merivale, *Pan the Goat-God*, Cambridge, MA, Harvard University Press, 1969, 1–42. This paved the way (eventually) for a much more glorious place for him in modern literature.

161. This image is on the frontispieces to Robert Fludd, *Utriusque cosmi historia*, Oppenheim, 1617; and Athansius Kircher, *Ars magica lucis et umbrae*, Rome, 1646.

162. A story told in Hutton, *Triumph of the Moon*, 32–42. The parallel burgeoning of the literary cult of Pan is on pp. 43–51.

163. For which see the works of Owen Davies and myself, cited in n. 120.

INDEX

Note: Page references in italics refer to illustrations.

Index created by Meg Davies (Fellow of the Society of Indexers)